# STRAY BULLETS®

BOOM BOOM
Palace
LIVE NUDE GIRLS
24hrs

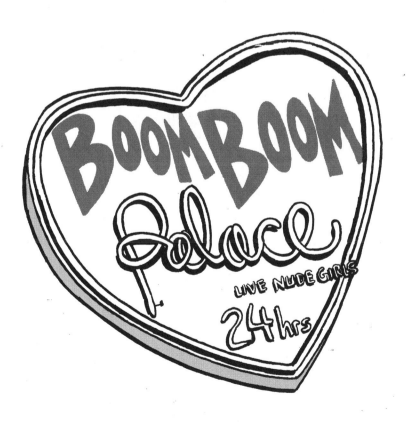

# STR
# BU

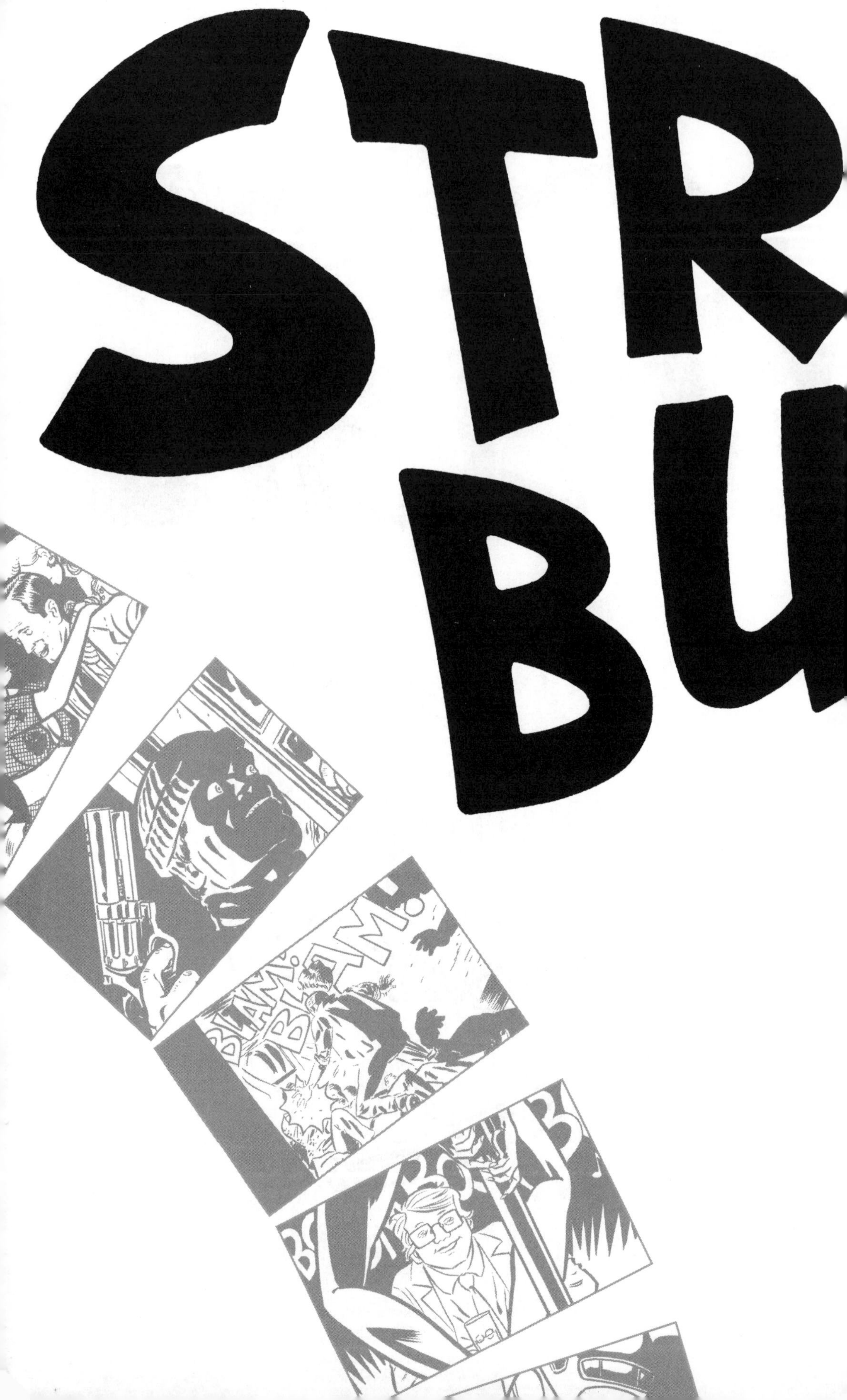
BLAM!
BLAM!

# AY
# LETS

VOLUME THREE

## "OTHER PEOPLE"

by

DAVID LAPHAM

# STRAY BULLETS: OTHER PEOPLE

by

## DAVID LAPHAM

•

### PRODUCED AND EDITED BY

## MARIA LAPHAM

AN

**ELCAPITÁN**

PRODUCTION

STRAY BULLETS #15-22 ORIGINALLY PUBLISHED AND EDITED BY
**MARIA LAPHAM**

SERIES DESIGN BY
**DAVID LAPHAM    MARIA LAPHAM**

COPY EDITED BY
**DEBORAH PURCELL**

COVER COLORS BY
**DAVID LAPHAM    SARAH DYER**

**IMAGE COMICS, INC.**
**Robert Kirkman** – Chief Operating Officer
**Erik Larsen** – Chief Financial Officer
**Todd McFarlane** – President
**Marc Silvestri** – Chief Executive Officer
**Jim Valentino** – Vice-President

**Eric Stephenson** – Publisher
**Corey Murphy** – Director of Sales
**Jeremy Sullivan** – Director of Digital Sales
**Kat Salazar** – Director of PR & Marketing
**Emily Miller** – Director of Operations
**Branwyn Bigglestone** – Senior Accounts Manager
**Sarah Mello** – Accounts Manager
**Drew Gill** – Art Director
**Jonathan Chan** – Production Manager
**Meredith Wallace** – Print Manager
**Randy Okamura** – Marketing Production Designer
**David Brothers** – Branding Manager
**Ally Power** – Content Manager
**Addison Duke** – Production Artist
**Vincent Kukua** – Production Artist
**Sasha Head** – Production Artist
**Tricia Ramos** – Production Artist
**Emilio Bautista** – Sales Assistant
**Jessica Ambriz** – Administrative Assistant
**IMAGECOMICS.COM**

ISBN: 978-1-63215-482-8    PRINTED IN CANADA

# CONTENTS

BLAM!
"sniff"
"sniff"

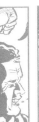

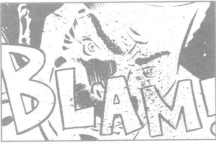

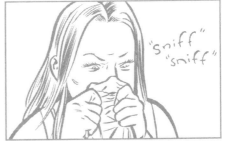

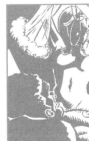

# STRAY BULLETS

"Winners are winners.  Losers are losers.  You can't win them all.  God bless them all."

JOHN R. GOTS

# 1

## "SEX and VIOLENCE"
### (part 1)

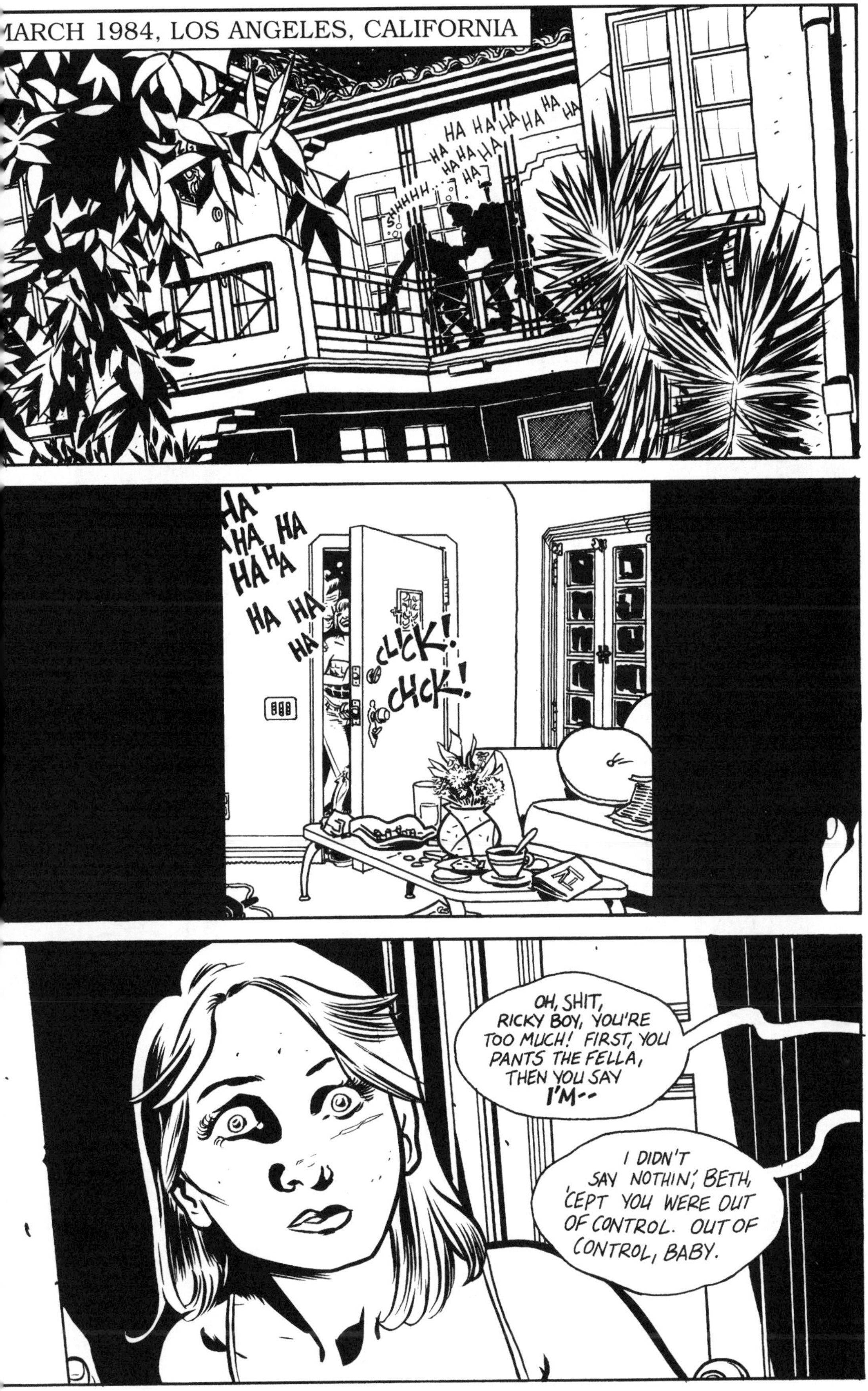

MARCH 1984, LOS ANGELES, CALIFORNIA
HA HA HA HA HA HA HA HA HA HA HA
SHHHHH...!
HA HA HA HA HA HA HA HA
CLICK! CHCK!
OH, SHIT, RICKY BOY, YOU'RE TOO MUCH! FIRST, YOU PANTS THE FELLA, THEN YOU SAY I'M--
I DIDN'T SAY NOTHIN', BETH, 'CEPT YOU WERE OUT OF CONTROL. OUT OF CONTROL, BABY.

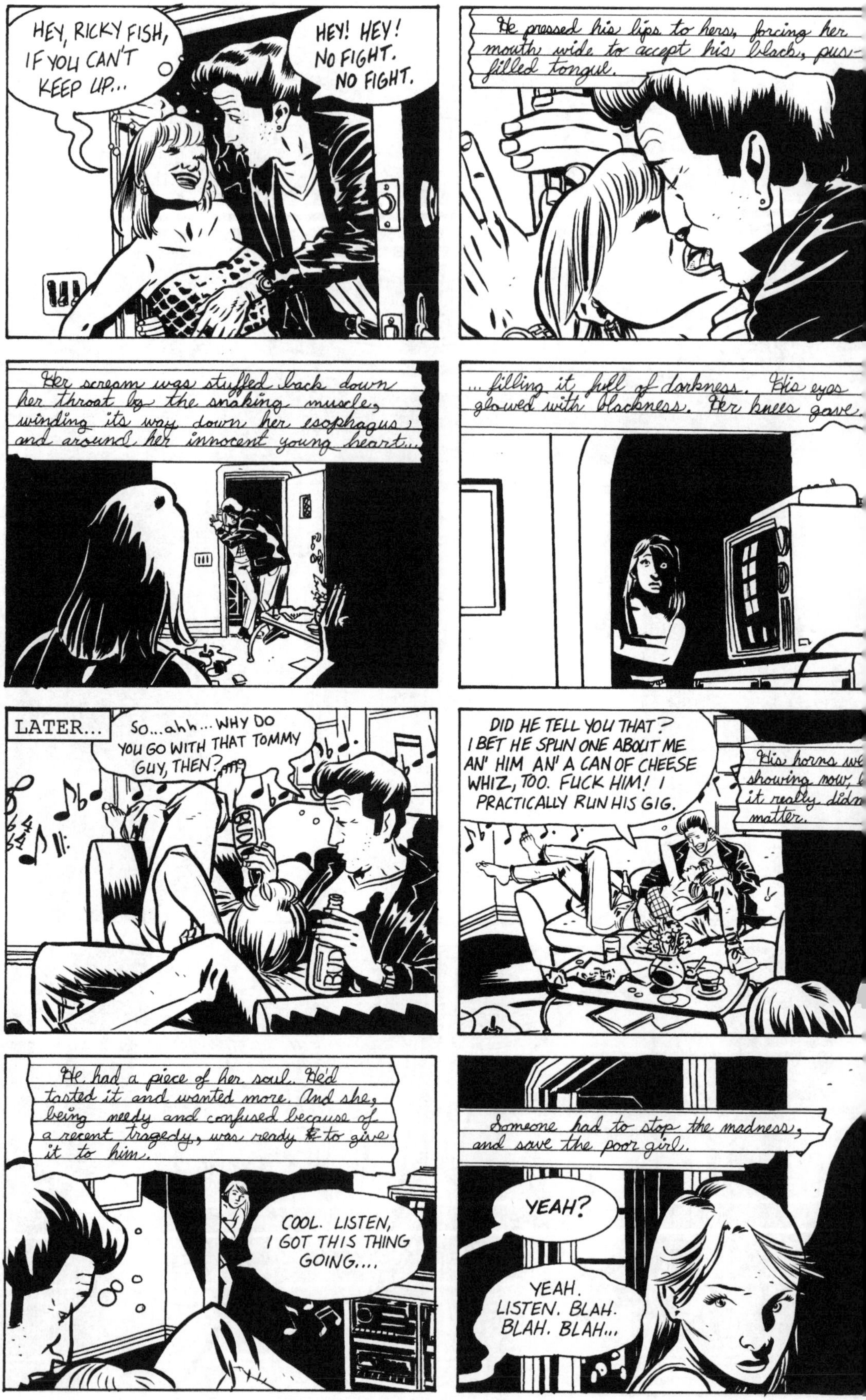

HEY, RICKY FISH, IF YOU CAN'T KEEP UP...
HEY! HEY! NO FIGHT. NO FIGHT.
He pressed his lips to hers, forcing her mouth wide to accept his black, pus-filled tongue.
Her scream was stuffed back down her throat by the snaking muscle, winding its way down her esophagus and around her innocent young heart...
...filling it full of darkness. His eyes glowed with blackness. Her knees gave.
LATER...
SO...ahh...WHY DO YOU GO WITH THAT TOMMY GUY, THEN?
DID HE TELL YOU THAT? I BET HE SPUN ONE ABOUT ME AN' HIM AN' A CAN OF CHEESE WHIZ, TOO. FUCK HIM! I PRACTICALLY RUN HIS GIG.
His horns we
showing now,
it really didn
matter.
He had a piece of her soul. He'd tasted it and wanted more. And she, being needy and confused because of a recent tragedy, was ready to give it to him.
COOL. LISTEN, I GOT THIS THING GOING....
Someone had to stop the madness, and save the poor girl.
YEAH?
YEAH. LISTEN. BLAH. BLAH. BLAH...

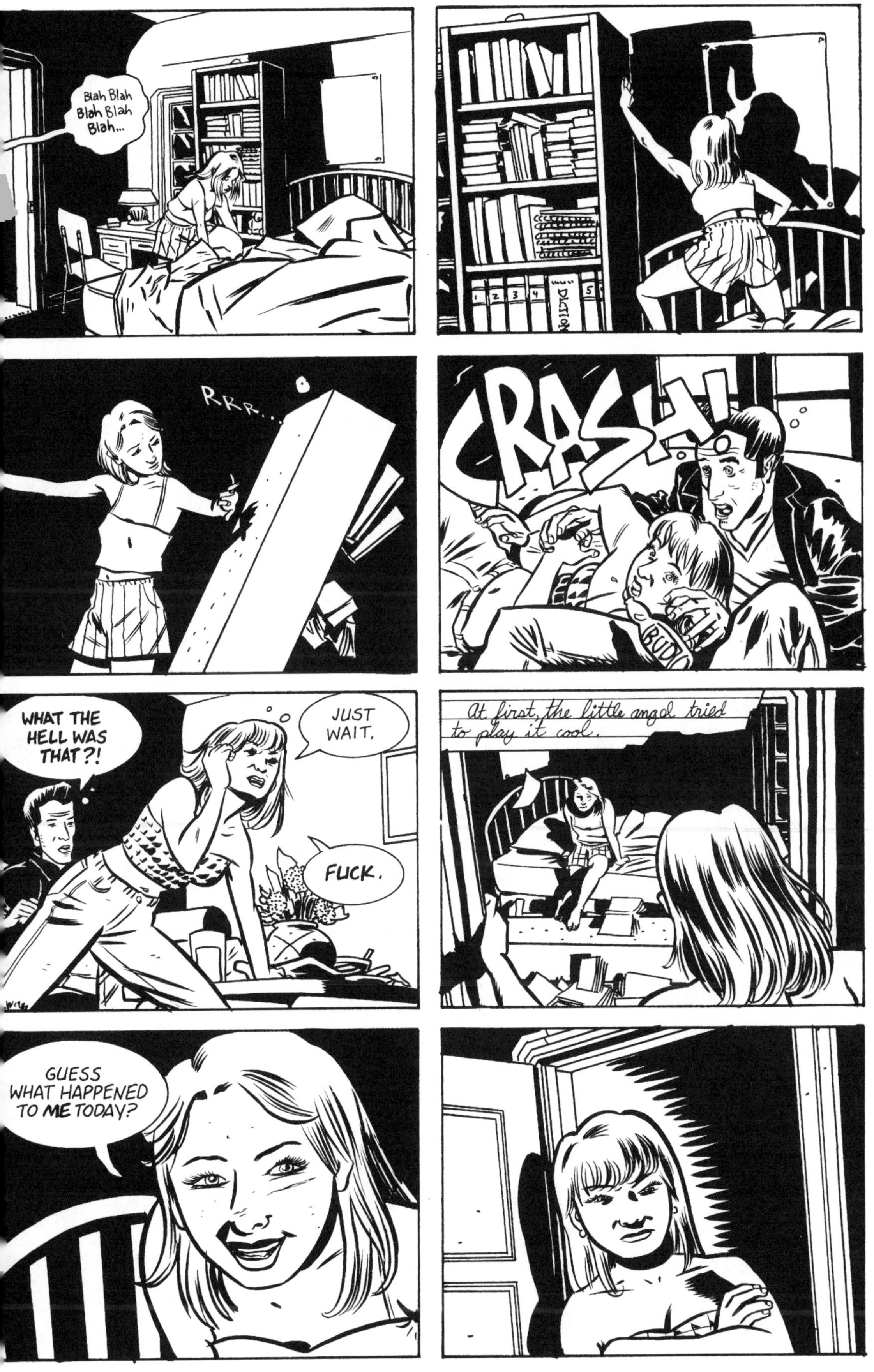
Blah Blah Blah Blah Blah...
RRR...
CRASH!
BUD
WHAT THE HELL WAS THAT?!
JUST WAIT.
FUCK.
At first, the little angel tried to play it cool.
GUESS WHAT HAPPENED TO ME TODAY?

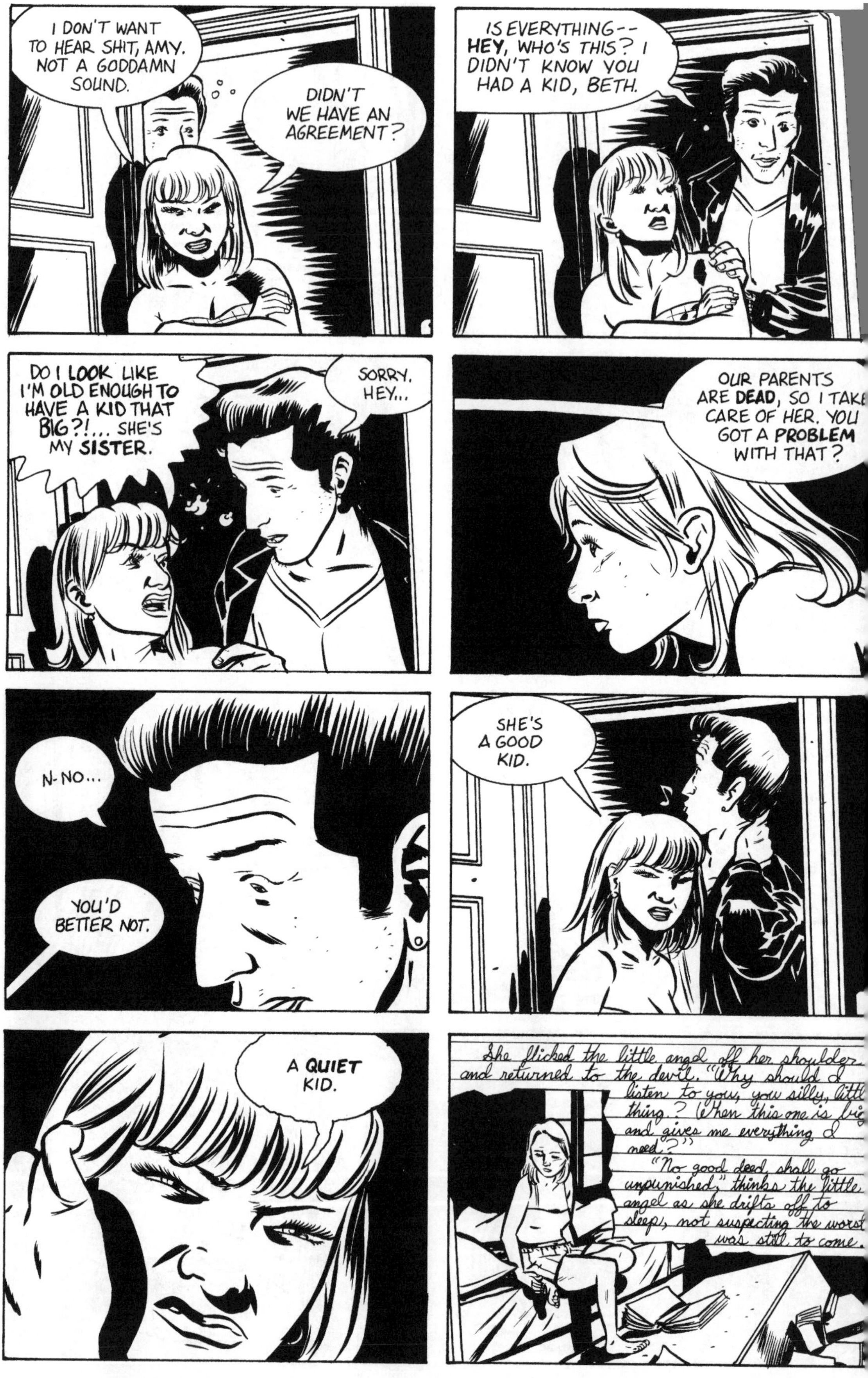
I DON'T WANT TO HEAR SHIT, AMY. NOT A GODDAMN SOUND.
DIDN'T WE HAVE AN AGREEMENT?
IS EVERYTHING-- HEY, WHO'S THIS? I DIDN'T KNOW YOU HAD A KID, BETH.
DO I LOOK LIKE I'M OLD ENOUGH TO HAVE A KID THAT BIG?!... SHE'S MY SISTER.
SORRY. HEY...
OUR PARENTS ARE DEAD, SO I TAKE CARE OF HER. YOU GOT A PROBLEM WITH THAT?
N-NO...
YOU'D BETTER NOT.
SHE'S A GOOD KID.
A QUIET KID.
She flicked the little angel off her shoulder and returned to the devil. "Why should I listen to you, you silly, little thing? When this one is big and gives me everything I need?"
"No good deed shall go unpunished," thinks the little angel as she drifts off to sleep, not suspecting the worst was still to come.

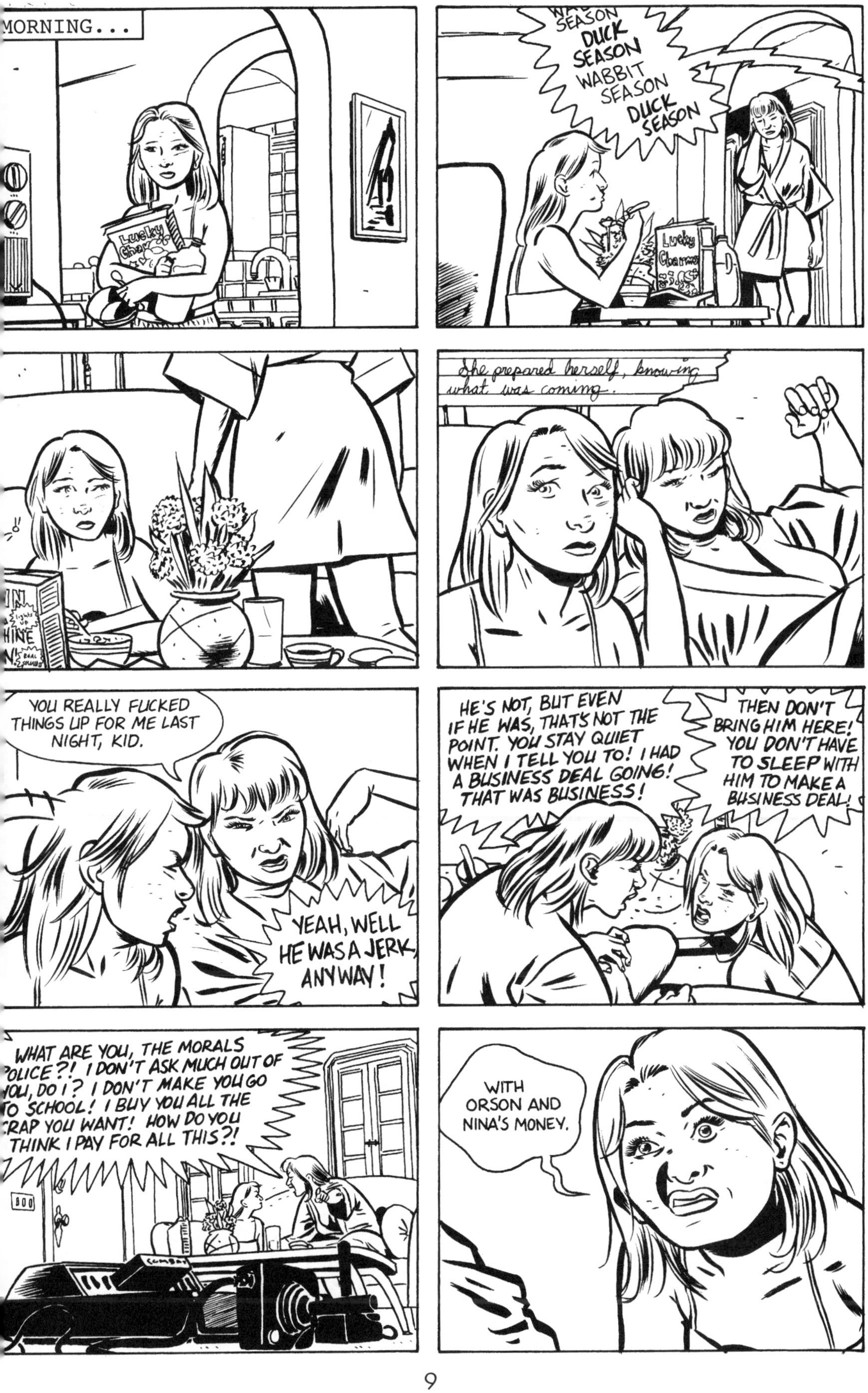
MORNING...
WABBIT SEASON
DUCK SEASON
WABBIT SEASON
DUCK SEASON
She prepared herself, knowing what was coming.
YOU REALLY FUCKED THINGS UP FOR ME LAST NIGHT, KID.
YEAH, WELL HE WAS A JERK, ANYWAY!
HE'S NOT, BUT EVEN IF HE WAS, THAT'S NOT THE POINT. YOU STAY QUIET WHEN I TELL YOU TO! I HAD A BUSINESS DEAL GOING! THAT WAS BUSINESS!
THEN DON'T BRING HIM HERE! YOU DON'T HAVE TO SLEEP WITH HIM TO MAKE A BUSINESS DEAL!
WHAT ARE YOU, THE MORALS POLICE?! I DON'T ASK MUCH OUT OF YOU, DO I? I DON'T MAKE YOU GO TO SCHOOL! I BUY YOU ALL THE CRAP YOU WANT! HOW DO YOU THINK I PAY FOR ALL THIS?!
WITH ORSON AND NINA'S MONEY.

YOU LITTLE SHIT! DON'T PLAY THAT CARD ON ME! I WAS A LOT CLOSER TO THEM THAN YOU! I DON'T GIVE A DAMN IF YOU UNDERSTAND, YOU DO IT CUZ I TELL YOU TO!

THAT'S A REALLY GOOD REASON.

YOU'RE DAMN RIGHT IT IS! RICKY LEFT NOT FIVE MINUTES AFTER YOUR LITTLE EPISODE!

DON'T YOU SMILE!

YOU THINK I WON'T BELT YOU IN THE MOUTH?!

YOU CAN'T HIDE BEHIND THAT LITTLE KID CRAP WITH ME! I REMEMBER THIRTEEN, AND BELIEVE ME, BABY, I WAS A HELL OF A LOT SHARPER THAN YOU!

KRICK

AHH!

OH, NO!

I'M GOING OUT. YOU CLEAN THAT UP, AND REARRANGE YOUR ATTITUDE BY THE TIME I GET HOME.

OR ELSE.

Realizing the dumb bitch was beyond hope, the little angel knew it was time to get the hell away from this stupid, stupid, retarded place.

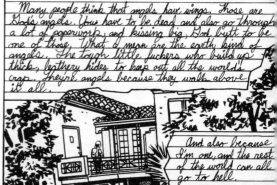

Many people think that angels have wings. Those are God's angels. You have to be dead and also go through a lot of paperwork, and kissing big, God butt to be one of those. What I mean are the earthy kind of angels. The tough little fuckers who build up thick, leathery hides to keep out all the world's crap. They're angels because they walk above it all.

And also because I'm one, and the rest of the world can all go to hell.

10

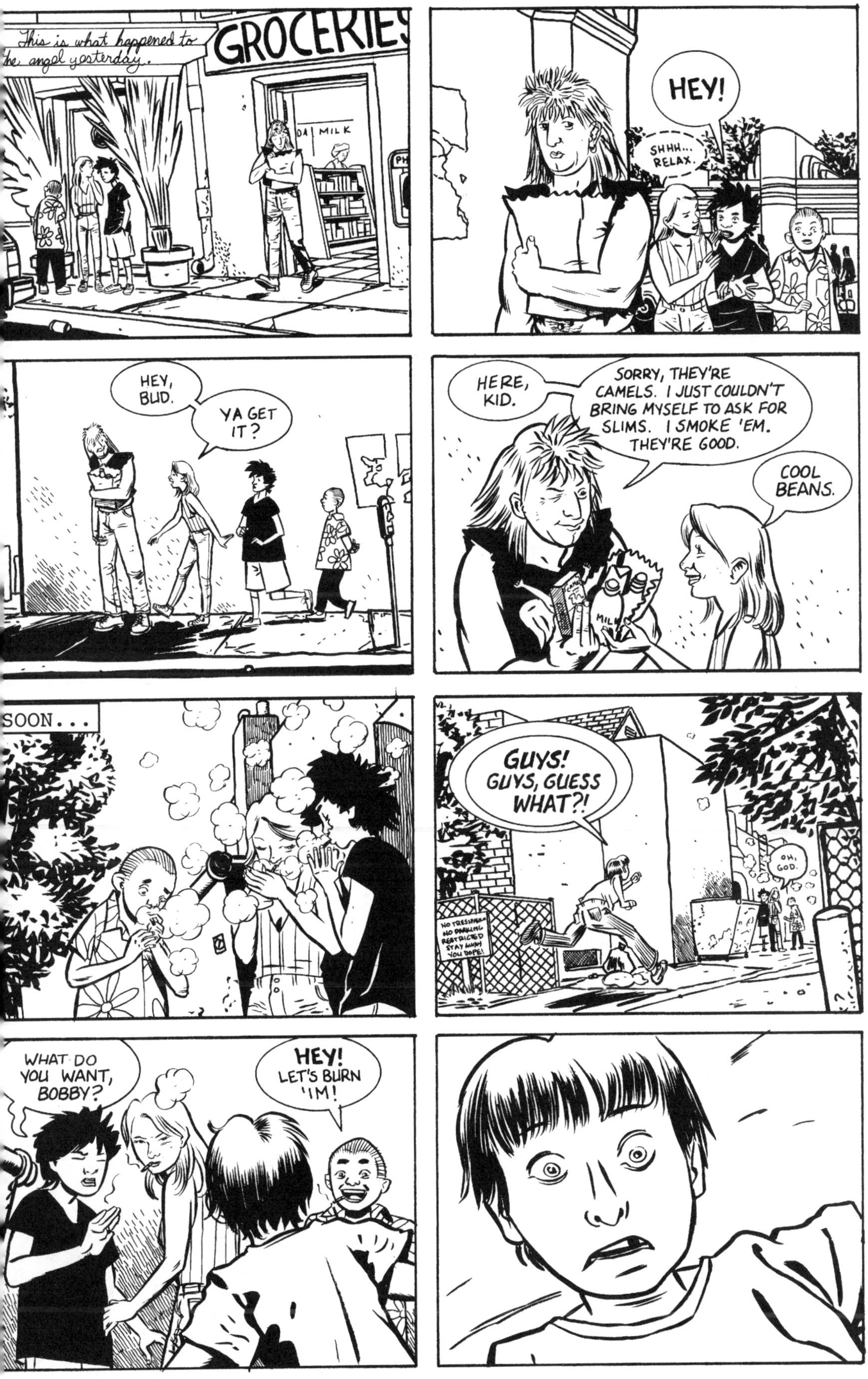
This is what happened to the angel yesterday.
GROCERIES
DA MILK
HEY!
SHHH... RELAX.
HEY, BUD.
YA GET IT?
HERE, KID.
SORRY, THEY'RE CAMELS. I JUST COULDN'T BRING MYSELF TO ASK FOR SLIMS. I SMOKE 'EM. THEY'RE GOOD.
COOL BEANS.
SOON...
GUYS! GUYS, GUESS WHAT?!
OH, GOD.
NO TRESSPASSING NO PARKING RESTRICTED STAY AWAY YOU DOPE!
WHAT DO YOU WANT, BOBBY?
HEY! LET'S BURN 'IM!

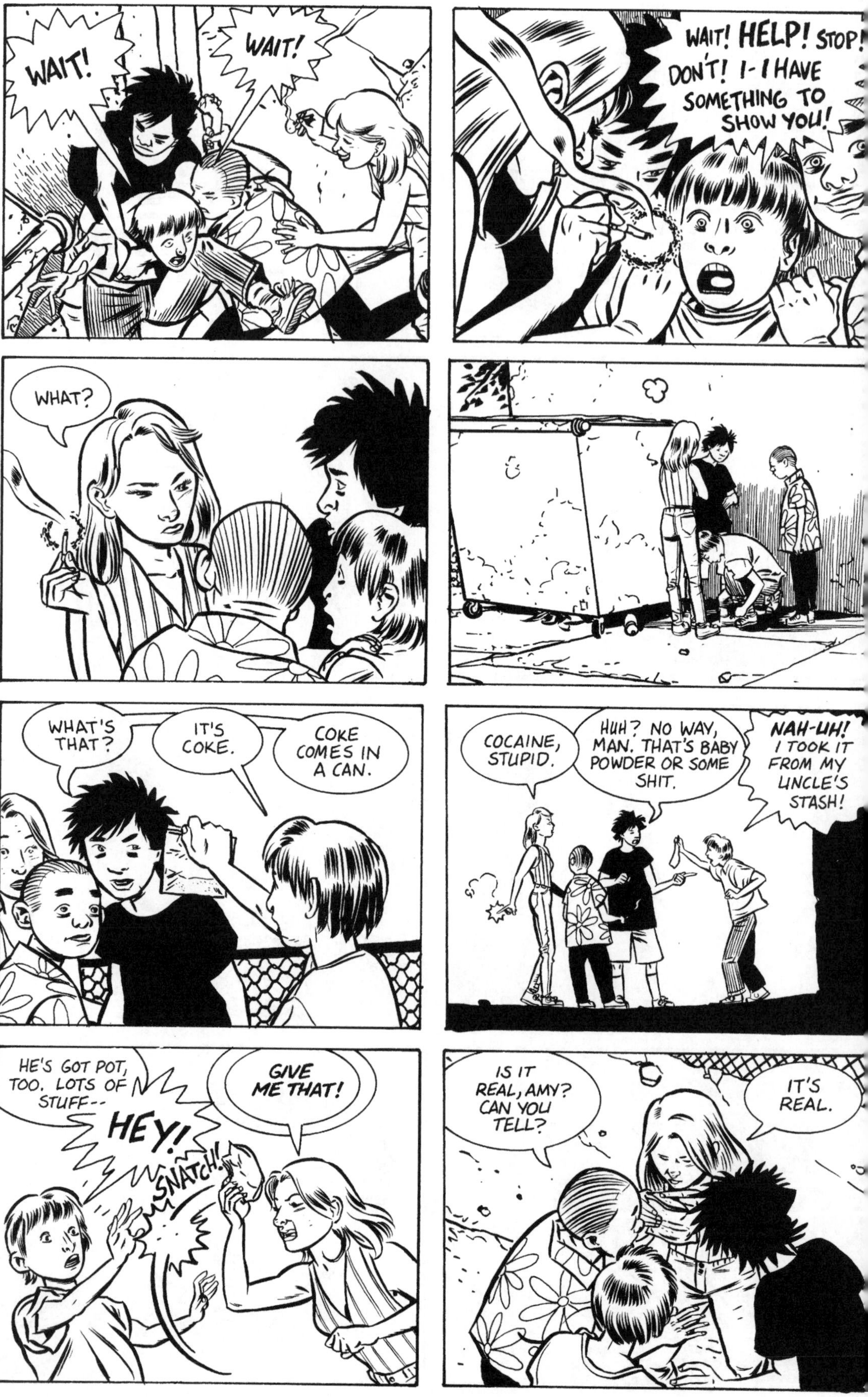
WAIT!
WAIT!
WAIT! HELP! STOP! DON'T! I-I HAVE SOMETHING TO SHOW YOU!
WHAT?
WHAT'S THAT?
IT'S COKE.
COKE COMES IN A CAN.
COCAINE, STUPID.
HUH? NO WAY, MAN. THAT'S BABY POWDER OR SOME SHIT.
NAH-UH! I TOOK IT FROM MY UNCLE'S STASH!
HE'S GOT POT, TOO. LOTS OF STUFF--
HEY!
SNATCH!
GIVE ME THAT!
IS IT REAL, AMY? CAN YOU TELL?
IT'S REAL.

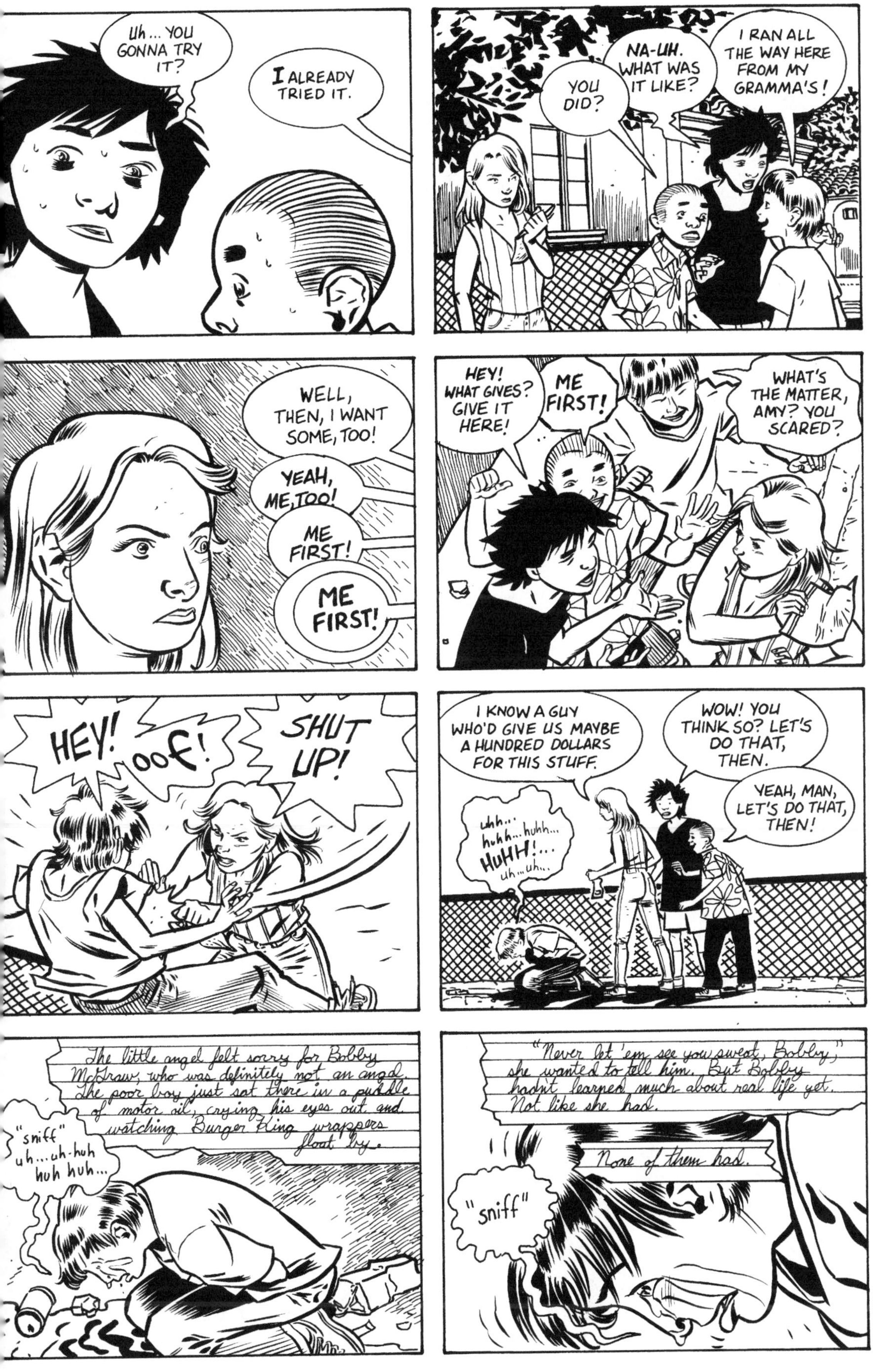

Uh... YOU GONNA TRY IT?
I ALREADY TRIED IT.
YOU DID?
NA-UH. WHAT WAS IT LIKE?
I RAN ALL THE WAY HERE FROM MY GRAMMA'S!
WELL, THEN, I WANT SOME, TOO!
YEAH, ME, TOO!
ME FIRST!
ME FIRST!
HEY! WHAT GIVES? GIVE IT HERE!
ME FIRST!
WHAT'S THE MATTER, AMY? YOU SCARED?
HEY!
OOF!
SHUT UP!
I KNOW A GUY WHO'D GIVE US MAYBE A HUNDRED DOLLARS FOR THIS STUFF.
WOW! YOU THINK SO? LET'S DO THAT, THEN.
YEAH, MAN, LET'S DO THAT, THEN!
uhh... huhh... huhh... HUHH!... uh... uh...
The little angel felt sorry for Bobby McGraw, who was definitely not an angel. The poor boy just sat there in a puddle of motor oil, crying his eyes out and watching Burger King wrappers float by.
"sniff" uh... uh-huh huh huh...
"Never let 'em see you sweat, Bobby," she wanted to tell him. But Bobby hadn't learned much about real life yet. Not like she had.
None of them had.
"sniff"

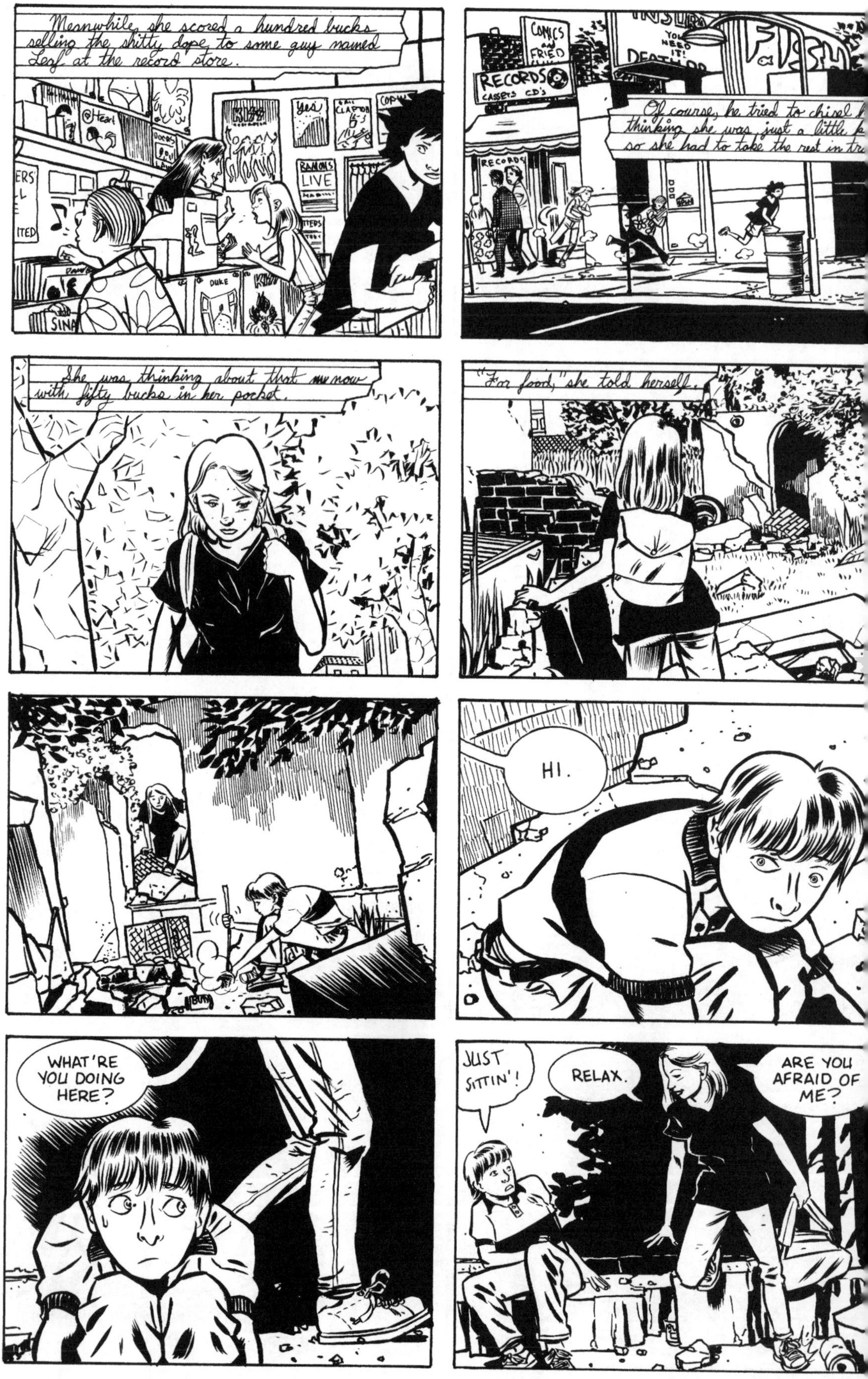

Meanwhile, she scored a hundred bucks selling the shitty dope to some guy named Leaf at the record store.
COMICS and FRIED
RECORDS CASSETS CD's
Of course, he tried to chisel
thinking she was just a little
so she had to take the rest in
She was thinking about that now with fifty bucks in her pocket.
"For food," she told herself.
HI.
WHAT'RE YOU DOING HERE?
JUST SITTIN'!
RELAX.
ARE YOU AFRAID OF ME?

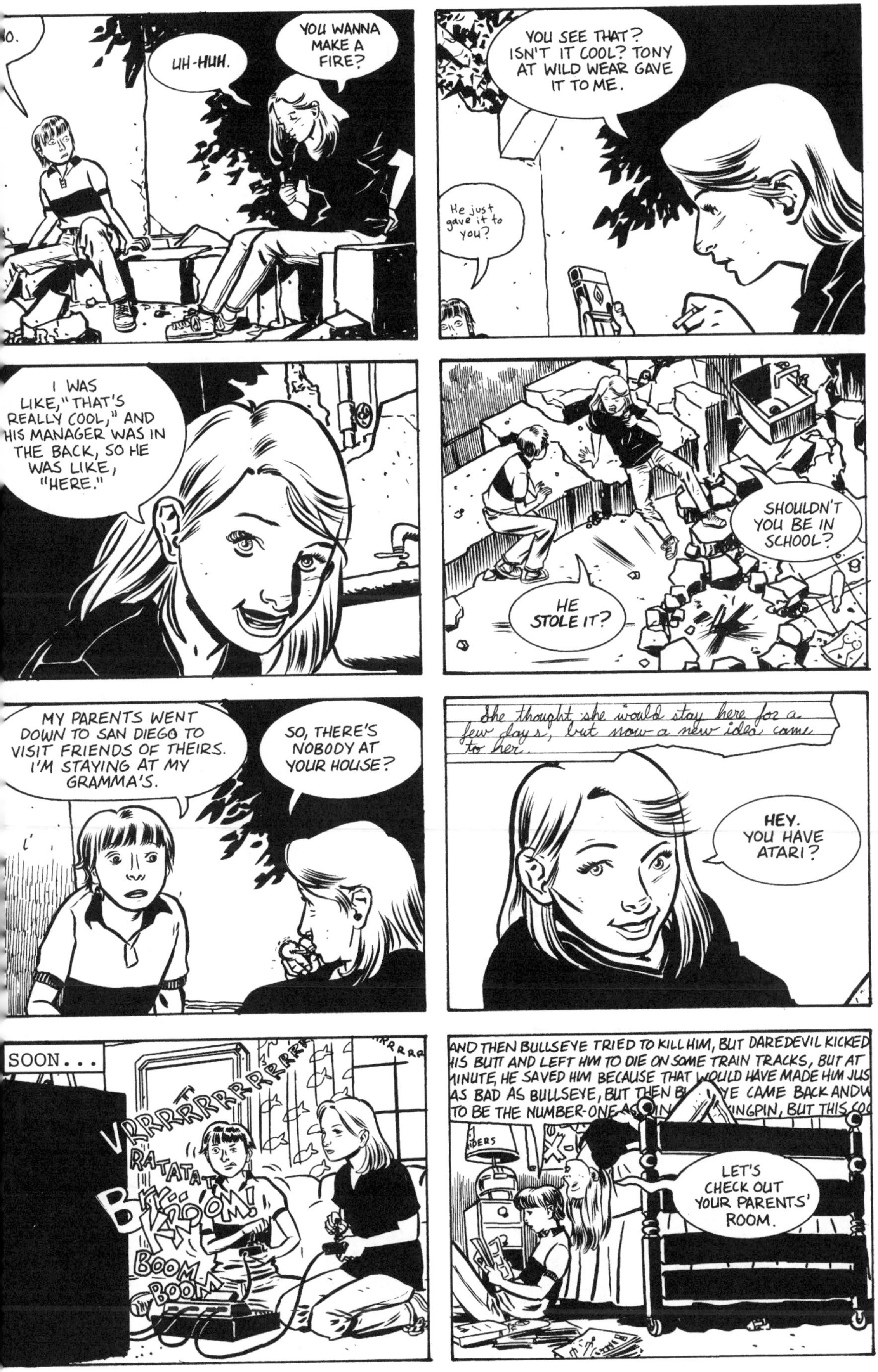

O.
UH-HUH.
YOU WANNA MAKE A FIRE?
YOU SEE THAT? ISN'T IT COOL? TONY AT WILD WEAR GAVE IT TO ME.
He just gave it to you?
I WAS LIKE, "THAT'S REALLY COOL," AND HIS MANAGER WAS IN THE BACK, SO HE WAS LIKE, "HERE."
HE STOLE IT?
SHOULDN'T YOU BE IN SCHOOL?
MY PARENTS WENT DOWN TO SAN DIEGO TO VISIT FRIENDS OF THEIRS. I'M STAYING AT MY GRAMMA'S.
SO, THERE'S NOBODY AT YOUR HOUSE?
She thought she would stay here for a few days, but now a new idea came to her.
HEY. YOU HAVE ATARI?
SOON...
VRRRRTRRRRRRRRRRR
RRRR
RATATATAT
BKKOOM!
BOOM
BOOM
AND THEN BULLSEYE TRIED TO KILL HIM, BUT DAREDEVIL KICKED HIS BUTT AND LEFT HIM TO DIE ON SOME TRAIN TRACKS, BUT AT
MINUTE, HE SAVED HIM BECAUSE THAT WOULD HAVE MADE HIM
AS BAD AS BULLSEYE, BUT THEN
YE CAME BACK AND
TO BE THE NUMBER-ONE
INGPIN, BUT THIS
LET'S CHECK OUT YOUR PARENTS' ROOM.

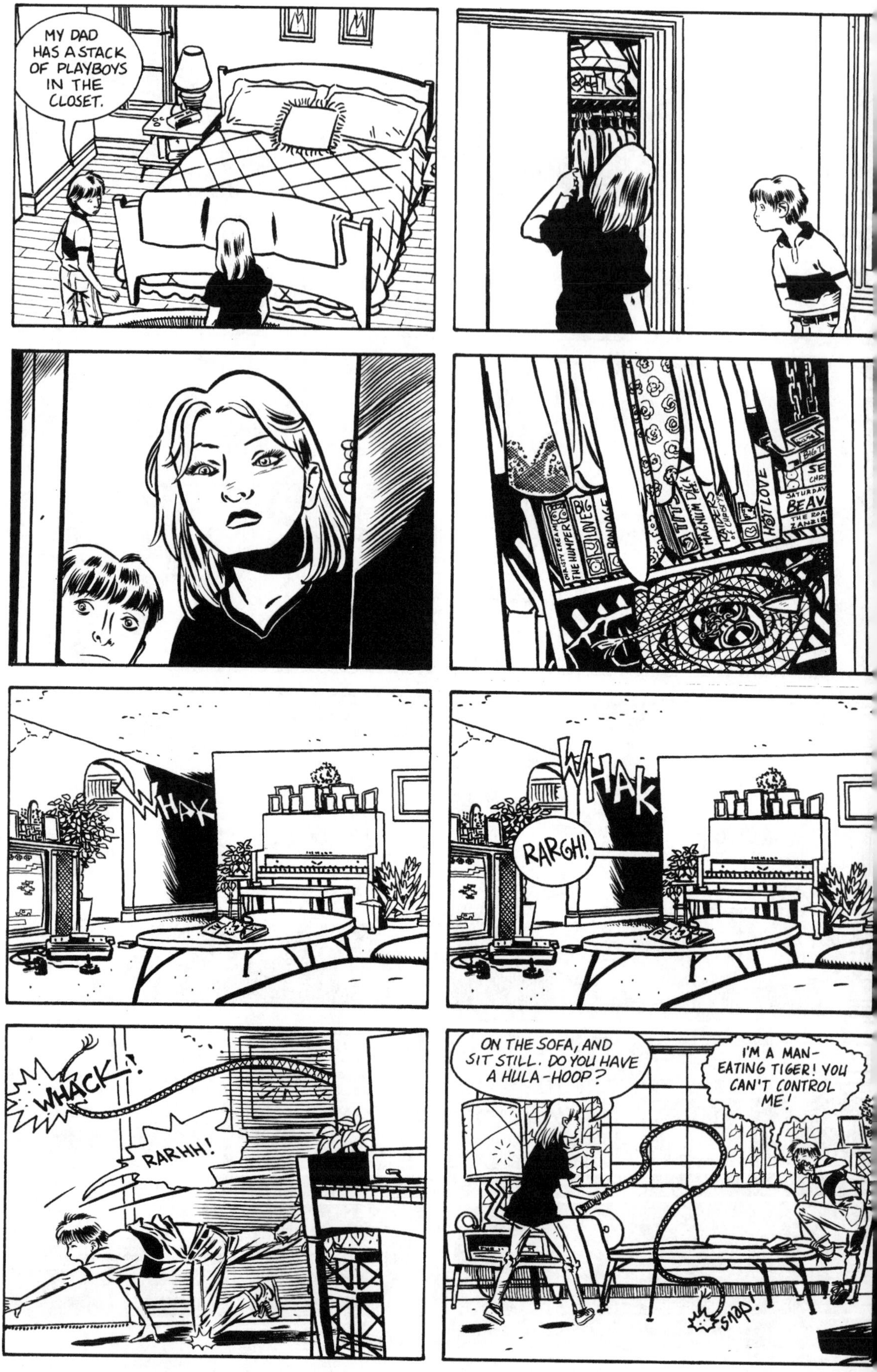

MY DAD HAS A STACK OF PLAYBOYS IN THE CLOSET.
THE HUMPER
HOT LOVE
WHAK
WHAK
RARGH!
WHACK!
RARHH!
ON THE SOFA, AND SIT STILL. DO YOU HAVE A HULA-HOOP?
I'M A MAN-EATING TIGER! YOU CAN'T CONTROL ME!
SNAP!

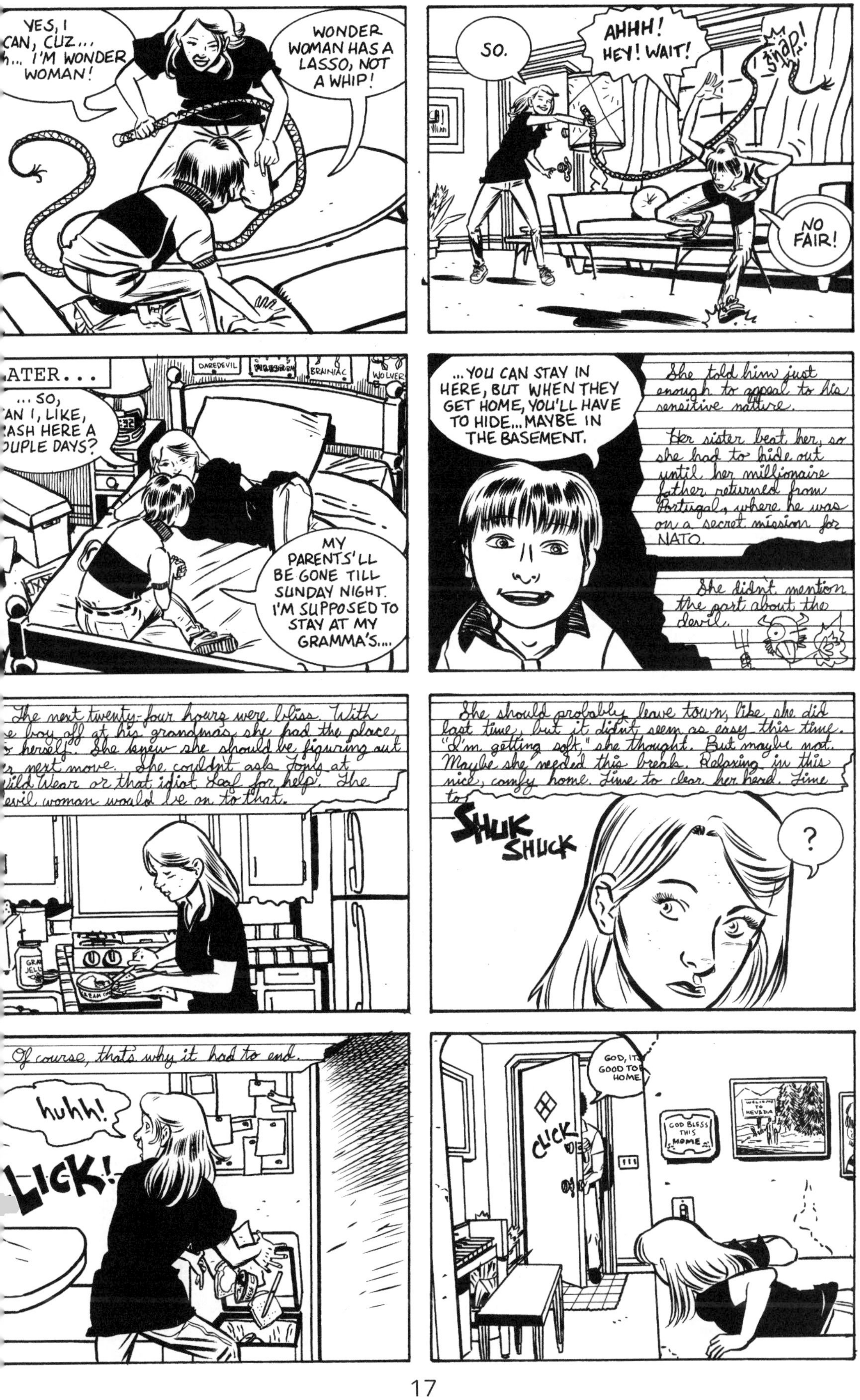
YES, I CAN, CUZ... h... I'M WONDER WOMAN!
WONDER WOMAN HAS A LASSO, NOT A WHIP!
SO.
AHHH! HEY! WAIT!
SNAP!
NO FAIR!
ATER...
DAREDEVIL
BRAINIAC
WOLVER
... SO, AN I, LIKE, ASH HERE A OUPLE DAYS?
MY PARENTS'LL BE GONE TILL SUNDAY NIGHT. I'M SUPPOSED TO STAY AT MY GRAMMA'S....
...YOU CAN STAY IN HERE, BUT WHEN THEY GET HOME, YOU'LL HAVE TO HIDE... MAYBE IN THE BASEMENT.
She told him just enough to appeal to his sensitive nature.
Her sister beat her, so she had to hide out until her millionaire father returned from Portugal, where he was on a secret mission for NATO.
She didn't mention the part about the devil.
The next twenty-four hours were bliss. With e boy off at his grandma's, she had the place o herself. She knew she should be figuring out r next move. She couldn't ask Tony at ild Wear or that idiot Loaf for help. The evil woman would be on to that.
She should probably leave town, like she did last time, but it didn't seem as easy this time. "I'm getting soft" she thought. But maybe not. Maybe she needed this break. Relaxing in this nice, comfy home. Time to clear her head. Time to...
SHUK SHUCK
?
Of course, that's why it had to end.
huhh!
LICK!
GOD, IT GOOD TO HOME.
CLICK
GOD BLESS THIS HOME
WELCOME TO NEVADA

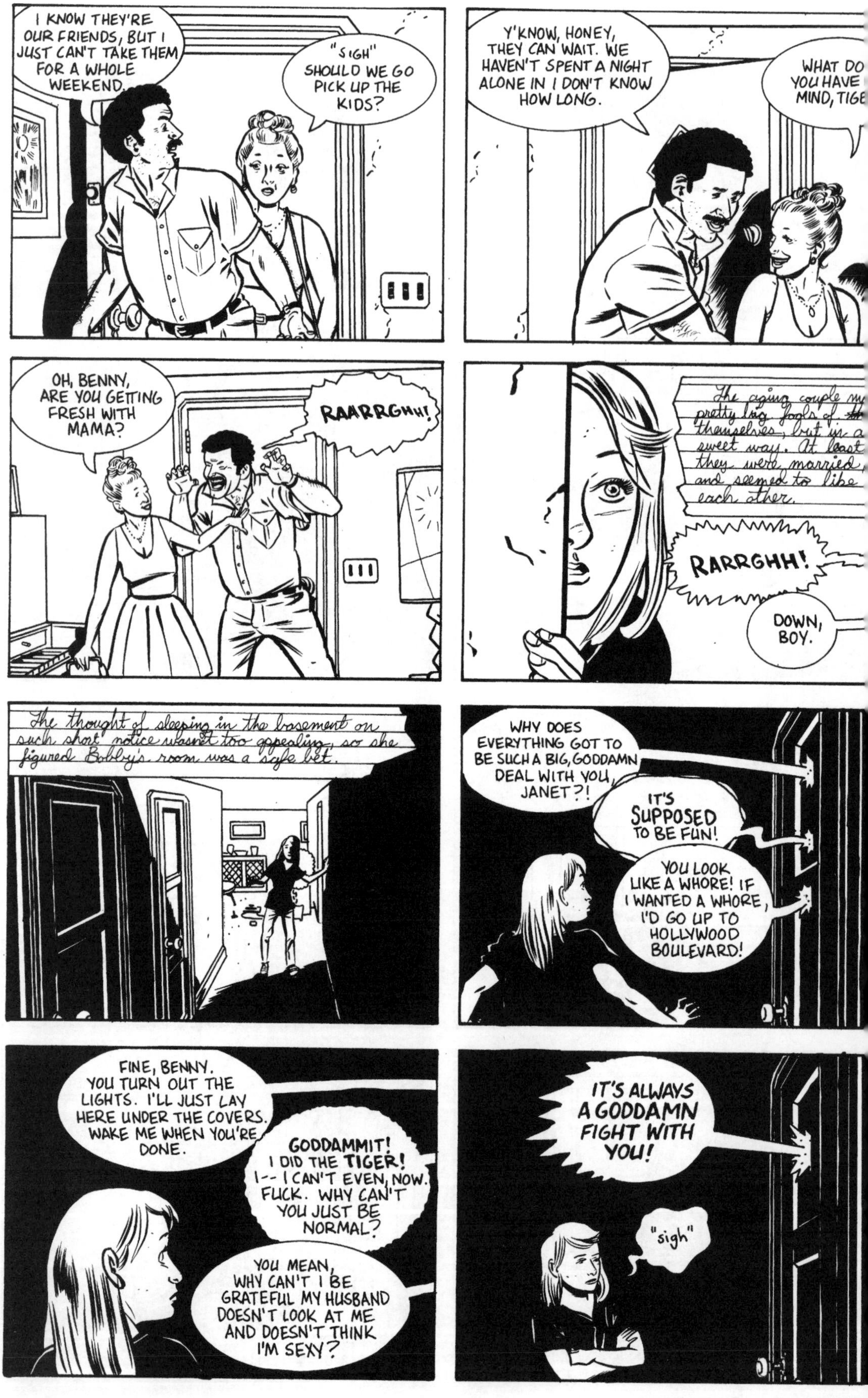
I KNOW THEY'RE OUR FRIENDS, BUT I JUST CAN'T TAKE THEM FOR A WHOLE WEEKEND.
"SIGH" SHOULD WE GO PICK UP THE KIDS?
Y'KNOW, HONEY, THEY CAN WAIT. WE HAVEN'T SPENT A NIGHT ALONE IN I DON'T KNOW HOW LONG.
WHAT DO YOU HAVE MIND, TIGE
OH, BENNY, ARE YOU GETTING FRESH WITH MAMA?
RAARRGHH!
The aging couple m pretty big fools of themselves, but in a sweet way. At least they were married, and seemed to like each other.
RARRGHH!
DOWN, BOY.
The thought of sleeping in the basement on such short notice wasn't too appealing, so she figured Bobby's room was a safe bet.
WHY DOES EVERYTHING GOT TO BE SUCH A BIG, GODDAMN DEAL WITH YOU, JANET?!
IT'S SUPPOSED TO BE FUN!
YOU LOOK LIKE A WHORE! IF I WANTED A WHORE, I'D GO UP TO HOLLYWOOD BOULEVARD!
FINE, BENNY. YOU TURN OUT THE LIGHTS. I'LL JUST LAY HERE UNDER THE COVERS. WAKE ME WHEN YOU'RE DONE.
GODDAMMIT! I DID THE TIGER! I-- I CAN'T EVEN, NOW. FUCK. WHY CAN'T YOU JUST BE NORMAL?
YOU MEAN, WHY CAN'T I BE GRATEFUL MY HUSBAND DOESN'T LOOK AT ME AND DOESN'T THINK I'M SEXY?
IT'S ALWAYS A GODDAMN FIGHT WITH YOU!
"sigh"

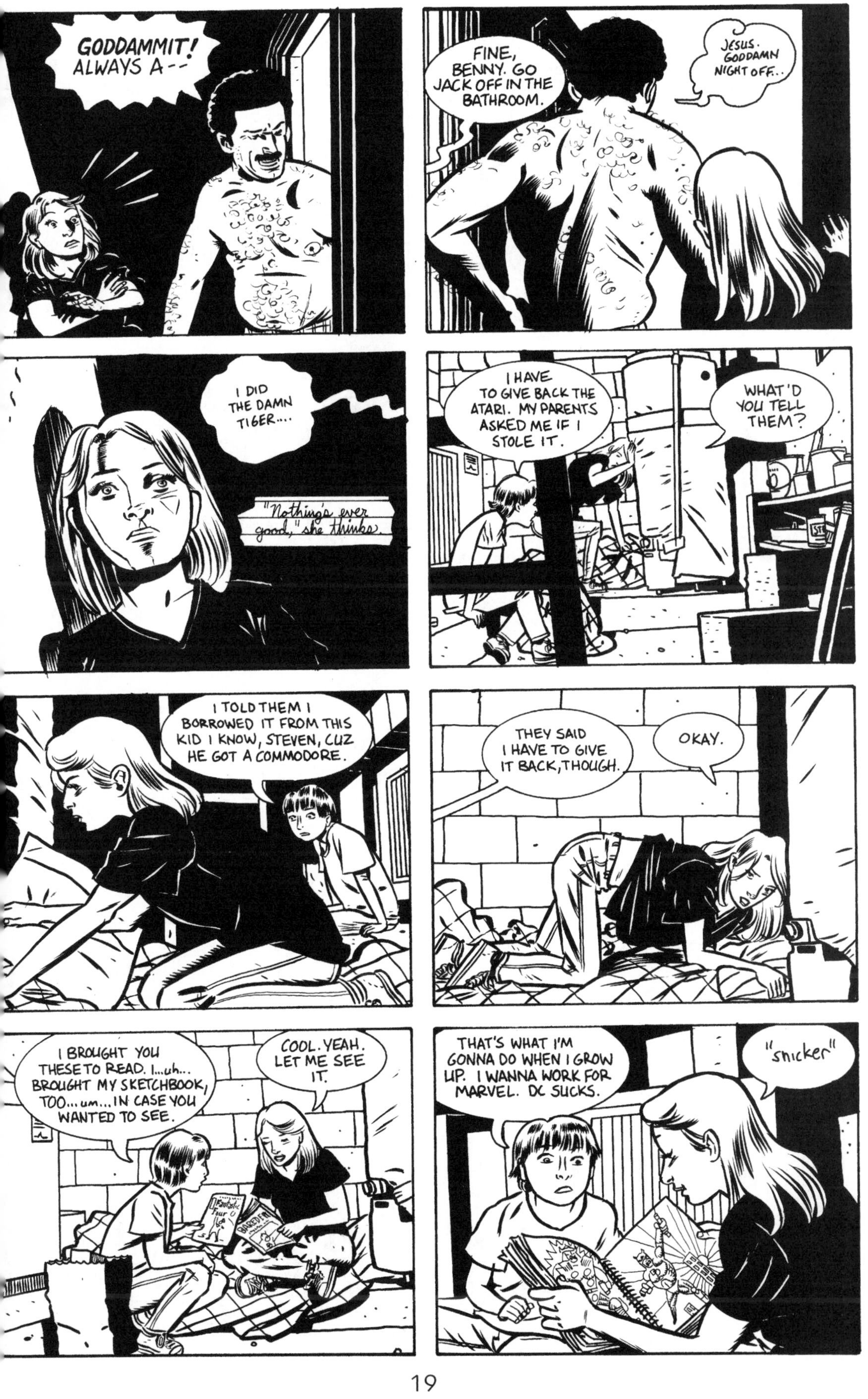
GODDAMMIT! ALWAYS A--
FINE, BENNY. GO JACK OFF IN THE BATHROOM.
JESUS. GODDAMN NIGHT OFF...
I DID THE DAMN TIGER....
"Nothing's ever good," she thinks
I HAVE TO GIVE BACK THE ATARI. MY PARENTS ASKED ME IF I STOLE IT.
WHAT'D YOU TELL THEM?
I TOLD THEM I BORROWED IT FROM THIS KID I KNOW, STEVEN, CUZ HE GOT A COMMODORE.
THEY SAID I HAVE TO GIVE IT BACK, THOUGH.
OKAY.
I BROUGHT YOU THESE TO READ. I...uh... BROUGHT MY SKETCHBOOK, TOO... um... IN CASE YOU WANTED TO SEE.
COOL. YEAH. LET ME SEE IT.
THAT'S WHAT I'M GONNA DO WHEN I GROW UP. I WANNA WORK FOR MARVEL. DC SUCKS.
"snicker"

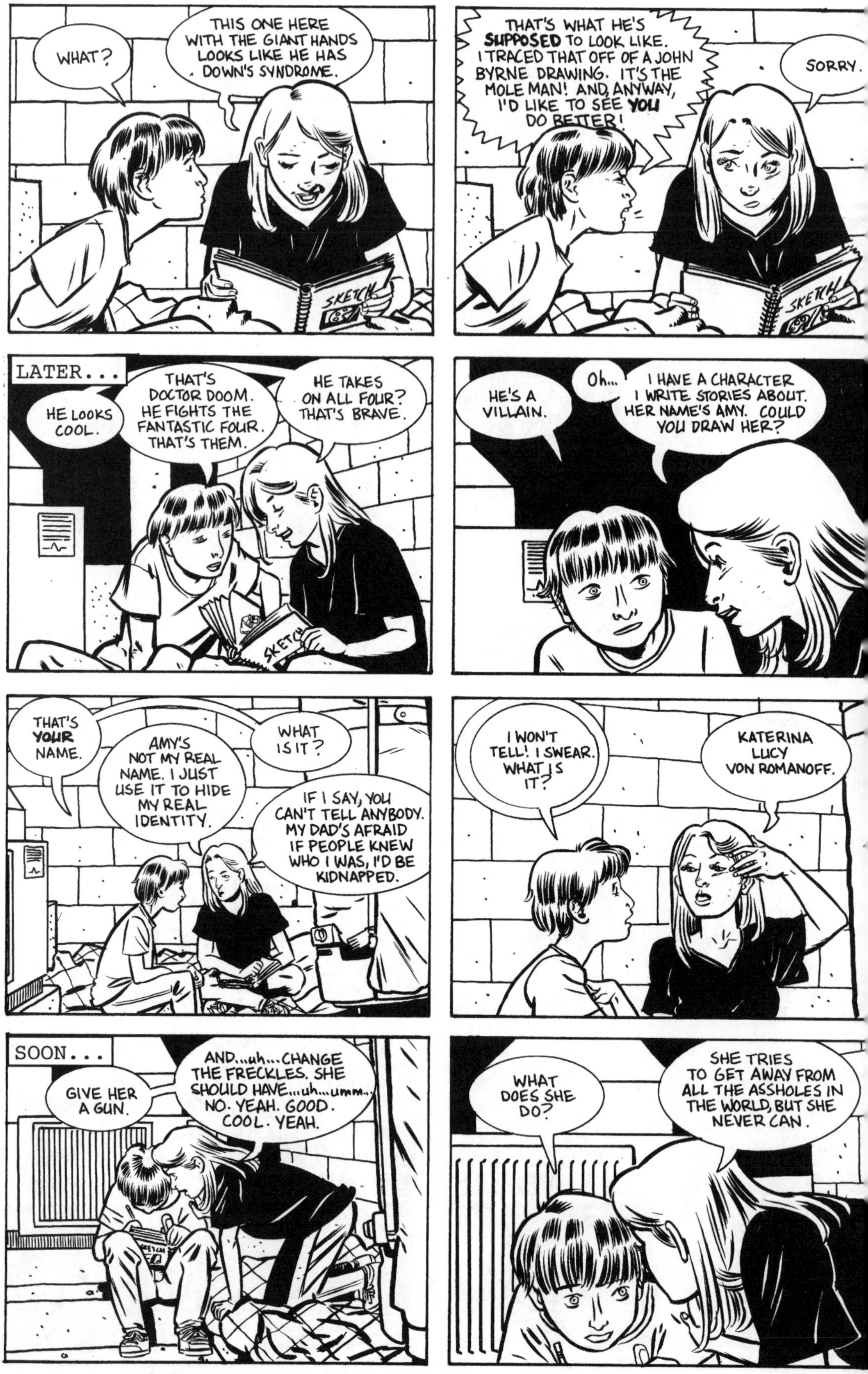
WHAT?
THIS ONE HERE WITH THE GIANT HANDS LOOKS LIKE HE HAS DOWN'S SYNDROME.
THAT'S WHAT HE'S SUPPOSED TO LOOK LIKE. I TRACED THAT OFF OF A JOHN BYRNE DRAWING. IT'S THE MOLE MAN! AND, ANYWAY, I'D LIKE TO SEE YOU DO BETTER!
SORRY.
SKETCH
LATER...
HE LOOKS COOL.
THAT'S DOCTOR DOOM. HE FIGHTS THE FANTASTIC FOUR. THAT'S THEM.
HE TAKES ON ALL FOUR? THAT'S BRAVE.
HE'S A VILLAIN.
Oh...
I HAVE A CHARACTER I WRITE STORIES ABOUT. HER NAME'S AMY. COULD YOU DRAW HER?
THAT'S YOUR NAME.
AMY'S NOT MY REAL NAME. I JUST USE IT TO HIDE MY REAL IDENTITY.
WHAT IS IT?
IF I SAY, YOU CAN'T TELL ANYBODY. MY DAD'S AFRAID IF PEOPLE KNEW WHO I WAS, I'D BE KIDNAPPED.
I WON'T TELL! I SWEAR. WHAT IS IT?
KATERINA LUCY VON ROMANOFF.
SOON...
GIVE HER A GUN.
AND...uh...CHANGE THE FRECKLES. SHE SHOULD HAVE...uh...umm... NO. YEAH. GOOD. COOL. YEAH.
WHAT DOES SHE DO?
SHE TRIES TO GET AWAY FROM ALL THE ASSHOLES IN THE WORLD, BUT SHE NEVER CAN.

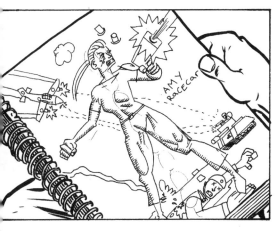

SHOULD I MAKE THE GUN BIGGER?

COLOR HER BOOTS IN BLACK.

HEY! WE SHOULD MAKE OUR OWN COMIC. WE COULD GET RICH.

NO WAY! I WOULDN'T MAKE MY STORIES INTO COMICS. THEY'RE TOO IMPORTANT. WORDS ARE BEAUTIFUL. THEY REVEAL THE CHARACTER'S INNER SOUL. COMICS ARE JUST SILLY.

ARE NOT.

DON'T BE STUPID. COMICS HAVE PICTURES.

SO?

PICTURES ARE FOR ILLITERATE MORONS.

COMICS ARE JUST AS GOOD AS BOOKS!

IN YOUR COMICS, FOUR GOOD GUYS GANG UP ON ONE BAD GUY, WHO ISN'T EVEN AS POWERFUL AS ONE OF THEM.

THAT'S CUZ HE'S AN EVIL GENIUS. HE'S SMARTER THAN THEY ARE!

I REST MY CASE.

YOU DO NOT! YOU CAN'T DO THAT! COMICS ARE BETTER THAN BOOKS. THEY—THEY ARE!!!

YOU DON' KNOW WHA TALKING YOU DO

HEY!

YOU'RE SUCH A KID!

Still, he was giving her refuge, so she lightened up on him and made him happy by making a big deal out of his crude drawing.

21

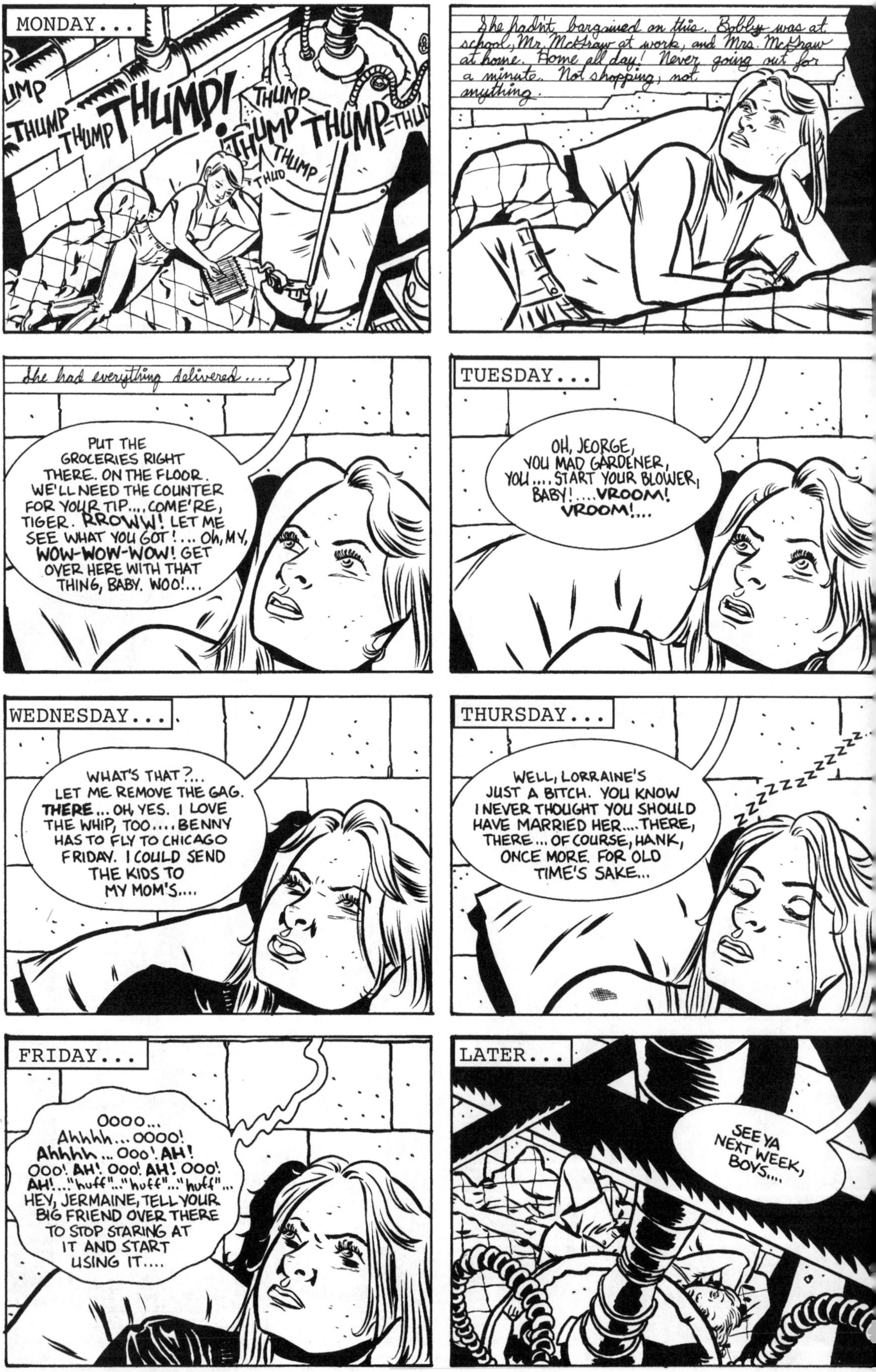
MONDAY...
THUMP THUMP THUMP THUMP! THUMP THUMP THUMP THUMP THUMP THUD THUD
She hadn't bargained on this. Bobby was at school, Mr. McGraw at work, and Mrs. McGraw at home. Home all day! Never going out for a minute. Not shopping, not anything.
She had everything delivered....
PUT THE GROCERIES RIGHT THERE. ON THE FLOOR. WE'LL NEED THE COUNTER FOR YOUR TIP.... COME'RE, TIGER. RROWW! LET ME SEE WHAT YOU GOT!... OH, MY, WOW-WOW-WOW! GET OVER HERE WITH THAT THING, BABY. WOO!...
TUESDAY...
OH, JEORGE, YOU MAD GARDENER, YOU.... START YOUR BLOWER, BABY!....VROOM! VROOM!...
WEDNESDAY...
WHAT'S THAT?... LET ME REMOVE THE GAG. THERE... OH, YES. I LOVE THE WHIP, TOO.... BENNY HAS TO FLY TO CHICAGO FRIDAY. I COULD SEND THE KIDS TO MY MOM'S....
THURSDAY...
WELL, LORRAINE'S JUST A BITCH. YOU KNOW I NEVER THOUGHT YOU SHOULD HAVE MARRIED HER.... THERE, THERE... OF COURSE, HANK, ONCE MORE. FOR OLD TIME'S SAKE...
ZZZZZZZZZZZ...
FRIDAY...
OOOO... AHHHH... OOOO! AHHHH... OOO! AH! OOO! AH! OOO! AH! OOO! AH!..."HUFF"..."HUFF"..."HUFF"... HEY, JERMAINE, TELL YOUR BIG FRIEND OVER THERE TO STOP STARING AT IT AND START USING IT....
LATER...
SEE YA NEXT WEEK, BOYS....

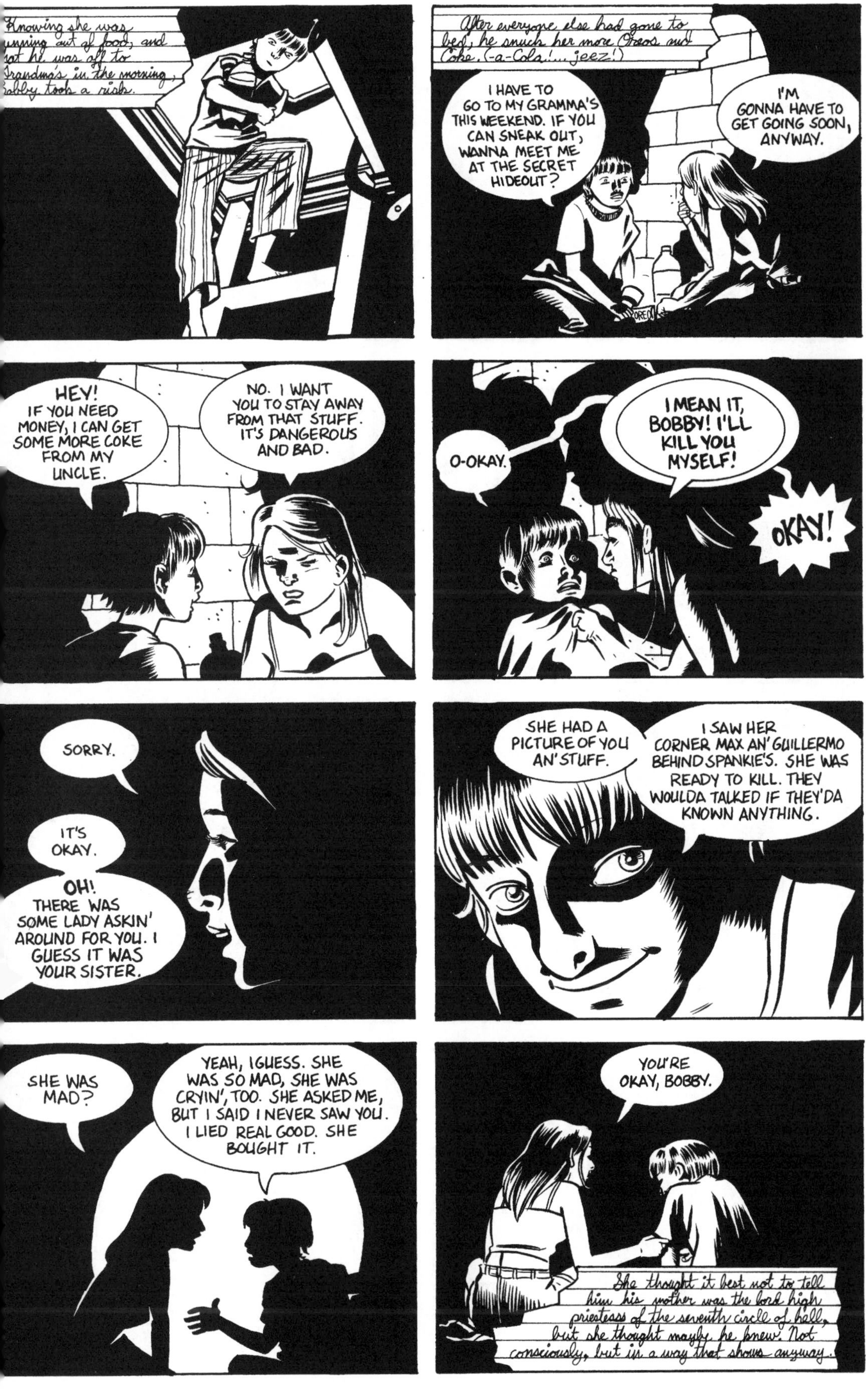
Knowing she was
unning out of food, and
hat he was off to
Grandma's in the morning,
obby took a risk.
After everyone else had gone to bed, he snuck her more Oreos and Coke. (-a-Cola!... jeez!)
I HAVE TO GO TO MY GRAMMA'S THIS WEEKEND. IF YOU CAN SNEAK OUT, WANNA MEET ME AT THE SECRET HIDEOUT?
I'M GONNA HAVE TO GET GOING SOON, ANYWAY.
OREO
HEY! IF YOU NEED MONEY, I CAN GET SOME MORE COKE FROM MY UNCLE.
NO. I WANT YOU TO STAY AWAY FROM THAT STUFF. IT'S DANGEROUS AND BAD.
O-OKAY.
I MEAN IT, BOBBY! I'LL KILL YOU MYSELF!
OKAY!
SORRY.
IT'S OKAY.
OH! THERE WAS SOME LADY ASKIN' AROUND FOR YOU. I GUESS IT WAS YOUR SISTER.
SHE HAD A PICTURE OF YOU AN' STUFF.
I SAW HER CORNER MAX AN' GUILLERMO BEHIND SPANKIE'S. SHE WAS READY TO KILL. THEY WOULDA TALKED IF THEY'DA KNOWN ANYTHING.
SHE WAS MAD?
YEAH, I GUESS. SHE WAS SO MAD, SHE WAS CRYIN', TOO. SHE ASKED ME, BUT I SAID I NEVER SAW YOU. I LIED REAL GOOD. SHE BOUGHT IT.
YOU'RE OKAY, BOBBY.
She thought it best not to tell him his mother was the lord high priestess of the seventh circle of hell, but she thought maybe he knew. Not consciously, but in a way that shows anyway.

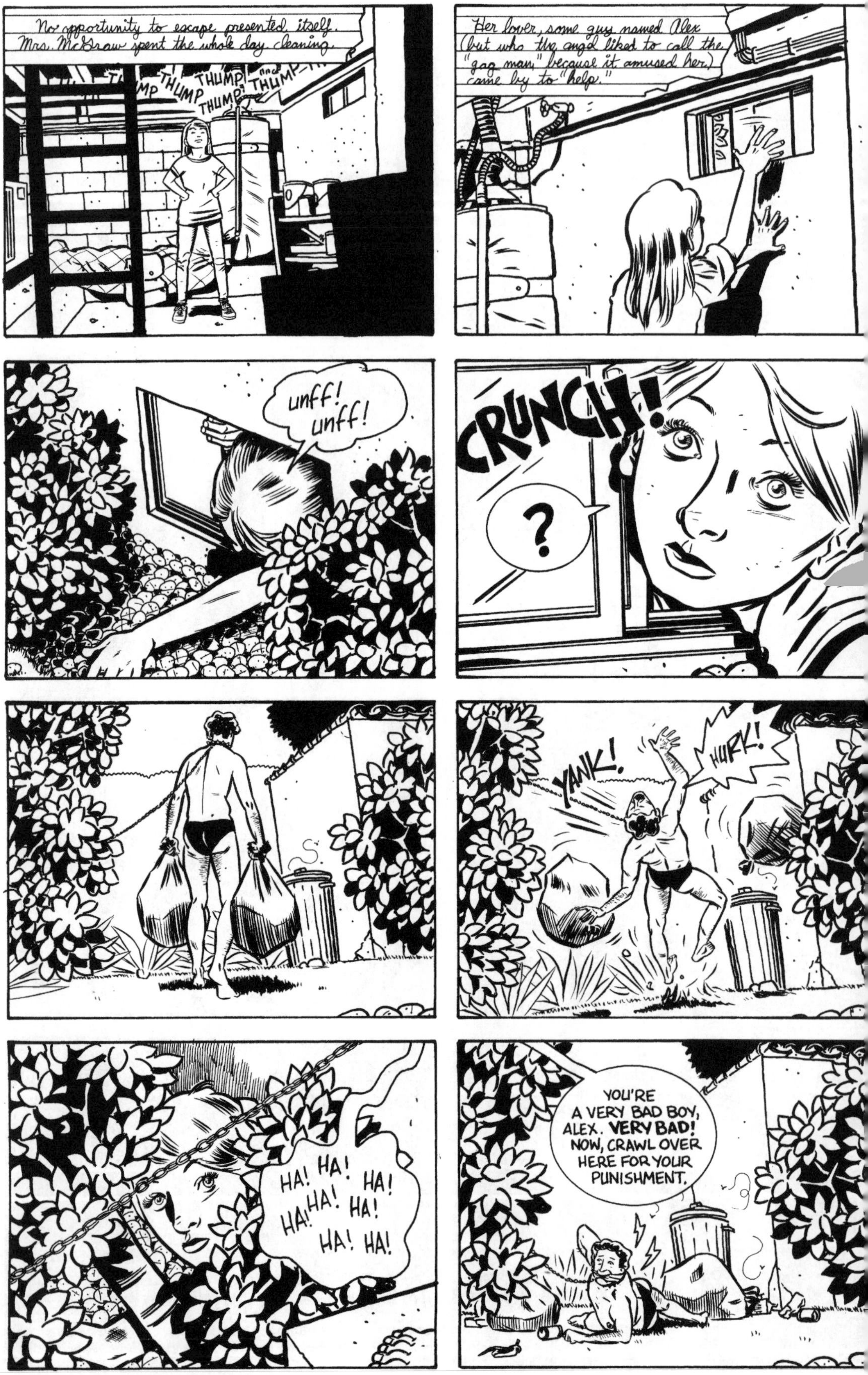
No opportunity to escape presented itself. Mrs. McGraw spent the whole day cleaning.
THUMP THUMP THUMP THUMP and THUMP
Her lover, some guy named Alex (but who the angel liked to call the "gag man," because it amused her) came by to "help."
unff! unff!
CRUNCH!
?
YANK!
HURK!
HA! HA! HA! HA! HA! HA! HA! HA!
YOU'RE A VERY BAD BOY, ALEX. VERY BAD! NOW, CRAWL OVER HERE FOR YOUR PUNISHMENT.

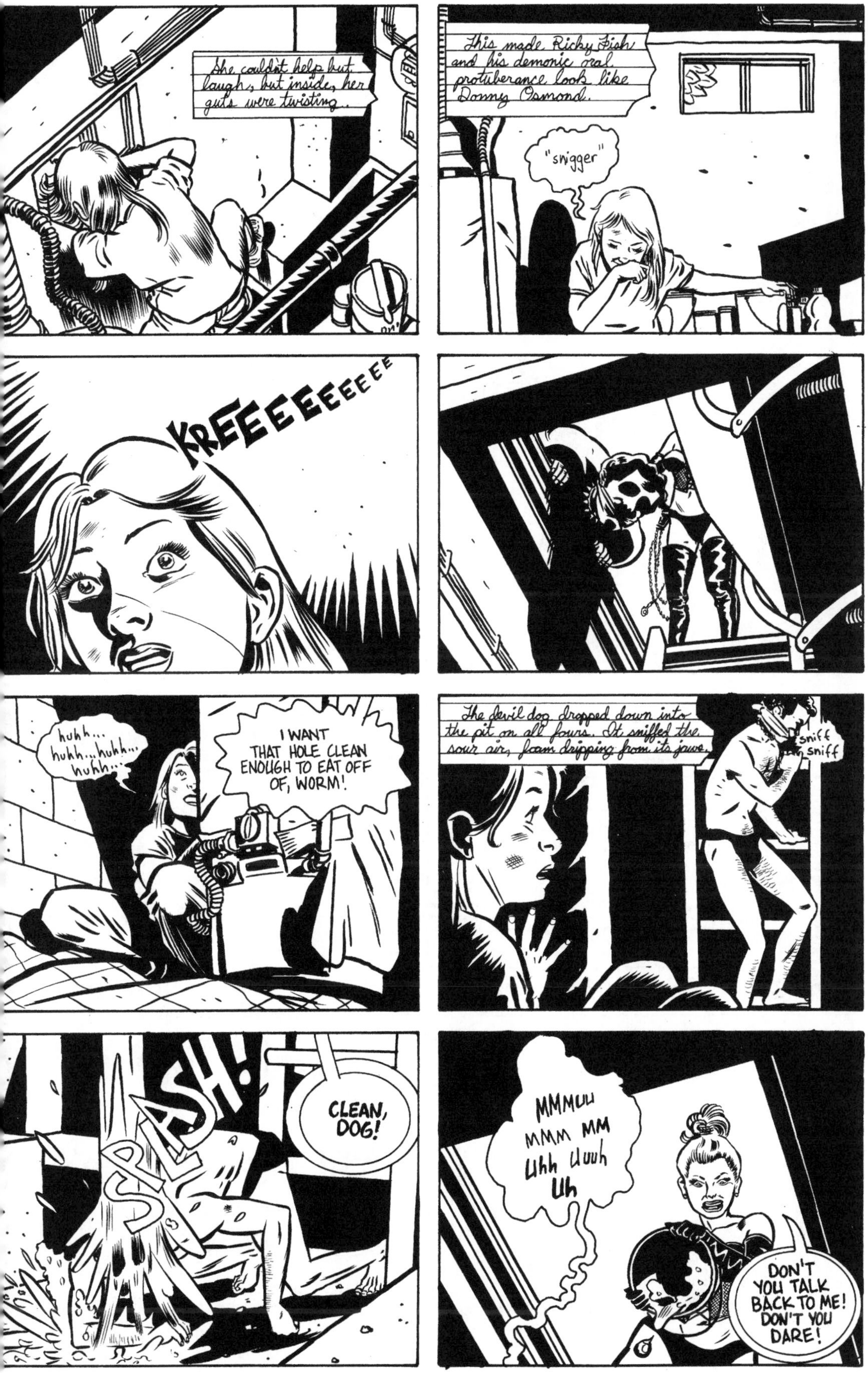
She couldn't help but laugh, but inside, her guts were twisting.
This made Ricky Fish and his demonic oral protuberance look like Donny Osmond.
"snigger"
KREEEEEEEEEE
huhh... huhh...huhh... huhh...
I WANT THAT HOLE CLEAN ENOUGH TO EAT OFF OF, WORM!
The devil dog dropped down into the pit on all fours. It sniffed the sour air, foam dripping from its jaws.
sniff sniff
SPLASH!
CLEAN, DOG!
MMMUU MMM MM Uhh Uuuh Uh
DON'T YOU TALK BACK TO ME! DON'T YOU DARE!

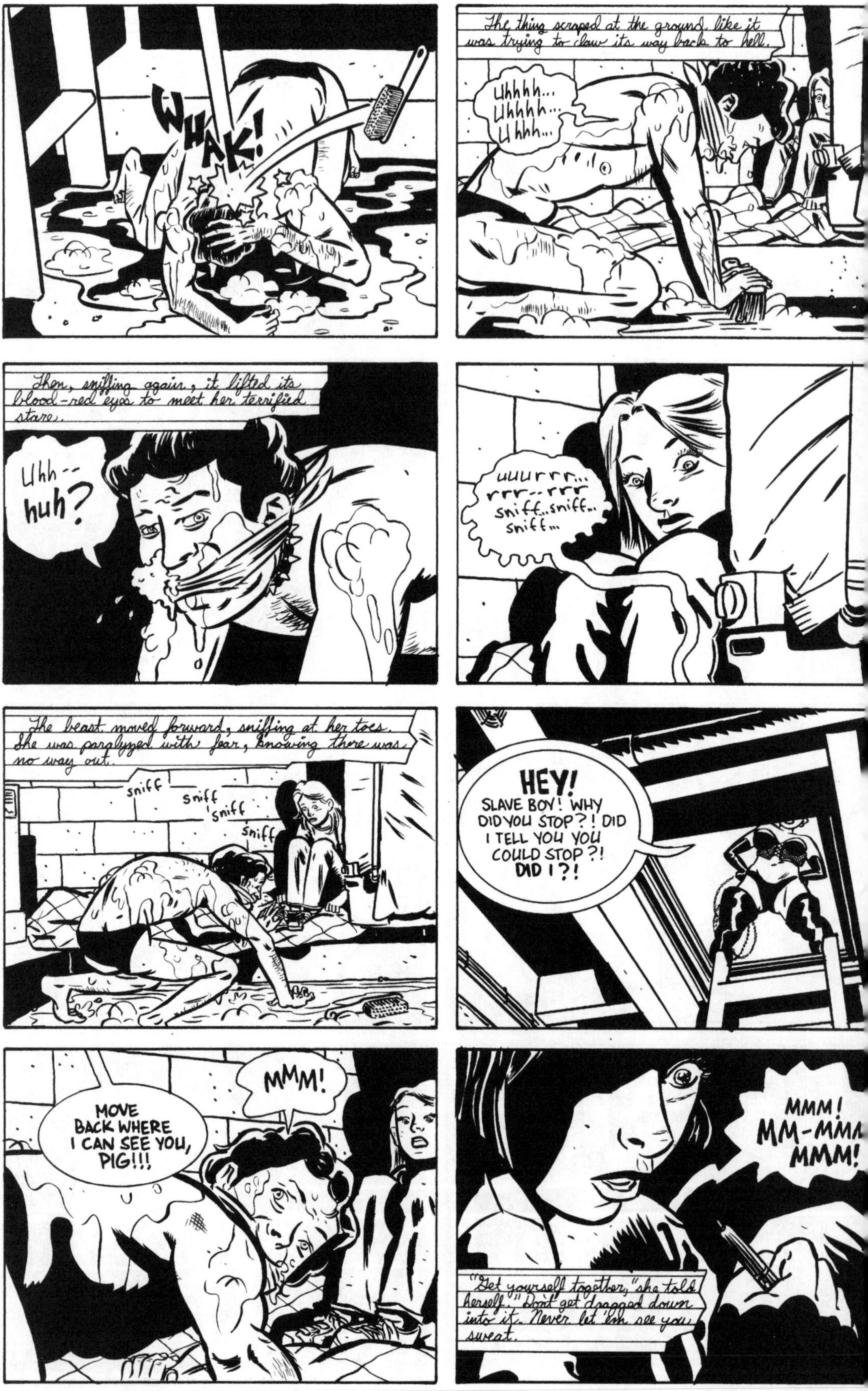
WHAK!
The thing scraped at the ground like it was trying to claw its way back to hell.
Uhhhh... Uhhhh... Uhhh...
Then, sniffing again, it lifted its blood-red eyes to meet her terrified stare.
Uhh-- huh?
uuurrr... rrr--rrr sniff...sniff... sniff...
The beast moved forward, sniffing at her toes. She was paralyzed with fear, knowing there was no way out.
sniff
sniff
sniff
sniff
HEY! SLAVE BOY! WHY DID YOU STOP?! DID I TELL YOU YOU COULD STOP?! DID I?!
MOVE BACK WHERE I CAN SEE YOU, PIG!!!
MMM!
MMM! MM-MMM MMM!
"Get yourself together," she told herself. "Don't get dragged down into it. Never let 'em see you sweat.

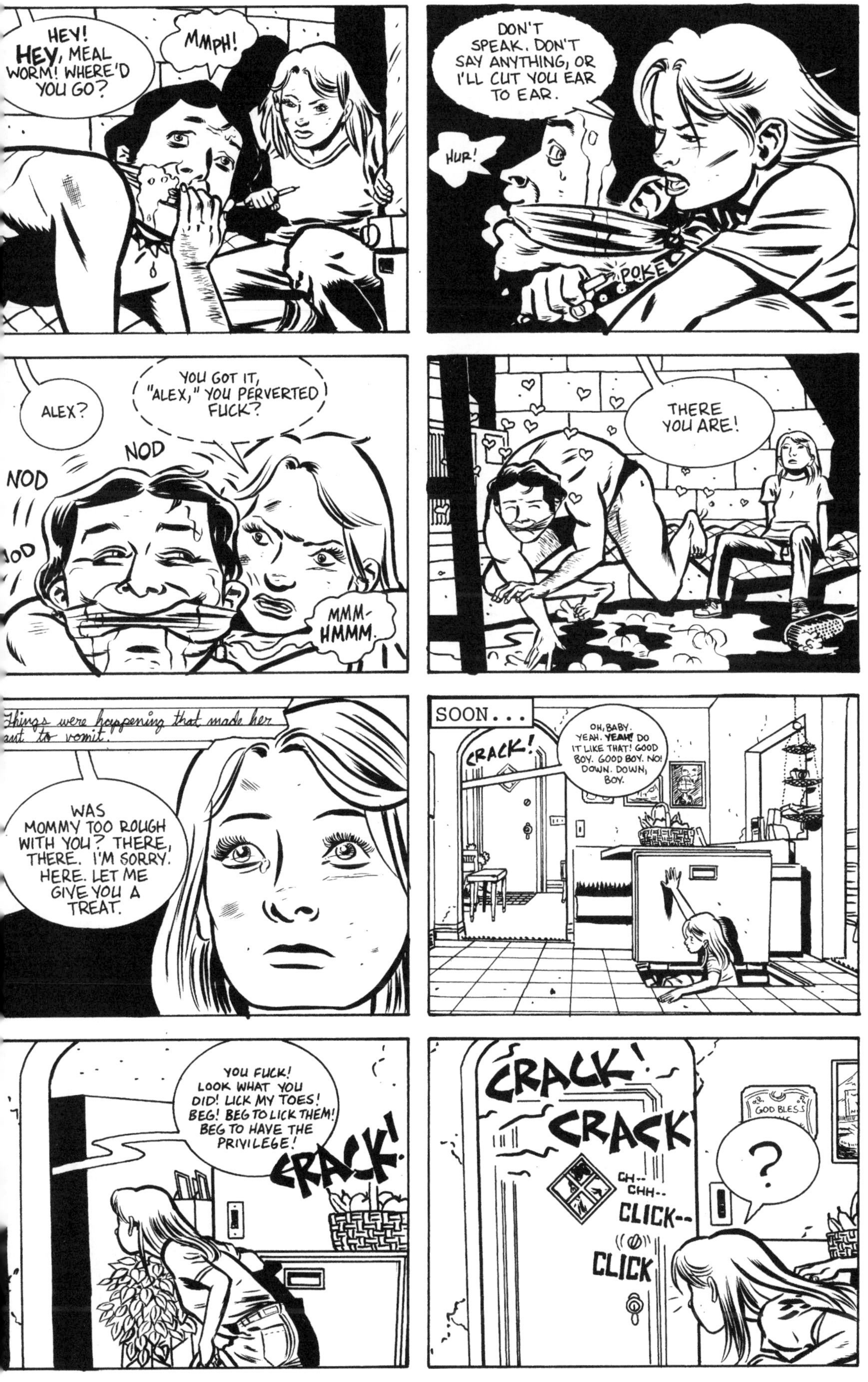
HEY! HEY, MEAL WORM! WHERE'D YOU GO?
MMPH!
DON'T SPEAK. DON'T SAY ANYTHING, OR I'LL CUT YOU EAR TO EAR.
HUR!
POKE
ALEX?
YOU GOT IT, "ALEX," YOU PERVERTED FUCK?
NOD
NOD
MMM-HMMM.
THERE YOU ARE!
hings were happening that made her
ant to vomit.
WAS MOMMY TOO ROUGH WITH YOU? THERE, THERE. I'M SORRY. HERE. LET ME GIVE YOU A TREAT.
SOON...
CRACK!
OH, BABY. YEAH. YEAH! DO IT LIKE THAT! GOOD BOY. GOOD BOY. NO! DOWN. DOWN, BOY.
YOU FUCK! LOOK WHAT YOU DID! LICK MY TOES! BEG! BEG TO LICK THEM! BEG TO HAVE THE PRIVILEGE!
CRACK!
CRACK!
CRACK
CH-- CHH--
CLICK--
CLICK
GOD BLESS
?

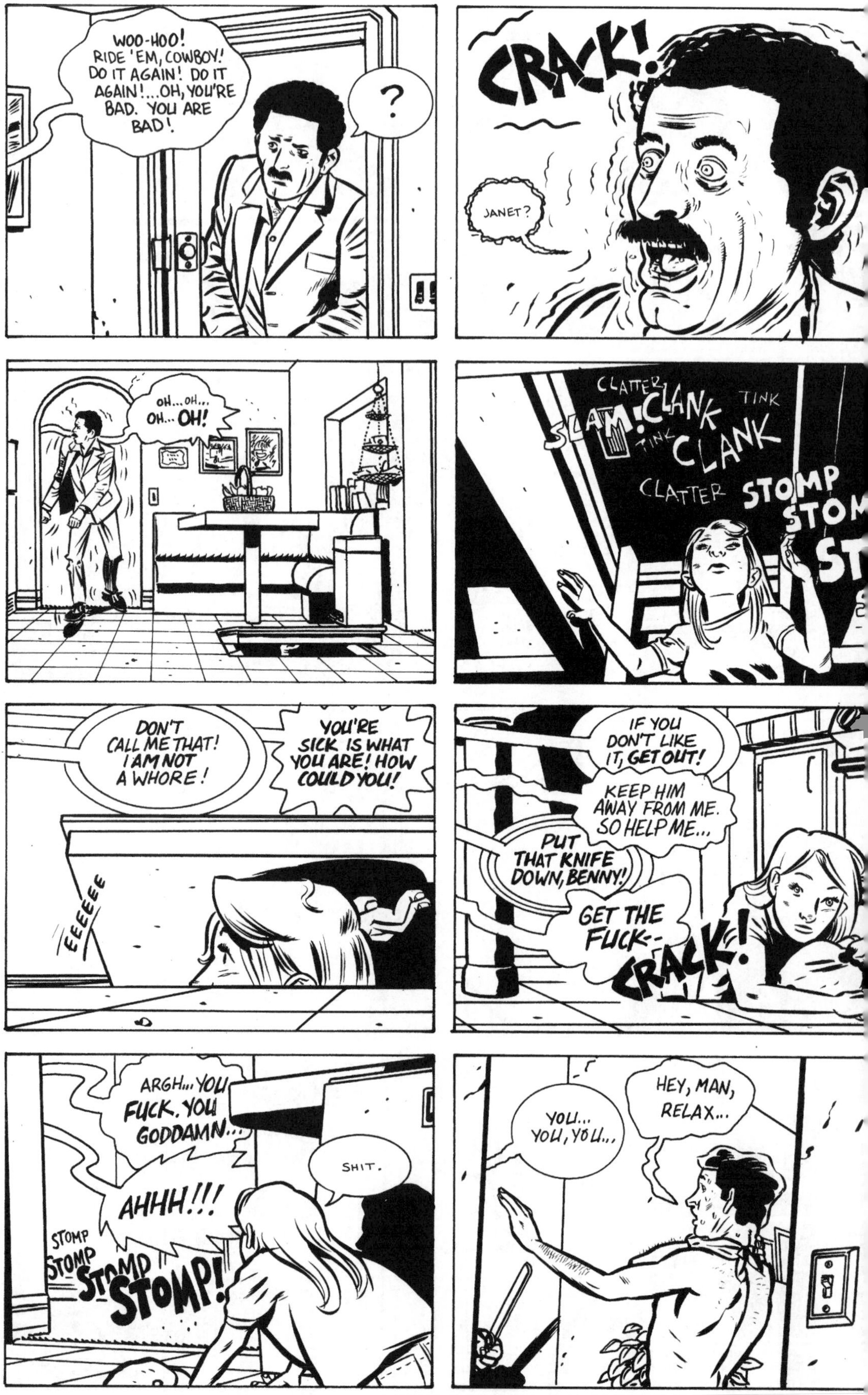
WOO-HOO! RIDE 'EM, COWBOY! DO IT AGAIN! DO IT AGAIN!...OH, YOU'RE BAD. YOU ARE BAD!
?
CRACK!
JANET?
OH...OH... OH... OH!
CLATTER
SLAM!
CLANK
TINK
TINK
CLANK
CLATTER
STOMP
DON'T CALL ME THAT! I AM NOT A WHORE!
YOU'RE SICK IS WHAT YOU ARE! HOW COULD YOU!
EEEEEEE
IF YOU DON'T LIKE IT, GET OUT!
KEEP HIM AWAY FROM ME. SO HELP ME...
PUT THAT KNIFE DOWN, BENNY!
GET THE FUCK-
CRACK!
ARGH... YOU FUCK. YOU GODDAMN...
AHHH!!!
SHIT.
STOMP
STOMP
STOMP
STOMP!
YOU... YOU, YOU...
HEY, MAN, RELAX...

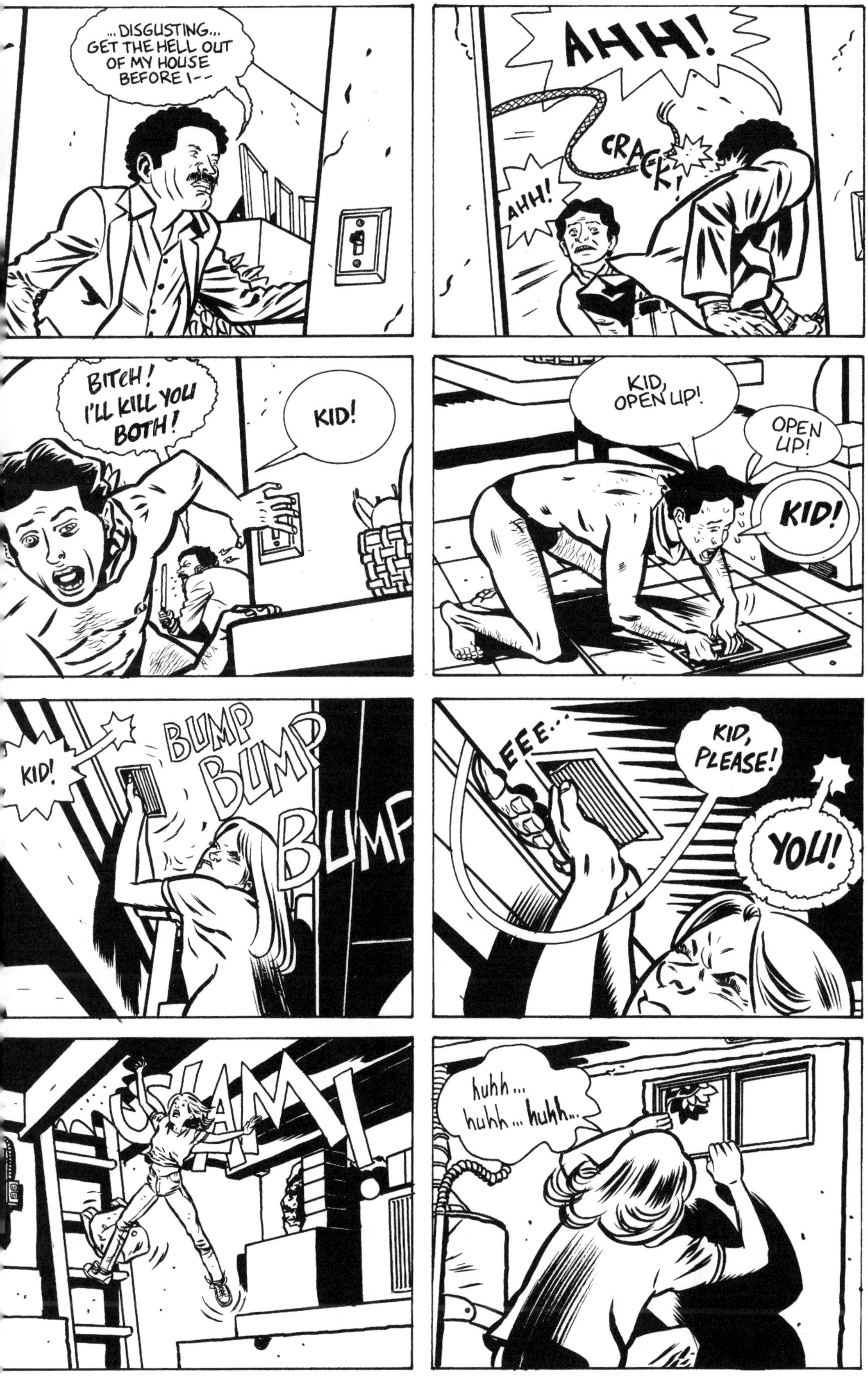
...DISGUSTING... GET THE HELL OUT OF MY HOUSE BEFORE I--
AHH!
CRACK!
AHH!
BITCH! I'LL KILL YOU BOTH!
KID!
KID, OPEN UP!
OPEN UP!
KID!
KID!
BUMP
BUMP
BUMP
EEE...
KID, PLEASE!
YOU!
SLAM!
huhh... huhh... huhh...

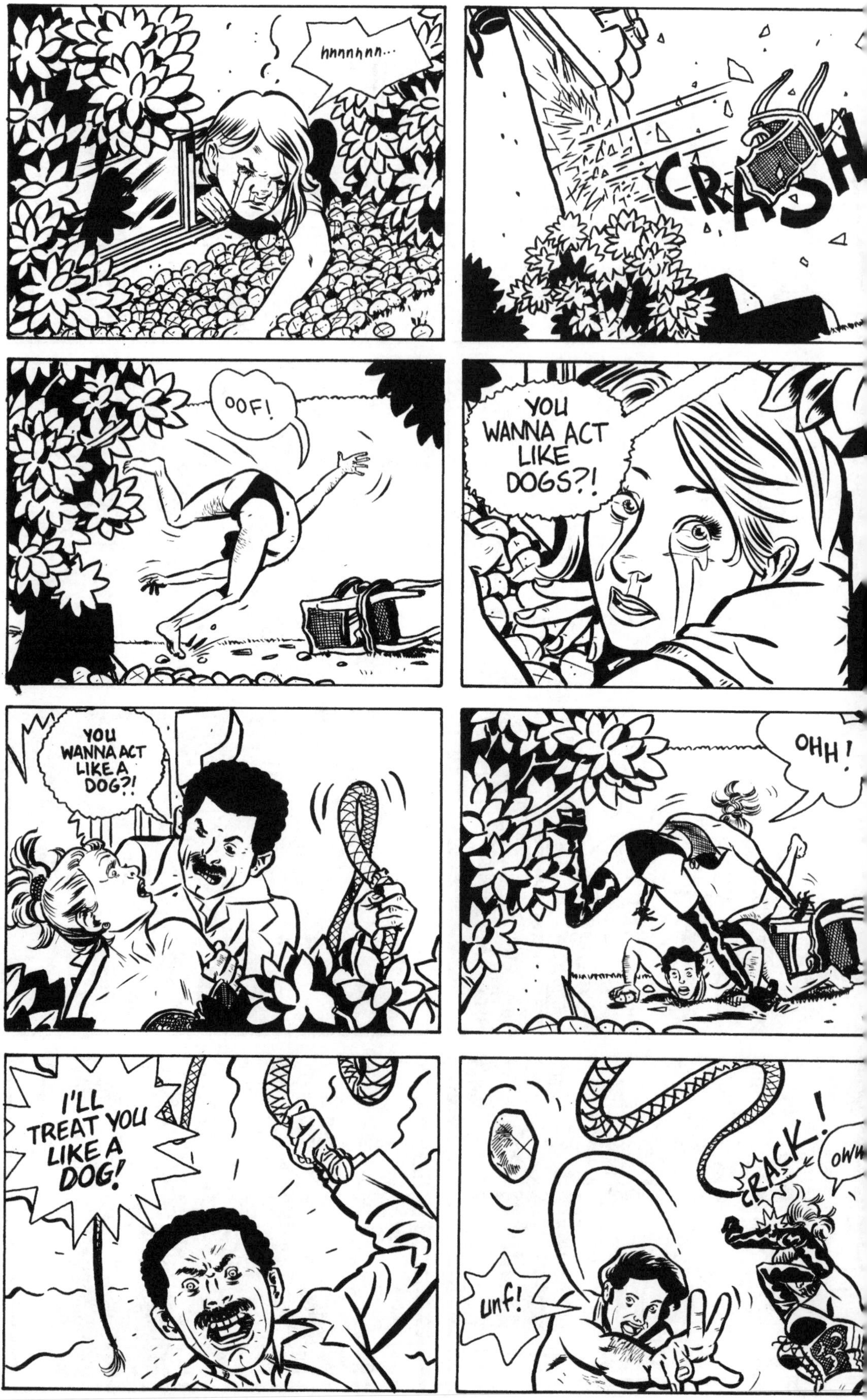
hnnnhnn...
CRASH
OOF!
YOU WANNA ACT LIKE DOGS?!
YOU WANNA ACT LIKE A DOG?!
OHH!
I'LL TREAT YOU LIKE A DOG!
CRACK!
unf!

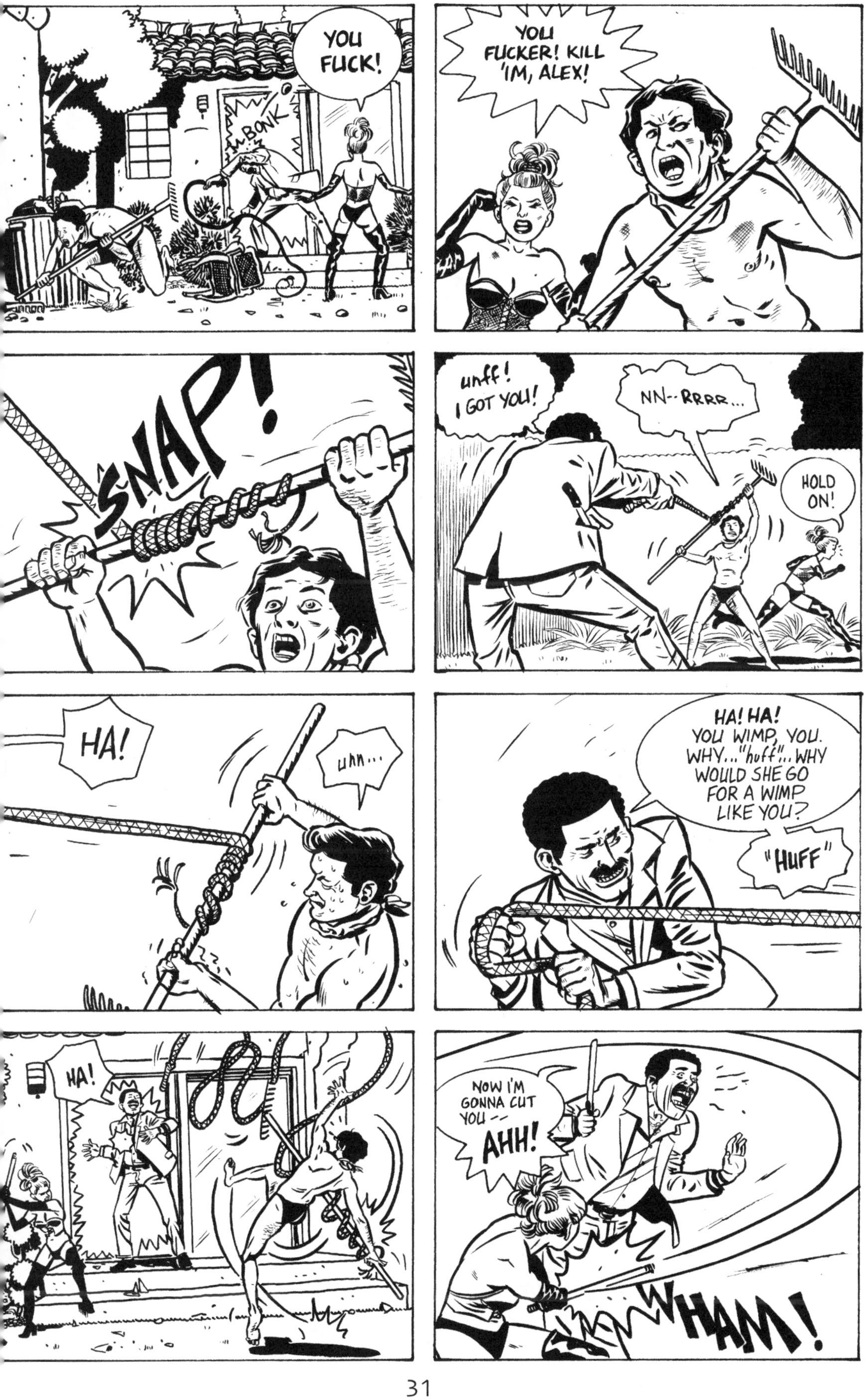
YOU FUCK!
BONK
YOU FUCKER! KILL 'IM, ALEX!
SNAP!
unff! I GOT YOU!
NN--RRRR...
HOLD ON!
HA!
uhn...
HA! HA! YOU WIMP, YOU. WHY..."huff"...WHY WOULD SHE GO FOR A WIMP LIKE YOU?
"HUFF"
HA!
NOW I'M GONNA CUT YOU --
AHH!
WHAM!

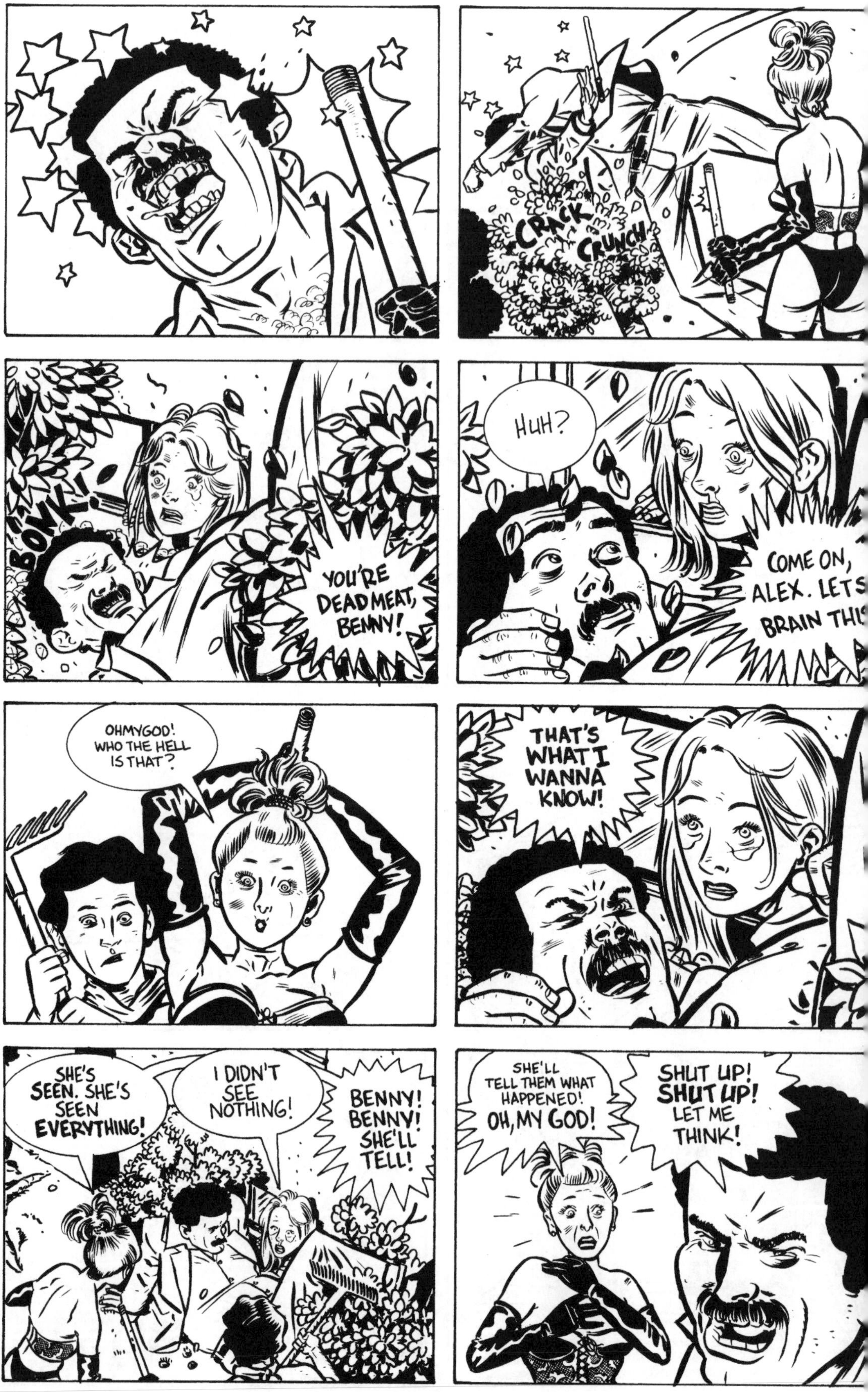
CRACK
CRUNCH
BONK!
YOU'RE DEADMEAT, BENNY!
HUH?
COME ON, ALEX. LETS BRAIN THI
OHMYGOD! WHO THE HELL IS THAT?
THAT'S WHAT I WANNA KNOW!
SHE'S SEEN. SHE'S SEEN EVERYTHING!
I DIDN'T SEE NOTHING!
BENNY! BENNY! SHE'LL TELL!
SHE'LL TELL THEM WHAT HAPPENED! OH, MY GOD!
SHUT UP! SHUT UP! LET ME THINK!

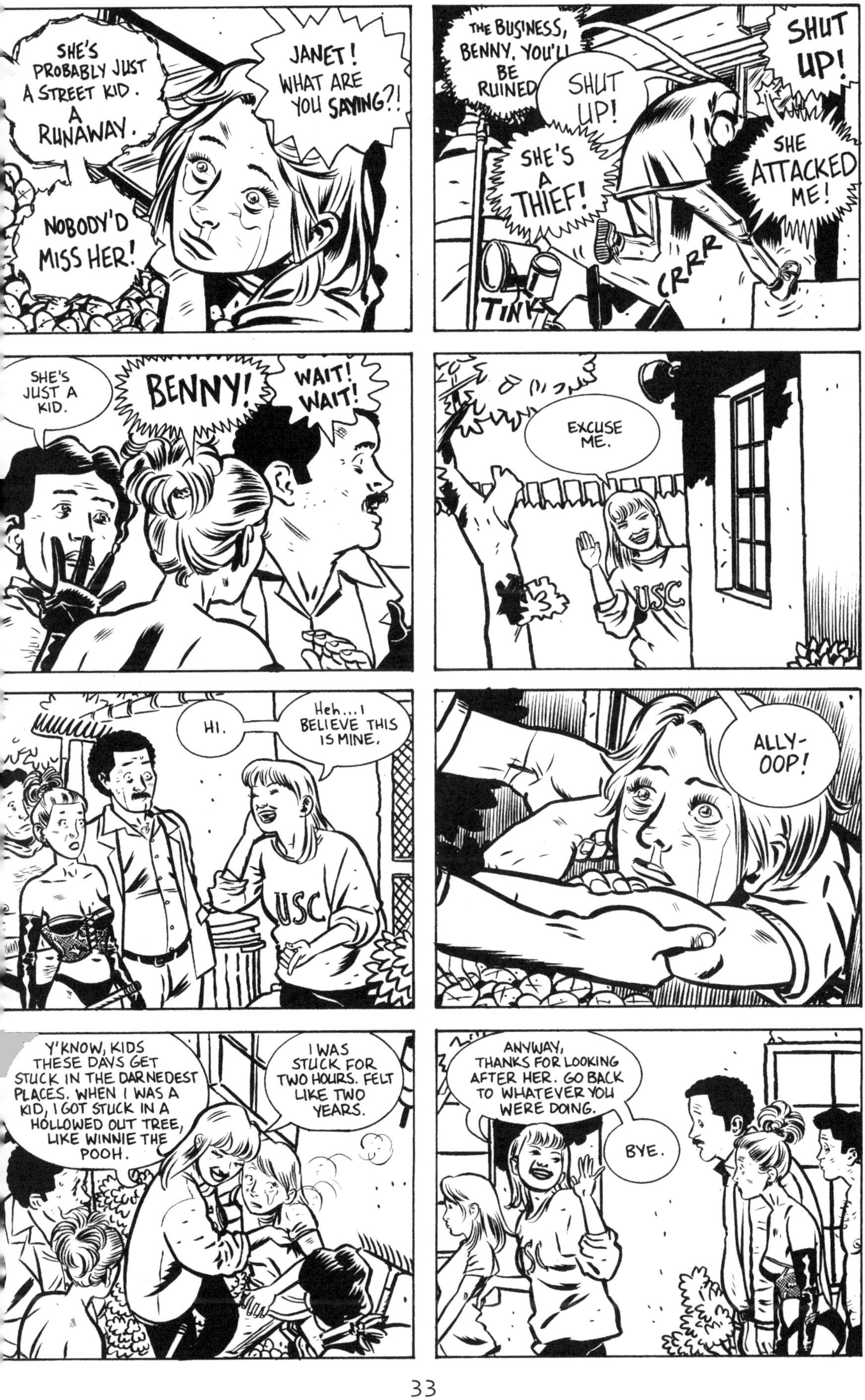
SHE'S PROBABLY JUST A STREET KID. A RUNAWAY.
NOBODY'D MISS HER!
JANET! WHAT ARE YOU SAYING?!
THE BUSINESS, BENNY. YOU'LL BE RUINED
SHUT UP!
SHE'S A THIEF!
SHUT UP!
SHE ATTACKED ME!
CRRR
TINK
SHE'S JUST A KID.
BENNY!
WAIT! WAIT!
EXCUSE ME.
HI.
Heh... I BELIEVE THIS IS MINE.
USC
ALLY-OOP!
Y'KNOW, KIDS THESE DAYS GET STUCK IN THE DARNEDEST PLACES. WHEN I WAS A KID, I GOT STUCK IN A HOLLOWED OUT TREE, LIKE WINNIE THE POOH.
I WAS STUCK FOR TWO HOURS. FELT LIKE TWO YEARS.
ANYWAY, THANKS FOR LOOKING AFTER HER. GO BACK TO WHATEVER YOU WERE DOING.
BYE.

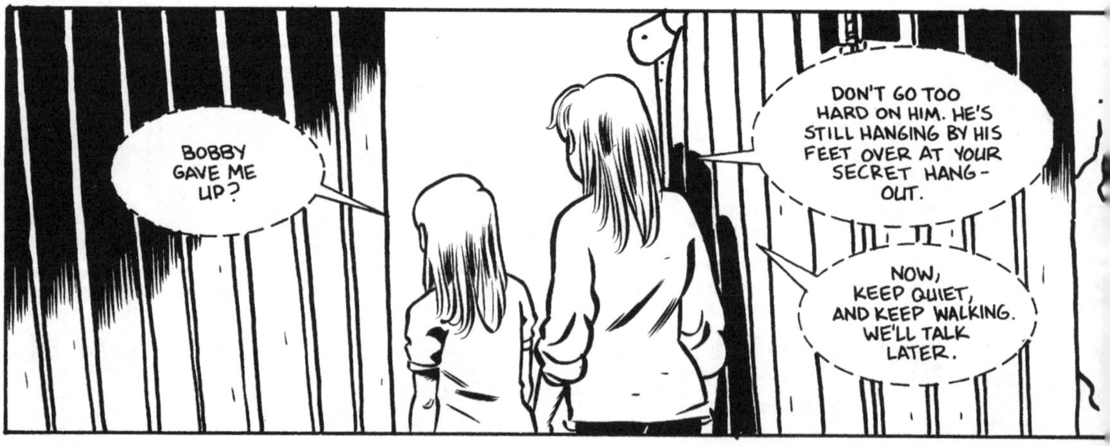
BOBBY GAVE ME UP?
DON'T GO TOO HARD ON HIM. HE'S STILL HANGING BY HIS FEET OVER AT YOUR SECRET HANG-OUT.
NOW, KEEP QUIET, AND KEEP WALKING. WE'LL TALK LATER.

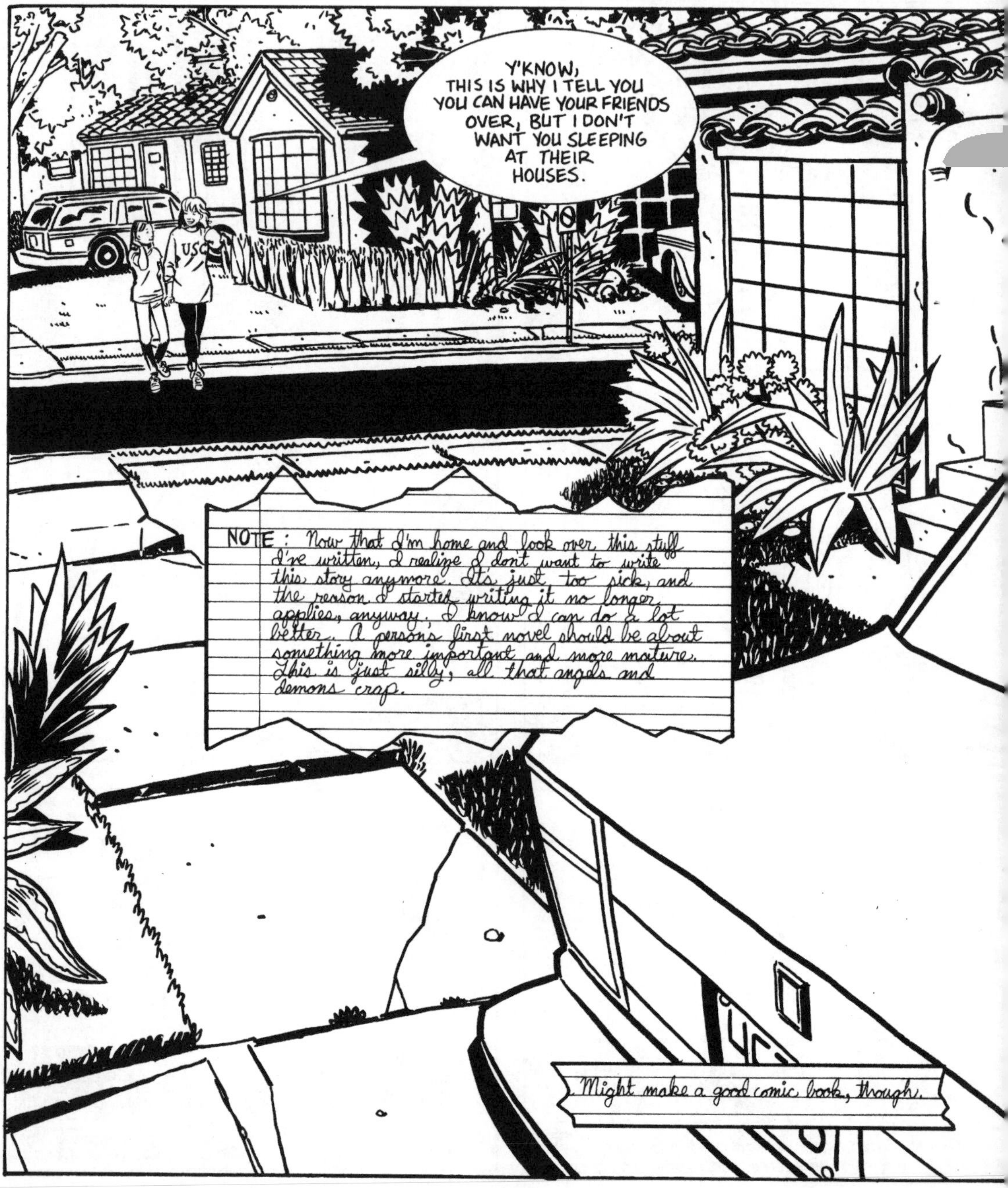
Y'KNOW, THIS IS WHY I TELL YOU YOU CAN HAVE YOUR FRIENDS OVER, BUT I DON'T WANT YOU SLEEPING AT THEIR HOUSES.
USC
NOTE: Now that I'm home and look over this stuff I've written, I realize I don't want to write this story anymore. It's just too sick, and the reason I started writing it no longer applies, anyway. I know I can do a lot better. A person's first novel should be about something more important and more mature. This is just silly, all that angels and demons crap.
Might make a good comic book, though.



THE END..

# 2

## "TWO-WEEK VACATION"

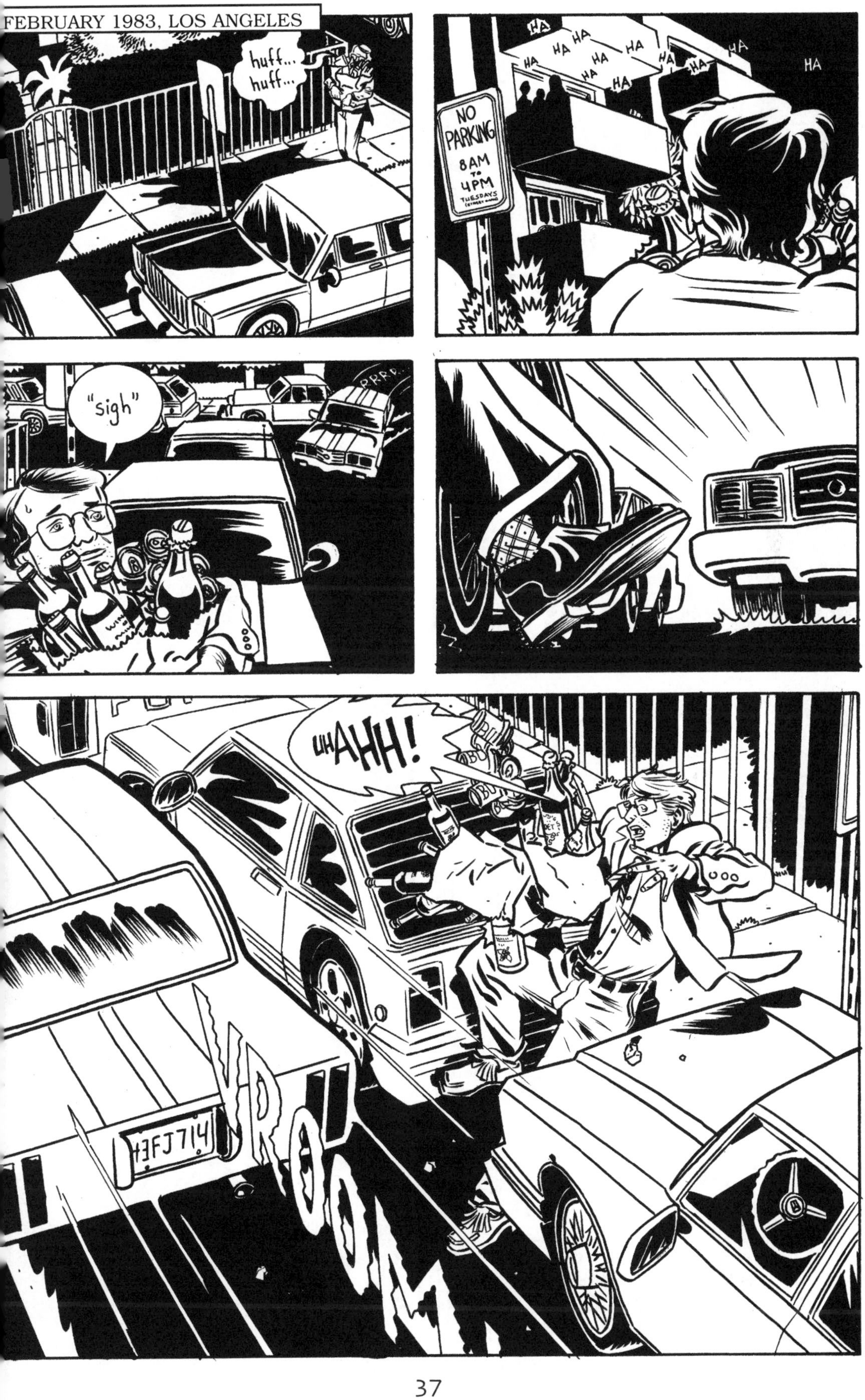
FEBRUARY 1983, LOS ANGELES
huff... huff...
HA HA HA HA HA HA HA HA HA HA HA HA
NO PARKING 8AM to 4PM TUESDAYS
"sigh"
PRRR
UHAHH!
VROOM

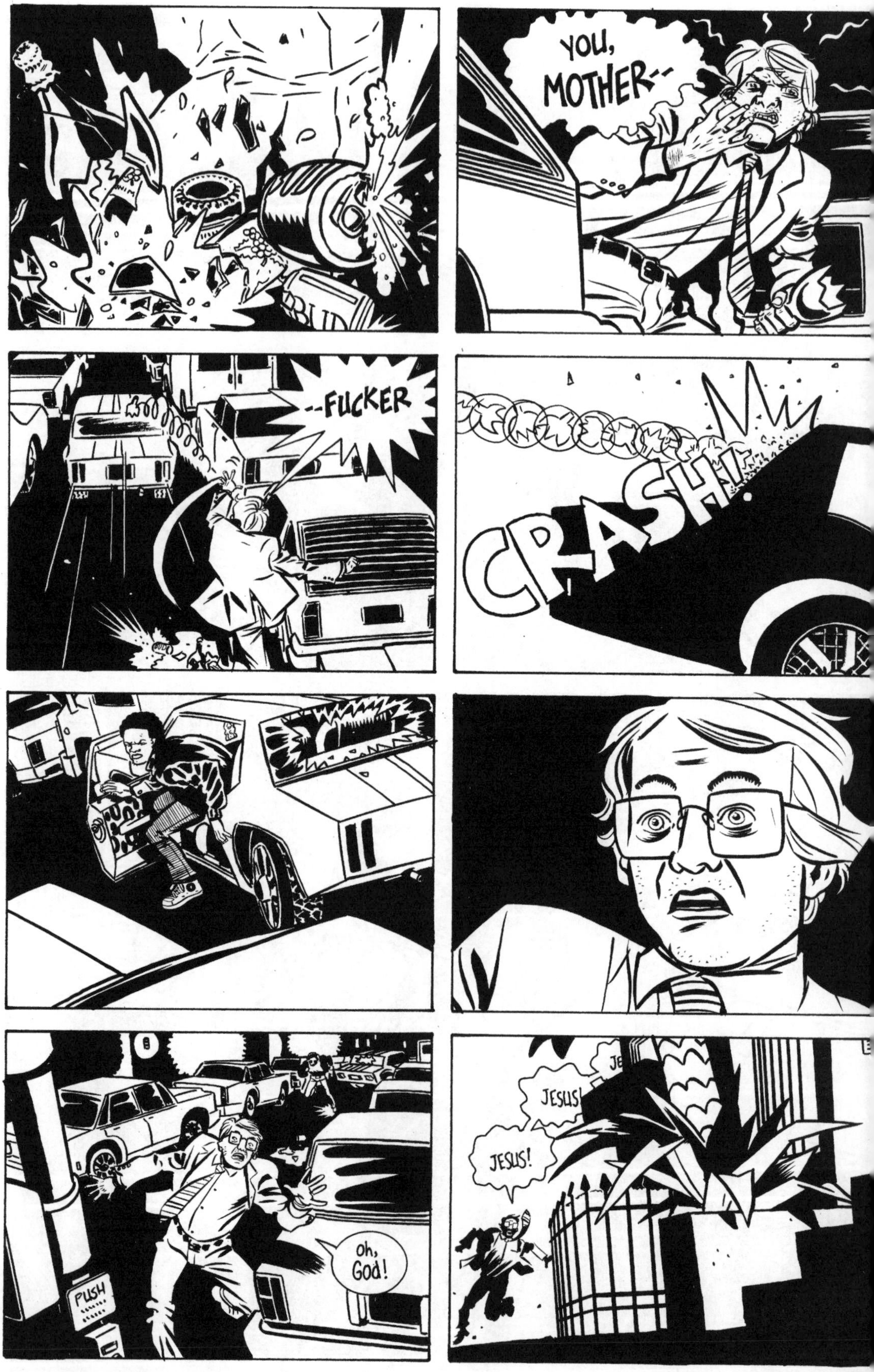
YOU, MOTHER--
--FUCKER
CRASH!
PUSH
Oh, God!
JESUS!
JESUS!

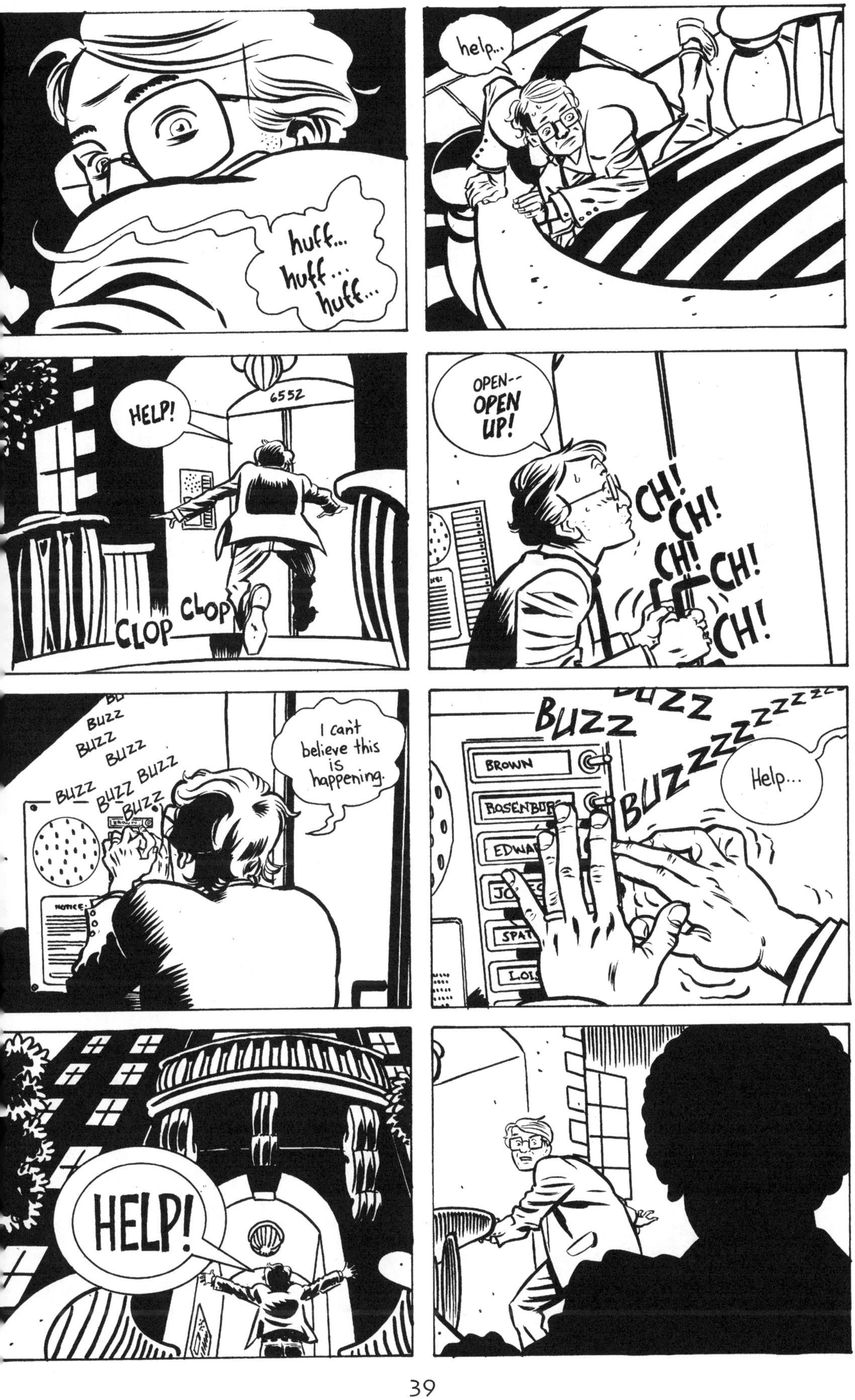
huff... huff... huff...
help...
HELP!
6552
CLOP CLOP
OPEN-- OPEN UP!
CH! CH! CH! CH! CH!
BUZZ BUZZ BUZZ BUZZ BUZZ BUZZ BUZZ
I can't believe this is happening.
BUZZ BUZZ BUZZZZZZZZZ
Help...
BROWN
ROSENB
HELP!

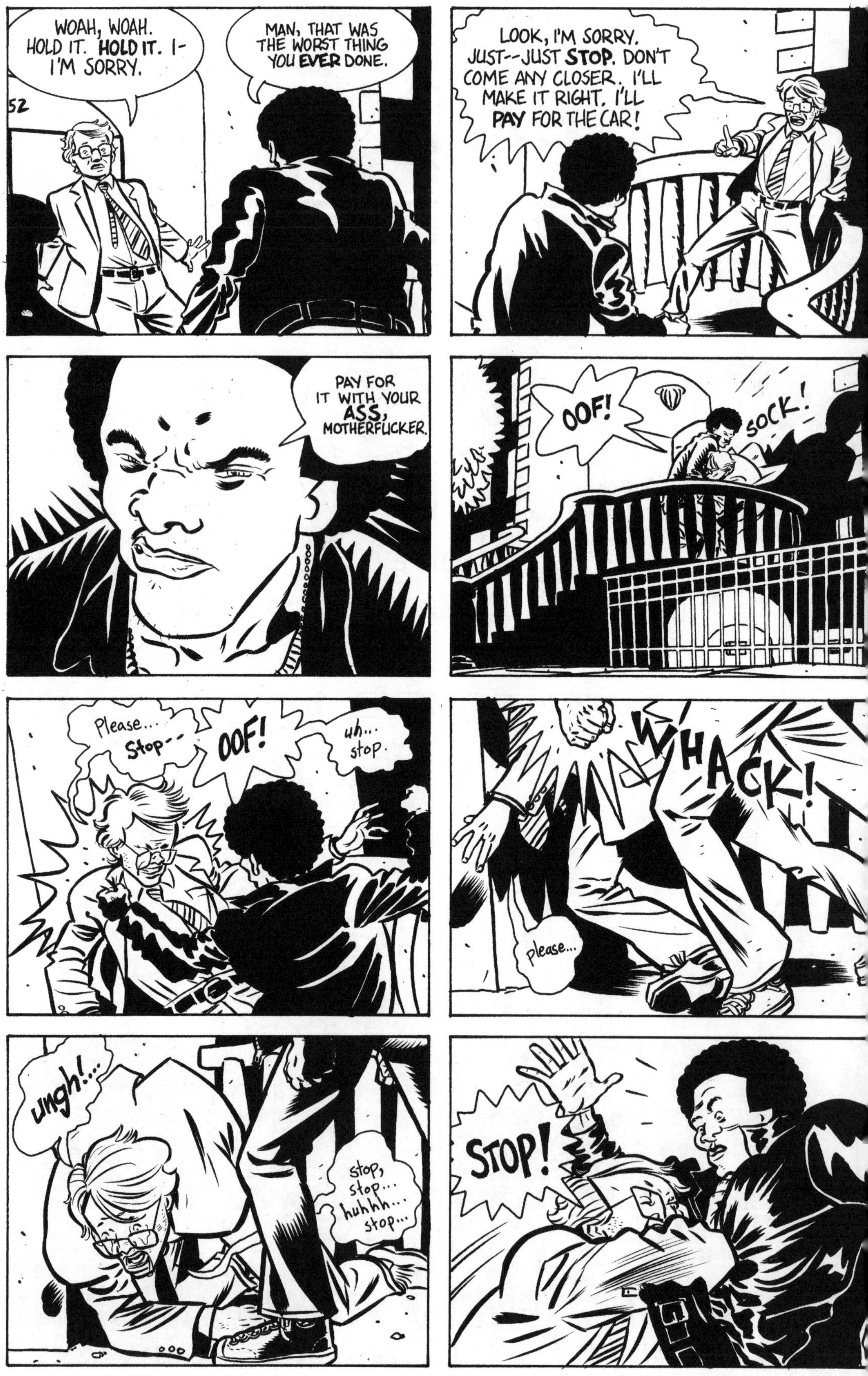
WOAH, WOAH. HOLD IT. HOLD IT. I- I'M SORRY.
MAN, THAT WAS THE WORST THING YOU EVER DONE.
52
LOOK, I'M SORRY. JUST--JUST STOP. DON'T COME ANY CLOSER. I'LL MAKE IT RIGHT. I'LL PAY FOR THE CAR!
PAY FOR IT WITH YOUR ASS, MOTHERFUCKER.
OOF!
SOCK!
Please... Stop--
OOF!
uh... stop.
WHACK!
please...
ungh!...
stop, stop... huhhh... stop...
STOP!

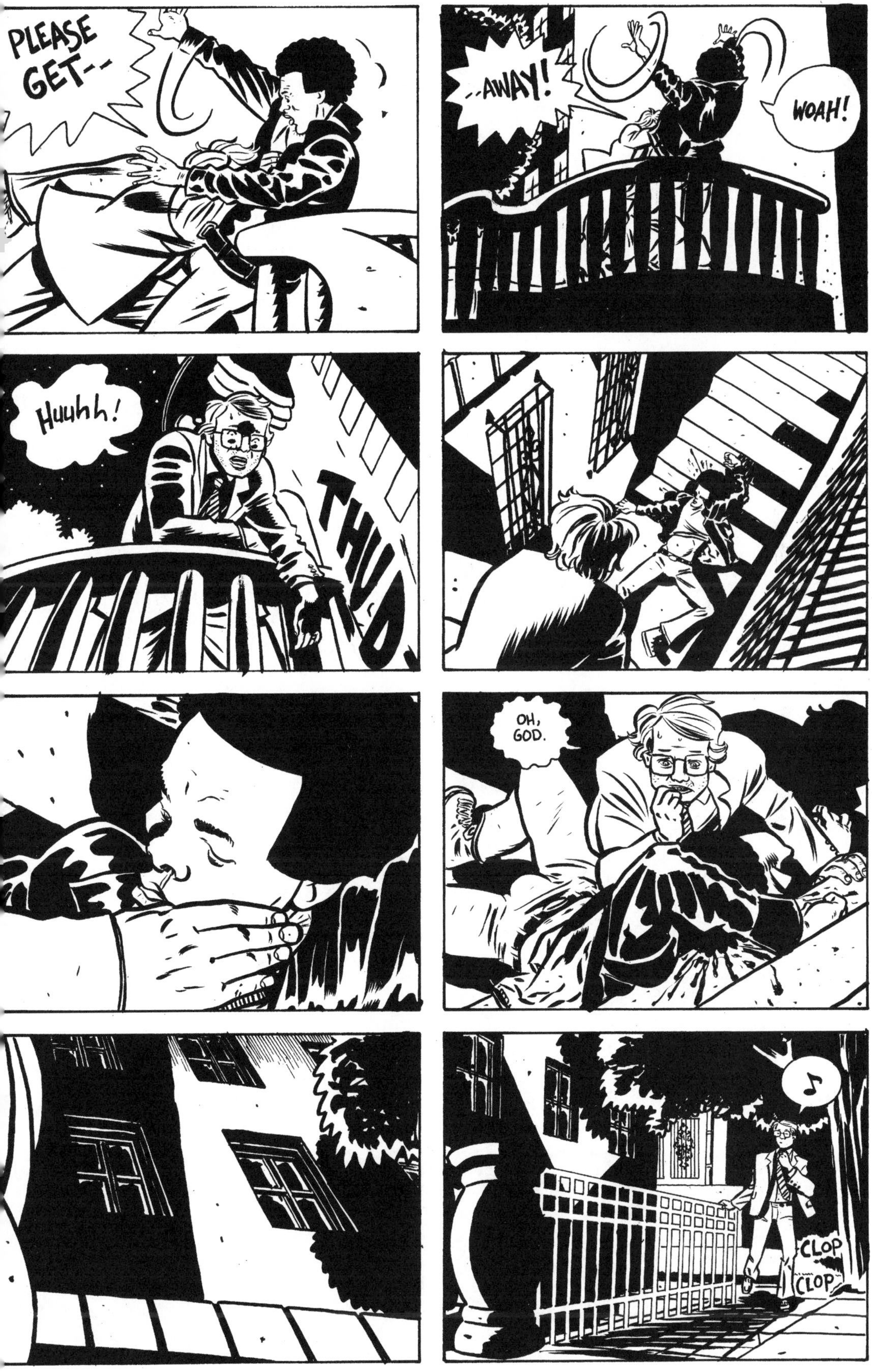
PLEASE GET--
--AWAY!
WOAH!
Huuhh!
THUD.
OH, GOD.
♪
CLOP
CLOP

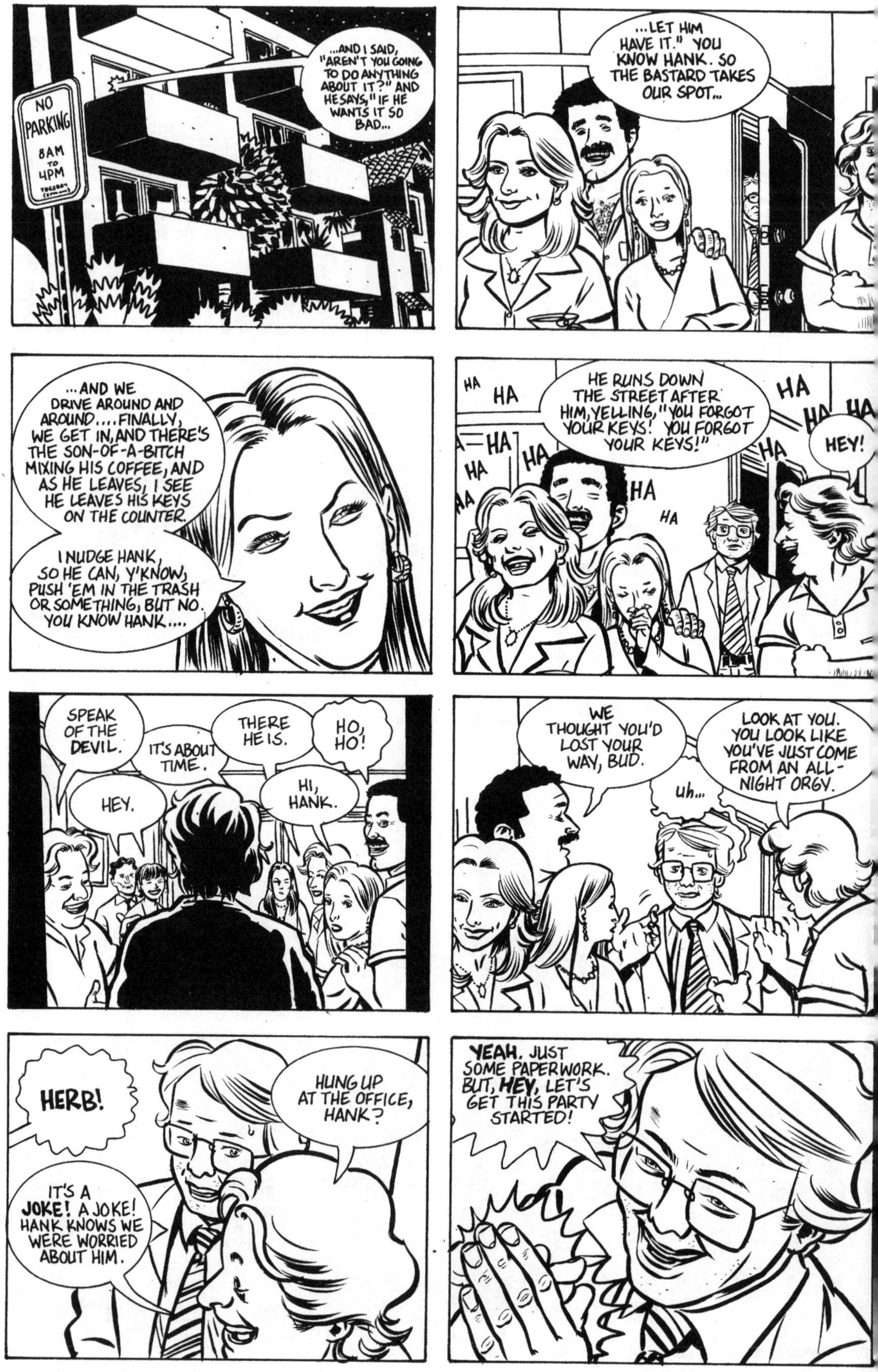
NO PARKING 8AM TO 4PM
...AND I SAID, "AREN'T YOU GOING TO DO ANYTHING ABOUT IT?" AND HE SAYS, "IF HE WANTS IT SO BAD...
...LET HIM HAVE IT." YOU KNOW HANK. SO THE BASTARD TAKES OUR SPOT...
...AND WE DRIVE AROUND AND AROUND.... FINALLY, WE GET IN, AND THERE'S THE SON-OF-A-BITCH MIXING HIS COFFEE, AND AS HE LEAVES, I SEE HE LEAVES HIS KEYS ON THE COUNTER.
I NUDGE HANK, SO HE CAN, Y'KNOW, PUSH 'EM IN THE TRASH OR SOMETHING, BUT NO. YOU KNOW HANK....
HE RUNS DOWN THE STREET AFTER HIM, YELLING, "YOU FORGOT YOUR KEYS! YOU FORGOT YOUR KEYS!"
HA HA HA HA HA HA HA HA HA HA HA HA
HEY!
SPEAK OF THE DEVIL.
IT'S ABOUT TIME.
THERE HE IS.
HO, HO!
HEY.
HI, HANK.
WE THOUGHT YOU'D LOST YOUR WAY, BUD.
uh...
LOOK AT YOU. YOU LOOK LIKE YOU'VE JUST COME FROM AN ALL-NIGHT ORGY.
HERB!
HUNG UP AT THE OFFICE, HANK?
IT'S A JOKE! A JOKE! HANK KNOWS WE WERE WORRIED ABOUT HIM.
YEAH. JUST SOME PAPERWORK. BUT, HEY, LET'S GET THIS PARTY STARTED!

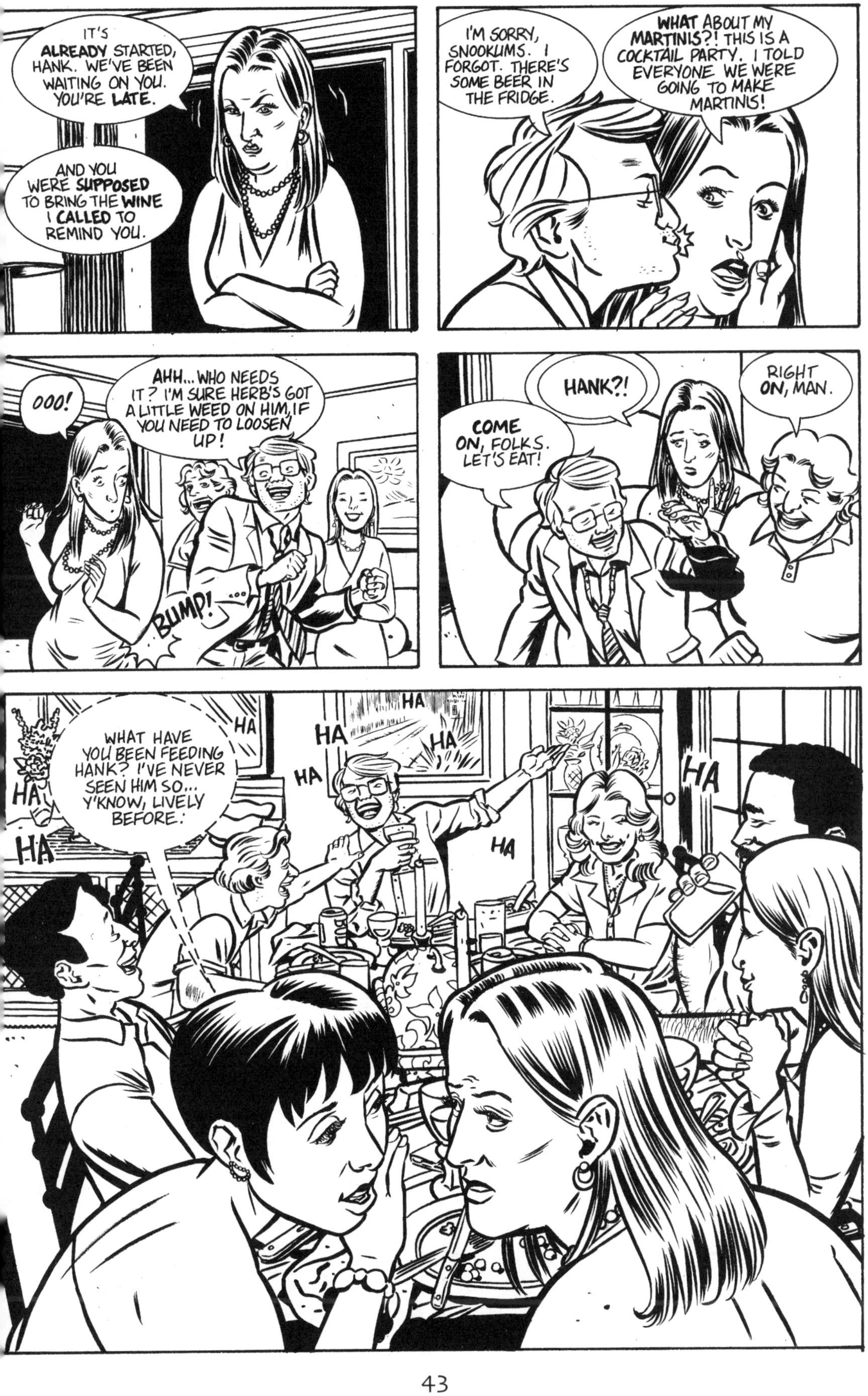
IT'S ALREADY STARTED, HANK. WE'VE BEEN WAITING ON YOU. YOU'RE LATE.
AND YOU WERE SUPPOSED TO BRING THE WINE I CALLED TO REMIND YOU.
I'M SORRY, SNOOKUMS. I FORGOT. THERE'S SOME BEER IN THE FRIDGE.
WHAT ABOUT MY MARTINIS?! THIS IS A COCKTAIL PARTY. I TOLD EVERYONE WE WERE GOING TO MAKE MARTINIS!
OOO!
AHH... WHO NEEDS IT? I'M SURE HERB'S GOT A LITTLE WEED ON HIM, IF YOU NEED TO LOOSEN UP!
BUMP!
HANK?!
RIGHT ON, MAN.
COME ON, FOLKS. LET'S EAT!
HA
HA
HA
HA
HA
HA
HA
HA
HA
WHAT HAVE YOU BEEN FEEDING HANK? I'VE NEVER SEEN HIM SO... Y'KNOW, LIVELY BEFORE.

LATER...

LOOKS LIKE THE HANKSTER AGAIN.

HEY, I THINK THE FIX IS IN.

DO THAT BIRD FLAPPING THING AGAIN, HANK.

HERE, HERE, HERBIE. GIMME.

HANK. HAVEN'T YOU HAD **ENOUGH** OF THAT YET, **HANK**?

OH, RELAX, LORRAINE. IT'S A **PARTY**. YOU WOULDN'T WANT EVERYONE HERE THINKING YOU WERE MARRIED TO A STUFFED SHIRT.

THAT DEPENDS ON WHAT IT WAS STUFFED WITH, HANK!

**HERB!**

HA! HA! HA! HA!

WHAT THE HELL IS THAT?

ONE FLEW OVER THE CUCKOO'S NEST!

HA! HA!

HE'S A BEE!

HA! NO!

HA!

WOAH!

SOUNDS LIKE...POT

ONE WORD! ONE WORD!

HA! WHA

BULLIT!

WAIT! NO! HA! NO!

HA!

**CLEOPATRA**

HA! H

LATER...

MORE BEER?

I HAVE TO GO IN TO THE OFFICE TOMORROW.

I'M BUSHED.

I THINK IT'S THAT TIME.

WAIT! NO ONE GOES HOME WITHOUT A PLATE!

YOU HAVE TO TAKE THIS, OR IT'LL ALL JUST GO TO WASTE. YOU CAN M SANDWICHES OR H FOR DINNER. BLA BLAH, BLAH...

HI, JANET. TIRED?

A LITTLE.

44

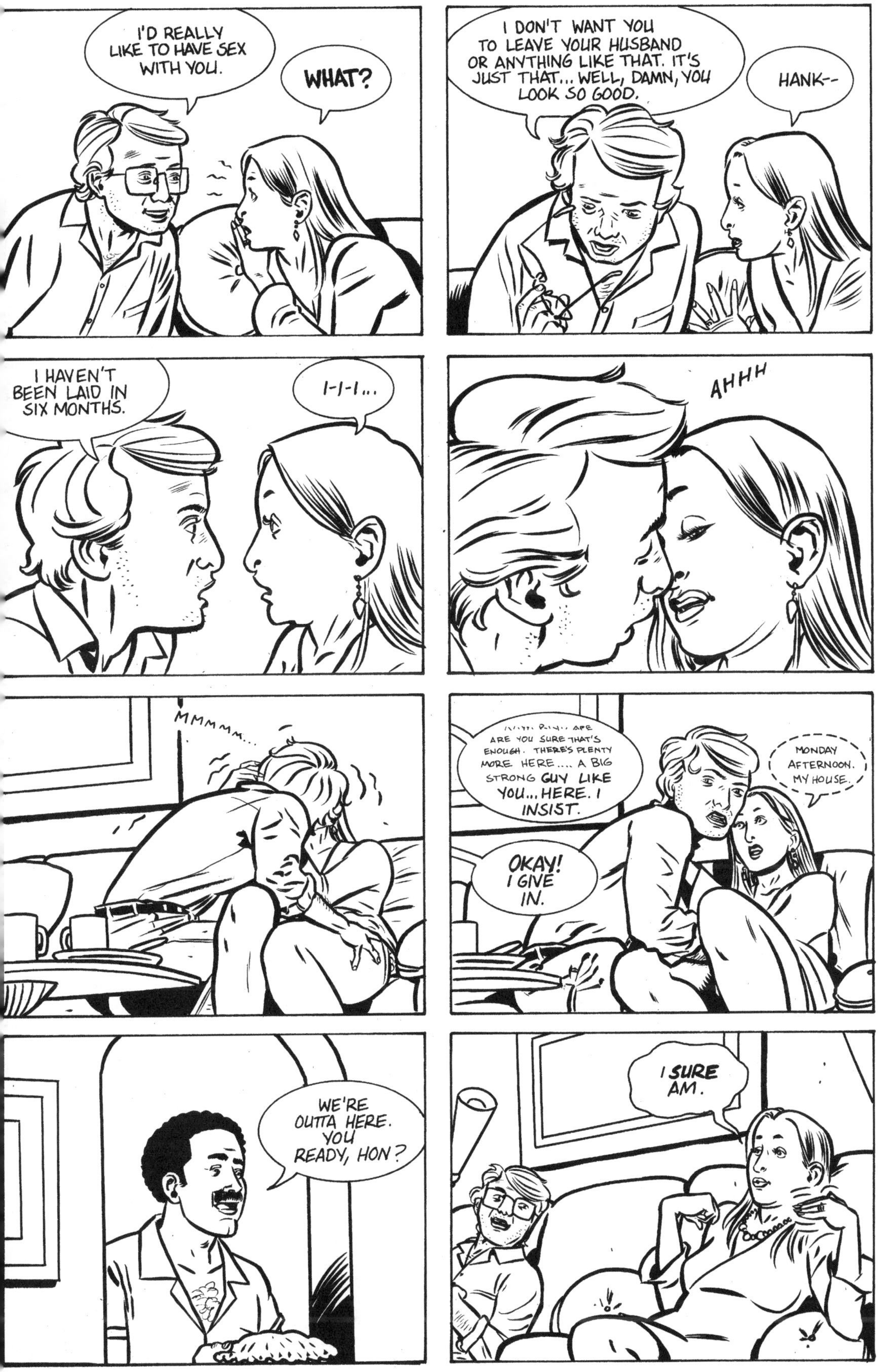
I'D REALLY LIKE TO HAVE SEX WITH YOU.
WHAT?
I DON'T WANT YOU TO LEAVE YOUR HUSBAND OR ANYTHING LIKE THAT. IT'S JUST THAT... WELL, DAMN, YOU LOOK SO GOOD.
HANK--
I HAVEN'T BEEN LAID IN SIX MONTHS.
I-I-I...
AHHH
MMMMM...
ARE YOU SURE THAT'S ENOUGH. THERE'S PLENTY MORE HERE.... A BIG STRONG GUY LIKE YOU... HERE. I INSIST.
MONDAY AFTERNOON. MY HOUSE.
OKAY! I GIVE IN.
WE'RE OUTTA HERE. YOU READY, HON?
I SURE AM.

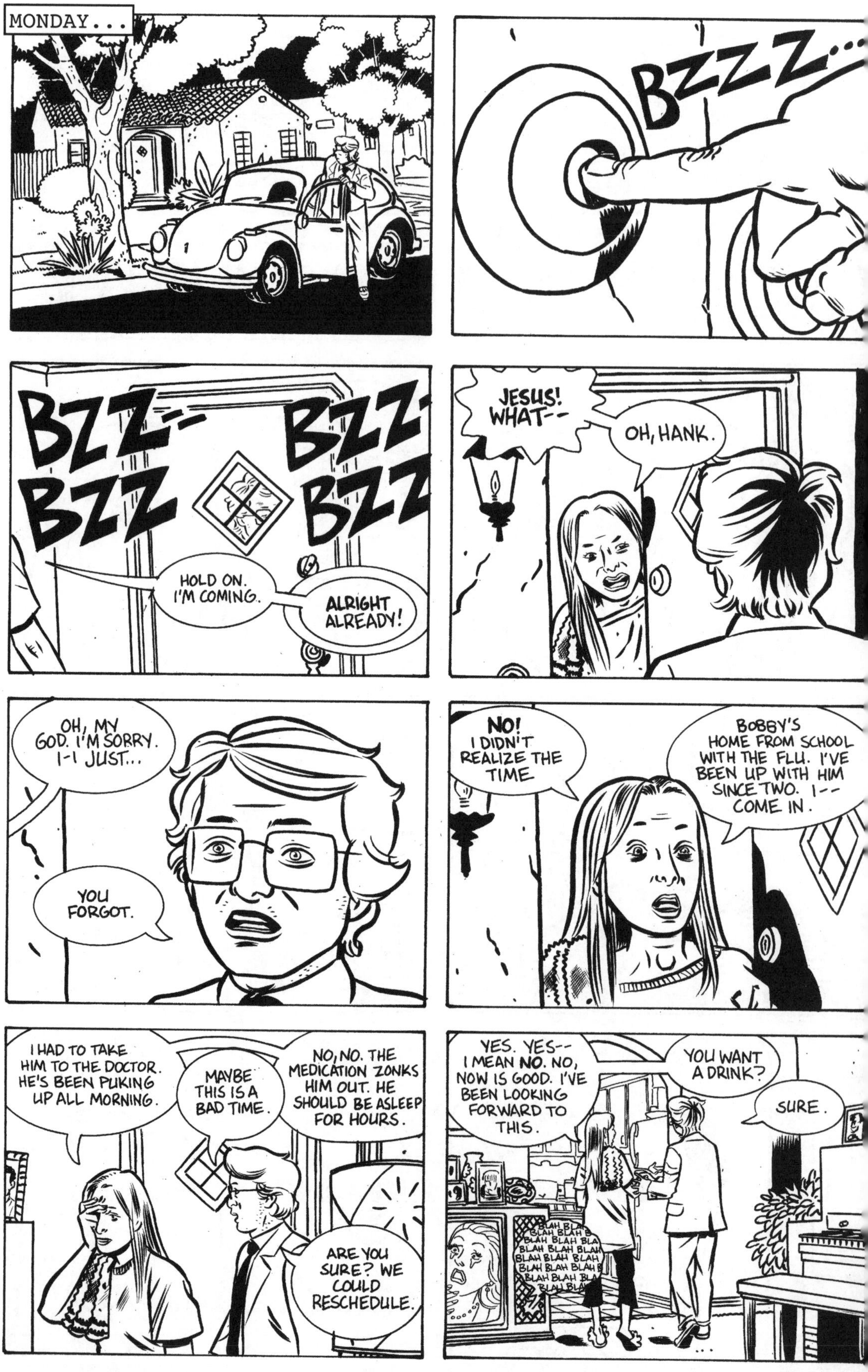
MONDAY...
BZZZ...
BZZ--
BZZ
BZZ-
BZZ
HOLD ON. I'M COMING.
ALRIGHT ALREADY!
JESUS! WHAT--
OH, HANK.
OH, MY GOD. I'M SORRY. I-I JUST...
YOU FORGOT.
NO! I DIDN'T REALIZE THE TIME
BOBBY'S HOME FROM SCHOOL WITH THE FLU. I'VE BEEN UP WITH HIM SINCE TWO. I-- COME IN.
I HAD TO TAKE HIM TO THE DOCTOR. HE'S BEEN PUKING UP ALL MORNING.
MAYBE THIS IS A BAD TIME.
NO, NO. THE MEDICATION ZONKS HIM OUT. HE SHOULD BE ASLEEP FOR HOURS.
ARE YOU SURE? WE COULD RESCHEDULE.
YES. YES-- I MEAN NO. NO, NOW IS GOOD. I'VE BEEN LOOKING FORWARD TO THIS.
YOU WANT A DRINK?
SURE.
BLAH BLAH BLAH BLAH BLAH BLAH BLAH BLAH BLAH BLAH BLAH BLAH

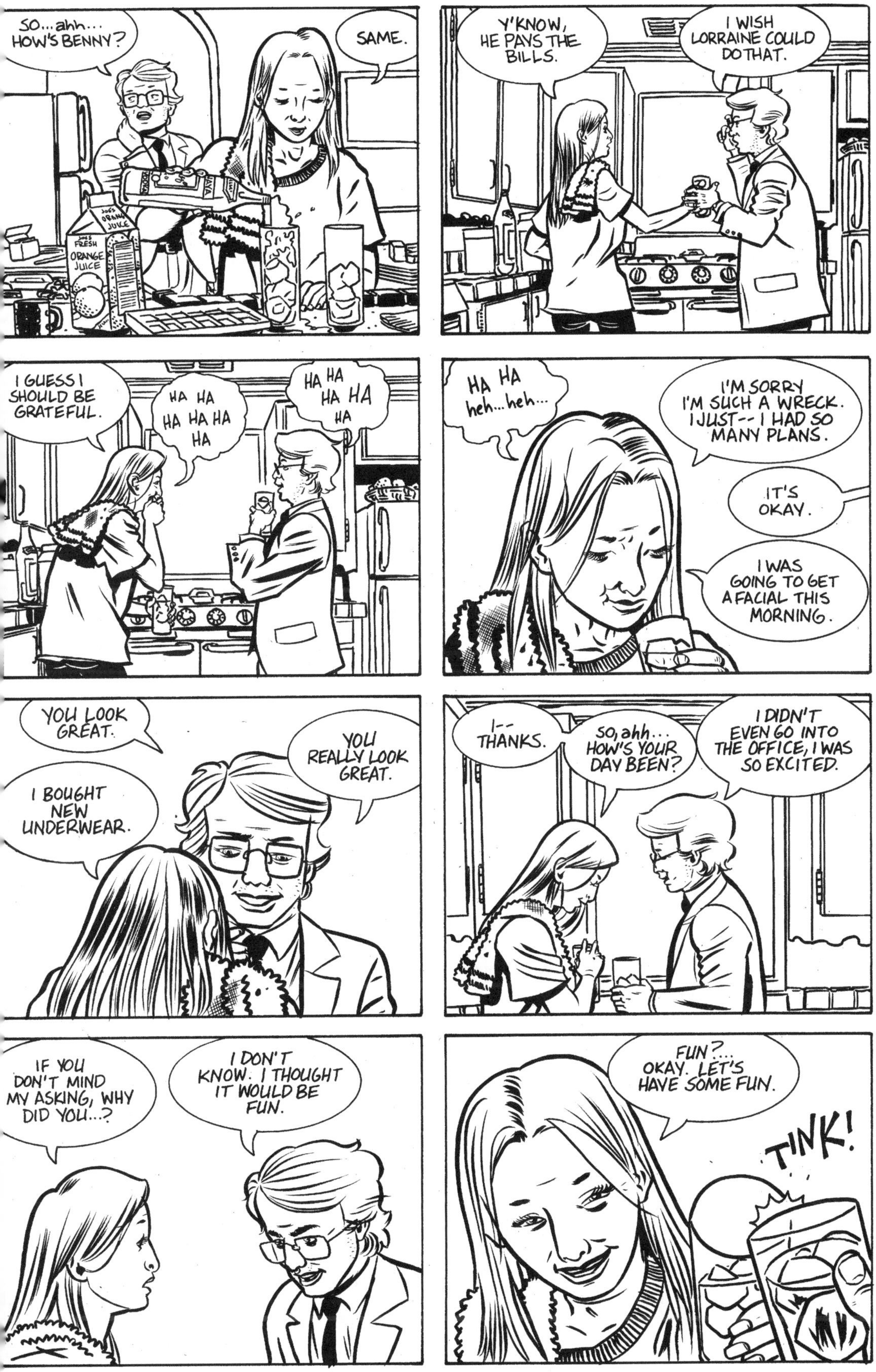
SO... ahh... HOW'S BENNY?
SAME.
Y'KNOW, HE PAYS THE BILLS.
I WISH LORRAINE COULD DO THAT.
I GUESS I SHOULD BE GRATEFUL.
HA HA HA HA HA HA
HA HA HA HA HA
HA HA heh... heh...
I'M SORRY I'M SUCH A WRECK. I JUST-- I HAD SO MANY PLANS.
IT'S OKAY.
I WAS GOING TO GET A FACIAL THIS MORNING.
YOU LOOK GREAT.
I BOUGHT NEW UNDERWEAR.
YOU REALLY LOOK GREAT.
I-- THANKS.
SO, ahh... HOW'S YOUR DAY BEEN?
I DIDN'T EVEN GO INTO THE OFFICE, I WAS SO EXCITED.
IF YOU DON'T MIND MY ASKING, WHY DID YOU...?
I DON'T KNOW. I THOUGHT IT WOULD BE FUN.
FUN?... OKAY. LET'S HAVE SOME FUN.
TINK!

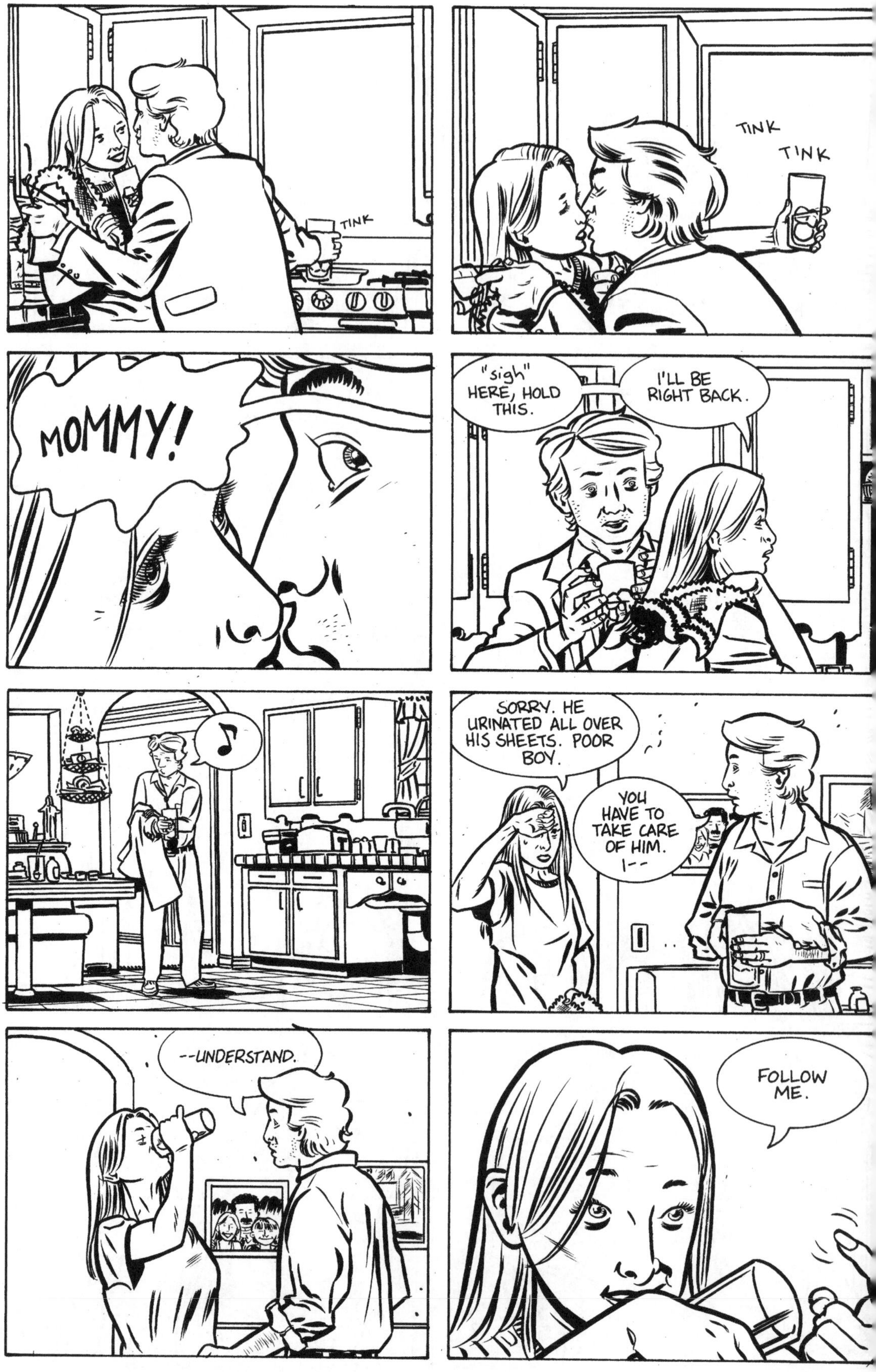
TINK
TINK
TINK
MOMMY!
"sigh" HERE, HOLD THIS.
I'LL BE RIGHT BACK.
♪
SORRY. HE URINATED ALL OVER HIS SHEETS. POOR BOY.
YOU HAVE TO TAKE CARE OF HIM. I--
--UNDERSTAND.
FOLLOW ME.

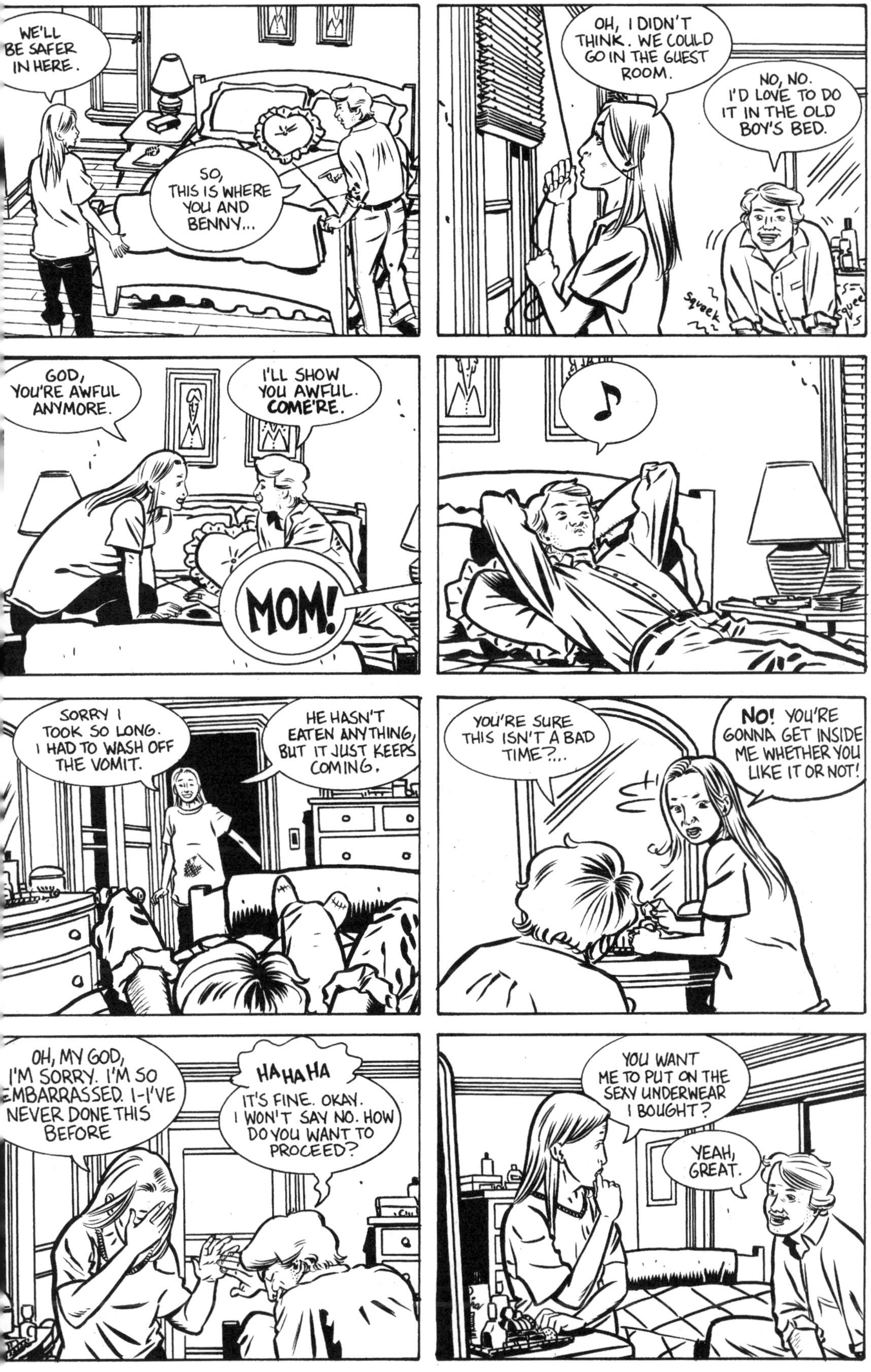
WE'LL BE SAFER IN HERE.
SO, THIS IS WHERE YOU AND BENNY...
OH, I DIDN'T THINK. WE COULD GO IN THE GUEST ROOM.
NO, NO. I'D LOVE TO DO IT IN THE OLD BOY'S BED.
squeek
squee
GOD, YOU'RE AWFUL ANYMORE.
I'LL SHOW YOU AWFUL. COME'RE.
MOM!
♪
SORRY I TOOK SO LONG. I HAD TO WASH OFF THE VOMIT.
HE HASN'T EATEN ANYTHING, BUT IT JUST KEEPS COMING.
YOU'RE SURE THIS ISN'T A BAD TIME?...
NO! YOU'RE GONNA GET INSIDE ME WHETHER YOU LIKE IT OR NOT!
OH, MY GOD, I'M SORRY. I'M SO EMBARRASSED. I-I'VE NEVER DONE THIS BEFORE
HA HA HA
IT'S FINE. OKAY. I WON'T SAY NO. HOW DO YOU WANT TO PROCEED?
YOU WANT ME TO PUT ON THE SEXY UNDERWEAR I BOUGHT?
YEAH, GREAT.

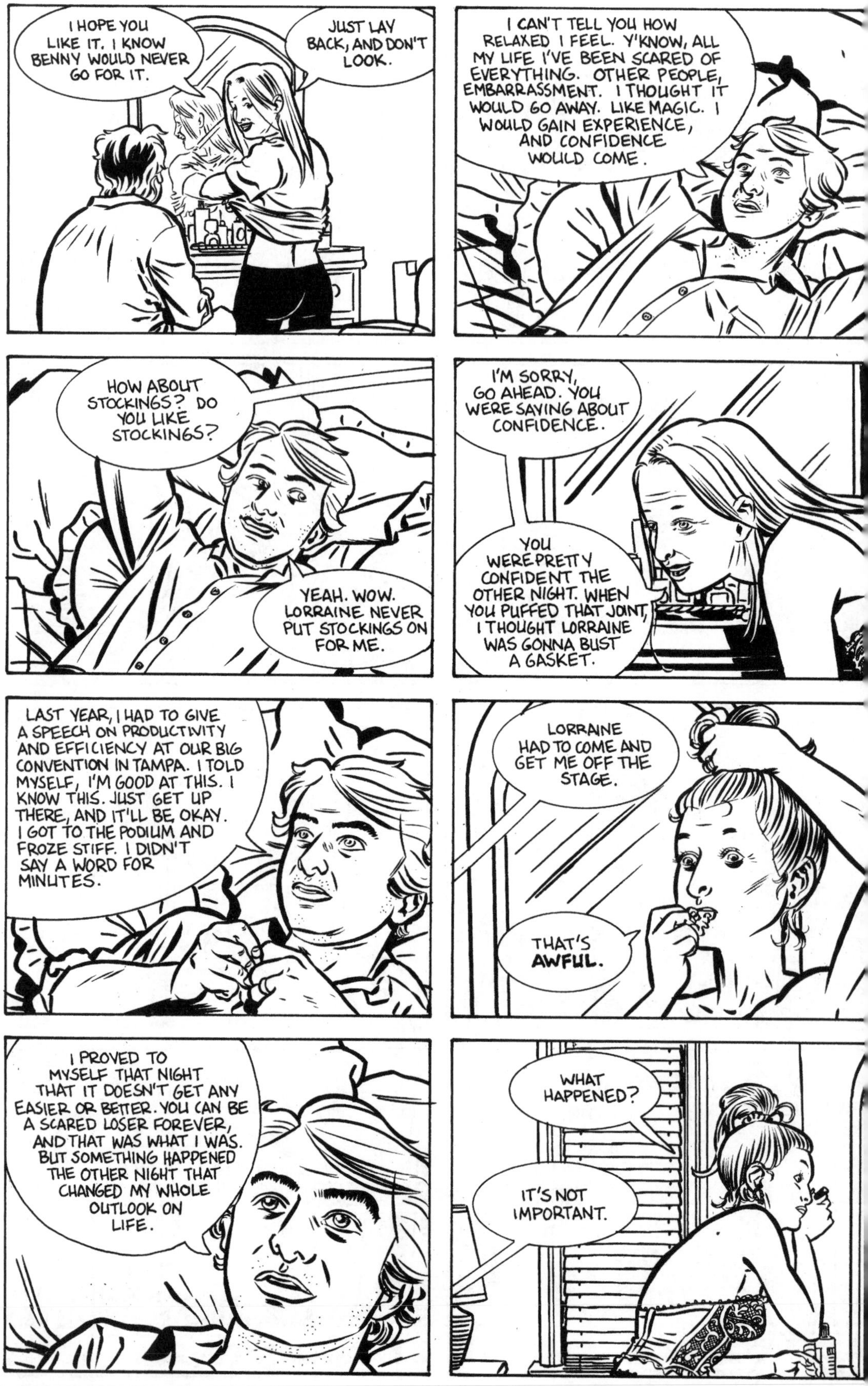
I HOPE YOU LIKE IT. I KNOW BENNY WOULD NEVER GO FOR IT.
JUST LAY BACK, AND DON'T LOOK.
I CAN'T TELL YOU HOW RELAXED I FEEL. Y'KNOW, ALL MY LIFE I'VE BEEN SCARED OF EVERYTHING. OTHER PEOPLE, EMBARRASSMENT. I THOUGHT IT WOULD GO AWAY. LIKE MAGIC. I WOULD GAIN EXPERIENCE, AND CONFIDENCE WOULD COME.
HOW ABOUT STOCKINGS? DO YOU LIKE STOCKINGS?
YEAH. WOW. LORRAINE NEVER PUT STOCKINGS ON FOR ME.
I'M SORRY, GO AHEAD. YOU WERE SAYING ABOUT CONFIDENCE.
YOU WERE PRETTY CONFIDENT THE OTHER NIGHT. WHEN YOU PUFFED THAT JOINT, I THOUGHT LORRAINE WAS GONNA BUST A GASKET.
LAST YEAR, I HAD TO GIVE A SPEECH ON PRODUCTIVITY AND EFFICIENCY AT OUR BIG CONVENTION IN TAMPA. I TOLD MYSELF, I'M GOOD AT THIS. I KNOW THIS. JUST GET UP THERE, AND IT'LL BE OKAY. I GOT TO THE PODIUM AND FROZE STIFF. I DIDN'T SAY A WORD FOR MINUTES.
LORRAINE HAD TO COME AND GET ME OFF THE STAGE.
THAT'S **AWFUL.**
I PROVED TO MYSELF THAT NIGHT THAT IT DOESN'T GET ANY EASIER OR BETTER. YOU CAN BE A SCARED LOSER FOREVER, AND THAT WAS WHAT I WAS. BUT SOMETHING HAPPENED THE OTHER NIGHT THAT CHANGED MY WHOLE OUTLOOK ON LIFE.
WHAT HAPPENED?
IT'S NOT IMPORTANT.

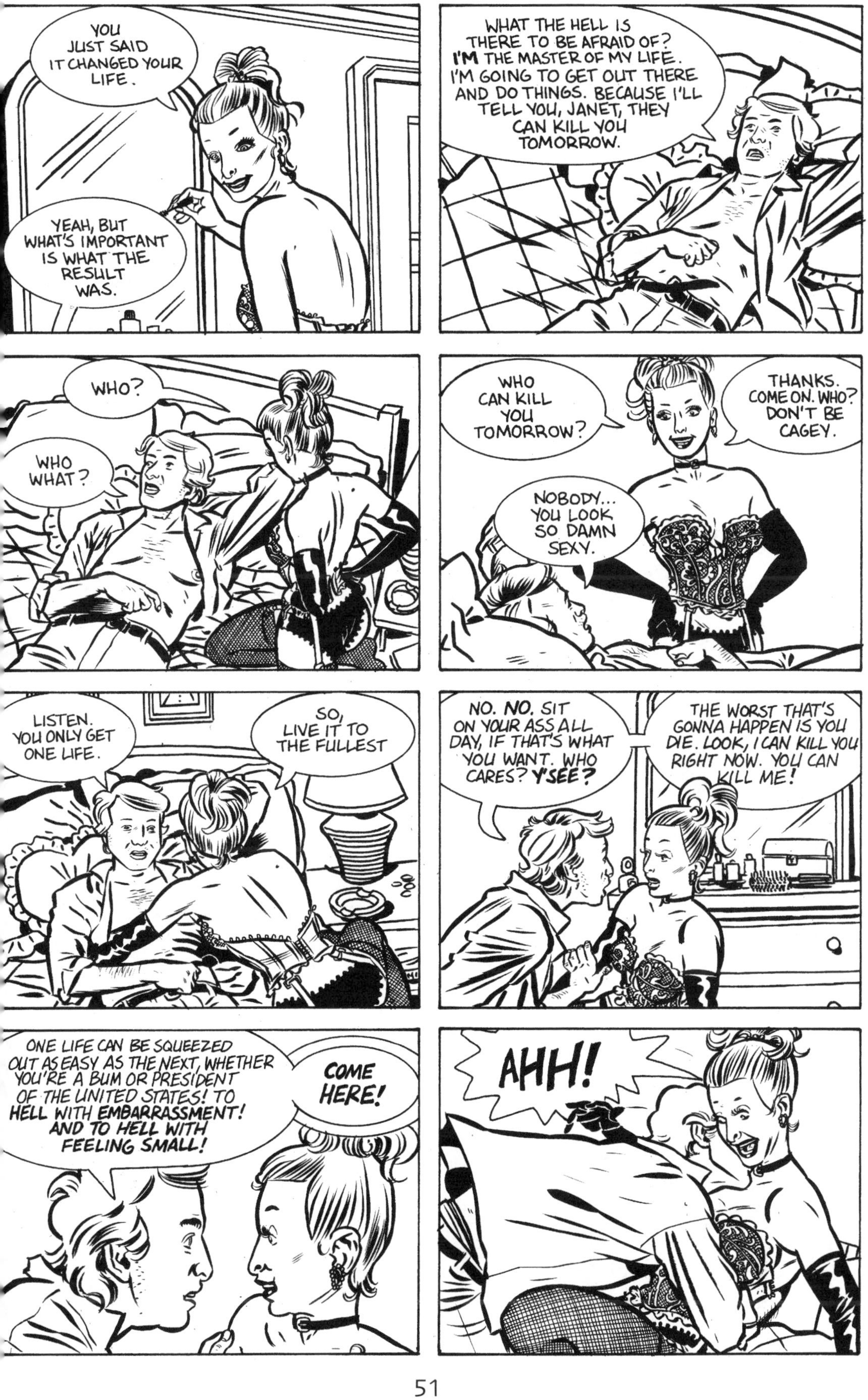
YOU JUST SAID IT CHANGED YOUR LIFE.
YEAH, BUT WHAT'S IMPORTANT IS WHAT THE RESULT WAS.
WHAT THE HELL IS THERE TO BE AFRAID OF? I'M THE MASTER OF MY LIFE. I'M GOING TO GET OUT THERE AND DO THINGS. BECAUSE I'LL TELL YOU, JANET, THEY CAN KILL YOU TOMORROW.
WHO?
WHO WHAT?
WHO CAN KILL YOU TOMORROW?
NOBODY... YOU LOOK SO DAMN SEXY.
THANKS. COME ON. WHO? DON'T BE CAGEY.
LISTEN. YOU ONLY GET ONE LIFE.
SO, LIVE IT TO THE FULLEST
NO. NO. SIT ON YOUR ASS ALL DAY, IF THAT'S WHAT YOU WANT. WHO CARES? Y'SEE?
THE WORST THAT'S GONNA HAPPEN IS YOU DIE. LOOK, I CAN KILL YOU RIGHT NOW. YOU CAN KILL ME!
ONE LIFE CAN BE SQUEEZED OUT AS EASY AS THE NEXT, WHETHER YOU'RE A BUM OR PRESIDENT OF THE UNITED STATES! TO HELL WITH EMBARRASSMENT! AND TO HELL WITH FEELING SMALL!
COME HERE!
AHH!

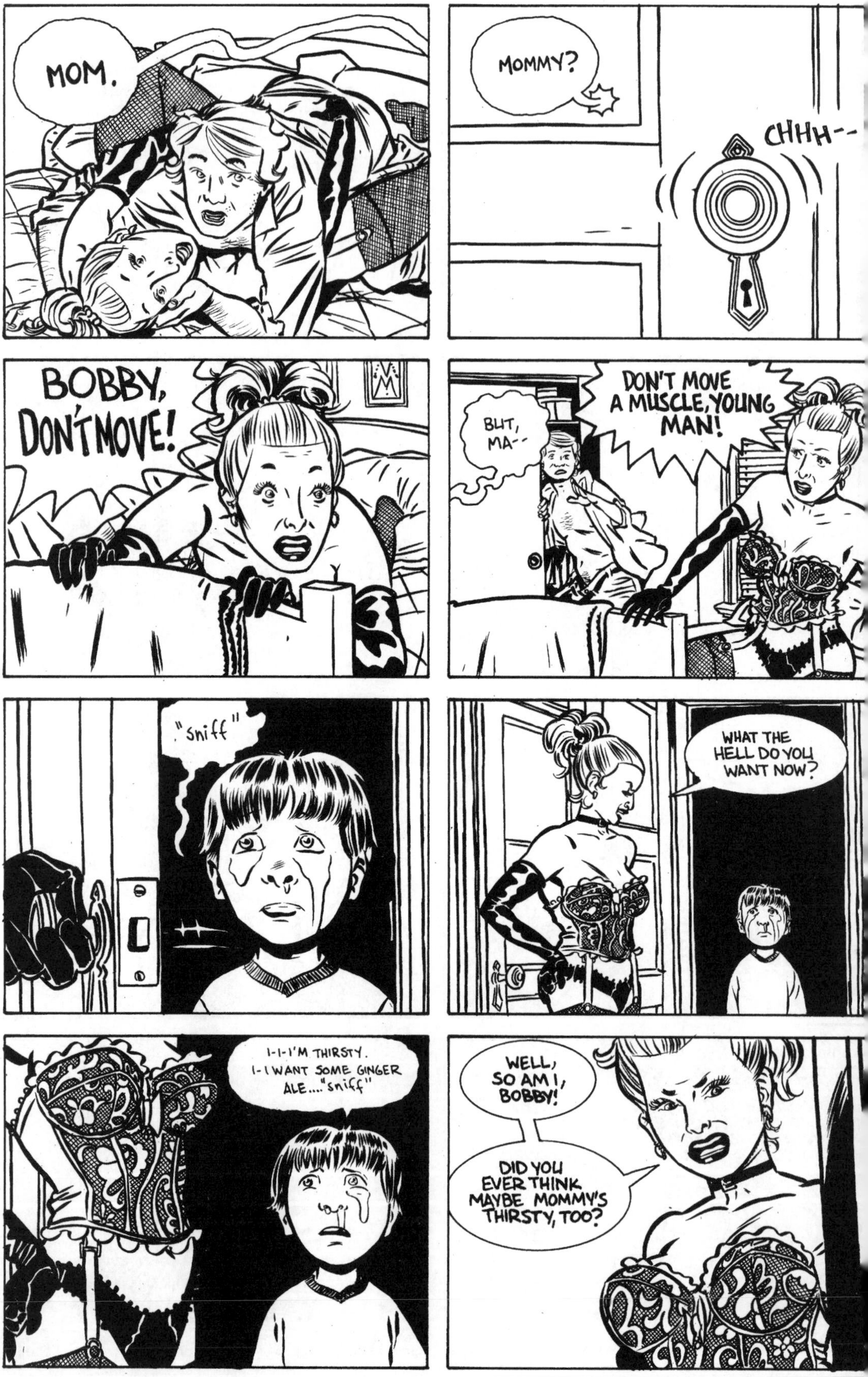
MOM.
MOMMY?
CHHH--
BOBBY, DON'T MOVE!
DON'T MOVE A MUSCLE, YOUNG MAN!
BUT, MA--
"sniff"
WHAT THE HELL DO YOU WANT NOW?
I-I-I'M THIRSTY. I-I WANT SOME GINGER ALE...."sniff"
WELL, SO AM I, BOBBY!
DID YOU EVER THINK MAYBE MOMMY'S THIRSTY, TOO?

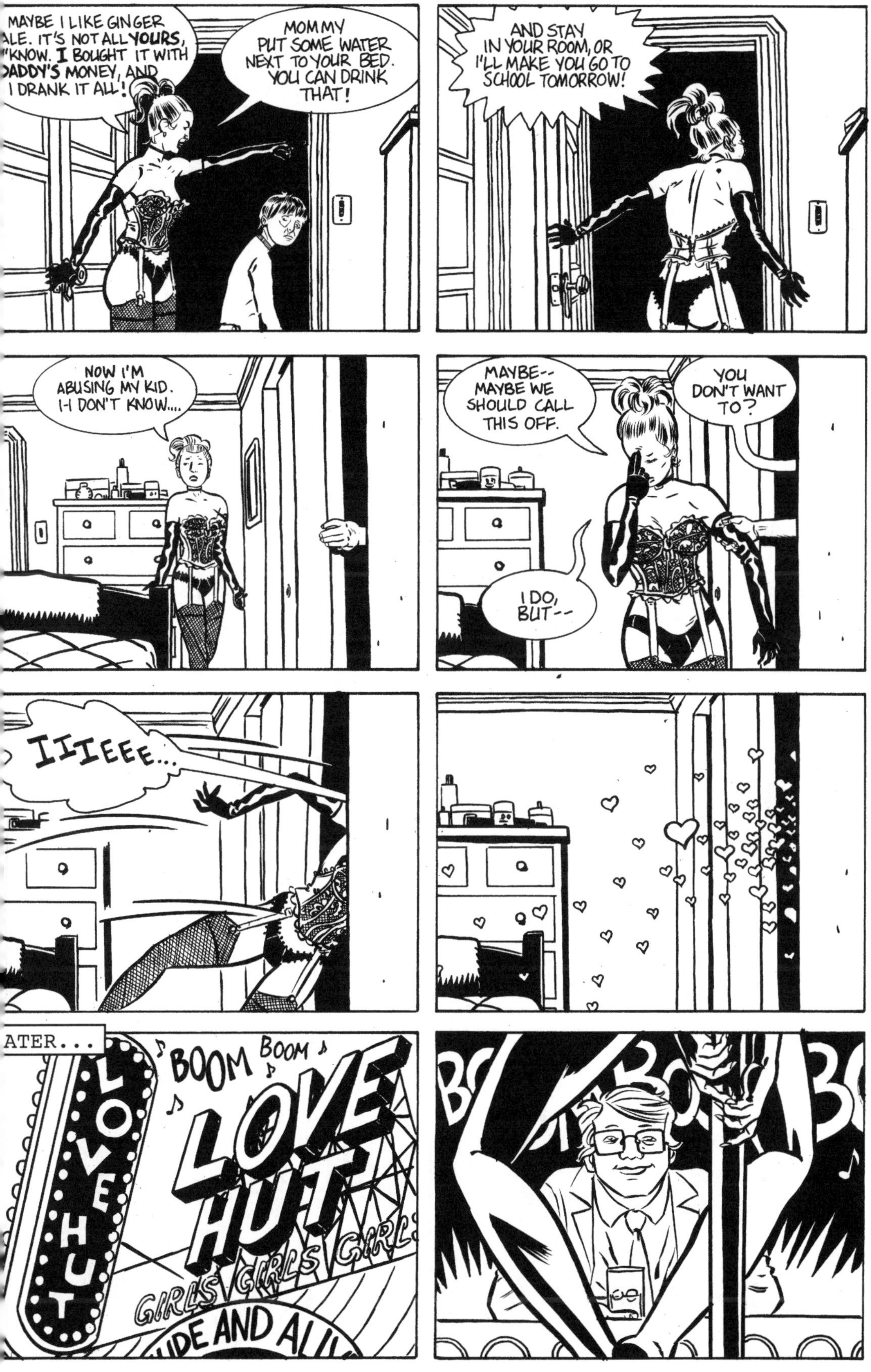

MAYBE I LIKE GINGER ALE. IT'S NOT ALL YOURS, Y'KNOW. I BOUGHT IT WITH DADDY'S MONEY, AND I DRANK IT ALL!
MOMMY PUT SOME WATER NEXT TO YOUR BED. YOU CAN DRINK THAT!
AND STAY IN YOUR ROOM, OR I'LL MAKE YOU GO TO SCHOOL TOMORROW!
NOW I'M ABUSING MY KID. I-I DON'T KNOW....
MAYBE-- MAYBE WE SHOULD CALL THIS OFF.
YOU DON'T WANT TO?
I DO, BUT--
IIIEEEE...
ATER...
LOVE HUT
BOOM BOOM
LOVE HUT
GIRLS GIRLS GIRLS
UDE AND AL

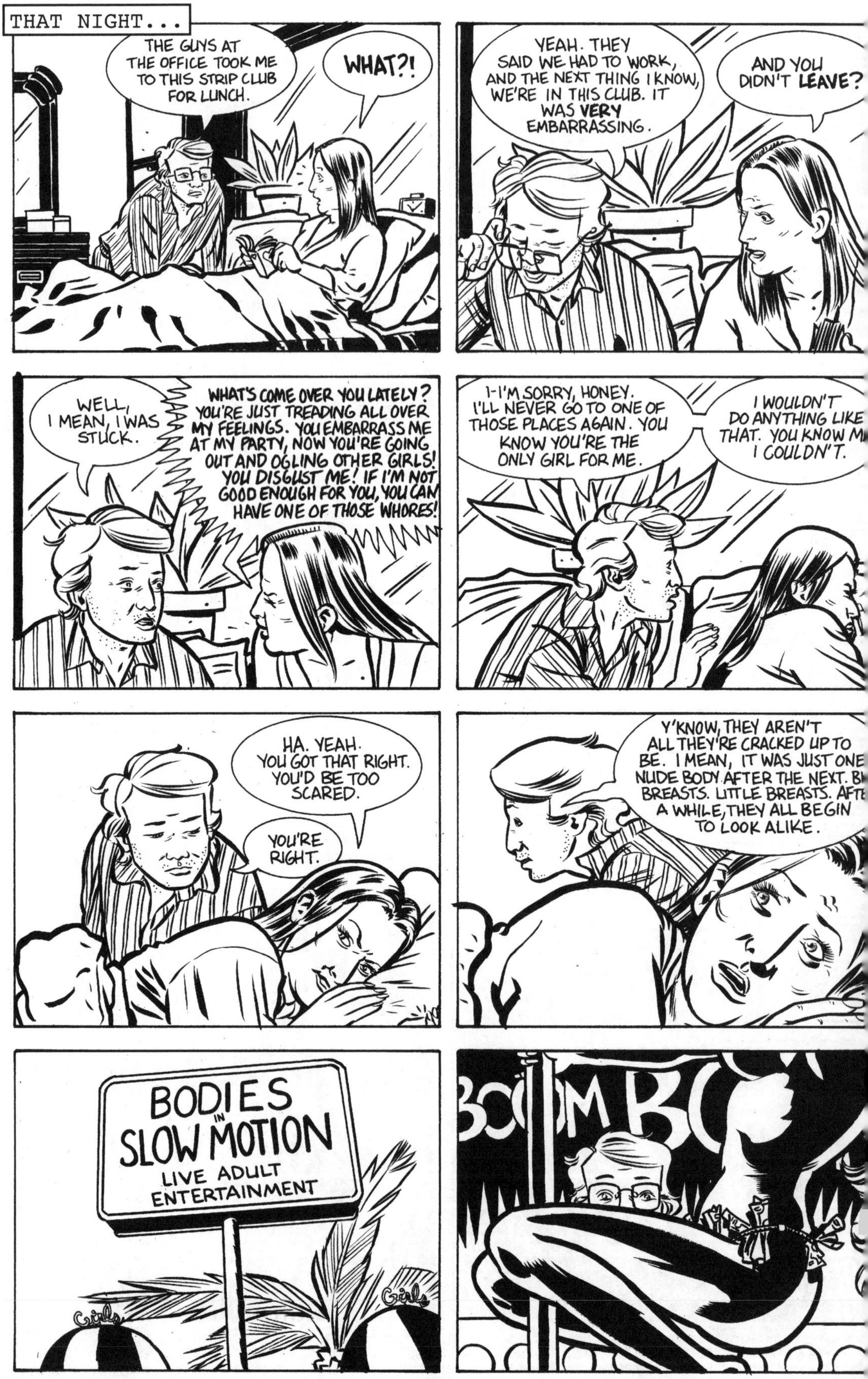
THAT NIGHT...
THE GUYS AT THE OFFICE TOOK ME TO THIS STRIP CLUB FOR LUNCH.
WHAT?!
YEAH. THEY SAID WE HAD TO WORK, AND THE NEXT THING I KNOW, WE'RE IN THIS CLUB. IT WAS VERY EMBARRASSING.
AND YOU DIDN'T LEAVE?
WELL, I MEAN, I WAS STUCK.
WHAT'S COME OVER YOU LATELY? YOU'RE JUST TREADING ALL OVER MY FEELINGS. YOU EMBARRASS ME AT MY PARTY, NOW YOU'RE GOING OUT AND OGLING OTHER GIRLS! YOU DISGUST ME! IF I'M NOT GOOD ENOUGH FOR YOU, YOU CAN HAVE ONE OF THOSE WHORES!
I-I'M SORRY, HONEY. I'LL NEVER GO TO ONE OF THOSE PLACES AGAIN. YOU KNOW YOU'RE THE ONLY GIRL FOR ME.
I WOULDN'T DO ANYTHING LIKE THAT. YOU KNOW M I COULDN'T.
HA. YEAH. YOU GOT THAT RIGHT. YOU'D BE TOO SCARED.
YOU'RE RIGHT.
Y'KNOW, THEY AREN'T ALL THEY'RE CRACKED UP TO BE. I MEAN, IT WAS JUST ONE NUDE BODY AFTER THE NEXT. B BREASTS. LITTLE BREASTS. AFT A WHILE, THEY ALL BEGIN TO LOOK ALIKE.
BODIES IN SLOW MOTION
LIVE ADULT ENTERTAINMENT
Girls
Girls
BOOM BO

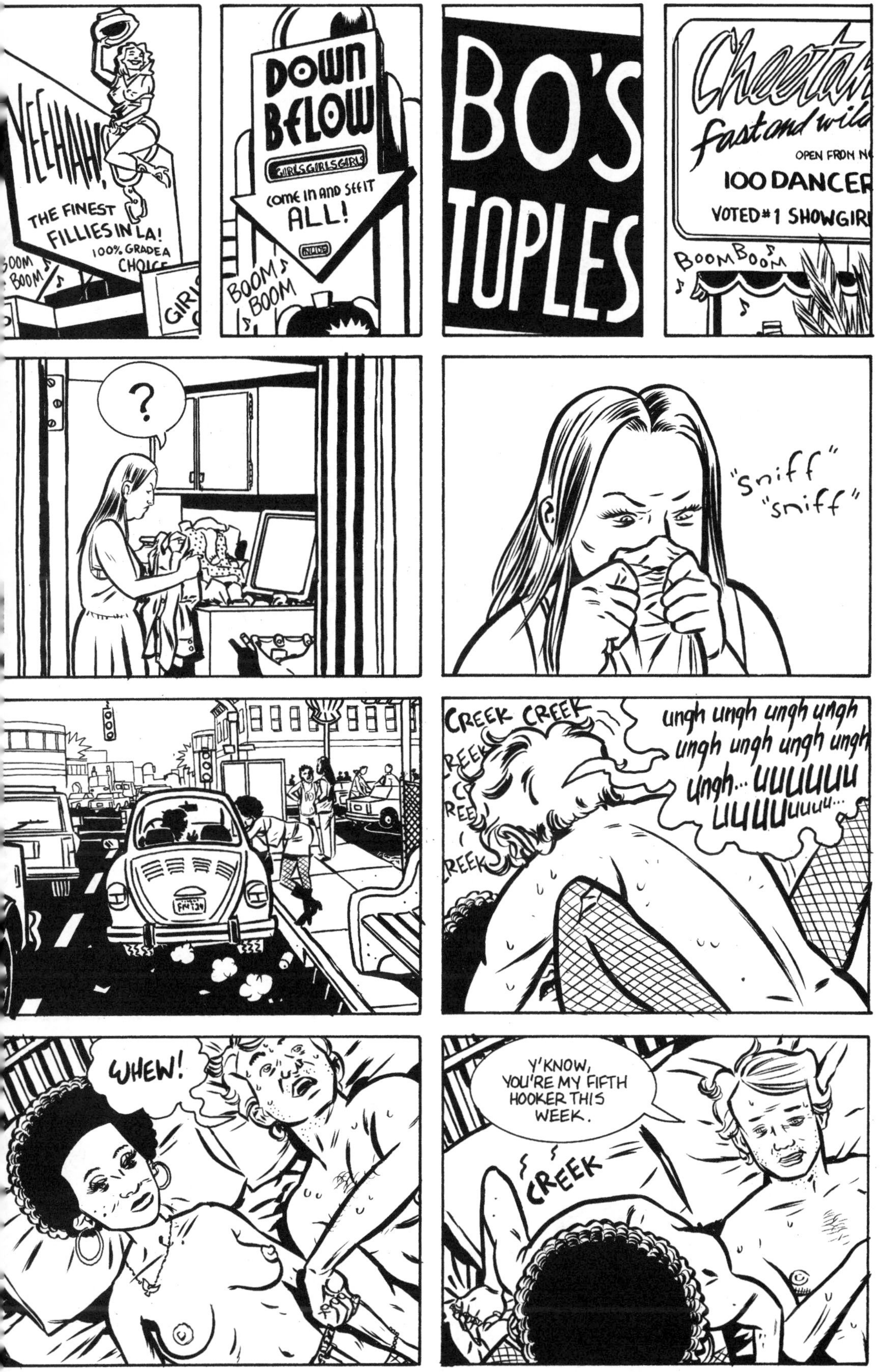
YEEHAW!
THE FINEST FILLIES IN LA!
100% GRADE A CHOICE
BOOM BOOM
DOWN BELOW
GIRLS GIRLS GIRLS
COME IN AND SEE IT ALL!
NUDE
BOOM BOOM
BO'S TOPLES
Cheetah
fast and wild
OPEN FROM N
100 DANCER
VOTED #1 SHOWGIRL
BOOM BOOM
?
"sniff" "sniff"
CREEK CREEK
CREEK CREEK CREEK
ungh ungh ungh ungh ungh ungh ungh ungh ungh... UUUUUU UUUUuuuu...
WHEW!
Y'KNOW, YOU'RE MY FIFTH HOOKER THIS WEEK.
CREEK

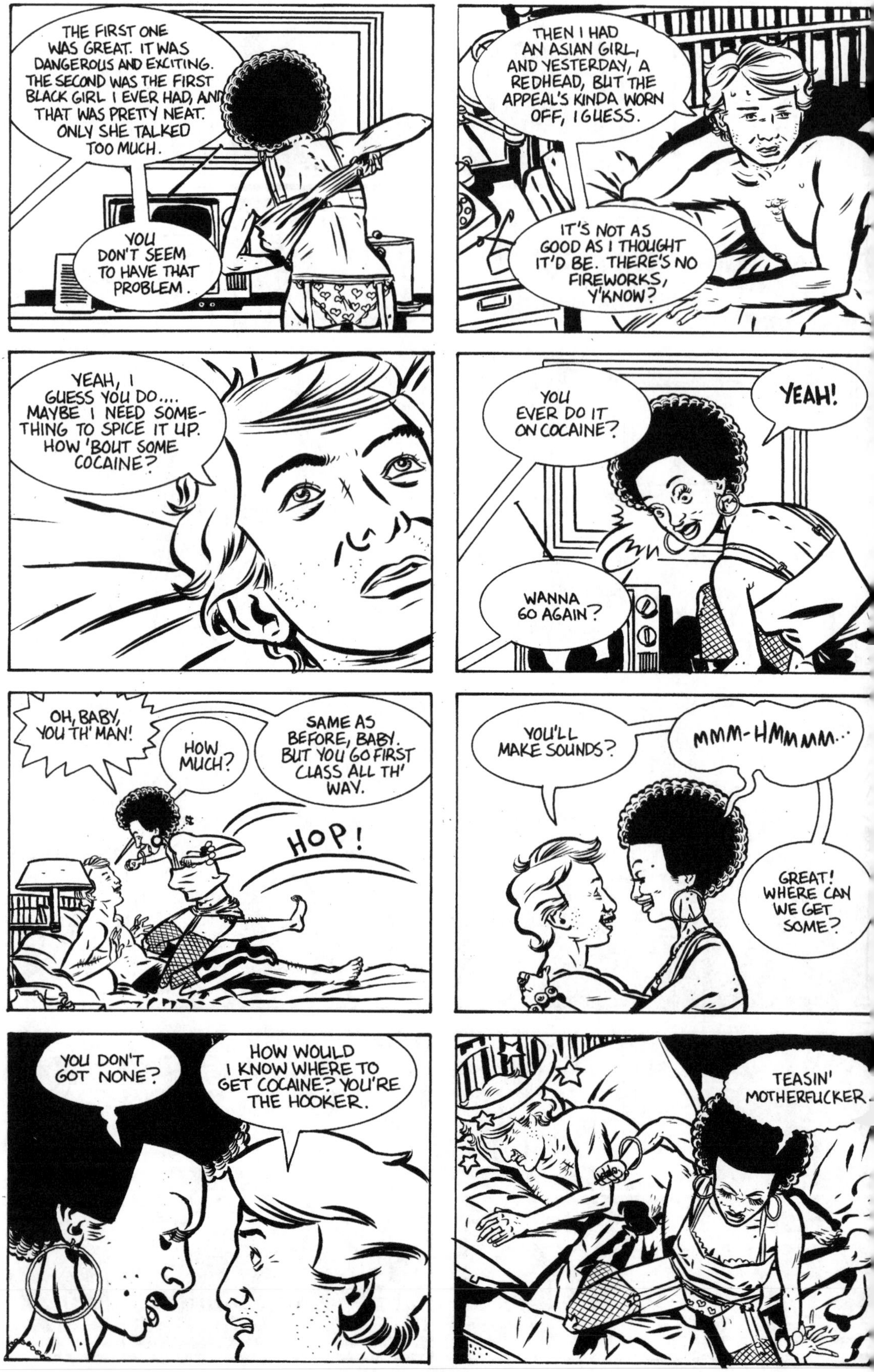
THE FIRST ONE WAS GREAT. IT WAS DANGEROUS AND EXCITING. THE SECOND WAS THE FIRST BLACK GIRL I EVER HAD, AND THAT WAS PRETTY NEAT. ONLY SHE TALKED TOO MUCH.
YOU DON'T SEEM TO HAVE THAT PROBLEM.
THEN I HAD AN ASIAN GIRL, AND YESTERDAY, A REDHEAD, BUT THE APPEAL'S KINDA WORN OFF, I GUESS.
IT'S NOT AS GOOD AS I THOUGHT IT'D BE. THERE'S NO FIREWORKS, Y'KNOW?
YEAH, I GUESS YOU DO.... MAYBE I NEED SOMETHING TO SPICE IT UP. HOW 'BOUT SOME COCAINE?
YOU EVER DO IT ON COCAINE?
YEAH!
WANNA GO AGAIN?
OH, BABY, YOU TH' MAN!
HOW MUCH?
SAME AS BEFORE, BABY. BUT YOU GO FIRST CLASS ALL TH' WAY.
HOP!
YOU'LL MAKE SOUNDS?
MMM-HMMMM...
GREAT! WHERE CAN WE GET SOME?
YOU DON'T GOT NONE?
HOW WOULD I KNOW WHERE TO GET COCAINE? YOU'RE THE HOOKER.
TEASIN' MOTHERFUCKER

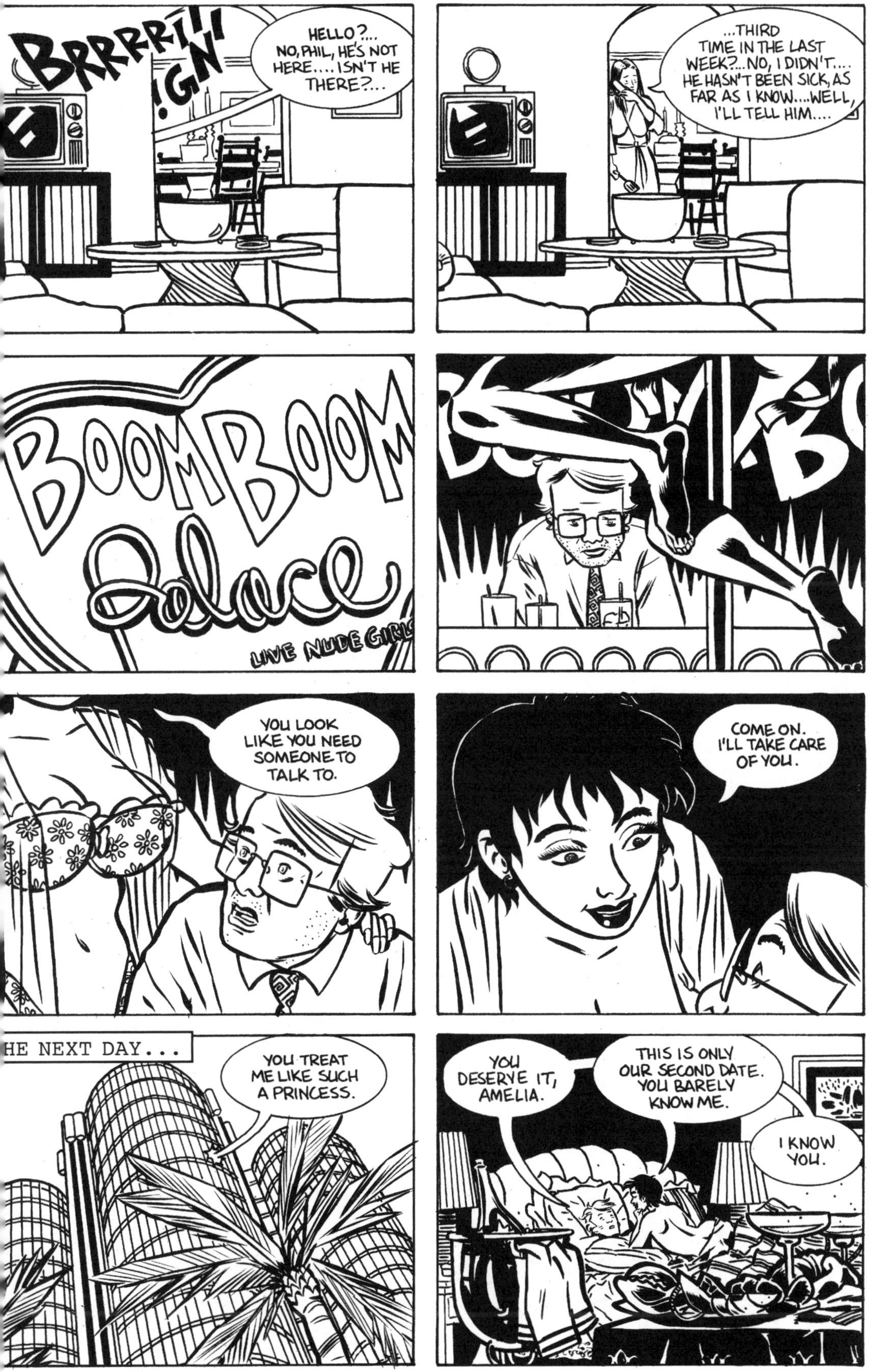
BRRRRI!!!GN!
HELLO?... NO, PHIL, HE'S NOT HERE.... ISN'T HE THERE?...
...THIRD TIME IN THE LAST WEEK?...NO, I DIDN'T.... HE HASN'T BEEN SICK, AS FAR AS I KNOW....WELL, I'LL TELL HIM....
BOOM BOOM Palace
LIVE NUDE GIRLS
YOU LOOK LIKE YOU NEED SOMEONE TO TALK TO.
COME ON. I'LL TAKE CARE OF YOU.
HE NEXT DAY...
YOU TREAT ME LIKE SUCH A PRINCESS.
YOU DESERVE IT, AMELIA.
THIS IS ONLY OUR SECOND DATE. YOU BARELY KNOW ME.
I KNOW YOU.

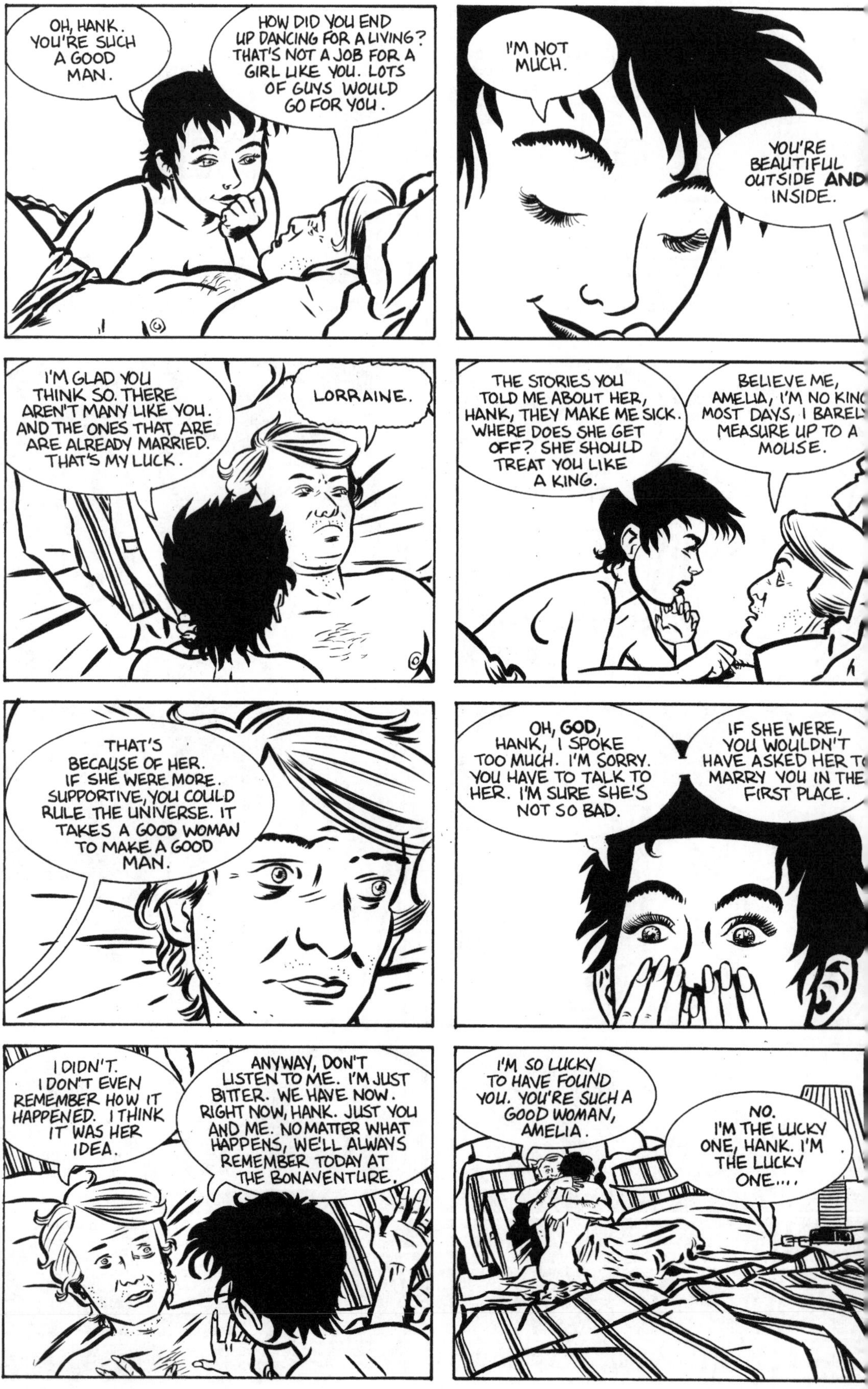
OH, HANK. YOU'RE SUCH A GOOD MAN.
HOW DID YOU END UP DANCING FOR A LIVING? THAT'S NOT A JOB FOR A GIRL LIKE YOU. LOTS OF GUYS WOULD GO FOR YOU.
I'M NOT MUCH.
YOU'RE BEAUTIFUL OUTSIDE **AND** INSIDE.
I'M GLAD YOU THINK SO. THERE AREN'T MANY LIKE YOU. AND THE ONES THAT ARE ARE ALREADY MARRIED. THAT'S MY LUCK.
LORRAINE.
THE STORIES YOU TOLD ME ABOUT HER, HANK, THEY MAKE ME SICK. WHERE DOES SHE GET OFF? SHE SHOULD TREAT YOU LIKE A KING.
BELIEVE ME, AMELIA, I'M NO KING. MOST DAYS, I BARELY MEASURE UP TO A MOUSE.
THAT'S BECAUSE OF HER. IF SHE WERE MORE SUPPORTIVE, YOU COULD RULE THE UNIVERSE. IT TAKES A GOOD WOMAN TO MAKE A GOOD MAN.
OH, **GOD**, HANK, I SPOKE TOO MUCH. I'M SORRY. YOU HAVE TO TALK TO HER. I'M SURE SHE'S NOT SO BAD.
IF SHE WERE, YOU WOULDN'T HAVE ASKED HER TO MARRY YOU IN THE FIRST PLACE.
I DIDN'T. I DON'T EVEN REMEMBER HOW IT HAPPENED. I THINK IT WAS HER IDEA.
ANYWAY, DON'T LISTEN TO ME. I'M JUST BITTER. WE HAVE NOW. RIGHT NOW, HANK. JUST YOU AND ME. NO MATTER WHAT HAPPENS, WE'LL ALWAYS REMEMBER TODAY AT THE BONAVENTURE.
I'M SO LUCKY TO HAVE FOUND YOU. YOU'RE SUCH A GOOD WOMAN, AMELIA.
NO. I'M THE LUCKY ONE, HANK. I'M THE LUCKY ONE....

THE NEXT DAY...

I'VE COMPLETELY FALLEN IN LOVE. SHE'S LIKE A MIRACLE SENT FROM HEAVEN.

YOU DON'T HAVE TO ASK MY PERMISSION, HANK. WHAT WE HAVE IS JUST FOR KICKS. I'D LIKE TO KEEP DOING IT, BUT YOU SEEM TO BE HEAD OVER HEELS FOR THIS GIRL.

I'M GOING TO LEAVE LORRAINE AND ASK HER TO MARRY ME.

SWEETIE, BELIEVE ME, THIS HAS NOTHING TO DO WITH LORRAINE. I'VE ALWAYS THOUGHT SHE WAS A ROTTEN BITCH.

BUT THIS IS ALL HAPPENING AWFULLY FAST.

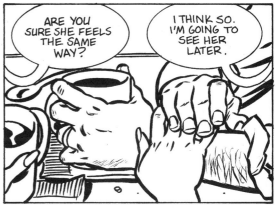

ARE YOU SURE SHE FEELS THE SAME WAY?

I THINK SO. I'M GOING TO SEE HER LATER.

...OON...

I CAN'T BELIEVE IT. YOU'D DO THAT FOR ME?

YOU'D LEAVE YOUR WIFE?

AMELIA, I DIDN'T KNOW WHAT WAS GOING ON IN MY LIFE. I'VE NEVER BEEN IN CONTROL.

I MARRIED A DOMINEERING BITCH, BECAUSE I WAS AFRAID TO MAKE ANY DECISIONS ON MY OWN. BUT THEN I MET YOU, AND EVERYTHING—THE MOON, THE STARS—THEY ALL CLICKED INTO PLACE.

FOR ME, TOO, HANK.

YOU LIBERATED ME. YOU FREED MY SOUL. I'LL MAKE YOU HAPPY, DEAREST. I SWEAR!

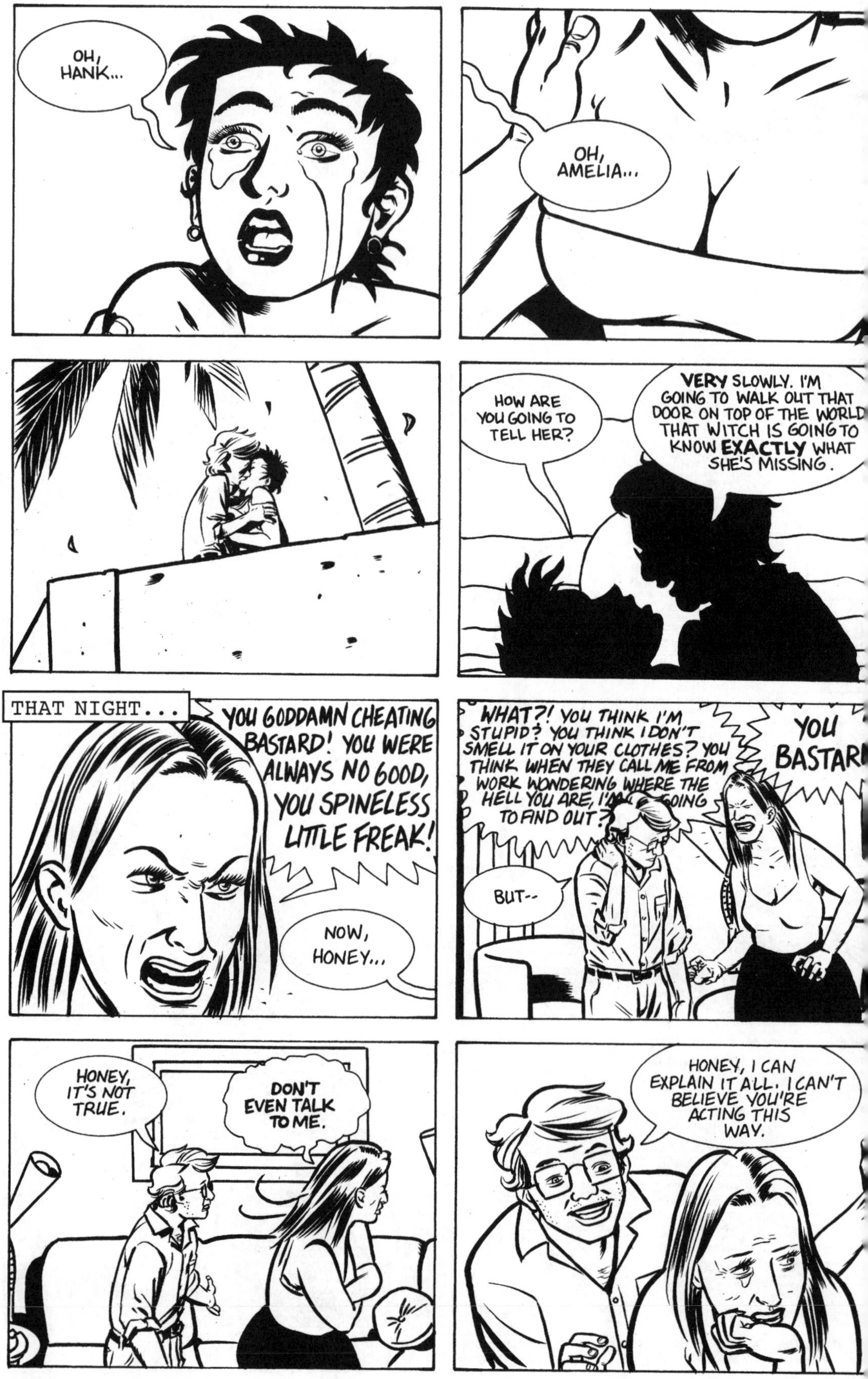

OH, HANK...
OH, AMELIA...
HOW ARE YOU GOING TO TELL HER?
VERY SLOWLY. I'M GOING TO WALK OUT THAT DOOR ON TOP OF THE WORLD THAT WITCH IS GOING TO KNOW EXACTLY WHAT SHE'S MISSING.
THAT NIGHT...
YOU GODDAMN CHEATING BASTARD! YOU WERE ALWAYS NO GOOD, YOU SPINELESS LITTLE FREAK!
NOW, HONEY...
WHAT?! YOU THINK I'M STUPID? YOU THINK I DON'T SMELL IT ON YOUR CLOTHES? YOU THINK WHEN THEY CALL ME FROM WORK WONDERING WHERE THE HELL YOU ARE, I'M NOT GOING TO FIND OUT?
YOU BASTAR
BUT--
HONEY, IT'S NOT TRUE.
DON'T EVEN TALK TO ME.
HONEY, I CAN EXPLAIN IT ALL. I CAN'T BELIEVE YOU'RE ACTING THIS WAY.

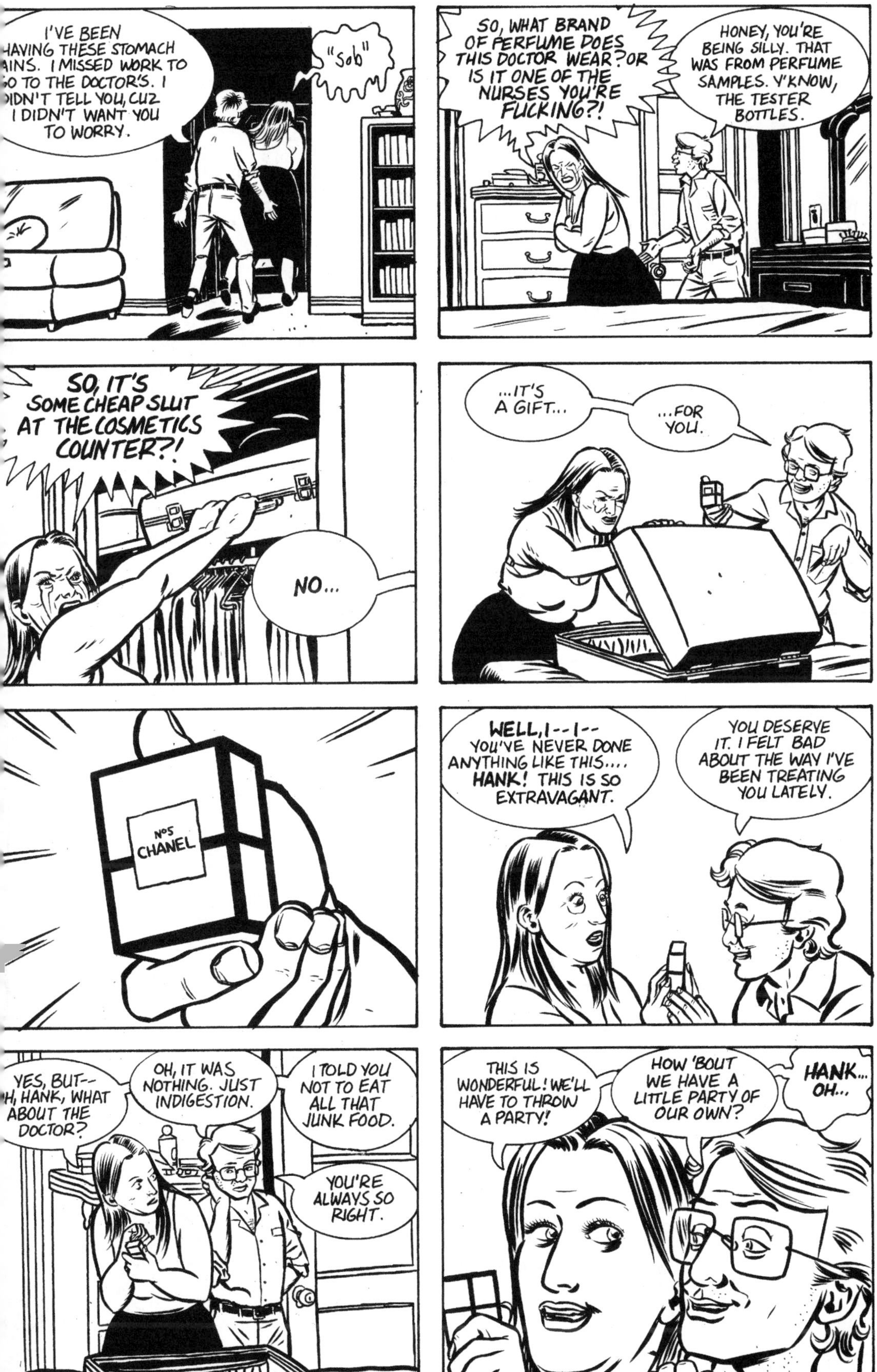
I'VE BEEN
HAVING THESE STOMACH
AINS. I MISSED WORK TO
O TO THE DOCTOR'S. I
IDN'T TELL YOU, CUZ
I DIDN'T WANT YOU
TO WORRY.
"Sob"
SO, WHAT BRAND OF PERFUME DOES THIS DOCTOR WEAR? OR IS IT ONE OF THE NURSES YOU'RE FUCKING?!
HONEY, YOU'RE BEING SILLY. THAT WAS FROM PERFUME SAMPLES. Y'KNOW, THE TESTER BOTTLES.
SO, IT'S SOME CHEAP SLUT AT THE COSMETICS COUNTER?!
NO...
...IT'S A GIFT...
...FOR YOU.
Nº5 CHANEL
WELL, I--I-- YOU'VE NEVER DONE ANYTHING LIKE THIS.... HANK! THIS IS SO EXTRAVAGANT.
YOU DESERVE IT. I FELT BAD ABOUT THE WAY I'VE BEEN TREATING YOU LATELY.
YES, BUT--
H, HANK, WHAT ABOUT THE DOCTOR?
OH, IT WAS NOTHING. JUST INDIGESTION.
I TOLD YOU NOT TO EAT ALL THAT JUNK FOOD.
YOU'RE ALWAYS SO RIGHT.
THIS IS WONDERFUL! WE'LL HAVE TO THROW A PARTY!
HOW 'BOUT WE HAVE A LITTLE PARTY OF OUR OWN?
HANK... OH...

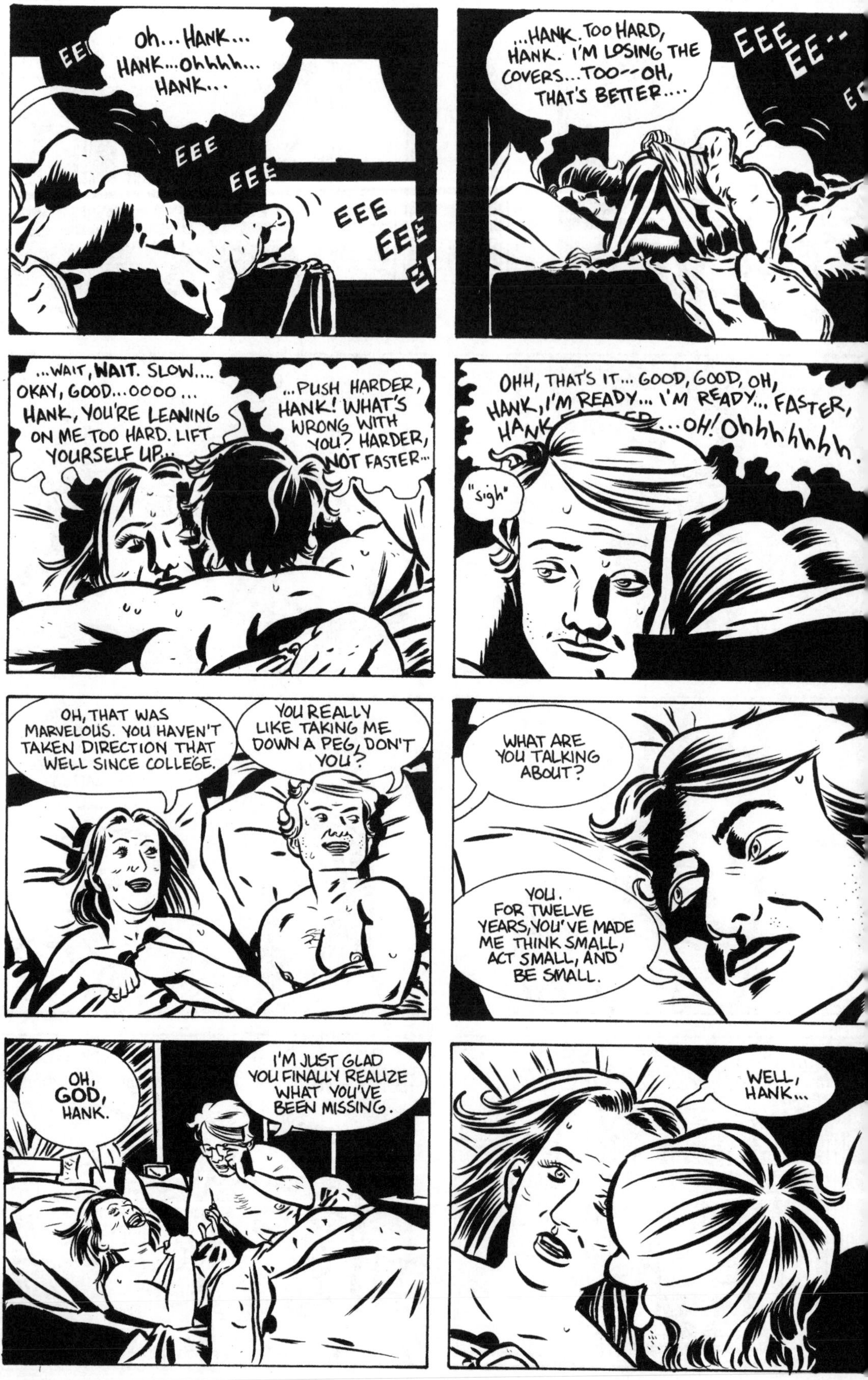
EEE
Oh... HANK... HANK...Ohhhh... HANK...
EEE
EEE
EEE
EEE
...HANK. TOO HARD, HANK. I'M LOSING THE COVERS...TOO--OH, THAT'S BETTER....
EEE EE..
...WAIT, WAIT. SLOW.... OKAY, GOOD...OOOO... HANK, YOU'RE LEANING ON ME TOO HARD. LIFT YOURSELF UP...
...PUSH HARDER, HANK! WHAT'S WRONG WITH YOU? HARDER, NOT FASTER...
OHH, THAT'S IT... GOOD, GOOD, OH, HANK, I'M READY... I'M READY... FASTER, HANK
...OH! Ohhhhhhh.
"sigh"
OH, THAT WAS MARVELOUS. YOU HAVEN'T TAKEN DIRECTION THAT WELL SINCE COLLEGE.
YOU REALLY LIKE TAKING ME DOWN A PEG, DON'T YOU?
WHAT ARE YOU TALKING ABOUT?
YOU. FOR TWELVE YEARS, YOU'VE MADE ME THINK SMALL, ACT SMALL, AND BE SMALL.
OH, GOD, HANK.
I'M JUST GLAD YOU FINALLY REALIZE WHAT YOU'VE BEEN MISSING.
WELL, HANK...

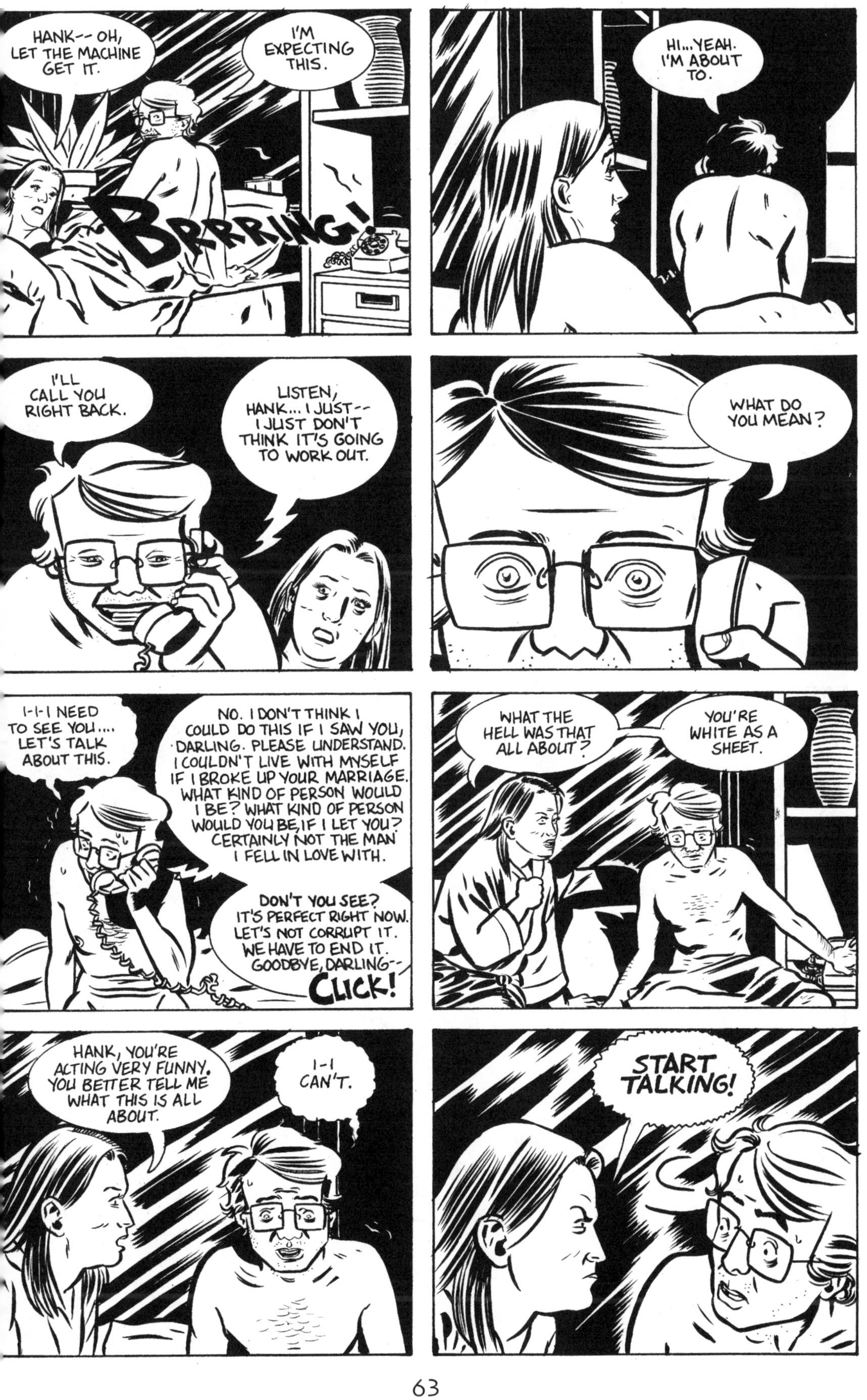
HANK-- OH, LET THE MACHINE GET IT.
I'M EXPECTING THIS.
BRRRING!
HI... YEAH. I'M ABOUT TO.
I'LL CALL YOU RIGHT BACK.
LISTEN, HANK... I JUST-- I JUST DON'T THINK IT'S GOING TO WORK OUT.
WHAT DO YOU MEAN?
I-I-I NEED TO SEE YOU.... LET'S TALK ABOUT THIS.
NO. I DON'T THINK I COULD DO THIS IF I SAW YOU, DARLING. PLEASE UNDERSTAND. I COULDN'T LIVE WITH MYSELF IF I BROKE UP YOUR MARRIAGE. WHAT KIND OF PERSON WOULD I BE? WHAT KIND OF PERSON WOULD YOU BE, IF I LET YOU? CERTAINLY NOT THE MAN I FELL IN LOVE WITH.
DON'T YOU SEE? IT'S PERFECT RIGHT NOW. LET'S NOT CORRUPT IT. WE HAVE TO END IT. GOODBYE, DARLING--
CLICK!
WHAT THE HELL WAS THAT ALL ABOUT?
YOU'RE WHITE AS A SHEET.
HANK, YOU'RE ACTING VERY FUNNY. YOU BETTER TELL ME WHAT THIS IS ALL ABOUT.
I-I CAN'T.
START TALKING!

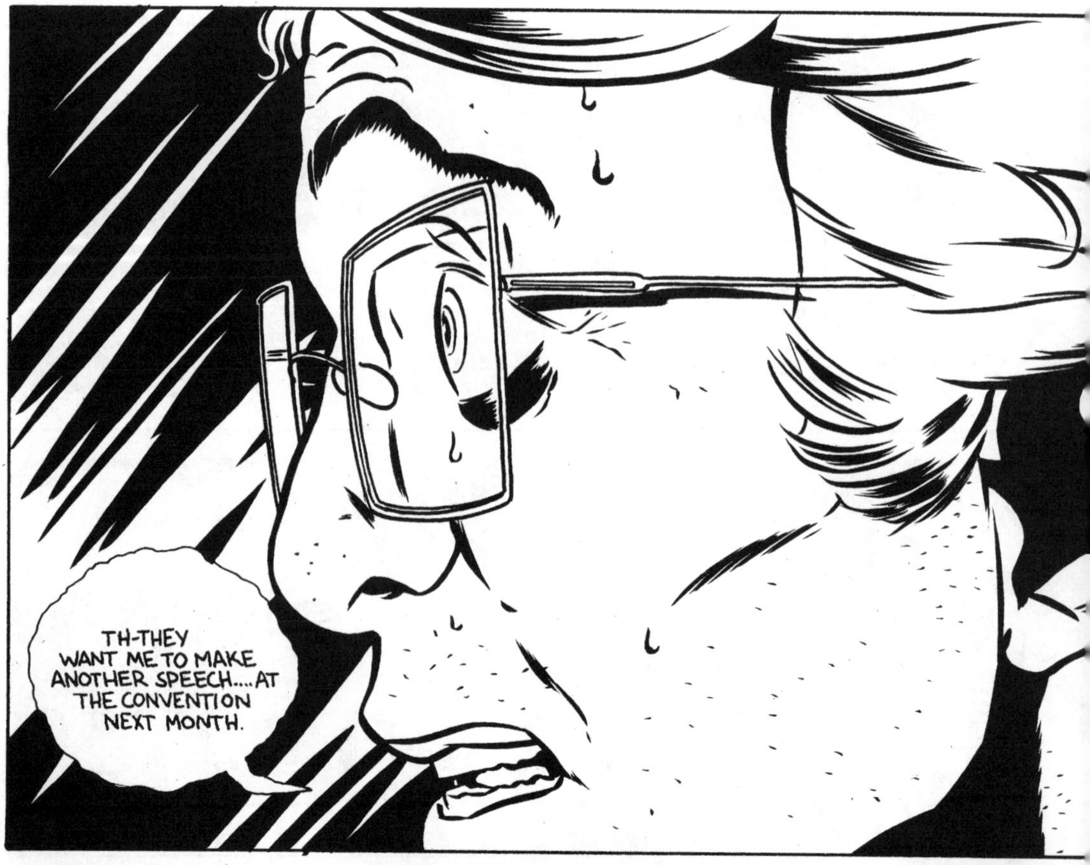
TH-THEY WANT ME TO MAKE ANOTHER SPEECH....AT THE CONVENTION NEXT MONTH.

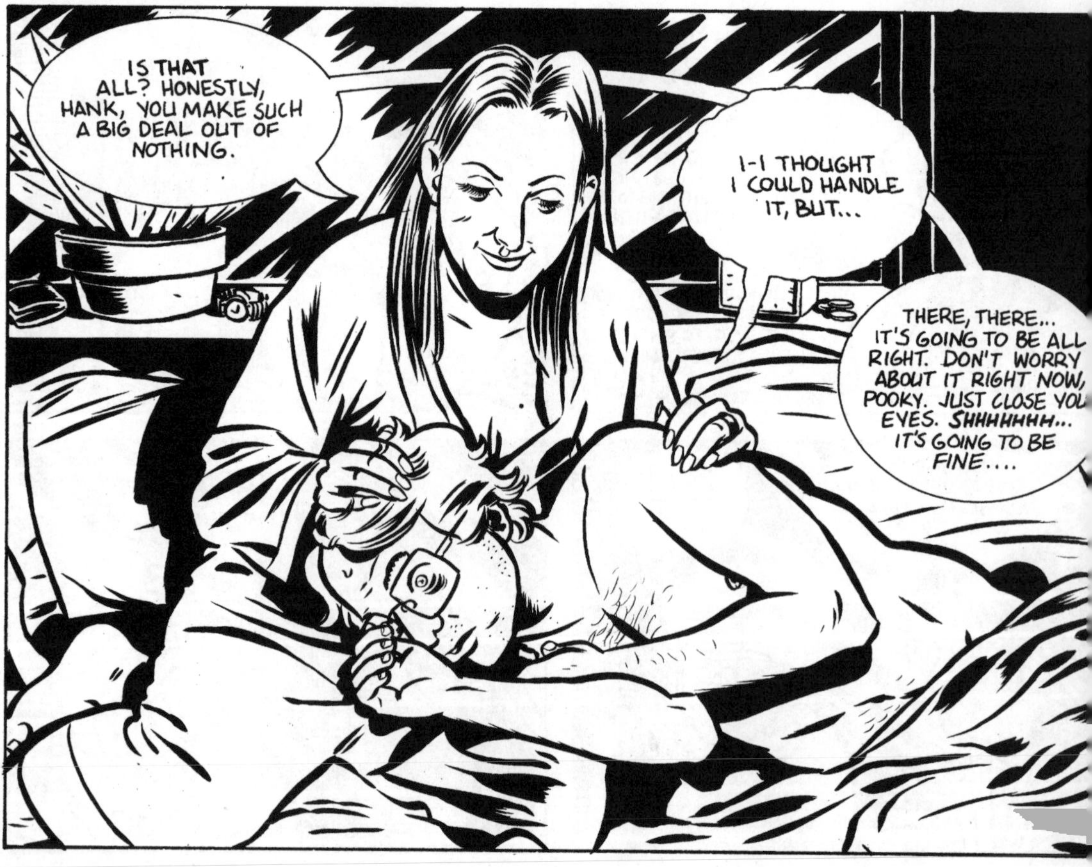
IS THAT ALL? HONESTLY, HANK, YOU MAKE SUCH A BIG DEAL OUT OF NOTHING.
I-I THOUGHT I COULD HANDLE IT, BUT...
THERE, THERE... IT'S GOING TO BE ALL RIGHT. DON'T WORRY ABOUT IT RIGHT NOW, POOKY. JUST CLOSE YOU EYES. SHHHHHHH... IT'S GOING TO BE FINE....



**THE END.**

# 3

## "While Ricky Fish Was Sleeping"

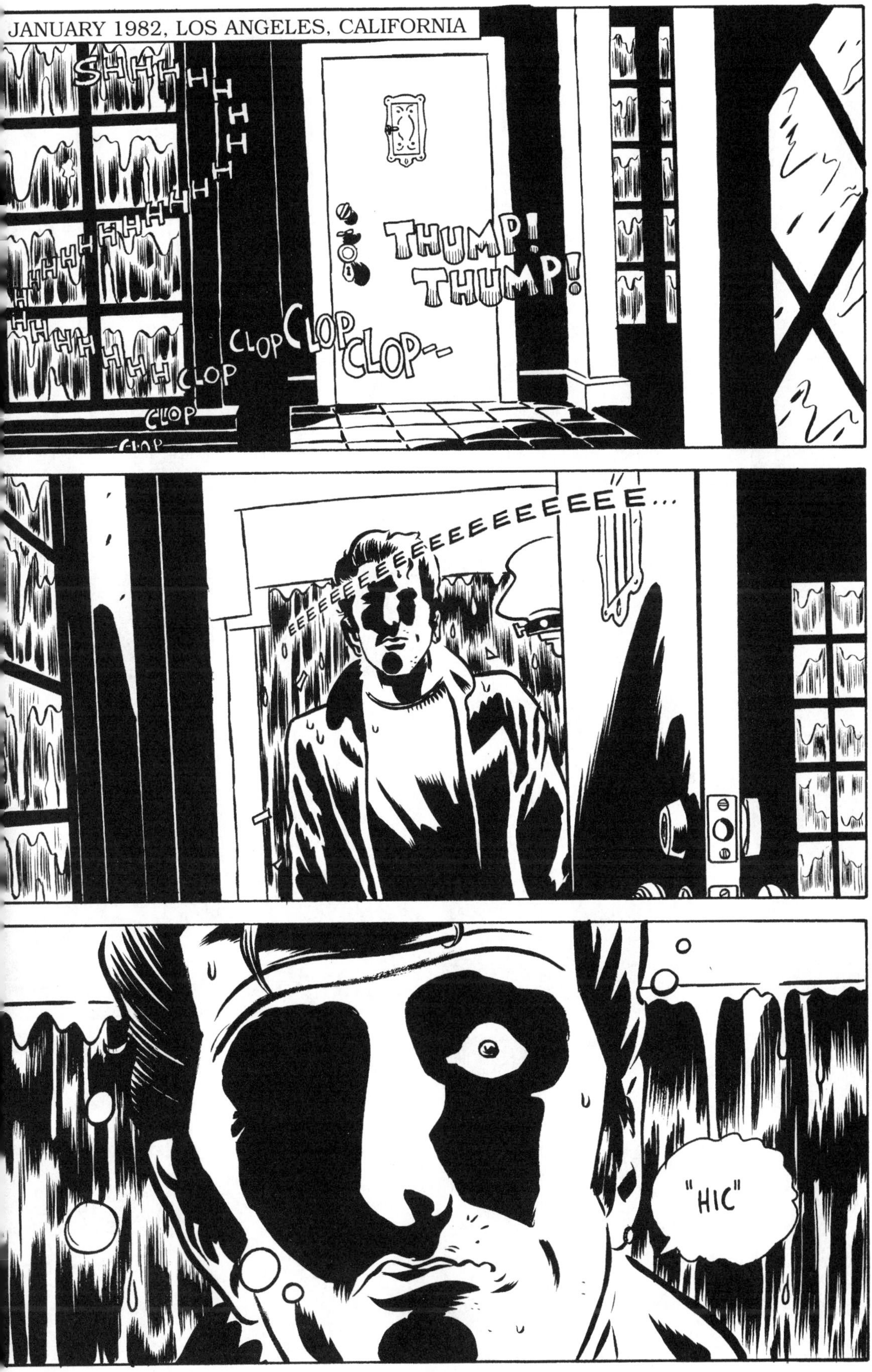
JANUARY 1982, LOS ANGELES, CALIFORNIA
SHHHHHHHHHHHHHHHHHHHHHHHHHHH
THUMP! THUMP!
CLOP CLOP CLOP--
CLOP CLOP CLOP
EEEEEEEEEEEEEEEEEEEEEEEEE...
"HIC"

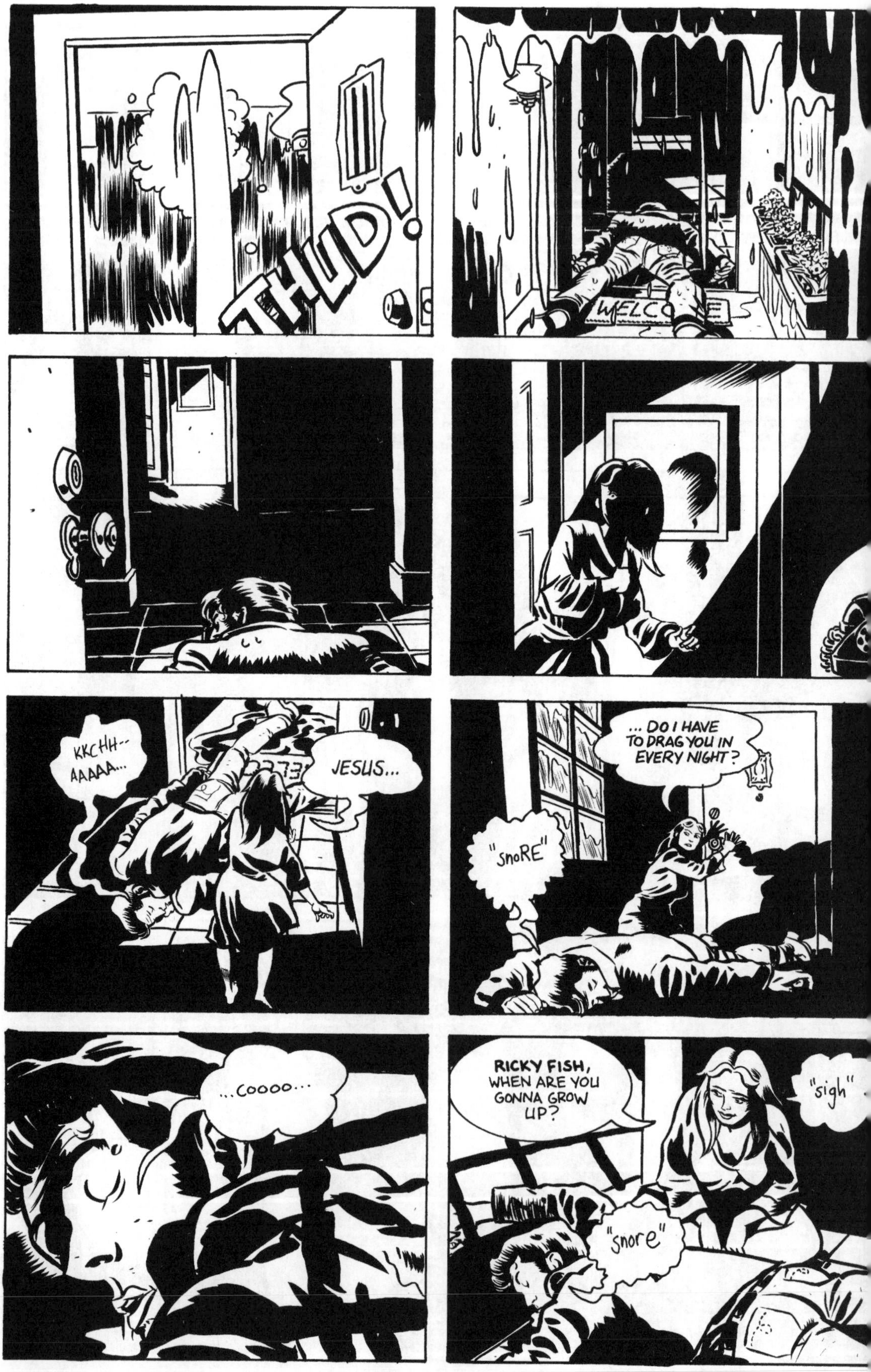
THUD!
WELCO E
KKCHH--
AAAAA...
JESUS...
... DO I HAVE TO DRAG YOU IN EVERY NIGHT?
"snoRE"
...COOOO...
RICKY FISH, WHEN ARE YOU GONNA GROW UP?
"sigh"
"snore"

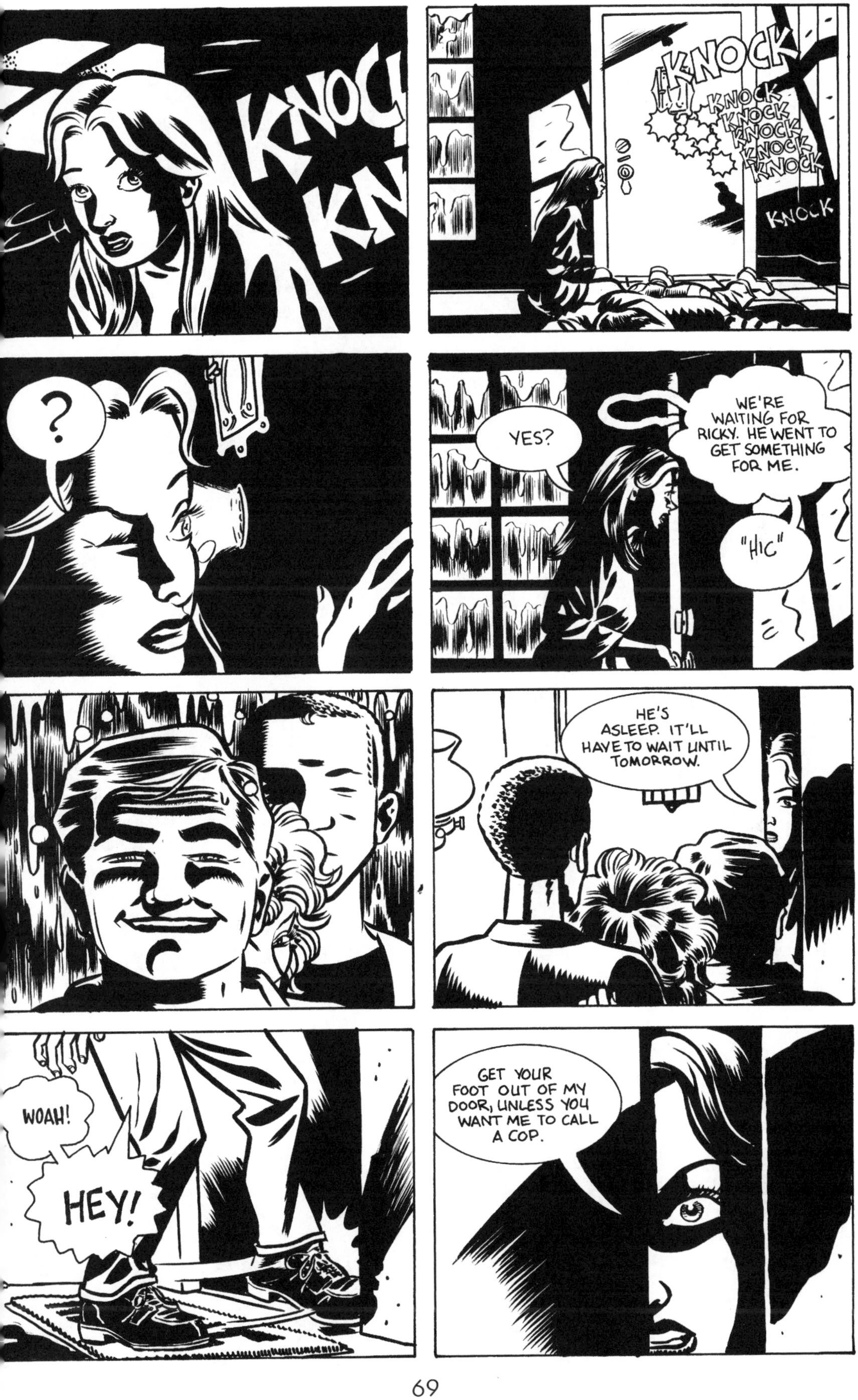
KNOC
KN
KNOCK
KNOCK
KNOCK
KNOCK
KNOCK
KNOCK
KNOCK
?
YES?
WE'RE WAITING FOR RICKY. HE WENT TO GET SOMETHING FOR ME.
"HIC"
HE'S ASLEEP. IT'LL HAVE TO WAIT UNTIL TOMORROW.
WOAH!
HEY!
GET YOUR FOOT OUT OF MY DOOR, UNLESS YOU WANT ME TO CALL A COP.

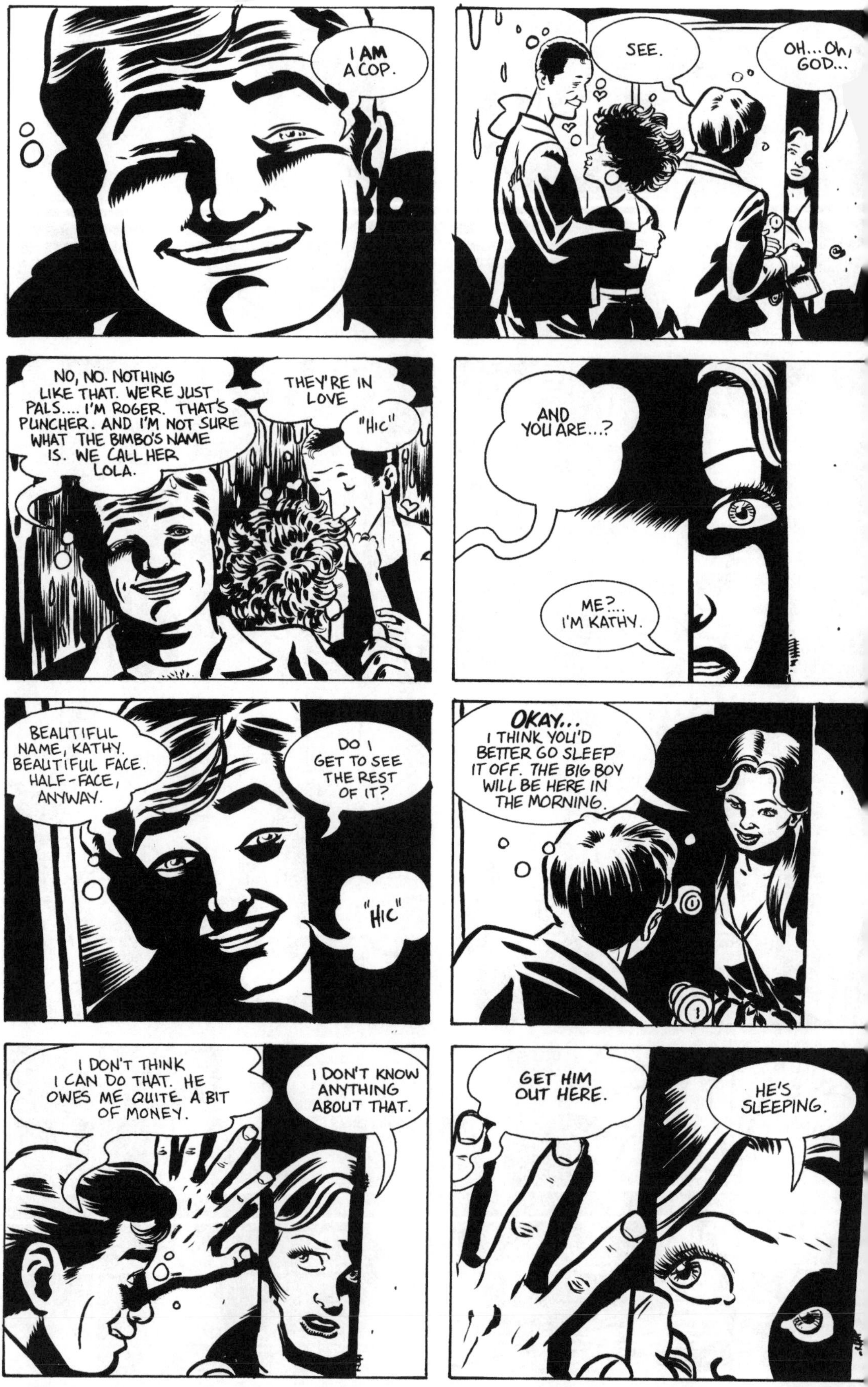
I AM A COP.
SEE.
OH... OH, GOD...
NO, NO. NOTHING LIKE THAT. WE'RE JUST PALS.... I'M ROGER. THAT'S PUNCHER. AND I'M NOT SURE WHAT THE BIMBO'S NAME IS. WE CALL HER LOLA.
THEY'RE IN LOVE
"HIC"
AND YOU ARE...?
ME?.... I'M KATHY.
BEAUTIFUL NAME, KATHY. BEAUTIFUL FACE. HALF-FACE, ANYWAY.
DO I GET TO SEE THE REST OF IT?
"HIC"
OKAY... I THINK YOU'D BETTER GO SLEEP IT OFF. THE BIG BOY WILL BE HERE IN THE MORNING.
I DON'T THINK I CAN DO THAT. HE OWES ME QUITE A BIT OF MONEY.
I DON'T KNOW ANYTHING ABOUT THAT.
GET HIM OUT HERE.
HE'S SLEEPING.

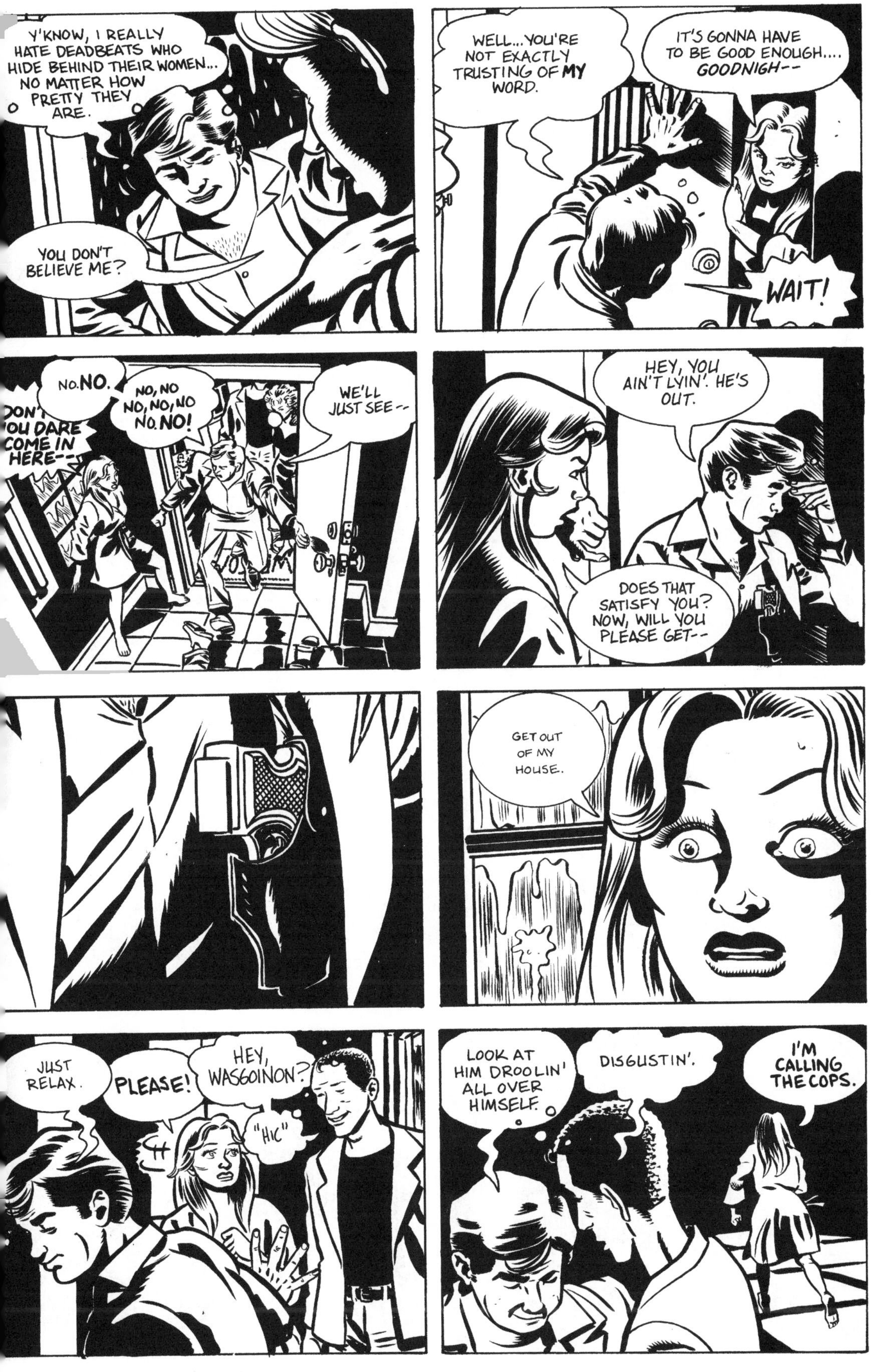
Y'KNOW, I REALLY HATE DEADBEATS WHO HIDE BEHIND THEIR WOMEN... NO MATTER HOW PRETTY THEY ARE.
YOU DON'T BELIEVE ME?
WELL... YOU'RE NOT EXACTLY TRUSTING OF MY WORD.
IT'S GONNA HAVE TO BE GOOD ENOUGH.... GOODNIGH--
WAIT!
DON'T YOU DARE COME IN HERE--
NO. NO.
NO, NO NO, NO, NO NO. NO!
WE'LL JUST SEE--
HEY, YOU AIN'T LYIN'. HE'S OUT.
DOES THAT SATISFY YOU? NOW, WILL YOU PLEASE GET--
GET OUT OF MY HOUSE.
JUST RELAX.
PLEASE!
HEY, WASGOINON?
"HIC"
LOOK AT HIM DROOLIN' ALL OVER HIMSELF.
DISGUSTIN'.
I'M CALLING THE COPS.

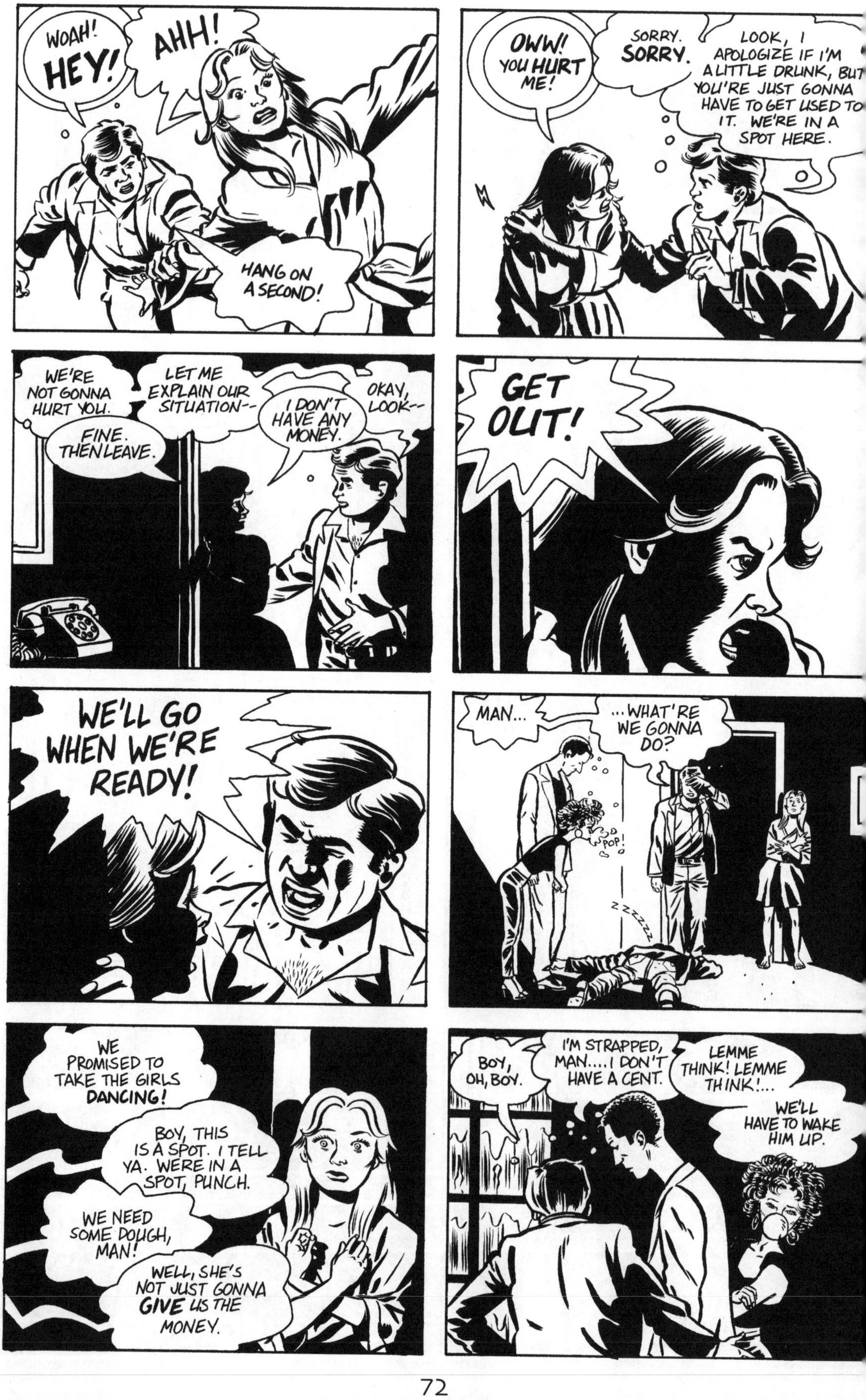
WOAH! HEY!
AHH!
HANG ON A SECOND!
OWW! YOU HURT ME!
SORRY. SORRY.
LOOK, I APOLOGIZE IF I'M A LITTLE DRUNK, BUT YOU'RE JUST GONNA HAVE TO GET USED TO IT. WE'RE IN A SPOT HERE.
WE'RE NOT GONNA HURT YOU.
LET ME EXPLAIN OUR SITUATION--
FINE. THEN LEAVE.
I DON'T HAVE ANY MONEY.
OKAY, LOOK--
GET OUT!
WE'LL GO WHEN WE'RE READY!
MAN...
...WHAT'RE WE GONNA DO?
POP!
ZZZZZZ
WE PROMISED TO TAKE THE GIRLS DANCING!
BOY, THIS IS A SPOT. I TELL YA. WERE IN A SPOT, PUNCH.
WE NEED SOME DOUGH, MAN!
WELL, SHE'S NOT JUST GONNA GIVE US THE MONEY.
BOY, OH, BOY.
I'M STRAPPED, MAN.... I DON'T HAVE A CENT.
LEMME THINK! LEMME THINK!...
WE'LL HAVE TO WAKE HIM UP.

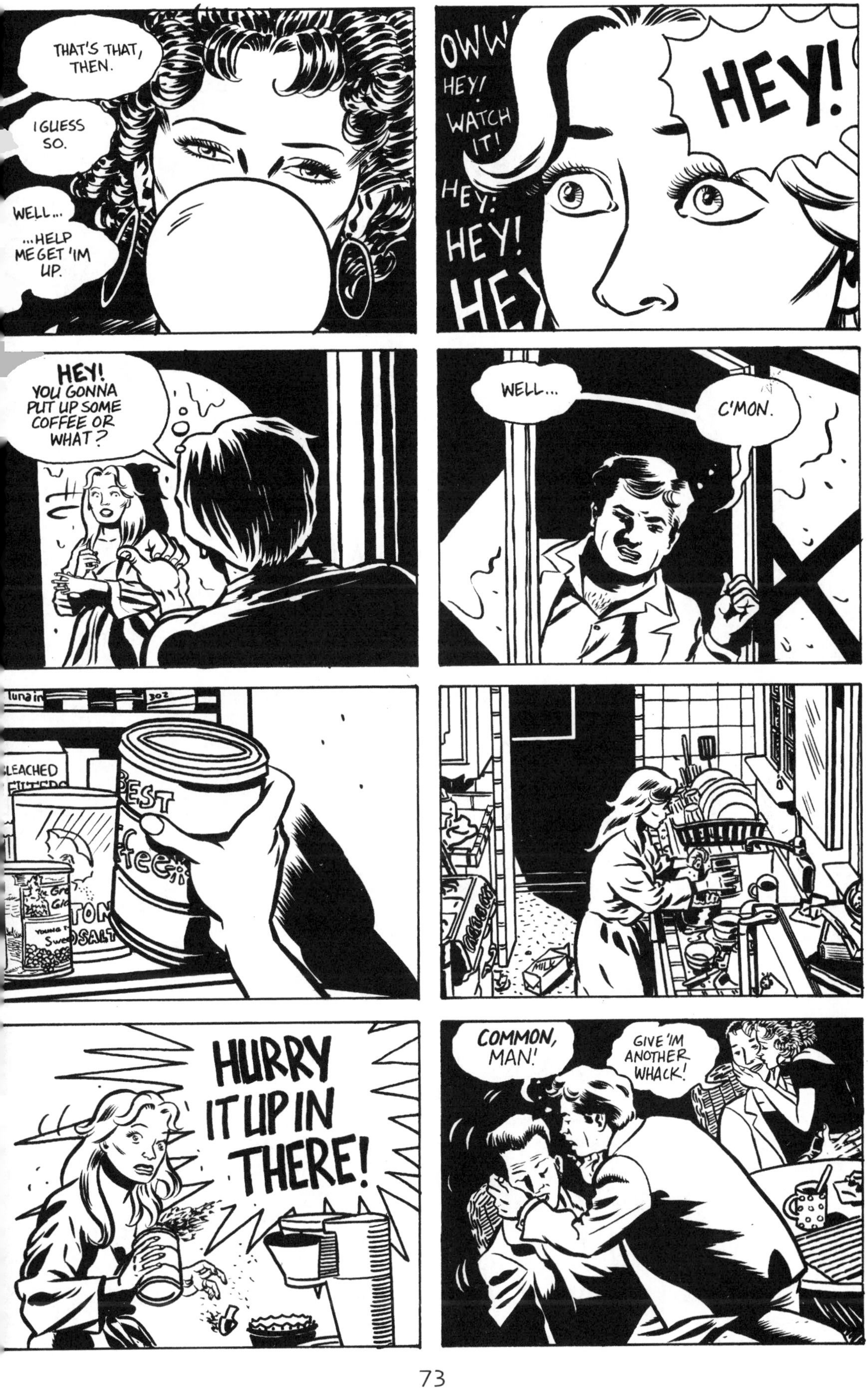
THAT'S THAT, THEN.
I GUESS SO.
WELL...
...HELP ME GET 'IM UP.
OWW
HEY! WATCH IT!
HEY!
HEY!
HEY!
HEY!
HEY! YOU GONNA PUT UP SOME COFFEE OR WHAT?
WELL...
C'MON.
BLEACHED
BEST
MILK
HURRY IT UP IN THERE!
COMMON, MAN!
GIVE 'IM ANOTHER WHACK!

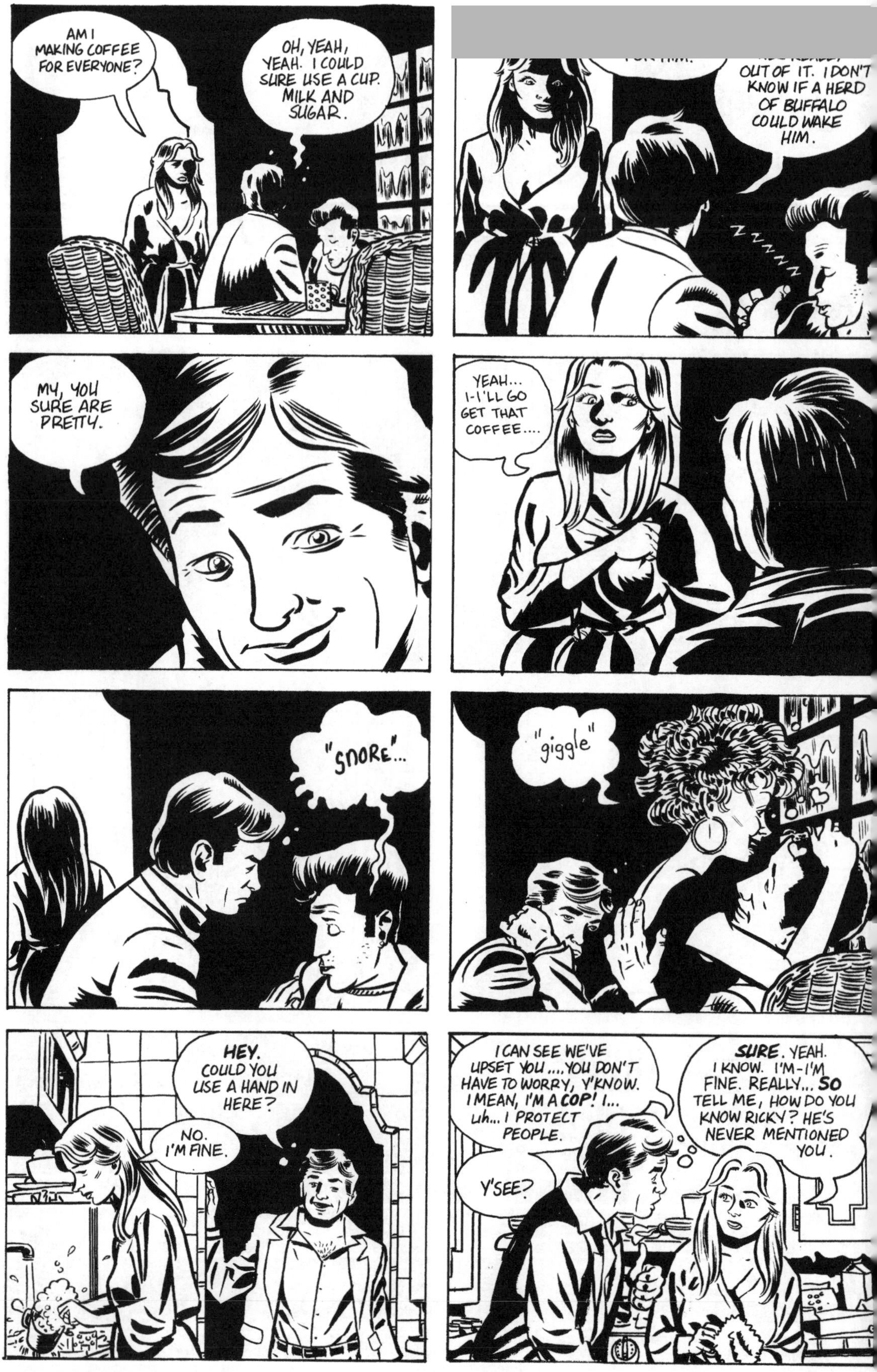
AM I MAKING COFFEE FOR EVERYONE?
OH, YEAH, YEAH. I COULD SURE USE A CUP. MILK AND SUGAR.
OUT OF IT. I DON'T KNOW IF A HERD OF BUFFALO COULD WAKE HIM.
Z Z Z Z Z
MY, YOU SURE ARE PRETTY.
YEAH... I-I'LL GO GET THAT COFFEE....
"SNORE"...
"giggle"
HEY. COULD YOU USE A HAND IN HERE?
NO. I'M FINE.
I CAN SEE WE'VE UPSET YOU.... YOU DON'T HAVE TO WORRY, Y'KNOW. I MEAN, I'M A COP! I... uh... I PROTECT PEOPLE.
Y'SEE?
SURE. YEAH. I KNOW. I'M-I'M FINE. REALLY... SO TELL ME, HOW DO YOU KNOW RICKY? HE'S NEVER MENTIONED YOU.

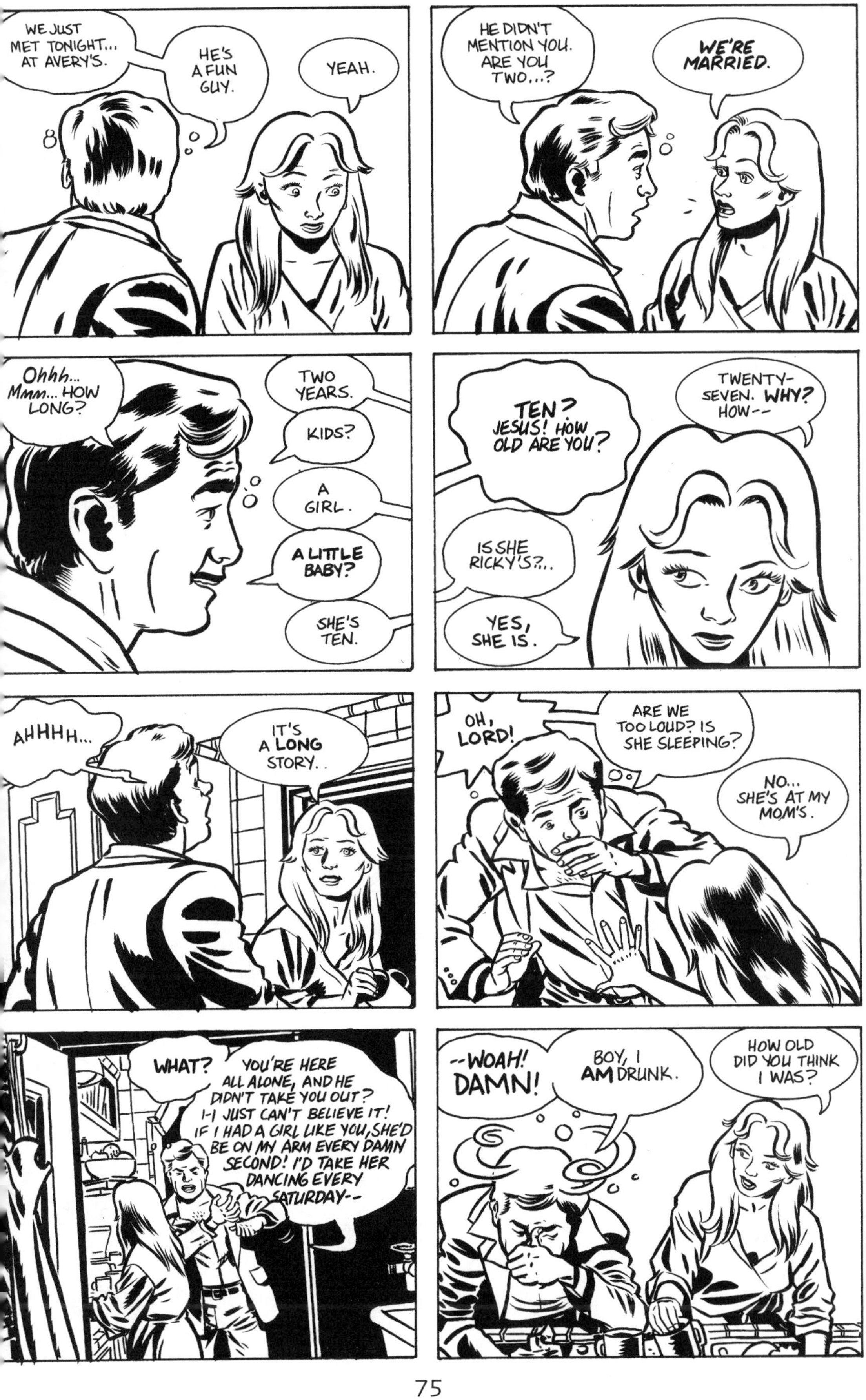
WE JUST MET TONIGHT... AT AVERY'S.
HE'S A FUN GUY.
YEAH.
HE DIDN'T MENTION YOU. ARE YOU TWO...?
WE'RE MARRIED.
Ohhh... Mmm... HOW LONG?
TWO YEARS.
KIDS?
A GIRL.
A LITTLE BABY?
SHE'S TEN.
TEN? JESUS! HOW OLD ARE YOU?
TWENTY-SEVEN. WHY? HOW--
IS SHE RICKY'S?..
YES, SHE IS.
AHHHH...
IT'S A LONG STORY..
OH, LORD!
ARE WE TOO LOUD? IS SHE SLEEPING?
NO... SHE'S AT MY MOM'S.
WHAT?
YOU'RE HERE ALL ALONE, AND HE DIDN'T TAKE YOU OUT? I-I JUST CAN'T BELIEVE IT! IF I HAD A GIRL LIKE YOU, SHE'D BE ON MY ARM EVERY DAMN SECOND! I'D TAKE HER DANCING EVERY SATURDAY--
--WOAH! DAMN!
BOY, I AM DRUNK.
HOW OLD DID YOU THINK I WAS?

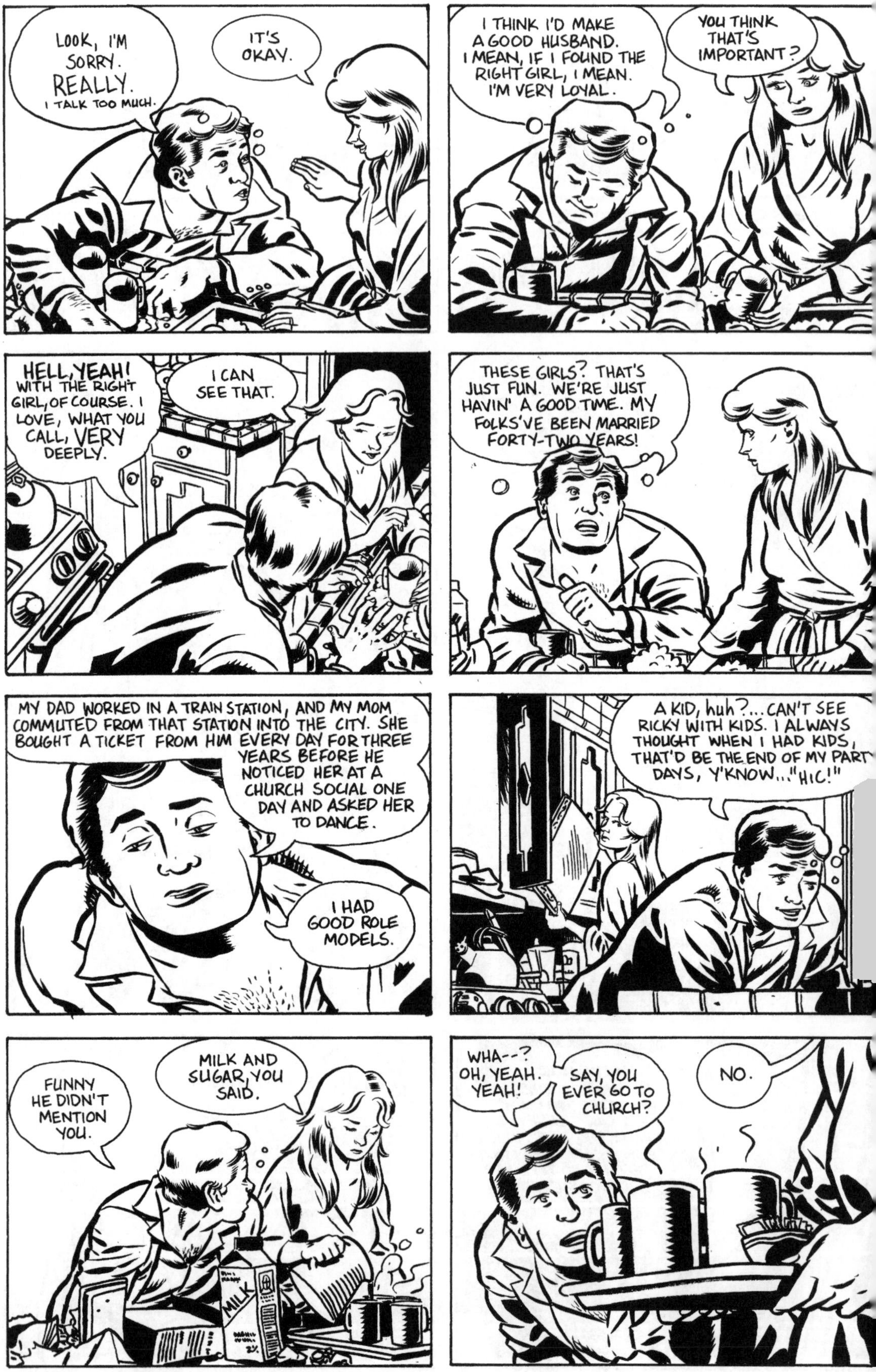
LOOK, I'M SORRY. REALLY. I TALK TOO MUCH.
IT'S OKAY.
I THINK I'D MAKE A GOOD HUSBAND. I MEAN, IF I FOUND THE RIGHT GIRL, I MEAN. I'M VERY LOYAL.
YOU THINK THAT'S IMPORTANT?
HELL, YEAH! WITH THE RIGHT GIRL, OF COURSE. I LOVE, WHAT YOU CALL, VERY DEEPLY.
I CAN SEE THAT.
THESE GIRLS? THAT'S JUST FUN. WE'RE JUST HAVIN' A GOOD TIME. MY FOLKS'VE BEEN MARRIED FORTY-TWO YEARS!
MY DAD WORKED IN A TRAIN STATION, AND MY MOM COMMUTED FROM THAT STATION INTO THE CITY. SHE BOUGHT A TICKET FROM HIM EVERY DAY FOR THREE YEARS BEFORE HE NOTICED HER AT A CHURCH SOCIAL ONE DAY AND ASKED HER TO DANCE.
I HAD GOOD ROLE MODELS.
A KID, huh?... CAN'T SEE RICKY WITH KIDS. I ALWAYS THOUGHT WHEN I HAD KIDS, THAT'D BE THE END OF MY PARTY DAYS, Y'KNOW..."HIC!"
FUNNY HE DIDN'T MENTION YOU.
MILK AND SUGAR, YOU SAID.
MILK
WHA--? OH, YEAH. YEAH!
SAY, YOU EVER GO TO CHURCH?
NO.

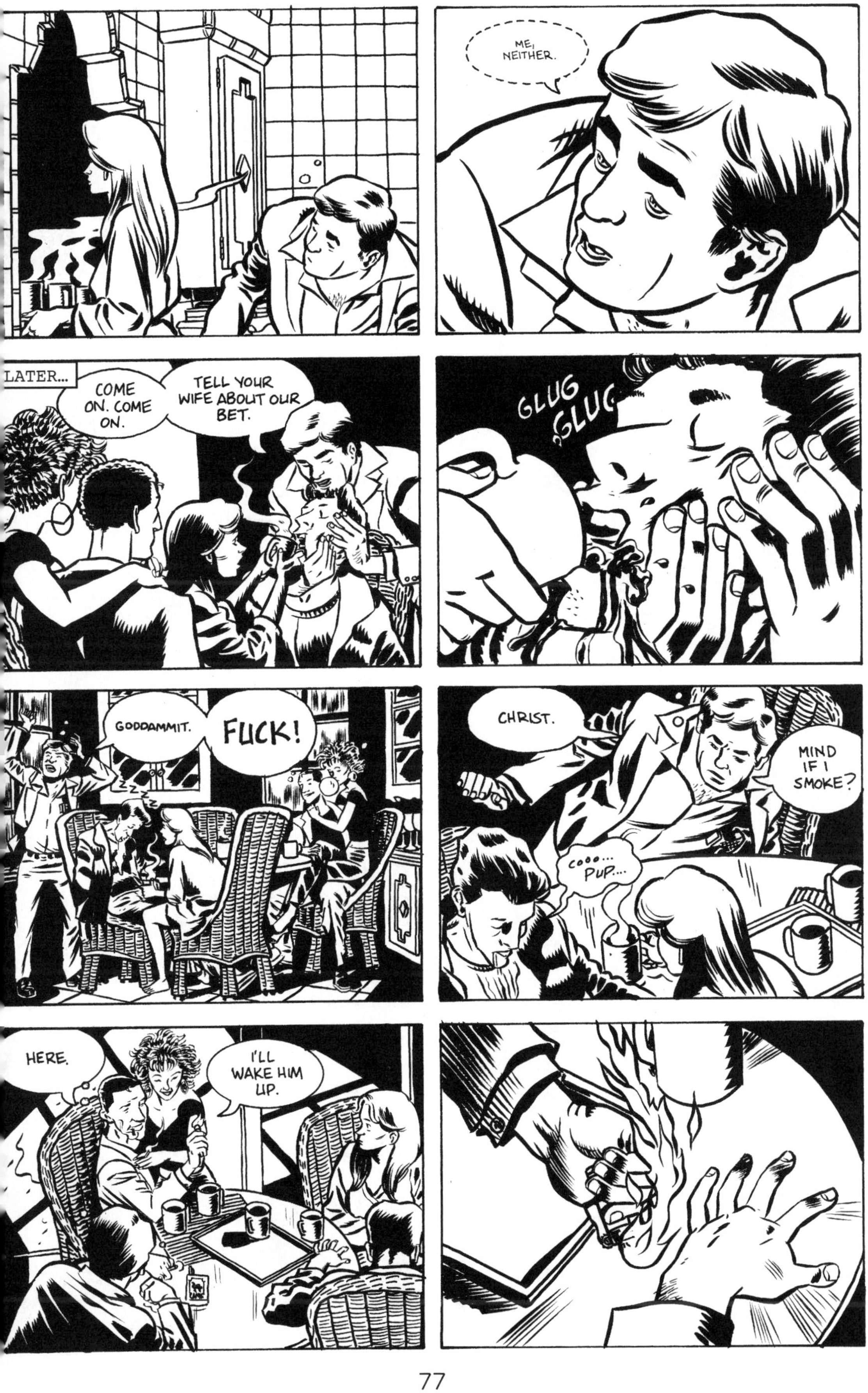
ME, NEITHER.
LATER...
COME ON. COME ON.
TELL YOUR WIFE ABOUT OUR BET.
GLUG GLUG
GODDAMMIT.
FUCK!
CHRIST.
MIND IF I SMOKE?
COOO... PUP...
HERE.
I'LL WAKE HIM UP.

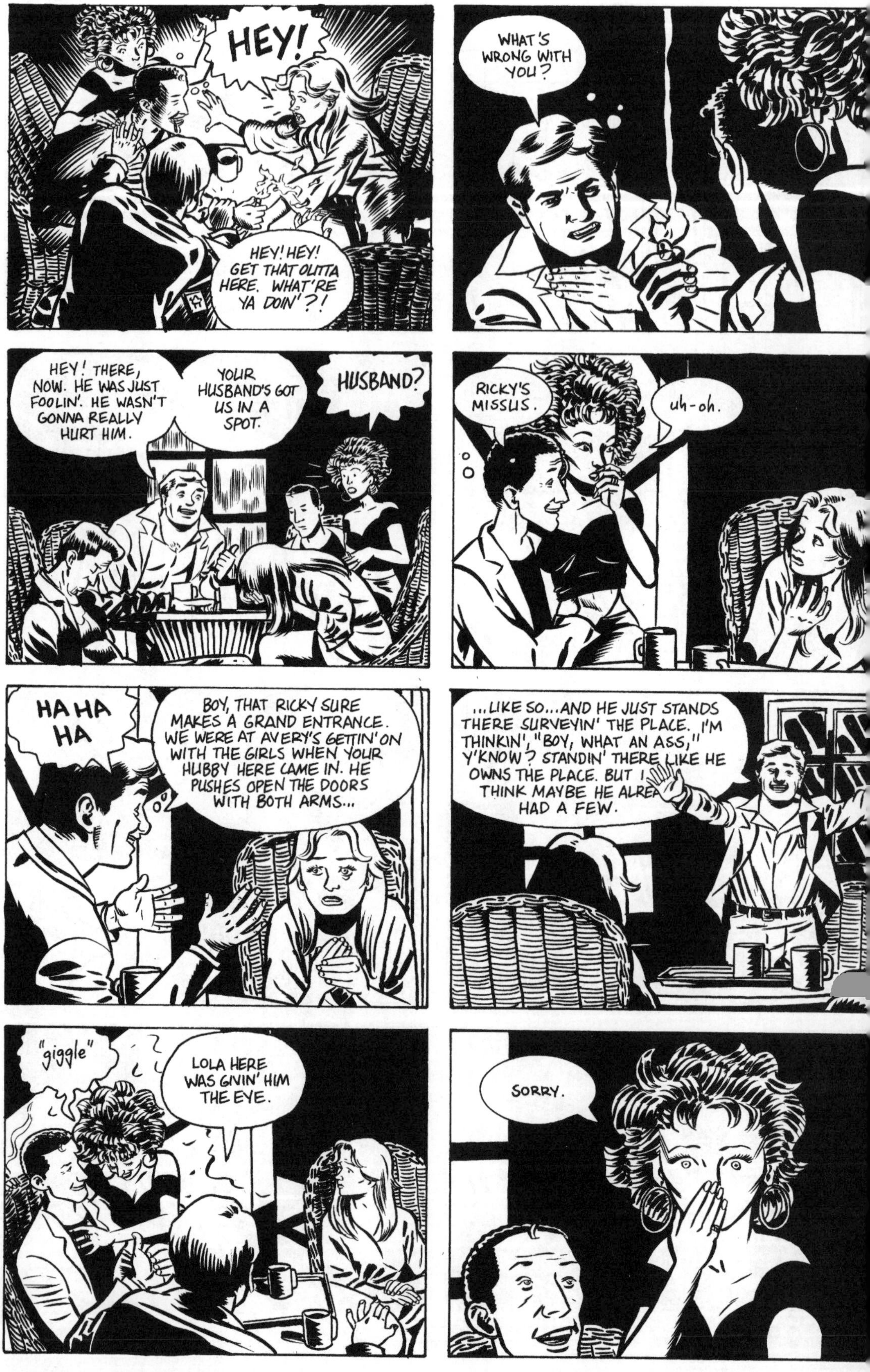
HEY!
HEY! HEY! GET THAT OUTTA HERE. WHAT'RE YA DOIN'?!
WHAT'S WRONG WITH YOU?
HEY! THERE, NOW. HE WAS JUST FOOLIN'. HE WASN'T GONNA REALLY HURT HIM.
YOUR HUSBAND'S GOT US IN A SPOT.
HUSBAND?
RICKY'S MISSUS.
uh-oh.
HA HA HA
BOY, THAT RICKY SURE MAKES A GRAND ENTRANCE. WE WERE AT AVERY'S GETTIN' ON WITH THE GIRLS WHEN YOUR HUBBY HERE CAME IN. HE PUSHES OPEN THE DOORS WITH BOTH ARMS...
...LIKE SO...AND HE JUST STANDS THERE SURVEYIN' THE PLACE. I'M THINKIN', "BOY, WHAT AN ASS," Y'KNOW? STANDIN' THERE LIKE HE OWNS THE PLACE. BUT I THINK MAYBE HE ALRE HAD A FEW.
"giggle"
LOLA HERE WAS GIVIN' HIM THE EYE.
SORRY.

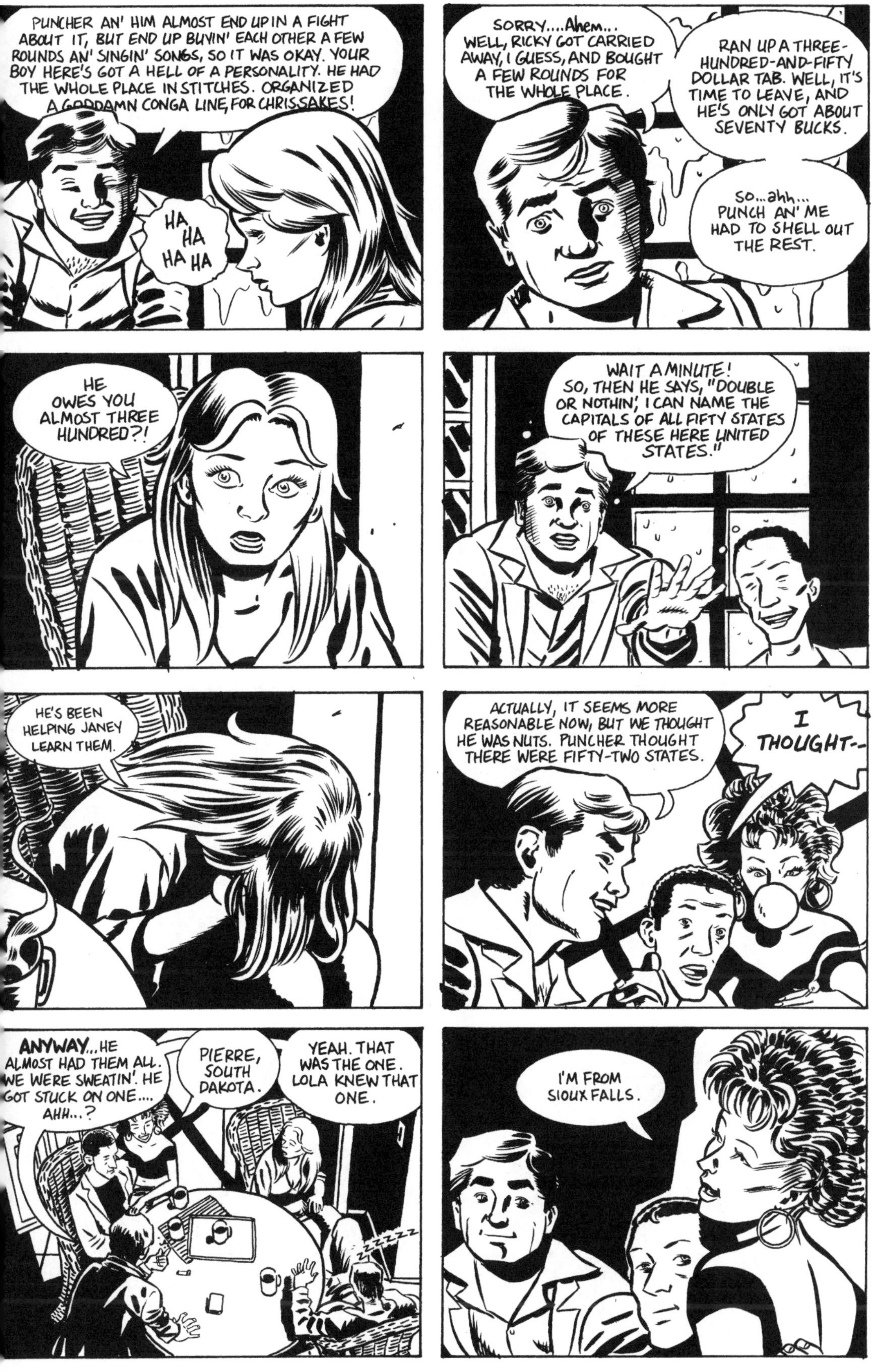
PUNCHER AN' HIM ALMOST END UP IN A FIGHT ABOUT IT, BUT END UP BUYIN' EACH OTHER A FEW ROUNDS AN' SINGIN' SONGS, SO IT WAS OKAY. YOUR BOY HERE'S GOT A HELL OF A PERSONALITY. HE HAD THE WHOLE PLACE IN STITCHES. ORGANIZED A GODDAMN CONGA LINE, FOR CHRISSAKES!
HA HA HA HA
SORRY....Ahem... WELL, RICKY GOT CARRIED AWAY, I GUESS, AND BOUGHT A FEW ROUNDS FOR THE WHOLE PLACE.
RAN UP A THREE-HUNDRED-AND-FIFTY DOLLAR TAB. WELL, IT'S TIME TO LEAVE, AND HE'S ONLY GOT ABOUT SEVENTY BUCKS.
SO...ahh... PUNCH AN' ME HAD TO SHELL OUT THE REST.
HE OWES YOU ALMOST THREE HUNDRED?!
WAIT A MINUTE! SO, THEN HE SAYS, "DOUBLE OR NOTHIN', I CAN NAME THE CAPITALS OF ALL FIFTY STATES OF THESE HERE UNITED STATES."
HE'S BEEN HELPING JANEY LEARN THEM.
ACTUALLY, IT SEEMS MORE REASONABLE NOW, BUT WE THOUGHT HE WAS NUTS. PUNCHER THOUGHT THERE WERE FIFTY-TWO STATES.
I THOUGHT--
ANYWAY...HE ALMOST HAD THEM ALL. WE WERE SWEATIN'. HE GOT STUCK ON ONE.... AHH...?
PIERRE, SOUTH DAKOTA.
YEAH. THAT WAS THE ONE. LOLA KNEW THAT ONE.
ZZZZZZ
I'M FROM SIOUX FALLS.

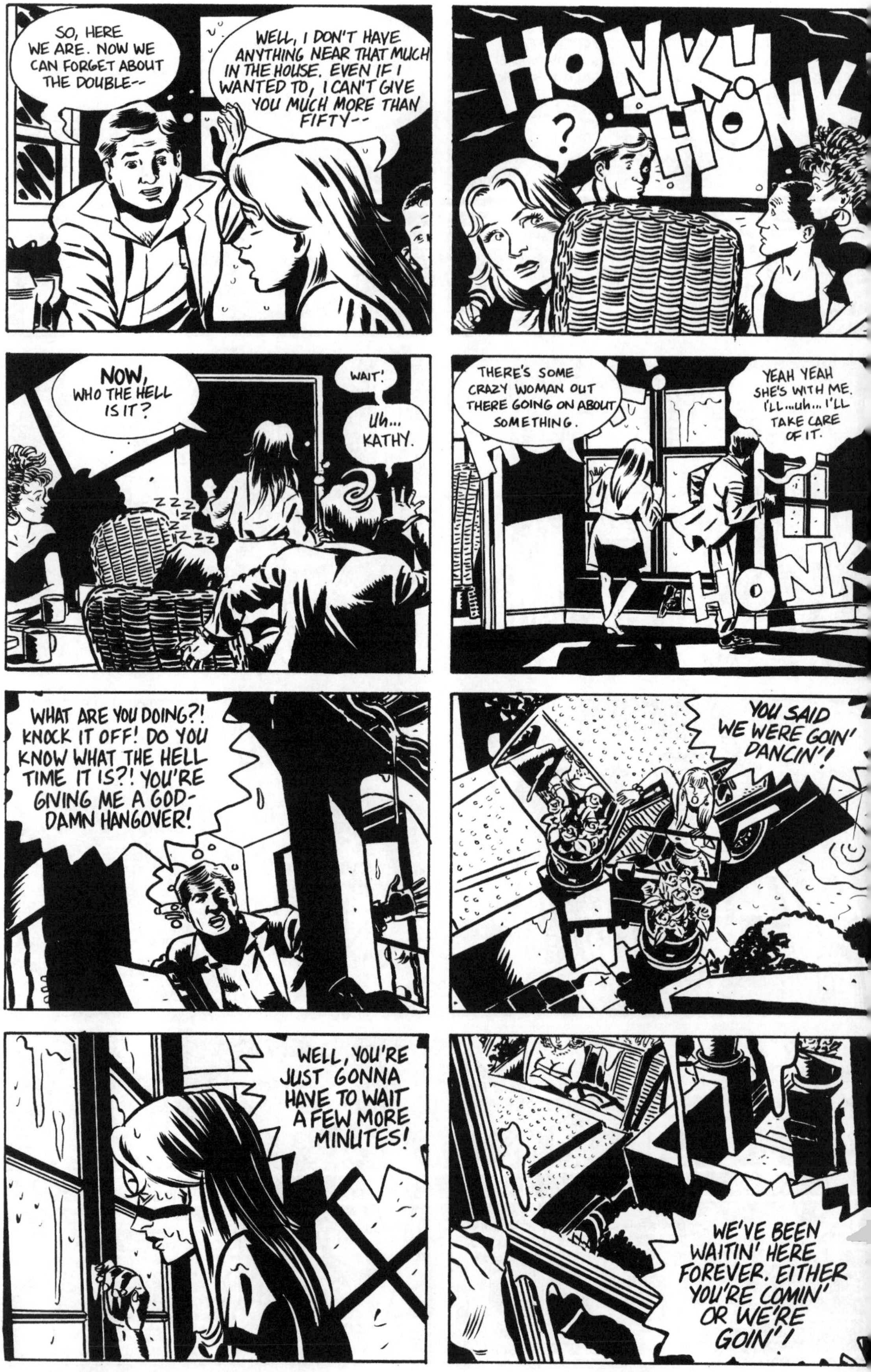
SO, HERE WE ARE. NOW WE CAN FORGET ABOUT THE DOUBLE--
WELL, I DON'T HAVE ANYTHING NEAR THAT MUCH IN THE HOUSE. EVEN IF I WANTED TO, I CAN'T GIVE YOU MUCH MORE THAN FIFTY--
HONK! HONK
?
NOW, WHO THE HELL IS IT?
WAIT!
Uh... KATHY.
Z Z Z Z Z Z Z Z
THERE'S SOME CRAZY WOMAN OUT THERE GOING ON ABOUT SOMETHING.
YEAH YEAH SHE'S WITH ME. I'LL...uh... I'LL TAKE CARE OF IT.
HONK
WHAT ARE YOU DOING?! KNOCK IT OFF! DO YOU KNOW WHAT THE HELL TIME IT IS?! YOU'RE GIVING ME A GOD-DAMN HANGOVER!
YOU SAID WE WERE GOIN' DANCIN'!
WELL, YOU'RE JUST GONNA HAVE TO WAIT A FEW MORE MINUTES!
WE'VE BEEN WAITIN' HERE FOREVER. EITHER YOU'RE COMIN' OR WE'RE GOIN'!

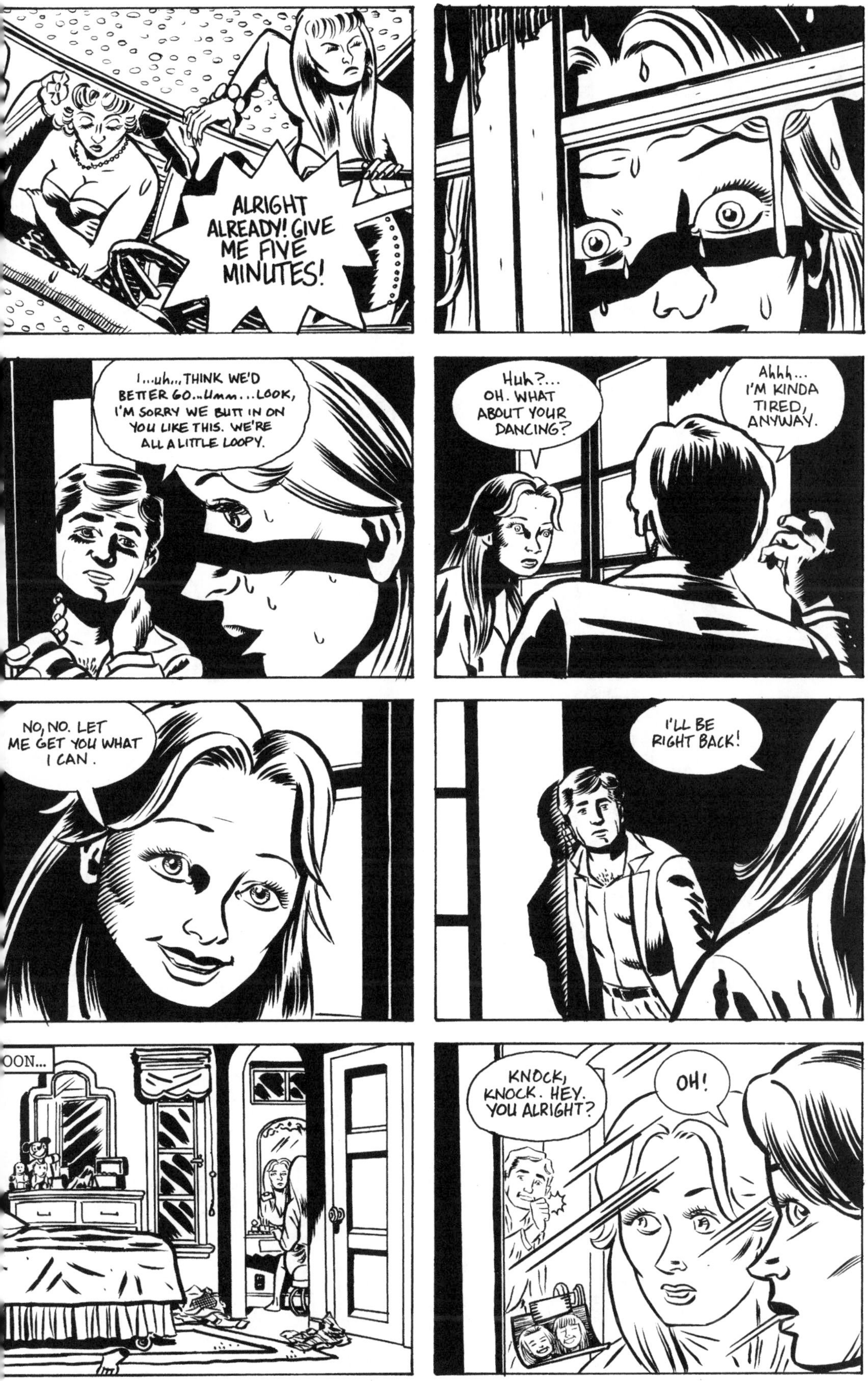
ALRIGHT ALREADY! GIVE ME FIVE MINUTES!
I...uh...THINK WE'D BETTER GO...Umm...LOOK, I'M SORRY WE BUTT IN ON YOU LIKE THIS. WE'RE ALL A LITTLE LOOPY.
Huh?... OH. WHAT ABOUT YOUR DANCING?
Ahhh... I'M KINDA TIRED, ANYWAY.
NO, NO. LET ME GET YOU WHAT I CAN.
I'LL BE RIGHT BACK!
OON...
KNOCK, KNOCK. HEY. YOU ALRIGHT?
OH!

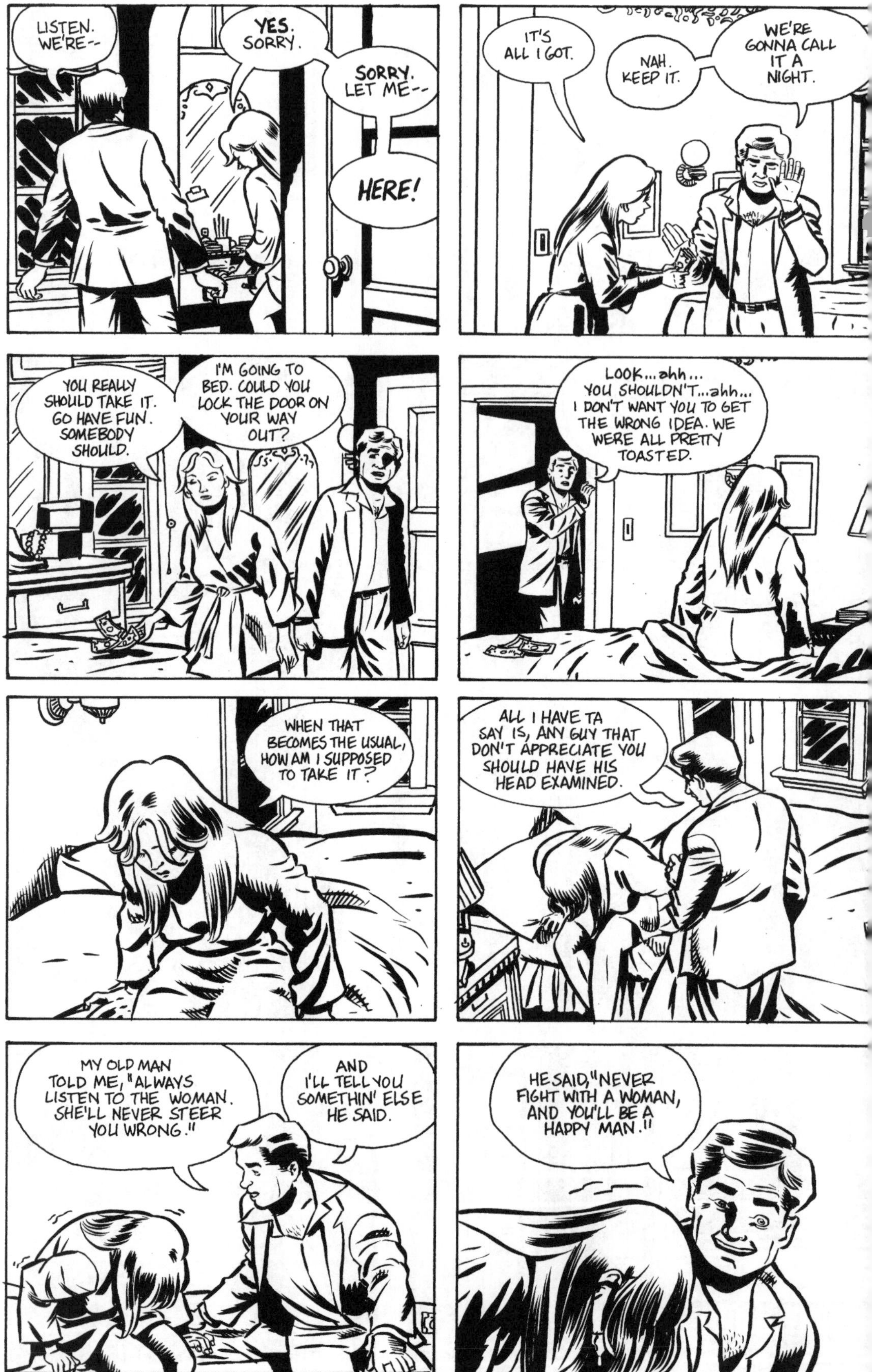
LISTEN. WE'RE--
YES. SORRY.
SORRY. LET ME--
HERE!
IT'S ALL I GOT.
NAH. KEEP IT.
WE'RE GONNA CALL IT A NIGHT.
YOU REALLY SHOULD TAKE IT. GO HAVE FUN. SOMEBODY SHOULD.
I'M GOING TO BED. COULD YOU LOCK THE DOOR ON YOUR WAY OUT?
LOOK...ahh... YOU SHOULDN'T...ahh... I DON'T WANT YOU TO GET THE WRONG IDEA. WE WERE ALL PRETTY TOASTED.
WHEN THAT BECOMES THE USUAL, HOW AM I SUPPOSED TO TAKE IT?
ALL I HAVE TA SAY IS, ANY GUY THAT DON'T APPRECIATE YOU SHOULD HAVE HIS HEAD EXAMINED.
MY OLD MAN TOLD ME, "ALWAYS LISTEN TO THE WOMAN. SHE'LL NEVER STEER YOU WRONG."
AND I'LL TELL YOU SOMETHIN' ELSE HE SAID.
HE SAID, "NEVER FIGHT WITH A WOMAN, AND YOU'LL BE A HAPPY MAN."

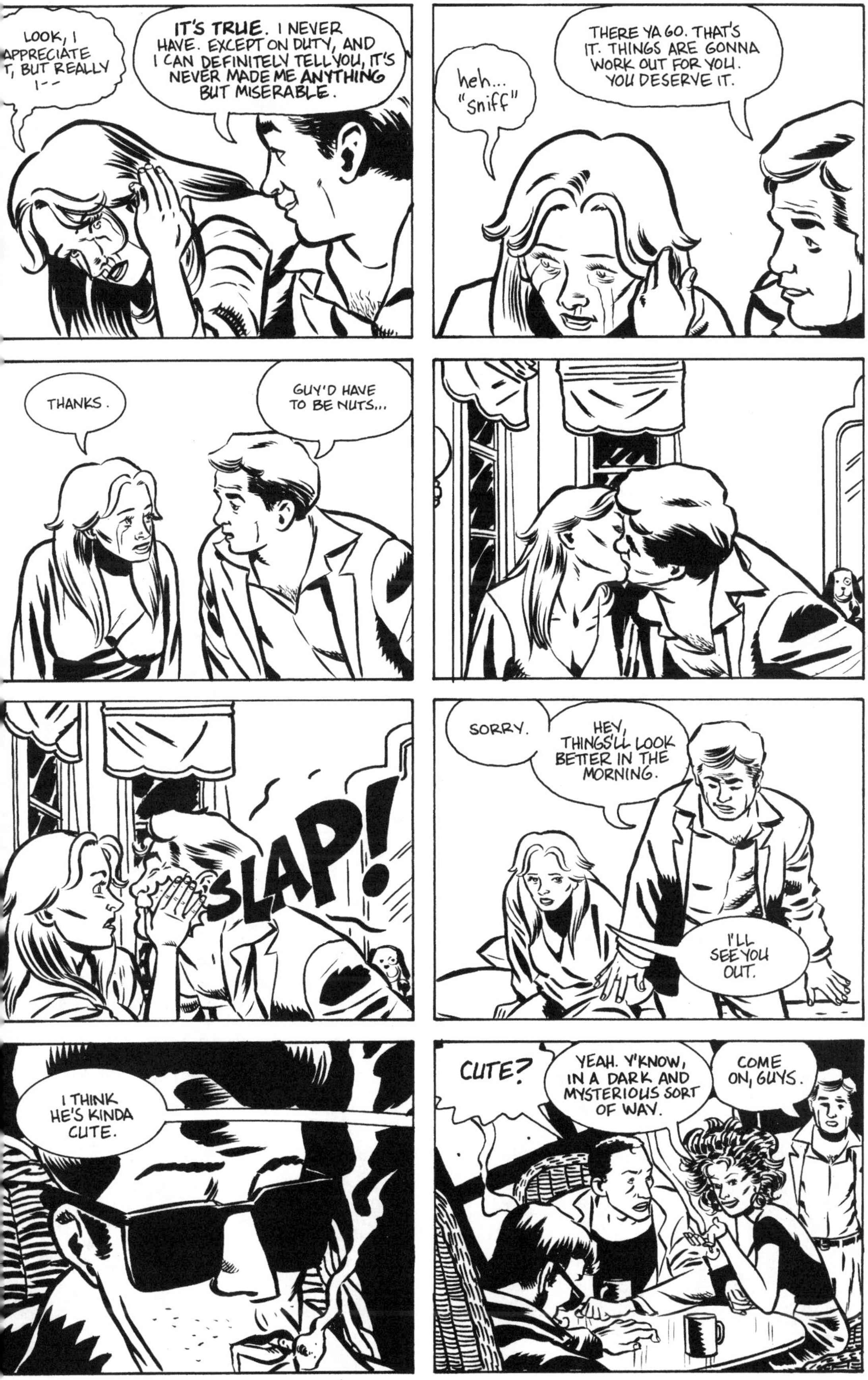
LOOK, I APPRECIATE IT, BUT REALLY I--
IT'S TRUE. I NEVER HAVE. EXCEPT ON DUTY, AND I CAN DEFINITELY TELL YOU, IT'S NEVER MADE ME ANYTHING BUT MISERABLE.
heh... "sniff"
THERE YA GO. THAT'S IT. THINGS ARE GONNA WORK OUT FOR YOU. YOU DESERVE IT.
THANKS.
GUY'D HAVE TO BE NUTS...
SLAP!
SORRY.
HEY, THINGS'LL LOOK BETTER IN THE MORNING.
I'LL SEE YOU OUT.
I THINK HE'S KINDA CUTE.
CUTE?
YEAH. Y'KNOW, IN A DARK AND MYSTERIOUS SORT OF WAY.
COME ON, GUYS.

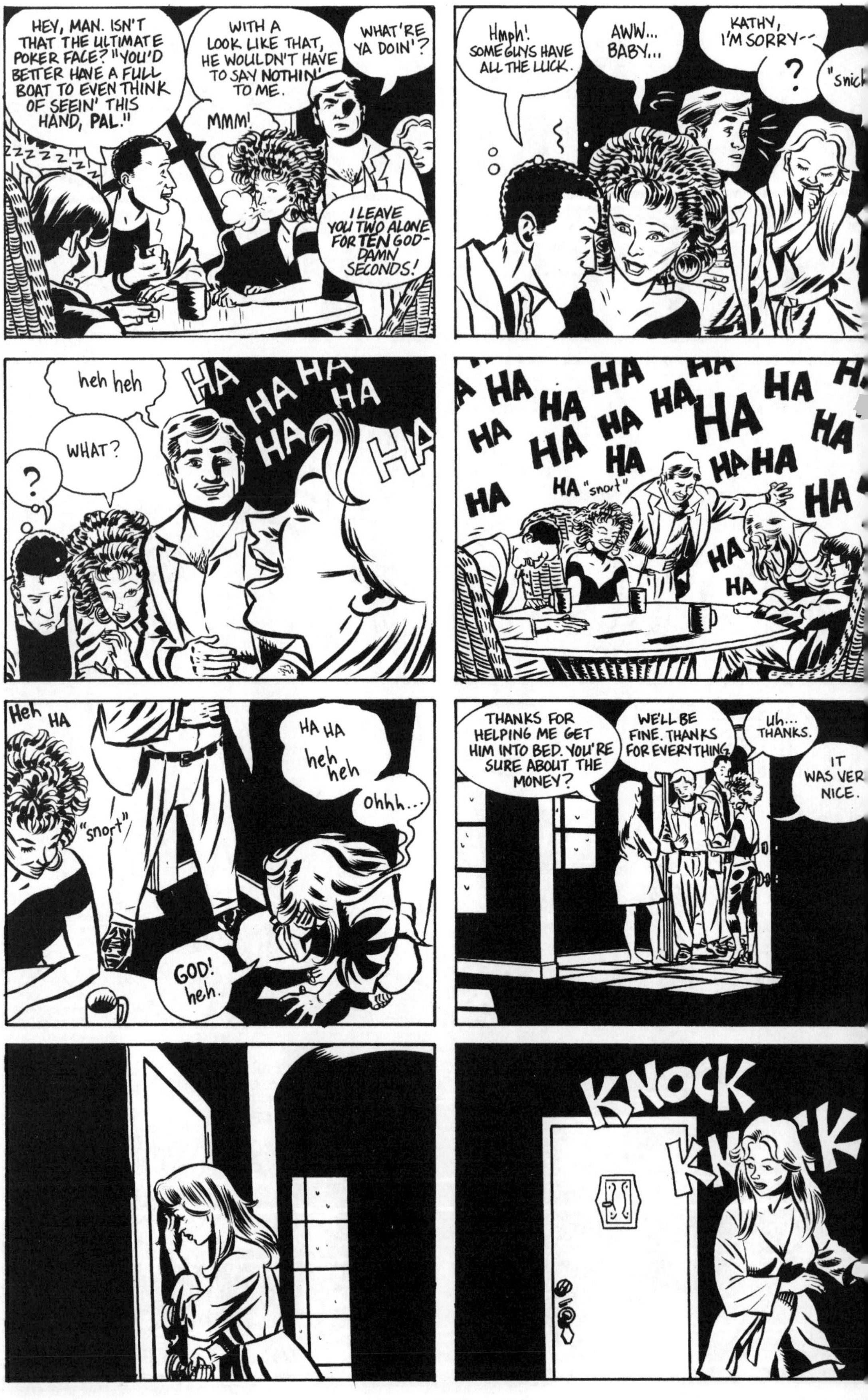
HEY, MAN. ISN'T THAT THE ULTIMATE POKER FACE? "YOU'D BETTER HAVE A FULL BOAT TO EVEN THINK OF SEEIN' THIS HAND, PAL."
ZZZZZZZ
WITH A LOOK LIKE THAT, HE WOULDN'T HAVE TO SAY NOTHIN' TO ME.
MMM!
WHAT'RE YA DOIN'?
I LEAVE YOU TWO ALONE FOR TEN GOD-DAMN SECONDS!
Hmph! SOME GUYS HAVE ALL THE LUCK.
AWW... BABY...
KATHY, I'M SORRY--
?
"Snick
heh heh
WHAT?
?
HA HA HA HA HA HA
HA HA HA HA HA HA HA HA HA HA HA HA HA HA HA HA
HA "snort"
HA HA
Heh HA
"snort"
HA HA heh heh
Ohhh...
GOD! heh.
THANKS FOR HELPING ME GET HIM INTO BED. YOU'RE SURE ABOUT THE MONEY?
WE'LL BE FINE. THANKS FOR EVERYTHING.
Uh... THANKS.
IT WAS VER NICE.
KNOCK
KNOCK

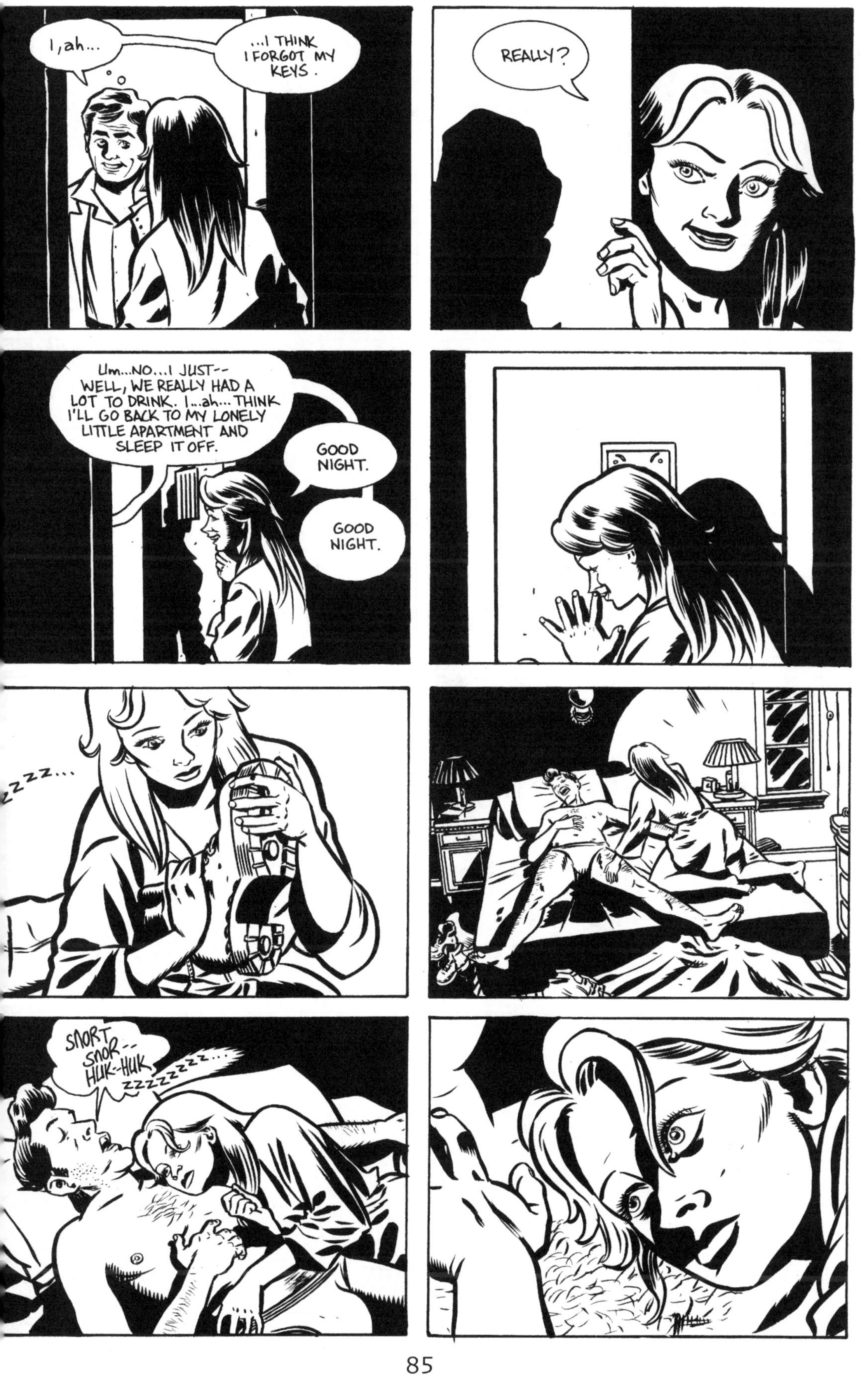
I, ah...
...I THINK I FORGOT MY KEYS.
REALLY?
Um...NO...I JUST-- WELL, WE REALLY HAD A LOT TO DRINK.. I...ah...THINK I'LL GO BACK TO MY LONELY LITTLE APARTMENT AND SLEEP IT OFF.
GOOD NIGHT.
GOOD NIGHT.
zzzz...
SNORT SNOR-- HUK-HUK zzzzzzz...

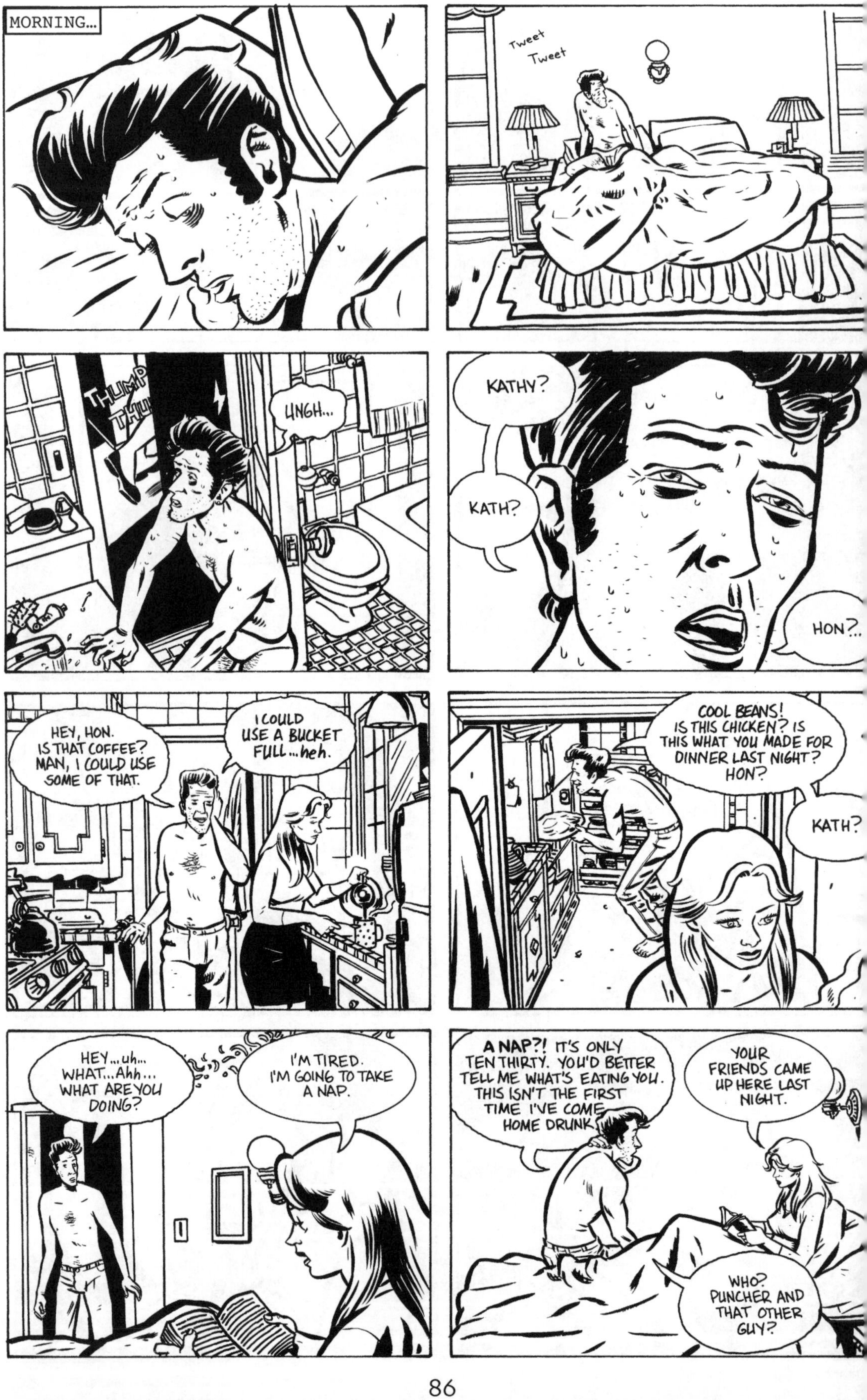

MORNING...
Tweet
Tweet
THUMP
THU
UNGH...
KATHY?
KATH?
HON?...
HEY, HON. IS THAT COFFEE? MAN, I COULD USE SOME OF THAT.
I COULD USE A BUCKET FULL...heh.
COOL BEANS! IS THIS CHICKEN? IS THIS WHAT YOU MADE FOR DINNER LAST NIGHT? HON?
KATH?
HEY...uh... WHAT...Ahh... WHAT ARE YOU DOING?
I'M TIRED. I'M GOING TO TAKE A NAP.
A NAP?! IT'S ONLY TEN THIRTY. YOU'D BETTER TELL ME WHAT'S EATING YOU. THIS ISN'T THE FIRST TIME I'VE COME HOME DRUNK.
YOUR FRIENDS CAME UP HERE LAST NIGHT.
WHO? PUNCHER AND THAT OTHER GUY?

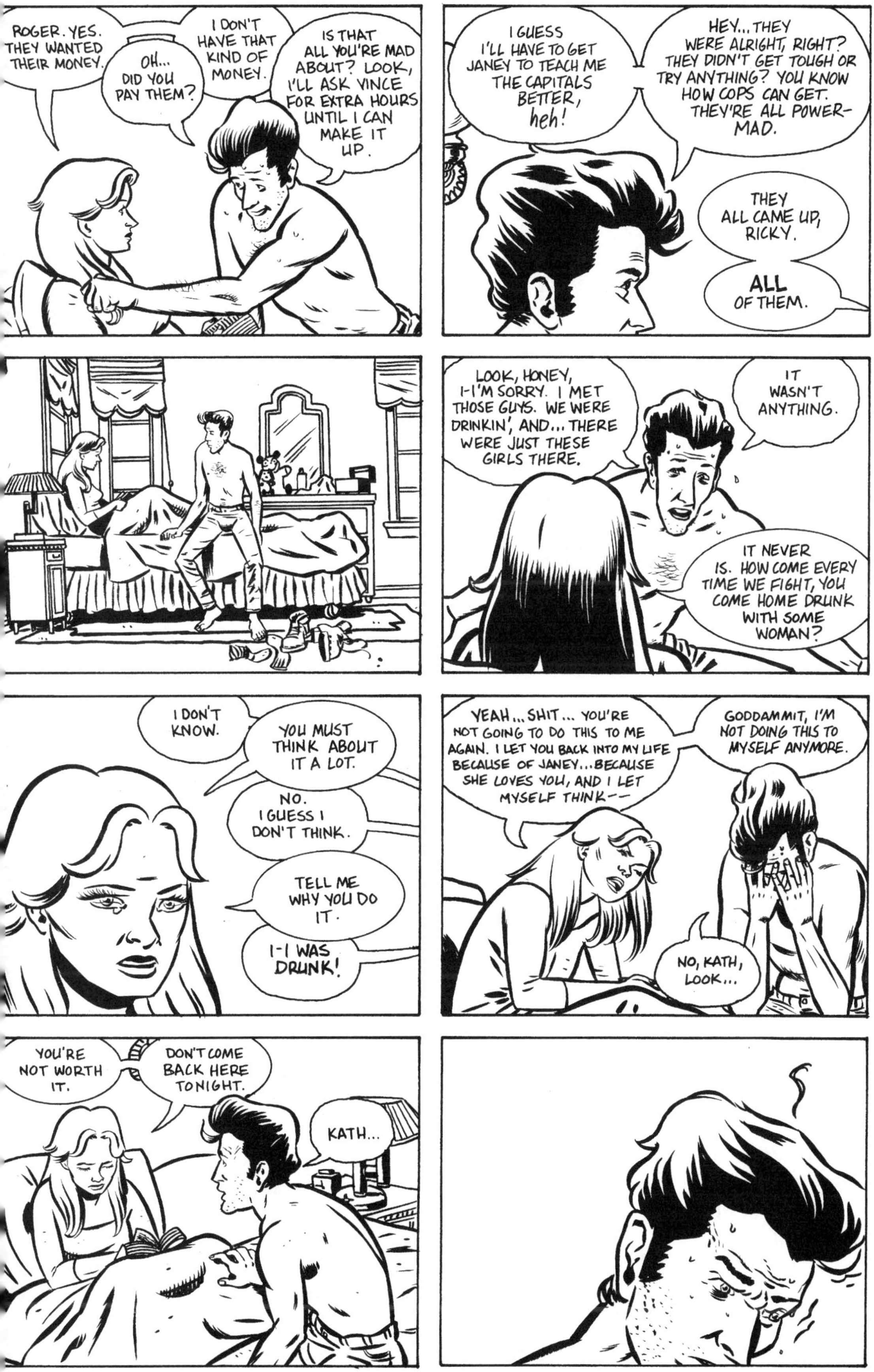
ROGER. YES. THEY WANTED THEIR MONEY.
OH... DID YOU PAY THEM?
I DON'T HAVE THAT KIND OF MONEY.
IS THAT ALL YOU'RE MAD ABOUT? LOOK, I'LL ASK VINCE FOR EXTRA HOURS UNTIL I CAN MAKE IT UP.
I GUESS I'LL HAVE TO GET JANEY TO TEACH ME THE CAPITALS BETTER, heh!
HEY... THEY WERE ALRIGHT, RIGHT? THEY DIDN'T GET TOUGH OR TRY ANYTHING? YOU KNOW HOW COPS CAN GET. THEY'RE ALL POWER-MAD.
THEY ALL CAME UP, RICKY.
ALL OF THEM.
LOOK, HONEY, I-I'M SORRY. I MET THOSE GUYS. WE WERE DRINKIN', AND... THERE WERE JUST THESE GIRLS THERE.
IT WASN'T ANYTHING.
IT NEVER IS. HOW COME EVERY TIME WE FIGHT, YOU COME HOME DRUNK WITH SOME WOMAN?
I DON'T KNOW.
YOU MUST THINK ABOUT IT A LOT.
NO. I GUESS I DON'T THINK.
TELL ME WHY YOU DO IT.
I-I WAS DRUNK!
YEAH... SHIT... YOU'RE NOT GOING TO DO THIS TO ME AGAIN. I LET YOU BACK INTO MY LIFE BECAUSE OF JANEY... BECAUSE SHE LOVES YOU, AND I LET MYSELF THINK--
GODDAMMIT, I'M NOT DOING THIS TO MYSELF ANYMORE.
NO, KATH, LOOK...
YOU'RE NOT WORTH IT.
DON'T COME BACK HERE TONIGHT.
KATH...

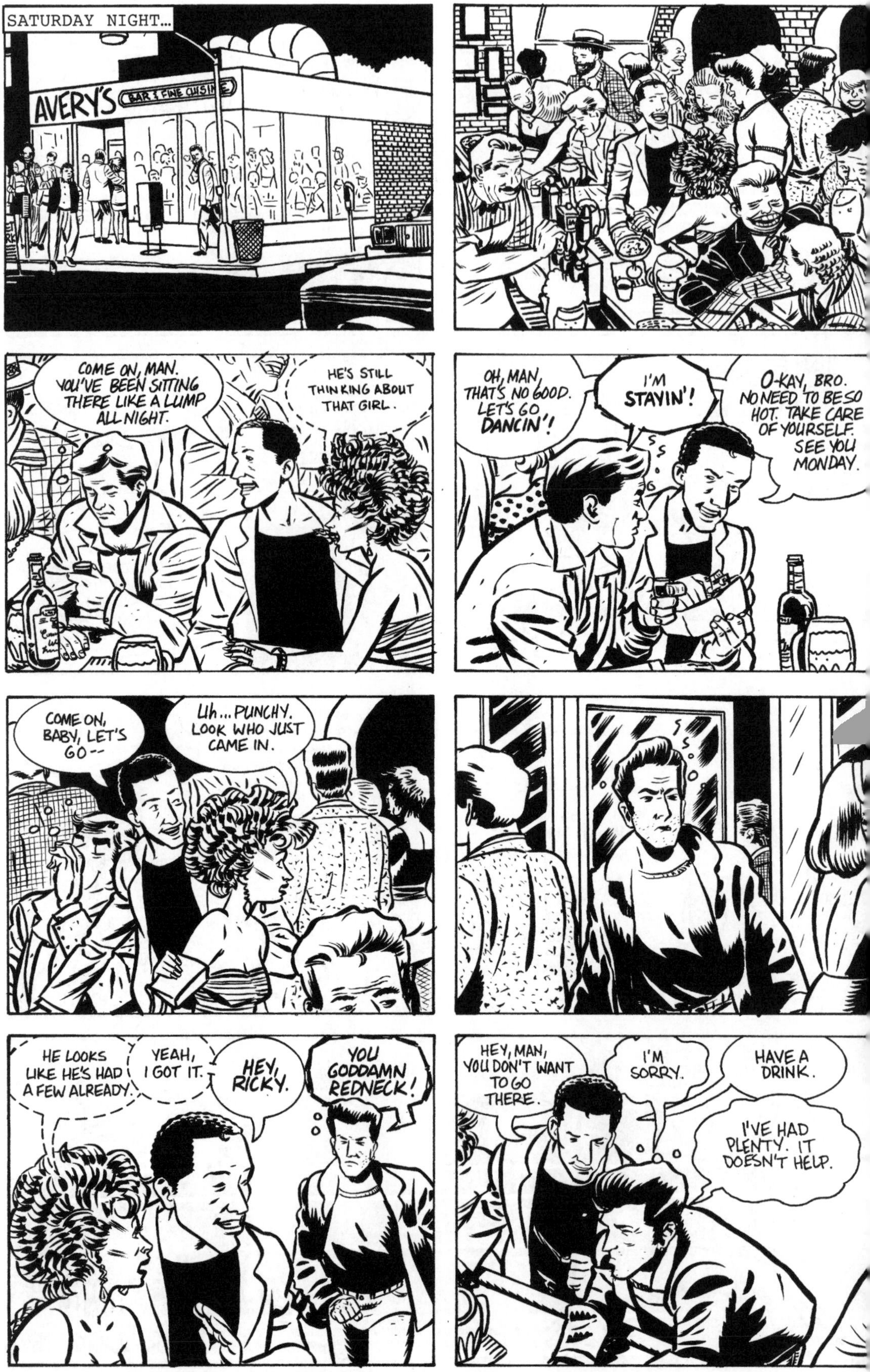
SATURDAY NIGHT...
AVERY'S
BAR & FINE CUISINE
COME ON, MAN. YOU'VE BEEN SITTING THERE LIKE A LUMP ALL NIGHT.
HE'S STILL THINKING ABOUT THAT GIRL.
OH, MAN, THAT'S NO GOOD. LET'S GO DANCIN'!
I'M STAYIN'!
O-KAY, BRO. NO NEED TO BE SO HOT. TAKE CARE OF YOURSELF. SEE YOU MONDAY.
COME ON, BABY, LET'S GO--
Uh... PUNCHY. LOOK WHO JUST CAME IN.
HE LOOKS LIKE HE'S HAD A FEW ALREADY.
YEAH, I GOT IT.
HEY, RICKY.
YOU GODDAMN REDNECK!
HEY, MAN, YOU DON'T WANT TO GO THERE.
I'M SORRY.
HAVE A DRINK.
I'VE HAD PLENTY. IT DOESN'T HELP.

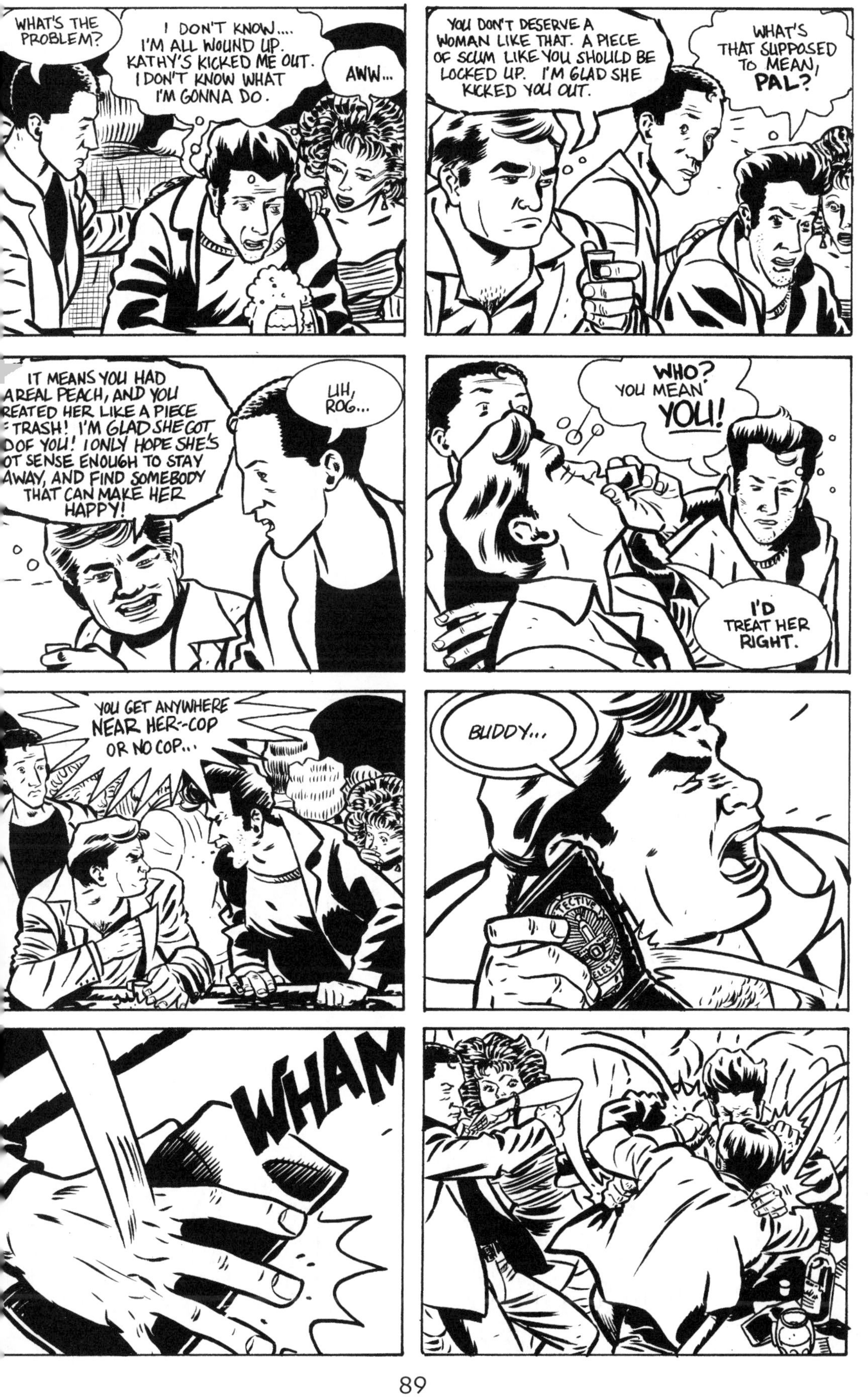
WHAT'S THE PROBLEM?
I DON'T KNOW.... I'M ALL WOUND UP. KATHY'S KICKED ME OUT. I DON'T KNOW WHAT I'M GONNA DO.
AWW...
YOU DON'T DESERVE A WOMAN LIKE THAT. A PIECE OF SCUM LIKE YOU SHOULD BE LOCKED UP. I'M GLAD SHE KICKED YOU OUT.
WHAT'S THAT SUPPOSED TO MEAN, PAL?
IT MEANS YOU HAD A REAL PEACH, AND YOU REATED HER LIKE A PIECE TRASH! I'M GLAD SHE GOT D OF YOU! I ONLY HOPE SHE'S OT SENSE ENOUGH TO STAY AWAY, AND FIND SOMEBODY THAT CAN MAKE HER HAPPY!
UH, ROG...
WHO? YOU MEAN YOU!
I'D TREAT HER RIGHT.
YOU GET ANYWHERE NEAR HER--COP OR NO COP...
BUDDY...
WHAM

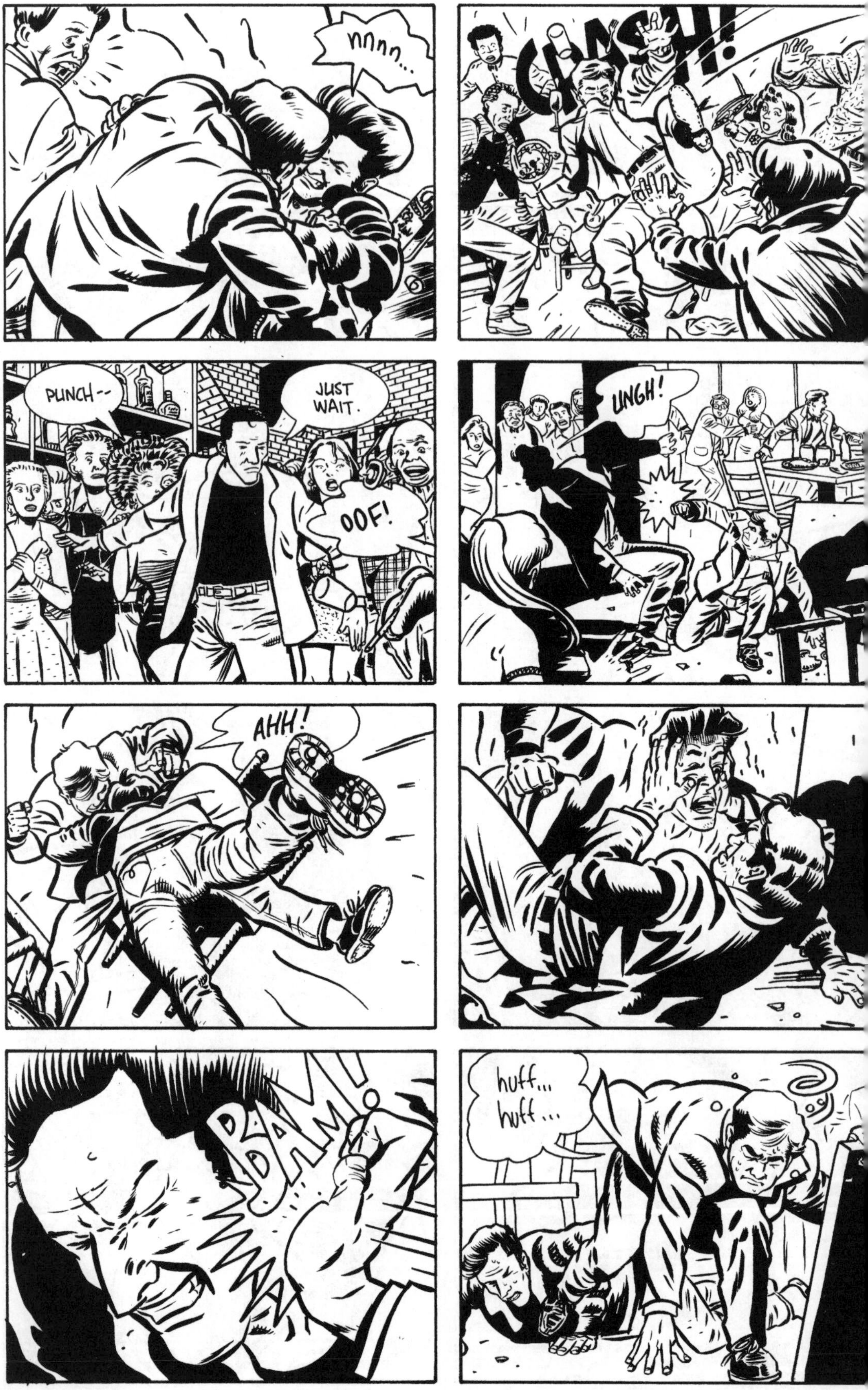
nnnn...
CRASH!!
PUNCH--
JUST WAIT.
OOF!
UNGH!
AHH!
BAM!
huff...
huff...

UHH!

huhh huhh huhh

uhnn...

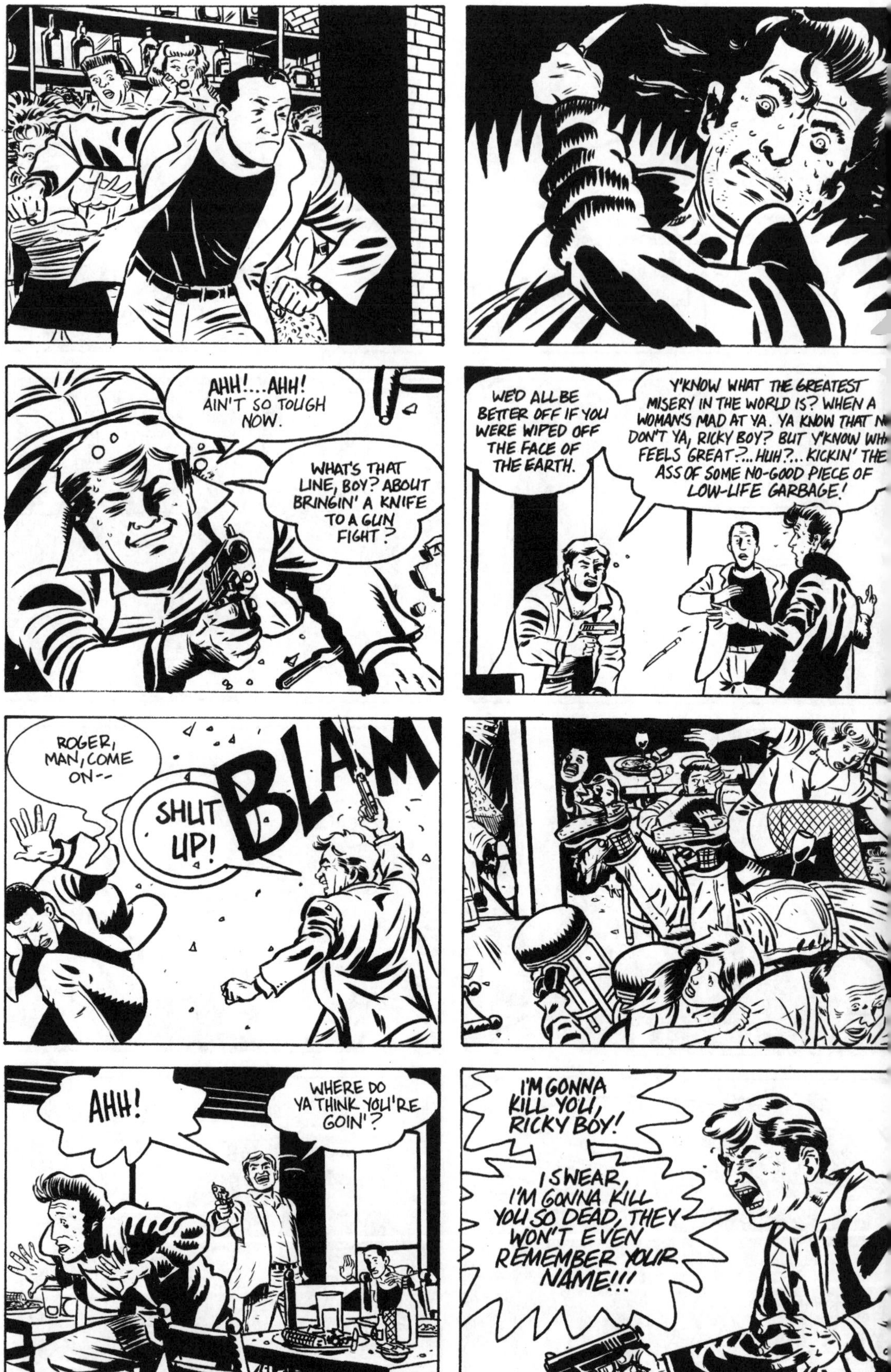
AHH!...AHH! AIN'T SO TOUGH NOW.
WHAT'S THAT LINE, BOY? ABOUT BRINGIN' A KNIFE TO A GUN FIGHT?
WE'D ALL BE BETTER OFF IF YOU WERE WIPED OFF THE FACE OF THE EARTH.
Y'KNOW WHAT THE GREATEST MISERY IN THE WORLD IS? WHEN A WOMAN'S MAD AT YA. YA KNOW THAT N DON'T YA, RICKY BOY? BUT Y'KNOW WH FEELS GREAT?...HUH?... KICKIN' THE ASS OF SOME NO-GOOD PIECE OF LOW-LIFE GARBAGE!
ROGER, MAN, COME ON--
SHUT UP!
BLAM
AHH!
WHERE DO YA THINK YOU'RE GOIN'?
I'M GONNA KILL YOU, RICKY BOY!
I SWEAR, I'M GONNA KILL YOU SO DEAD, THEY WON'T EVEN REMEMBER YOUR NAME!!!

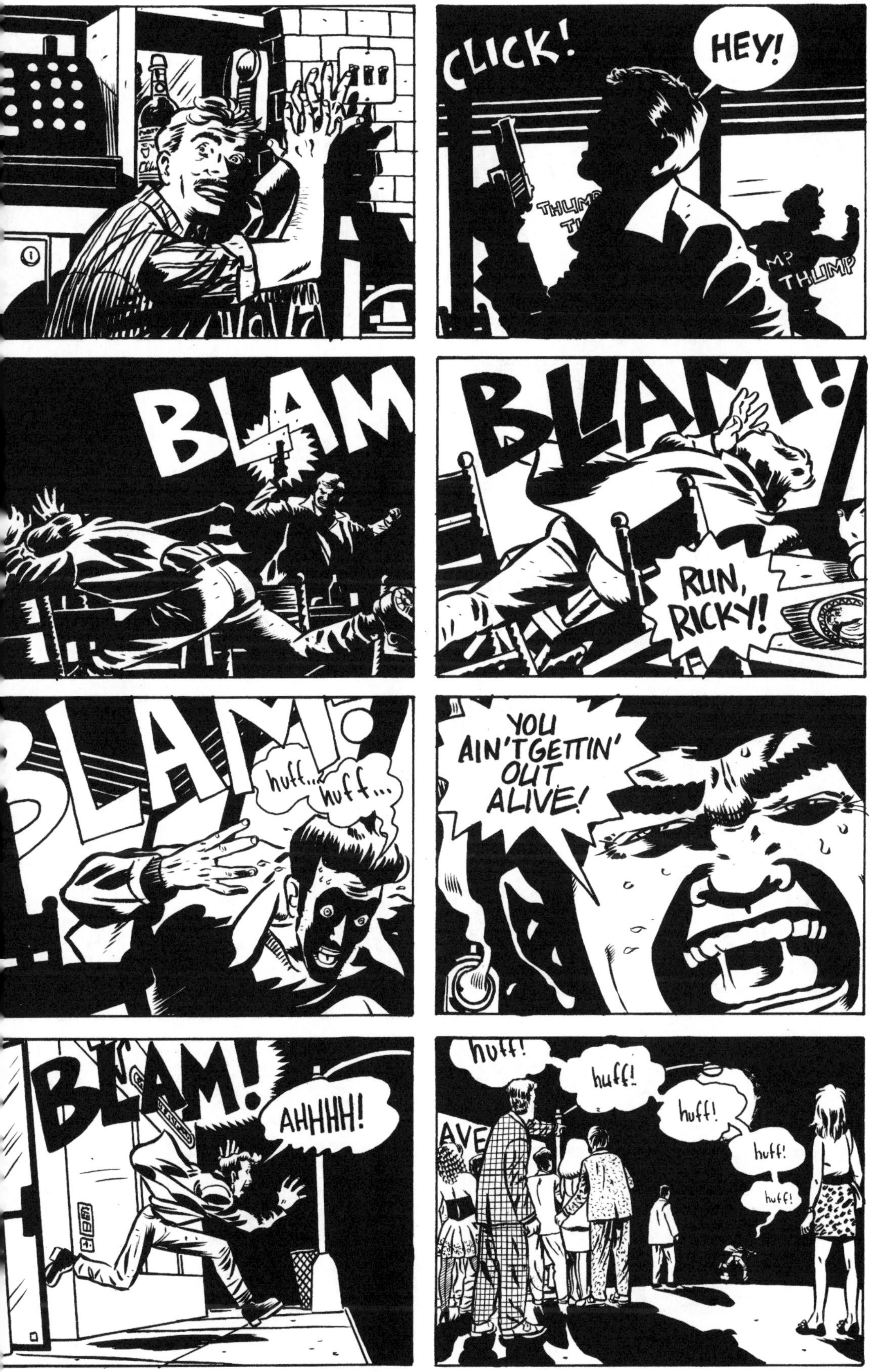
CLICK!
HEY!
THUMP THUMP
BLAM
BLAM!
RUN, RICKY!
BLAM!
huff... huff...
YOU AIN'T GETTIN' OUT ALIVE!
BLAM!
AHHHH!
AVE
huff!
huff!
huff!
huff!
huff!

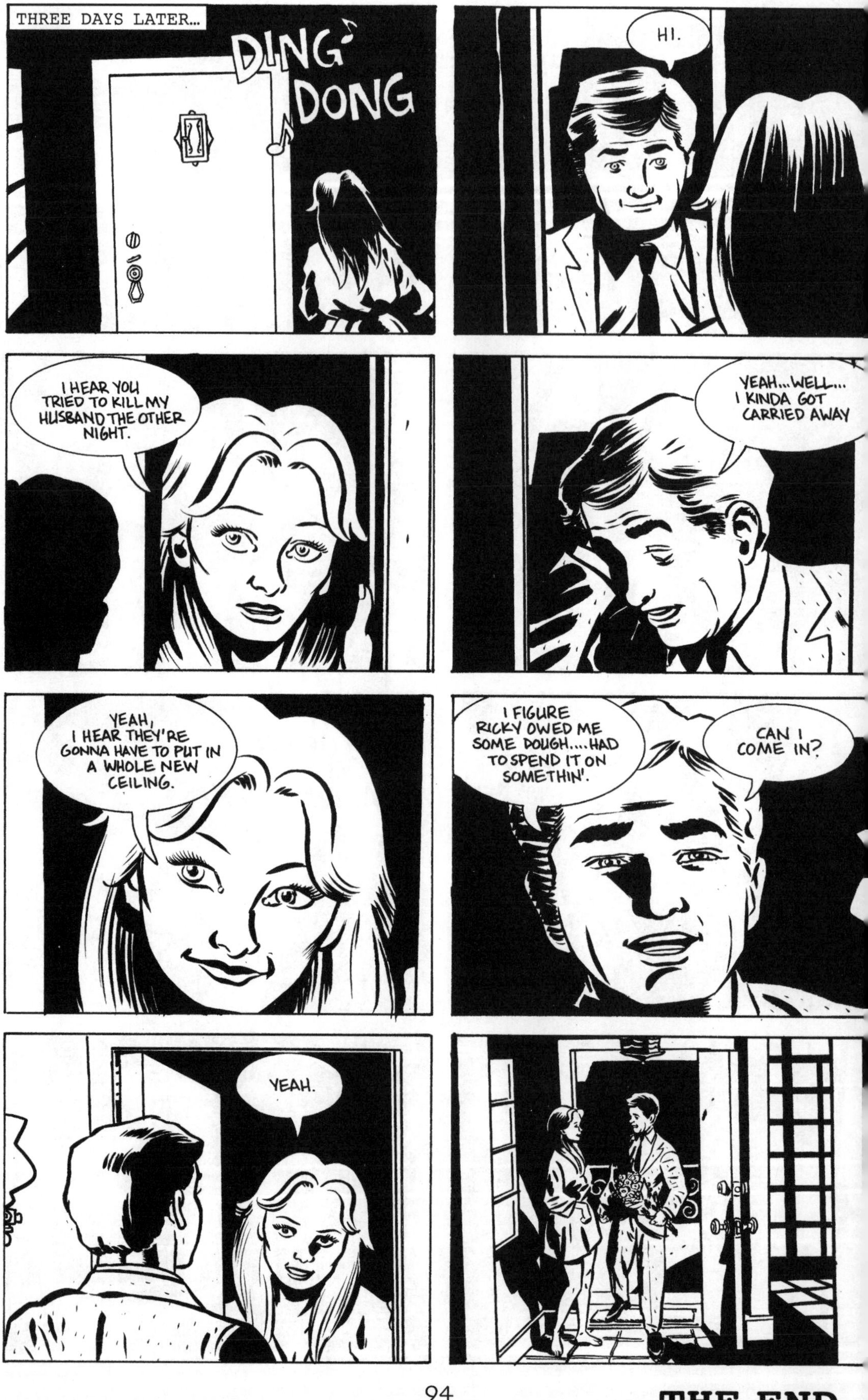
THREE DAYS LATER...
DING DONG
HI.
I HEAR YOU TRIED TO KILL MY HUSBAND THE OTHER NIGHT.
YEAH...WELL... I KINDA GOT CARRIED AWAY
YEAH, I HEAR THEY'RE GONNA HAVE TO PUT IN A WHOLE NEW CEILING.
I FIGURE RICKY OWED ME SOME DOUGH....HAD TO SPEND IT ON SOMETHIN'.
CAN I COME IN?
YEAH.



**THE END...**

# 4

## "SEX and VIOLENCE"
### (part 2)

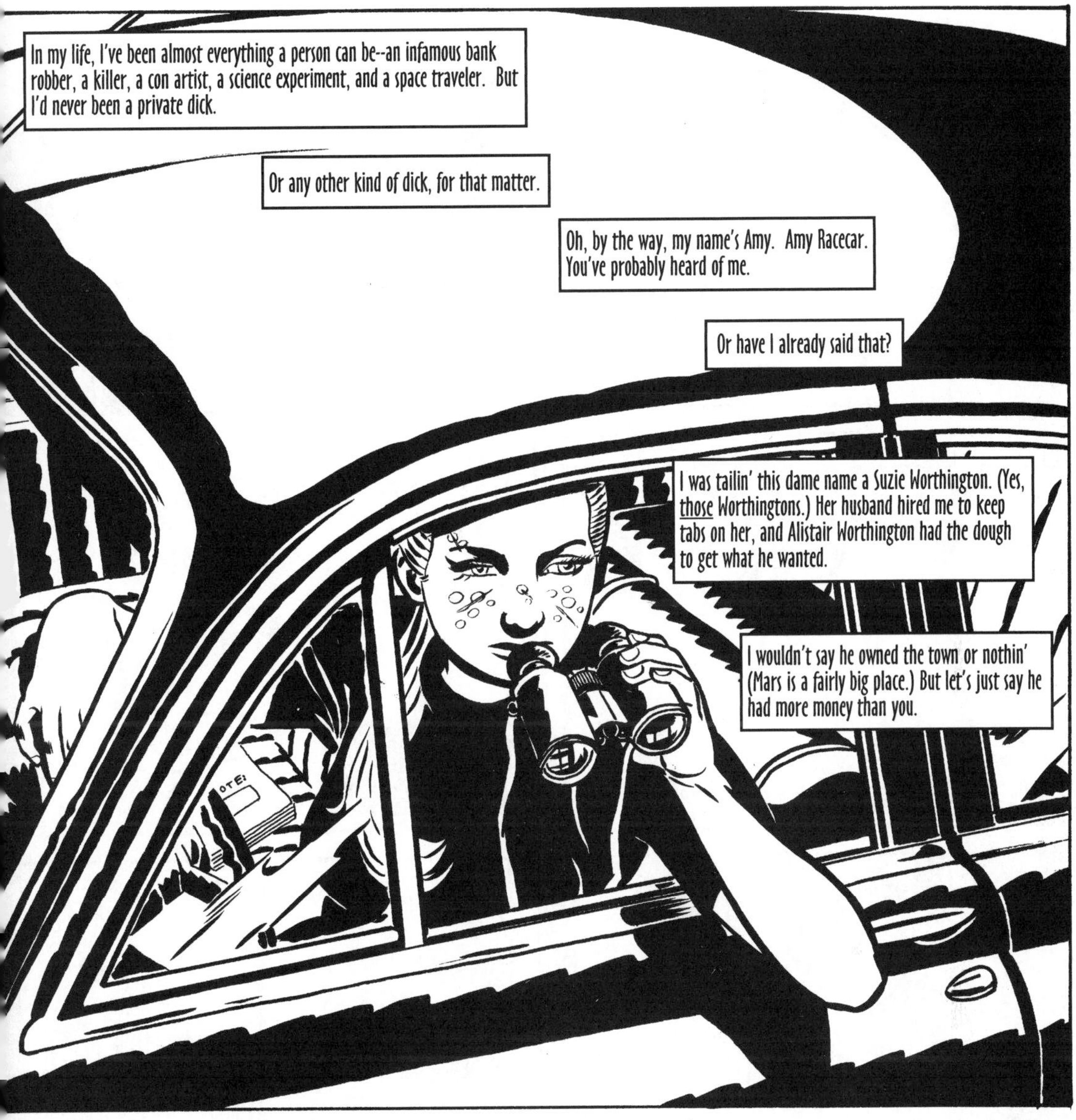
In my life, I've been almost everything a person can be--an infamous bank robber, a killer, a con artist, a science experiment, and a space traveler. But I'd never been a private dick.
Or any other kind of dick, for that matter.
Oh, by the way, my name's Amy. Amy Racecar. You've probably heard of me.
Or have I already said that?
I was tailin' this dame name a Suzie Worthington. (Yes, those Worthingtons.) Her husband hired me to keep tabs on her, and Alistair Worthington had the dough to get what he wanted.
I wouldn't say he owned the town or nothin' (Mars is a fairly big place.) But let's just say he had more money than you.

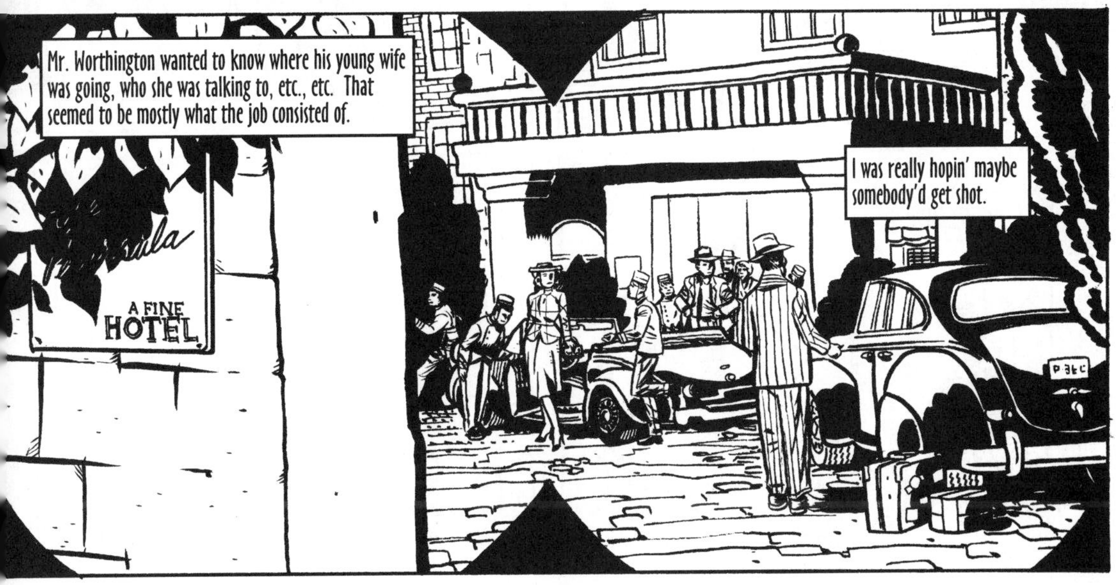
Mr. Worthington wanted to know where his young wife was going, who she was talking to, etc., etc. That seemed to be mostly what the job consisted of.
I was really hopin' maybe somebody'd get shot.
A FINE HOTEL

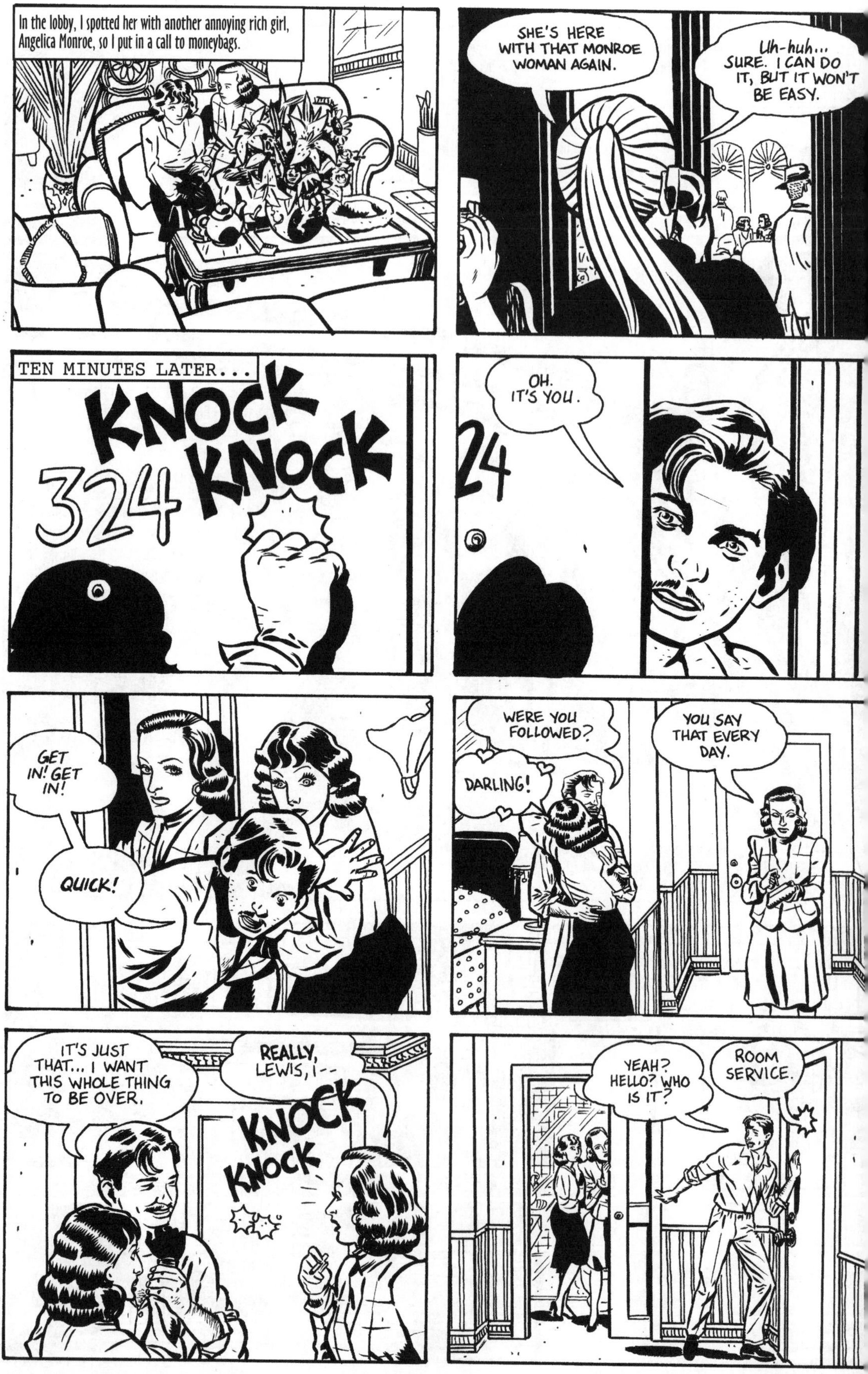
In the lobby, I spotted her with another annoying rich girl, Angelica Monroe, so I put in a call to moneybags.
SHE'S HERE WITH THAT MONROE WOMAN AGAIN.
Uh-huh... SURE. I CAN DO IT, BUT IT WON'T BE EASY.
TEN MINUTES LATER...
KNOCK KNOCK
324
OH. IT'S YOU.
24
GET IN! GET IN!
QUICK!
WERE YOU FOLLOWED?
DARLING!
YOU SAY THAT EVERY DAY.
IT'S JUST THAT... I WANT THIS WHOLE THING TO BE OVER.
REALLY, LEWIS, I--
KNOCK KNOCK
YEAH? HELLO? WHO IS IT?
ROOM SERVICE.

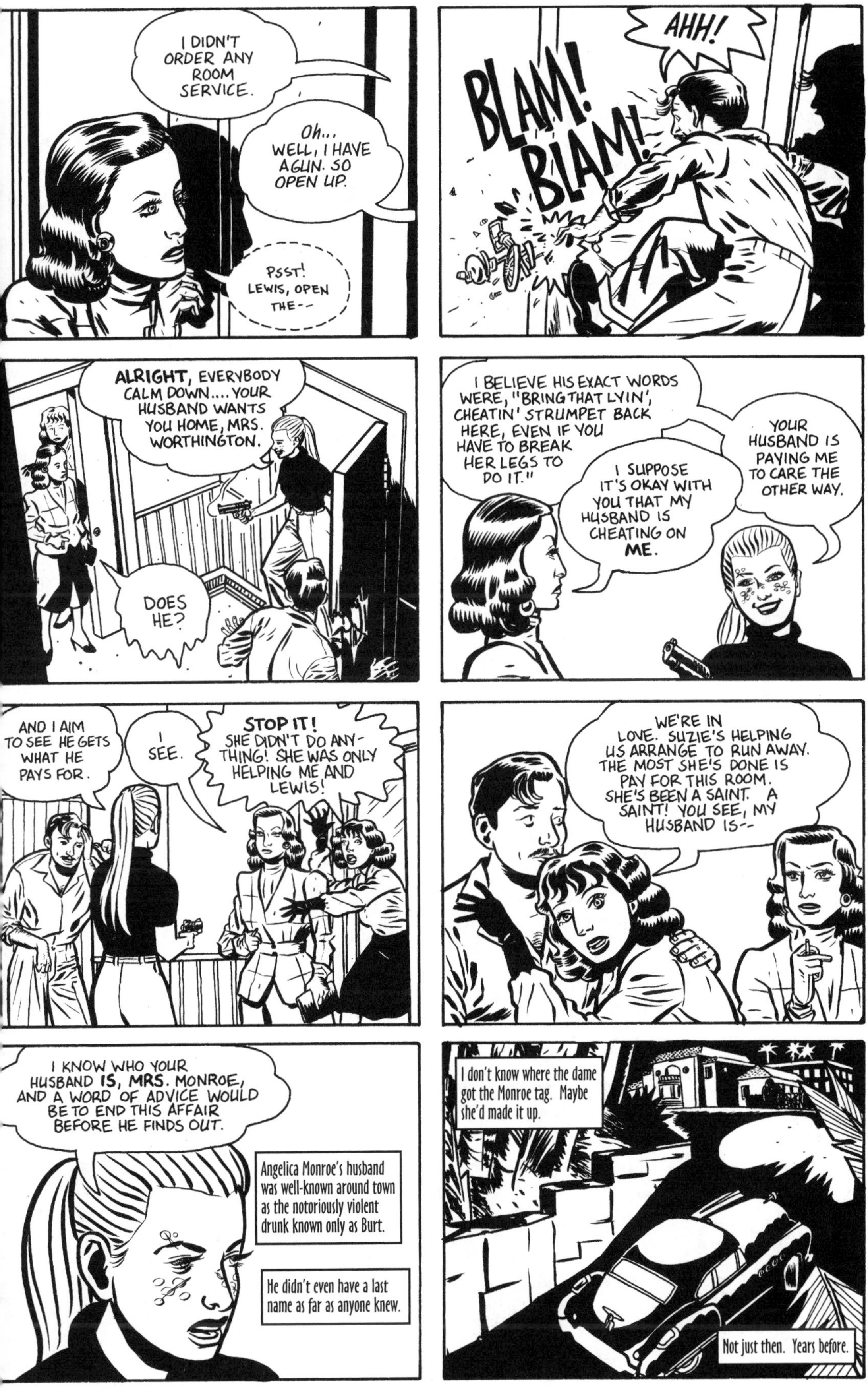
I DIDN'T ORDER ANY ROOM SERVICE.
Oh... WELL, I HAVE A GUN. SO OPEN UP.
PSST! LEWIS, OPEN THE--
AHH!
BLAM! BLAM!
ALRIGHT, EVERYBODY CALM DOWN.... YOUR HUSBAND WANTS YOU HOME, MRS. WORTHINGTON.
DOES HE?
I BELIEVE HIS EXACT WORDS WERE, "BRING THAT LYIN', CHEATIN' STRUMPET BACK HERE, EVEN IF YOU HAVE TO BREAK HER LEGS TO DO IT."
I SUPPOSE IT'S OKAY WITH YOU THAT MY HUSBAND IS CHEATING ON ME.
YOUR HUSBAND IS PAYING ME TO CARE THE OTHER WAY.
AND I AIM TO SEE HE GETS WHAT HE PAYS FOR.
I SEE.
STOP IT! SHE DIDN'T DO ANY-THING! SHE WAS ONLY HELPING ME AND LEWIS!
WE'RE IN LOVE. SUZIE'S HELPING US ARRANGE TO RUN AWAY. THE MOST SHE'S DONE IS PAY FOR THIS ROOM. SHE'S BEEN A SAINT. A SAINT! YOU SEE, MY HUSBAND IS--
I KNOW WHO YOUR HUSBAND IS, MRS. MONROE, AND A WORD OF ADVICE WOULD BE TO END THIS AFFAIR BEFORE HE FINDS OUT.
Angelica Monroe's husband was well-known around town as the notoriously violent drunk known only as Burt.
He didn't even have a last name as far as anyone knew.
I don't know where the dame got the Monroe tag. Maybe she'd made it up.
Not just then. Years before.

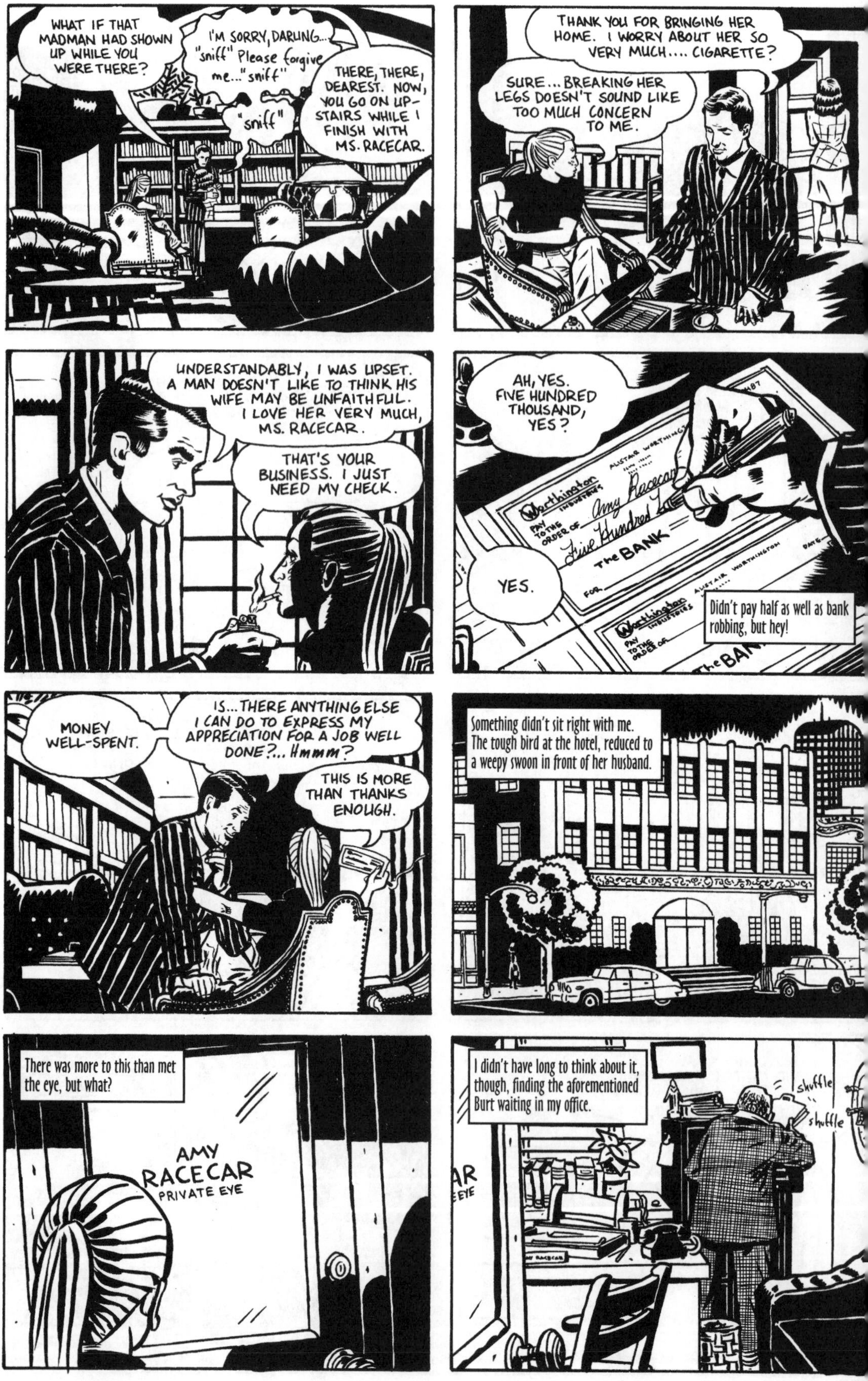
WHAT IF THAT MADMAN HAD SHOWN UP WHILE YOU WERE THERE?
I'M SORRY, DARLING... "sniff" Please forgive me..."sniff"
"sniff"
THERE, THERE, DEAREST. NOW, YOU GO ON UPSTAIRS WHILE I FINISH WITH MS. RACECAR.
THANK YOU FOR BRINGING HER HOME. I WORRY ABOUT HER SO VERY MUCH.... CIGARETTE?
SURE... BREAKING HER LEGS DOESN'T SOUND LIKE TOO MUCH CONCERN TO ME.
UNDERSTANDABLY, I WAS UPSET. A MAN DOESN'T LIKE TO THINK HIS WIFE MAY BE UNFAITHFUL. I LOVE HER VERY MUCH, MS. RACECAR.
THAT'S YOUR BUSINESS. I JUST NEED MY CHECK.
AH, YES. FIVE HUNDRED THOUSAND, YES?
YES.
Worthington Industries
PAY TO THE ORDER OF Amy Racecar
Five Hundred
THE BANK
Didn't pay half as well as bank robbing, but hey!
MONEY WELL-SPENT.
IS... THERE ANYTHING ELSE I CAN DO TO EXPRESS MY APPRECIATION FOR A JOB WELL DONE?... Hmmm?
THIS IS MORE THAN THANKS ENOUGH.
Something didn't sit right with me. The tough bird at the hotel, reduced to a weepy swoon in front of her husband.
There was more to this than met the eye, but what?
AMY RACECAR PRIVATE EYE
I didn't have long to think about it, though, finding the aforementioned Burt waiting in my office.
shuffle
shuffle

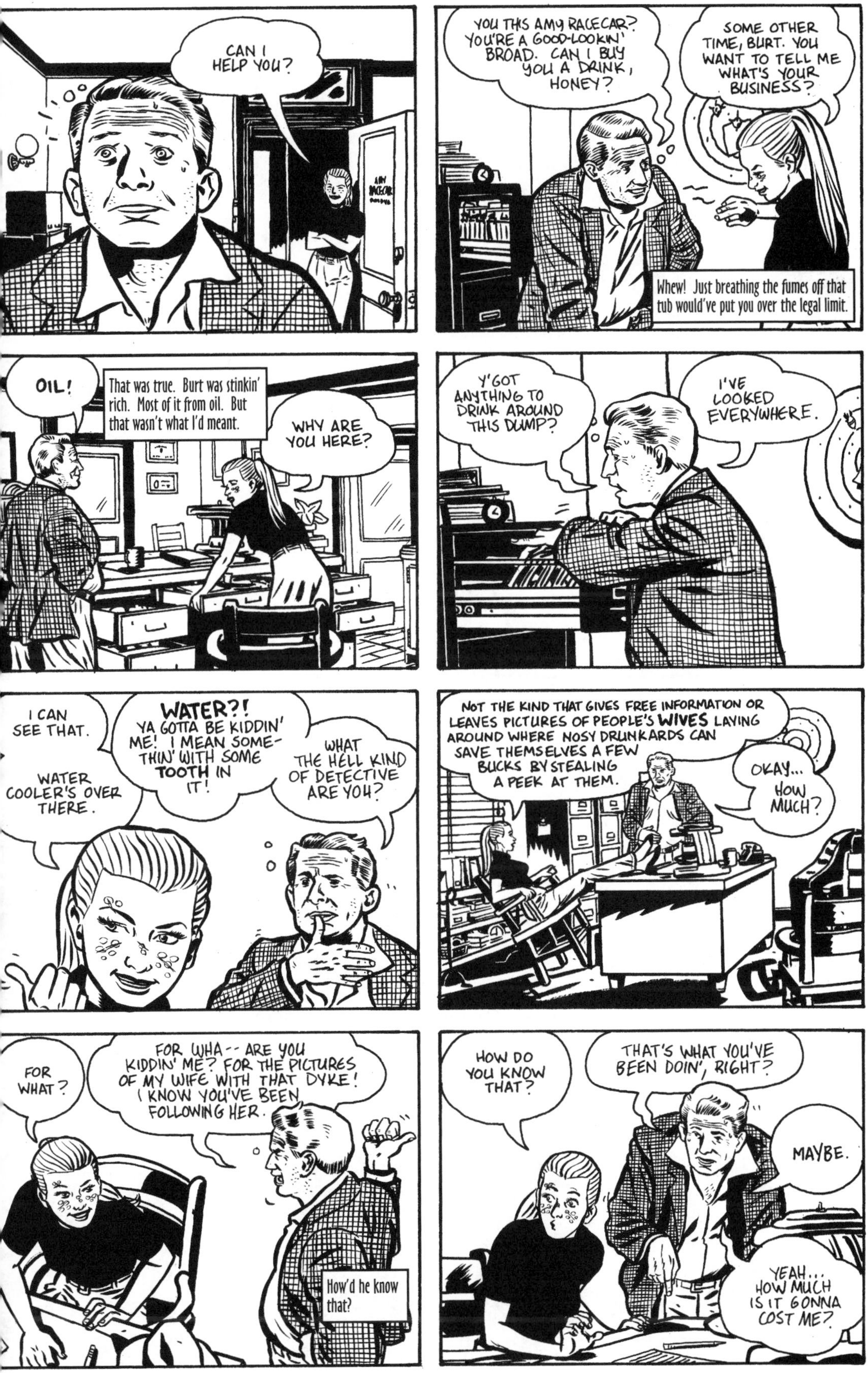
CAN I HELP YOU?
AMY RACECAR
YOU THIS AMY RACECAR? YOU'RE A GOOD-LOOKIN' BROAD. CAN I BUY YOU A DRINK, HONEY?
SOME OTHER TIME, BURT. YOU WANT TO TELL ME WHAT'S YOUR BUSINESS?
Whew! Just breathing the fumes off that tub would've put you over the legal limit.
OIL!
That was true. Burt was stinkin' rich. Most of it from oil. But that wasn't what I'd meant.
WHY ARE YOU HERE?
Y'GOT ANYTHING TO DRINK AROUND THIS DUMP?
I'VE LOOKED EVERYWHERE.
I CAN SEE THAT.
WATER COOLER'S OVER THERE.
WATER?! YA GOTTA BE KIDDIN' ME! I MEAN SOME-THIN' WITH SOME TOOTH IN IT!
WHAT THE HELL KIND OF DETECTIVE ARE YOU?
NOT THE KIND THAT GIVES FREE INFORMATION OR LEAVES PICTURES OF PEOPLE'S WIVES LAYING AROUND WHERE NOSY DRUNKARDS CAN SAVE THEMSELVES A FEW BUCKS BY STEALING A PEEK AT THEM.
OKAY... HOW MUCH?
FOR WHAT?
FOR WHA-- ARE YOU KIDDIN' ME? FOR THE PICTURES OF MY WIFE WITH THAT DYKE! I KNOW YOU'VE BEEN FOLLOWING HER.
How'd he know that?
HOW DO YOU KNOW THAT?
THAT'S WHAT YOU'VE BEEN DOIN', RIGHT?
MAYBE.
YEAH... HOW MUCH IS IT GONNA COST ME?

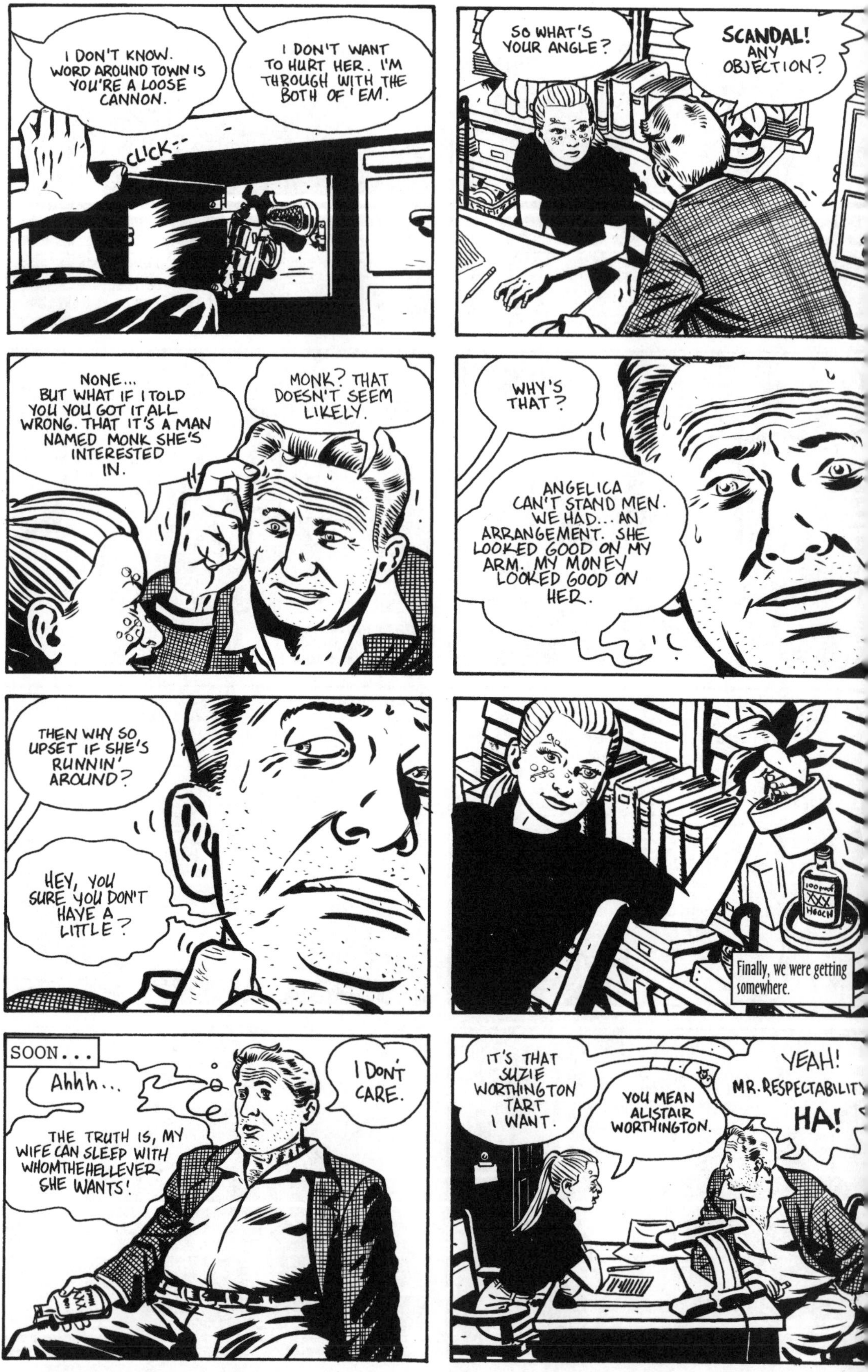
I DON'T KNOW. WORD AROUND TOWN IS YOU'RE A LOOSE CANNON.
I DON'T WANT TO HURT HER. I'M THROUGH WITH THE BOTH OF 'EM.
CLICK--
SO WHAT'S YOUR ANGLE?
SCANDAL! ANY OBJECTION?
NONE... BUT WHAT IF I TOLD YOU YOU GOT IT ALL WRONG. THAT IT'S A MAN NAMED MONK SHE'S INTERESTED IN.
MONK? THAT DOESN'T SEEM LIKELY.
WHY'S THAT?
ANGELICA CAN'T STAND MEN. WE HAD... AN ARRANGEMENT. SHE LOOKED GOOD ON MY ARM. MY MONEY LOOKED GOOD ON HER.
THEN WHY SO UPSET IF SHE'S RUNNIN' AROUND?
HEY, YOU SURE YOU DON'T HAVE A LITTLE?
100 proof XXX HOOCH
Finally, we were getting somewhere.
SOON...
Ahhh...
I DON'T CARE.
THE TRUTH IS, MY WIFE CAN SLEEP WITH WHOMTHEHELLEVER SHE WANTS!
IT'S THAT SUZIE WORTHINGTON TART I WANT.
YOU MEAN ALISTAIR WORTHINGTON.
YEAH! MR. RESPECTABILITY HA!

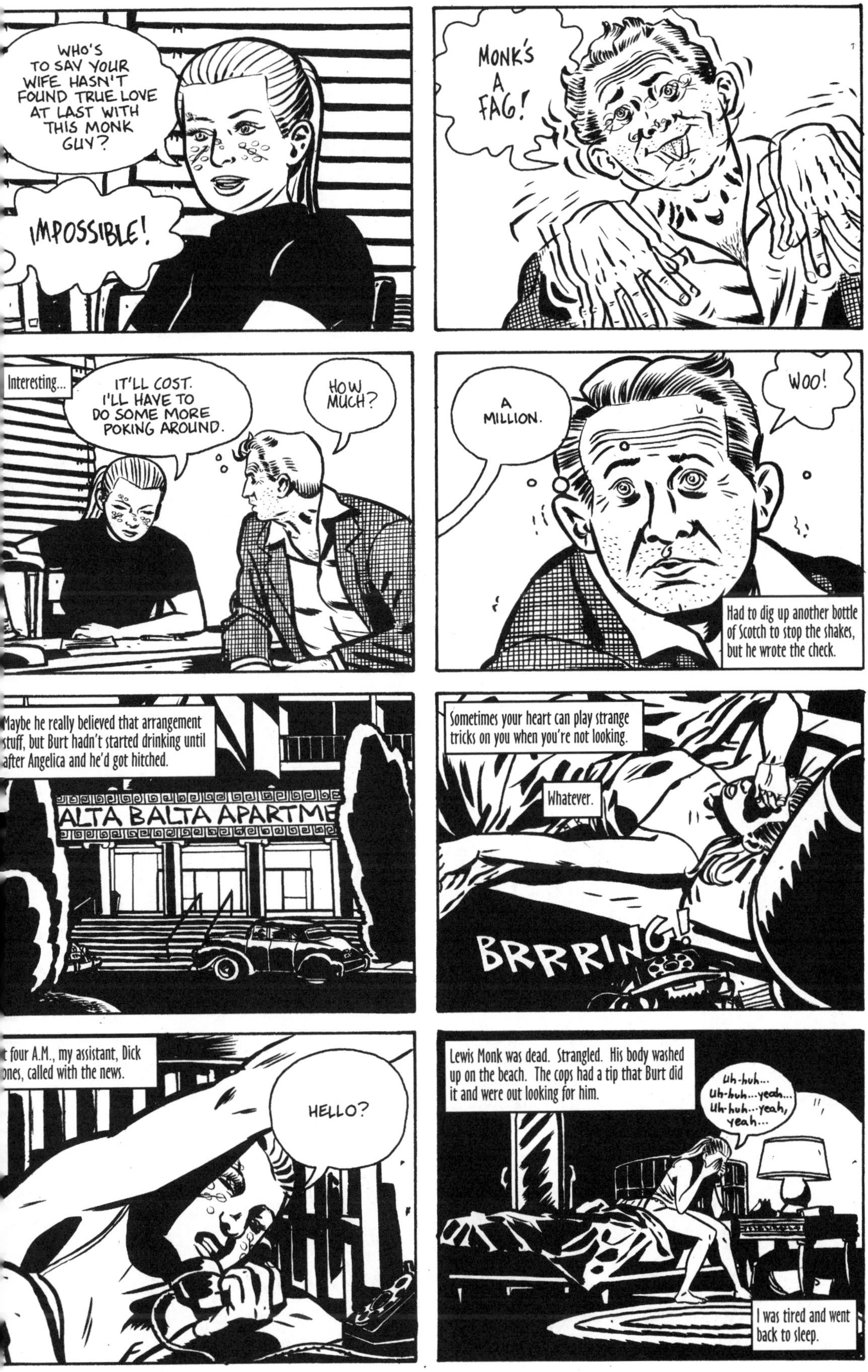
WHO'S TO SAY YOUR WIFE HASN'T FOUND TRUE LOVE AT LAST WITH THIS MONK GUY?
IMPOSSIBLE!
MONK'S A FAG!
Interesting...
IT'LL COST. I'LL HAVE TO DO SOME MORE POKING AROUND.
HOW MUCH?
A MILLION.
WOO!
Had to dig up another bottle of Scotch to stop the shakes, but he wrote the check.
Maybe he really believed that arrangement stuff, but Burt hadn't started drinking until after Angelica and he'd got hitched.
ALTA BALTA APARTME
Sometimes your heart can play strange tricks on you when you're not looking.
Whatever.
BRRRING!
t four A.M., my assistant, Dick ones, called with the news.
HELLO?
Lewis Monk was dead. Strangled. His body washed up on the beach. The cops had a tip that Burt did it and were out looking for him.
Uh-huh... Uh-huh...yeah... Uh-huh...yeah, yeah...
I was tired and went back to sleep.

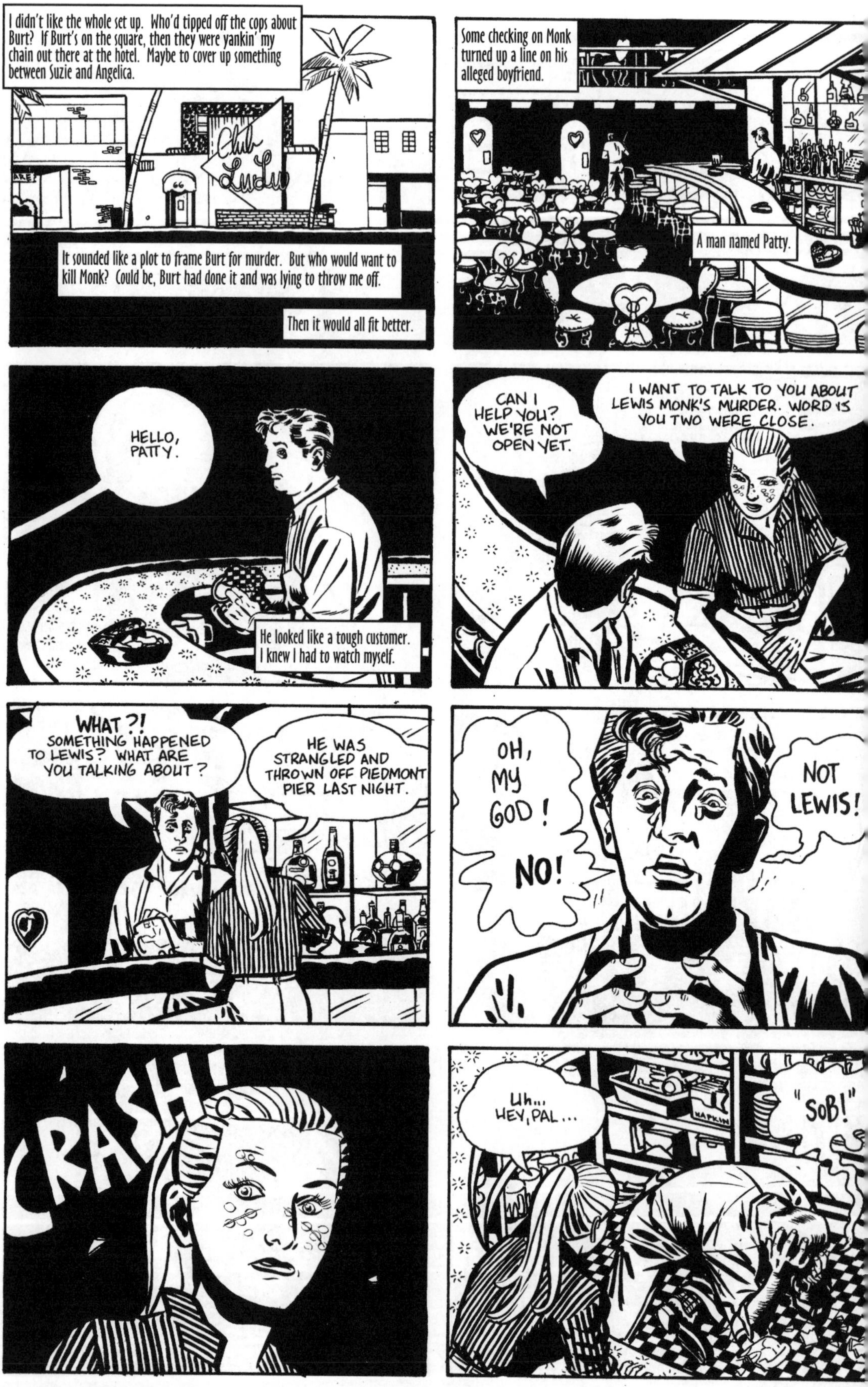
I didn't like the whole set up. Who'd tipped off the cops about Burt? If Burt's on the square, then they were yankin' my chain out there at the hotel. Maybe to cover up something between Suzie and Angelica.
Club Lulu
It sounded like a plot to frame Burt for murder. But who would want to kill Monk? Could be, Burt had done it and was lying to throw me off.
Then it would all fit better.
Some checking on Monk turned up a line on his alleged boyfriend.
A man named Patty.
HELLO, PATTY.
He looked like a tough customer. I knew I had to watch myself.
CAN I HELP YOU? WE'RE NOT OPEN YET.
I WANT TO TALK TO YOU ABOUT LEWIS MONK'S MURDER. WORD IS YOU TWO WERE CLOSE.
WHAT?! SOMETHING HAPPENED TO LEWIS? WHAT ARE YOU TALKING ABOUT?
HE WAS STRANGLED AND THROWN OFF PIEDMONT PIER LAST NIGHT.
OH, MY GOD! NO!
NOT LEWIS!
CRASH!
UH... HEY, PAL...
"SOB!"

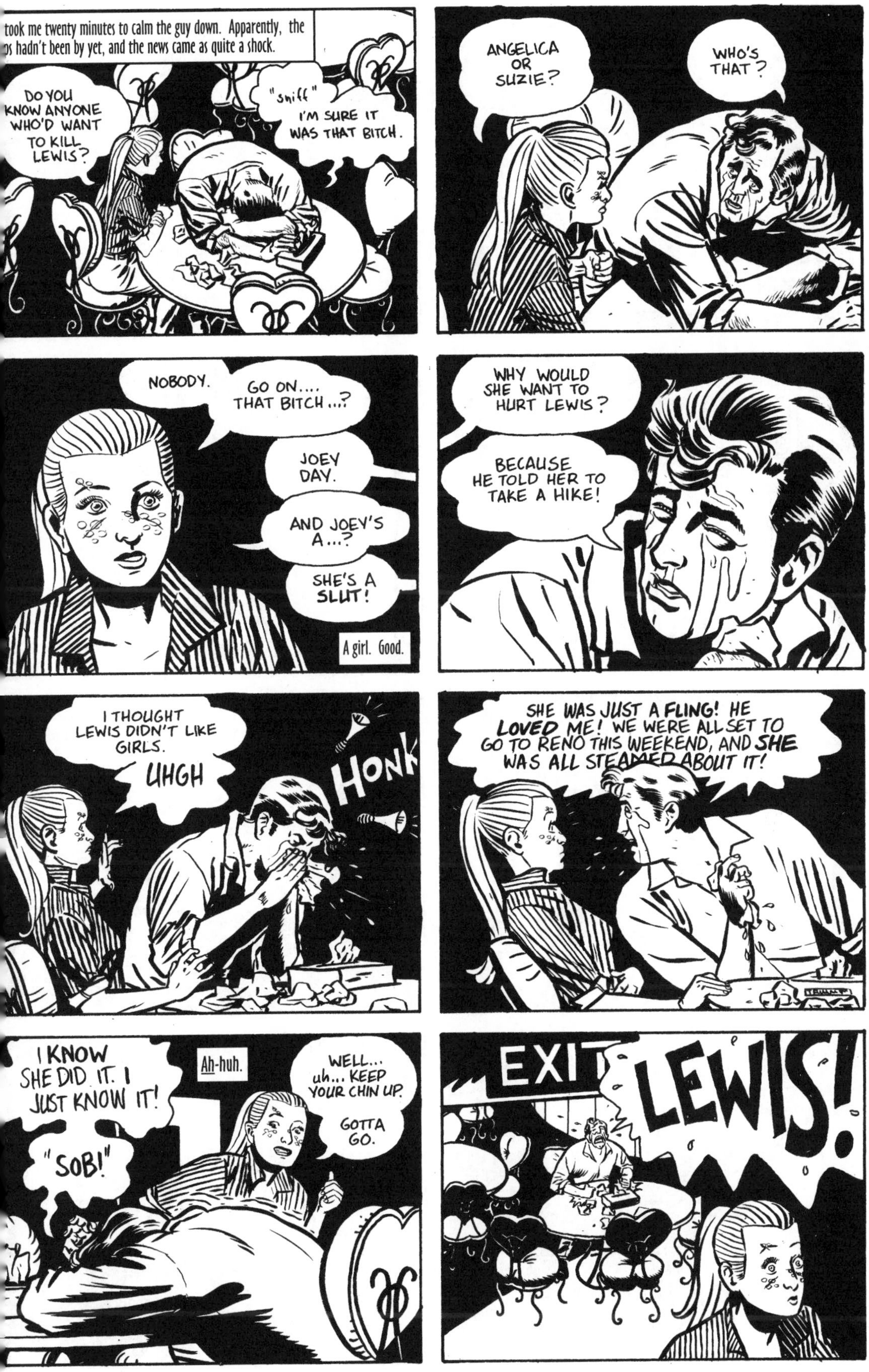
took me twenty minutes to calm the guy down. Apparently, the
ps hadn't been by yet, and the news came as quite a shock.
DO YOU KNOW ANYONE WHO'D WANT TO KILL LEWIS?
"sniff" I'M SURE IT WAS THAT BITCH.
ANGELICA OR SUZIE?
WHO'S THAT?
NOBODY.
GO ON.... THAT BITCH...?
JOEY DAY.
AND JOEY'S A...?
SHE'S A SLUT!
A girl. Good.
WHY WOULD SHE WANT TO HURT LEWIS?
BECAUSE HE TOLD HER TO TAKE A HIKE!
I THOUGHT LEWIS DIDN'T LIKE GIRLS.
UHGH
HONK
SHE WAS JUST A FLING! HE LOVED ME! WE WERE ALL SET TO GO TO RENO THIS WEEKEND, AND SHE WAS ALL STEAMED ABOUT IT!
I KNOW SHE DID IT. I JUST KNOW IT!
Ah-huh.
WELL... uh... KEEP YOUR CHIN UP.
GOTTA GO.
"SOB!"
EXIT
LEWIS!

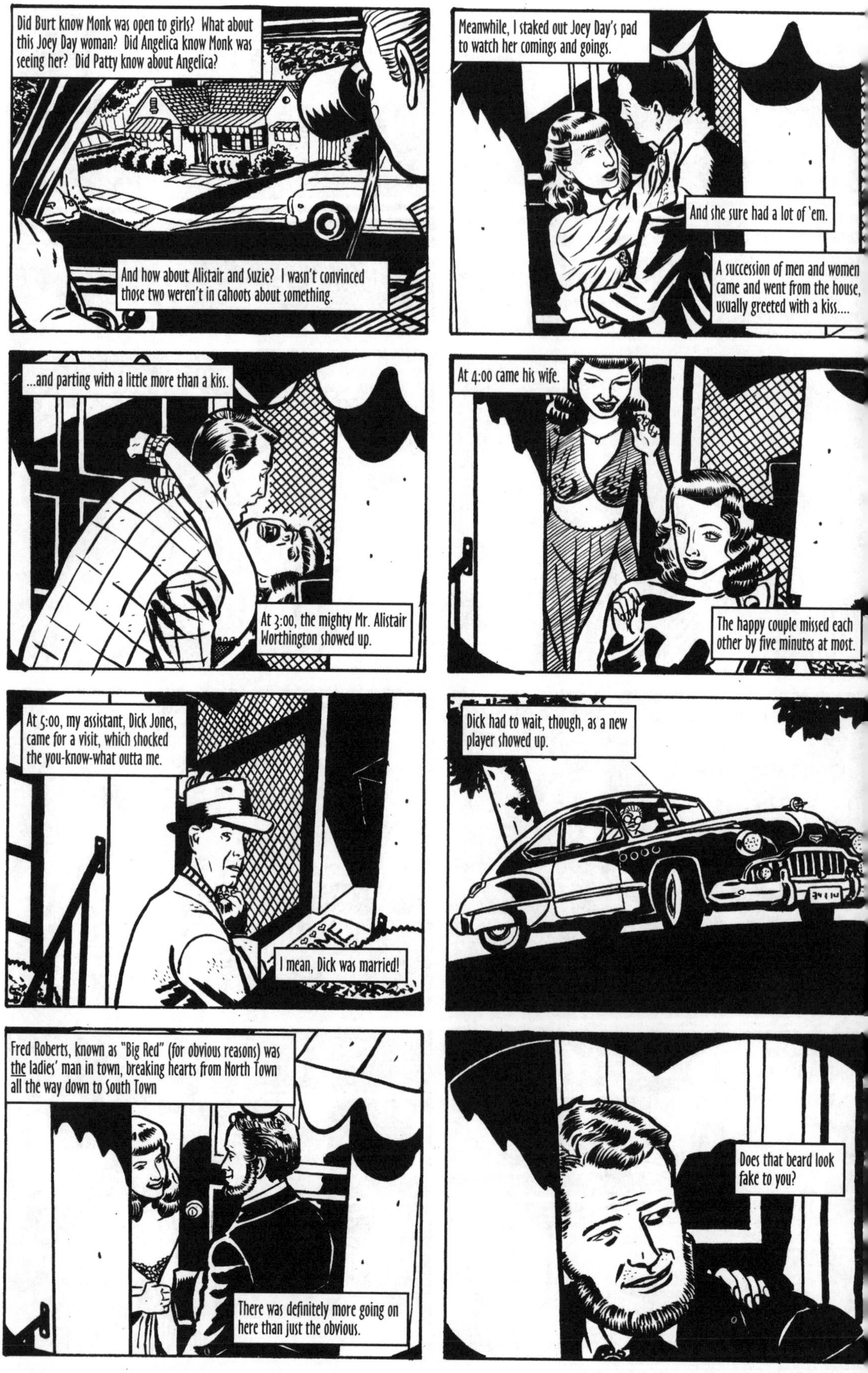
Did Burt know Monk was open to girls? What about this Joey Day woman? Did Angelica know Monk was seeing her? Did Patty know about Angelica?
And how about Alistair and Suzie? I wasn't convinced those two weren't in cahoots about something.
Meanwhile, I staked out Joey Day's pad to watch her comings and goings.
And she sure had a lot of 'em.
A succession of men and women came and went from the house, usually greeted with a kiss....
...and parting with a little more than a kiss.
At 3:00, the mighty Mr. Alistair Worthington showed up.
At 4:00 came his wife.
The happy couple missed each other by five minutes at most.
At 5:00, my assistant, Dick Jones, came for a visit, which shocked the you-know-what outta me.
I mean, Dick was married!
Dick had to wait, though, as a new player showed up.
Fred Roberts, known as "Big Red" (for obvious reasons) was the ladies' man in town, breaking hearts from North Town all the way down to South Town
There was definitely more going on here than just the obvious.
Does that beard look fake to you?

followed Big Red downtown to a eedy little dive called Friday's 49.

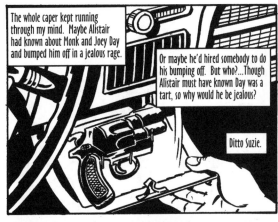

The whole caper kept running through my mind. Maybe Alistair had known about Monk and Joey Day and bumped him off in a jealous rage.

Or maybe he'd hired somebody to do his bumping off. But who?...Though Alistair must have known Day was a tart, so why would he be jealous?

Ditto Suzie.

And who else had been visiting Day for an afternoon whoop-de-do?

I was hoping Big Red could provide some answers.

DID YOU GET IT?!

YEAH, YEAH, I GOT IT. DAT BASTARD WON'T BE BOTHERIN' YA AGAIN.

PRIVATE

YOU'RE SURE THIS IS THE ONLY COPY?

THE ONLY COPY OF WHAT?

"gasp!"

WHAT'S ON THE CELLULOID, FRED?

AMY!

STAY OUTTA DIS, SHAMUS. IT AIN'T GOT NOTHIN' TA DO WIT YOU.

IS THAT ANY WAY TO TALK TO A WOMAN WHO CAN BEAT YOU SILLY? I HAVE A GOOD MIND TO BOX YOUR EARS.

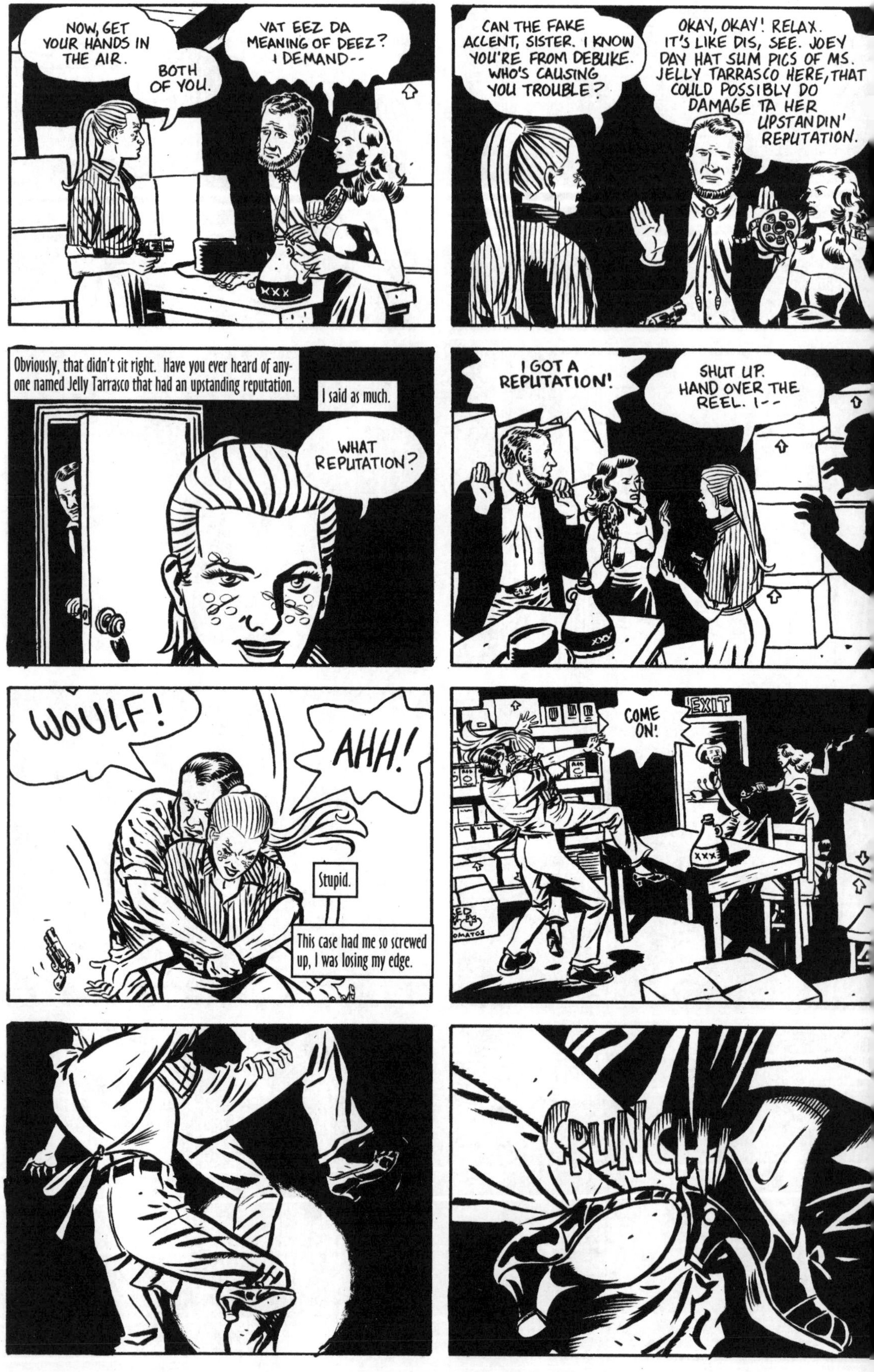

NOW, GET YOUR HANDS IN THE AIR.
BOTH OF YOU.
VAT EEZ DA MEANING OF DEEZ? I DEMAND--
CAN THE FAKE ACCENT, SISTER. I KNOW YOU'RE FROM DEBUKE. WHO'S CAUSING YOU TROUBLE?
OKAY, OKAY! RELAX. IT'S LIKE DIS, SEE. JOEY DAY HAT SUM PICS OF MS. JELLY TARRASCO HERE, THAT COULD POSSIBLY DO DAMAGE TA HER UPSTANDIN' REPUTATION.
Obviously, that didn't sit right. Have you ever heard of anyone named Jelly Tarrasco that had an upstanding reputation.
I said as much.
WHAT REPUTATION?
I GOT A REPUTATION!
SHUT UP. HAND OVER THE REEL. I--
WOULF!
AHH!
Stupid.
This case had me so screwed up, I was losing my edge.
COME ON!
EXIT
XXX
CRUNCH!

huuu...

AAAAHHHHHHHHHHH

There wasn't time to finish him off.

I made a note to come back later.

Damn.

I think I broke my heel.

I couldn't pick up a line on Red or Jelly. I needed to know what was on that reel, or, more specifically, who was on it. Alistair? Angelica? Suzie? Patty? Burt? Who? The answer might be the key to this whole mess.

DING DONG!

First, though, I had some personal business to take care of.

Dick Jones had been my partner since the day I hit town three weeks before. He and his wife Jane, were just about the only people in this world I didn't hate. Seeing him at Joey Day's love pad just didn't fit with the Dick I knew. I went to his house to talk with him....Jane answered.

HELLO?

OH, AMY!

HI, JANE. DICK AROUND?

NO!

I MEAN...um...HOW ARE YOU?...um...DICK? I-I THOUGHT HE WAS WORKING LATE.

ALL-NIGHT STAKEOUT, HE SAID.

That cheating bastard. I HATE men!

OH! OH, YEAH, I REMEMBER NOW.

ALL-NIGHT STAKEOUT...Ha, Ha, HOW SILLY OF ME.

SORRY TO BOTHER YOU, JANE....Ha, Ha...

I couldn't believe I was covering up for that--I just wanted to scream....

OH...ahh... THAT'S OKAY.... WELL, GOODBYE--

AARGH!

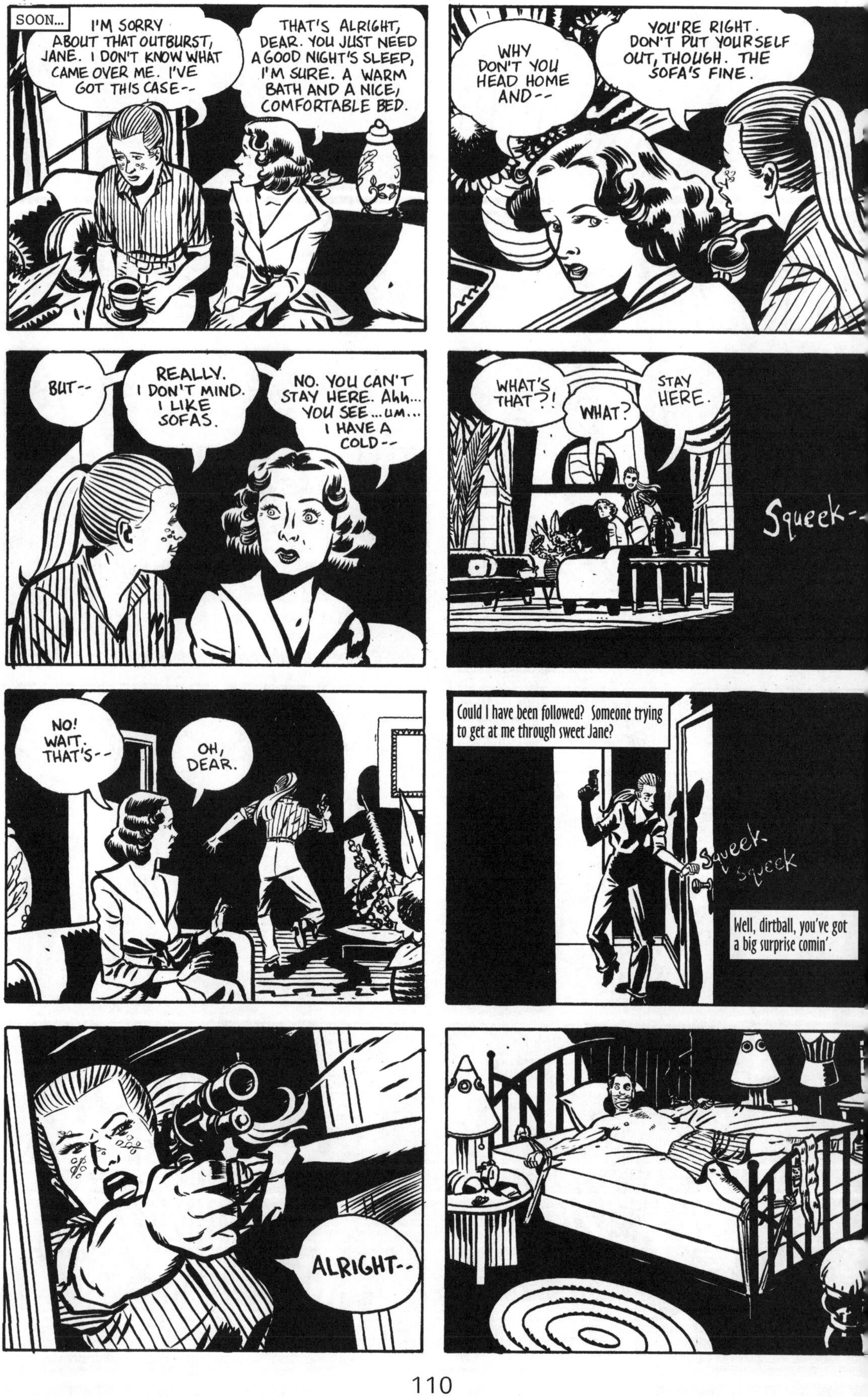
SOON...
I'M SORRY ABOUT THAT OUTBURST, JANE. I DON'T KNOW WHAT CAME OVER ME. I'VE GOT THIS CASE--
THAT'S ALRIGHT, DEAR. YOU JUST NEED A GOOD NIGHT'S SLEEP, I'M SURE. A WARM BATH AND A NICE, COMFORTABLE BED.
WHY DON'T YOU HEAD HOME AND--
YOU'RE RIGHT. DON'T PUT YOURSELF OUT, THOUGH. THE SOFA'S FINE.
BUT--
REALLY. I DON'T MIND. I LIKE SOFAS.
NO. YOU CAN'T STAY HERE. Ahh... YOU SEE...um... I HAVE A COLD--
WHAT'S THAT?!
WHAT?
STAY HERE.
Squeek--
NO! WAIT. THAT'S--
OH, DEAR.
Could I have been followed? Someone trying to get at me through sweet Jane?
Squeek
Squeek
Well, dirtball, you've got a big surprise comin'.
ALRIGHT--

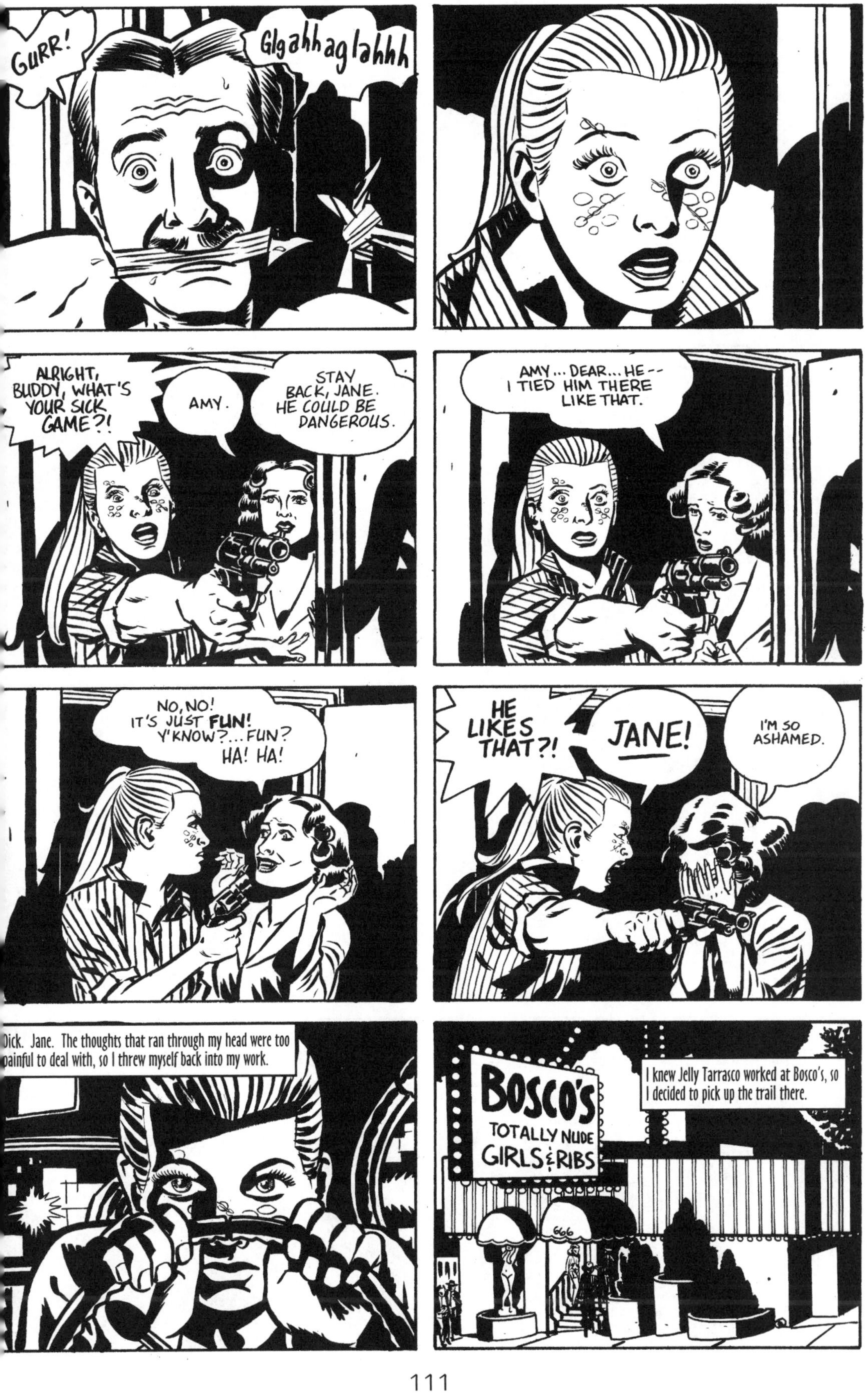
GURR!
Glgahhaglahhh
ALRIGHT, BUDDY, WHAT'S YOUR SICK GAME?!
AMY.
STAY BACK, JANE. HE COULD BE DANGEROUS.
AMY... DEAR... HE-- I TIED HIM THERE LIKE THAT.
NO, NO! IT'S JUST FUN! Y'KNOW?... FUN? HA! HA!
HE LIKES THAT?!
JANE!
I'M SO ASHAMED.
Dick. Jane. The thoughts that ran through my head were too painful to deal with, so I threw myself back into my work.
BOSCO'S
TOTALLY NUDE
GIRLS & RIBS
666
I knew Jelly Tarrasco worked at Bosco's, so I decided to pick up the trail there.

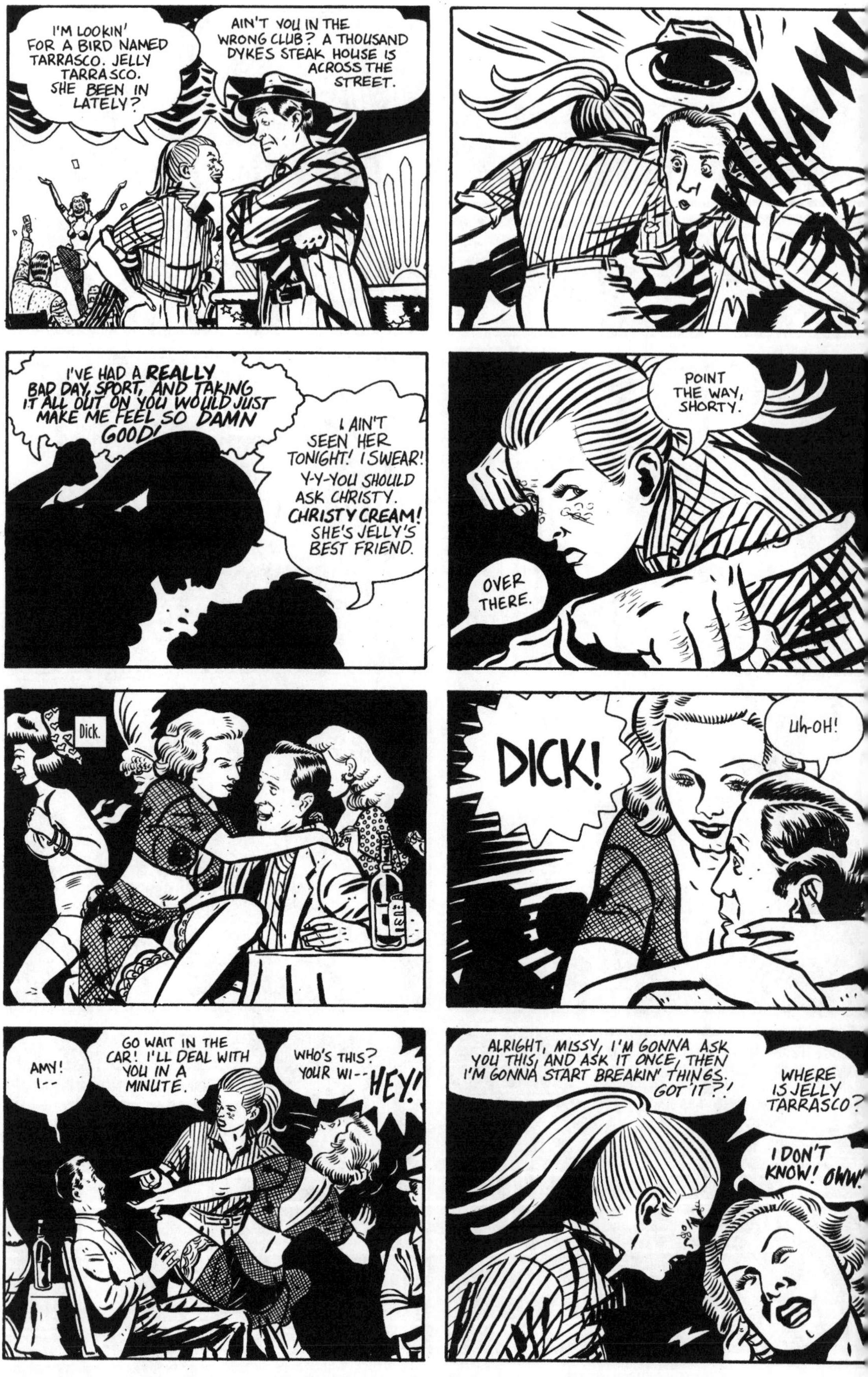

I'M LOOKIN' FOR A BIRD NAMED TARRASCO. JELLY TARRASCO. SHE BEEN IN LATELY?
AIN'T YOU IN THE WRONG CLUB? A THOUSAND DYKES STEAK HOUSE IS ACROSS THE STREET.
I'VE HAD A REALLY BAD DAY, SPORT, AND TAKING IT ALL OUT ON YOU WOULD JUST MAKE ME FEEL SO DAMN GOOD!
I AIN'T SEEN HER TONIGHT! I SWEAR! Y-Y-YOU SHOULD ASK CHRISTY. CHRISTY CREAM! SHE'S JELLY'S BEST FRIEND.
POINT THE WAY, SHORTY.
OVER THERE.
Dick.
DICK!
Uh-OH!
AMY! I--
GO WAIT IN THE CAR! I'LL DEAL WITH YOU IN A MINUTE.
WHO'S THIS? YOUR WI--
HEY!
ALRIGHT, MISSY, I'M GONNA ASK YOU THIS, AND ASK IT ONCE, THEN I'M GONNA START BREAKIN' THINGS. GOT IT?!
WHERE IS JELLY TARRASCO?
I DON'T KNOW! OWW!

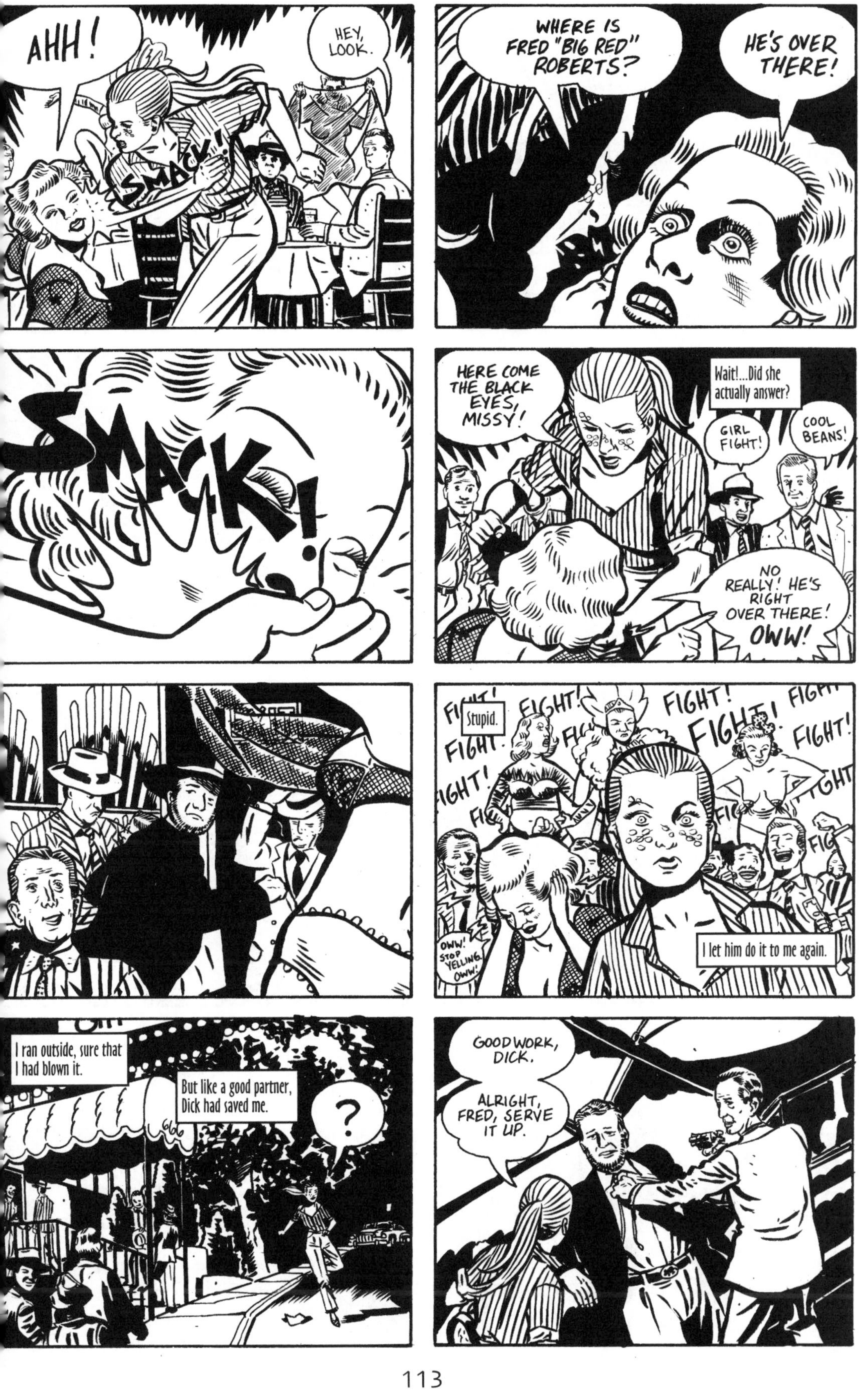
AHH!
HEY, LOOK.
SMACK!
WHERE IS FRED "BIG RED" ROBERTS?
HE'S OVER THERE!
SMACK!
HERE COME THE BLACK EYES, MISSY!
Wait!...Did she actually answer?
GIRL FIGHT!
COOL BEANS!
NO REALLY! HE'S RIGHT OVER THERE! OWW!
Stupid.
FIGHT! FIGHT! FIGHT! FIGHT! FIGHT! FIGHT! FIGHT!
OWW! STOP YELLING. OWW!
I let him do it to me again.
I ran outside, sure that I had blown it.
But like a good partner, Dick had saved me.
?
GOOD WORK, DICK.
ALRIGHT, FRED, SERVE IT UP.

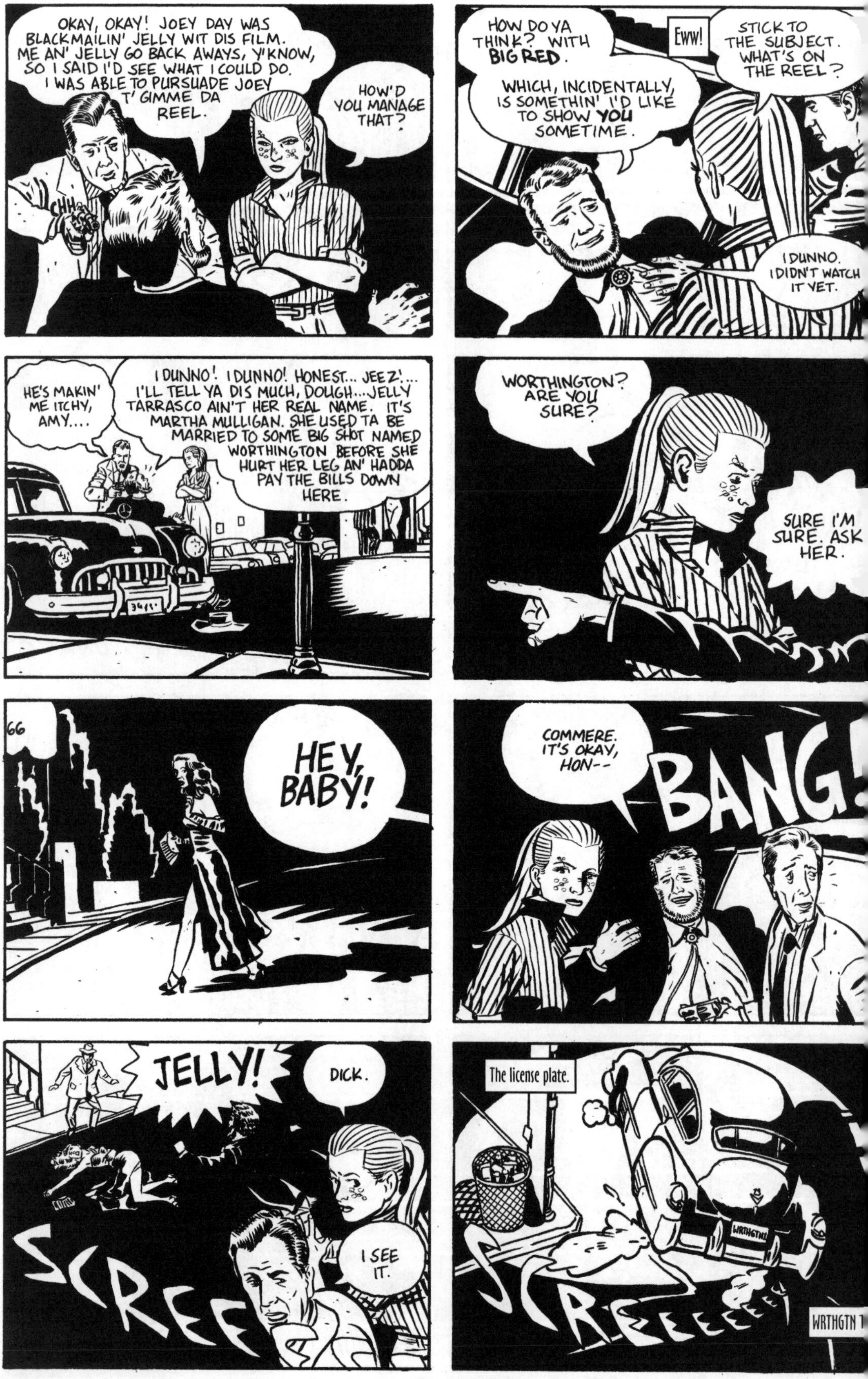

OKAY, OKAY! JOEY DAY WAS BLACKMAILIN' JELLY WIT DIS FILM. ME AN' JELLY GO BACK AWAYS, Y'KNOW, SO I SAID I'D SEE WHAT I COULD DO. I WAS ABLE TO PURSUADE JOEY T' GIMME DA REEL.
CHH
HOW'D YOU MANAGE THAT?
HOW DO YA THINK? WITH BIG RED.
WHICH, INCIDENTALLY, IS SOMETHIN' I'D LIKE TO SHOW YOU SOMETIME.
Eww!
STICK TO THE SUBJECT. WHAT'S ON THE REEL?
I DUNNO. I DIDN'T WATCH IT YET.
HE'S MAKIN' ME ITCHY, AMY....
I DUNNO! I DUNNO! HONEST... JEEZ!... I'LL TELL YA DIS MUCH, DOUGH... JELLY TARRASCO AIN'T HER REAL NAME. IT'S MARTHA MULLIGAN. SHE USED TA BE MARRIED TO SOME BIG SHOT NAMED WORTHINGTON BEFORE SHE HURT HER LEG AN' HADDA PAY THE BILLS DOWN HERE.
WORTHINGTON? ARE YOU SURE?
SURE I'M SURE. ASK HER.
66
HEY, BABY!
COMMERE. IT'S OKAY, HON--
BANG!
JELLY!
DICK.
I SEE IT.
SCREE
The license plate.
WRTHGTN
SCREEEEE
WRTHGTN 1

SOON...

I DON'T KNOW, AMY. A MAN GETS TO BE MY AGE, AND HE WANTS SOME EXCITEMENT.

YOU WANT EXCITEMENT? I'LL SHOOT YOU.

I KNOW....I KNOW.... YOU WON'T TELL JANE, WILL YOU?

NO... IN SPITE OF EVERYTHING, I THINK YOU TWO REALLY DESERVE EACH OTHER.

"sigh"

THANKS. YOU'RE THE BEST.

WATCH IT.

SO... ahh... WHAT HAVE WE GOT?

THERE'S A DEAD GUY NAMED LEWIS MONK WHO MAY HAVE BEEN KILLED BY BURT, THE TOWN MILLIONAIRE DRUNK. BURT'S WIFE, ANGELICA, WAS SUPPOSEDLY SET TO RUN OFF WITH MONK. A TRIP THAT SUZIE WORTHINGTON, WIFE OF THE MILLIONAIRE ALISTAIR WORTHINGTON, WAS GENEROUSLY HELPING TO ARRANGE...

... PRESUMABLY FOR THE CAUSE OF TRUE LOVE-- A CONCEPT I'M RAPIDLY LOSING FAITH IN. ALISTAIR WORTHINGTON HIRED ME TO FIND OUT WHAT HIS WIFE WOULD BE UP TO, THINKING SHE AND MONK WERE INVOLVED-- THOUGH WHEN THE TWO WERE REUNITED, THEY WENT THROUGH GREAT PAINS TO CONVINCE ME OF THEIR GREAT LOVE FOR ONE ANOTHER, AND OF THE MURDEROUS INTENTIONS OF ANGELICA'S HUSBAND BURT.

SOUNDS LIKE A SETUP.

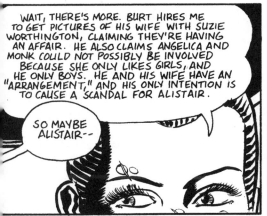

WAIT, THERE'S MORE. BURT HIRES ME TO GET PICTURES OF HIS WIFE WITH SUZIE WORTHINGTON, CLAIMING THEY'RE HAVING AN AFFAIR. HE ALSO CLAIMS ANGELICA AND MONK COULD NOT POSSIBLY BE INVOLVED BECAUSE SHE ONLY LIKES GIRLS, AND HE ONLY BOYS. HE AND HIS WIFE HAVE AN "ARRANGEMENT," AND HIS ONLY INTENTION IS TO CAUSE A SCANDAL FOR ALISTAIR.

SO MAYBE ALISTAIR--

HOLD YOUR HORSES! I'M NOT THROUGH. TO COMPLICATE MATTERS, IT TURNS OUT MONK SEEMED TO BE CHANGING HIS MIND ABOUT THE OPPOSITE SEX AFTER A FEW VISITS TO THE TOWN PIT STOP, JOEY DAY. I WAS TOLD THIS BY A JEALOUS BOYFRIEND NAMED PATTY.

SO YOU THINK MAYBE HE--

ALSO VISITING MS. DAY WERE BOTH ALISTAIR AND SUZIE WORTHINGTON...

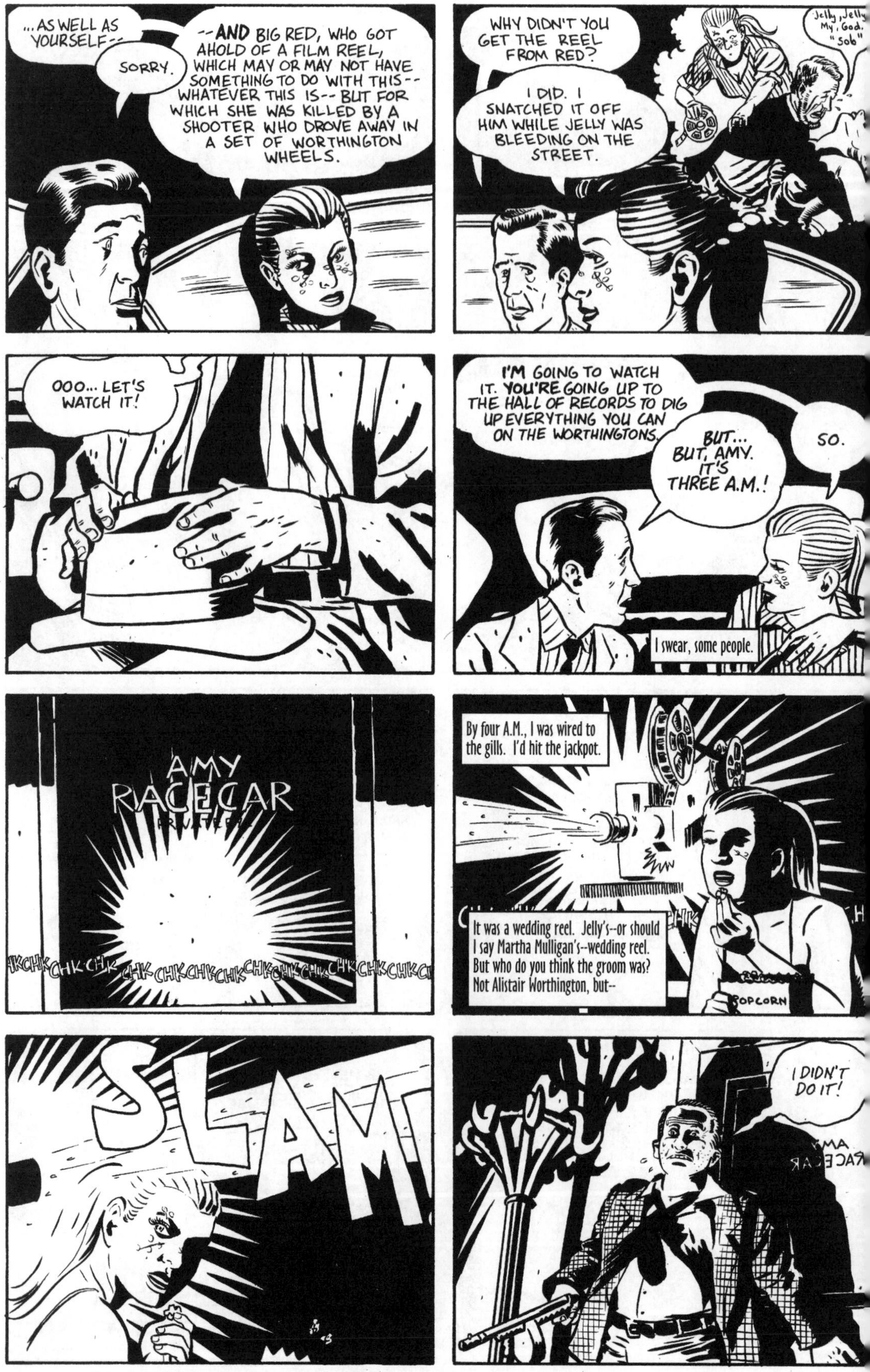
...AS WELL AS YOURSELF--
SORRY.
--AND BIG RED, WHO GOT AHOLD OF A FILM REEL, WHICH MAY OR MAY NOT HAVE SOMETHING TO DO WITH THIS-- WHATEVER THIS IS-- BUT FOR WHICH SHE WAS KILLED BY A SHOOTER WHO DROVE AWAY IN A SET OF WORTHINGTON WHEELS.
WHY DIDN'T YOU GET THE REEL FROM RED?
I DID. I SNATCHED IT OFF HIM WHILE JELLY WAS BLEEDING ON THE STREET.
Jelly, Jelly My, God. "Sob"
OOO... LET'S WATCH IT!
I'M GOING TO WATCH IT. YOU'RE GOING UP TO THE HALL OF RECORDS TO DIG UP EVERYTHING YOU CAN ON THE WORTHINGTONS.
BUT... BUT, AMY. IT'S THREE A.M.!
SO.
I swear, some people.
AMY RACECAR
CHK CHK CHK CHK CHK CHK CHK CHK CHK CHK CHK CHK CHK
By four A.M., I was wired to the gills. I'd hit the jackpot.
It was a wedding reel. Jelly's--or should I say Martha Mulligan's--wedding reel. But who do you think the groom was? Not Alistair Worthington, but--
POPCORN
SLAM
I DIDN'T DO IT!

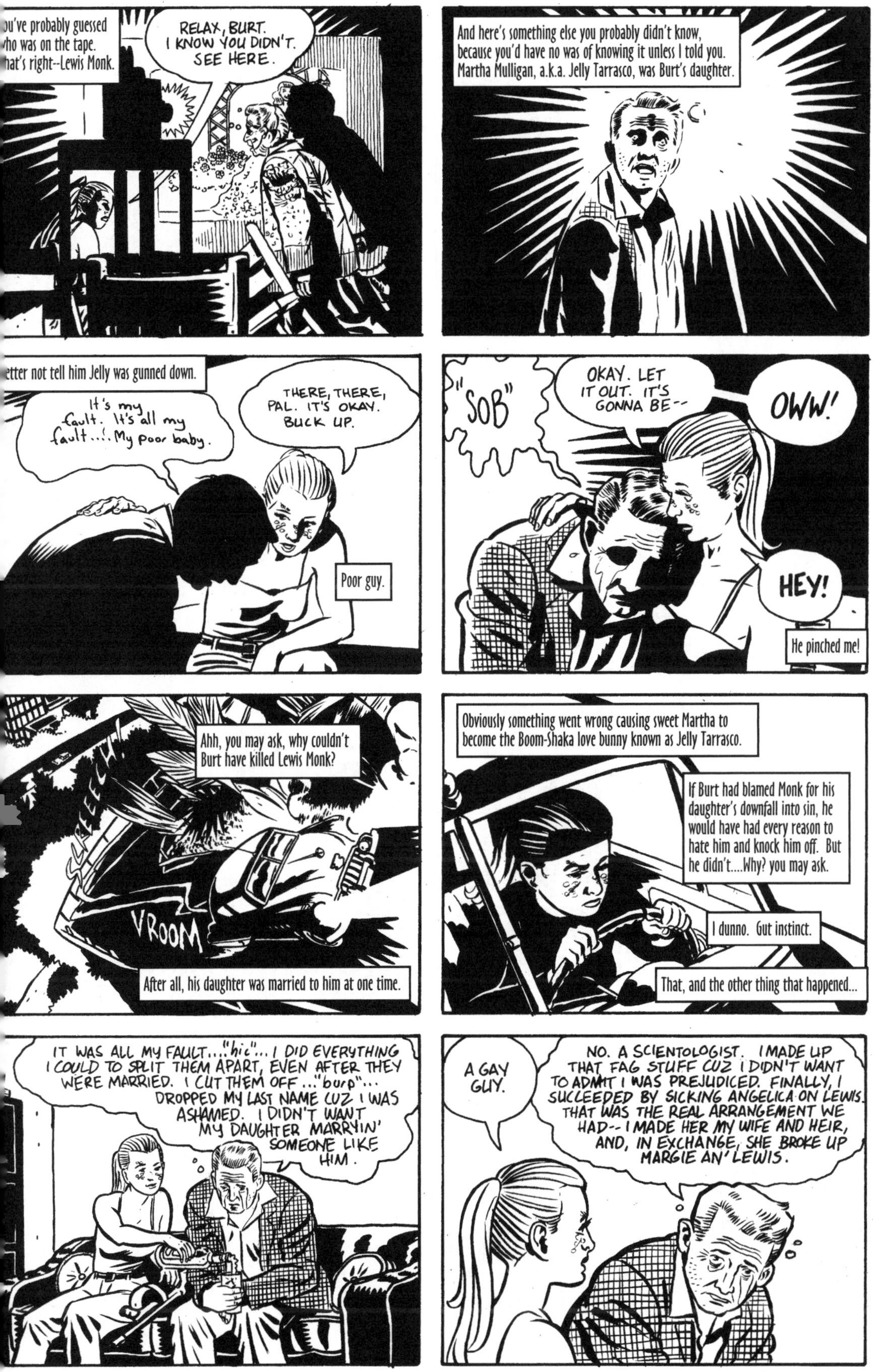

ou've probably guessed who was on the tape. hat's right--Lewis Monk.
RELAX, BURT. I KNOW YOU DIDN'T. SEE HERE.
And here's something else you probably didn't know, because you'd have no was of knowing it unless I told you. Martha Mulligan, a.k.a. Jelly Tarrasco, was Burt's daughter.
etter not tell him Jelly was gunned down.
It's my fault. It's all my fault...! My poor baby.
THERE, THERE, PAL. IT'S OKAY. BUCK UP.
Poor guy.
"SOB"
OKAY. LET IT OUT. IT'S GONNA BE--
OWW!
HEY!
He pinched me!
Ahh, you may ask, why couldn't Burt have killed Lewis Monk?
VROOM
After all, his daughter was married to him at one time.
Obviously something went wrong causing sweet Martha to become the Boom-Shaka love bunny known as Jelly Tarrasco.
If Burt had blamed Monk for his daughter's downfall into sin, he would have had every reason to hate him and knock him off. But he didn't....Why? you may ask.
I dunno. Gut instinct.
That, and the other thing that happened...
IT WAS ALL MY FAULT..."hic"... I DID EVERYTHING I COULD TO SPLIT THEM APART, EVEN AFTER THEY WERE MARRIED. I CUT THEM OFF..."burp"... DROPPED MY LAST NAME CUZ I WAS ASHAMED. I DIDN'T WANT MY DAUGHTER MARRYIN' SOMEONE LIKE HIM.
A GAY GUY.
NO. A SCIENTOLOGIST. I MADE UP THAT FAG STUFF CUZ I DIDN'T WANT TO ADMIT I WAS PREJUDICED. FINALLY, I SUCCEEDED BY SICKING ANGELICA ON LEWIS. THAT WAS THE REAL ARRANGEMENT WE HAD--I MADE HER MY WIFE AND HEIR, AND, IN EXCHANGE, SHE BROKE UP MARGIE AN' LEWIS.

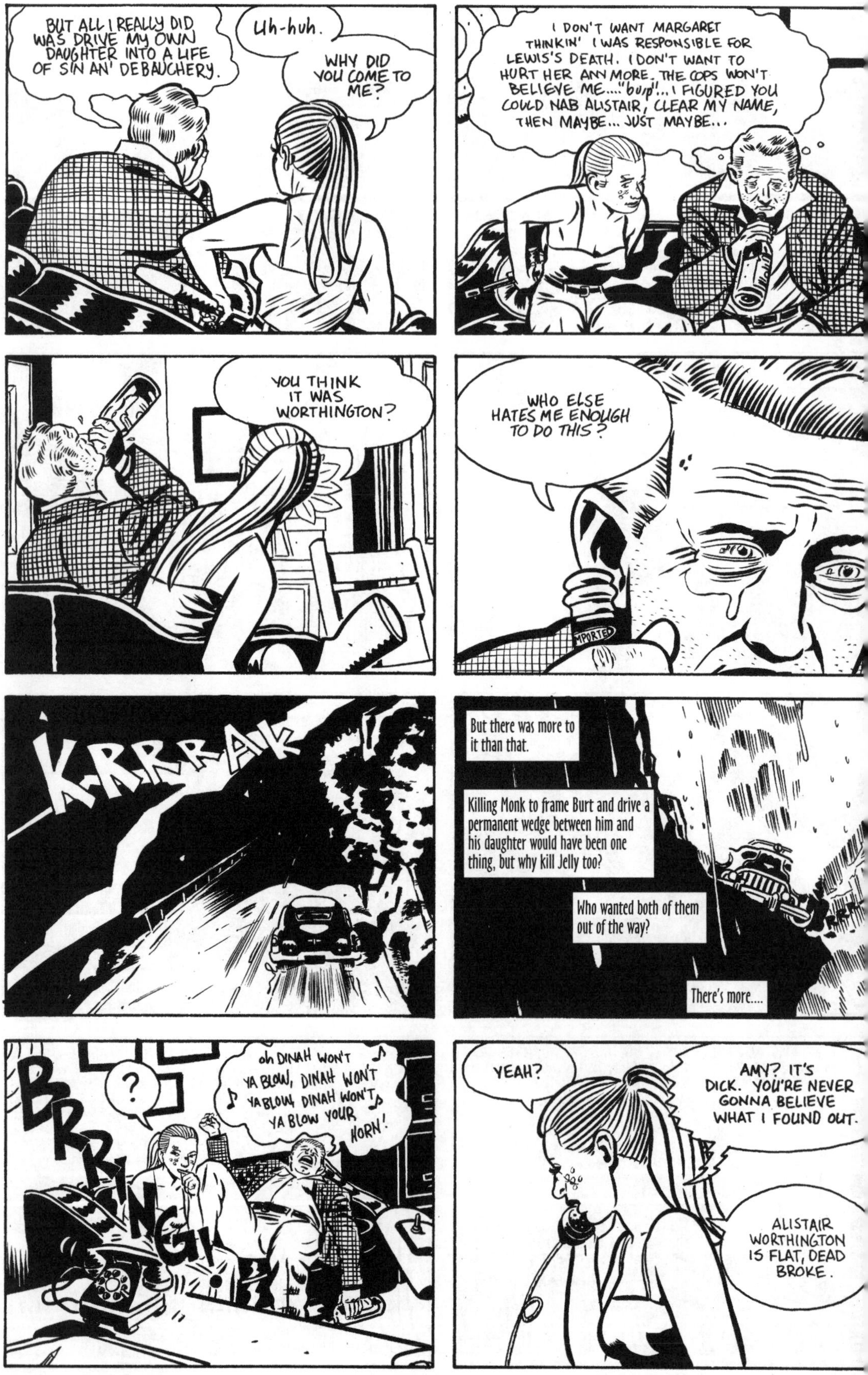
BUT ALL I REALLY DID WAS DRIVE MY OWN DAUGHTER INTO A LIFE OF SIN AN' DEBAUCHERY.
Uh-huh.
WHY DID YOU COME TO ME?
I DON'T WANT MARGARET THINKIN' I WAS RESPONSIBLE FOR LEWIS'S DEATH. I DON'T WANT TO HURT HER ANY MORE. THE COPS WON'T BELIEVE ME...."burp"... I FIGURED YOU COULD NAB ALISTAIR, CLEAR MY NAME, THEN MAYBE... JUST MAYBE...
YOU THINK IT WAS WORTHINGTON?
WHO ELSE HATES ME ENOUGH TO DO THIS?
IMPORTED
KRRRAK
But there was more to it than that.
Killing Monk to frame Burt and drive a permanent wedge between him and his daughter would have been one thing, but why kill Jelly too?
Who wanted both of them out of the way?
There's more....
BRRING!
?
oh DINAH WON'T YA BLOW, DINAH WON'T YA BLOW, DINAH WON'T YA BLOW YOUR HORN!
YEAH?
AMY? IT'S DICK. YOU'RE NEVER GONNA BELIEVE WHAT I FOUND OUT.
ALISTAIR WORTHINGTON IS FLAT, DEAD BROKE.

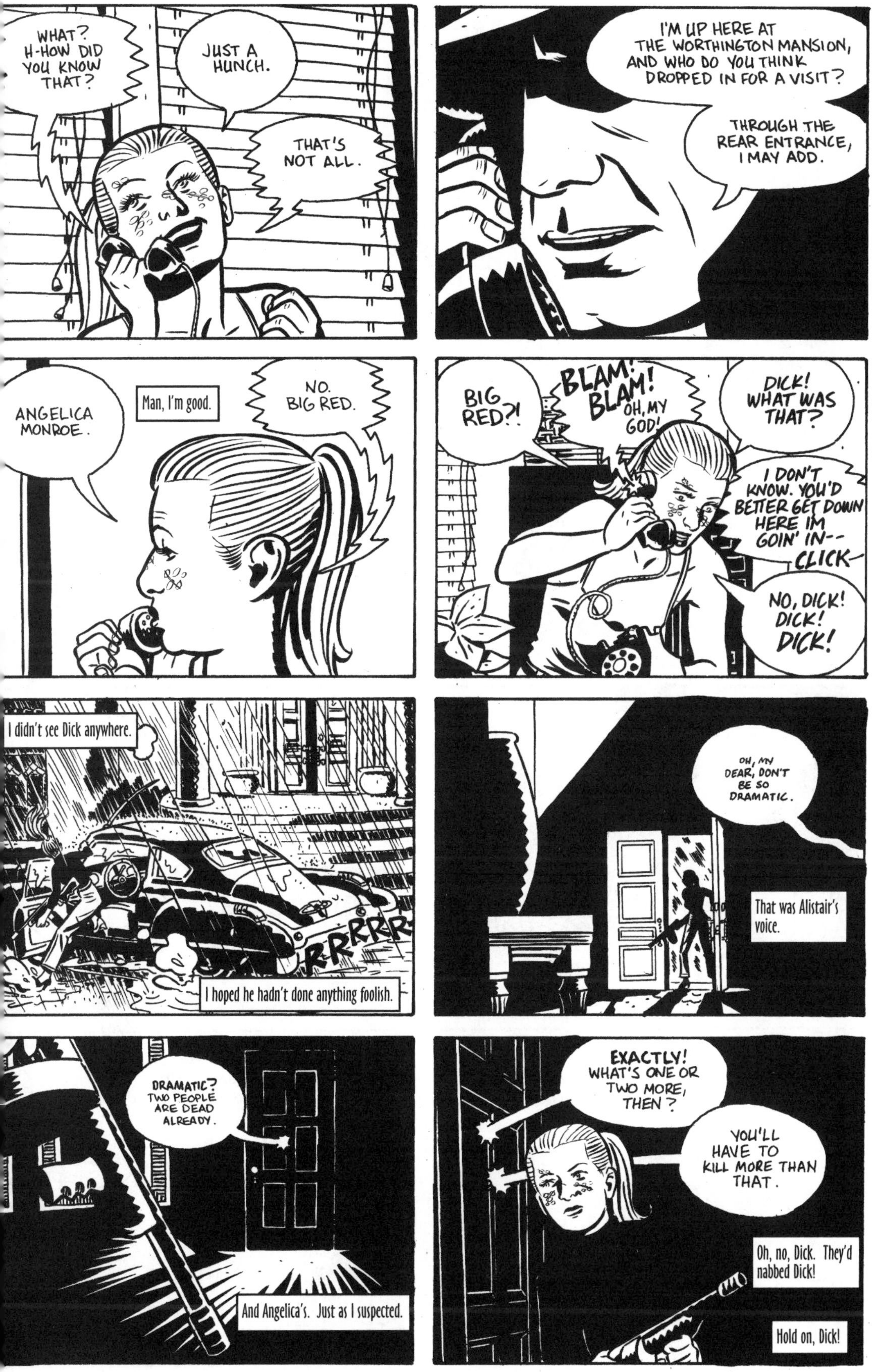
WHAT? H-HOW DID YOU KNOW THAT?
JUST A HUNCH.
THAT'S NOT ALL.
I'M UP HERE AT THE WORTHINGTON MANSION, AND WHO DO YOU THINK DROPPED IN FOR A VISIT?
THROUGH THE REAR ENTRANCE, I MAY ADD.
ANGELICA MONROE.
Man, I'm good.
NO. BIG RED.
BIG RED?!
BLAM! BLAM! OH, MY GOD!
DICK! WHAT WAS THAT?
I DON'T KNOW. YOU'D BETTER GET DOWN HERE IM GOIN' IN--
CLICK
NO, DICK! DICK! DICK!
I didn't see Dick anywhere.
RRRRR
I hoped he hadn't done anything foolish.
OH, MY DEAR, DON'T BE SO DRAMATIC.
That was Alistair's voice.
DRAMATIC? TWO PEOPLE ARE DEAD ALREADY.
And Angelica's. Just as I suspected.
EXACTLY! WHAT'S ONE OR TWO MORE, THEN?
YOU'LL HAVE TO KILL MORE THAN THAT.
Oh, no, Dick. They'd nabbed Dick!
Hold on, Dick!

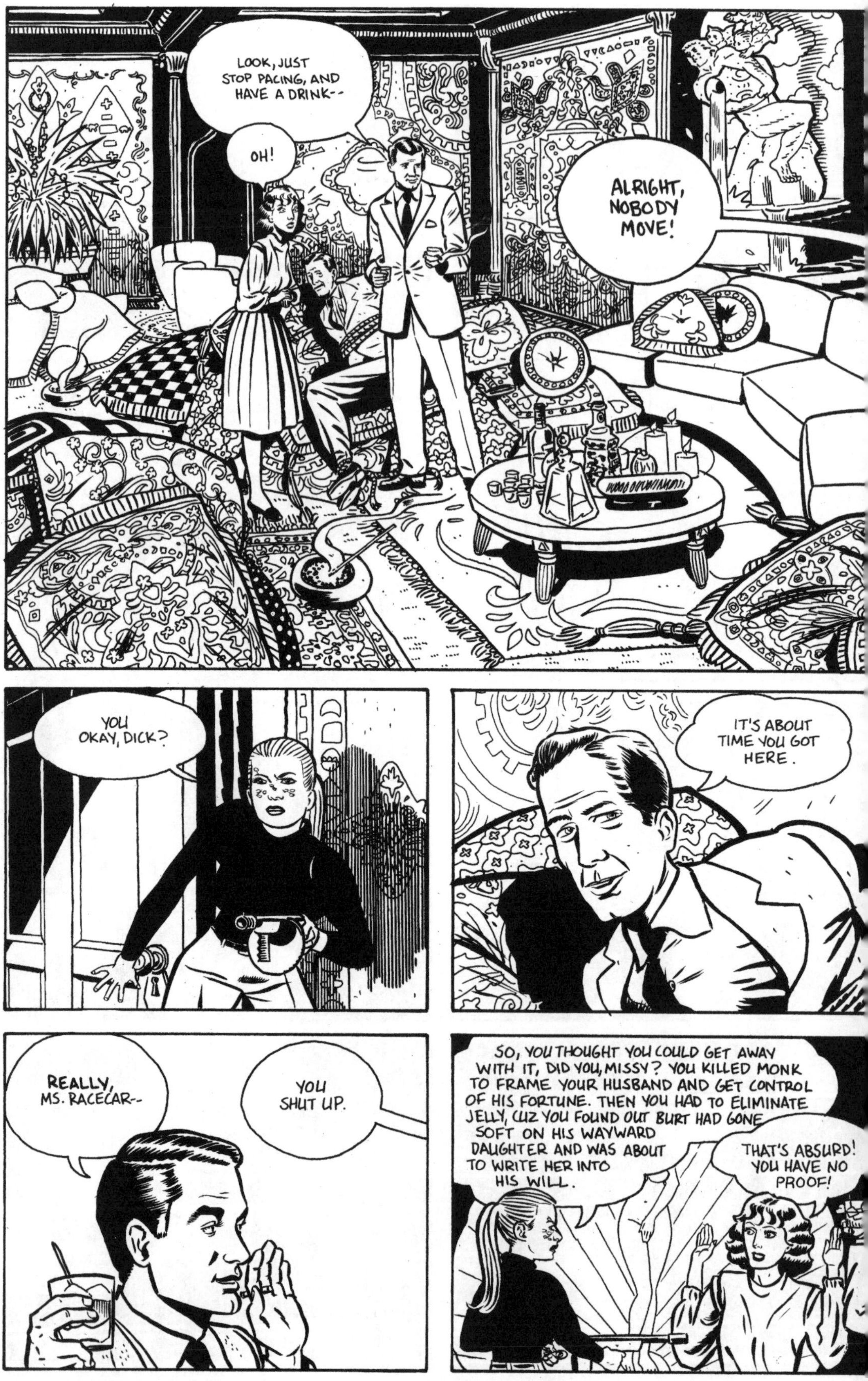
LOOK, JUST STOP PACING, AND HAVE A DRINK--
OH!
ALRIGHT, NOBODY MOVE!
YOU OKAY, DICK?
IT'S ABOUT TIME YOU GOT HERE.
REALLY, MS. RACECAR--
YOU SHUT UP.
SO, YOU THOUGHT YOU COULD GET AWAY WITH IT, DID YOU, MISSY? YOU KILLED MONK TO FRAME YOUR HUSBAND AND GET CONTROL OF HIS FORTUNE. THEN YOU HAD TO ELIMINATE JELLY, CUZ YOU FOUND OUT BURT HAD GONE SOFT ON HIS WAYWARD DAUGHTER AND WAS ABOUT TO WRITE HER INTO HIS WILL.
THAT'S ABSURD! YOU HAVE NO PROOF!

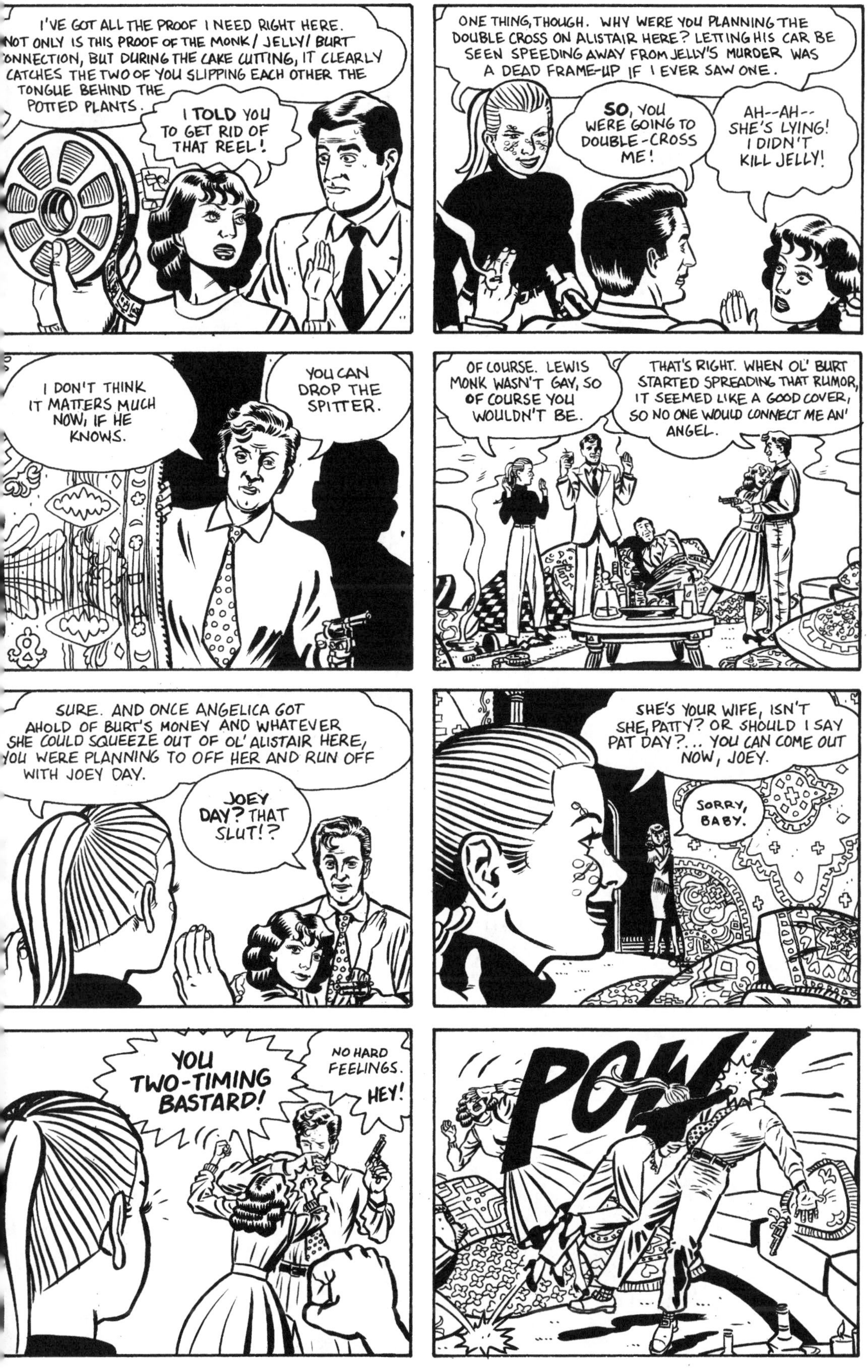
I'VE GOT ALL THE PROOF I NEED RIGHT HERE. NOT ONLY IS THIS PROOF OF THE MONK/ JELLY/ BURT CONNECTION, BUT DURING THE CAKE CUTTING, IT CLEARLY CATCHES THE TWO OF YOU SLIPPING EACH OTHER THE TONGUE BEHIND THE POTTED PLANTS.
I TOLD YOU TO GET RID OF THAT REEL!
ONE THING, THOUGH. WHY WERE YOU PLANNING THE DOUBLE CROSS ON ALISTAIR HERE? LETTING HIS CAR BE SEEN SPEEDING AWAY FROM JELLY'S MURDER WAS A DEAD FRAME-UP IF I EVER SAW ONE.
SO, YOU WERE GOING TO DOUBLE-CROSS ME!
AH--AH-- SHE'S LYING! I DIDN'T KILL JELLY!
I DON'T THINK IT MATTERS MUCH NOW, IF HE KNOWS.
YOU CAN DROP THE SPITTER.
OF COURSE. LEWIS MONK WASN'T GAY, SO OF COURSE YOU WOULDN'T BE.
THAT'S RIGHT. WHEN OL' BURT STARTED SPREADING THAT RUMOR, IT SEEMED LIKE A GOOD COVER, SO NO ONE WOULD CONNECT ME AN' ANGEL.
SURE. AND ONCE ANGELICA GOT AHOLD OF BURT'S MONEY AND WHATEVER SHE COULD SQUEEZE OUT OF OL' ALISTAIR HERE, YOU WERE PLANNING TO OFF HER AND RUN OFF WITH JOEY DAY.
JOEY DAY? THAT SLUT!?
SHE'S YOUR WIFE, ISN'T SHE, PATTY? OR SHOULD I SAY PAT DAY?... YOU CAN COME OUT NOW, JOEY.
SORRY, BABY.
YOU TWO-TIMING BASTARD!
NO HARD FEELINGS.
HEY!
POW!

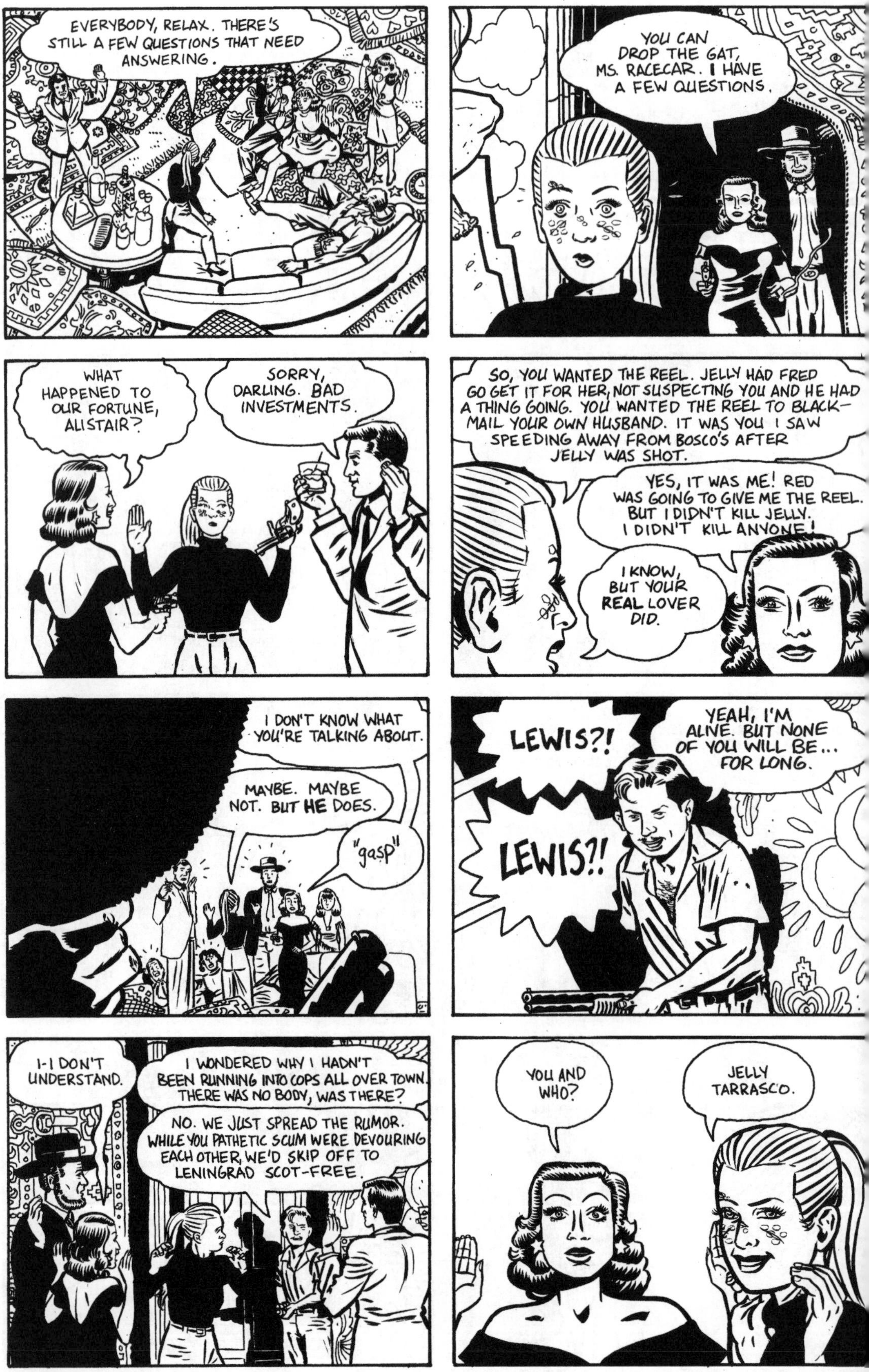
EVERYBODY, RELAX. THERE'S STILL A FEW QUESTIONS THAT NEED ANSWERING.
YOU CAN DROP THE GAT, MS. RACECAR. I HAVE A FEW QUESTIONS.
WHAT HAPPENED TO OUR FORTUNE, ALISTAIR?
SORRY, DARLING. BAD INVESTMENTS.
SO, YOU WANTED THE REEL. JELLY HAD FRED GO GET IT FOR HER, NOT SUSPECTING YOU AND HE HAD A THING GOING. YOU WANTED THE REEL TO BLACK-MAIL YOUR OWN HUSBAND. IT WAS YOU I SAW SPEEDING AWAY FROM BOSCO'S AFTER JELLY WAS SHOT.
YES, IT WAS ME! RED WAS GOING TO GIVE ME THE REEL. BUT I DIDN'T KILL JELLY. I DIDN'T KILL ANYONE!
I KNOW, BUT YOUR REAL LOVER DID.
I DON'T KNOW WHAT YOU'RE TALKING ABOUT.
MAYBE. MAYBE NOT. BUT HE DOES.
"gasp"
LEWIS?!
LEWIS?!
YEAH, I'M ALIVE. BUT NONE OF YOU WILL BE... FOR LONG.
I-I DON'T UNDERSTAND.
I WONDERED WHY I HADN'T BEEN RUNNING INTO COPS ALL OVER TOWN. THERE WAS NO BODY, WAS THERE?
NO. WE JUST SPREAD THE RUMOR. WHILE YOU PATHETIC SCUM WERE DEVOURING EACH OTHER, WE'D SKIP OFF TO LENINGRAD SCOT-FREE.
YOU AND WHO?
JELLY TARRASCO.

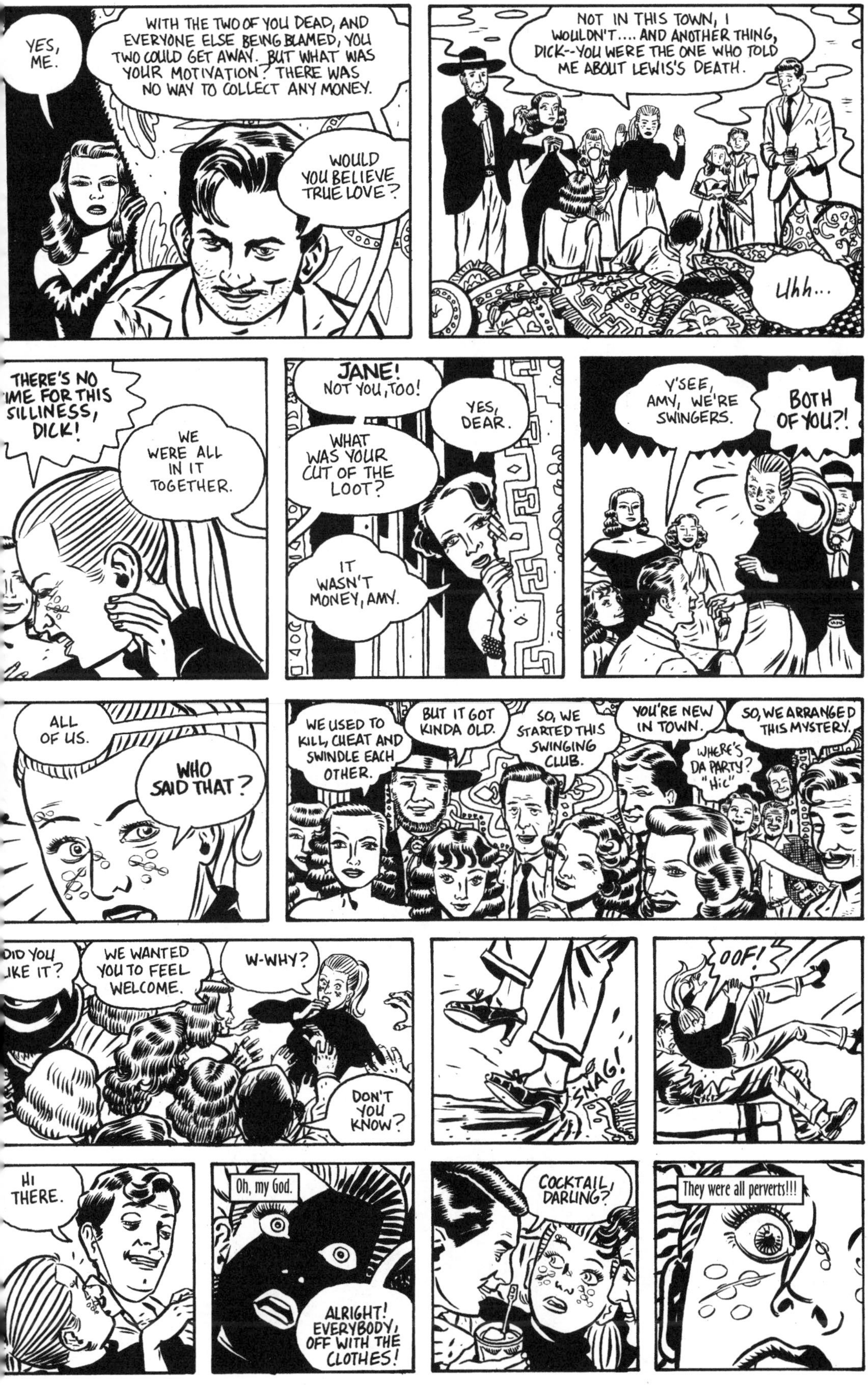
YES, ME.
WITH THE TWO OF YOU DEAD, AND EVERYONE ELSE BEING BLAMED, YOU TWO COULD GET AWAY. BUT WHAT WAS YOUR MOTIVATION? THERE WAS NO WAY TO COLLECT ANY MONEY.
WOULD YOU BELIEVE TRUE LOVE?
NOT IN THIS TOWN, I WOULDN'T.... AND ANOTHER THING, DICK--YOU WERE THE ONE WHO TOLD ME ABOUT LEWIS'S DEATH.
Uhh...
THERE'S NO TIME FOR THIS SILLINESS, DICK!
WE WERE ALL IN IT TOGETHER.
JANE! NOT YOU, TOO!
YES, DEAR.
WHAT WAS YOUR CUT OF THE LOOT?
IT WASN'T MONEY, AMY.
Y'SEE, AMY, WE'RE SWINGERS.
BOTH OF YOU?!
ALL OF US.
WHO SAID THAT?
WE USED TO KILL, CHEAT AND SWINDLE EACH OTHER.
BUT IT GOT KINDA OLD.
SO, WE STARTED THIS SWINGING CLUB.
YOU'RE NEW IN TOWN.
SO, WE ARRANGED THIS MYSTERY.
WHERE'S DA PARTY? "Hic"
DID YOU LIKE IT?
WE WANTED YOU TO FEEL WELCOME.
W-WHY?
DON'T YOU KNOW?
SNAG!
OOF!
HI THERE.
Oh, my God.
ALRIGHT! EVERYBODY, OFF WITH THE CLOTHES!
COCKTAIL, DARLING?
They were all perverts!!!

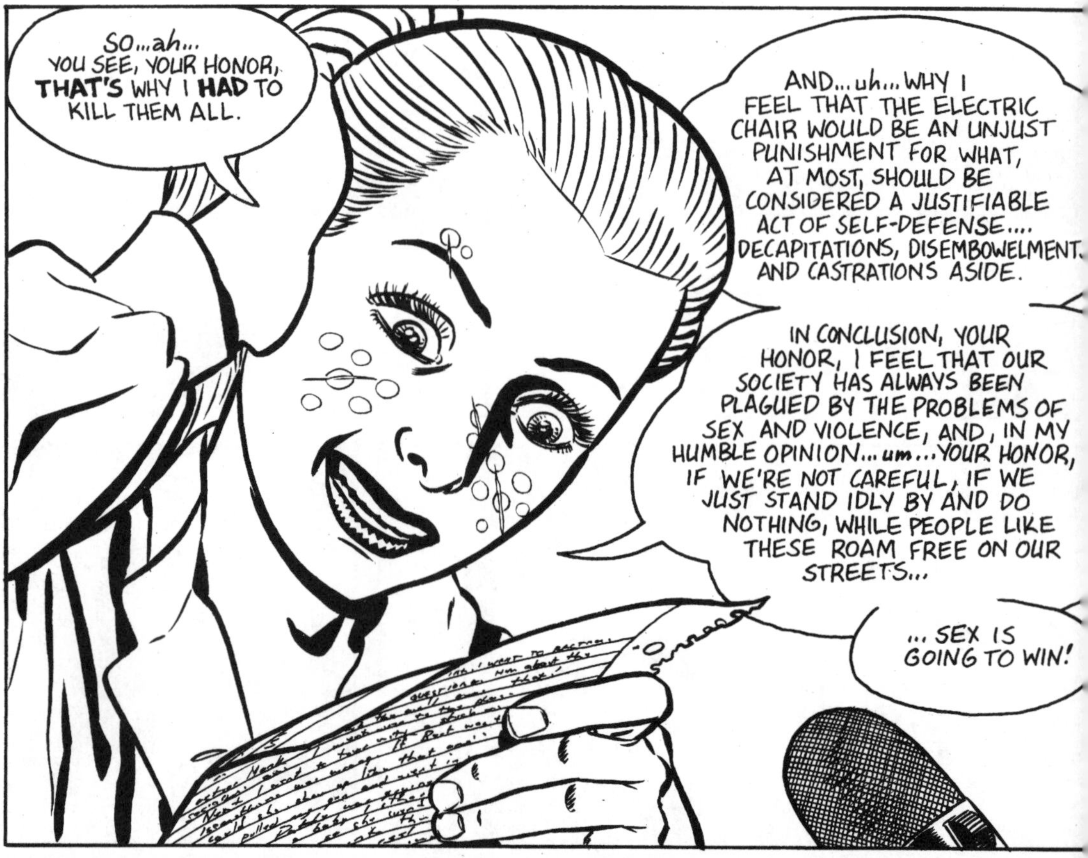
SO...ah... YOU SEE, YOUR HONOR, **THAT'S** WHY I **HAD** TO KILL THEM ALL.
AND...uh...WHY I FEEL THAT THE ELECTRIC CHAIR WOULD BE AN UNJUST PUNISHMENT FOR WHAT, AT MOST, SHOULD BE CONSIDERED A JUSTIFIABLE ACT OF SELF-DEFENSE.... DECAPITATIONS, DISEMBOWELMENT, AND CASTRATIONS ASIDE.
IN CONCLUSION, YOUR HONOR, I FEEL THAT OUR SOCIETY HAS ALWAYS BEEN PLAGUED BY THE PROBLEMS OF SEX AND VIOLENCE, AND, IN MY HUMBLE OPINION...*um*...YOUR HONOR, IF WE'RE NOT CAREFUL, IF WE JUST STAND IDLY BY AND DO NOTHING, WHILE PEOPLE LIKE THESE ROAM FREE ON OUR STREETS...
...SEX IS GOING TO WIN!

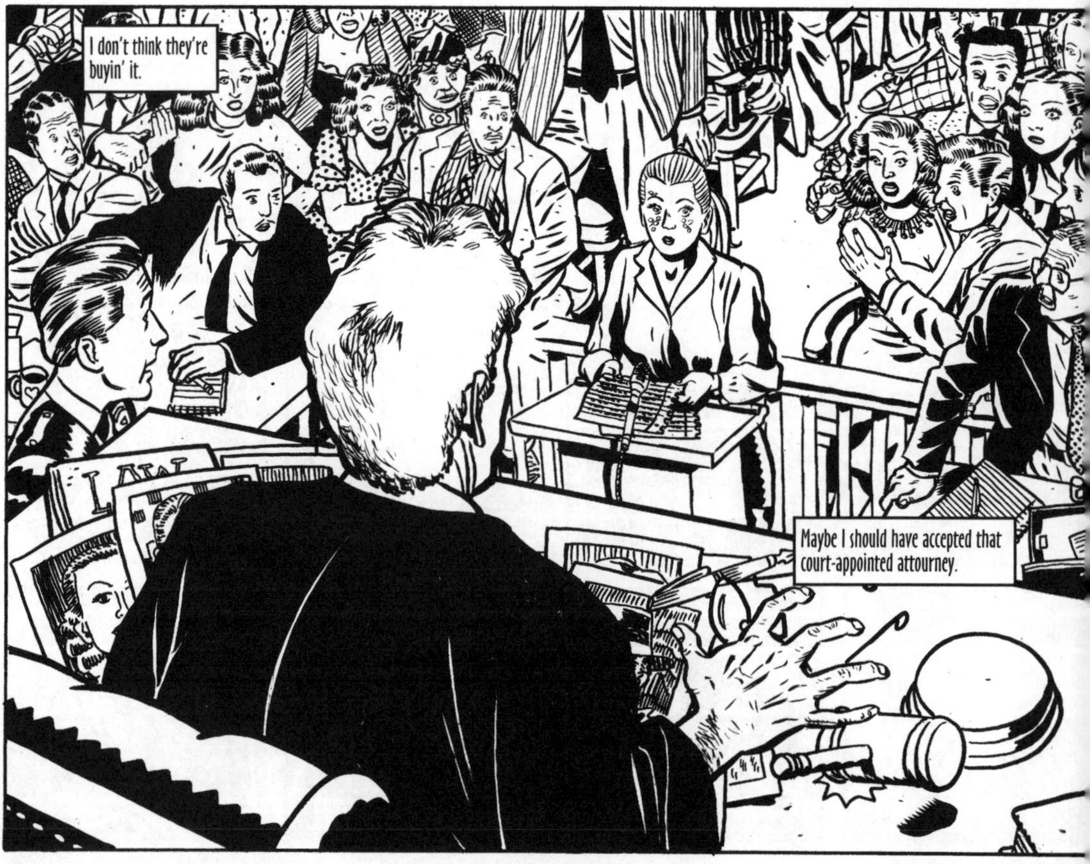
I don't think they're buyin' it.
Maybe I should have accepted that court-appointed attourney.



**THE END.**

# 5

## "LIVE NUDE GIRLS!"

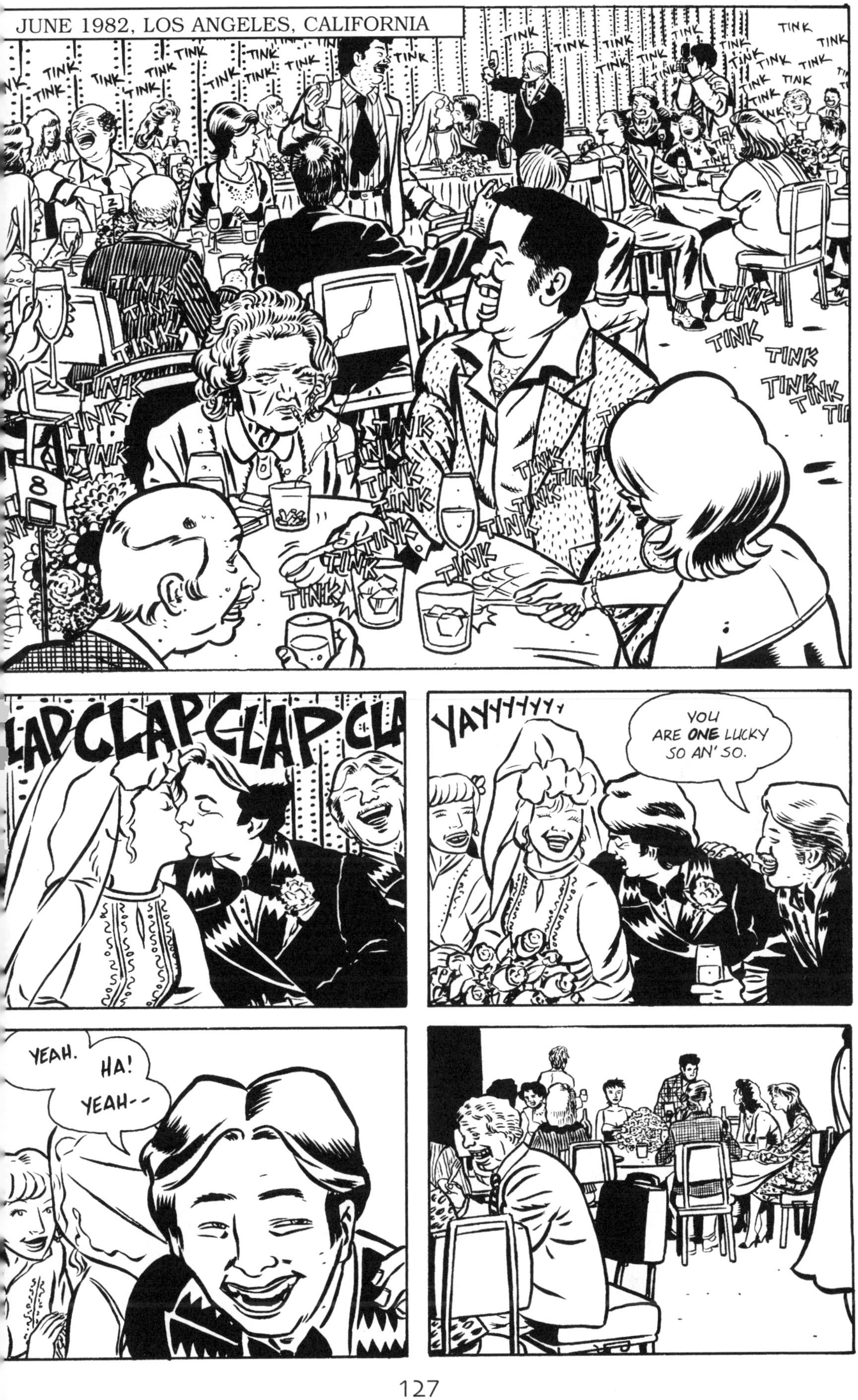
JUNE 1982, LOS ANGELES, CALIFORNIA
TINK TINK TINK TINK
CLAP CLAP CLAP
YAYYYYYY
YOU ARE ONE LUCKY SO AN' SO.
YEAH. HA! YEAH--

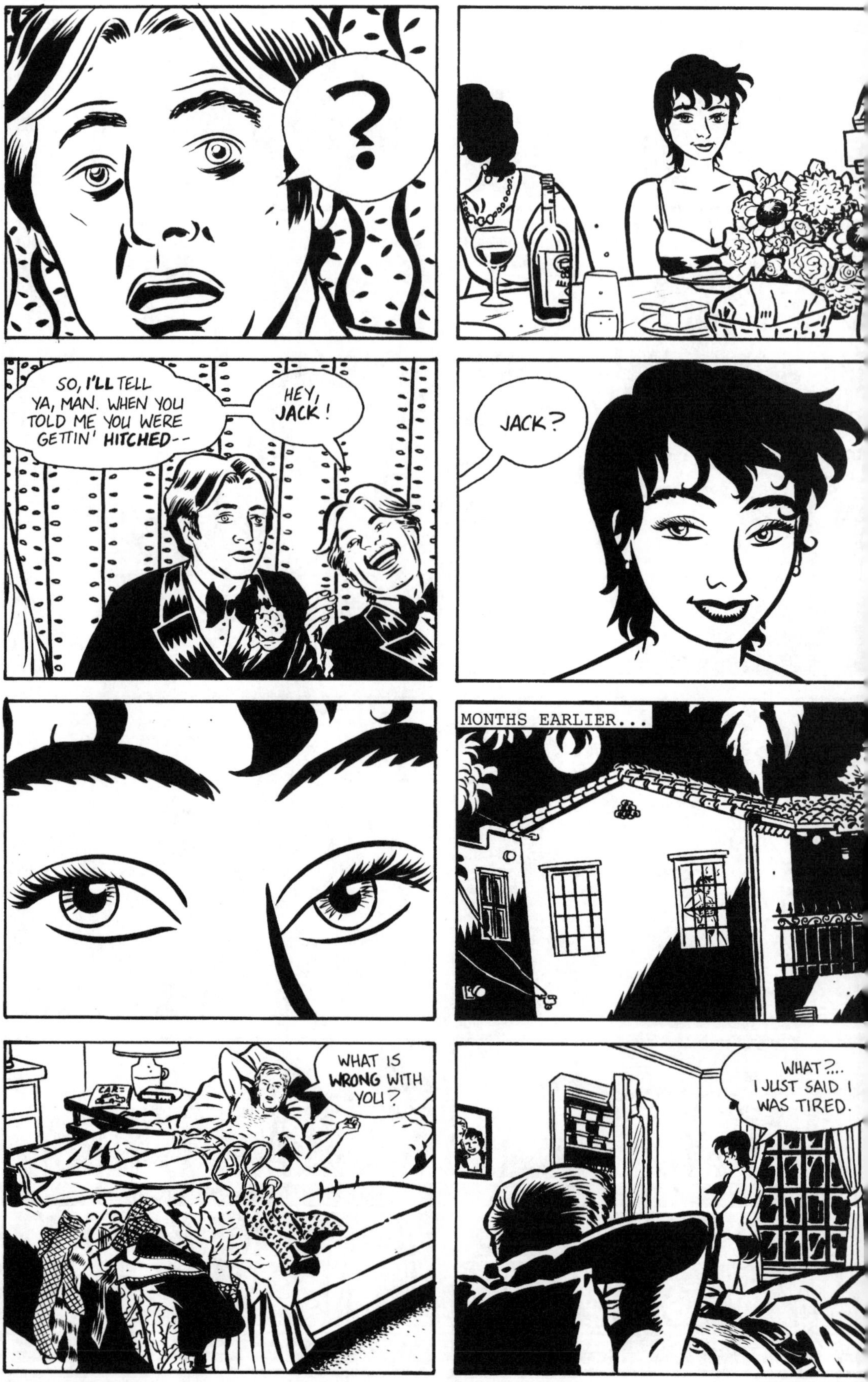
?
SO, I'LL TELL YA, MAN. WHEN YOU TOLD ME YOU WERE GETTIN' HITCHED--
HEY, JACK!
JACK?
MONTHS EARLIER...
WHAT IS WRONG WITH YOU?
WHAT?... I JUST SAID I WAS TIRED.

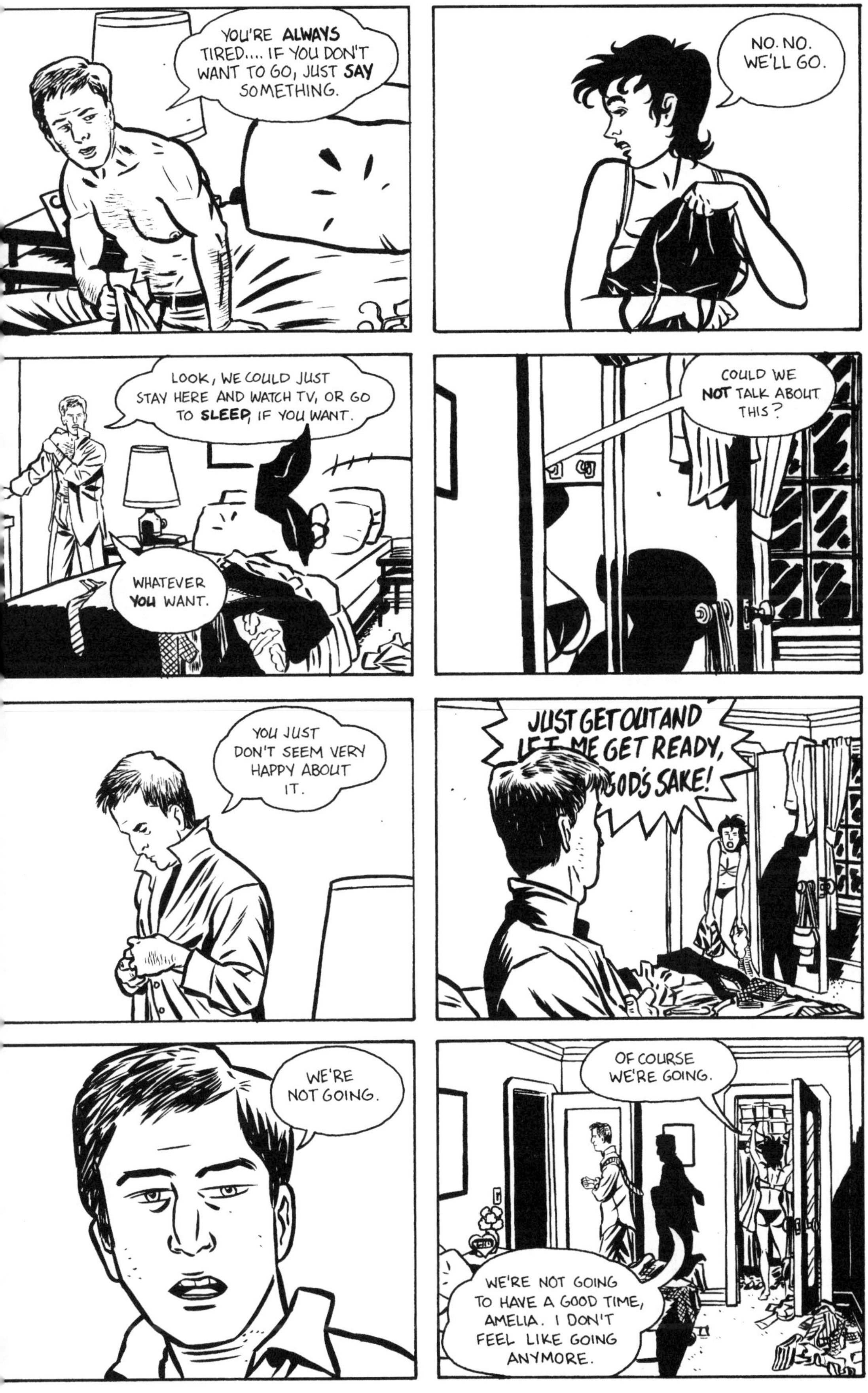
YOU'RE **ALWAYS** TIRED.... IF YOU DON'T WANT TO GO, JUST **SAY** SOMETHING.
NO. NO. WE'LL GO.
LOOK, WE COULD JUST STAY HERE AND WATCH TV, OR GO TO **SLEEP**, IF YOU WANT.
WHATEVER **YOU** WANT.
COULD WE **NOT** TALK ABOUT THIS?
YOU JUST DON'T SEEM VERY HAPPY ABOUT IT.
JUST GET OUT AND LET ME GET READY, FOR GOD'S SAKE!
WE'RE NOT GOING.
OF COURSE WE'RE GOING.
WE'RE NOT GOING TO HAVE A GOOD TIME, AMELIA. I DON'T FEEL LIKE GOING ANYMORE.

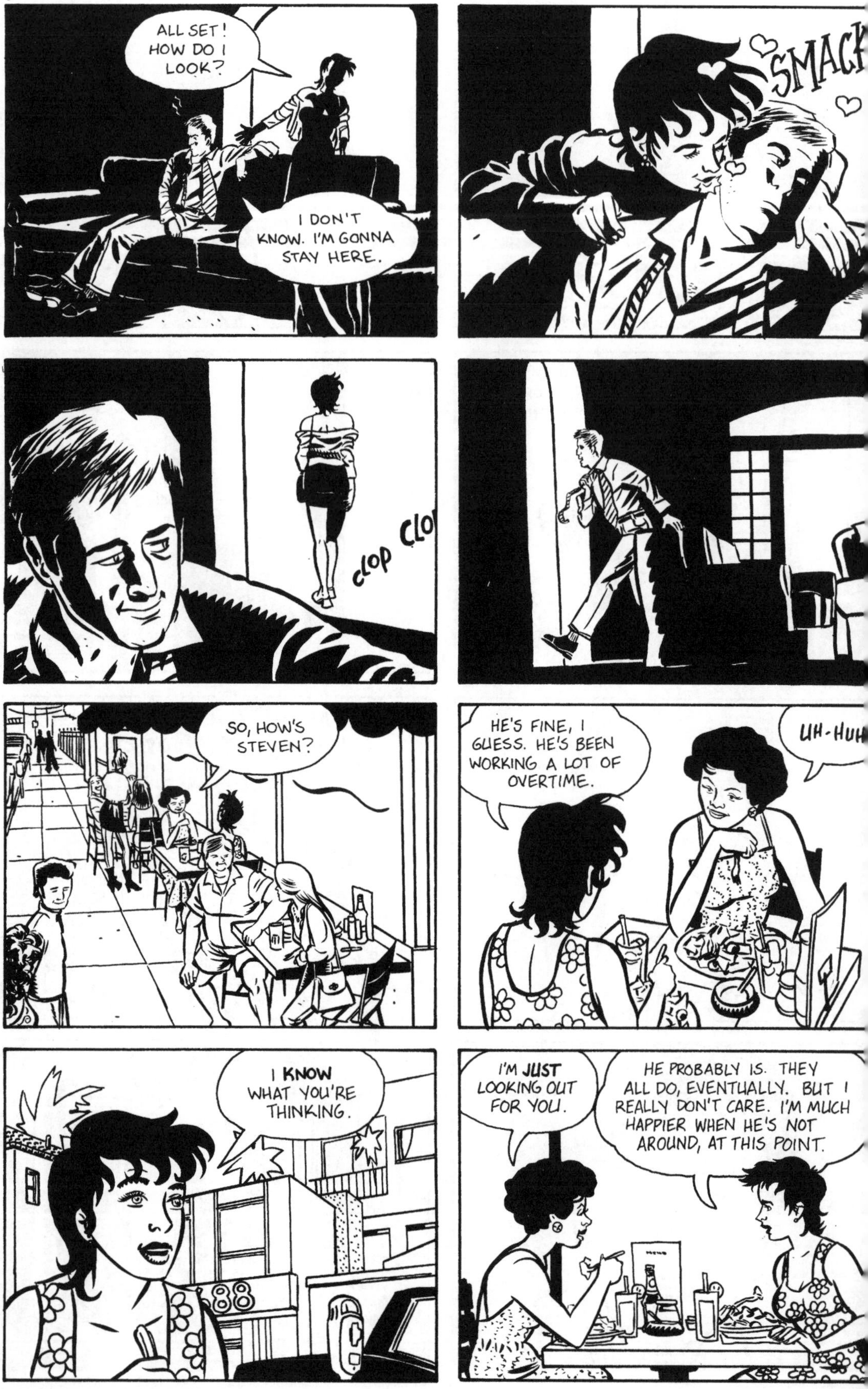
ALL SET! HOW DO I LOOK?
I DON'T KNOW. I'M GONNA STAY HERE.
SMACK
CLOP CLO
SO, HOW'S STEVEN?
HE'S FINE, I GUESS. HE'S BEEN WORKING A LOT OF OVERTIME.
UH-HUH
I KNOW WHAT YOU'RE THINKING.
88
I'M JUST LOOKING OUT FOR YOU.
HE PROBABLY IS. THEY ALL DO, EVENTUALLY. BUT I REALLY DON'T CARE. I'M MUCH HAPPIER WHEN HE'S NOT AROUND, AT THIS POINT.

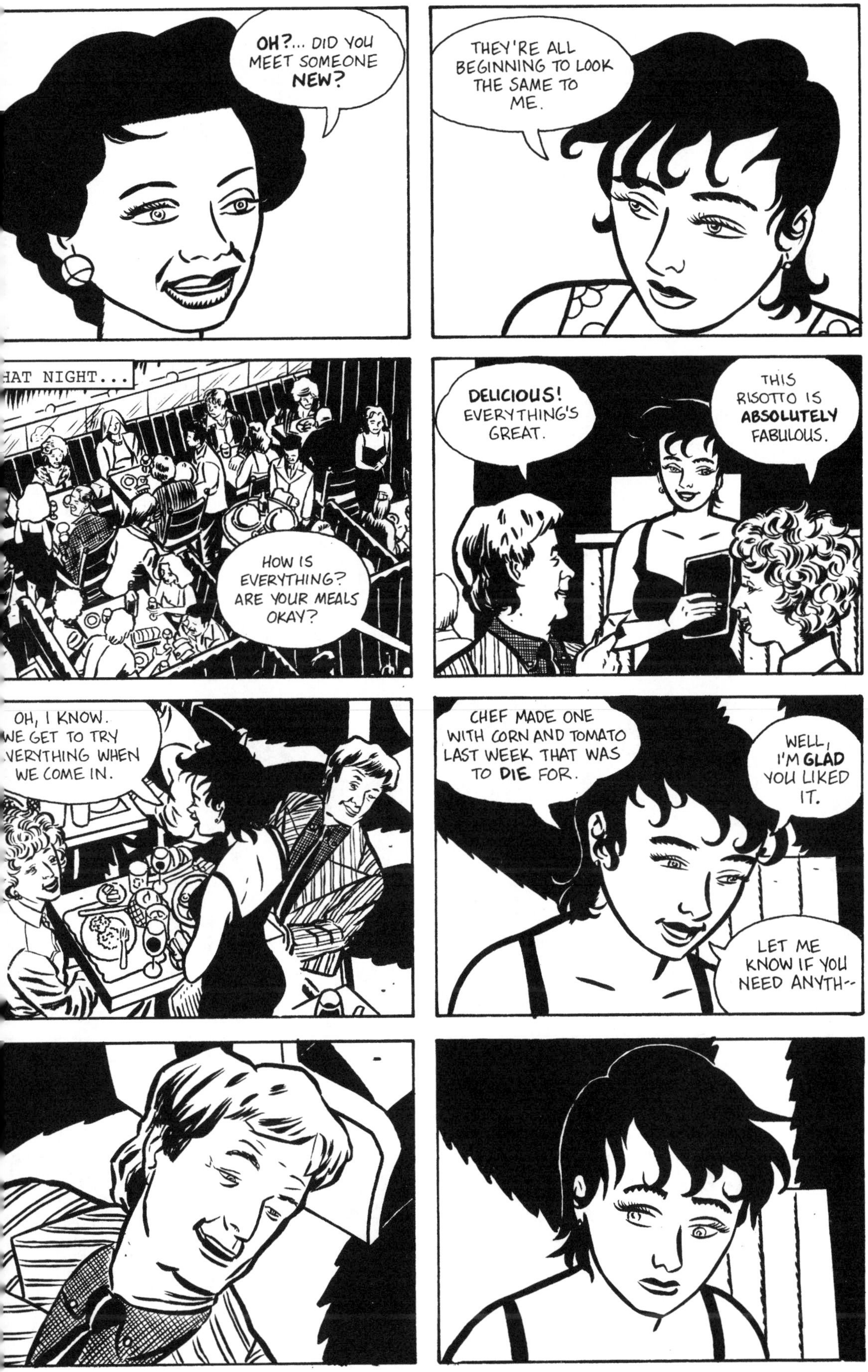

OH?... DID YOU MEET SOMEONE NEW?
THEY'RE ALL BEGINNING TO LOOK THE SAME TO ME.
HAT NIGHT...
HOW IS EVERYTHING? ARE YOUR MEALS OKAY?
DELICIOUS! EVERYTHING'S GREAT.
THIS RISOTTO IS ABSOLUTELY FABULOUS.
OH, I KNOW. WE GET TO TRY EVERYTHING WHEN WE COME IN.
CHEF MADE ONE WITH CORN AND TOMATO LAST WEEK THAT WAS TO DIE FOR.
WELL, I'M GLAD YOU LIKED IT.
LET ME KNOW IF YOU NEED ANYTH--

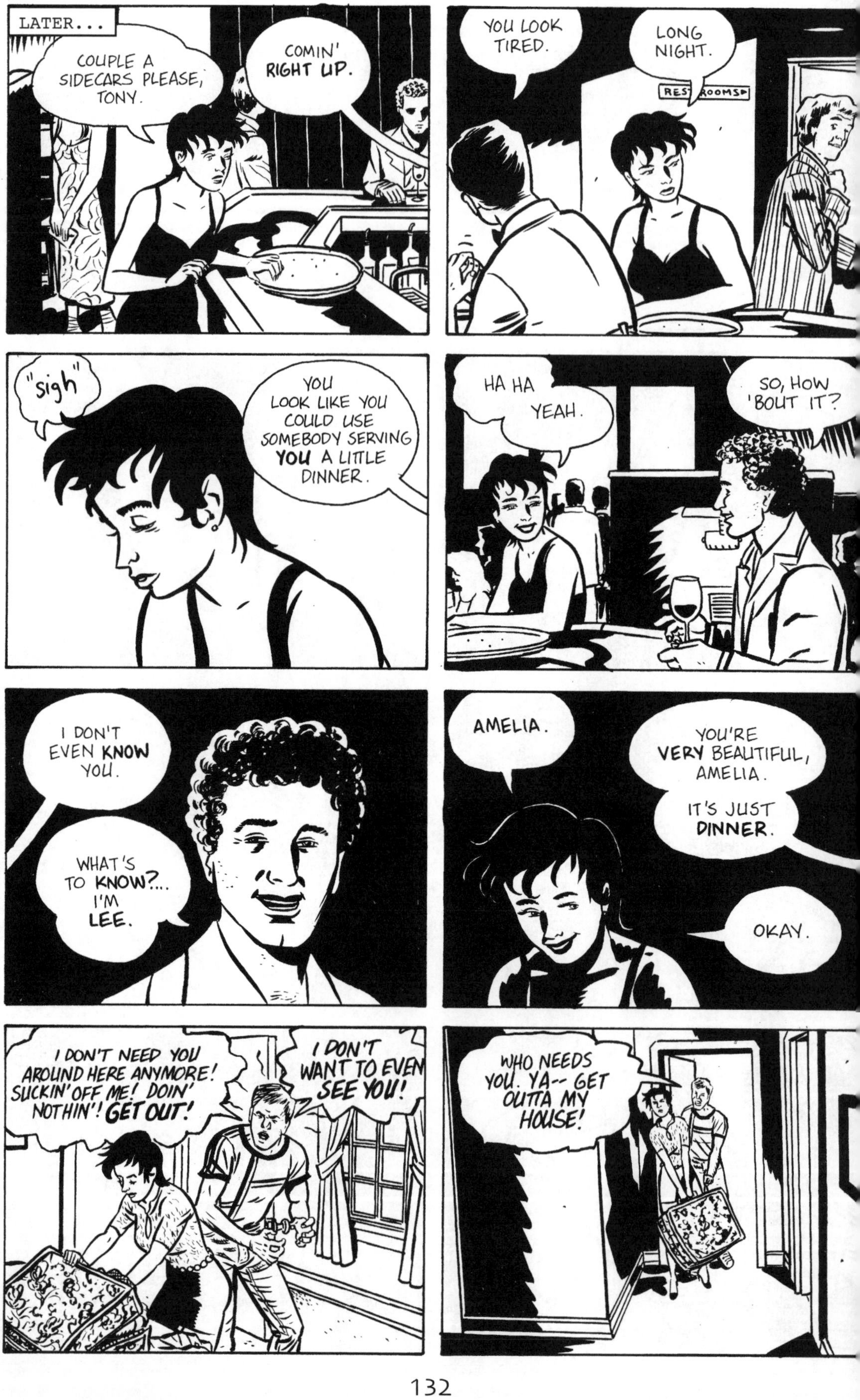
LATER...
COUPLE A SIDECARS PLEASE, TONY.
COMIN' RIGHT UP.
YOU LOOK TIRED.
LONG NIGHT.
RESTROOMS
"sigh"
YOU LOOK LIKE YOU COULD USE SOMEBODY SERVING YOU A LITTLE DINNER.
HA HA YEAH.
SO, HOW 'BOUT IT?
I DON'T EVEN KNOW YOU.
WHAT'S TO KNOW?... I'M LEE.
AMELIA.
YOU'RE VERY BEAUTIFUL, AMELIA.
IT'S JUST DINNER.
OKAY.
I DON'T NEED YOU AROUND HERE ANYMORE! SUCKIN' OFF ME! DOIN' NOTHIN'! GET OUT!
I DON'T WANT TO EVEN SEE YOU!
WHO NEEDS YOU. YA-- GET OUTTA MY HOUSE!

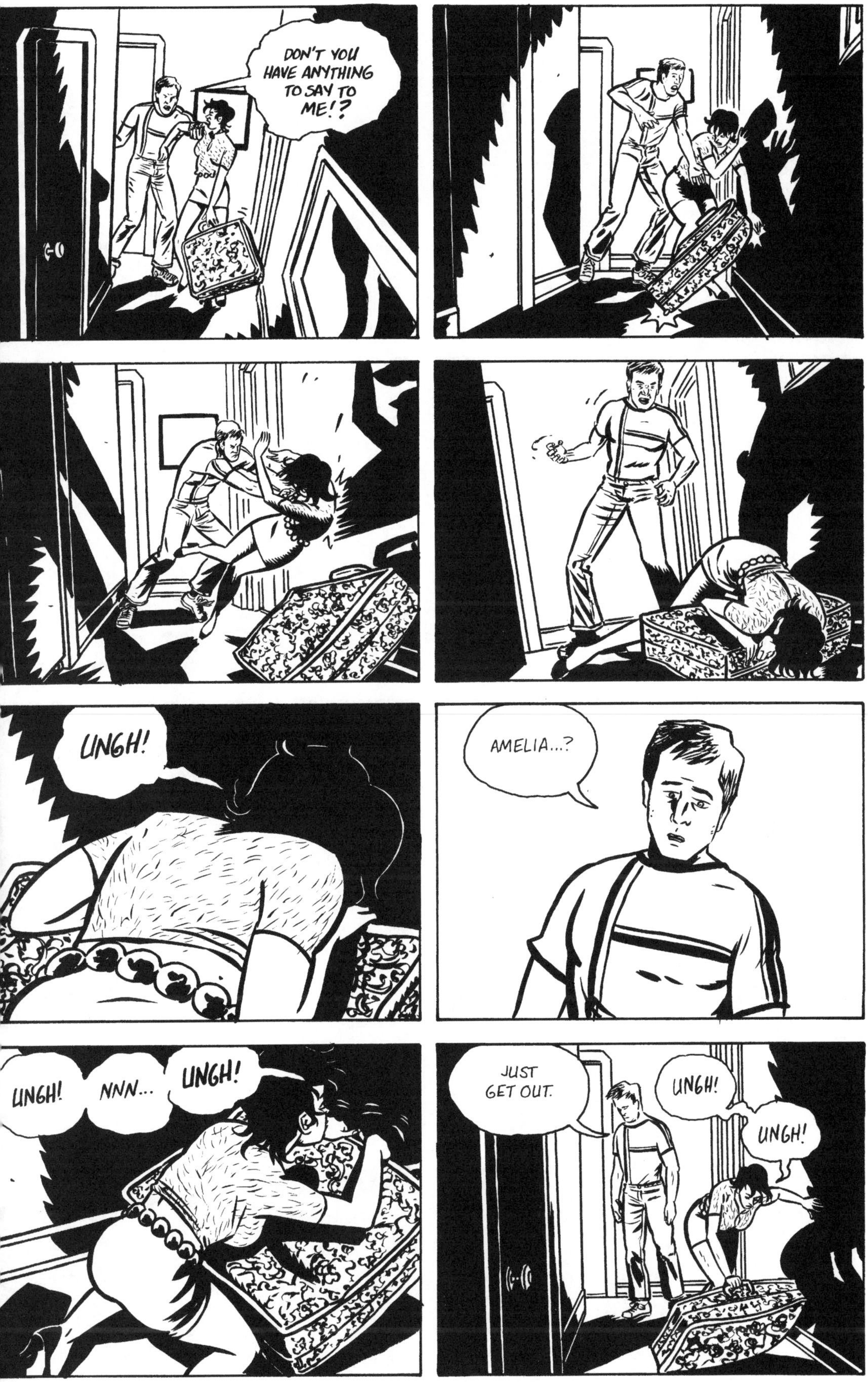
DON'T YOU HAVE ANYTHING TO SAY TO ME!?
UNGH!
AMELIA...?
UNGH!
NNN...
UNGH!
JUST GET OUT.
UNGH!
UNGH!

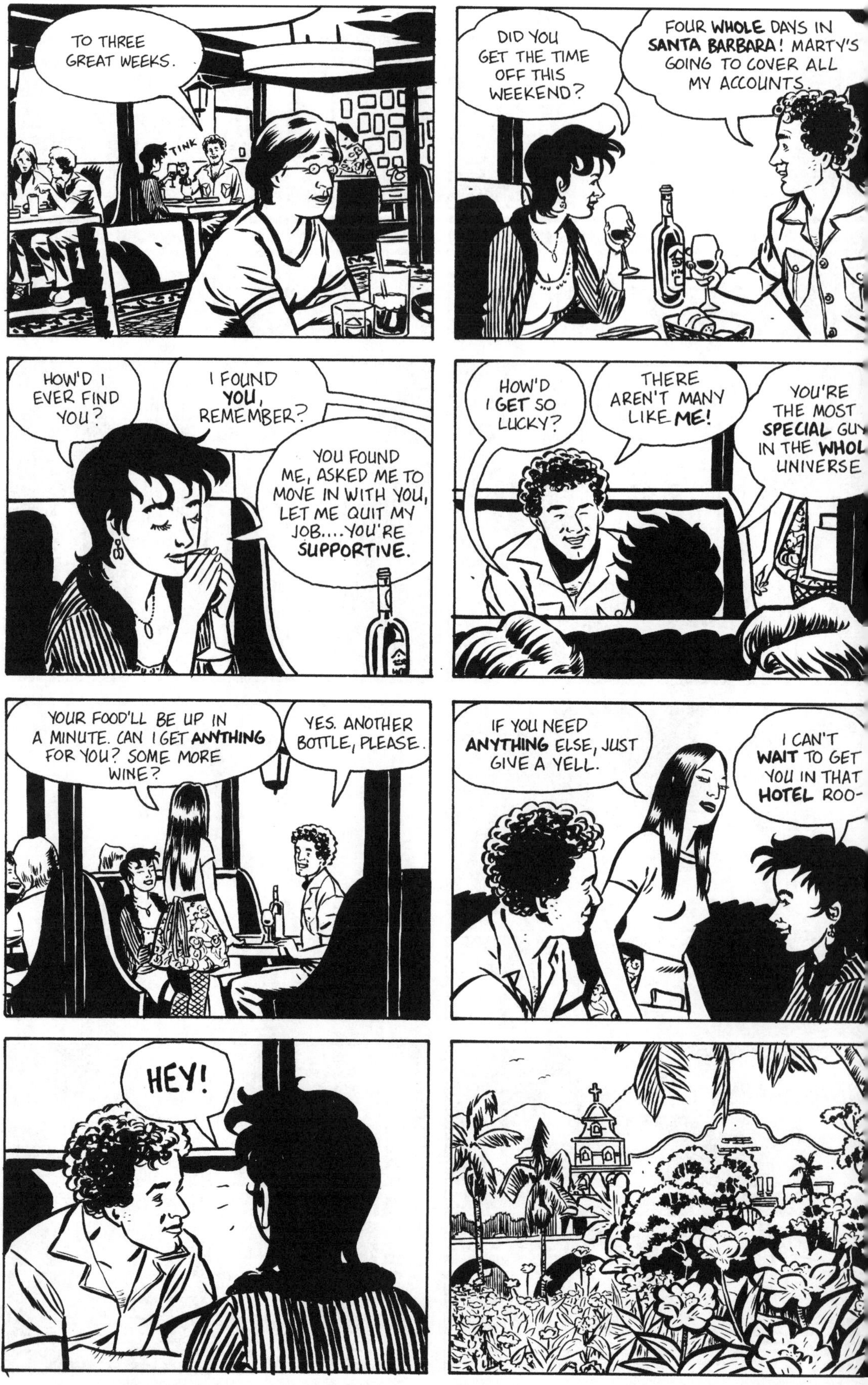

TO THREE GREAT WEEKS.
TINK
DID YOU GET THE TIME OFF THIS WEEKEND?
FOUR WHOLE DAYS IN SANTA BARBARA! MARTY'S GOING TO COVER ALL MY ACCOUNTS.
HOW'D I EVER FIND YOU?
I FOUND YOU, REMEMBER?
YOU FOUND ME, ASKED ME TO MOVE IN WITH YOU, LET ME QUIT MY JOB.... YOU'RE SUPPORTIVE.
HOW'D I GET SO LUCKY?
THERE AREN'T MANY LIKE ME!
YOU'RE THE MOST SPECIAL GU IN THE WHOL UNIVERSE
YOUR FOOD'LL BE UP IN A MINUTE. CAN I GET ANYTHING FOR YOU? SOME MORE WINE?
YES. ANOTHER BOTTLE, PLEASE.
IF YOU NEED ANYTHING ELSE, JUST GIVE A YELL.
I CAN'T WAIT TO GET YOU IN THAT HOTEL ROO-
HEY!

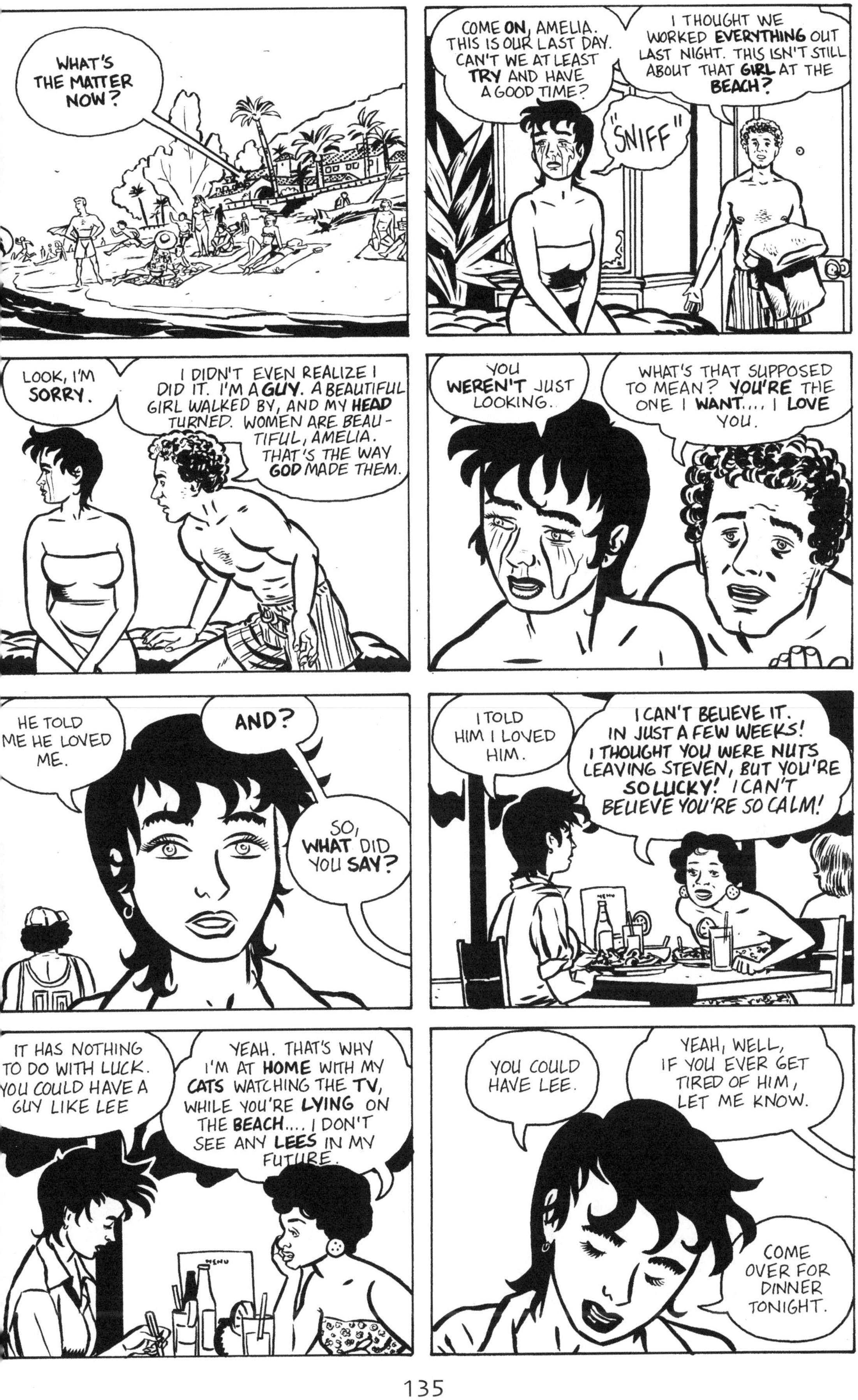
WHAT'S THE MATTER NOW?
COME ON, AMELIA. THIS IS OUR LAST DAY. CAN'T WE AT LEAST TRY AND HAVE A GOOD TIME?
I THOUGHT WE WORKED EVERYTHING OUT LAST NIGHT. THIS ISN'T STILL ABOUT THAT GIRL AT THE BEACH?
"SNIFF"
LOOK, I'M SORRY.
I DIDN'T EVEN REALIZE I DID IT. I'M A GUY. A BEAUTIFUL GIRL WALKED BY, AND MY HEAD TURNED. WOMEN ARE BEAUTIFUL, AMELIA. THAT'S THE WAY GOD MADE THEM.
YOU WEREN'T JUST LOOKING.
WHAT'S THAT SUPPOSED TO MEAN? YOU'RE THE ONE I WANT.... I LOVE YOU.
HE TOLD ME HE LOVED ME.
AND?
SO, WHAT DID YOU SAY?
I TOLD HIM I LOVED HIM.
I CAN'T BELIEVE IT. IN JUST A FEW WEEKS! I THOUGHT YOU WERE NUTS LEAVING STEVEN, BUT YOU'RE SO LUCKY! I CAN'T BELIEVE YOU'RE SO CALM!
MENU
IT HAS NOTHING TO DO WITH LUCK. YOU COULD HAVE A GUY LIKE LEE
YEAH. THAT'S WHY I'M AT HOME WITH MY CATS WATCHING THE TV, WHILE YOU'RE LYING ON THE BEACH.... I DON'T SEE ANY LEES IN MY FUTURE.
MENU
YOU COULD HAVE LEE.
YEAH, WELL, IF YOU EVER GET TIRED OF HIM, LET ME KNOW.
COME OVER FOR DINNER TONIGHT.

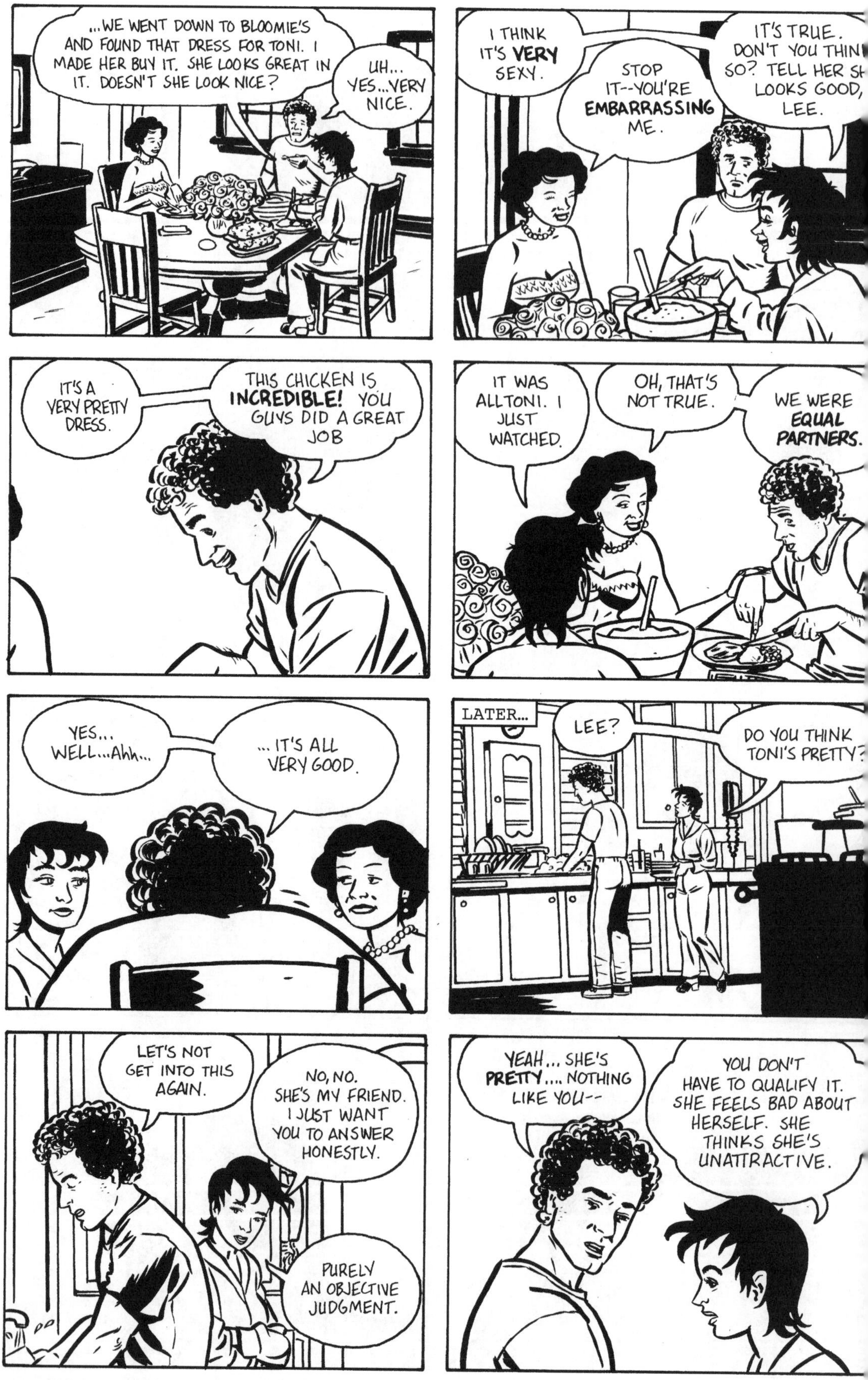
...WE WENT DOWN TO BLOOMIE'S AND FOUND THAT DRESS FOR TONI. I MADE HER BUY IT. SHE LOOKS GREAT IN IT. DOESN'T SHE LOOK NICE?
UH... YES...VERY NICE.
I THINK IT'S VERY SEXY.
STOP IT--YOU'RE EMBARRASSING ME.
IT'S TRUE. DON'T YOU THIN SO? TELL HER SH LOOKS GOOD, LEE.
IT'S A VERY PRETTY DRESS.
THIS CHICKEN IS INCREDIBLE! YOU GUYS DID A GREAT JOB
IT WAS ALLTONI. I JUST WATCHED.
OH, THAT'S NOT TRUE.
WE WERE EQUAL PARTNERS.
YES... WELL...Ahh...
...IT'S ALL VERY GOOD.
LATER...
LEE?
DO YOU THINK TONI'S PRETTY?
LET'S NOT GET INTO THIS AGAIN.
NO, NO. SHE'S MY FRIEND. I JUST WANT YOU TO ANSWER HONESTLY.
PURELY AN OBJECTIVE JUDGMENT.
YEAH... SHE'S PRETTY.... NOTHING LIKE YOU--
YOU DON'T HAVE TO QUALIFY IT. SHE FEELS BAD ABOUT HERSELF. SHE THINKS SHE'S UNATTRACTIVE.

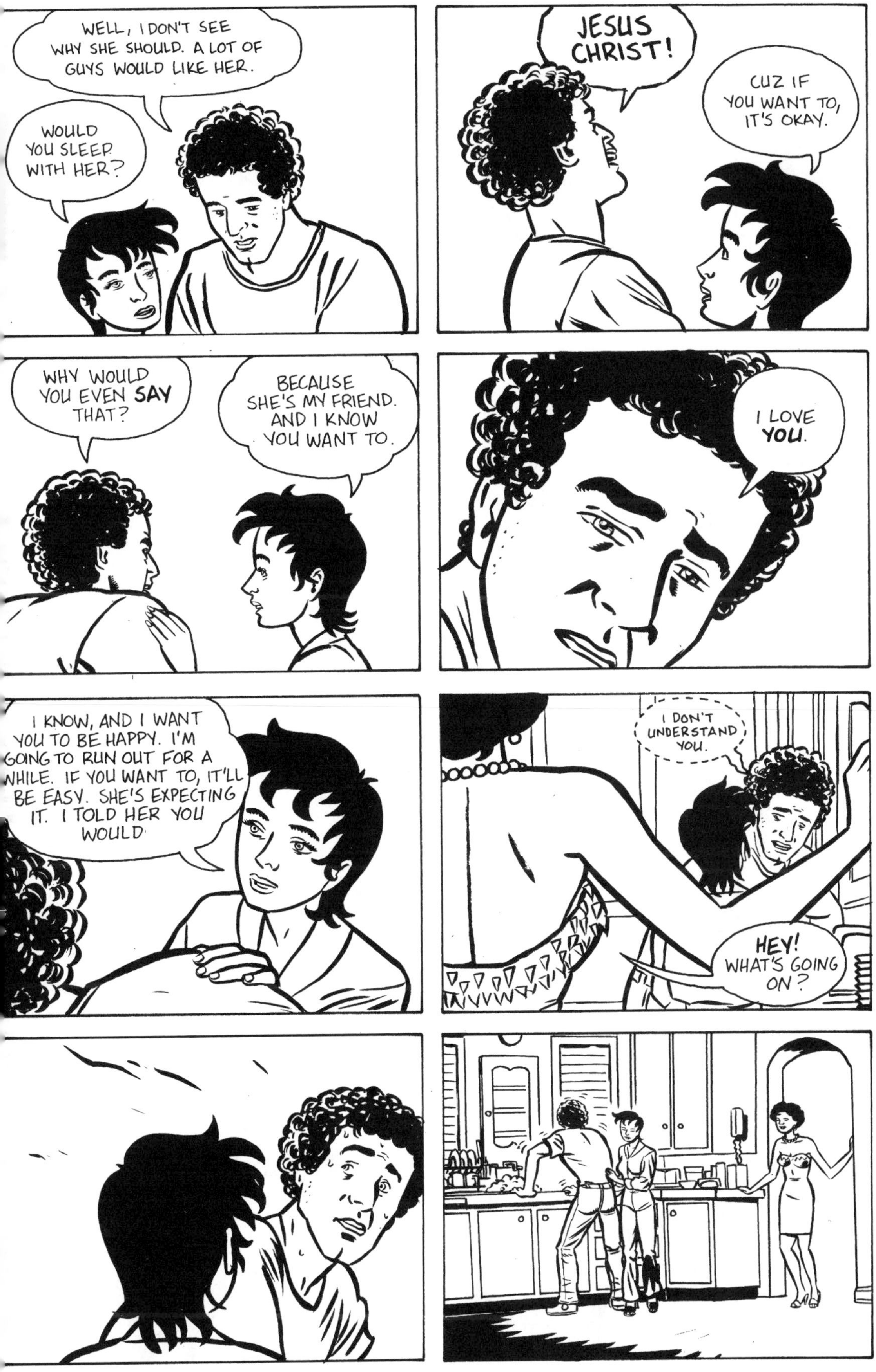

WELL, I DON'T SEE WHY SHE SHOULD. A LOT OF GUYS WOULD LIKE HER.
WOULD YOU SLEEP WITH HER?
JESUS CHRIST!
CUZ IF YOU WANT TO, IT'S OKAY.
WHY WOULD YOU EVEN SAY THAT?
BECAUSE SHE'S MY FRIEND. AND I KNOW YOU WANT TO.
I LOVE YOU.
I KNOW, AND I WANT YOU TO BE HAPPY. I'M GOING TO RUN OUT FOR A WHILE. IF YOU WANT TO, IT'LL BE EASY. SHE'S EXPECTING IT. I TOLD HER YOU WOULD.
I DON'T UNDERSTAND YOU.
HEY! WHAT'S GOING ON?

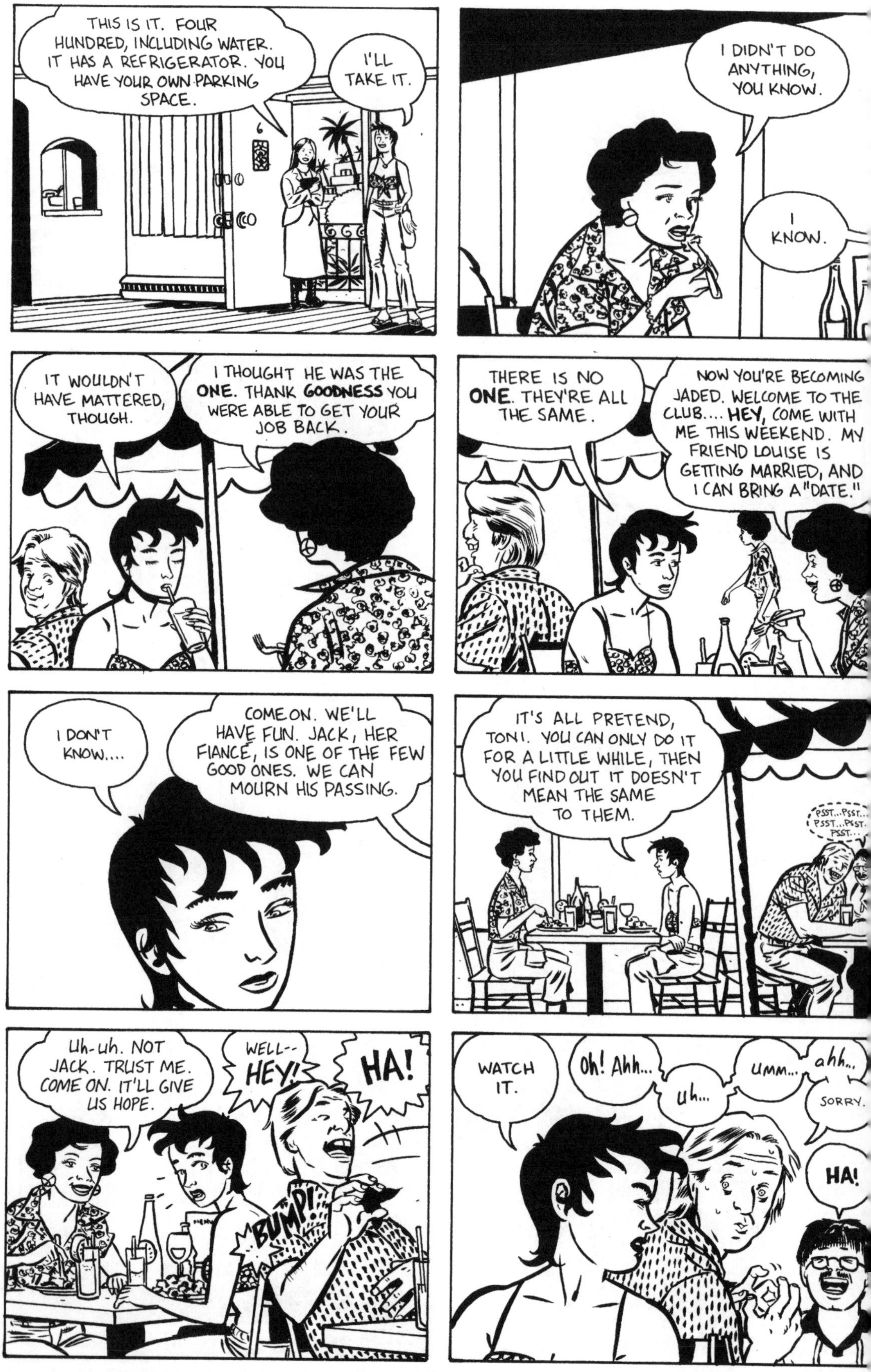
THIS IS IT. FOUR HUNDRED, INCLUDING WATER. IT HAS A REFRIGERATOR. YOU HAVE YOUR OWN PARKING SPACE.
I'LL TAKE IT.
I DIDN'T DO ANYTHING, YOU KNOW.
I KNOW.
IT WOULDN'T HAVE MATTERED, THOUGH.
I THOUGHT HE WAS THE ONE. THANK GOODNESS YOU WERE ABLE TO GET YOUR JOB BACK.
THERE IS NO ONE. THEY'RE ALL THE SAME.
NOW YOU'RE BECOMING JADED. WELCOME TO THE CLUB.... HEY, COME WITH ME THIS WEEKEND. MY FRIEND LOUISE IS GETTING MARRIED, AND I CAN BRING A "DATE."
I DON'T KNOW....
COME ON. WE'LL HAVE FUN. JACK, HER FIANCÉ, IS ONE OF THE FEW GOOD ONES. WE CAN MOURN HIS PASSING.
IT'S ALL PRETEND, TONI. YOU CAN ONLY DO IT FOR A LITTLE WHILE, THEN YOU FIND OUT IT DOESN'T MEAN THE SAME TO THEM.
PSST...PSST... PSST...PSST. PSST...
Uh-uh. NOT JACK. TRUST ME. COME ON. IT'LL GIVE US HOPE.
WELL-- HEY!
HA!
BUMP!
WATCH IT.
Oh! Ahh...
uh...
umm...
ahh...
SORRY.
HA!

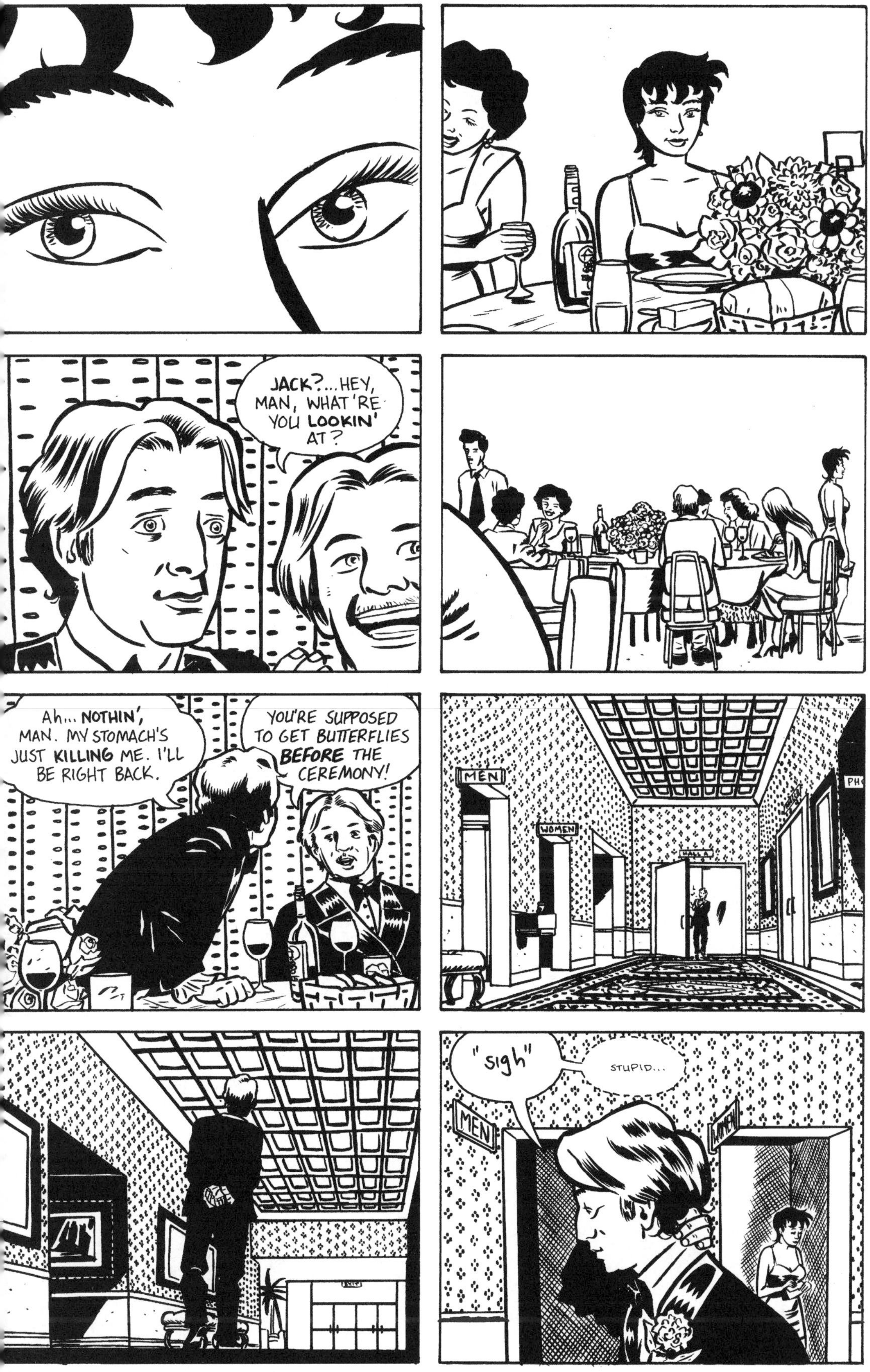
JACK?... HEY, MAN, WHAT'RE YOU LOOKIN' AT?
Ah... NOTHIN', MAN. MY STOMACH'S JUST KILLING ME. I'LL BE RIGHT BACK.
YOU'RE SUPPOSED TO GET BUTTERFLIES BEFORE THE CEREMONY!
MEN
WOMEN
"sigh"
STUPID...
MEN
WOMEN

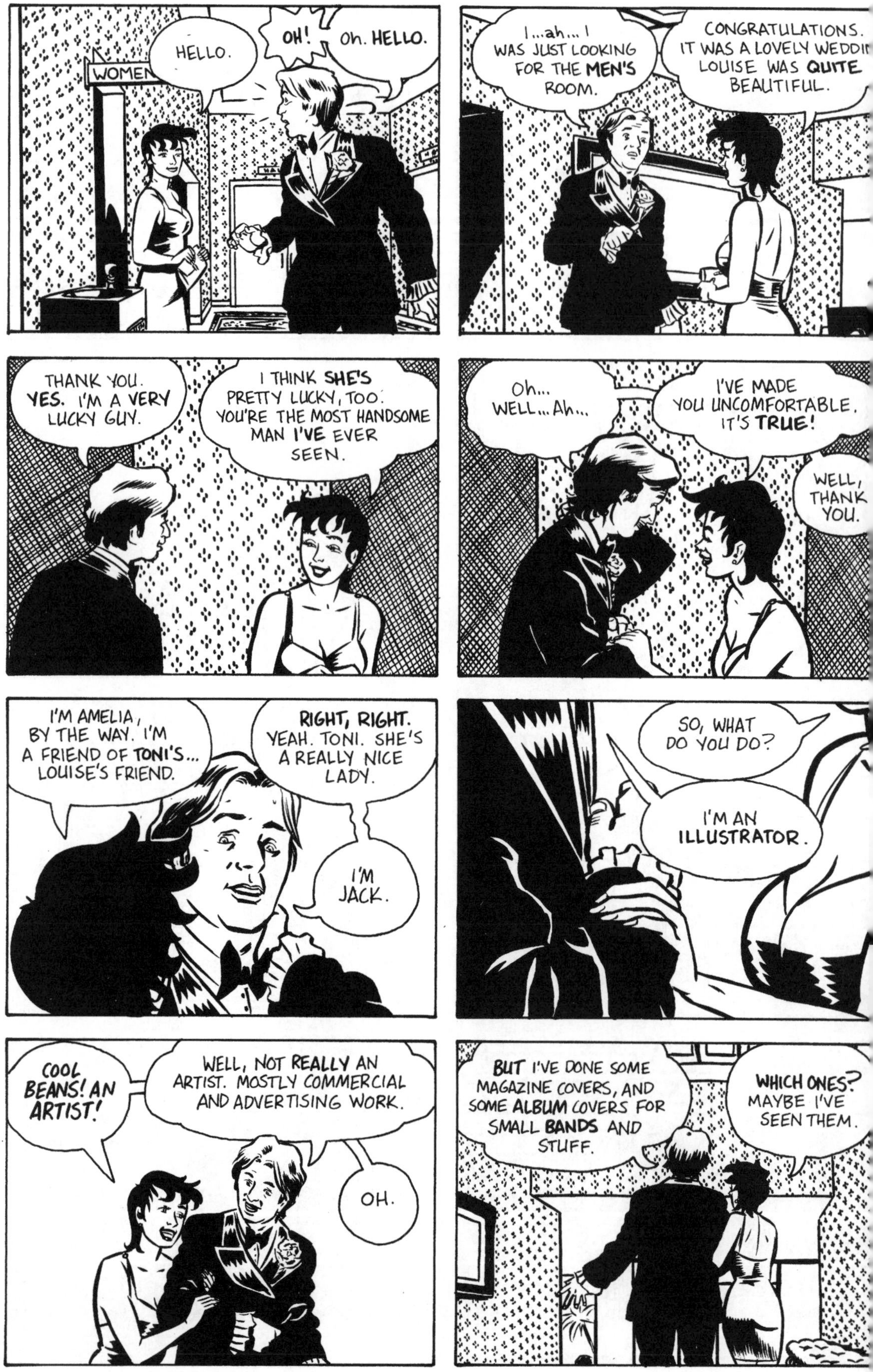
HELLO.
OH!
Oh. HELLO.
WOMEN
I...ah... I WAS JUST LOOKING FOR THE MEN'S ROOM.
CONGRATULATIONS. IT WAS A LOVELY WEDDI LOUISE WAS QUITE BEAUTIFUL.
THANK YOU. YES. I'M A VERY LUCKY GUY.
I THINK SHE'S PRETTY LUCKY, TOO. YOU'RE THE MOST HANDSOME MAN I'VE EVER SEEN.
Oh... WELL... Ah...
I'VE MADE YOU UNCOMFORTABLE. IT'S TRUE!
WELL, THANK YOU.
I'M AMELIA, BY THE WAY. I'M A FRIEND OF TONI'S... LOUISE'S FRIEND.
RIGHT, RIGHT. YEAH. TONI. SHE'S A REALLY NICE LADY.
I'M JACK.
SO, WHAT DO YOU DO?
I'M AN ILLUSTRATOR.
COOL BEANS! AN ARTIST!
WELL, NOT REALLY AN ARTIST. MOSTLY COMMERCIAL AND ADVERTISING WORK.
OH.
BUT I'VE DONE SOME MAGAZINE COVERS, AND SOME ALBUM COVERS FOR SMALL BANDS AND STUFF.
WHICH ONES? MAYBE I'VE SEEN THEM.

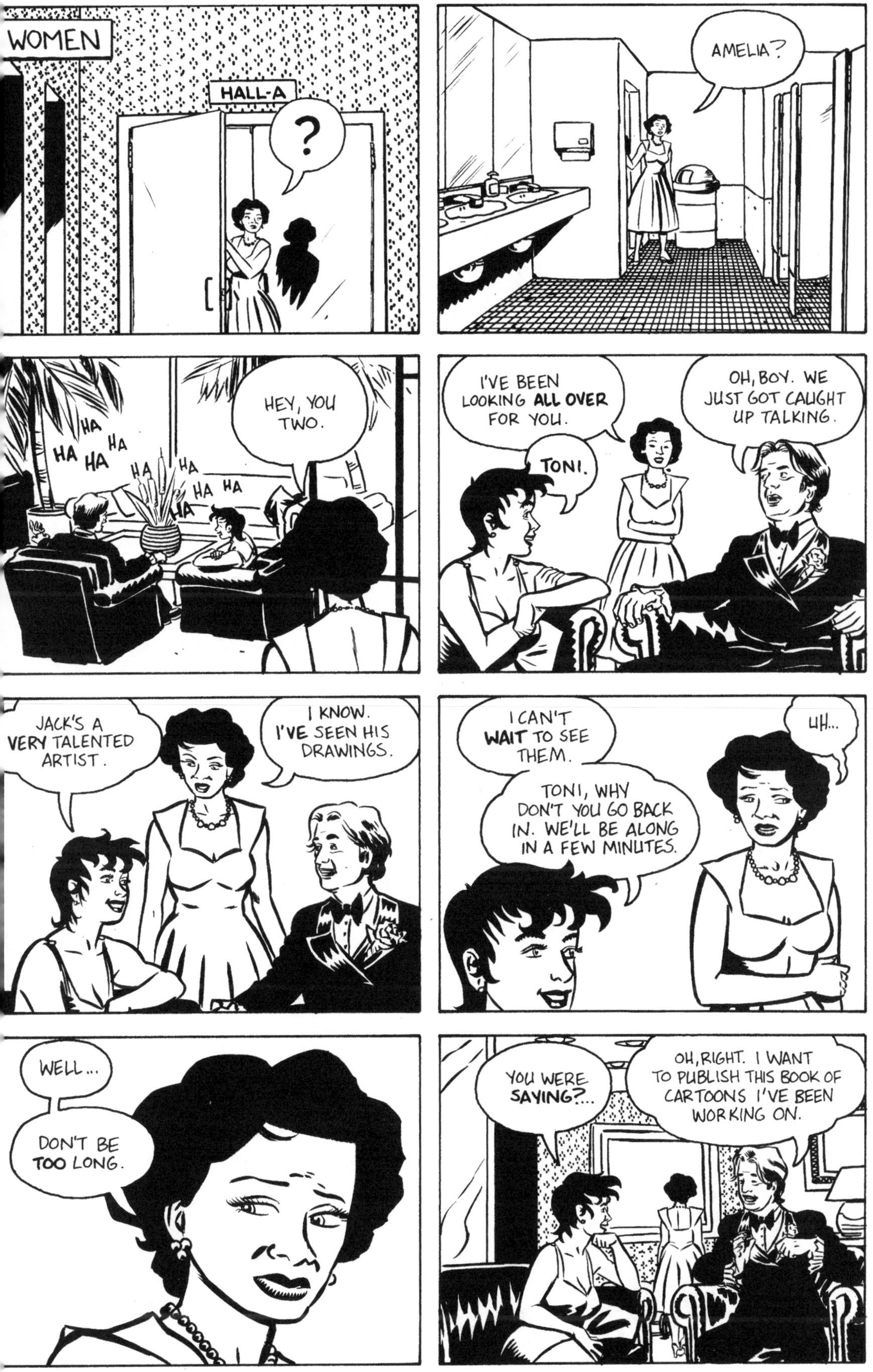
WOMEN
HALL-A
?
AMELIA?
HA HA HA HA HA HA HA HA HA HA
HEY, YOU TWO.
I'VE BEEN LOOKING **ALL OVER** FOR YOU.
TONI.
OH, BOY. WE JUST GOT CAUGHT UP TALKING.
JACK'S A **VERY** TALENTED ARTIST.
I KNOW. **I'VE** SEEN HIS DRAWINGS.
I CAN'T **WAIT** TO SEE THEM.
TONI, WHY DON'T YOU GO BACK IN. WE'LL BE ALONG IN A FEW MINUTES.
UH...
WELL...
DON'T BE **TOO** LONG.
YOU WERE **SAYING?**...
OH, RIGHT. I WANT TO PUBLISH THIS BOOK OF CARTOONS I'VE BEEN WORKING ON.

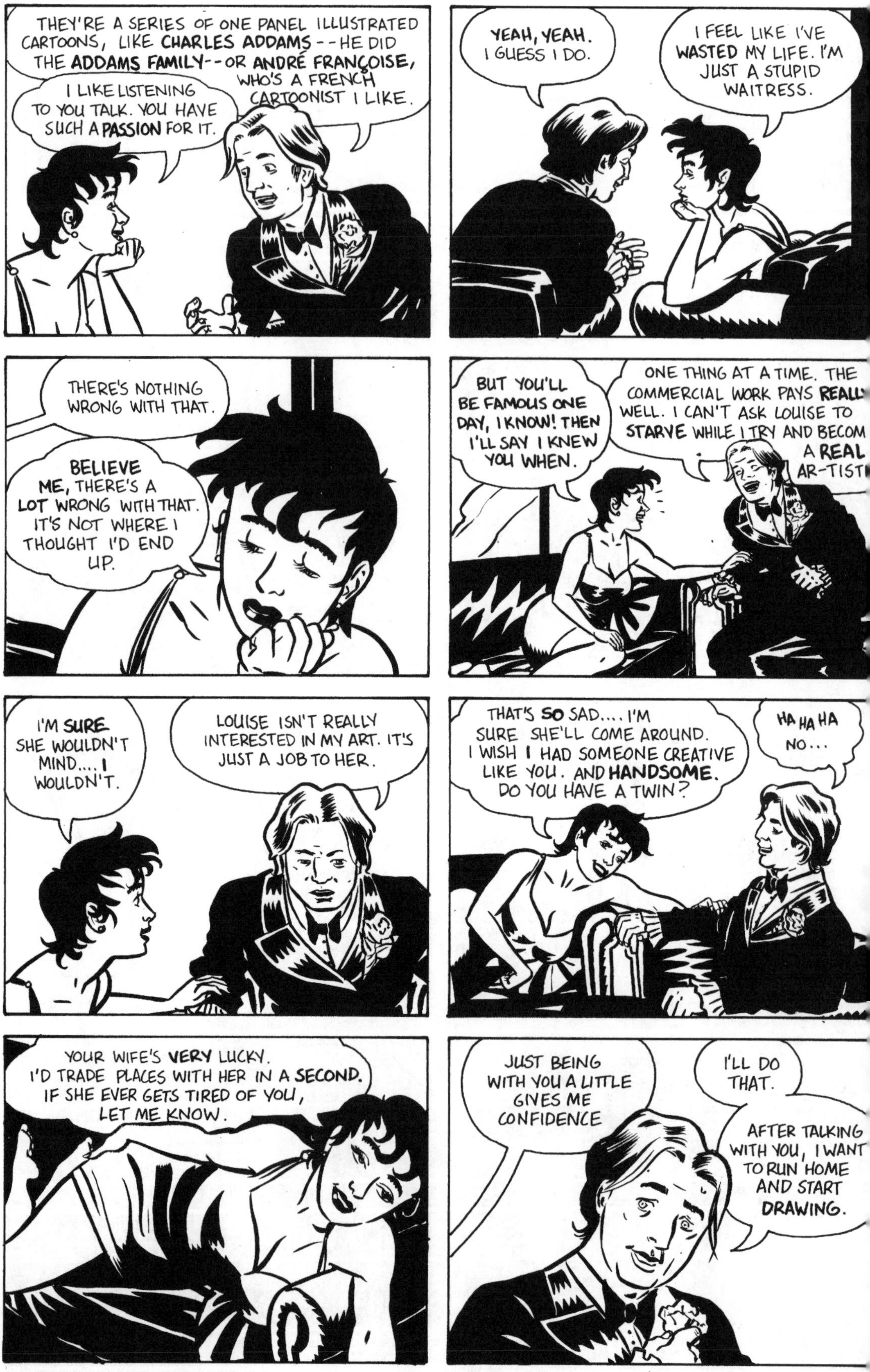
THEY'RE A SERIES OF ONE PANEL ILLUSTRATED CARTOONS, LIKE CHARLES ADDAMS --HE DID THE ADDAMS FAMILY--OR ANDRÉ FRANÇOISE, WHO'S A FRENCH CARTOONIST I LIKE.
I LIKE LISTENING TO YOU TALK. YOU HAVE SUCH A PASSION FOR IT.
YEAH, YEAH. I GUESS I DO.
I FEEL LIKE I'VE WASTED MY LIFE. I'M JUST A STUPID WAITRESS.
THERE'S NOTHING WRONG WITH THAT.
BELIEVE ME, THERE'S A LOT WRONG WITH THAT. IT'S NOT WHERE I THOUGHT I'D END UP.
BUT YOU'LL BE FAMOUS ONE DAY, I KNOW! THEN I'LL SAY I KNEW YOU WHEN.
ONE THING AT A TIME. THE COMMERCIAL WORK PAYS REALL WELL. I CAN'T ASK LOUISE TO STARVE WHILE I TRY AND BECOM A REAL AR-TIST
I'M SURE SHE WOULDN'T MIND.... I WOULDN'T.
LOUISE ISN'T REALLY INTERESTED IN MY ART. IT'S JUST A JOB TO HER.
THAT'S SO SAD.... I'M SURE SHE'LL COME AROUND. I WISH I HAD SOMEONE CREATIVE LIKE YOU. AND HANDSOME. DO YOU HAVE A TWIN?
HA HA HA NO...
YOUR WIFE'S VERY LUCKY. I'D TRADE PLACES WITH HER IN A SECOND. IF SHE EVER GETS TIRED OF YOU, LET ME KNOW.
JUST BEING WITH YOU A LITTLE GIVES ME CONFIDENCE
I'LL DO THAT.
AFTER TALKING WITH YOU, I WANT TO RUN HOME AND START DRAWING.

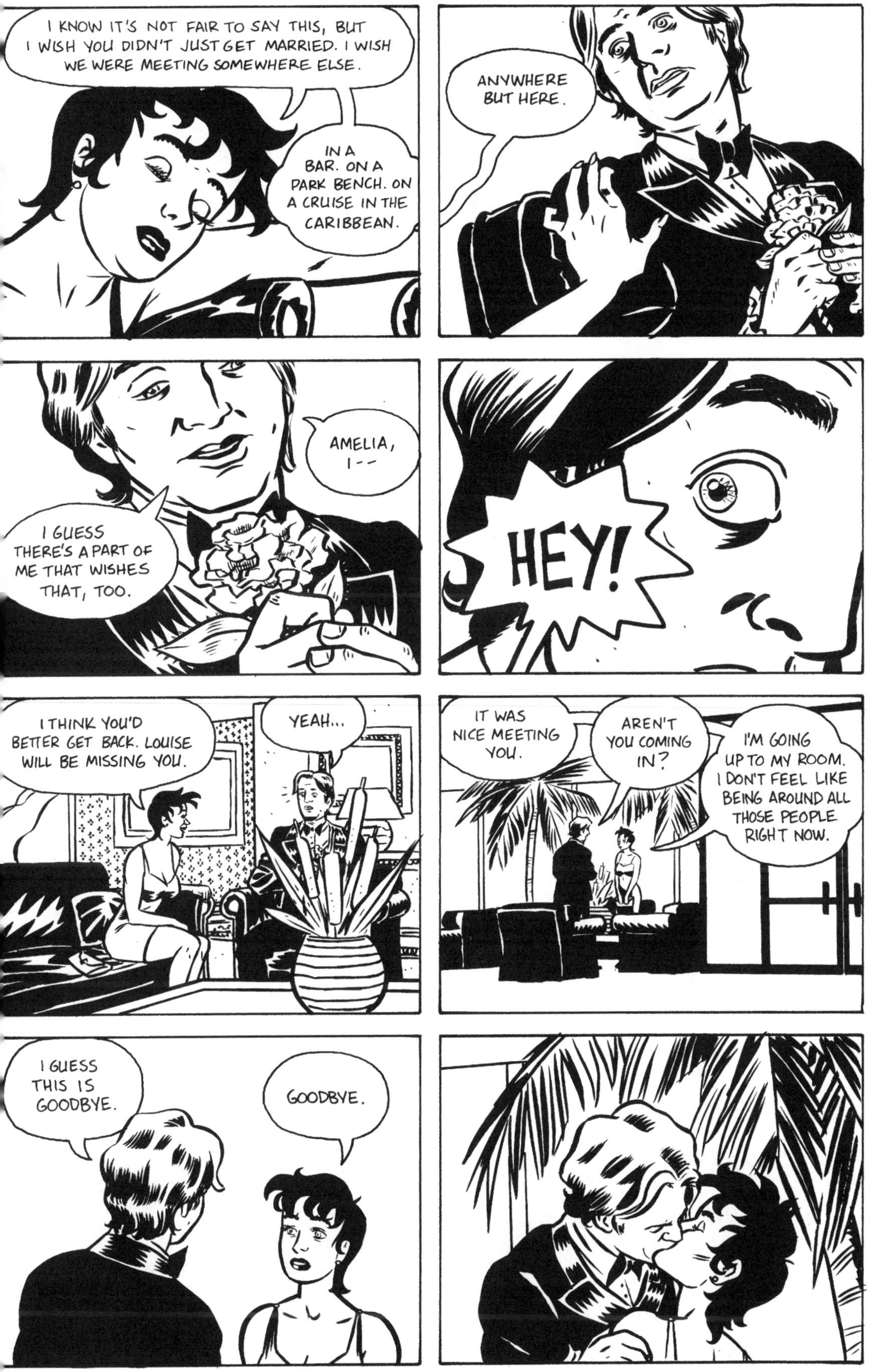
I KNOW IT'S NOT FAIR TO SAY THIS, BUT I WISH YOU DIDN'T JUST GET MARRIED. I WISH WE WERE MEETING SOMEWHERE ELSE.
IN A BAR. ON A PARK BENCH. ON A CRUISE IN THE CARIBBEAN.
ANYWHERE BUT HERE.
AMELIA, I--
I GUESS THERE'S A PART OF ME THAT WISHES THAT, TOO.
HEY!
I THINK YOU'D BETTER GET BACK. LOUISE WILL BE MISSING YOU.
YEAH...
IT WAS NICE MEETING YOU.
AREN'T YOU COMING IN?
I'M GOING UP TO MY ROOM. I DON'T FEEL LIKE BEING AROUND ALL THOSE PEOPLE RIGHT NOW.
I GUESS THIS IS GOODBYE.
GOODBYE.

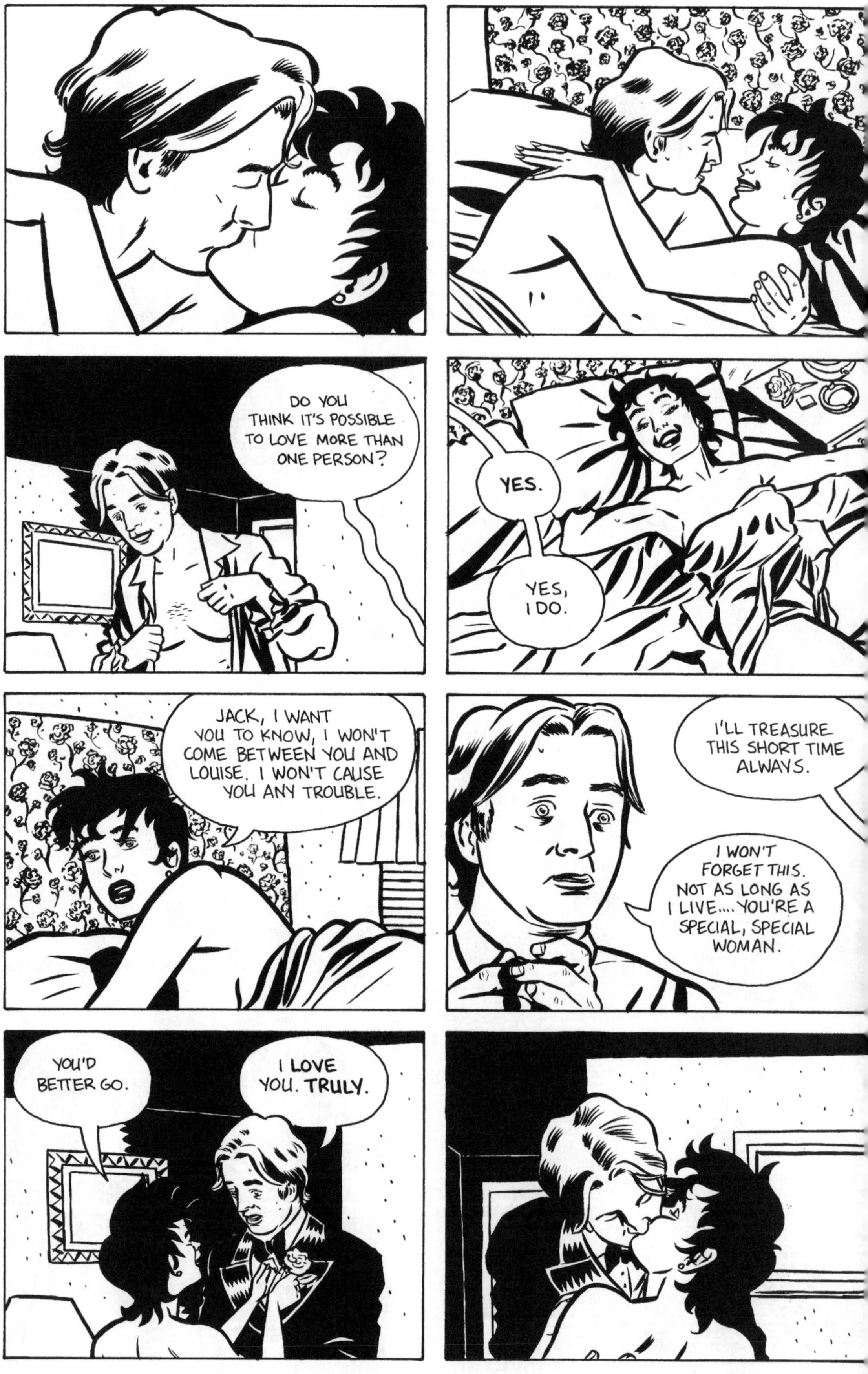
DO YOU THINK IT'S POSSIBLE TO LOVE MORE THAN ONE PERSON?
YES.
YES, I DO.
JACK, I WANT YOU TO KNOW, I WON'T COME BETWEEN YOU AND LOUISE. I WON'T CAUSE YOU ANY TROUBLE.
I'LL TREASURE THIS SHORT TIME ALWAYS.
I WON'T FORGET THIS. NOT AS LONG AS I LIVE.... YOU'RE A SPECIAL, SPECIAL WOMAN.
YOU'D BETTER GO.
I LOVE YOU. TRULY.

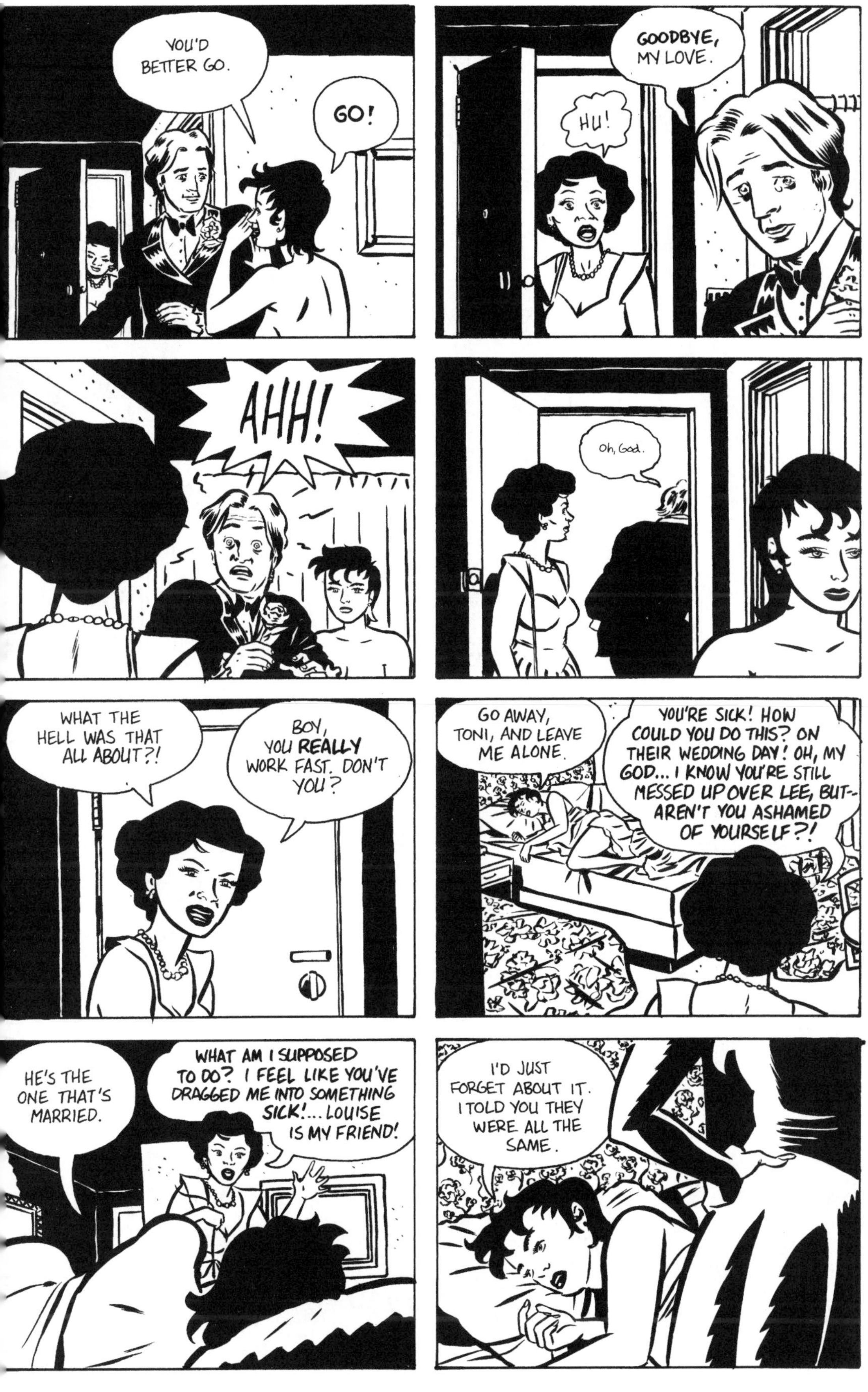

YOU'D BETTER GO.
GO!
GOODBYE, MY LOVE.
HU!
AHH!
Oh, God.
WHAT THE HELL WAS THAT ALL ABOUT?!
BOY, YOU **REALLY** WORK FAST. DON'T YOU?
GO AWAY, TONI, AND LEAVE ME ALONE.
YOU'RE SICK! HOW COULD YOU DO THIS? ON THEIR WEDDING DAY! OH, MY GOD... I KNOW YOU'RE STILL MESSED UP OVER LEE, BUT-- AREN'T YOU ASHAMED OF YOURSELF?!
HE'S THE ONE THAT'S MARRIED.
WHAT AM I SUPPOSED TO DO? I FEEL LIKE YOU'VE DRAGGED ME INTO SOMETHING SICK!... LOUISE IS MY FRIEND!
I'D JUST FORGET ABOUT IT. I TOLD YOU THEY WERE ALL THE SAME.

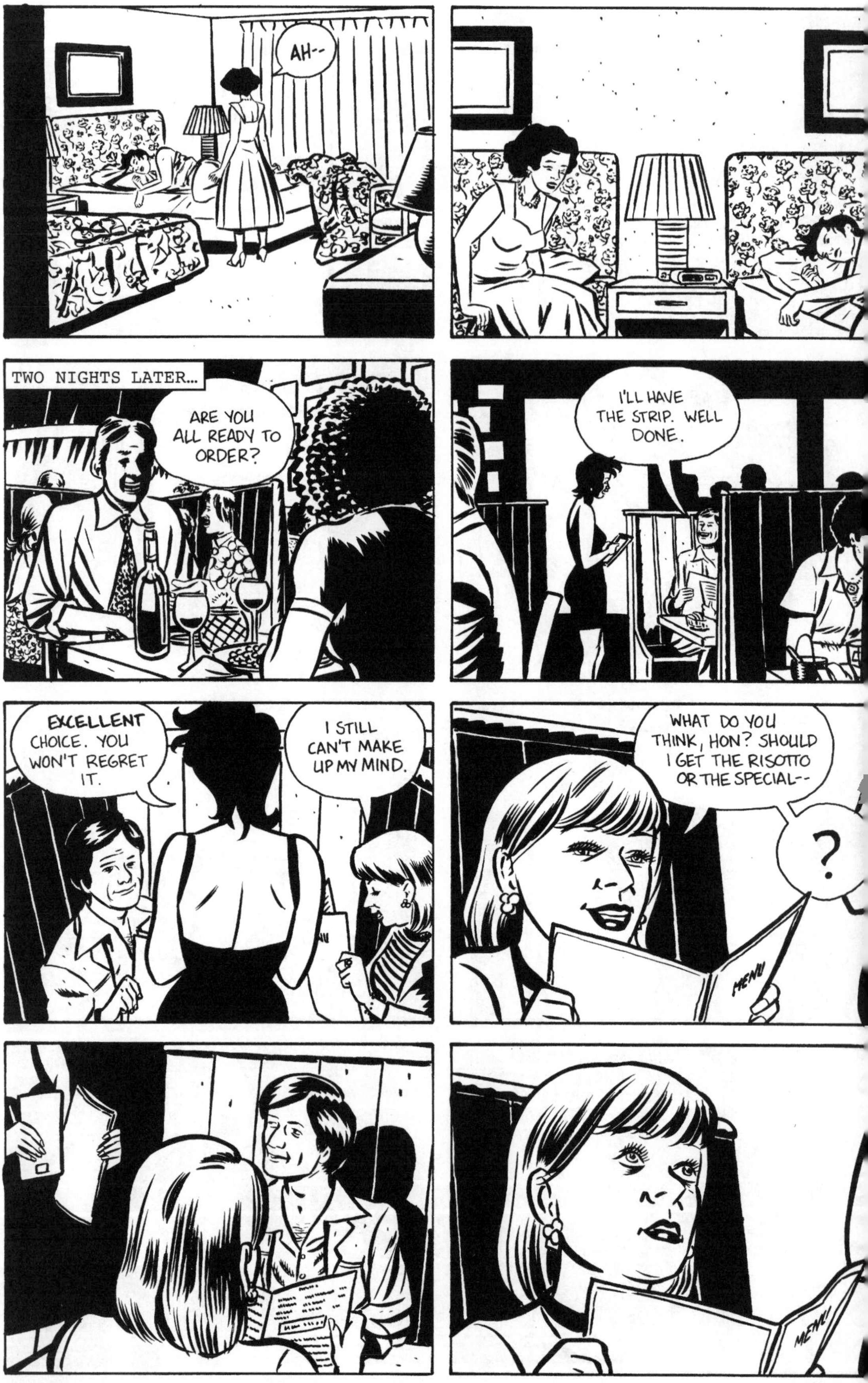
AH--
TWO NIGHTS LATER...
ARE YOU ALL READY TO ORDER?
I'LL HAVE THE STRIP. WELL DONE.
EXCELLENT CHOICE. YOU WON'T REGRET IT.
I STILL CAN'T MAKE UP MY MIND.
WHAT DO YOU THINK, HON? SHOULD I GET THE RISOTTO OR THE SPECIAL--
?
MENU
MENU

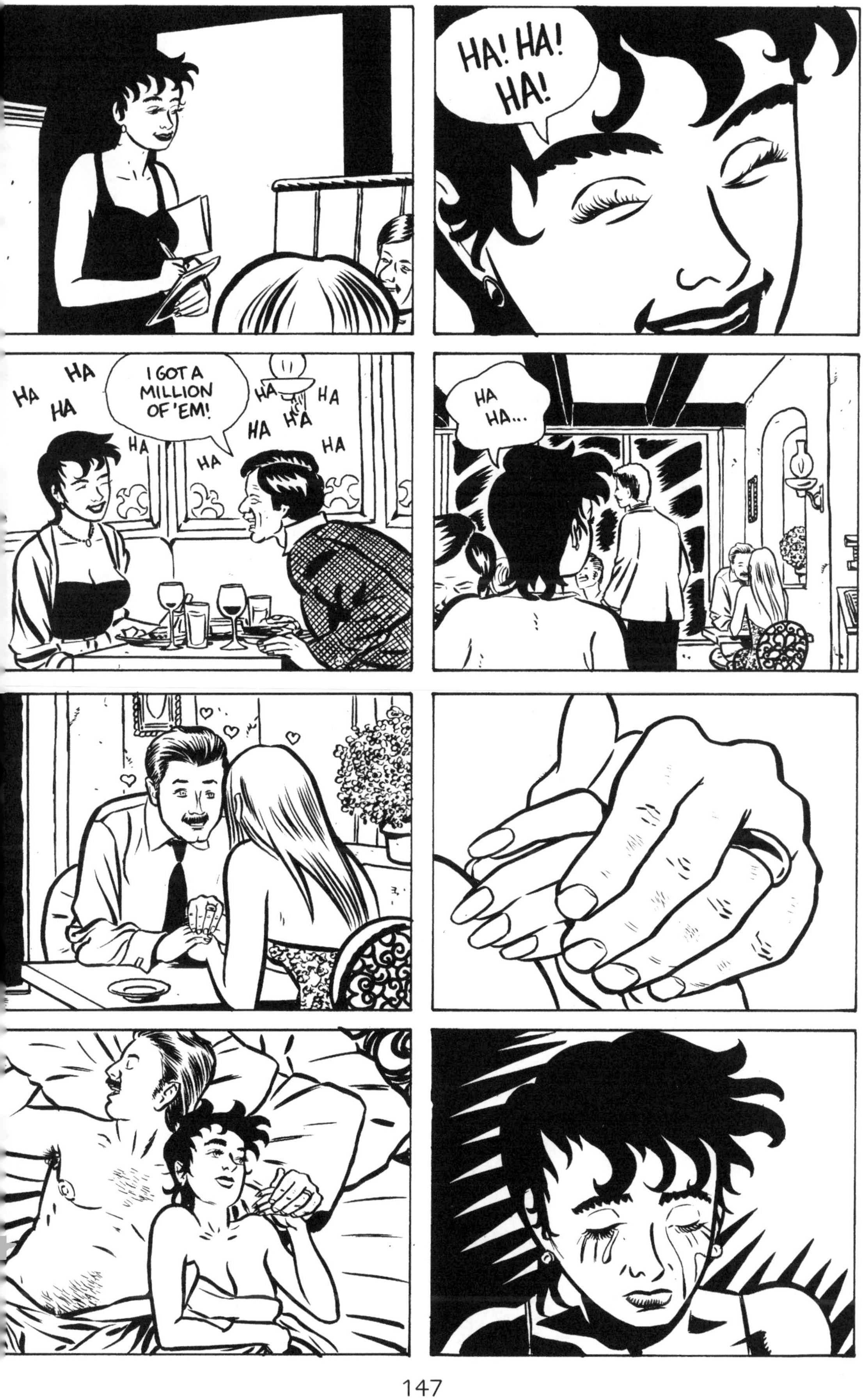
HA! HA! HA!
HA HA HA
I GOT A MILLION OF 'EM!
HA HA HA HA HA HA HA HA
HA HA...

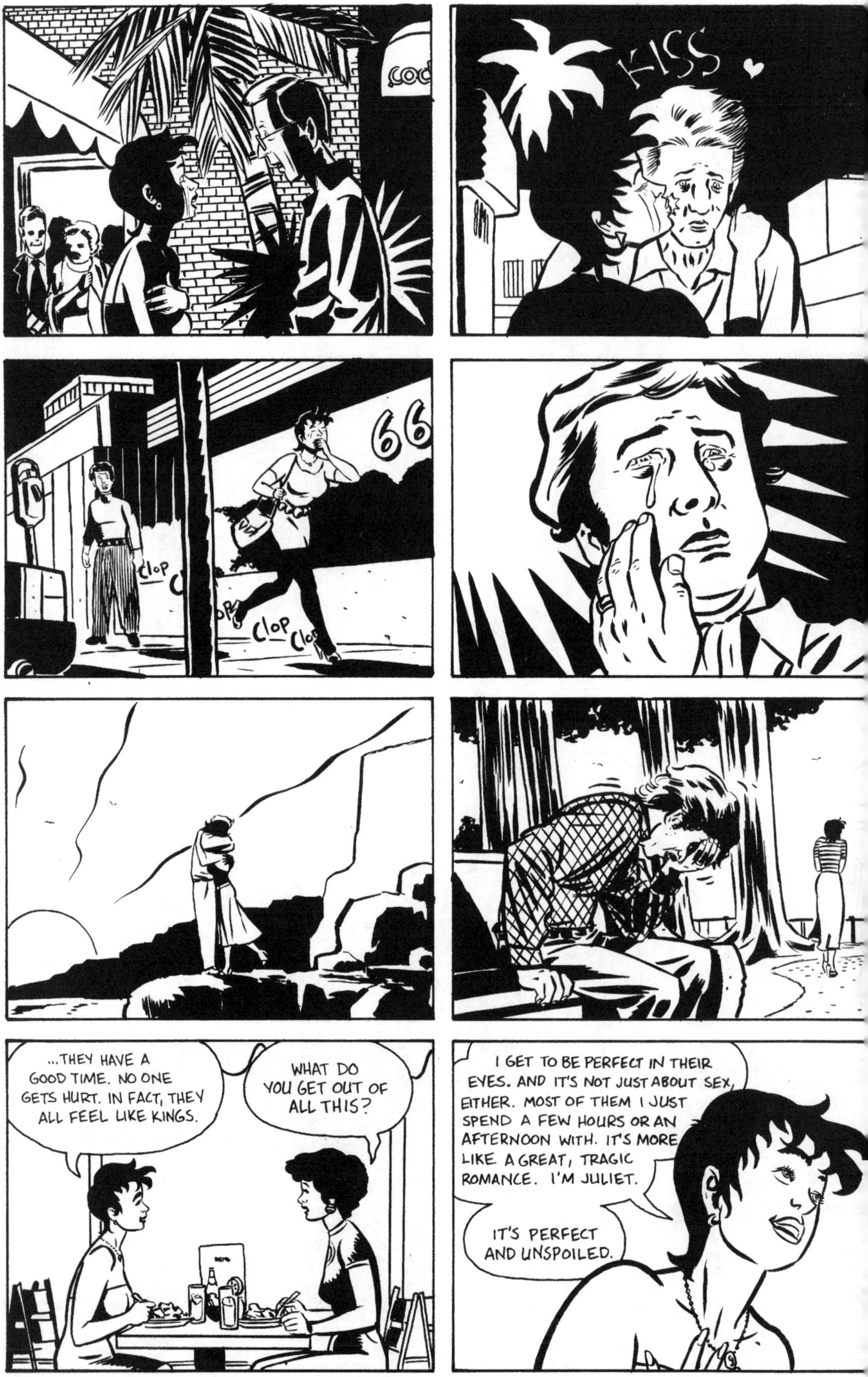

KISS
Clop
Clop
Clop
Clop
...THEY HAVE A GOOD TIME. NO ONE GETS HURT. IN FACT, THEY ALL FEEL LIKE KINGS.
WHAT DO YOU GET OUT OF ALL THIS?
I GET TO BE PERFECT IN THEIR EYES. AND IT'S NOT JUST ABOUT SEX, EITHER. MOST OF THEM I JUST SPEND A FEW HOURS OR AN AFTERNOON WITH. IT'S MORE LIKE A GREAT, TRAGIC ROMANCE. I'M JULIET.
IT'S PERFECT AND UNSPOILED.

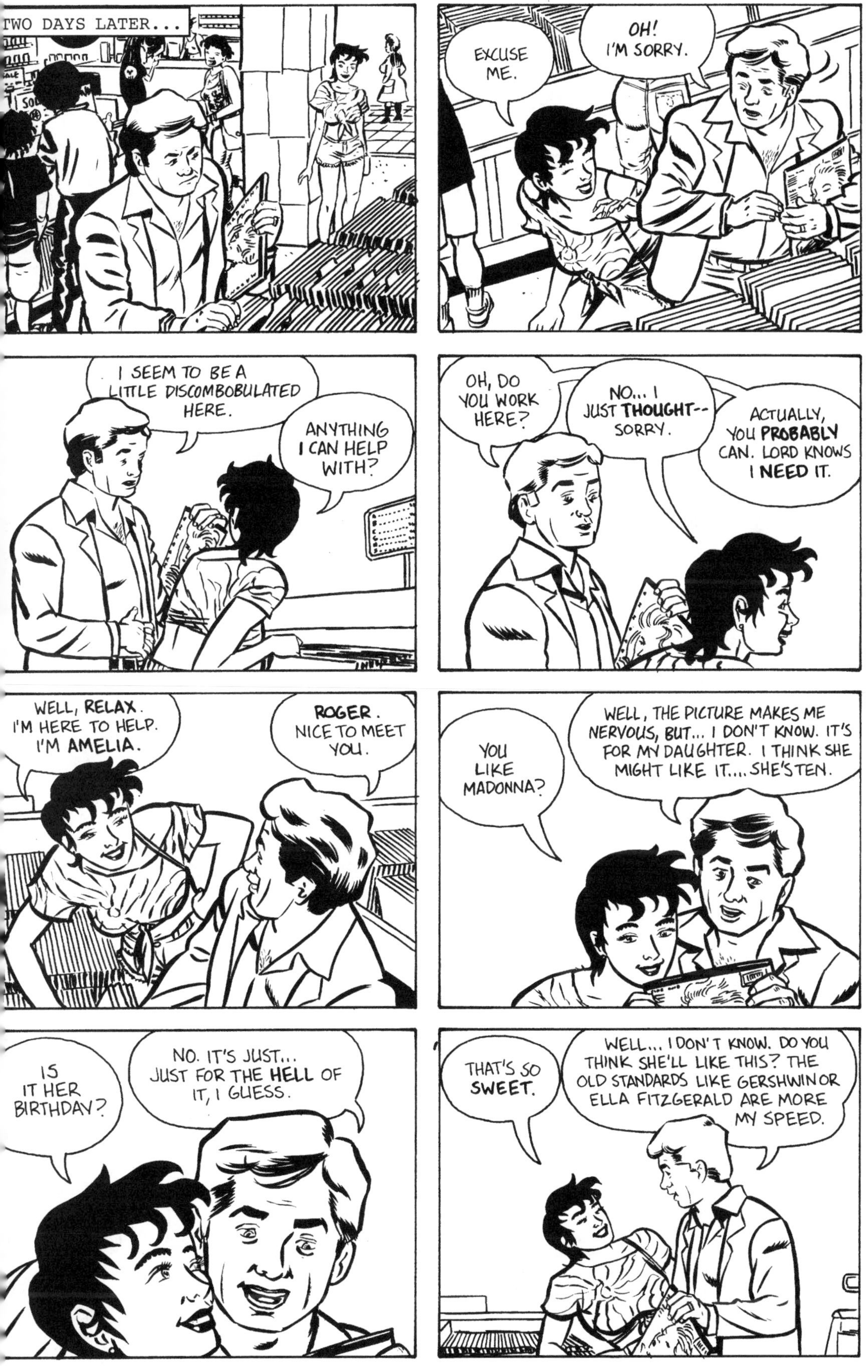
TWO DAYS LATER...
EXCUSE ME.
OH! I'M SORRY.
I SEEM TO BE A LITTLE DISCOMBOBULATED HERE.
ANYTHING I CAN HELP WITH?
OH, DO YOU WORK HERE?
NO... I JUST THOUGHT-- SORRY.
ACTUALLY, YOU PROBABLY CAN. LORD KNOWS I NEED IT.
WELL, RELAX. I'M HERE TO HELP. I'M AMELIA.
ROGER. NICE TO MEET YOU.
YOU LIKE MADONNA?
WELL, THE PICTURE MAKES ME NERVOUS, BUT... I DON'T KNOW. IT'S FOR MY DAUGHTER. I THINK SHE MIGHT LIKE IT.... SHE'S TEN.
IS IT HER BIRTHDAY?
NO. IT'S JUST... JUST FOR THE HELL OF IT, I GUESS.
THAT'S SO SWEET.
WELL... I DON'T KNOW. DO YOU THINK SHE'LL LIKE THIS? THE OLD STANDARDS LIKE GERSHWIN OR ELLA FITZGERALD ARE MORE MY SPEED.

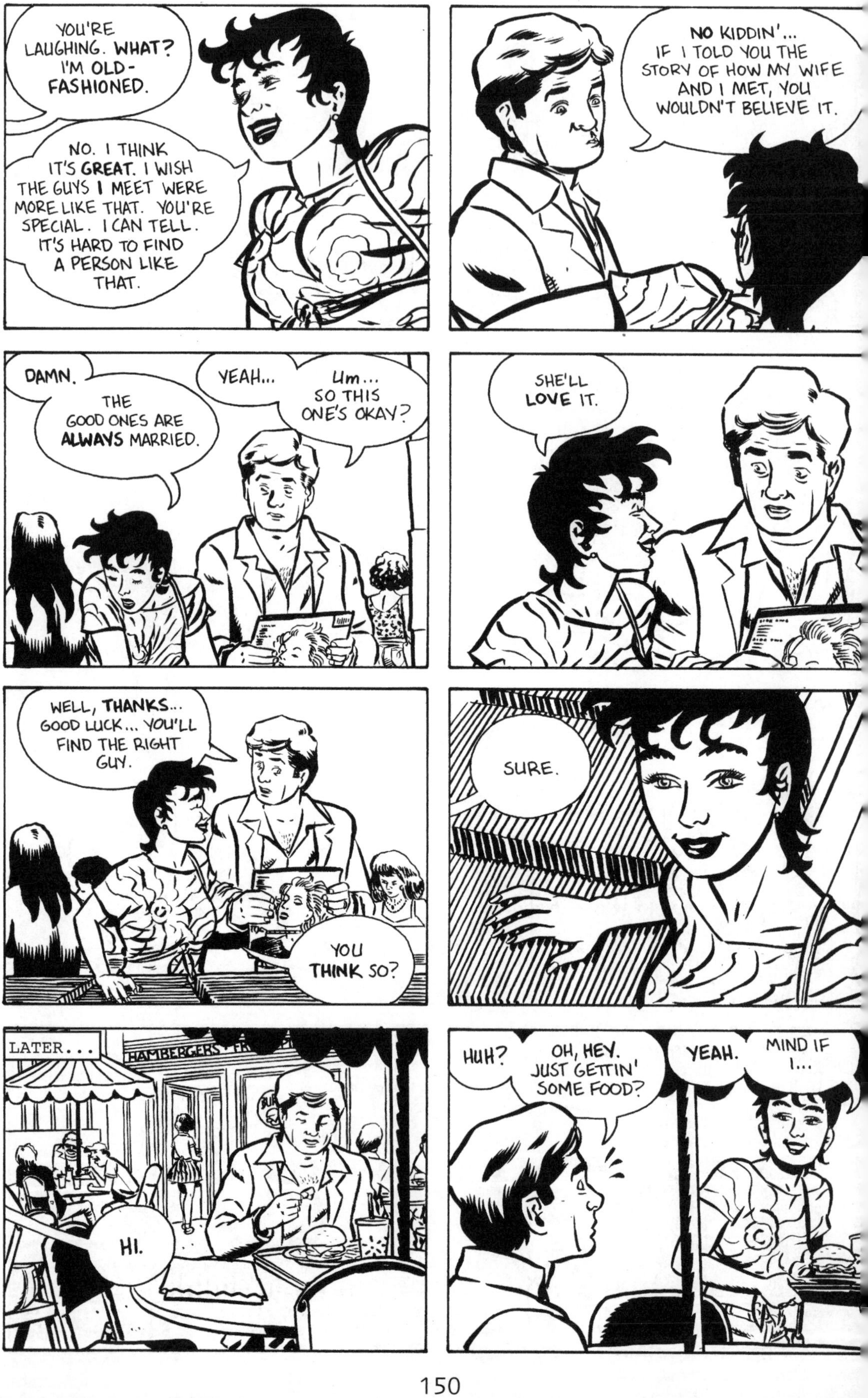
YOU'RE LAUGHING. WHAT? I'M OLD-FASHIONED.
NO. I THINK IT'S GREAT. I WISH THE GUYS I MEET WERE MORE LIKE THAT. YOU'RE SPECIAL. I CAN TELL. IT'S HARD TO FIND A PERSON LIKE THAT.
NO KIDDIN'... IF I TOLD YOU THE STORY OF HOW MY WIFE AND I MET, YOU WOULDN'T BELIEVE IT.
DAMN.
THE GOOD ONES ARE ALWAYS MARRIED.
YEAH...
UM... SO THIS ONE'S OKAY?
SHE'LL LOVE IT.
WELL, THANKS... GOOD LUCK... YOU'LL FIND THE RIGHT GUY.
YOU THINK SO?
SURE.
LATER...
HAMBERGERS
HI.
HUH?
OH, HEY. JUST GETTIN' SOME FOOD?
YEAH.
MIND IF I...

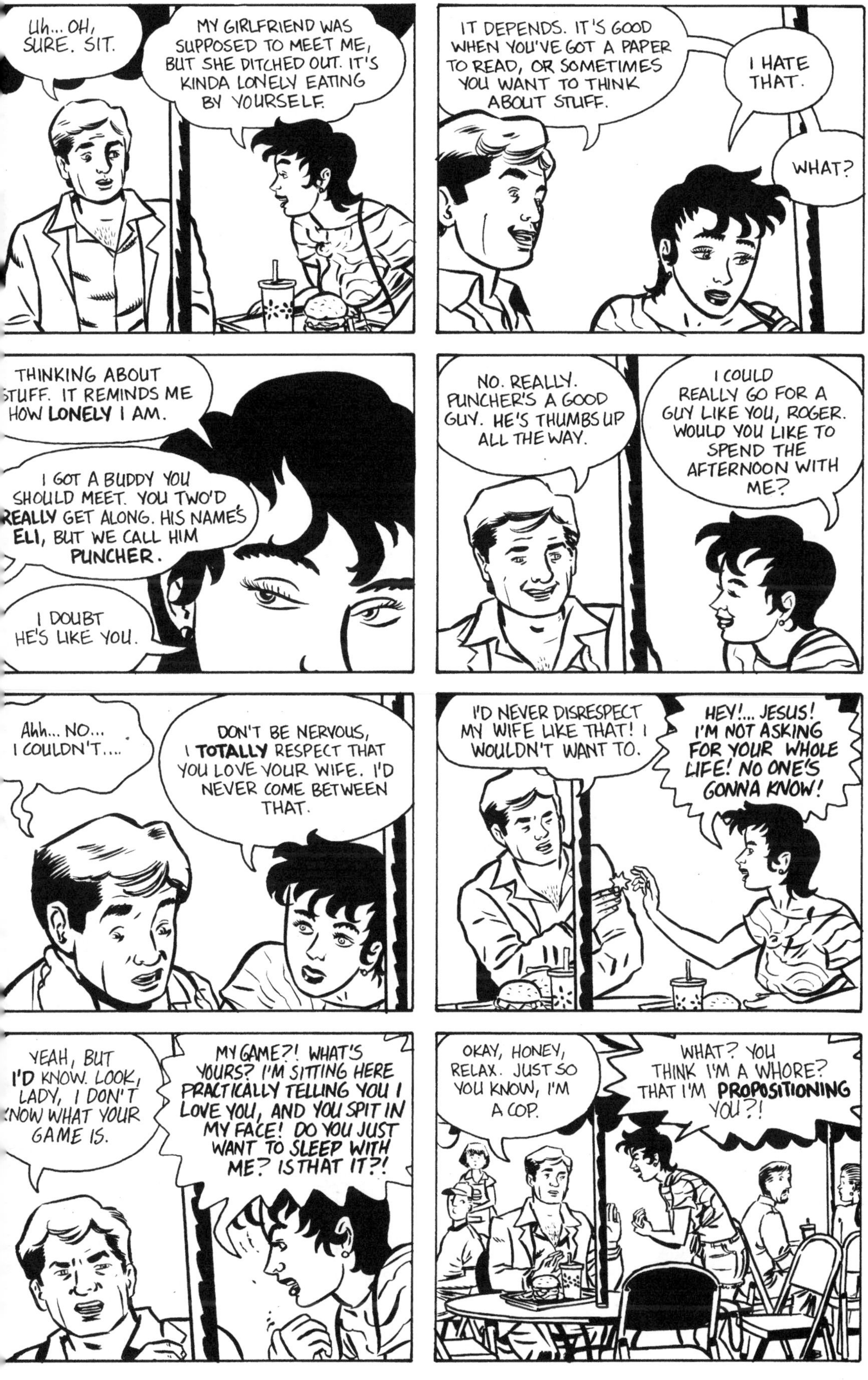

Uh... OH, SURE. SIT.
MY GIRLFRIEND WAS SUPPOSED TO MEET ME, BUT SHE DITCHED OUT. IT'S KINDA LONELY EATING BY YOURSELF.
IT DEPENDS. IT'S GOOD WHEN YOU'VE GOT A PAPER TO READ, OR SOMETIMES YOU WANT TO THINK ABOUT STUFF.
I HATE THAT.
WHAT?
THINKING ABOUT STUFF. IT REMINDS ME HOW LONELY I AM.
I GOT A BUDDY YOU SHOULD MEET. YOU TWO'D REALLY GET ALONG. HIS NAME'S ELI, BUT WE CALL HIM PUNCHER.
I DOUBT HE'S LIKE YOU.
NO. REALLY. PUNCHER'S A GOOD GUY. HE'S THUMBS UP ALL THE WAY.
I COULD REALLY GO FOR A GUY LIKE YOU, ROGER. WOULD YOU LIKE TO SPEND THE AFTERNOON WITH ME?
Ahh... NO... I COULDN'T....
DON'T BE NERVOUS, I TOTALLY RESPECT THAT YOU LOVE YOUR WIFE. I'D NEVER COME BETWEEN THAT.
I'D NEVER DISRESPECT MY WIFE LIKE THAT! I WOULDN'T WANT TO.
HEY!... JESUS! I'M NOT ASKING FOR YOUR WHOLE LIFE! NO ONE'S GONNA KNOW!
YEAH, BUT I'D KNOW. LOOK, LADY, I DON'T KNOW WHAT YOUR GAME IS.
MY GAME?! WHAT'S YOURS? I'M SITTING HERE PRACTICALLY TELLING YOU I LOVE YOU, AND YOU SPIT IN MY FACE! DO YOU JUST WANT TO SLEEP WITH ME? IS THAT IT?!
OKAY, HONEY, RELAX. JUST SO YOU KNOW, I'M A COP.
WHAT? YOU THINK I'M A WHORE? THAT I'M PROPOSITIONING YOU?!

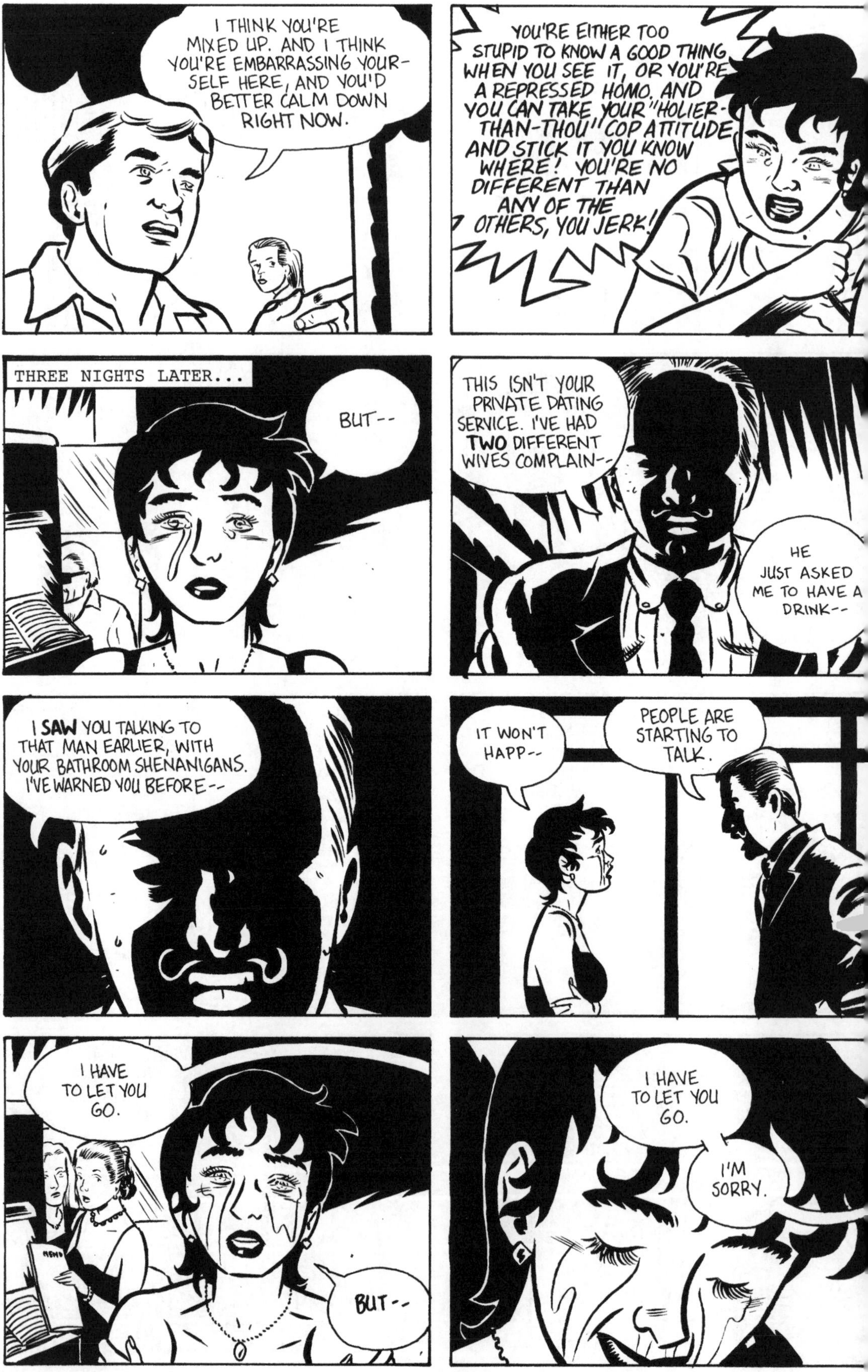
I THINK YOU'RE MIXED UP. AND I THINK YOU'RE EMBARRASSING YOURSELF HERE, AND YOU'D BETTER CALM DOWN RIGHT NOW.
YOU'RE EITHER TOO STUPID TO KNOW A GOOD THING WHEN YOU SEE IT, OR YOU'RE A REPRESSED HOMO. AND YOU CAN TAKE YOUR "HOLIER-THAN-THOU" COP ATTITUDE AND STICK IT YOU KNOW WHERE! YOU'RE NO DIFFERENT THAN ANY OF THE OTHERS, YOU JERK!
THREE NIGHTS LATER...
BUT--
THIS ISN'T YOUR PRIVATE DATING SERVICE. I'VE HAD **TWO** DIFFERENT WIVES COMPLAIN--
HE JUST ASKED ME TO HAVE A DRINK--
I **SAW** YOU TALKING TO THAT MAN EARLIER, WITH YOUR BATHROOM SHENANIGANS. I'VE WARNED YOU BEFORE--
IT WON'T HAPP--
PEOPLE ARE STARTING TO TALK.
I HAVE TO LET YOU GO.
BUT--
I HAVE TO LET YOU GO.
I'M SORRY.

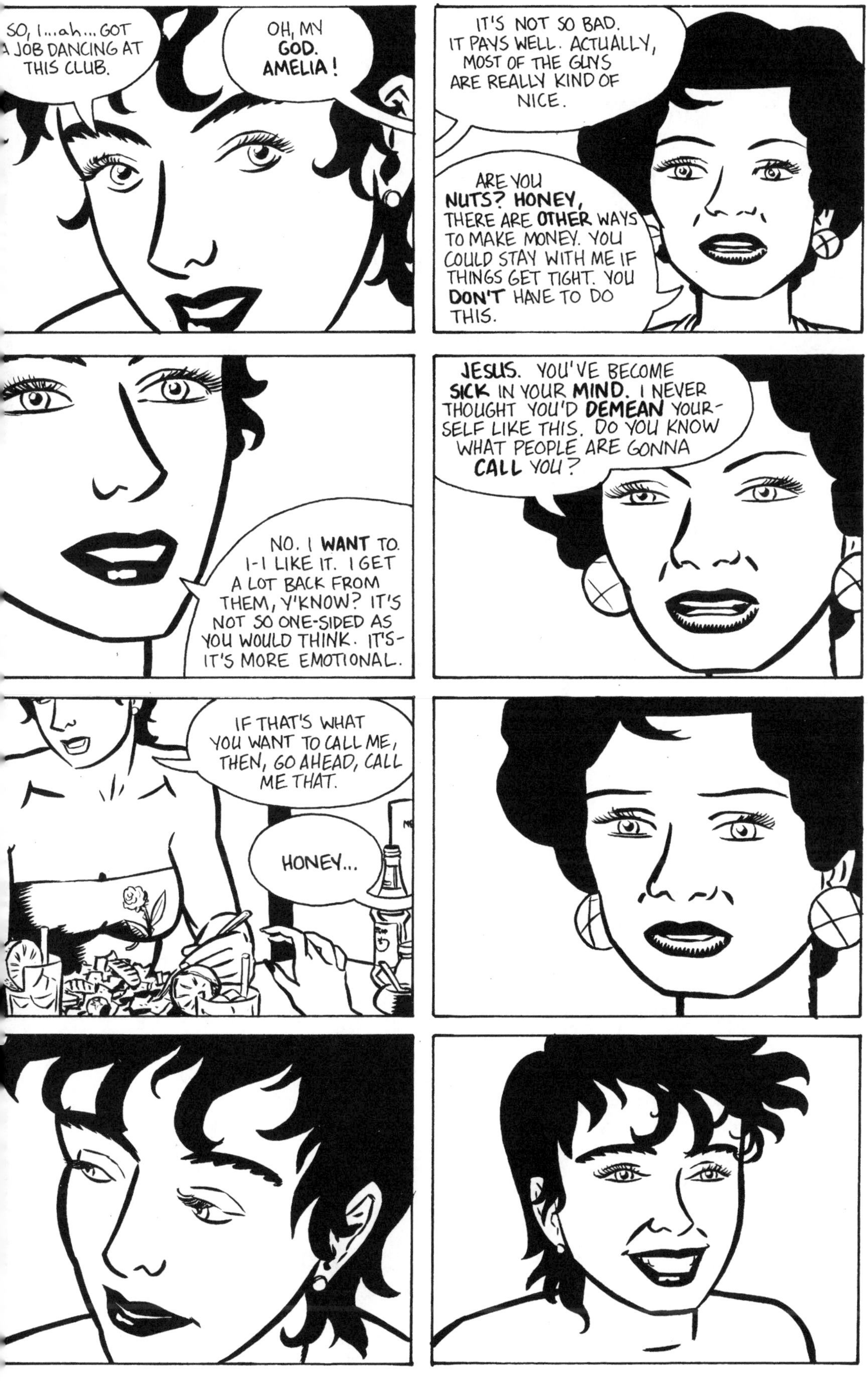
SO, I...ah... GOT A JOB DANCING AT THIS CLUB.
OH, MY GOD. AMELIA!
IT'S NOT SO BAD. IT PAYS WELL. ACTUALLY, MOST OF THE GUYS ARE REALLY KIND OF NICE.
ARE YOU NUTS? HONEY, THERE ARE OTHER WAYS TO MAKE MONEY. YOU COULD STAY WITH ME IF THINGS GET TIGHT. YOU DON'T HAVE TO DO THIS.
NO. I WANT TO. I-I LIKE IT. I GET A LOT BACK FROM THEM, Y'KNOW? IT'S NOT SO ONE-SIDED AS YOU WOULD THINK. IT'S-IT'S MORE EMOTIONAL.
JESUS. YOU'VE BECOME SICK IN YOUR MIND. I NEVER THOUGHT YOU'D DEMEAN YOURSELF LIKE THIS. DO YOU KNOW WHAT PEOPLE ARE GONNA CALL YOU?
IF THAT'S WHAT YOU WANT TO CALL ME, THEN, GO AHEAD, CALL ME THAT.
HONEY...

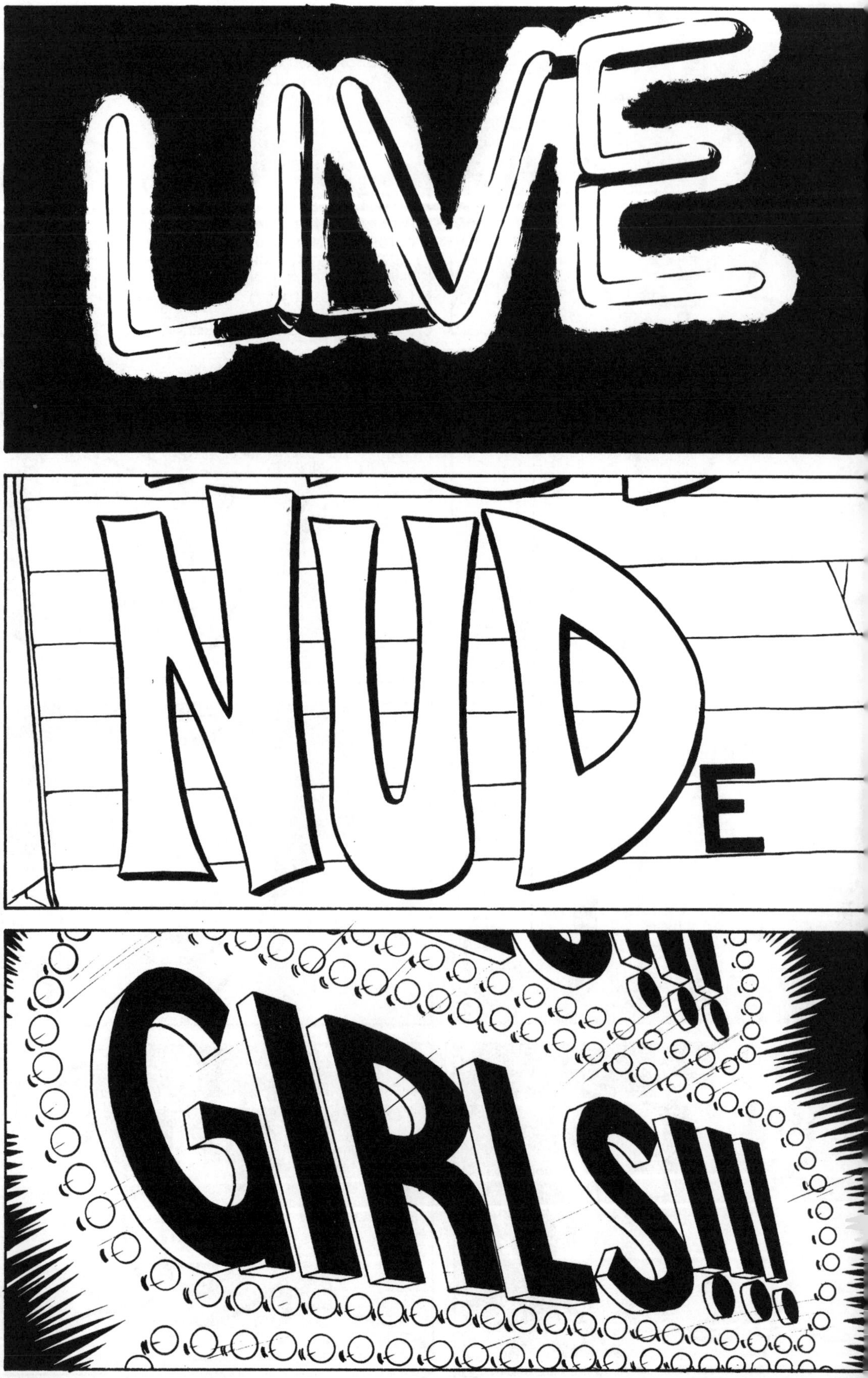
LIVE
NUDE
GIRLS!!!



THE END.

# "MOTEL"

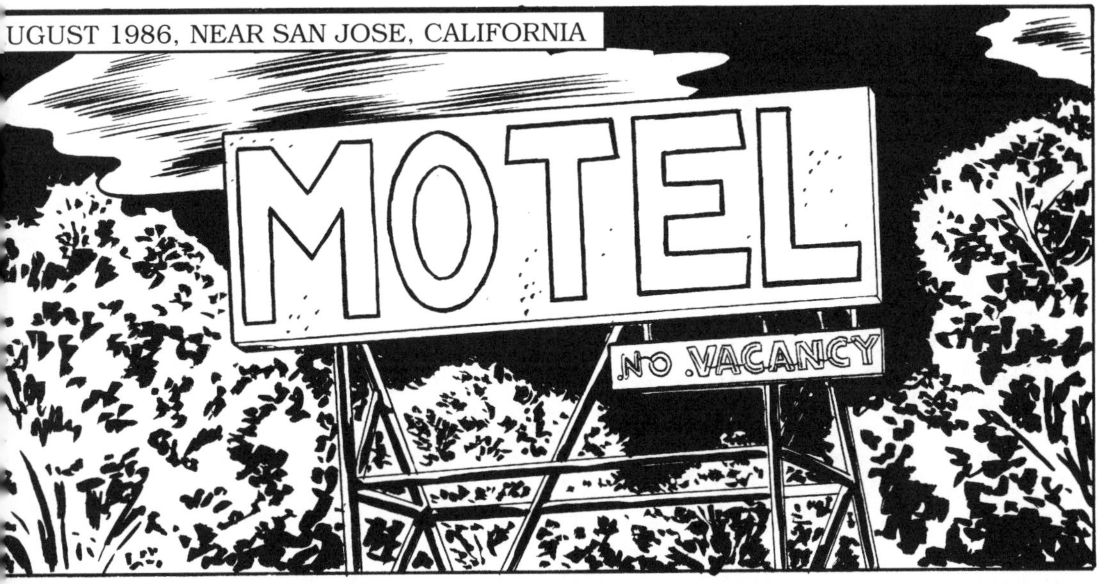
UGUST 1986, NEAR SAN JOSE, CALIFORNIA
MOTEL
NO VACANCY

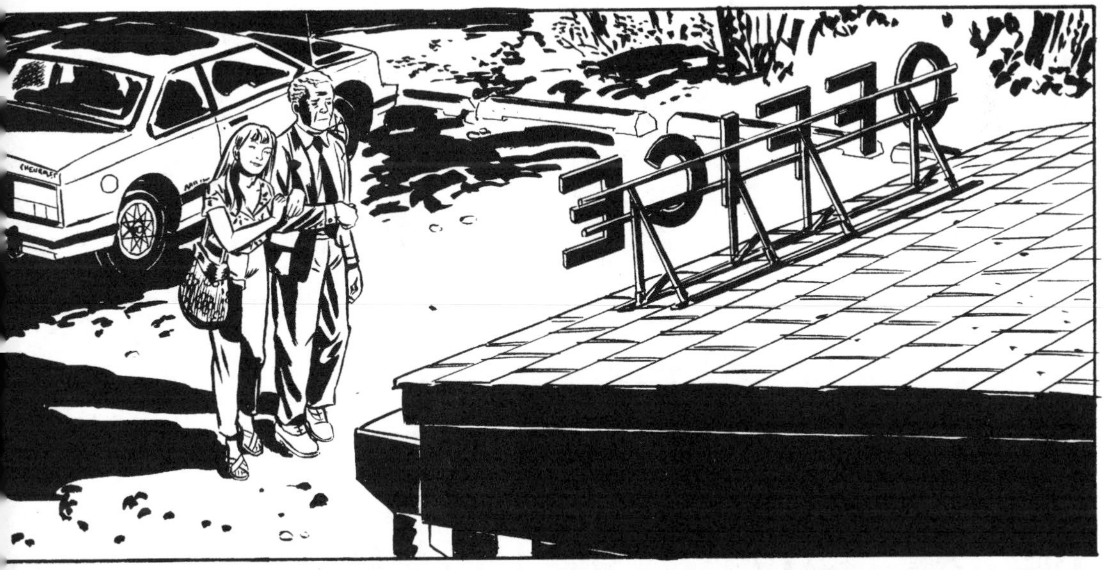
OFFICE

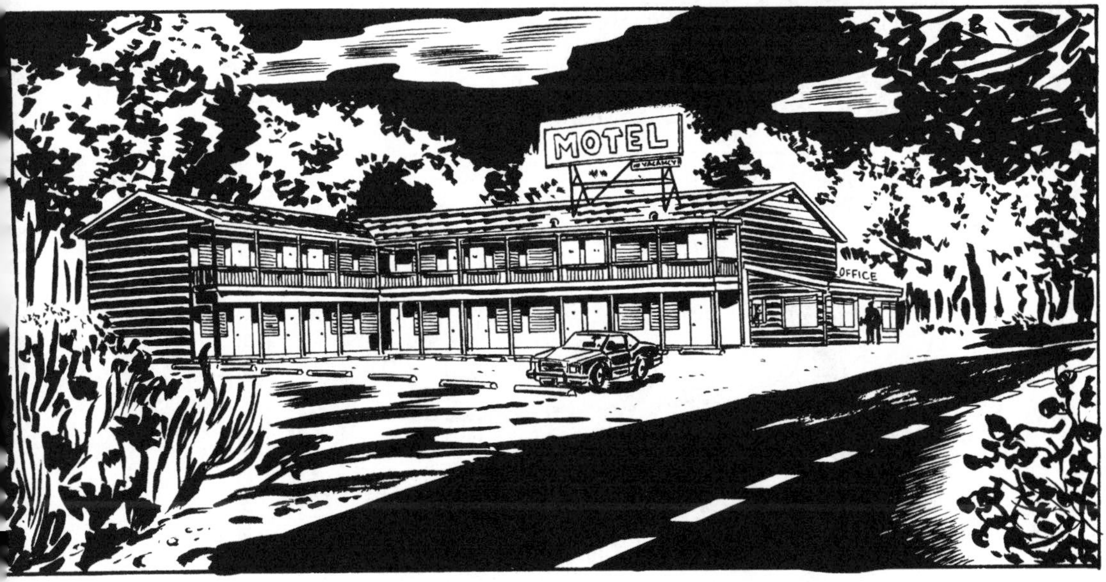
MOTEL
OFFICE

WELL, HELLO, MRS. SMITH...

...MR. SMITH.

HELLO, FRANK. HOW ARE YOU TONIGHT?

GETTIN' BY... SORRY ABOUT THE HEAT.

WE'RE NOT GOING TO LET ANYTHING SPOIL THIS NIGHT.

THAT'S THE SPIRIT. YOU'VE GOT A GOOD ONE THERE, MR. SMITH. DON'T LET 'ER GET AWAY.

Mmm....

MY WIFE TOOK OFF TO HER MOTHER'S. THEY GOT THE AIR CONDITIONING. I'LL BE LUCKY TO SEE HER 'FORE THIS HEAT BREAKS.

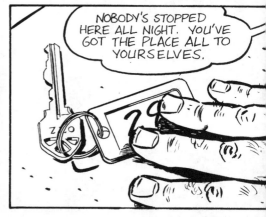

NOBODY'S STOPPED HERE ALL NIGHT. YOU'VE GOT THE PLACE ALL TO YOURSELVES.

THAT'S FINE WITH ME.

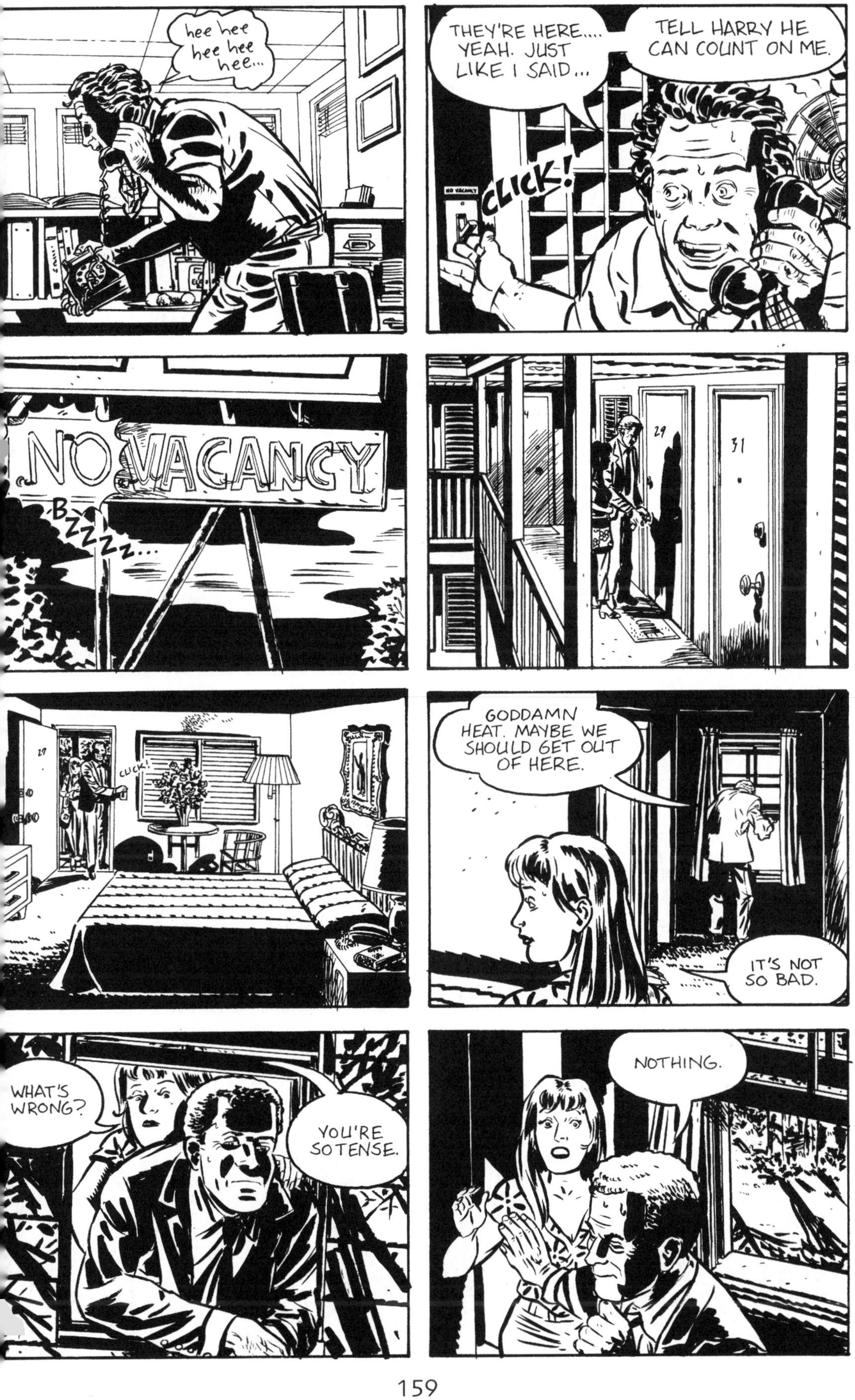
hee hee
hee hee
hee...
THEY'RE HERE.... YEAH. JUST LIKE I SAID...
TELL HARRY HE CAN COUNT ON ME.
NO VACANCY
CLICK!
NO VACANCY
BZZZZ...
29
31
29
CLICK!
GODDAMN HEAT. MAYBE WE SHOULD GET OUT OF HERE.
IT'S NOT SO BAD.
WHAT'S WRONG?
YOU'RE SO TENSE.
NOTHING.

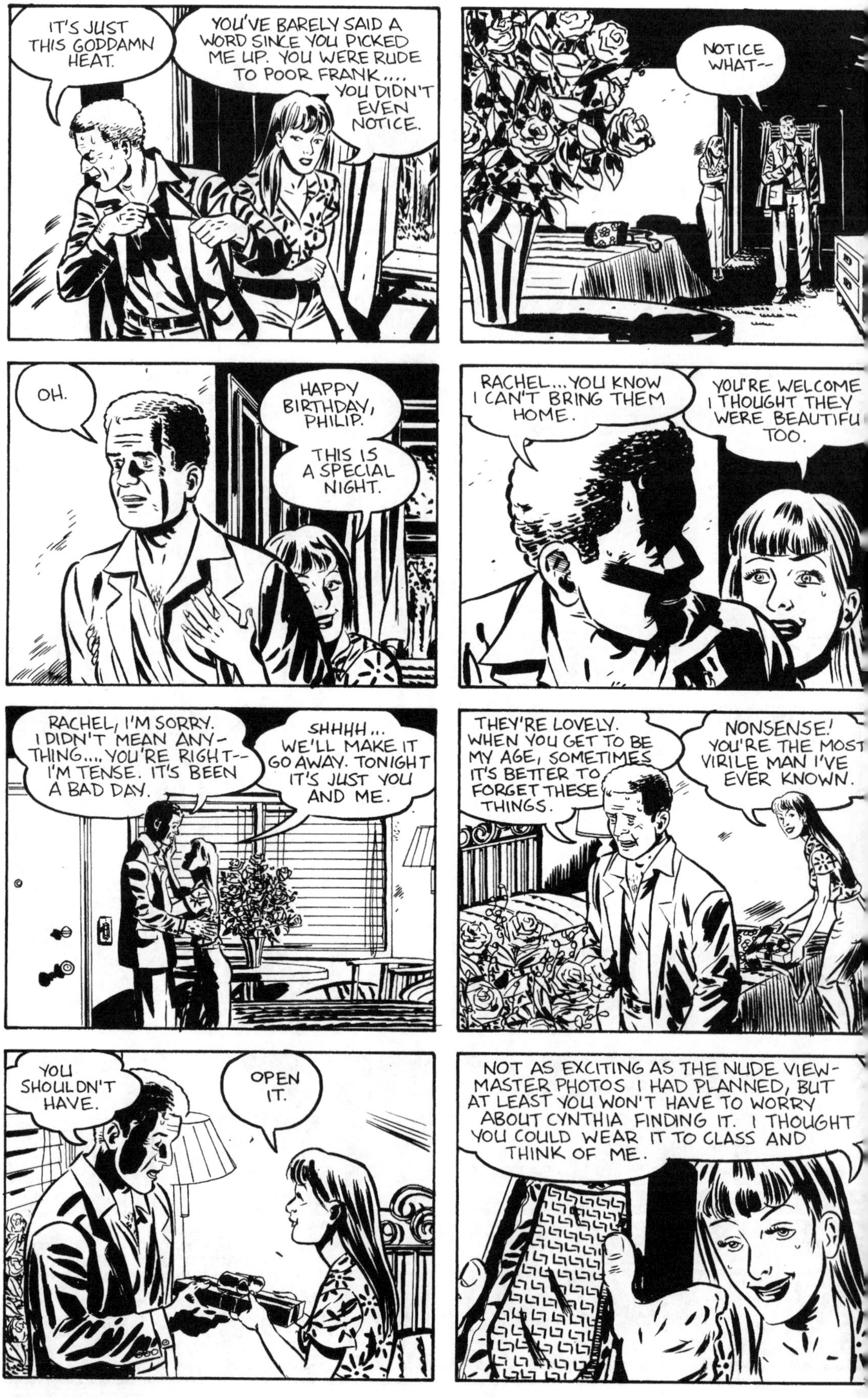
IT'S JUST THIS GODDAMN HEAT.
YOU'VE BARELY SAID A WORD SINCE YOU PICKED ME UP. YOU WERE RUDE TO POOR FRANK.... YOU DIDN'T EVEN NOTICE.
NOTICE WHAT--
OH.
HAPPY BIRTHDAY, PHILIP.
THIS IS A SPECIAL NIGHT.
RACHEL... YOU KNOW I CAN'T BRING THEM HOME.
YOU'RE WELCOME. I THOUGHT THEY WERE BEAUTIFU TOO.
RACHEL, I'M SORRY. I DIDN'T MEAN ANYTHING.... YOU'RE RIGHT-- I'M TENSE. IT'S BEEN A BAD DAY.
SHHHH... WE'LL MAKE IT GO AWAY. TONIGHT IT'S JUST YOU AND ME.
THEY'RE LOVELY. WHEN YOU GET TO BE MY AGE, SOMETIMES IT'S BETTER TO FORGET THESE THINGS.
NONSENSE! YOU'RE THE MOST VIRILE MAN I'VE EVER KNOWN.
YOU SHOULDN'T HAVE.
OPEN IT.
NOT AS EXCITING AS THE NUDE VIEW-MASTER PHOTOS I HAD PLANNED, BUT AT LEAST YOU WON'T HAVE TO WORRY ABOUT CYNTHIA FINDING IT. I THOUGHT YOU COULD WEAR IT TO CLASS AND THINK OF ME.

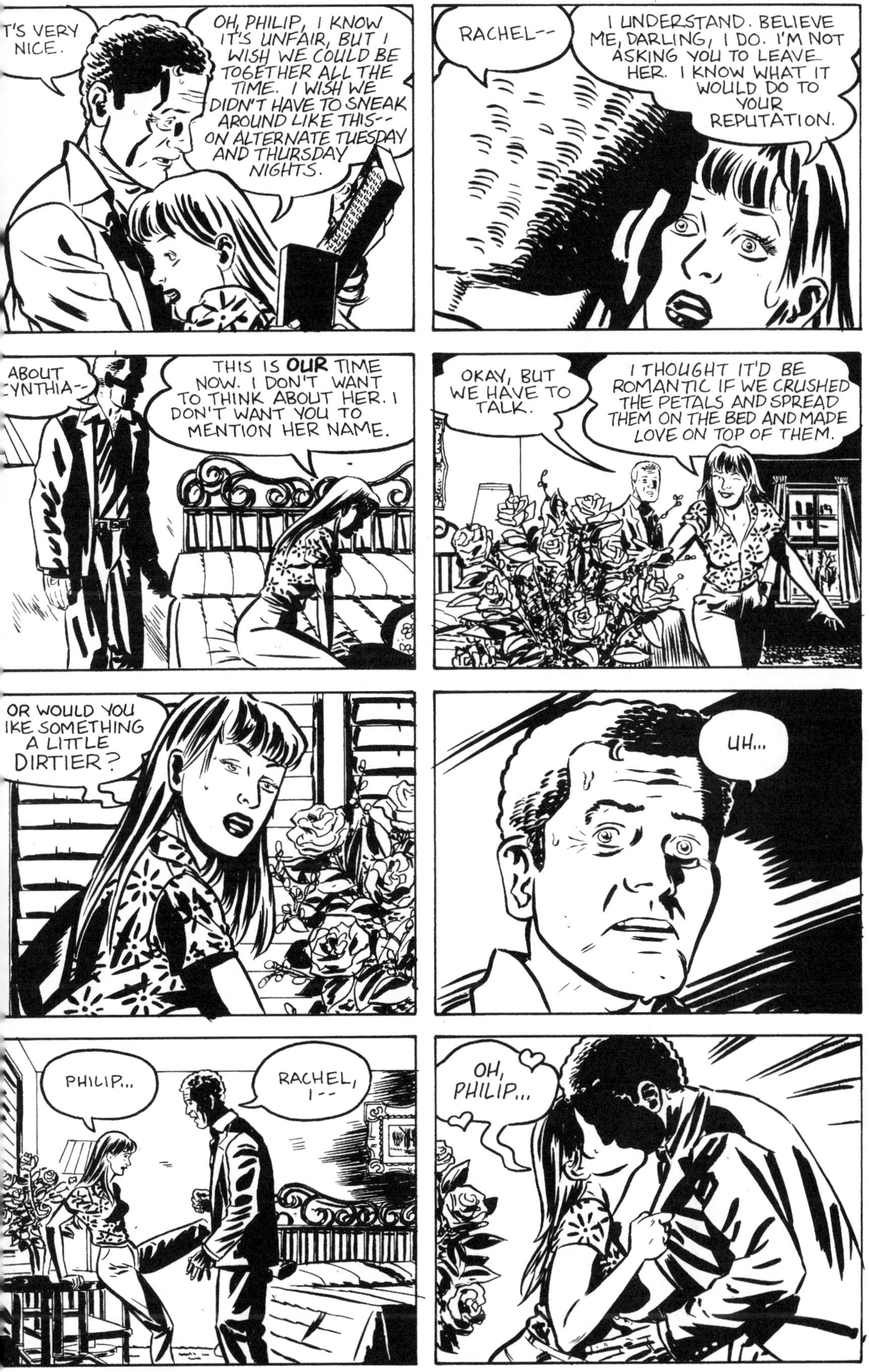
T'S VERY NICE.
OH, PHILIP, I KNOW IT'S UNFAIR, BUT I WISH WE COULD BE TOGETHER ALL THE TIME. I WISH WE DIDN'T HAVE TO SNEAK AROUND LIKE THIS-- ON ALTERNATE TUESDAY AND THURSDAY NIGHTS.
RACHEL--
I UNDERSTAND. BELIEVE ME, DARLING, I DO. I'M NOT ASKING YOU TO LEAVE HER. I KNOW WHAT IT WOULD DO TO YOUR REPUTATION.
ABOUT CYNTHIA--
THIS IS OUR TIME NOW. I DON'T WANT TO THINK ABOUT HER. I DON'T WANT YOU TO MENTION HER NAME.
OKAY, BUT WE HAVE TO TALK.
I THOUGHT IT'D BE ROMANTIC IF WE CRUSHED THE PETALS AND SPREAD THEM ON THE BED AND MADE LOVE ON TOP OF THEM.
OR WOULD YOU LIKE SOMETHING A LITTLE DIRTIER?
UH...
PHILIP...
RACHEL, I--
OH, PHILIP...

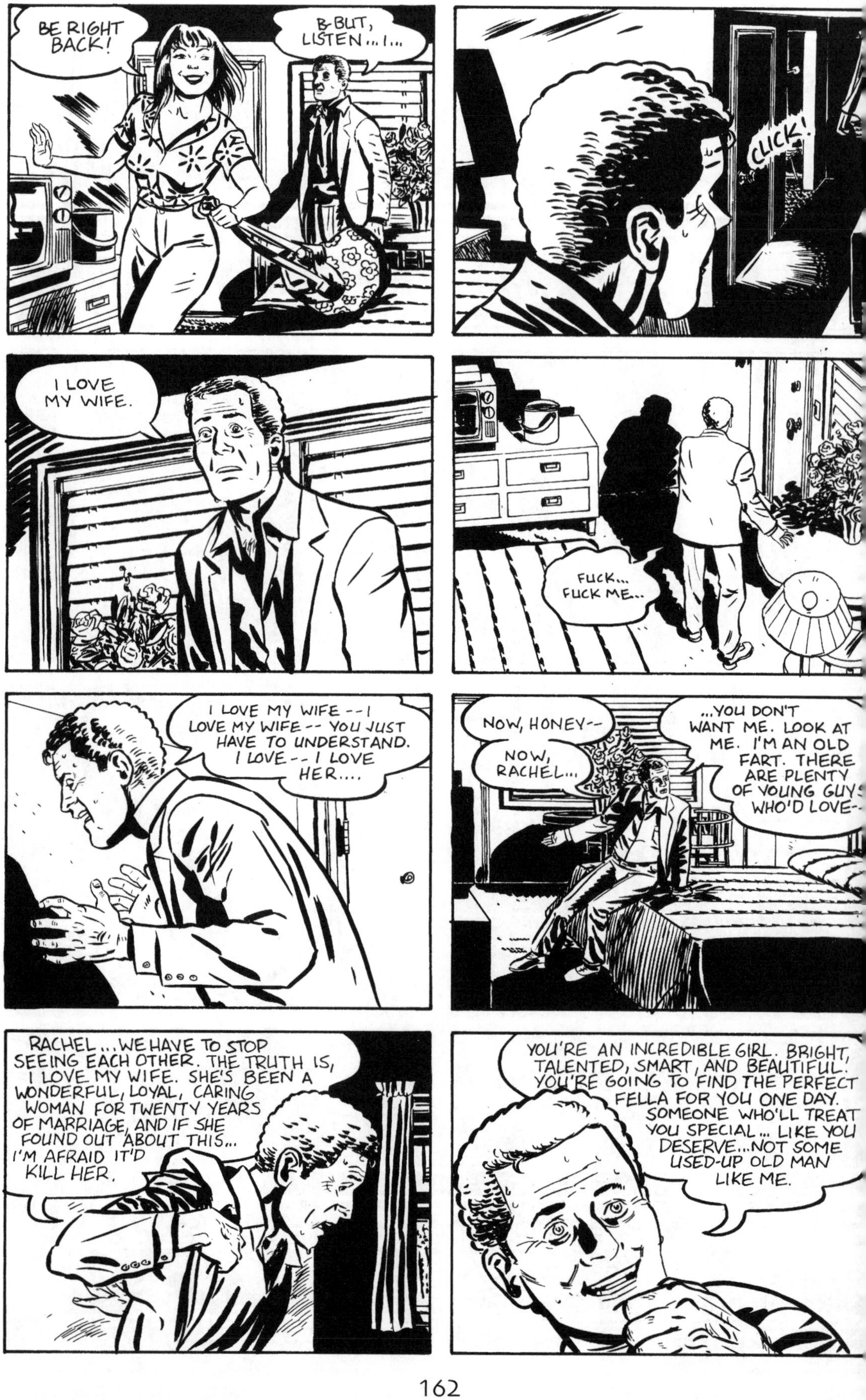
BE RIGHT BACK!
B-BUT, LISTEN...I...
CLICK!
I LOVE MY WIFE.
FUCK... FUCK ME...
I LOVE MY WIFE--I LOVE MY WIFE-- YOU JUST HAVE TO UNDERSTAND. I LOVE--I LOVE HER....
NOW, HONEY--
NOW, RACHEL...
...YOU DON'T WANT ME. LOOK AT ME. I'M AN OLD FART. THERE ARE PLENTY OF YOUNG GUYS WHO'D LOVE--
RACHEL...WE HAVE TO STOP SEEING EACH OTHER. THE TRUTH IS, I LOVE MY WIFE. SHE'S BEEN A WONDERFUL, LOYAL, CARING WOMAN FOR TWENTY YEARS OF MARRIAGE, AND IF SHE FOUND OUT ABOUT THIS... I'M AFRAID IT'D KILL HER.
YOU'RE AN INCREDIBLE GIRL. BRIGHT, TALENTED, SMART, AND BEAUTIFUL. YOU'RE GOING TO FIND THE PERFECT FELLA FOR YOU ONE DAY. SOMEONE WHO'LL TREAT YOU SPECIAL... LIKE YOU DESERVE...NOT SOME USED-UP OLD MAN LIKE ME.

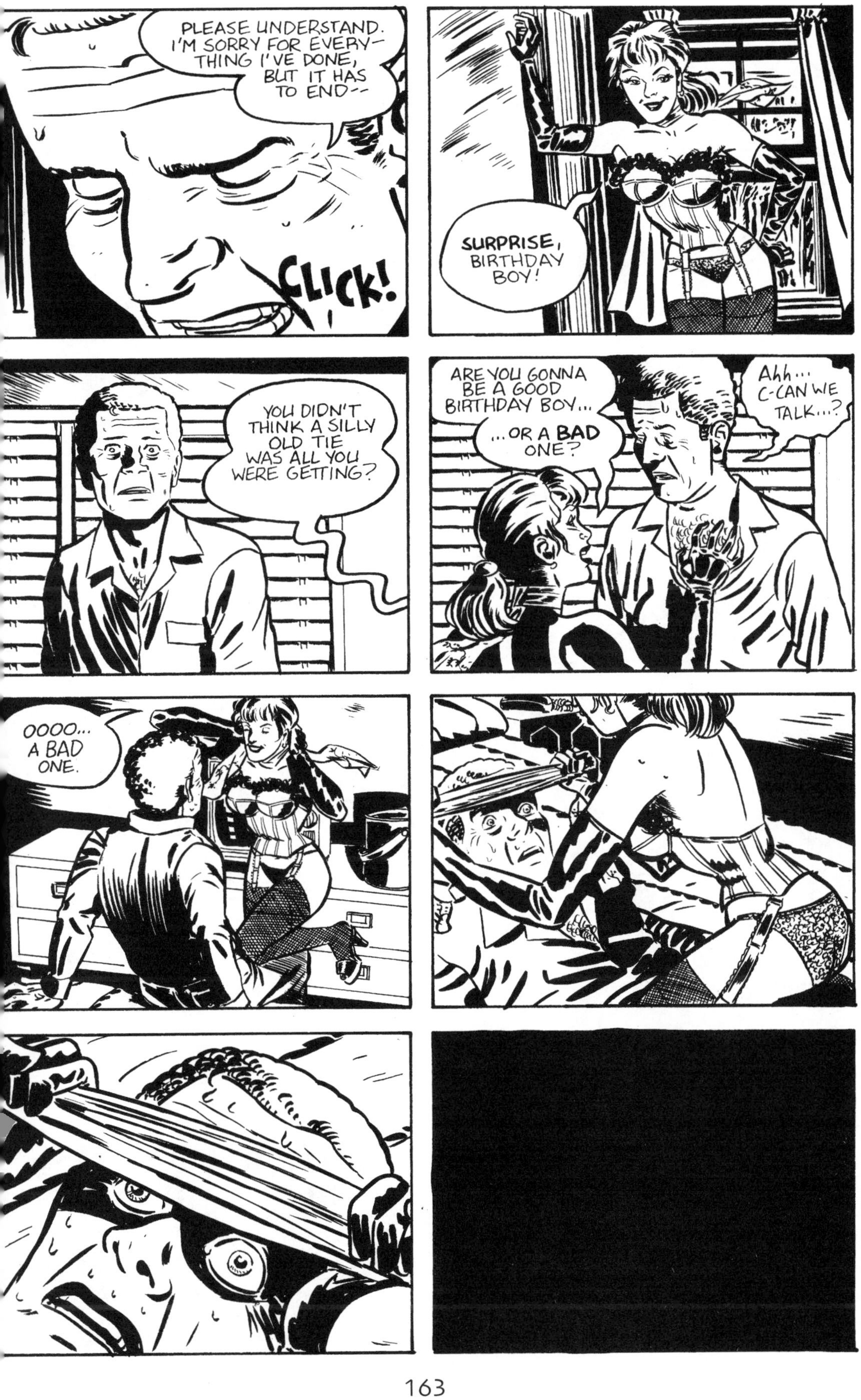
PLEASE UNDERSTAND. I'M SORRY FOR EVERYTHING I'VE DONE, BUT IT HAS TO END--
CLICK!
SURPRISE, BIRTHDAY BOY!
YOU DIDN'T THINK A SILLY OLD TIE WAS ALL YOU WERE GETTING?
ARE YOU GONNA BE A GOOD BIRTHDAY BOY...
...OR A BAD ONE?
Ahh... C-CAN WE TALK...?
OOOO... A BAD ONE.

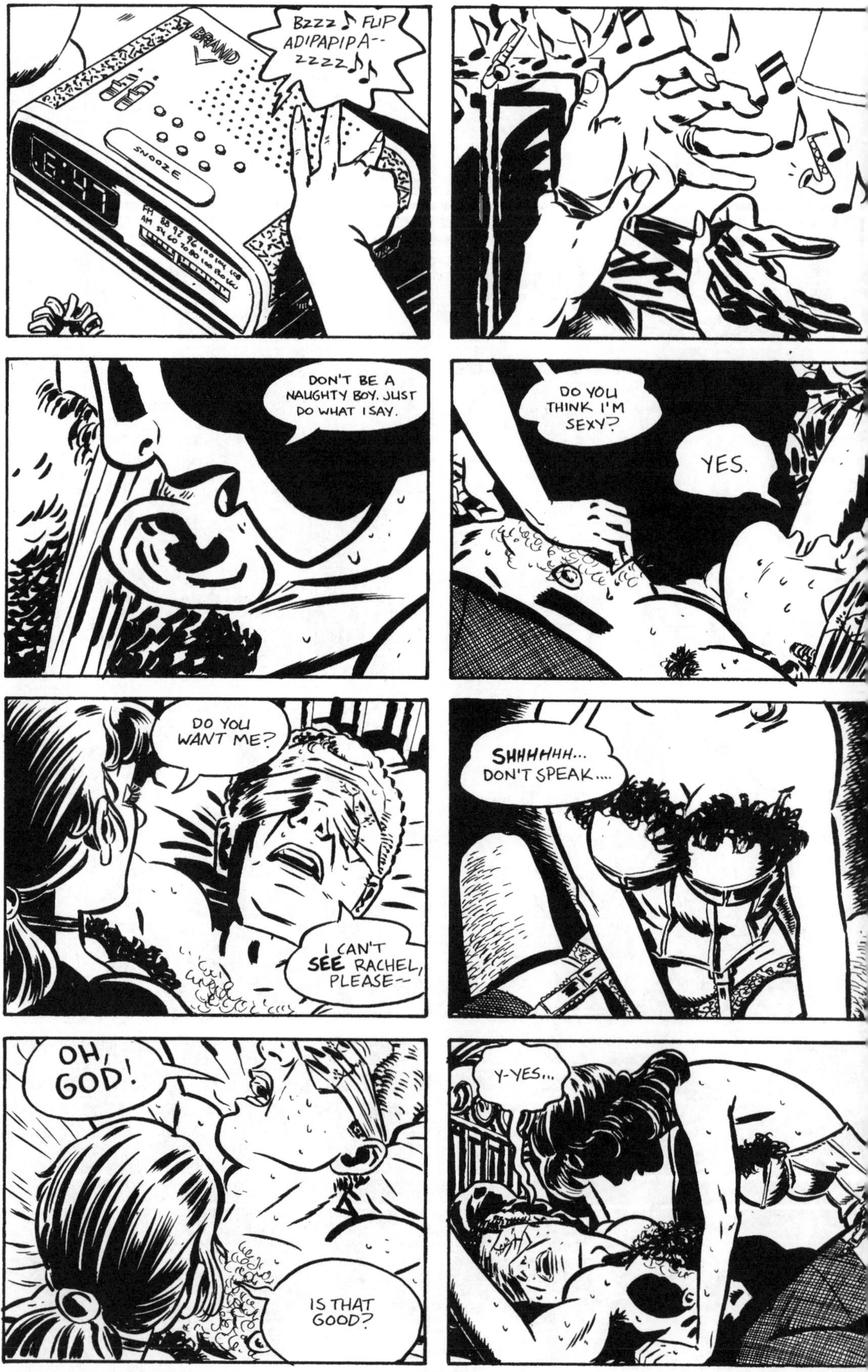
BRAND
SNOOZE
Bzzz♪ FLIP ADIPAPIPA-- zzzz♪♪
DON'T BE A NAUGHTY BOY. JUST DO WHAT I SAY.
DO YOU THINK I'M SEXY?
YES.
DO YOU WANT ME?
I CAN'T **SEE** RACHEL, PLEASE--
SHHHHHH... DON'T SPEAK....
OH, GOD!
IS THAT GOOD?
Y-YES...

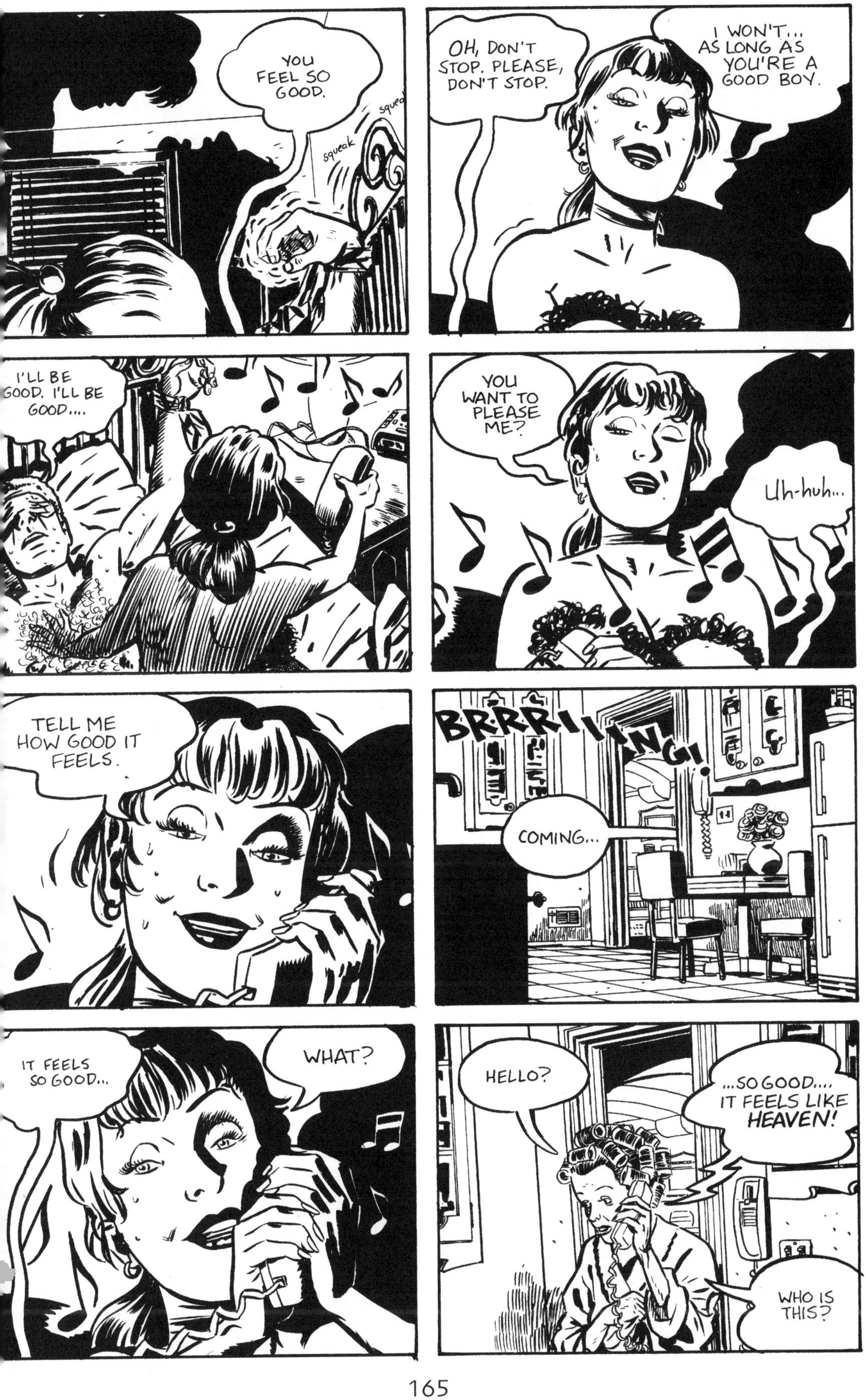
YOU FEEL SO GOOD.
squeak
squea
OH, DON'T STOP. PLEASE, DON'T STOP.
I WON'T... AS LONG AS YOU'RE A GOOD BOY.
I'LL BE GOOD. I'LL BE GOOD....
YOU WANT TO PLEASE ME?
Uh-huh...
TELL ME HOW GOOD IT FEELS.
BRRRIIING!
COMING...
IT FEELS SO GOOD...
WHAT?
HELLO?
...SO GOOD.... IT FEELS LIKE HEAVEN!
WHO IS THIS?

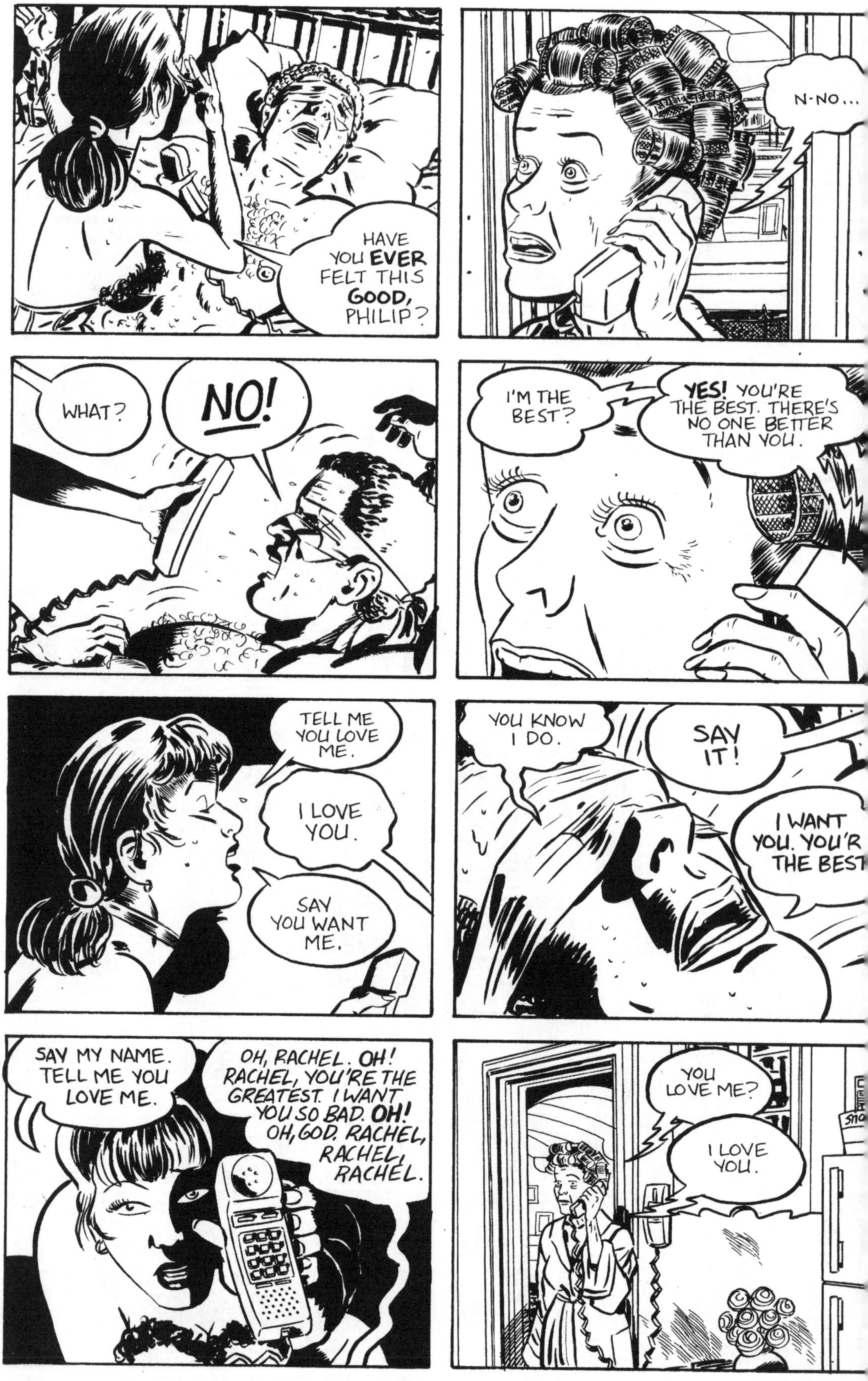
HAVE YOU EVER FELT THIS GOOD, PHILIP?
N-NO...
WHAT?
NO!
I'M THE BEST?
YES! YOU'RE THE BEST. THERE'S NO ONE BETTER THAN YOU.
TELL ME YOU LOVE ME.
I LOVE YOU.
SAY YOU WANT ME.
YOU KNOW I DO.
SAY IT!
I WANT YOU. YOU'R THE BEST
SAY MY NAME. TELL ME YOU LOVE ME.
OH, RACHEL. OH! RACHEL, YOU'RE THE GREATEST. I WANT YOU SO BAD. OH! OH, GOD. RACHEL, RACHEL, RACHEL.
YOU LOVE ME?
I LOVE YOU.

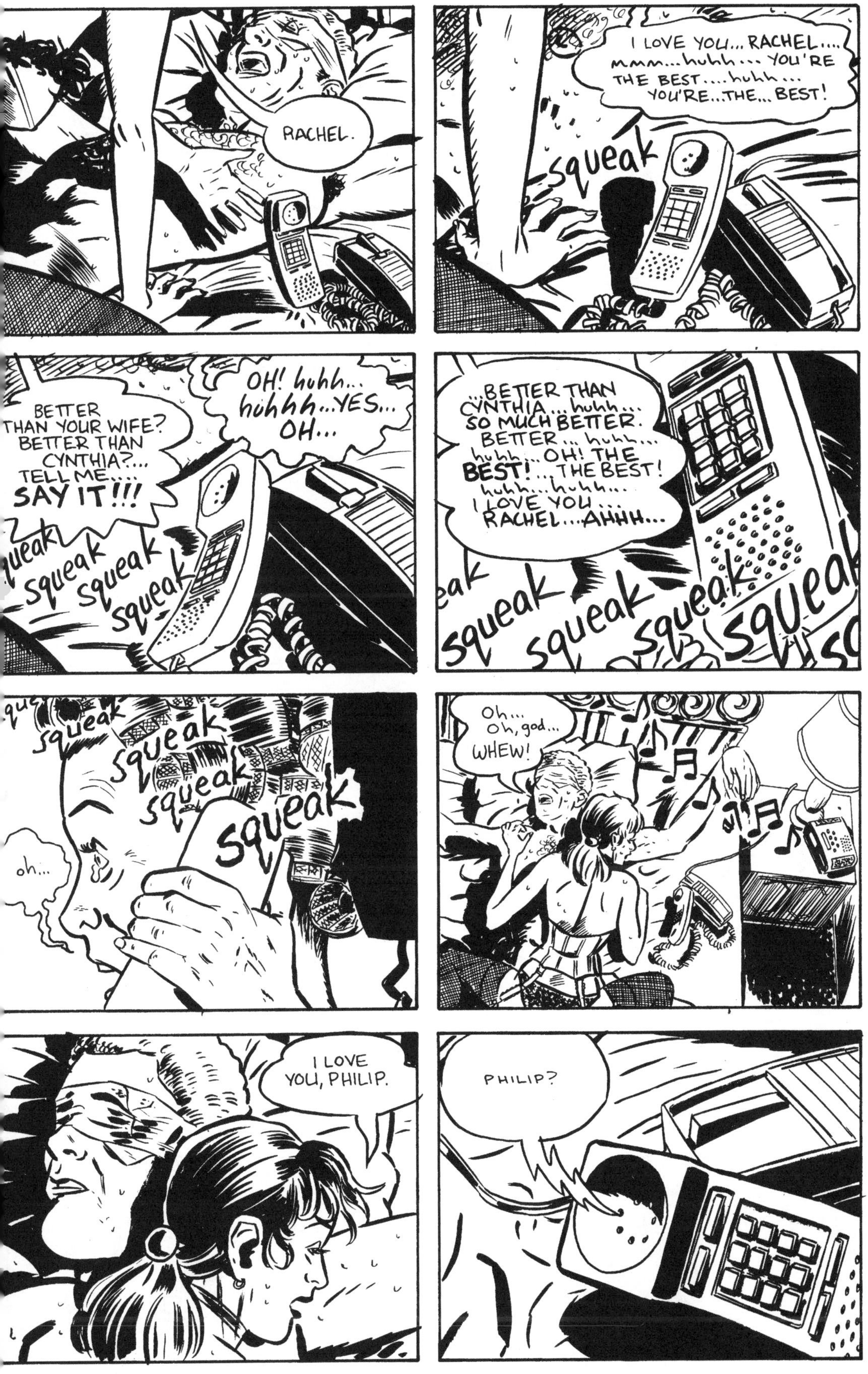
RACHEL.
I LOVE YOU... RACHEL.... mmm...huhh... YOU'RE THE BEST....huhh... YOU'RE...THE... BEST!
squeak
BETTER THAN YOUR WIFE? BETTER THAN CYNTHIA?... TELL ME.... SAY IT!!!
OH! huhh... huhhh...YES... OH...
squeak
squeak
squeak
squeak
...BETTER THAN CYNTHIA... huhh... SO MUCH BETTER. BETTER... huhh... huhh...OH! THE BEST!...THE BEST! huhh...huhh... I LOVE YOU... RACHEL...AHHH...
squeak
squeak
squeak
squeak
squeak
squeak
squeak
oh...
squeak
Oh... Oh, god... WHEW!
I LOVE YOU, PHILIP.
PHILIP?

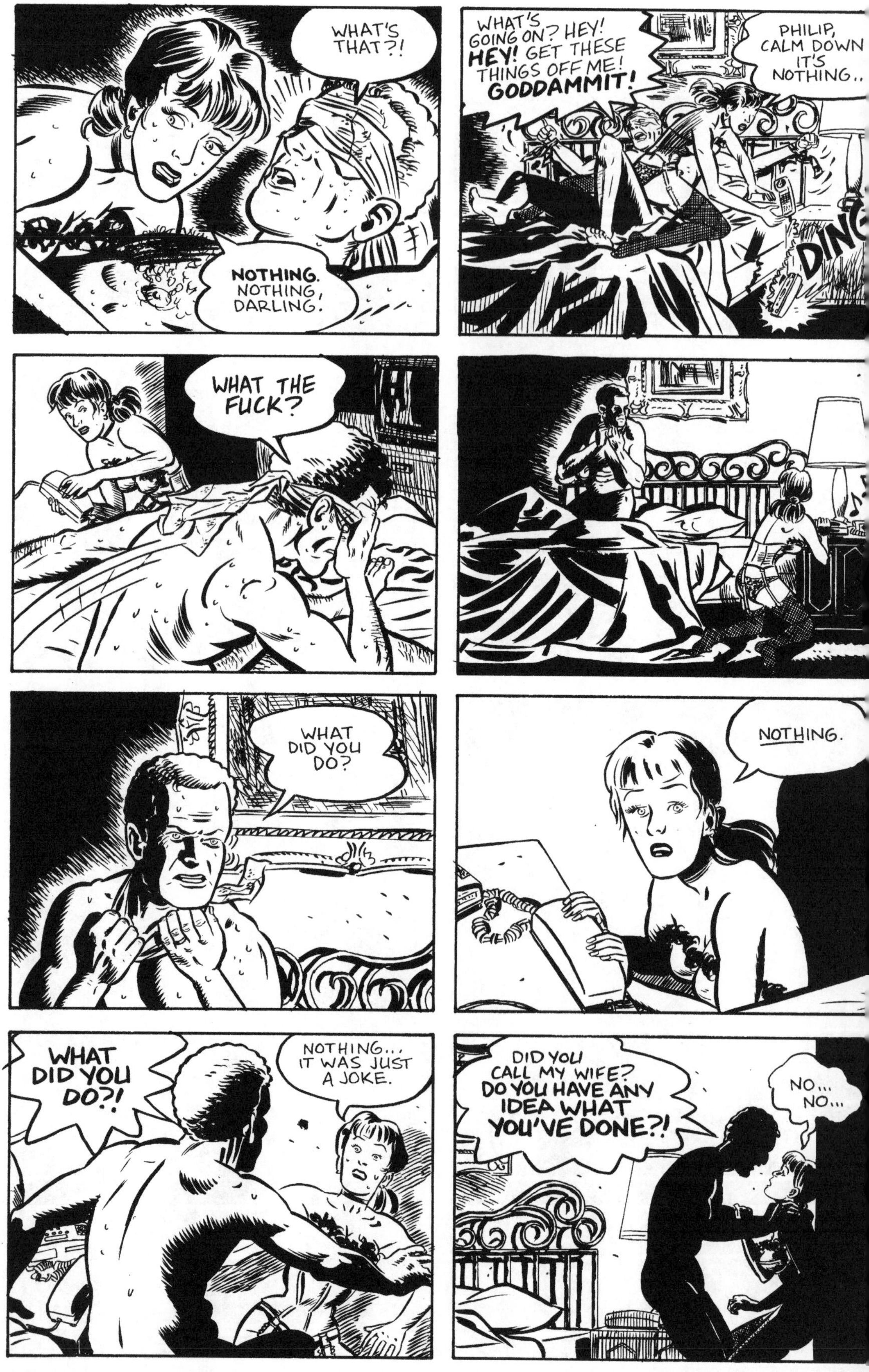

WHAT'S THAT?!
NOTHING. NOTHING, DARLING.
WHAT'S GOING ON? HEY! HEY! GET THESE THINGS OFF ME! GODDAMMIT!
PHILIP, CALM DOWN IT'S NOTHING..
WHAT THE FUCK?
WHAT DID YOU DO?
NOTHING.
WHAT DID YOU DO?!
NOTHING... IT WAS JUST A JOKE.
DID YOU CALL MY WIFE? DO YOU HAVE ANY IDEA WHAT YOU'VE DONE?!
NO... NO...

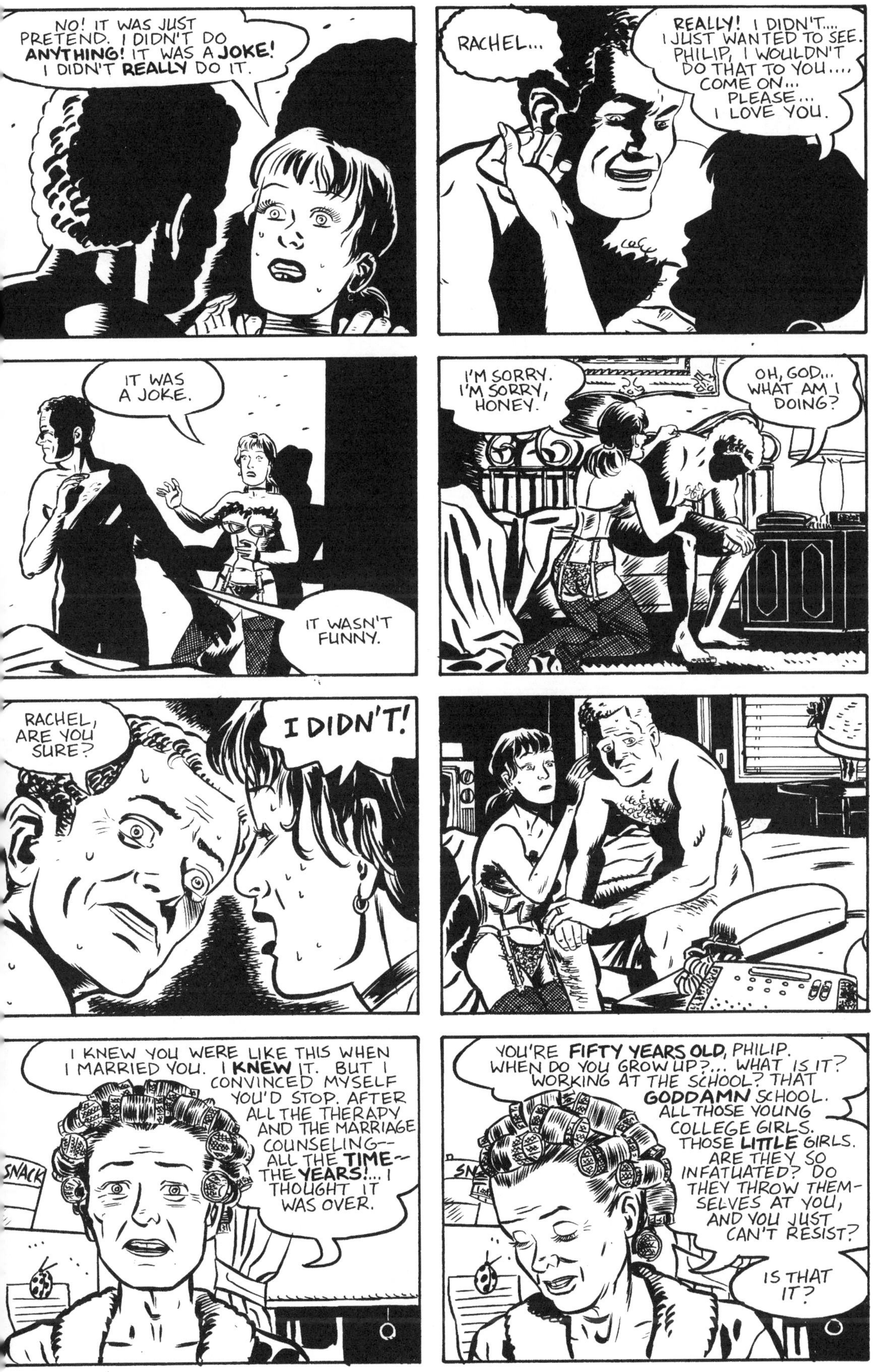
NO! IT WAS JUST PRETEND. I DIDN'T DO **ANYTHING!** IT WAS A **JOKE!** I DIDN'T **REALLY** DO IT.
RACHEL...
**REALLY!** I DIDN'T.... I JUST WANTED TO SEE. PHILIP, I WOULDN'T DO THAT TO YOU...., COME ON... PLEASE... I LOVE YOU.
IT WAS A JOKE.
IT WASN'T FUNNY.
I'M SORRY. I'M SORRY, HONEY.
OH, GOD... WHAT AM I DOING?
RACHEL, ARE YOU SURE?
I DIDN'T!
I KNEW YOU WERE LIKE THIS WHEN I MARRIED YOU. I **KNEW** IT. BUT I CONVINCED MYSELF YOU'D STOP. AFTER ALL THE THERAPY AND THE MARRIAGE COUNSELING-- ALL THE **TIME**-- THE **YEARS!**... I THOUGHT IT WAS OVER.
SNACK
YOU'RE **FIFTY YEARS OLD**, PHILIP. WHEN DO YOU GROW UP?... WHAT IS IT? WORKING AT THE SCHOOL? THAT **GODDAMN** SCHOOL. ALL THOSE YOUNG COLLEGE GIRLS. THOSE **LITTLE** GIRLS. ARE THEY SO INFATUATED? DO THEY THROW THEMSELVES AT YOU, AND YOU JUST CAN'T RESIST?
IS THAT IT?

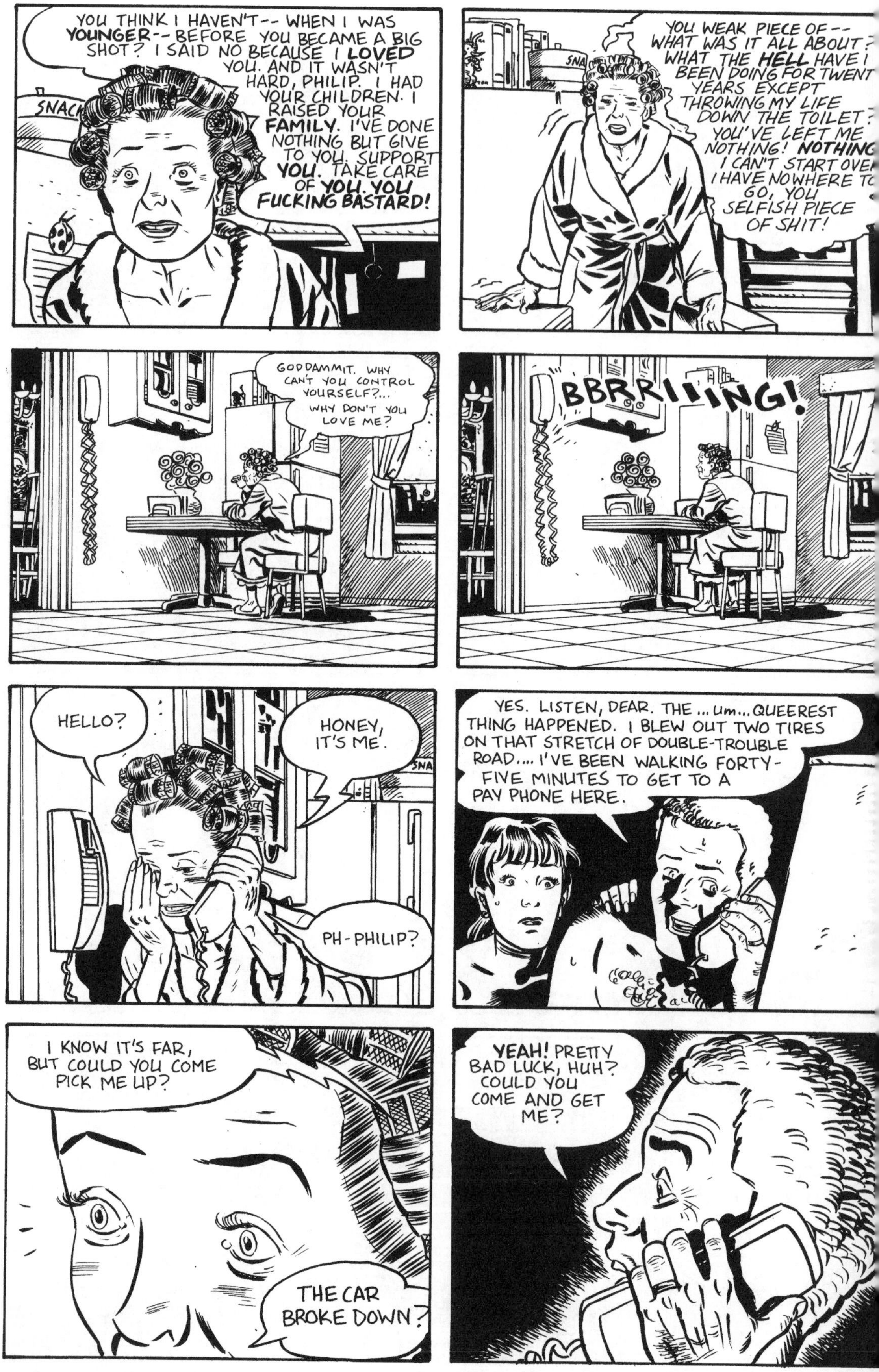

YOU THINK I HAVEN'T-- WHEN I WAS YOUNGER-- BEFORE YOU BECAME A BIG SHOT? I SAID NO BECAUSE I LOVED YOU. AND IT WASN'T HARD, PHILIP. I HAD YOUR CHILDREN. I RAISED YOUR FAMILY. I'VE DONE NOTHING BUT GIVE TO YOU. SUPPORT YOU. TAKE CARE OF YOU. YOU FUCKING BASTARD!
YOU WEAK PIECE OF-- WHAT WAS IT ALL ABOUT? WHAT THE HELL HAVE I BEEN DOING FOR TWENTY YEARS EXCEPT THROWING MY LIFE DOWN THE TOILET? YOU'VE LEFT ME NOTHING! NOTHING! I CAN'T START OVER! I HAVE NOWHERE TO GO, YOU SELFISH PIECE OF SHIT!
GODDAMMIT. WHY CAN'T YOU CONTROL YOURSELF?... WHY DON'T YOU LOVE ME?
BBRRIIING!
HELLO?
HONEY, IT'S ME.
PH-PHILIP?
YES. LISTEN, DEAR. THE ... um... QUEEREST THING HAPPENED. I BLEW OUT TWO TIRES ON THAT STRETCH OF DOUBLE-TROUBLE ROAD.... I'VE BEEN WALKING FORTY-FIVE MINUTES TO GET TO A PAY PHONE HERE.
I KNOW IT'S FAR, BUT COULD YOU COME PICK ME UP?
THE CAR BROKE DOWN?
YEAH! PRETTY BAD LUCK, HUH? COULD YOU COME AND GET ME?

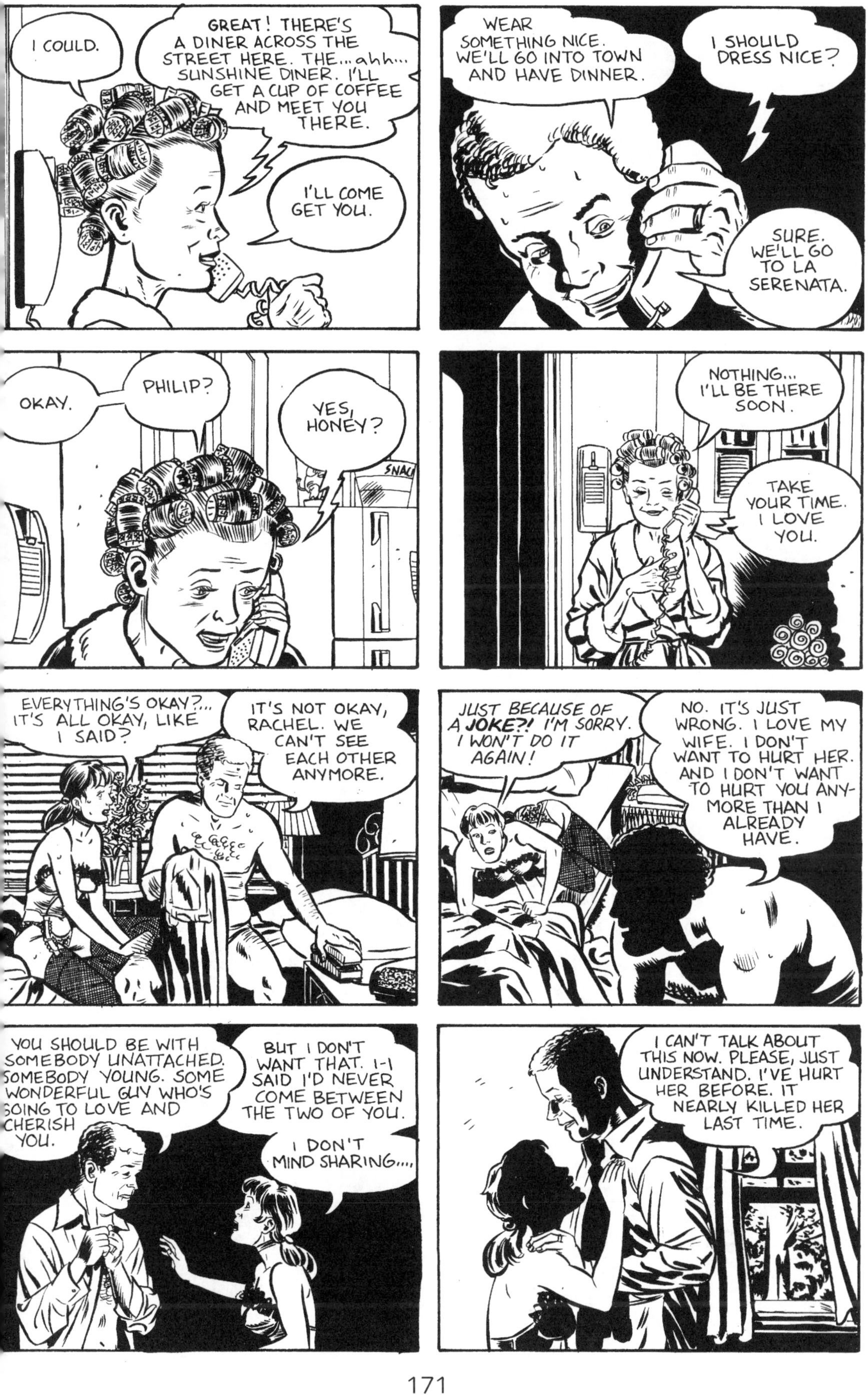
I COULD.
GREAT! THERE'S A DINER ACROSS THE STREET HERE. THE... ahh... SUNSHINE DINER. I'LL GET A CUP OF COFFEE AND MEET YOU THERE.
I'LL COME GET YOU.
WEAR SOMETHING NICE. WE'LL GO INTO TOWN AND HAVE DINNER.
I SHOULD DRESS NICE?
SURE. WE'LL GO TO LA SERENATA.
OKAY.
PHILIP?
YES, HONEY?
NOTHING... I'LL BE THERE SOON.
TAKE YOUR TIME. I LOVE YOU.
EVERYTHING'S OKAY?... IT'S ALL OKAY, LIKE I SAID?
IT'S NOT OKAY, RACHEL. WE CAN'T SEE EACH OTHER ANYMORE.
JUST BECAUSE OF A JOKE?! I'M SORRY. I WON'T DO IT AGAIN!
NO. IT'S JUST WRONG. I LOVE MY WIFE. I DON'T WANT TO HURT HER. AND I DON'T WANT TO HURT YOU ANY-MORE THAN I ALREADY HAVE.
YOU SHOULD BE WITH SOMEBODY UNATTACHED. SOMEBODY YOUNG. SOME WONDERFUL GUY WHO'S GOING TO LOVE AND CHERISH YOU.
BUT I DON'T WANT THAT. I-I SAID I'D NEVER COME BETWEEN THE TWO OF YOU.
I DON'T MIND SHARING....
I CAN'T TALK ABOUT THIS NOW. PLEASE, JUST UNDERSTAND. I'VE HURT HER BEFORE. IT NEARLY KILLED HER LAST TIME.

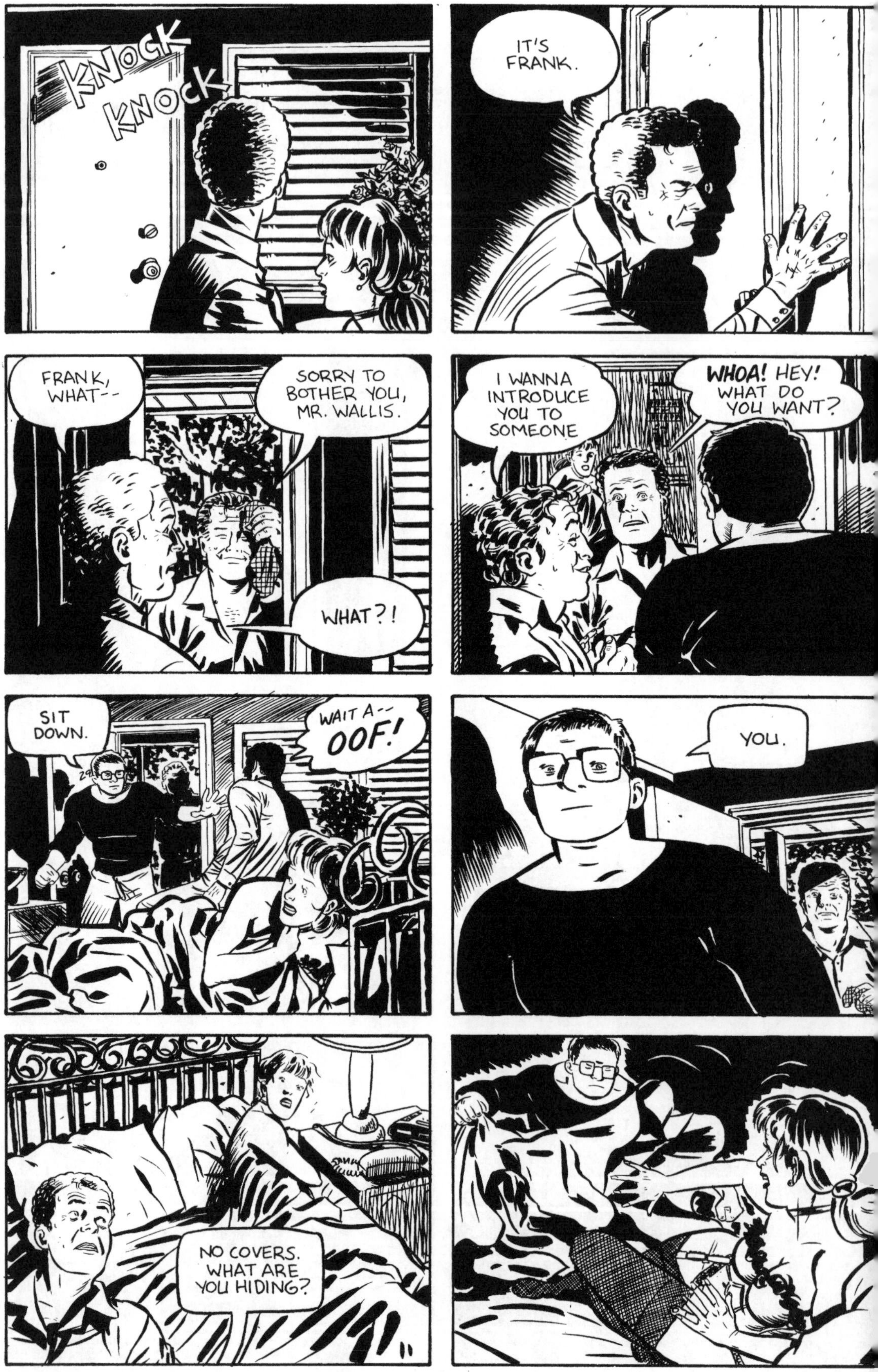
KNOCK KNOCK
IT'S FRANK.
FRANK, WHAT--
SORRY TO BOTHER YOU, MR. WALLIS.
WHAT?!
I WANNA INTRODUCE YOU TO SOMEONE
WHOA! HEY! WHAT DO YOU WANT?
SIT DOWN.
WAIT A-- OOF!
YOU.
NO COVERS. WHAT ARE YOU HIDING?

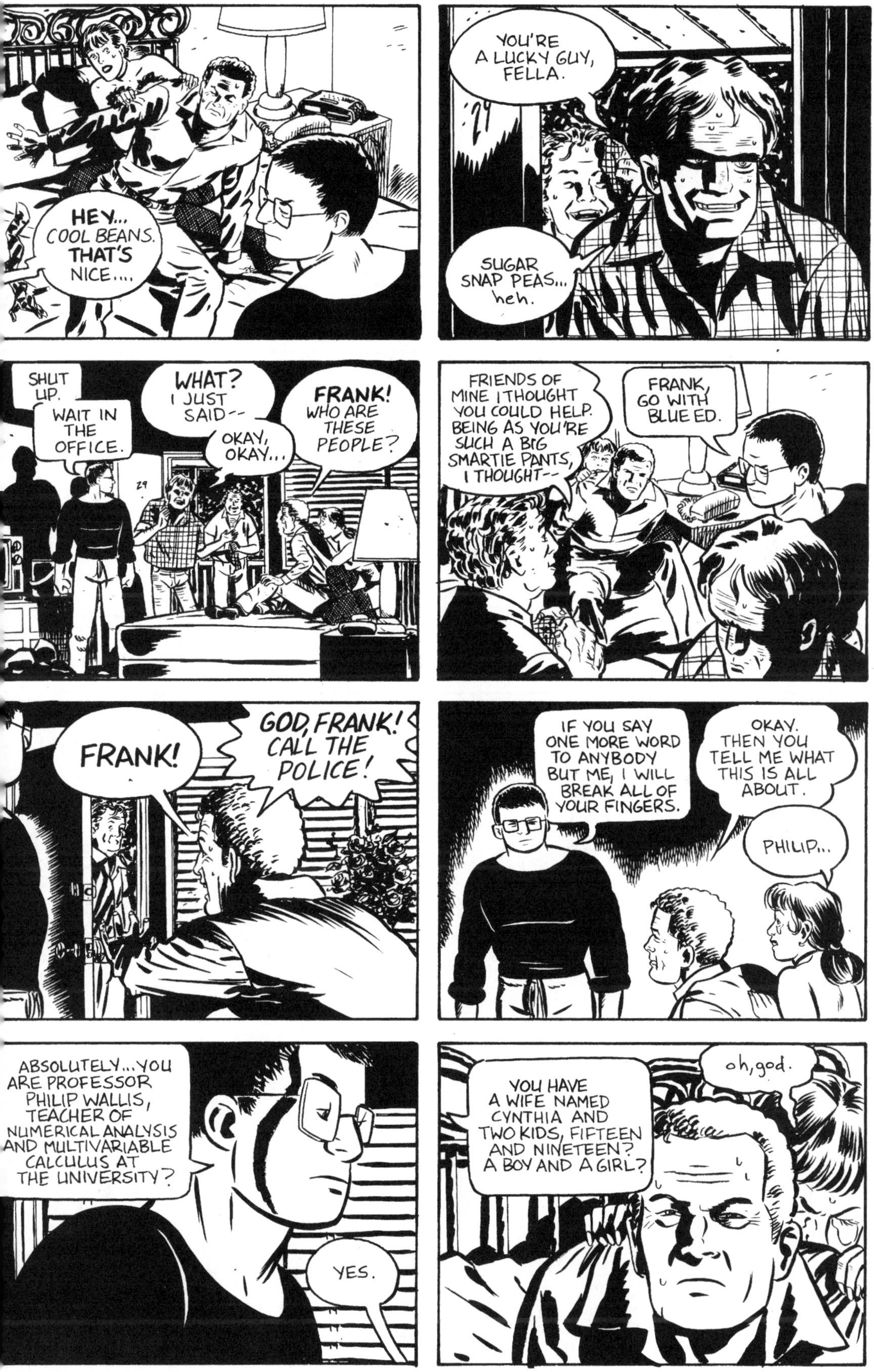
HEY... COOL BEANS. THAT'S NICE....
YOU'RE A LUCKY GUY, FELLA.
SUGAR SNAP PEAS... heh.
SHUT UP.
WAIT IN THE OFFICE.
WHAT? I JUST SAID--
OKAY, OKAY...
FRANK! WHO ARE THESE PEOPLE?
FRIENDS OF MINE I THOUGHT YOU COULD HELP. BEING AS YOU'RE SUCH A BIG SMARTIE PANTS, I THOUGHT--
FRANK, GO WITH BLUE ED.
FRANK!
GOD, FRANK! CALL THE POLICE!
IF YOU SAY ONE MORE WORD TO ANYBODY BUT ME, I WILL BREAK ALL OF YOUR FINGERS.
OKAY. THEN YOU TELL ME WHAT THIS IS ALL ABOUT.
PHILIP...
ABSOLUTELY... YOU ARE PROFESSOR PHILIP WALLIS, TEACHER OF NUMERICAL ANALYSIS AND MULTIVARIABLE CALCULUS AT THE UNIVERSITY?
YES.
YOU HAVE A WIFE NAMED CYNTHIA AND TWO KIDS, FIFTEEN AND NINETEEN? A BOY AND A GIRL?
oh, god.

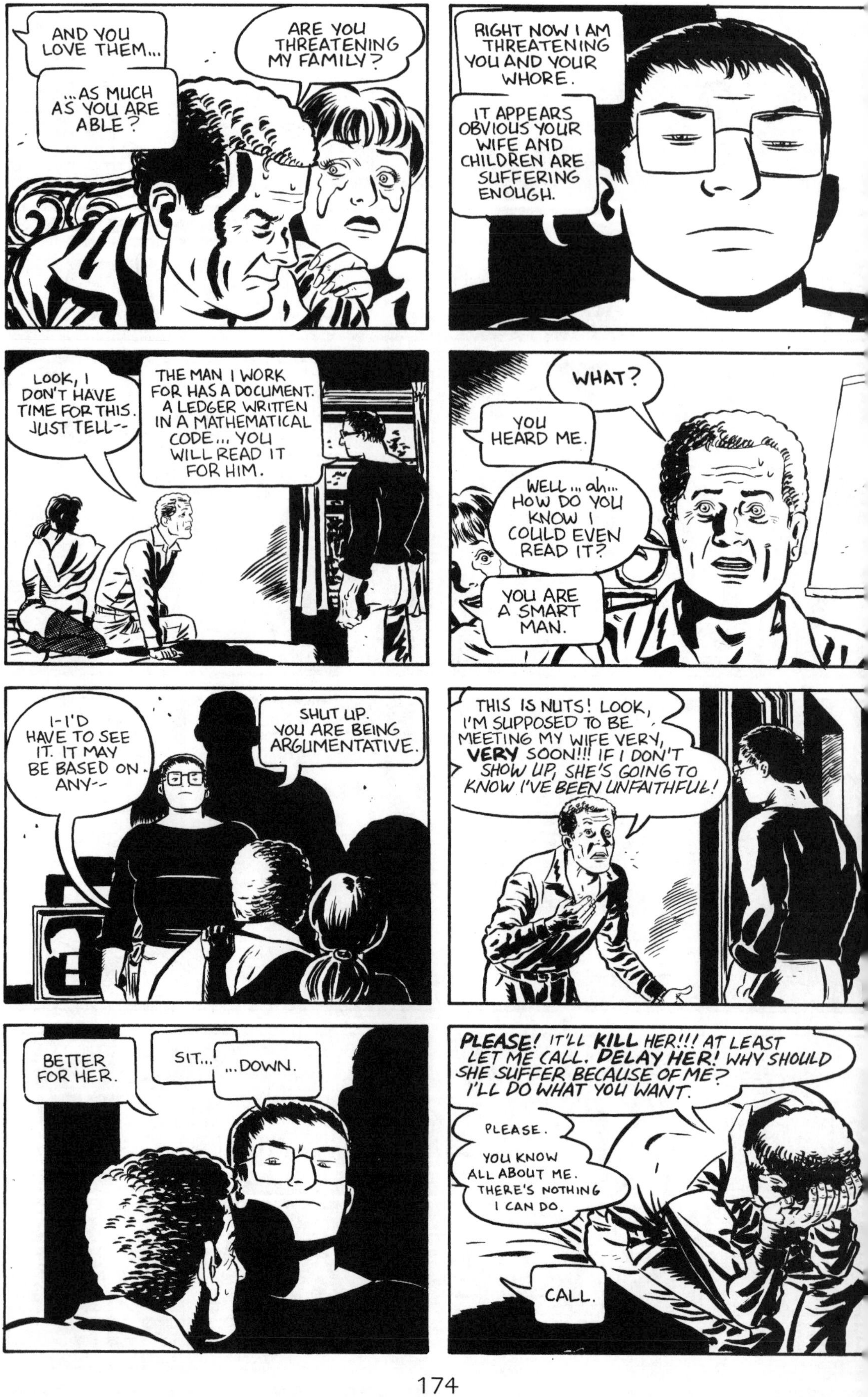
AND YOU LOVE THEM...
...AS MUCH AS YOU ARE ABLE?
ARE YOU THREATENING MY FAMILY?
RIGHT NOW I AM THREATENING YOU AND YOUR WHORE.
IT APPEARS OBVIOUS YOUR WIFE AND CHILDREN ARE SUFFERING ENOUGH.
LOOK, I DON'T HAVE TIME FOR THIS. JUST TELL--
THE MAN I WORK FOR HAS A DOCUMENT. A LEDGER WRITTEN IN A MATHEMATICAL CODE... YOU WILL READ IT FOR HIM.
WHAT?
YOU HEARD ME.
WELL... ah... HOW DO YOU KNOW I COULD EVEN READ IT?
YOU ARE A SMART MAN.
I-I'D HAVE TO SEE IT. IT MAY BE BASED ON ANY--
SHUT UP. YOU ARE BEING ARGUMENTATIVE.
THIS IS NUTS! LOOK, I'M SUPPOSED TO BE MEETING MY WIFE VERY, VERY SOON!!! IF I DON'T SHOW UP, SHE'S GOING TO KNOW I'VE BEEN UNFAITHFUL!
BETTER FOR HER.
SIT...
...DOWN.
PLEASE! IT'LL KILL HER!!! AT LEAST LET ME CALL. DELAY HER! WHY SHOULD SHE SUFFER BECAUSE OF ME? I'LL DO WHAT YOU WANT.
PLEASE.
YOU KNOW ALL ABOUT ME. THERE'S NOTHING I CAN DO.
CALL.

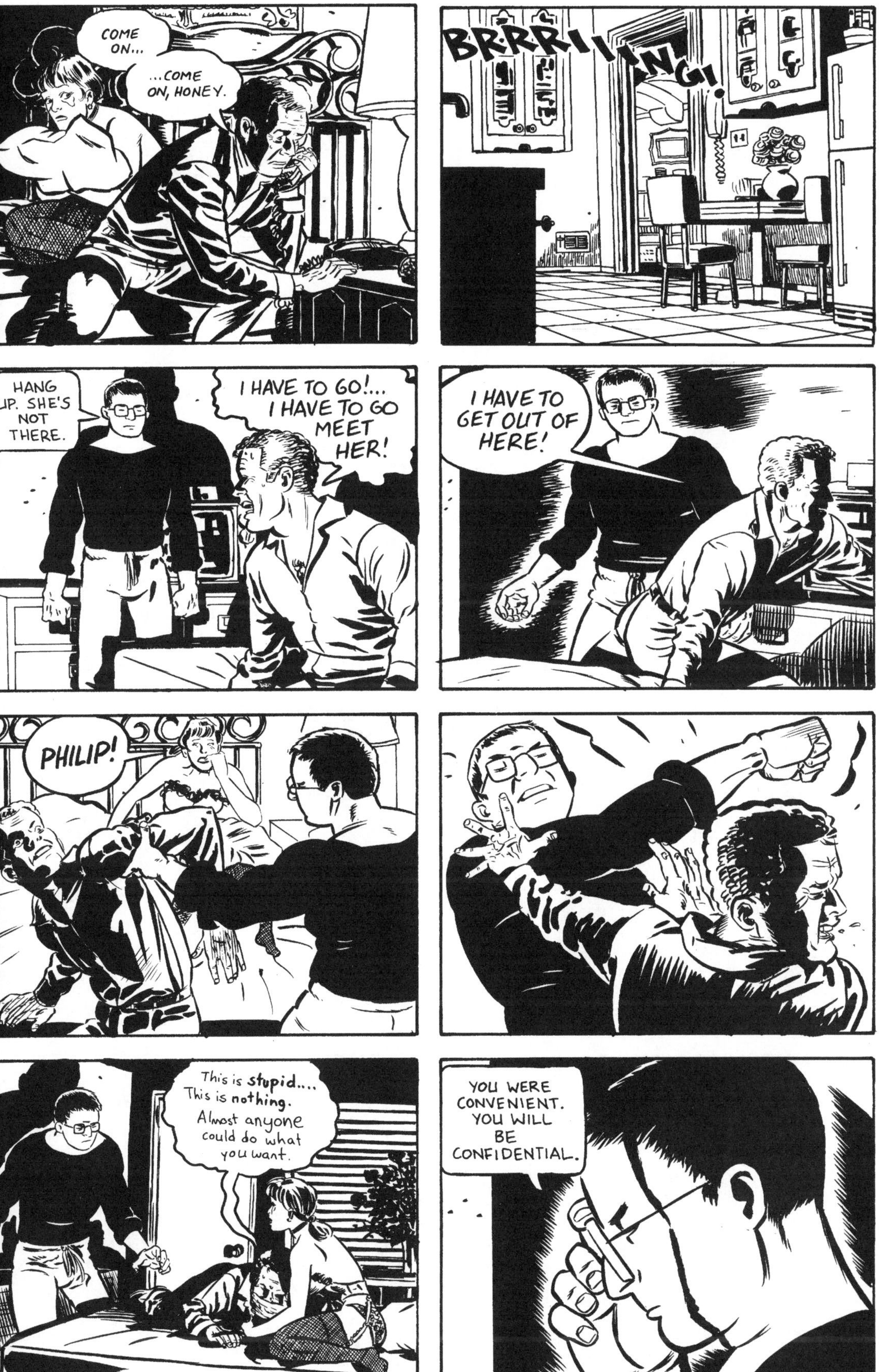
COME ON...
...COME ON, HONEY.
BRRRIIING!
HANG UP. SHE'S NOT THERE.
I HAVE TO GO!... I HAVE TO GO MEET HER!
I HAVE TO GET OUT OF HERE!
PHILIP!
This is stupid.... This is nothing. Almost anyone could do what you want.
YOU WERE CONVENIENT. YOU WILL BE CONFIDENTIAL.

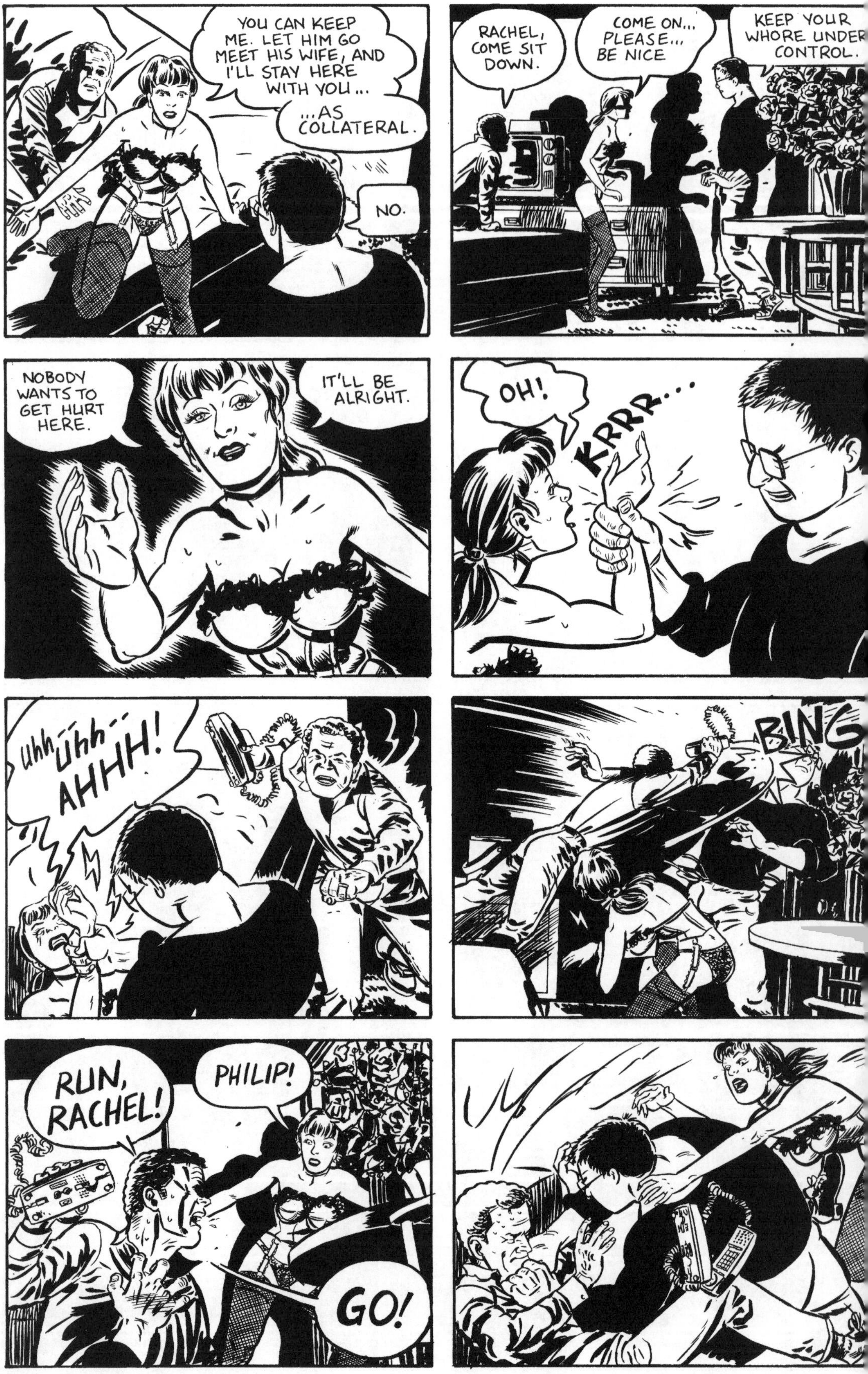
YOU CAN KEEP ME. LET HIM GO MEET HIS WIFE, AND I'LL STAY HERE WITH YOU...
...AS COLLATERAL.
NO.
RACHEL, COME SIT DOWN.
COME ON... PLEASE... BE NICE
KEEP YOUR WHORE UNDER CONTROL.
NOBODY WANTS TO GET HURT HERE.
IT'LL BE ALRIGHT.
OH!
KRRR...
uhh uhh AHHH!
BING
RUN, RACHEL!
PHILIP!
GO!

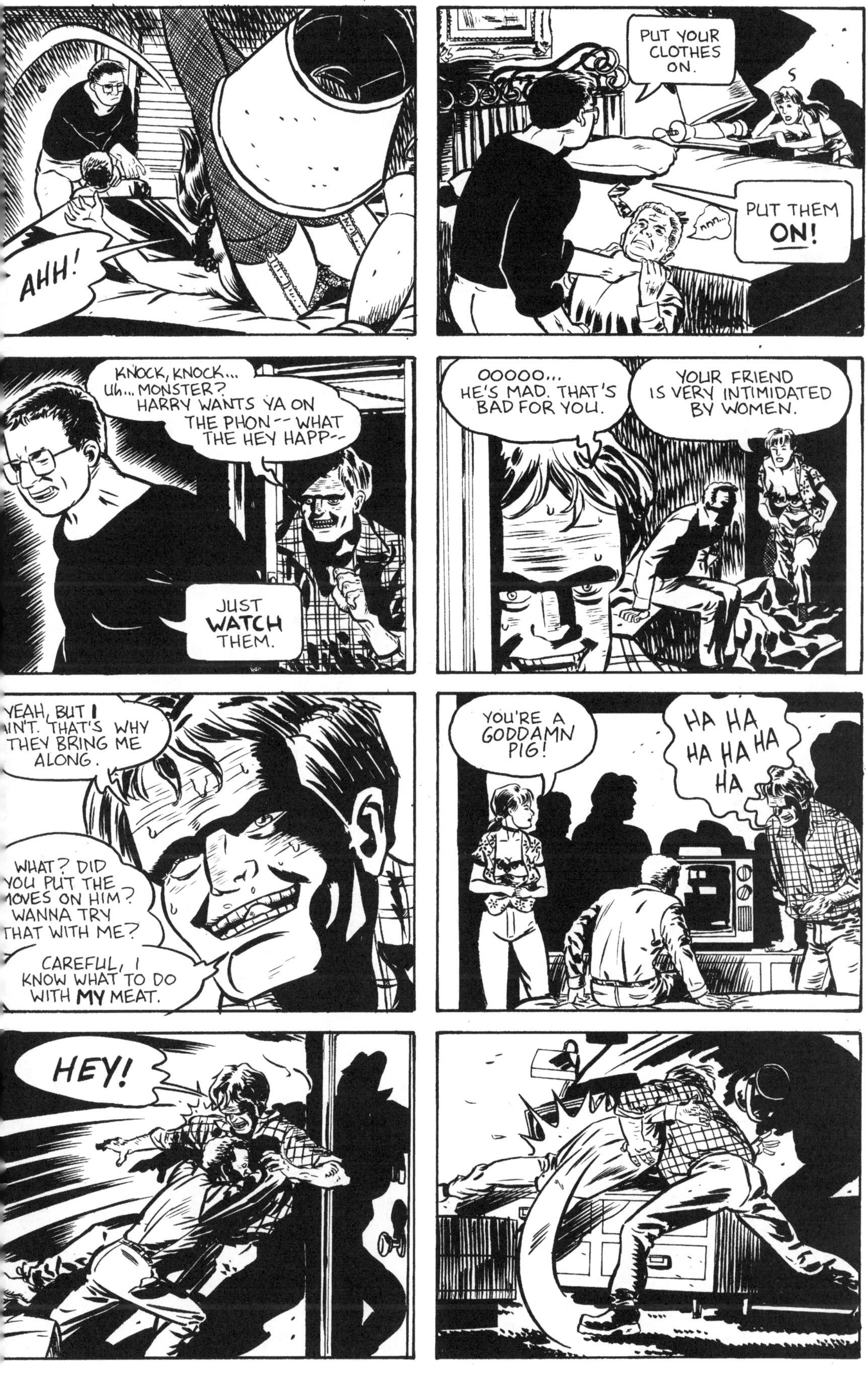
AHH!
PUT YOUR CLOTHES ON.
nnn...
PUT THEM ON!
KNOCK, KNOCK... Uh... MONSTER? HARRY WANTS YA ON THE PHON-- WHAT THE HEY HAPP--
JUST WATCH THEM.
OOOOO... HE'S MAD. THAT'S BAD FOR YOU.
YOUR FRIEND IS VERY INTIMIDATED BY WOMEN.
YEAH, BUT I AIN'T. THAT'S WHY THEY BRING ME ALONG.
WHAT? DID YOU PUT THE MOVES ON HIM? WANNA TRY THAT WITH ME?
CAREFUL, I KNOW WHAT TO DO WITH MY MEAT.
YOU'RE A GODDAMN PIG!
HA HA HA HA HA HA
HEY!

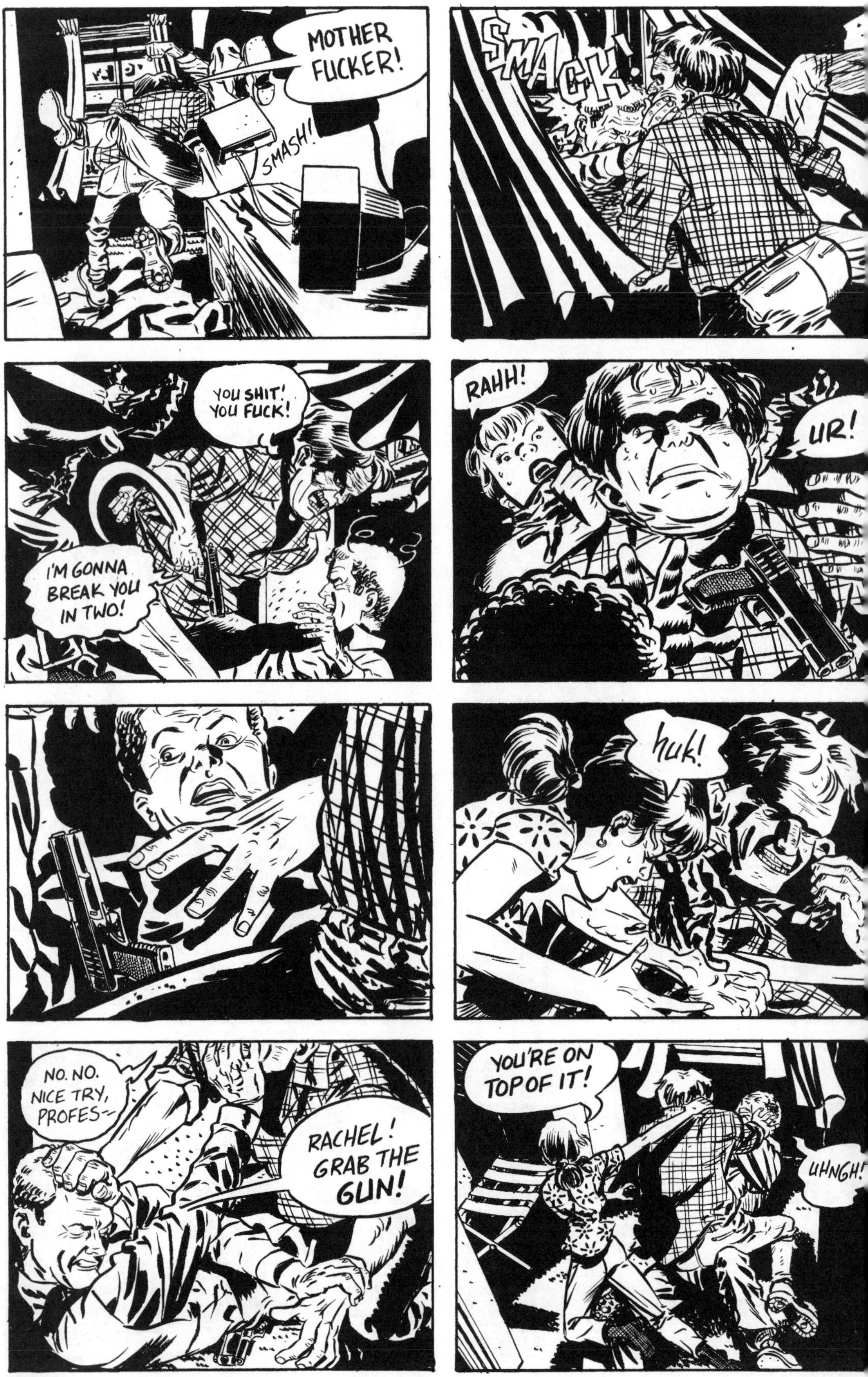
MOTHER FUCKER!
SMASH!
SMACK!
YOU SHIT! YOU FUCK!
I'M GONNA BREAK YOU IN TWO!
RAHH!
UR!
huk!
NO. NO. NICE TRY, PROFES--
RACHEL! GRAB THE GUN!
YOU'RE ON TOP OF IT!
UHNGH!

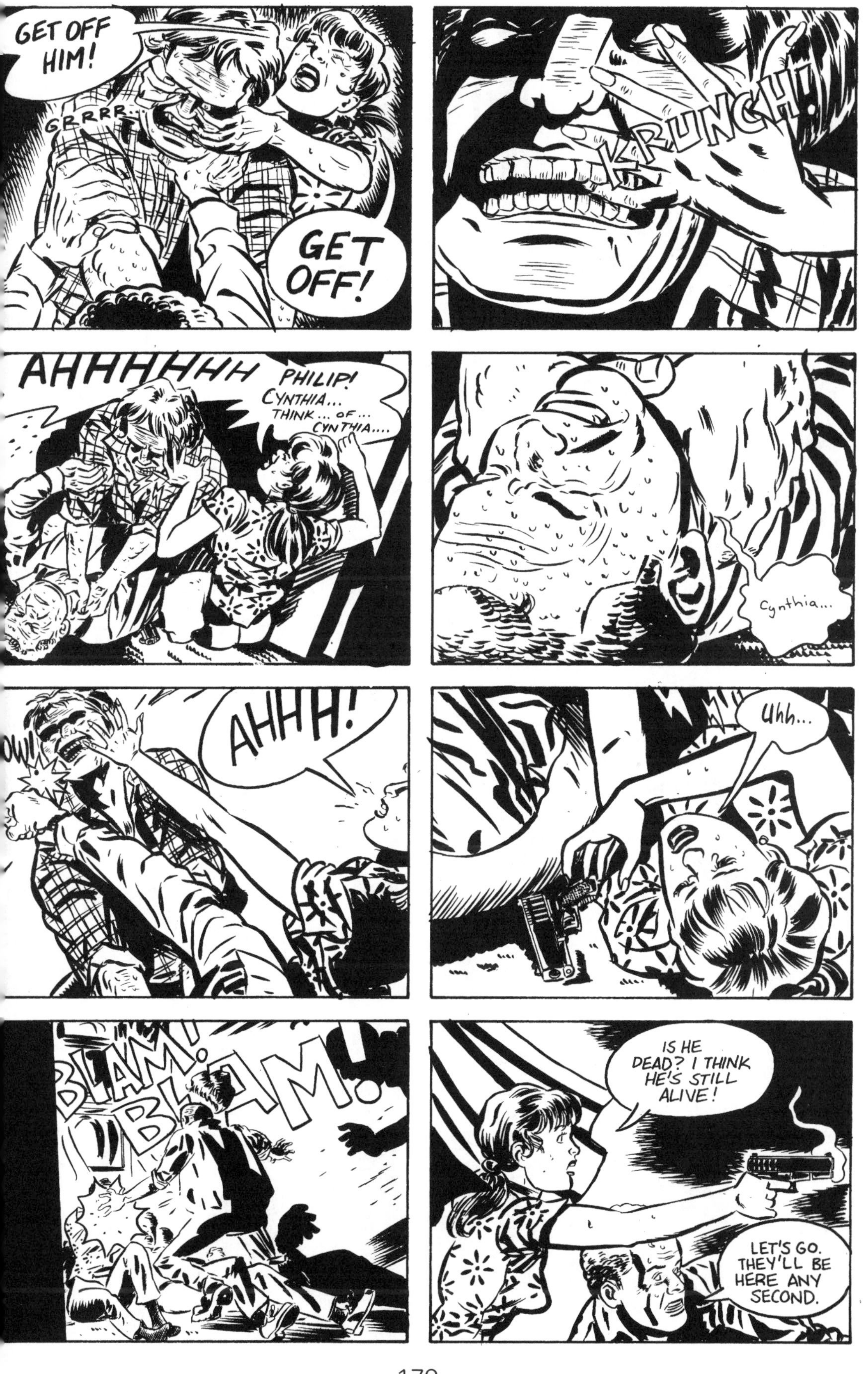
GET OFF HIM!
GRRRR
GET OFF!
KRUNCH!
AHHHHHH
PHILIP! CYNTHIA... THINK... OF... CYNTHIA....
Cynthia...
OW!
AHHH!
Uhh...
BLAM! BLAM!
IS HE DEAD? I THINK HE'S STILL ALIVE!
LET'S GO. THEY'LL BE HERE ANY SECOND.

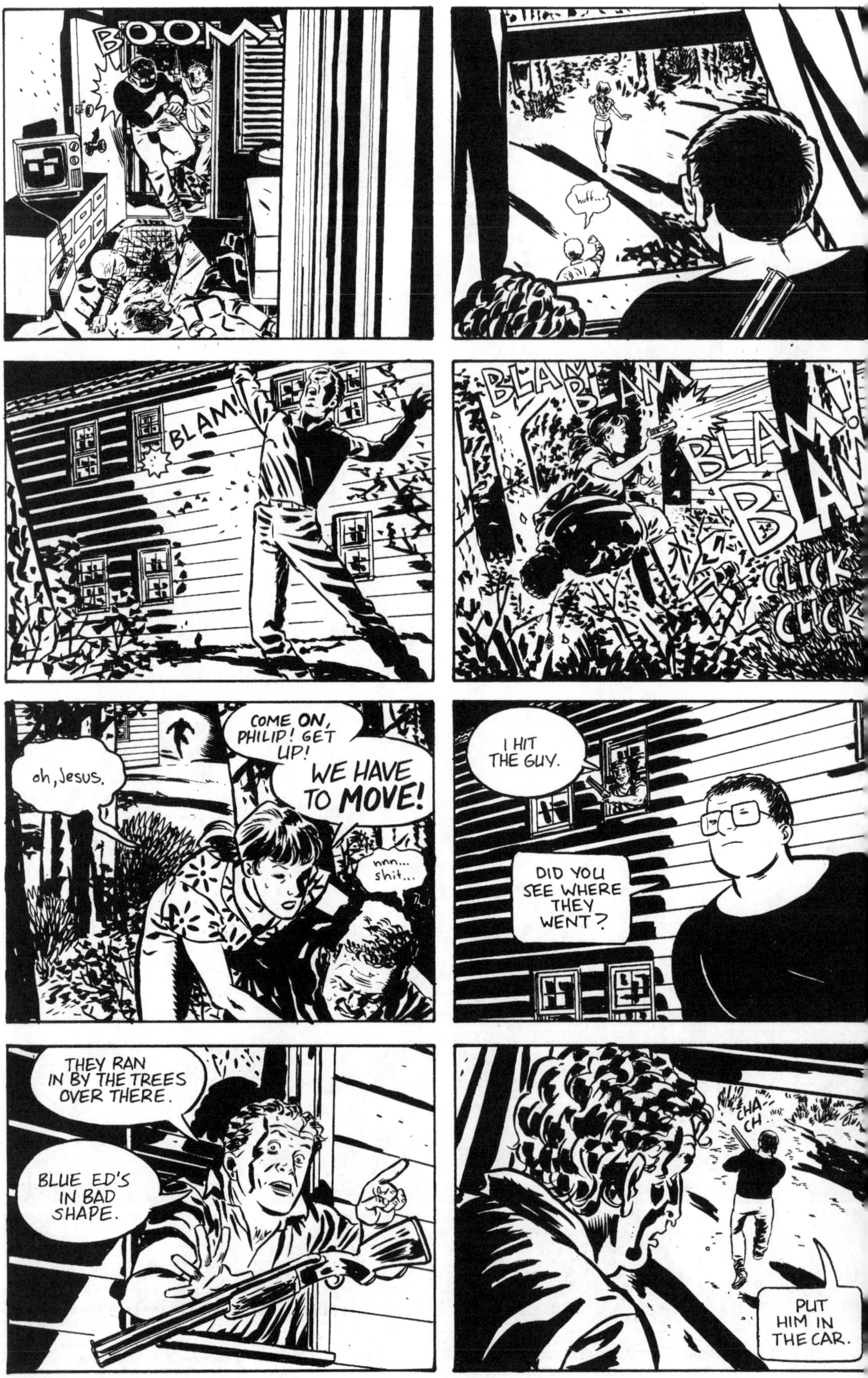
BOOM!
huff...
BLAM!
BLAM BLAM
BLAM!
BLAM!
BLAM
CLICK
CLICK
oh, Jesus.
COME ON, PHILIP! GET UP!
WE HAVE TO MOVE!
nnn... shit...
I HIT THE GUY.
DID YOU SEE WHERE THEY WENT?
THEY RAN IN BY THE TREES OVER THERE.
BLUE ED'S IN BAD SHAPE.
CHA CH
PUT HIM IN THE CAR.

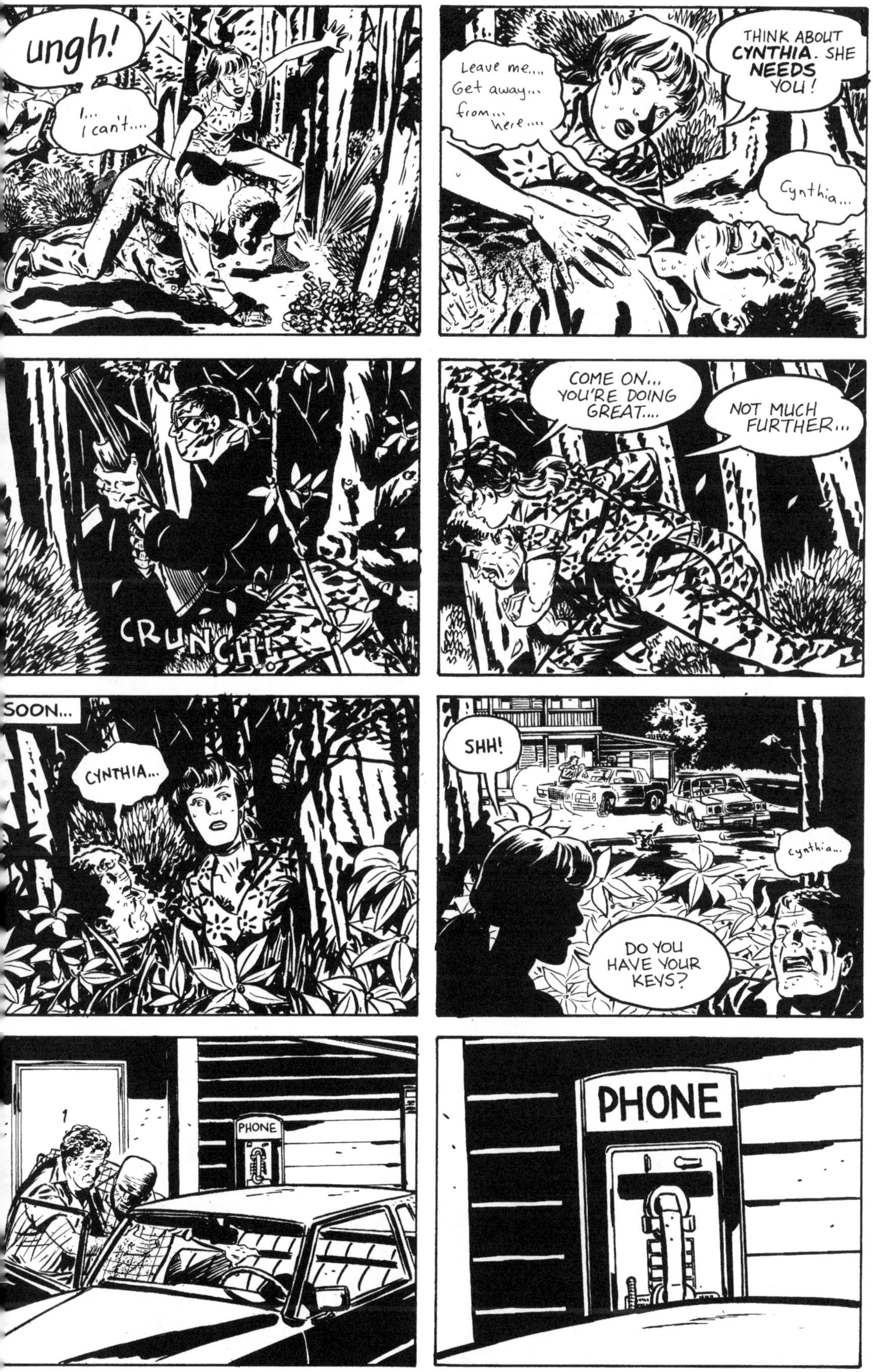

ungh!
I... I can't....
Leave me.... Get away... from... here....
THINK ABOUT CYNTHIA. SHE NEEDS YOU!
Cynthia...
CRUNCH!
COME ON... YOU'RE DOING GREAT....
NOT MUCH FURTHER...
SOON...
CYNTHIA...
SHH!
cynthia...
DO YOU HAVE YOUR KEYS?
PHONE
PHONE

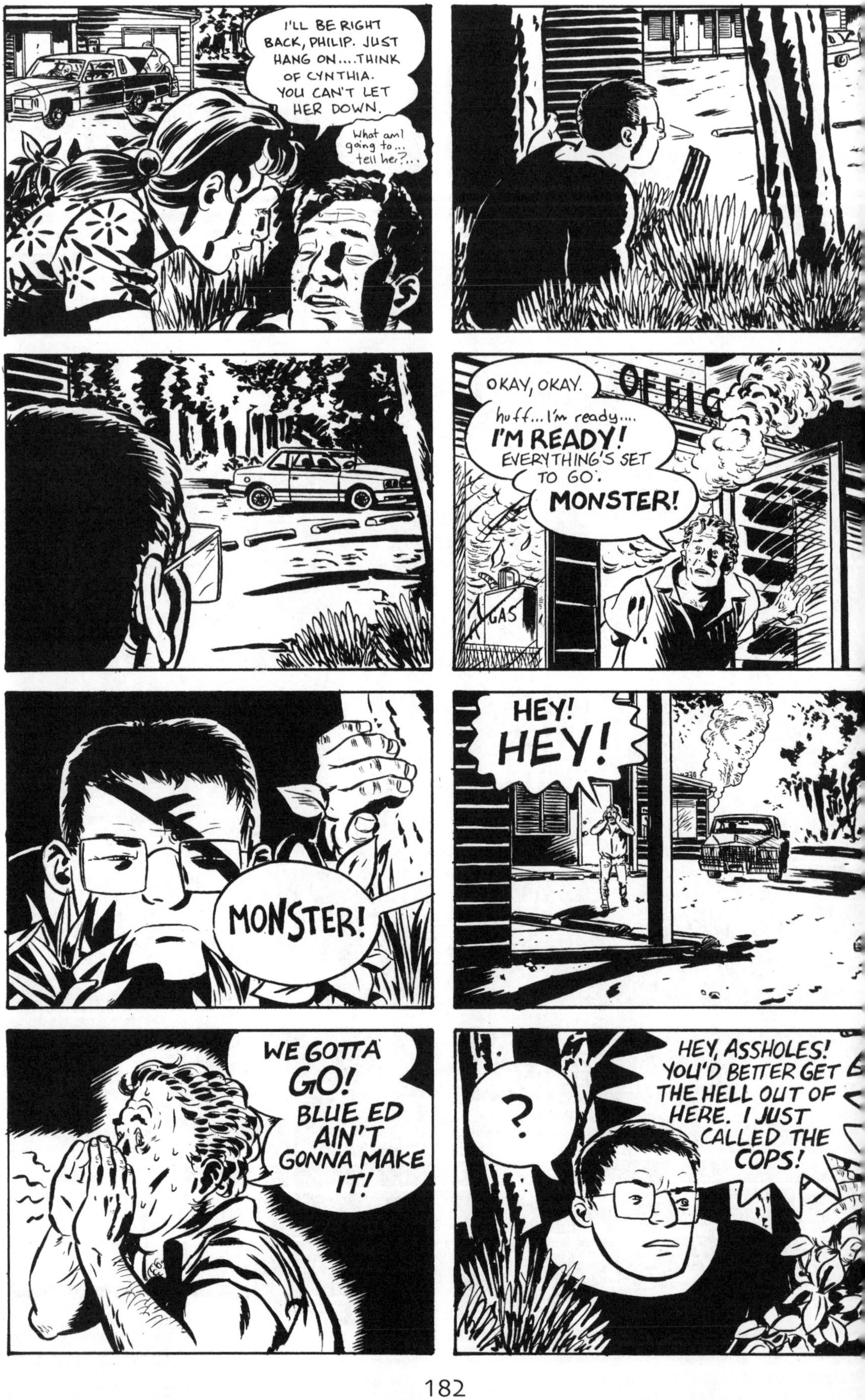
I'LL BE RIGHT BACK, PHILIP. JUST HANG ON....THINK OF CYNTHIA. YOU CAN'T LET HER DOWN.
What am I going to... tell her?...
OKAY, OKAY.
huff... I'm ready.... I'M READY! EVERYTHING'S SET TO GO.
MONSTER!
MONSTER!
HEY! HEY!
WE GOTTA GO! BLUE ED AIN'T GONNA MAKE IT!
?
HEY, ASSHOLES! YOU'D BETTER GET THE HELL OUT OF HERE. I JUST CALLED THE COPS!

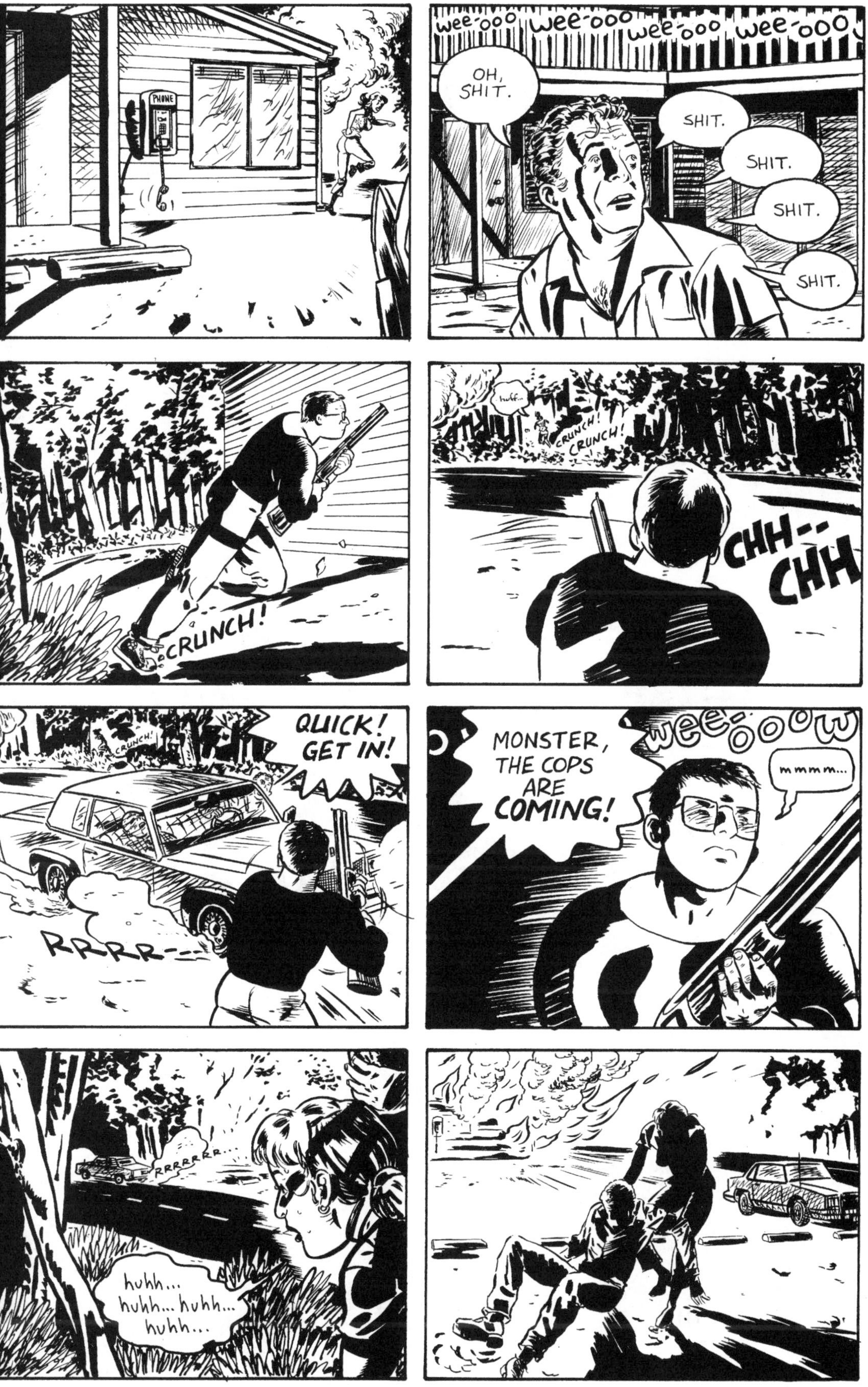
PHONE
wee-ooo wee-ooo wee-ooo wee-ooo
OH, SHIT.
SHIT.
SHIT.
SHIT.
SHIT.
CRUNCH!
huff...
CRUNCH! CRUNCH!
CHH-- CHH
CRUNCH!
QUICK! GET IN!
RRRR---
MONSTER, THE COPS ARE COMING!
wee-ooow
mmmm...
RRRRRRR...
huhh... huhh... huhh... huhh...

VROOM!
RRRRRR
What am I going to tell her?... What am I going to tell her?...
SHHHHH... DON'T SPEAK. JUST HANG ON. IT'LL BE OKAY.
IT'S GONNA BE OKAY.
MOTEL
wee-ooo wee-ooo wee-ooo
wee-ooo wee-ooo
POLICE



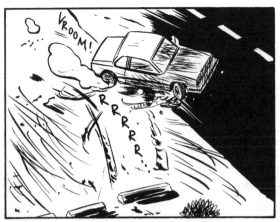

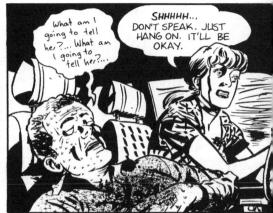

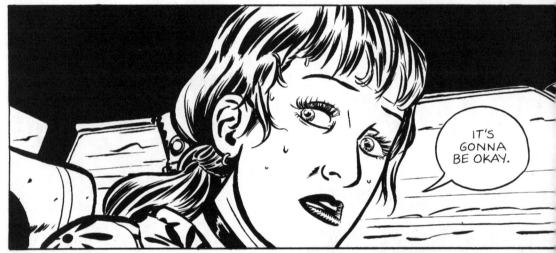

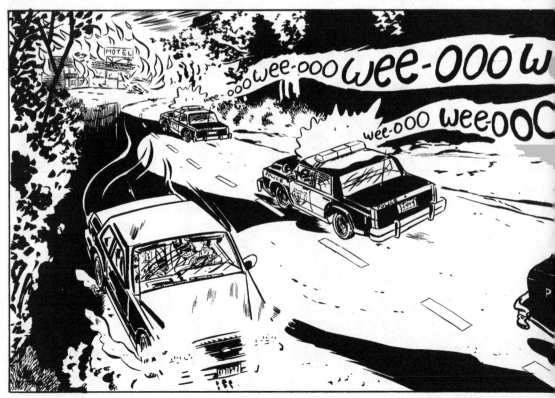

THE END.

# 7

## "LITTLE LOVE TRAGEDY"

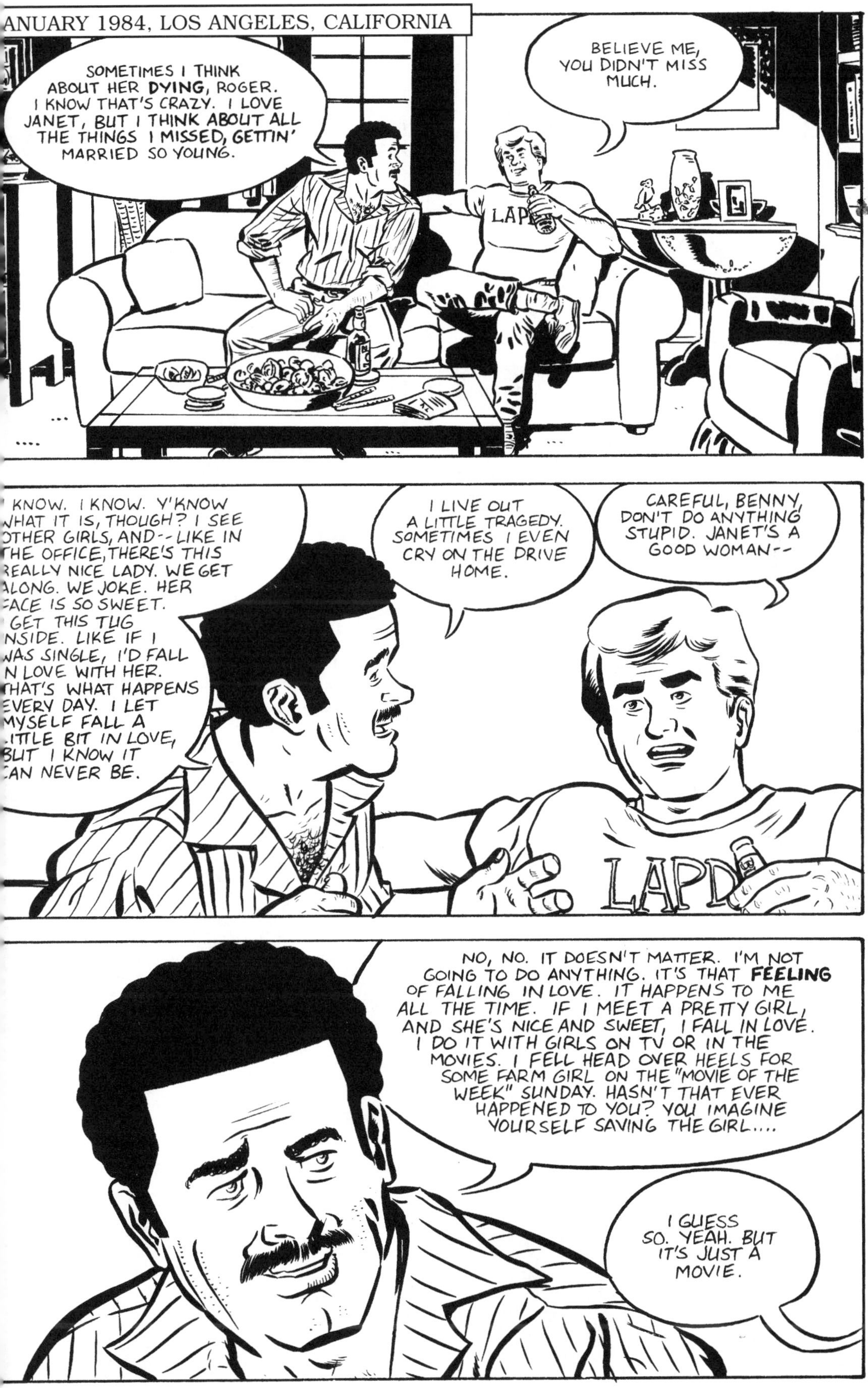
ANUARY 1984, LOS ANGELES, CALIFORNIA
SOMETIMES I THINK ABOUT HER **DYING**, ROGER. I KNOW THAT'S CRAZY. I LOVE JANET, BUT I THINK ABOUT ALL THE THINGS I MISSED, GETTIN' MARRIED SO YOUNG.
BELIEVE ME, YOU DIDN'T MISS MUCH.
LAPD
I KNOW. I KNOW. Y'KNOW WHAT IT IS, THOUGH? I SEE OTHER GIRLS, AND--LIKE IN THE OFFICE, THERE'S THIS REALLY NICE LADY. WE GET ALONG. WE JOKE. HER FACE IS SO SWEET. I GET THIS TUG INSIDE. LIKE IF I WAS SINGLE, I'D FALL IN LOVE WITH HER. THAT'S WHAT HAPPENS EVERY DAY. I LET MYSELF FALL A LITTLE BIT IN LOVE, BUT I KNOW IT CAN NEVER BE.
I LIVE OUT A LITTLE TRAGEDY. SOMETIMES I EVEN CRY ON THE DRIVE HOME.
CAREFUL, BENNY, DON'T DO ANYTHING STUPID. JANET'S A GOOD WOMAN--
LAPD
NO, NO. IT DOESN'T MATTER. I'M NOT GOING TO DO ANYTHING. IT'S THAT **FEELING** OF FALLING IN LOVE. IT HAPPENS TO ME ALL THE TIME. IF I MEET A PRETTY GIRL, AND SHE'S NICE AND SWEET, I FALL IN LOVE. I DO IT WITH GIRLS ON TV OR IN THE MOVIES. I FELL HEAD OVER HEELS FOR SOME FARM GIRL ON THE "MOVIE OF THE WEEK" SUNDAY. HASN'T THAT EVER HAPPENED TO YOU? YOU IMAGINE YOURSELF SAVING THE GIRL....
I GUESS SO. YEAH. BUT IT'S JUST A MOVIE.

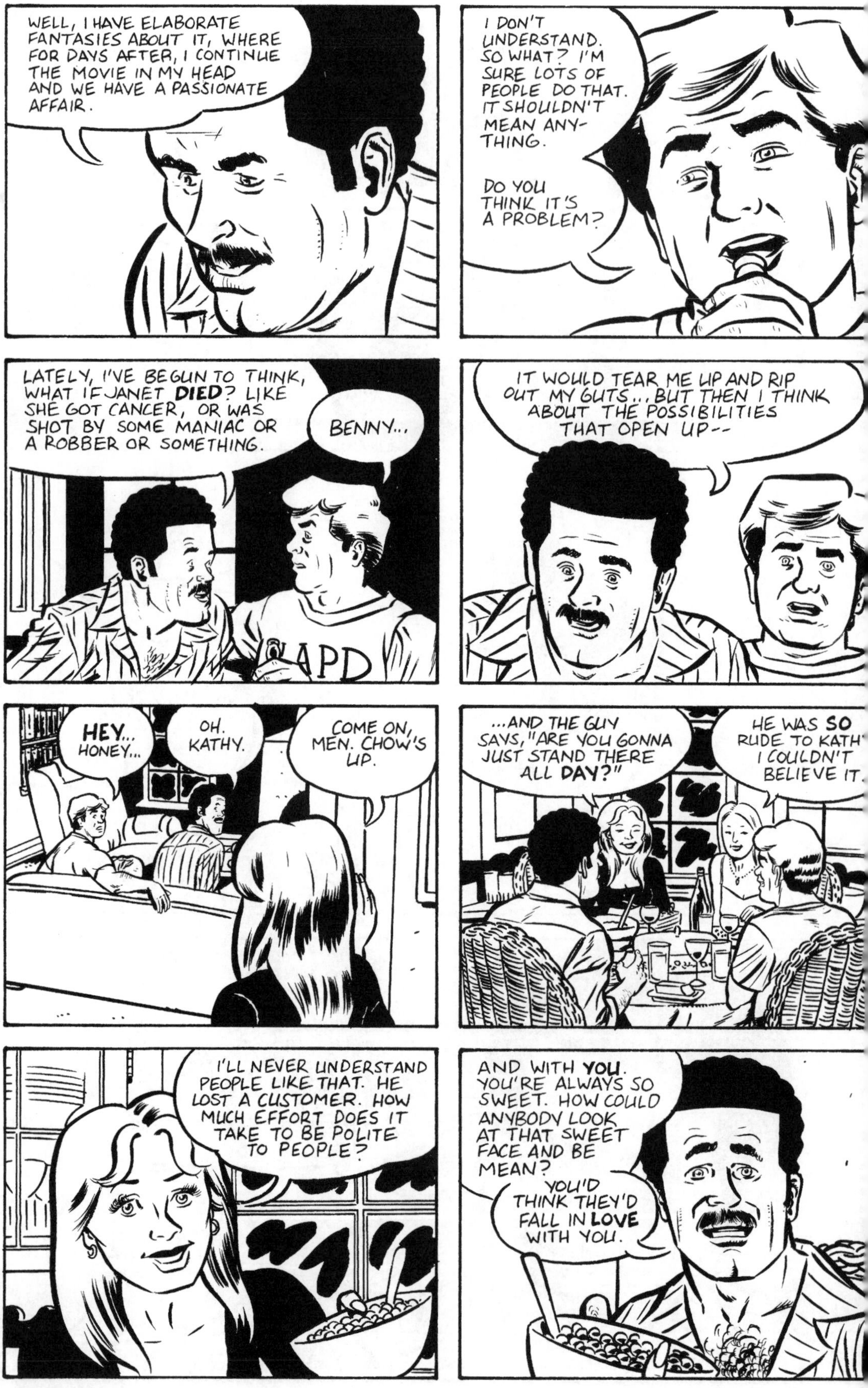
WELL, I HAVE ELABORATE FANTASIES ABOUT IT, WHERE FOR DAYS AFTER, I CONTINUE THE MOVIE IN MY HEAD AND WE HAVE A PASSIONATE AFFAIR.
I DON'T UNDERSTAND. SO WHAT? I'M SURE LOTS OF PEOPLE DO THAT. IT SHOULDN'T MEAN ANY-THING.
DO YOU THINK IT'S A PROBLEM?
LATELY, I'VE BEGUN TO THINK, WHAT IF JANET **DIED**? LIKE SHE GOT CANCER, OR WAS SHOT BY SOME MANIAC OR A ROBBER OR SOMETHING.
BENNY...
APD
IT WOULD TEAR ME UP AND RIP OUT MY GUTS... BUT THEN I THINK ABOUT THE POSSIBILITIES THAT OPEN UP--
**HEY**... HONEY...
OH. KATHY.
COME ON, MEN. CHOW'S UP.
...AND THE GUY SAYS, "ARE YOU GONNA JUST STAND THERE ALL **DAY**?"
HE WAS **SO** RUDE TO KATH I COULDN'T BELIEVE IT.
I'LL NEVER UNDERSTAND PEOPLE LIKE THAT. HE LOST A CUSTOMER. HOW MUCH EFFORT DOES IT TAKE TO BE POLITE TO PEOPLE?
AND WITH **YOU**. YOU'RE ALWAYS SO SWEET. HOW COULD ANYBODY LOOK AT THAT SWEET FACE AND BE MEAN?
YOU'D THINK THEY'D FALL IN **LOVE** WITH YOU.

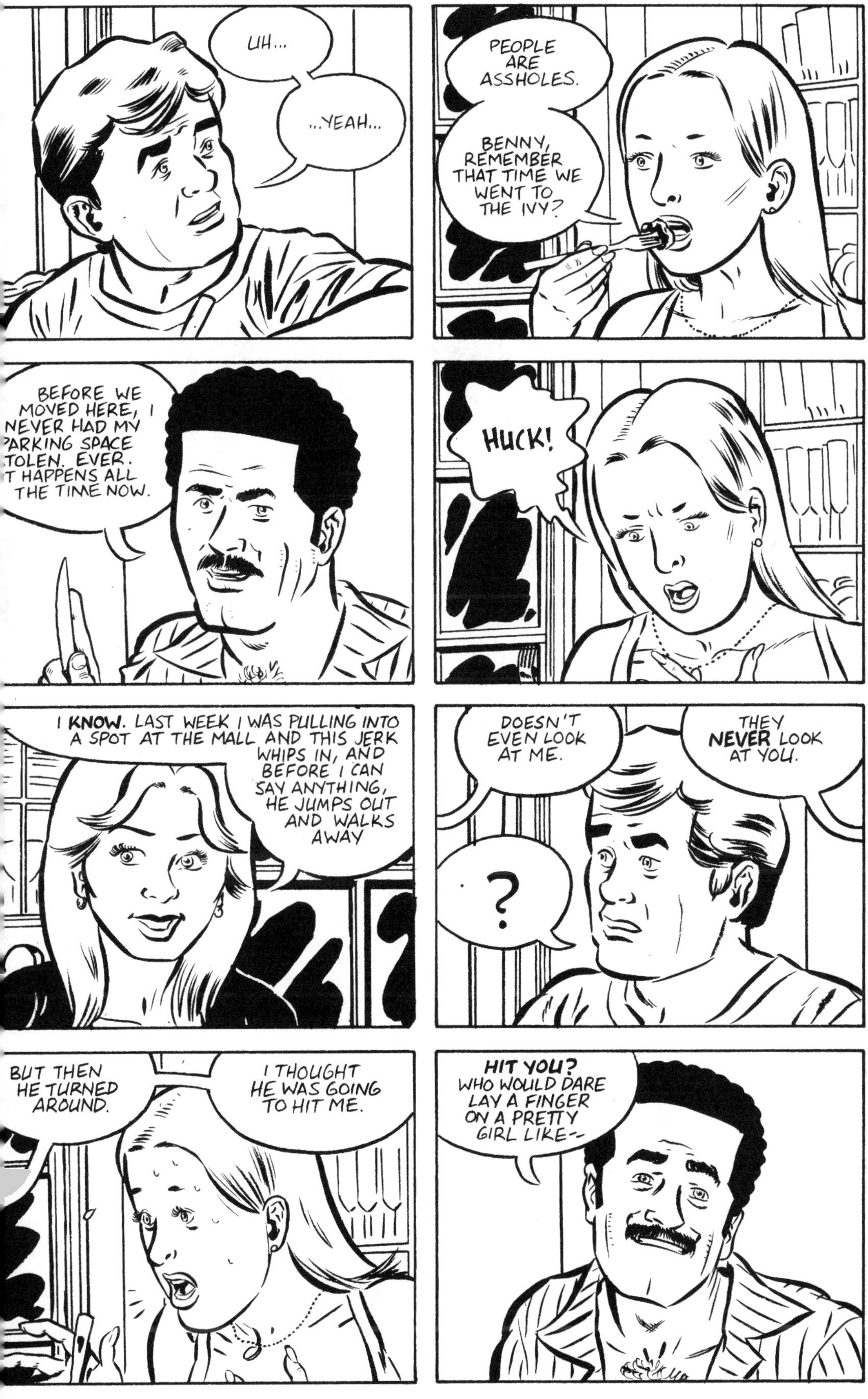
UH...
...YEAH...
PEOPLE ARE ASSHOLES.
BENNY, REMEMBER THAT TIME WE WENT TO THE IVY?
BEFORE WE MOVED HERE, I NEVER HAD MY PARKING SPACE STOLEN. EVER. IT HAPPENS ALL THE TIME NOW.
HUCK!
I **KNOW.** LAST WEEK I WAS PULLING INTO A SPOT AT THE MALL AND THIS JERK WHIPS IN, AND BEFORE I CAN SAY ANYTHING, HE JUMPS OUT AND WALKS AWAY
DOESN'T EVEN LOOK AT ME.
THEY **NEVER** LOOK AT YOU.
?
BUT THEN HE TURNED AROUND.
I THOUGHT HE WAS GOING TO HIT ME.
**HIT YOU?** WHO WOULD DARE LAY A FINGER ON A PRETTY GIRL LIKE--

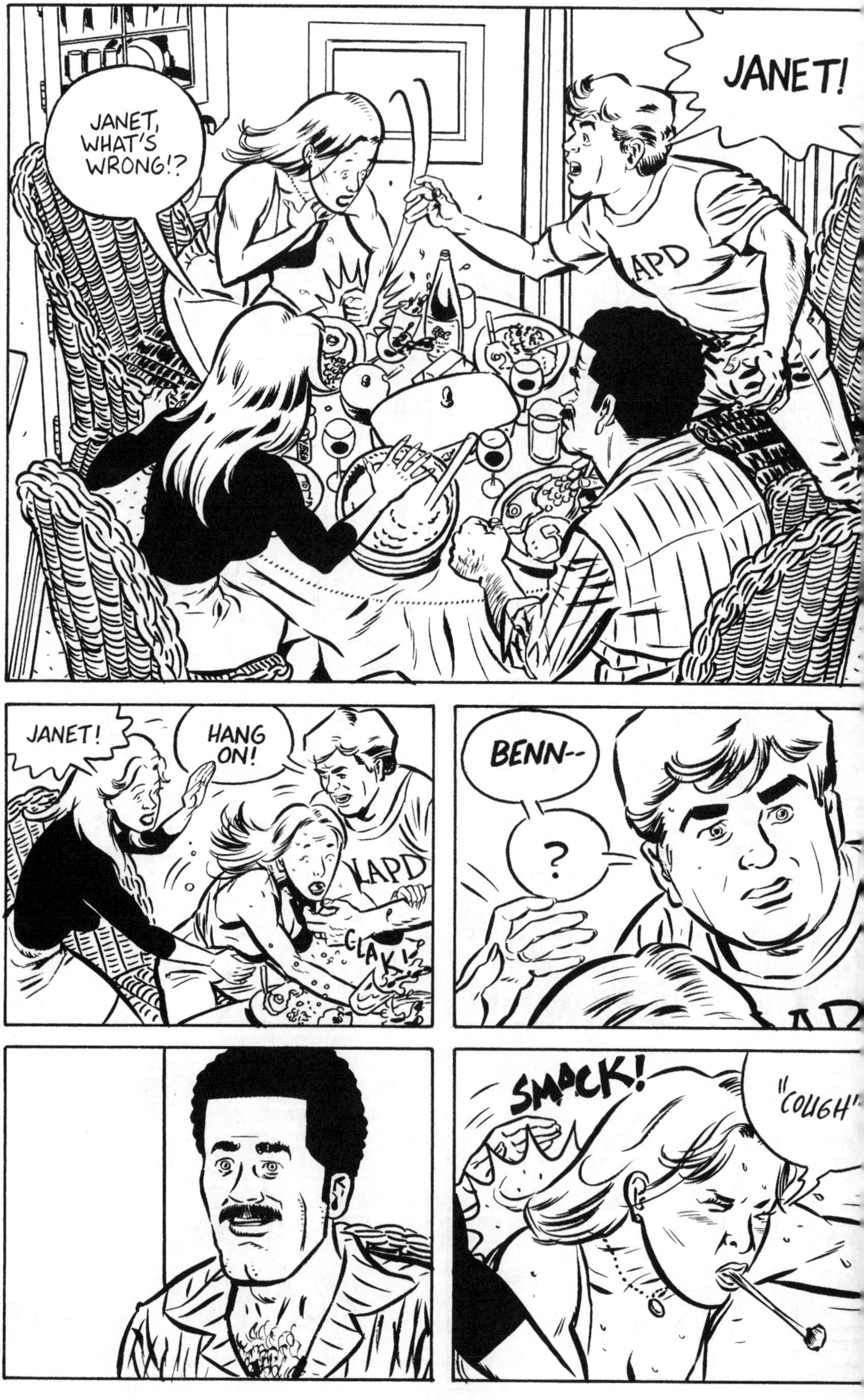
JANET, WHAT'S WRONG!?
JANET!
JANET!
HANG ON!
CLAK!
BENN--
?
SMACK!
"COUGH"

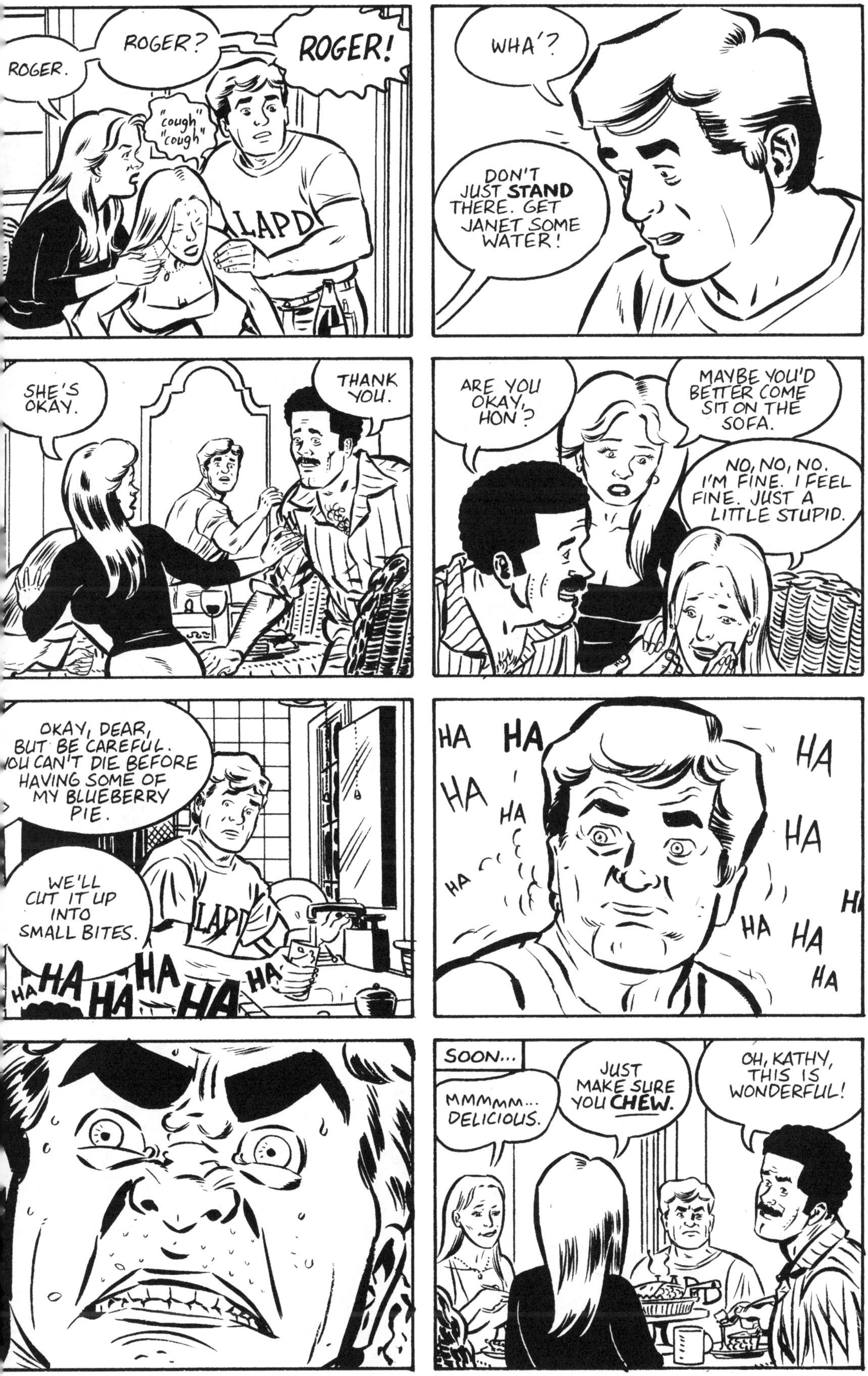
ROGER.
ROGER?
ROGER!
"cough" "cough"
LAPD
WHA'?
DON'T JUST STAND THERE. GET JANET SOME WATER!
SHE'S OKAY.
THANK YOU.
ARE YOU OKAY, HON?
MAYBE YOU'D BETTER COME SIT ON THE SOFA.
NO, NO, NO. I'M FINE. I FEEL FINE. JUST A LITTLE STUPID.
OKAY, DEAR, BUT BE CAREFUL. YOU CAN'T DIE BEFORE HAVING SOME OF MY BLUEBERRY PIE.
WE'LL CUT IT UP INTO SMALL BITES.
HA HA HA HA HA HA
HA HA HA HA HA HA HA HA HA HA HA
SOON...
MMMMM... DELICIOUS.
JUST MAKE SURE YOU CHEW.
OH, KATHY, THIS IS WONDERFUL!

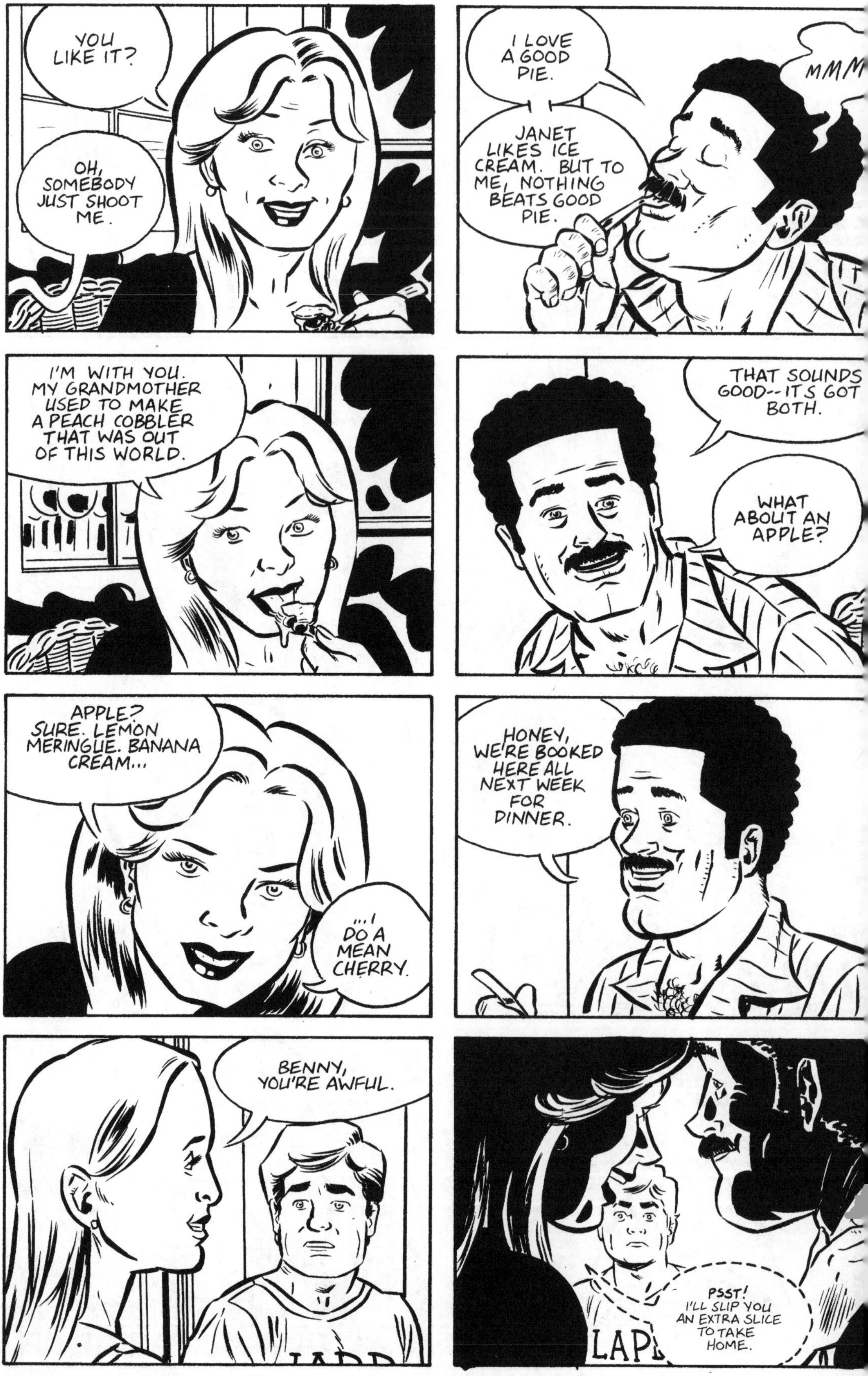
YOU LIKE IT?
OH, SOMEBODY JUST SHOOT ME.
I LOVE A GOOD PIE.
JANET LIKES ICE CREAM. BUT TO ME, NOTHING BEATS GOOD PIE.
MMM
I'M WITH YOU. MY GRANDMOTHER USED TO MAKE A PEACH COBBLER THAT WAS OUT OF THIS WORLD.
THAT SOUNDS GOOD--IT'S GOT BOTH.
WHAT ABOUT AN APPLE?
APPLE? SURE. LEMON MERINGUE. BANANA CREAM...
...I DO A MEAN CHERRY.
HONEY, WE'RE BOOKED HERE ALL NEXT WEEK FOR DINNER.
BENNY, YOU'RE AWFUL.
PSST! I'LL SLIP YOU AN EXTRA SLICE TO TAKE HOME.

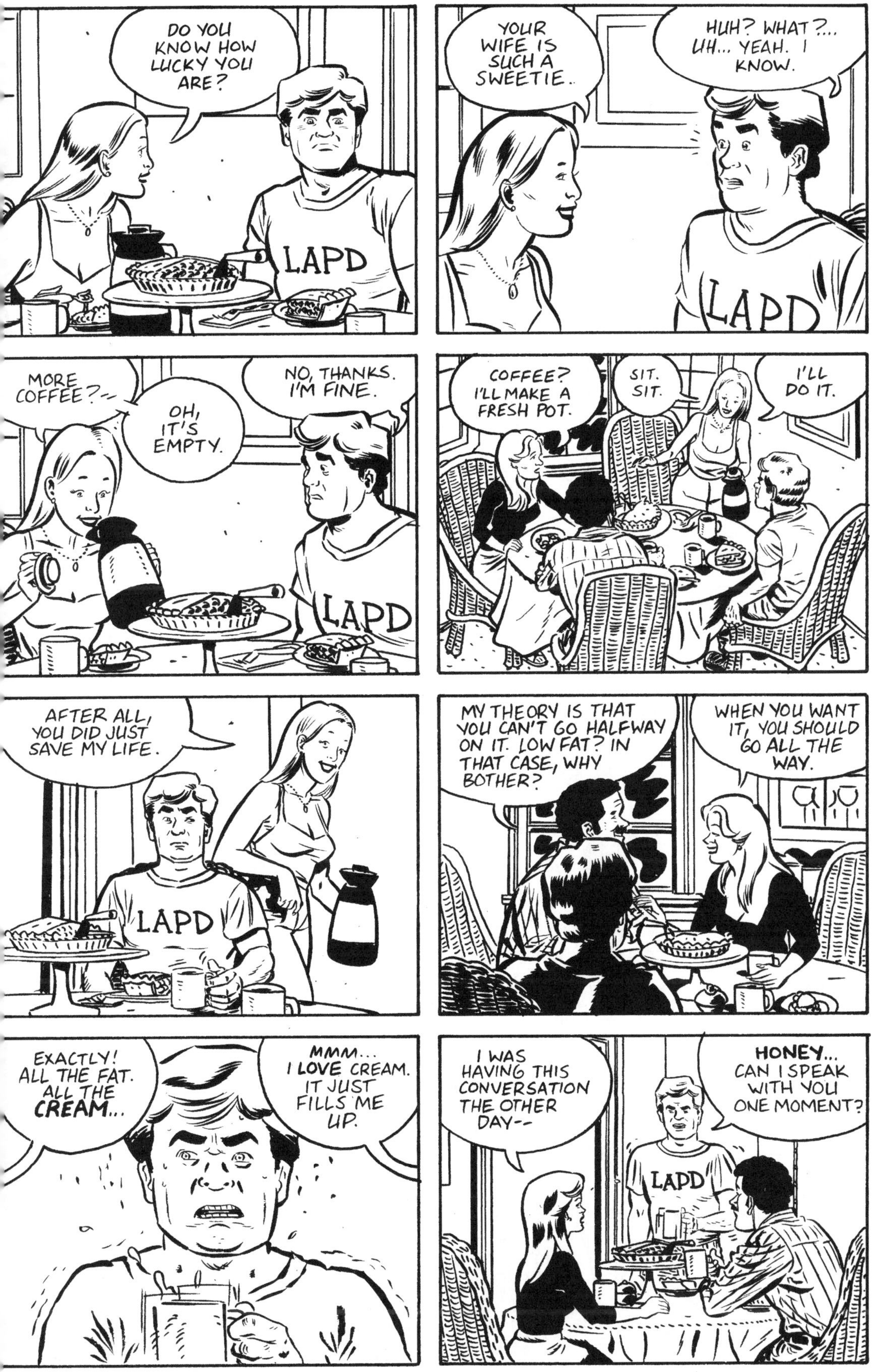
DO YOU KNOW HOW LUCKY YOU ARE?
LAPD
YOUR WIFE IS SUCH A SWEETIE..
HUH? WHAT?... UH... YEAH. I KNOW.
LAPD
MORE COFFEE?
OH, IT'S EMPTY.
NO, THANKS. I'M FINE.
LAPD
COFFEE? I'LL MAKE A FRESH POT.
SIT. SIT.
I'LL DO IT.
AFTER ALL, YOU DID JUST SAVE MY LIFE.
LAPD
MY THEORY IS THAT YOU CAN'T GO HALFWAY ON IT. LOW FAT? IN THAT CASE, WHY BOTHER?
WHEN YOU WANT IT, YOU SHOULD GO ALL THE WAY.
EXACTLY! ALL THE FAT. ALL THE CREAM...
MMM... I LOVE CREAM. IT JUST FILLS ME UP.
I WAS HAVING THIS CONVERSATION THE OTHER DAY--
HONEY... CAN I SPEAK WITH YOU ONE MOMENT?
LAPD

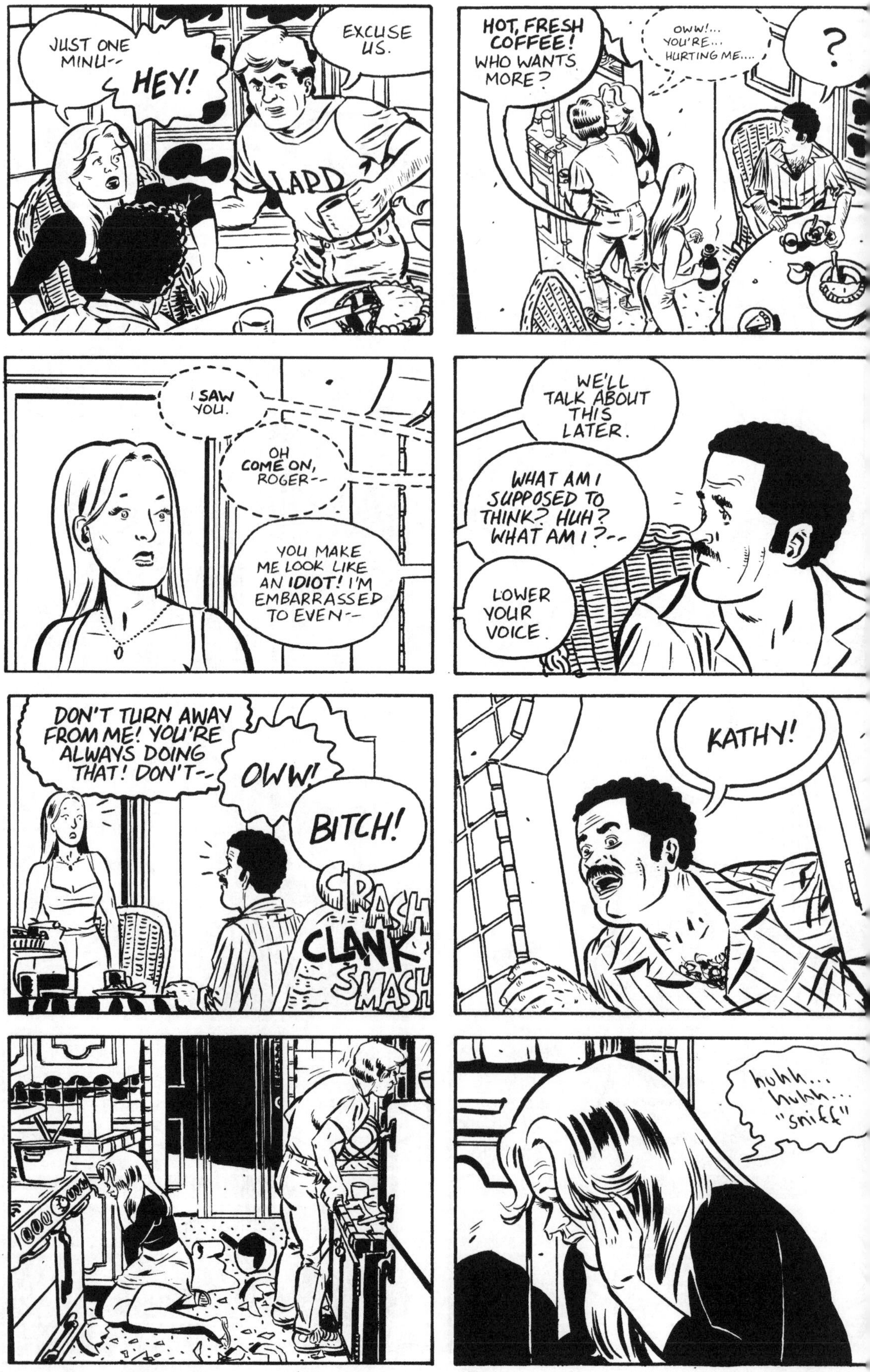
JUST ONE MINU--
HEY!
EXCUSE US.
LAPD
HOT, FRESH COFFEE! WHO WANTS MORE?
OWW!... YOU'RE... HURTING ME....
?
I SAW YOU.
OH COME ON, ROGER--
YOU MAKE ME LOOK LIKE AN IDIOT! I'M EMBARRASSED TO EVEN--
WE'LL TALK ABOUT THIS LATER.
WHAT AM I SUPPOSED TO THINK? HUH? WHAT AM I?--
LOWER YOUR VOICE.
DON'T TURN AWAY FROM ME! YOU'RE ALWAYS DOING THAT! DON'T--
OWW!
BITCH!
CRASH
CLANK
SMASH
KATHY!
huhh... huhh... "sniff"

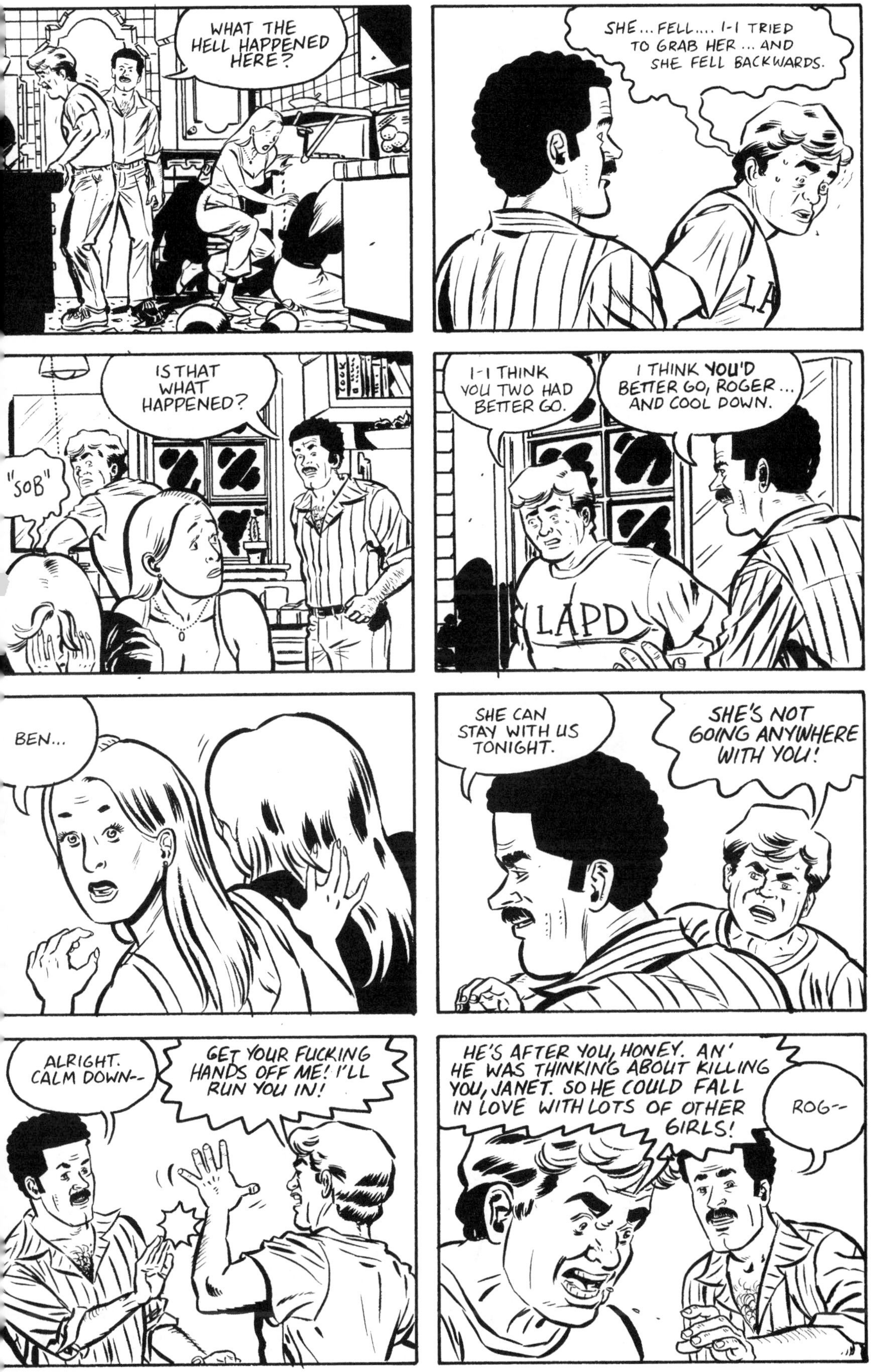
WHAT THE HELL HAPPENED HERE?
SHE... FELL.... I-I TRIED TO GRAB HER ... AND SHE FELL BACKWARDS.
IS THAT WHAT HAPPENED?
"SOB"
I-I THINK YOU TWO HAD BETTER GO.
I THINK YOU'D BETTER GO, ROGER... AND COOL DOWN.
LAPD
BEN...
SHE CAN STAY WITH US TONIGHT.
SHE'S NOT GOING ANYWHERE WITH YOU!
ALRIGHT. CALM DOWN--
GET YOUR FUCKING HANDS OFF ME! I'LL RUN YOU IN!
HE'S AFTER YOU, HONEY. AN' HE WAS THINKING ABOUT KILLING YOU, JANET. SO HE COULD FALL IN LOVE WITH LOTS OF OTHER GIRLS!
ROG--

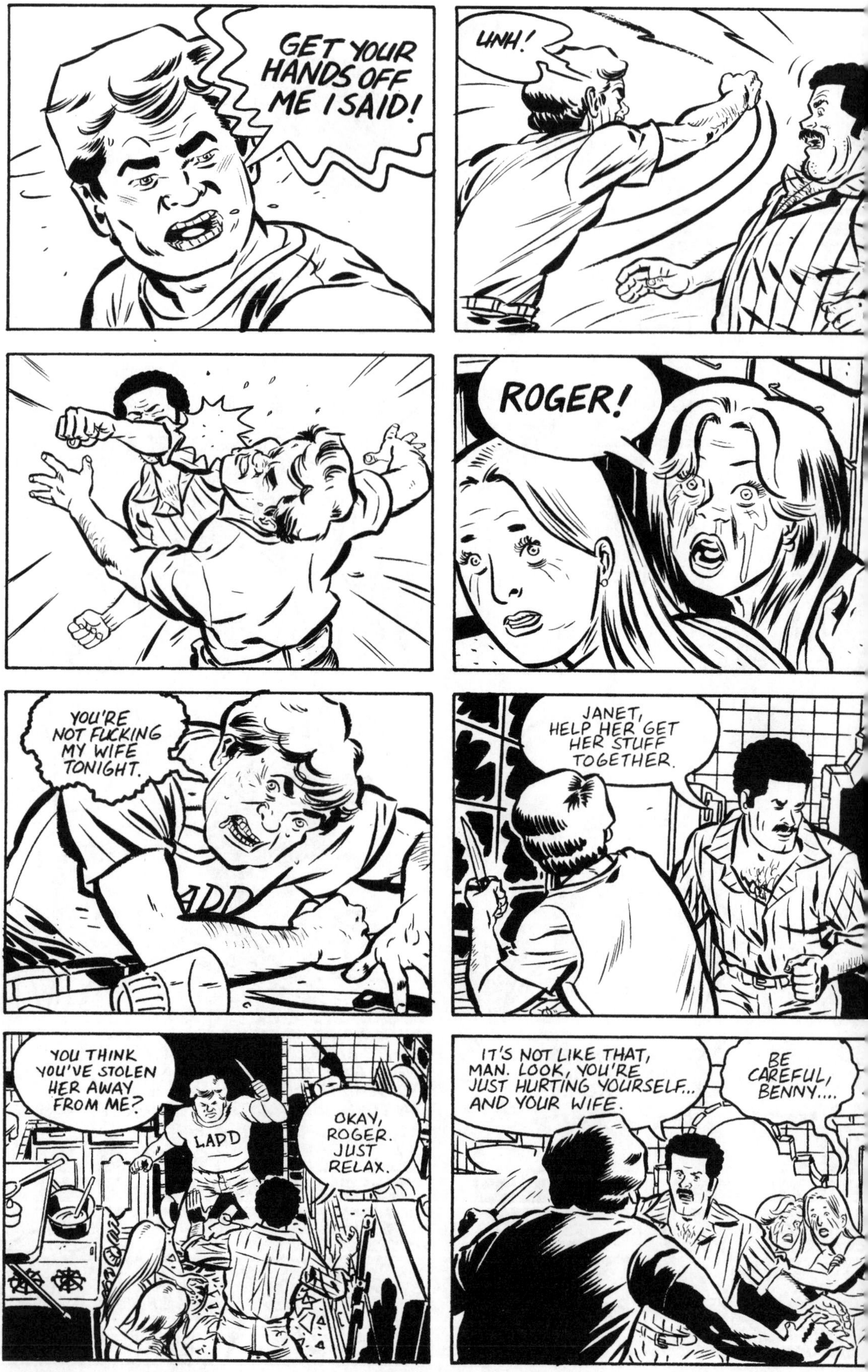
GET YOUR HANDS OFF ME I SAID!
UNH!
ROGER!
YOU'RE NOT FUCKING MY WIFE TONIGHT.
LADD
JANET, HELP HER GET HER STUFF TOGETHER.
YOU THINK YOU'VE STOLEN HER AWAY FROM ME?
LAPD
OKAY, ROGER. JUST RELAX.
IT'S NOT LIKE THAT, MAN. LOOK, YOU'RE JUST HURTING YOURSELF... AND YOUR WIFE.
BE CAREFUL, BENNY....

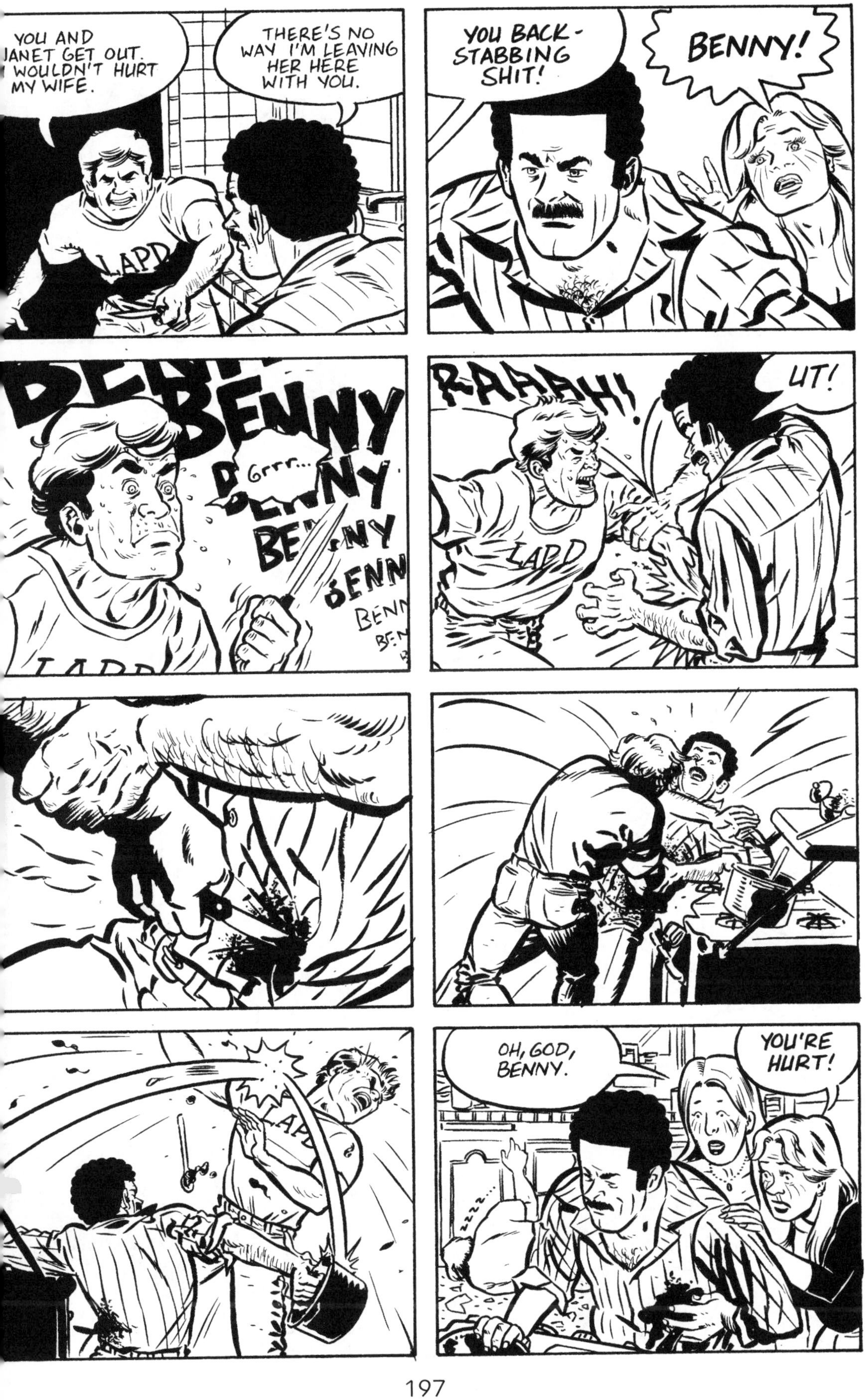
YOU AND JANET GET OUT. WOULDN'T HURT MY WIFE.
THERE'S NO WAY I'M LEAVING HER HERE WITH YOU.
LAPD
YOU BACK-STABBING SHIT!
BENNY!
BENNY
Grrr...
RAAAH!
UT!
LAPD
OH, GOD, BENNY.
YOU'RE HURT!

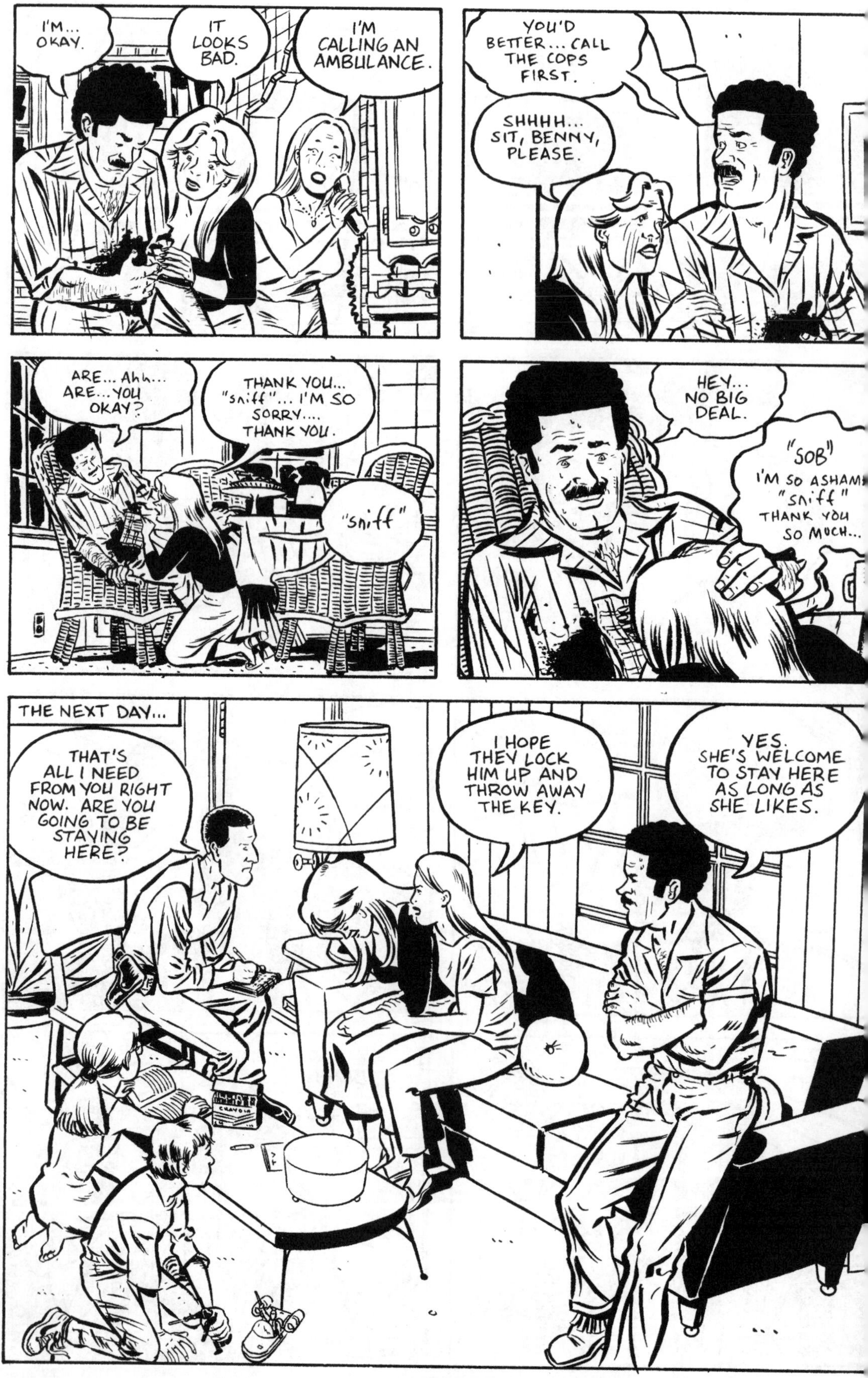

I'M... OKAY.
IT LOOKS BAD.
I'M CALLING AN AMBULANCE.
YOU'D BETTER... CALL THE COPS FIRST.
SHHHH... SIT, BENNY, PLEASE.
ARE... Ahh... ARE... YOU OKAY?
THANK YOU... "sniff"... I'M SO SORRY.... THANK YOU.
"sniff"
HEY... NO BIG DEAL.
"SOB" I'M SO ASHAM "sniff" THANK YOU SO MUCH...
THE NEXT DAY...
THAT'S ALL I NEED FROM YOU RIGHT NOW. ARE YOU GOING TO BE STAYING HERE?
I HOPE THEY LOCK HIM UP AND THROW AWAY THE KEY.
YES. SHE'S WELCOME TO STAY HERE AS LONG AS SHE LIKES.

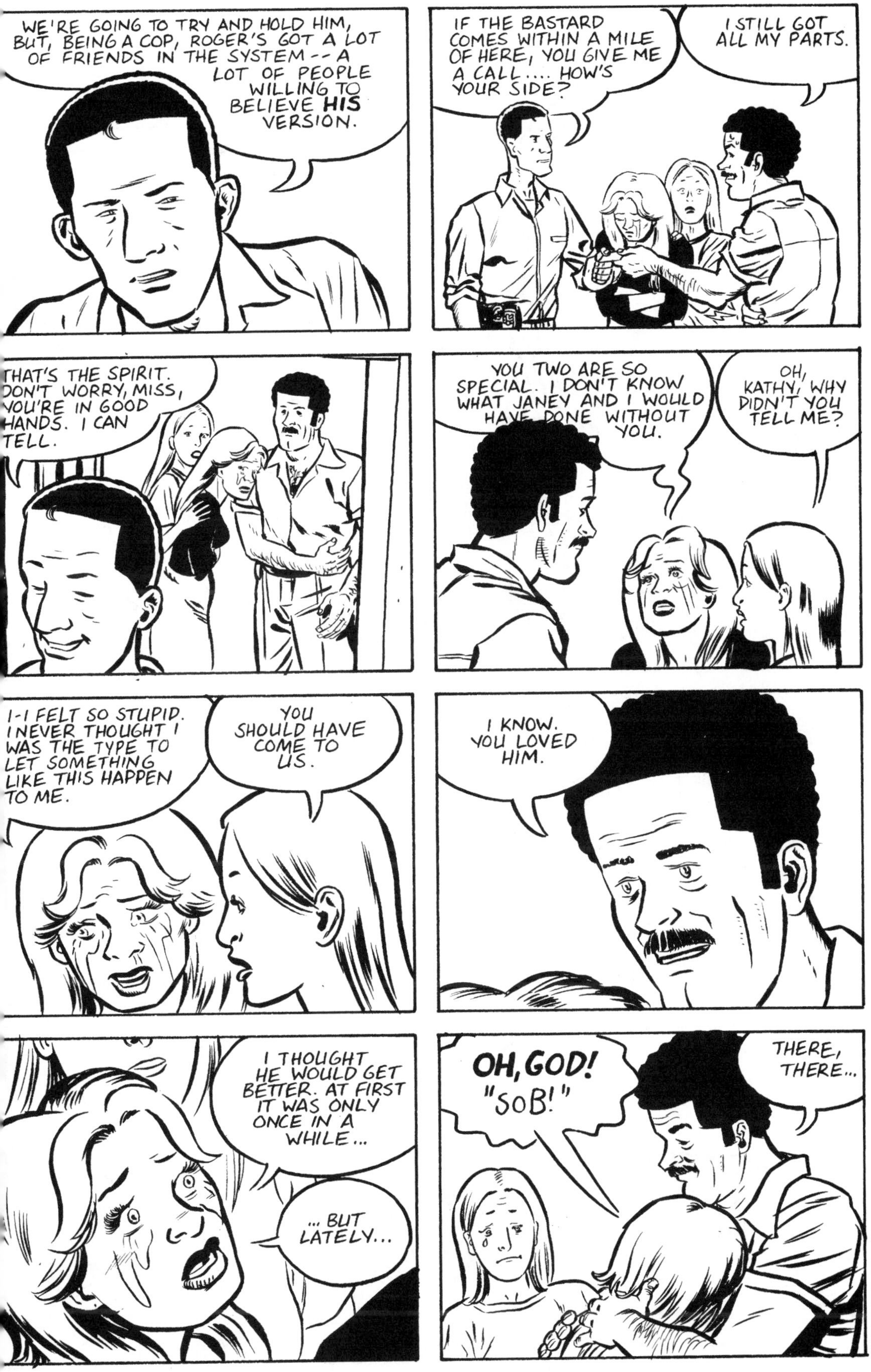

WE'RE GOING TO TRY AND HOLD HIM, BUT, BEING A COP, ROGER'S GOT A LOT OF FRIENDS IN THE SYSTEM -- A LOT OF PEOPLE WILLING TO BELIEVE **HIS** VERSION.
IF THE BASTARD COMES WITHIN A MILE OF HERE, YOU GIVE ME A CALL.... HOW'S YOUR SIDE?
I STILL GOT ALL MY PARTS.
THAT'S THE SPIRIT. DON'T WORRY, MISS, YOU'RE IN GOOD HANDS. I CAN TELL.
YOU TWO ARE SO SPECIAL. I DON'T KNOW WHAT JANEY AND I WOULD HAVE DONE WITHOUT YOU.
OH, KATHY, WHY DIDN'T YOU TELL ME?
I-I FELT SO STUPID. I NEVER THOUGHT I WAS THE TYPE TO LET SOMETHING LIKE THIS HAPPEN TO ME.
YOU SHOULD HAVE COME TO US.
I KNOW. YOU LOVED HIM.
I THOUGHT HE WOULD GET BETTER. AT FIRST IT WAS ONLY ONCE IN A WHILE...
... BUT LATELY...
**OH, GOD!**
"SOB!"
THERE, THERE...

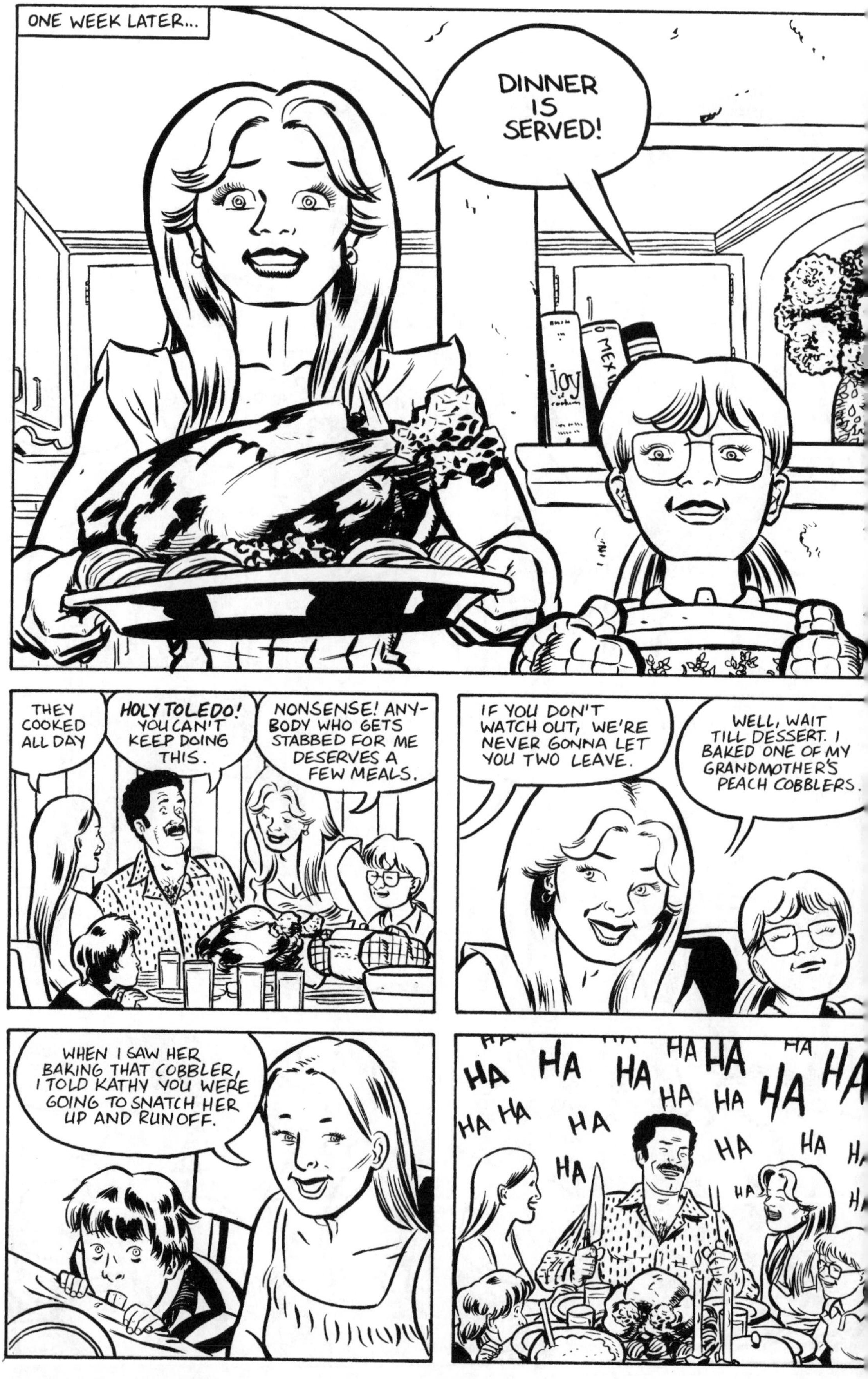
ONE WEEK LATER...
DINNER IS SERVED!
joy
MEX
THEY COOKED ALL DAY
HOLY TOLEDO! YOU CAN'T KEEP DOING THIS.
NONSENSE! ANYBODY WHO GETS STABBED FOR ME DESERVES A FEW MEALS.
IF YOU DON'T WATCH OUT, WE'RE NEVER GONNA LET YOU TWO LEAVE.
WELL, WAIT TILL DESSERT. I BAKED ONE OF MY GRANDMOTHER'S PEACH COBBLERS.
WHEN I SAW HER BAKING THAT COBBLER, I TOLD KATHY YOU WERE GOING TO SNATCH HER UP AND RUN OFF.
HA HA HA HA HA HA HA HA HA HA HA HA HA HA HA HA HA HA HA

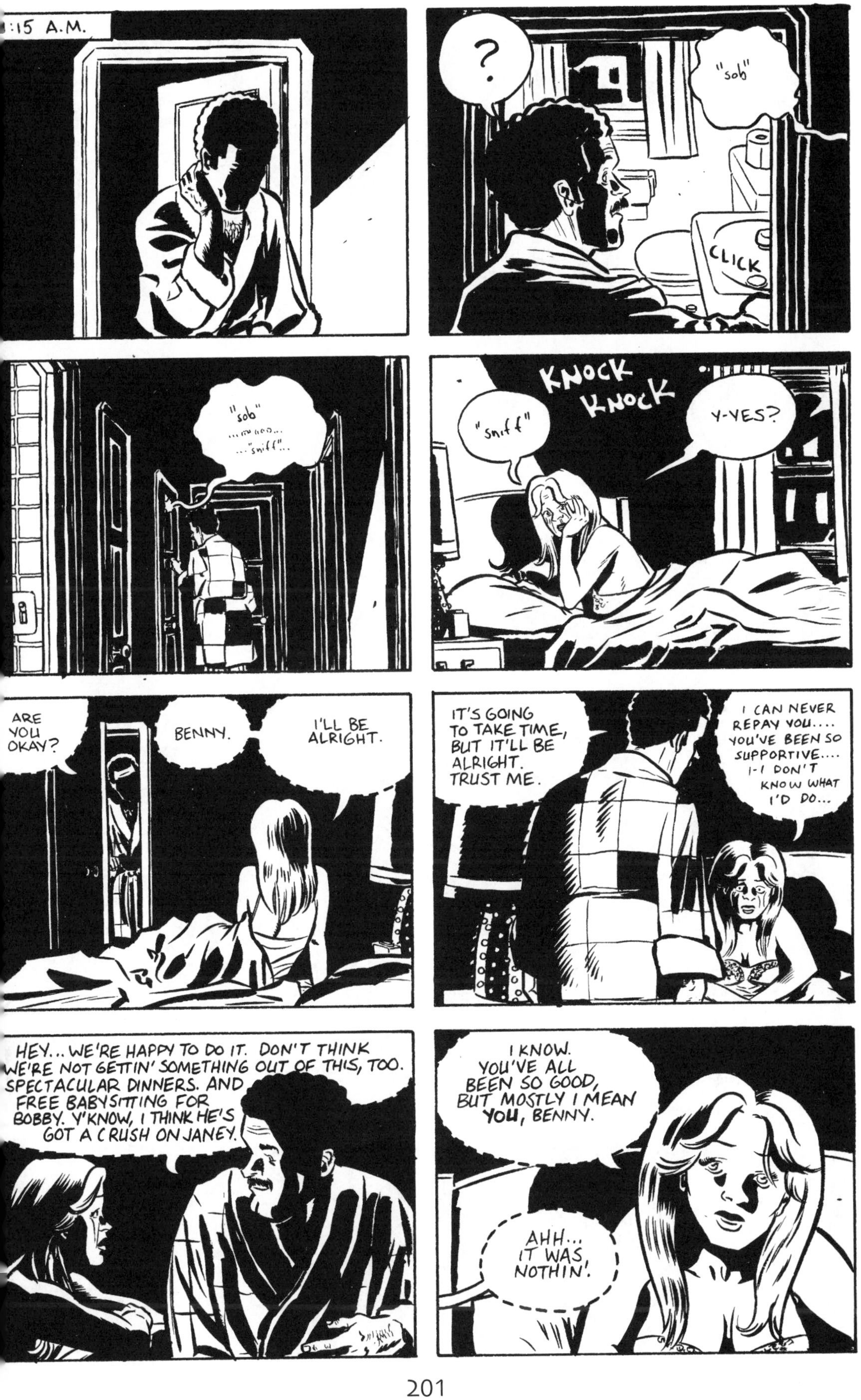
:15 A.M.
?
"sob"
CLICK
"sob"
..."sniff"...
KNOCK KNOCK
"sniff"
Y-YES?
ARE YOU OKAY?
BENNY.
I'LL BE ALRIGHT.
IT'S GOING TO TAKE TIME, BUT IT'LL BE ALRIGHT. TRUST ME.
I CAN NEVER REPAY YOU.... YOU'VE BEEN SO SUPPORTIVE.... I-I DON'T KNOW WHAT I'D DO...
HEY... WE'RE HAPPY TO DO IT. DON'T THINK WE'RE NOT GETTIN' SOMETHING OUT OF THIS, TOO. SPECTACULAR DINNERS. AND FREE BABYSITTING FOR BOBBY. Y'KNOW, I THINK HE'S GOT A CRUSH ON JANEY.
I KNOW. YOU'VE ALL BEEN SO GOOD, BUT MOSTLY I MEAN YOU, BENNY.
AHH... IT WAS NOTHIN'.

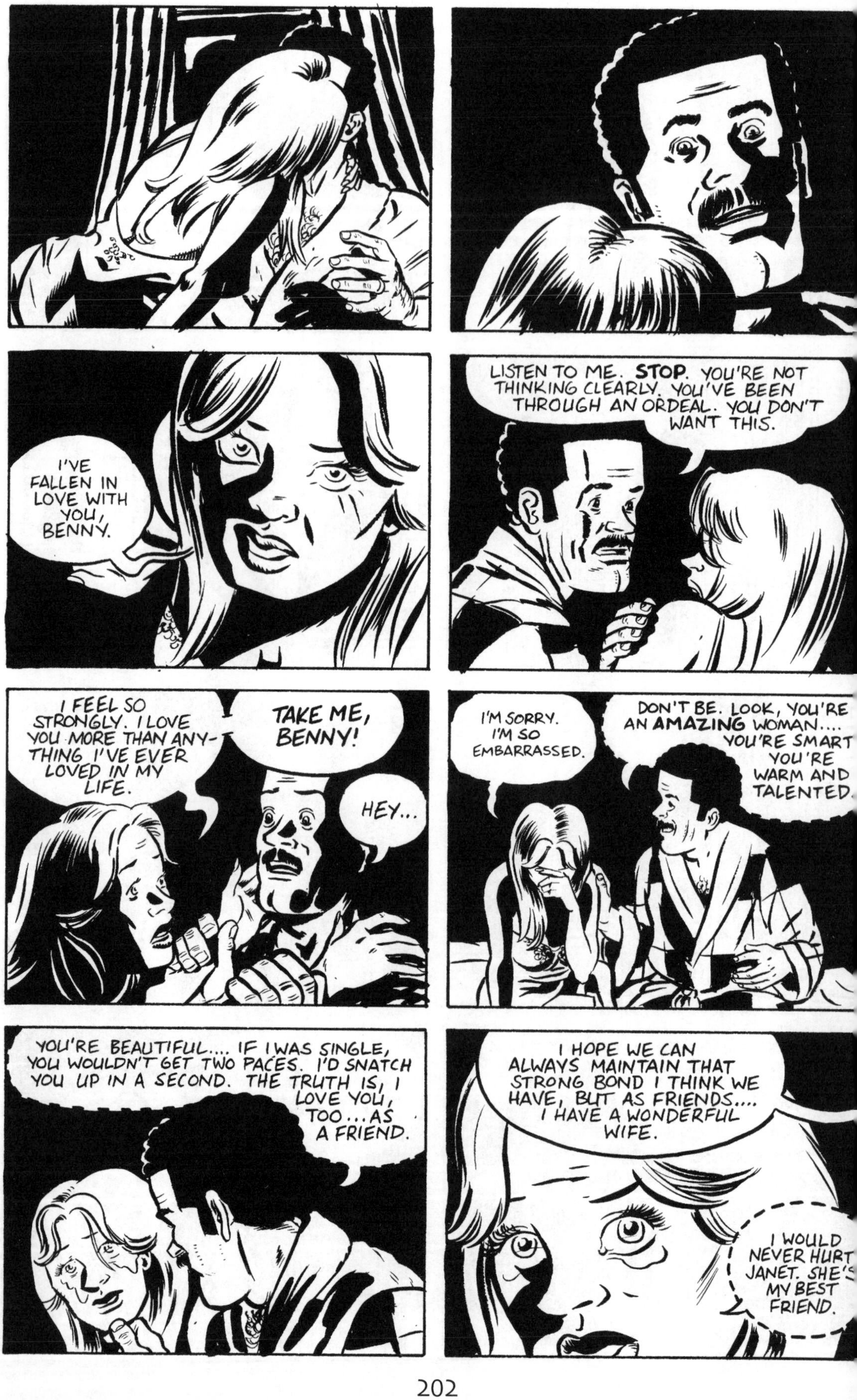
I'VE FALLEN IN LOVE WITH YOU, BENNY.
LISTEN TO ME. STOP. YOU'RE NOT THINKING CLEARLY. YOU'VE BEEN THROUGH AN ORDEAL. YOU DON'T WANT THIS.
I FEEL SO STRONGLY. I LOVE YOU MORE THAN ANYTHING I'VE EVER LOVED IN MY LIFE.
TAKE ME, BENNY!
HEY...
I'M SORRY. I'M SO EMBARRASSED.
DON'T BE. LOOK, YOU'RE AN AMAZING WOMAN.... YOU'RE SMART YOU'RE WARM AND TALENTED.
YOU'RE BEAUTIFUL.... IF I WAS SINGLE, YOU WOULDN'T GET TWO PACES. I'D SNATCH YOU UP IN A SECOND. THE TRUTH IS, I LOVE YOU, TOO...AS A FRIEND.
I HOPE WE CAN ALWAYS MAINTAIN THAT STRONG BOND I THINK WE HAVE, BUT AS FRIENDS.... I HAVE A WONDERFUL WIFE.
I WOULD NEVER HURT JANET. SHE'S MY BEST FRIEND.

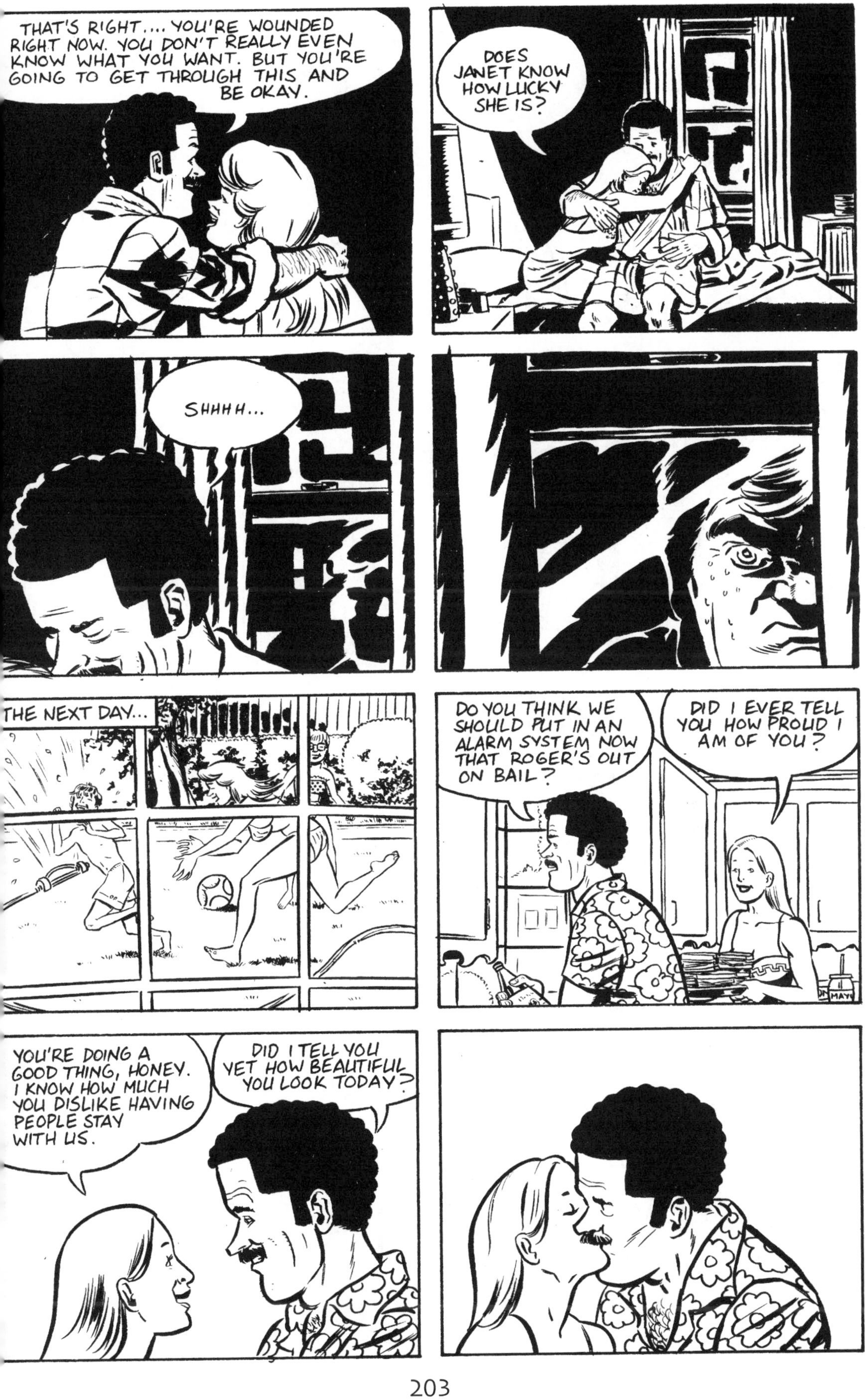
THAT'S RIGHT.... YOU'RE WOUNDED RIGHT NOW. YOU DON'T REALLY EVEN KNOW WHAT YOU WANT. BUT YOU'RE GOING TO GET THROUGH THIS AND BE OKAY.
DOES JANET KNOW HOW LUCKY SHE IS?
SHHHH...
THE NEXT DAY...
DO YOU THINK WE SHOULD PUT IN AN ALARM SYSTEM NOW THAT ROGER'S OUT ON BAIL?
DID I EVER TELL YOU HOW PROUD I AM OF YOU?
MAYO
YOU'RE DOING A GOOD THING, HONEY. I KNOW HOW MUCH YOU DISLIKE HAVING PEOPLE STAY WITH US.
DID I TELL YOU YET HOW BEAUTIFUL YOU LOOK TODAY?

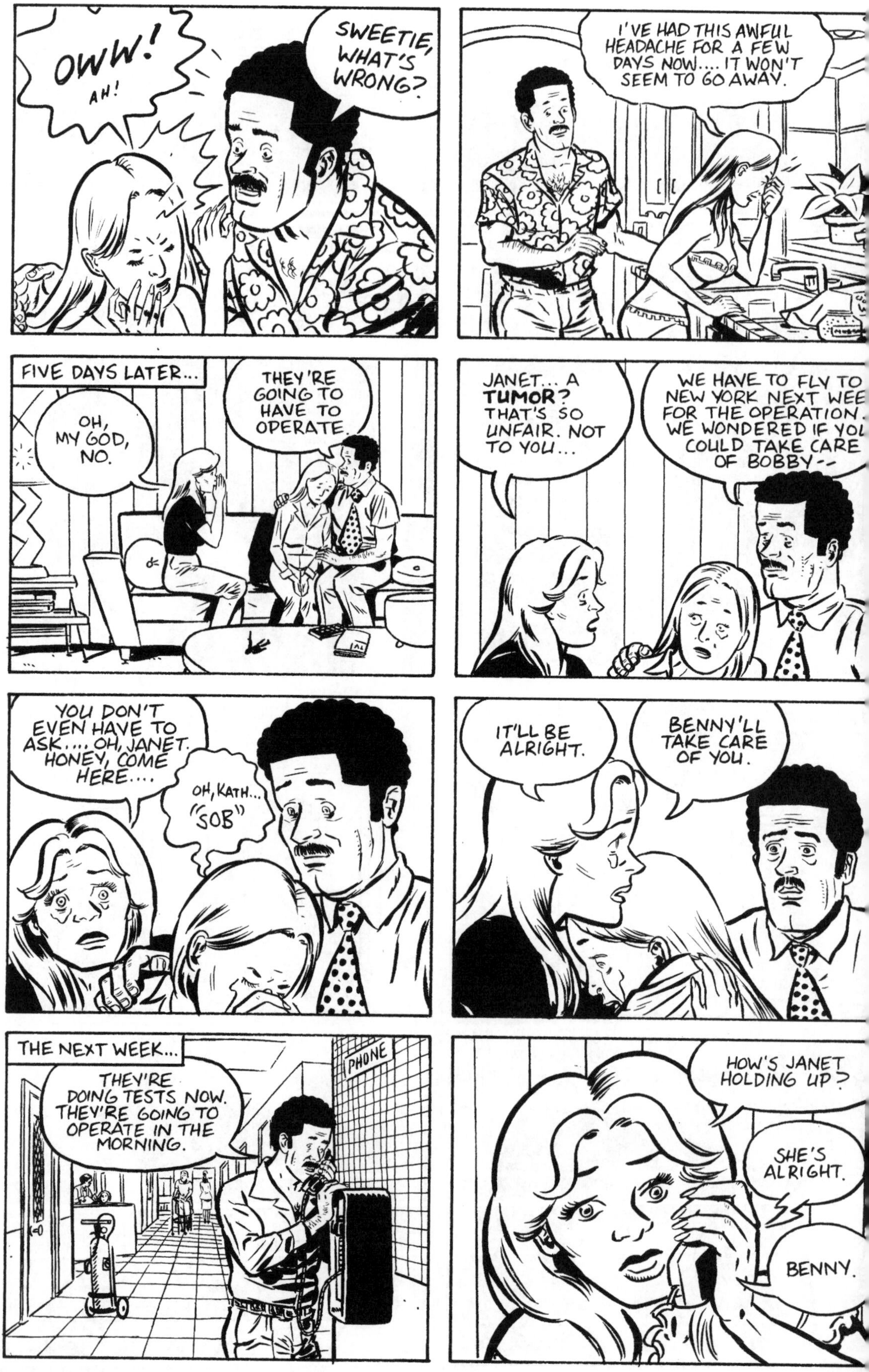
OWW!
AH!
SWEETIE, WHAT'S WRONG?
I'VE HAD THIS AWFUL HEADACHE FOR A FEW DAYS NOW.... IT WON'T SEEM TO GO AWAY.
FIVE DAYS LATER...
OH, MY GOD, NO.
THEY'RE GOING TO HAVE TO OPERATE.
JANET... A **TUMOR**? THAT'S SO UNFAIR. NOT TO YOU...
WE HAVE TO FLY TO NEW YORK NEXT WEE FOR THE OPERATION. WE WONDERED IF YOU COULD TAKE CARE OF BOBBY--
YOU DON'T EVEN HAVE TO ASK.... OH, JANET. HONEY, COME HERE....
OH, KATH... "SOB"
IT'LL BE ALRIGHT.
BENNY'LL TAKE CARE OF YOU.
THE NEXT WEEK...
PHONE
THEY'RE DOING TESTS NOW. THEY'RE GOING TO OPERATE IN THE MORNING.
HOW'S JANET HOLDING UP?
SHE'S ALRIGHT.
BENNY.

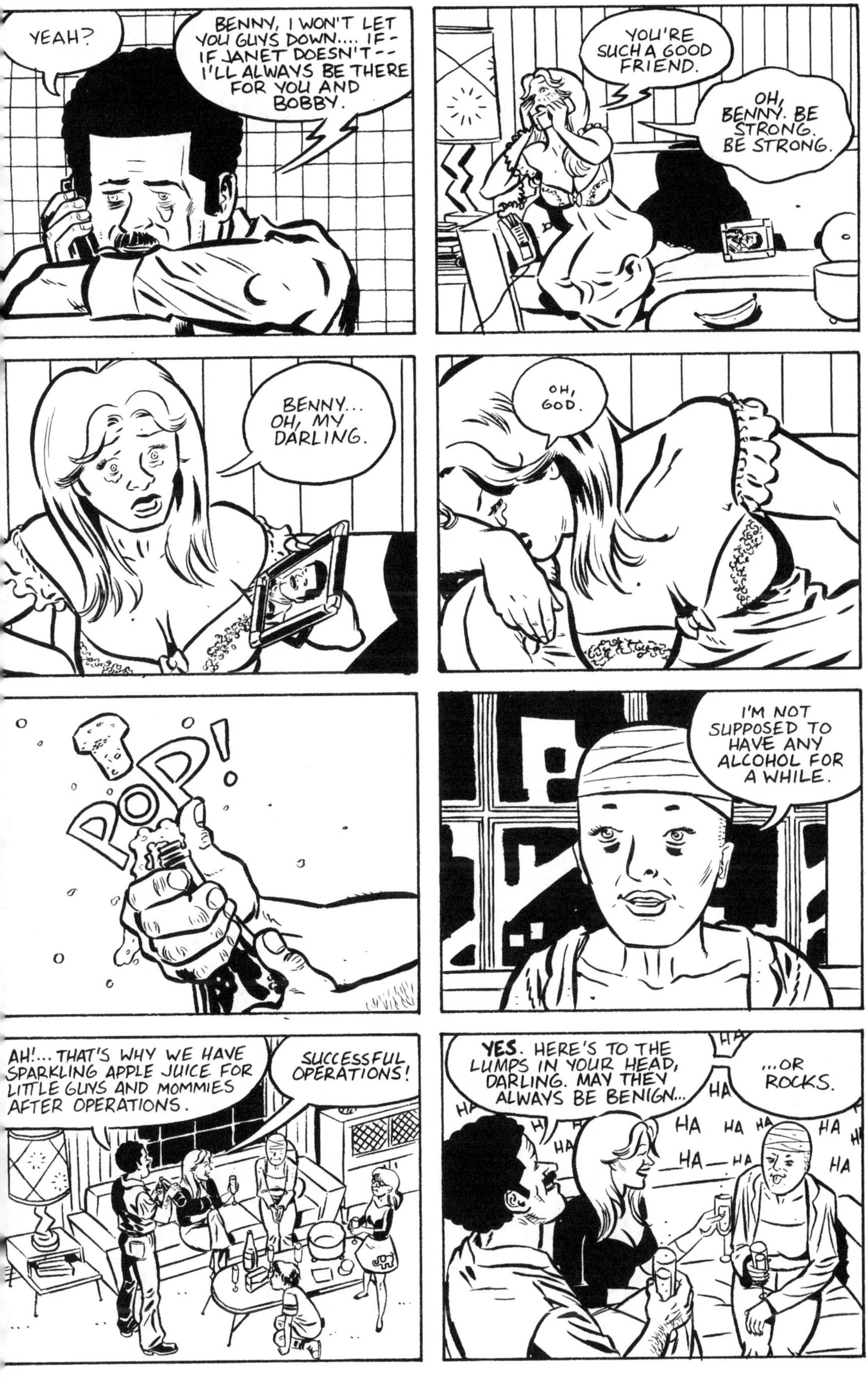
YEAH?
BENNY, I WON'T LET YOU GUYS DOWN.... IF- IF JANET DOESN'T-- I'LL ALWAYS BE THERE FOR YOU AND BOBBY.
YOU'RE SUCH A GOOD FRIEND.
OH, BENNY. BE STRONG. BE STRONG.
BENNY... OH, MY DARLING.
OH, GOD.
POP!
I'M NOT SUPPOSED TO HAVE ANY ALCOHOL FOR A WHILE.
AH!... THAT'S WHY WE HAVE SPARKLING APPLE JUICE FOR LITTLE GUYS AND MOMMIES AFTER OPERATIONS.
SUCCESSFUL OPERATIONS!
YES. HERE'S TO THE LUMPS IN YOUR HEAD, DARLING. MAY THEY ALWAYS BE BENIGN...
...OR ROCKS.
HA HA HA HA HA HA HA HA HA HA HA HA HA

LATER...

SKRRCH

SCRAPE

SCRRAPE

EEE...

BWAAA

???

THE ALARM!

OH, GOD. BENNY!

AAAAAH

WAAAH

JANET, LOOK OUT!

BLAM!

UNGH!

WAAAAA

WAAAH

HANG ON, HONEY!

UNNN...

BENNY! WHA--

GET THE KIDS AND STAY WITH JANET UNTIL THE POLICE COME!

BWAAAAAAAAA

155

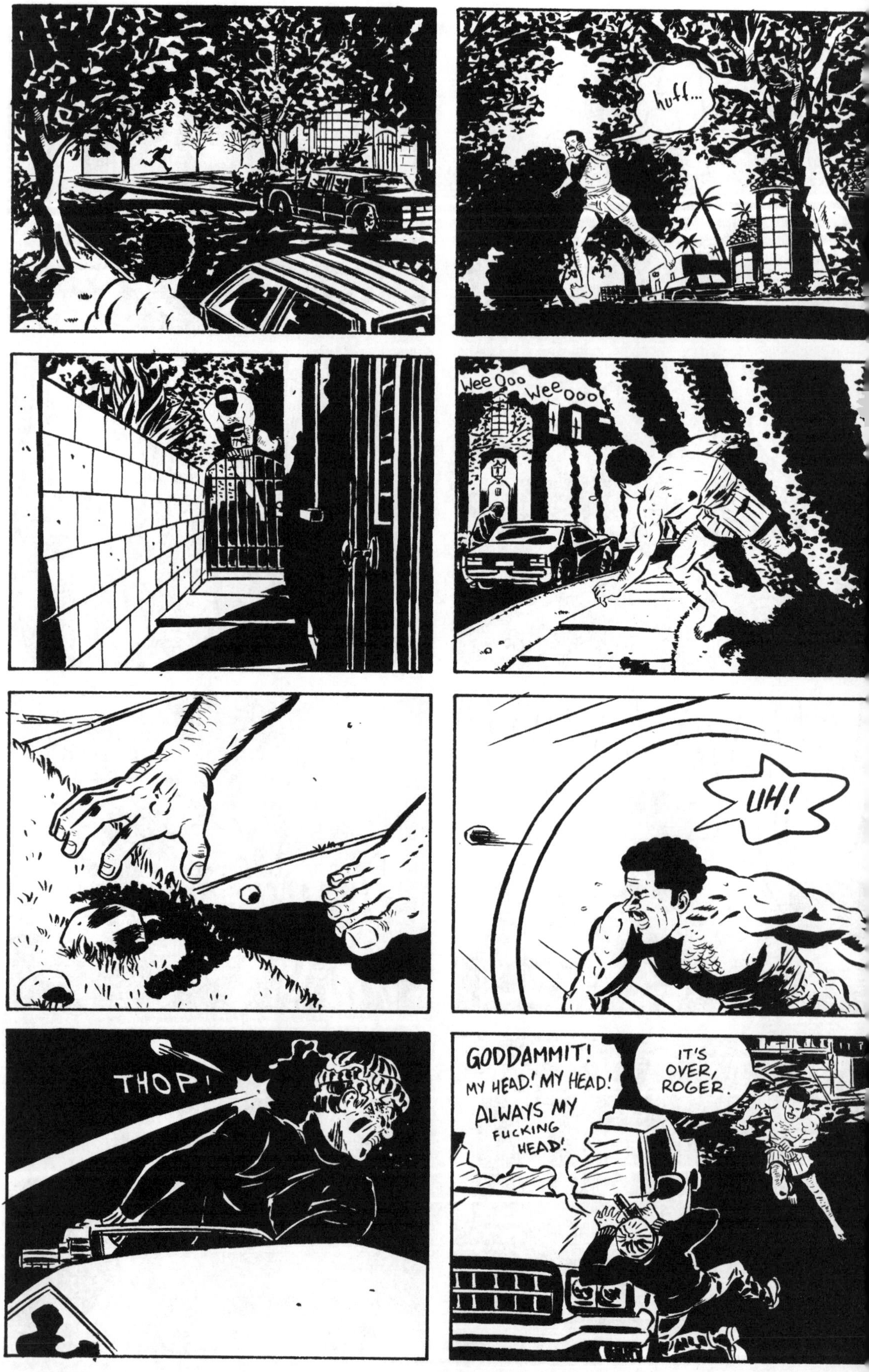
huff...
Wee ooo Wee ooo
UH!
THOP!
GODDAMMIT!
MY HEAD! MY HEAD!
ALWAYS MY FUCKING HEAD!
IT'S OVER, ROGER.

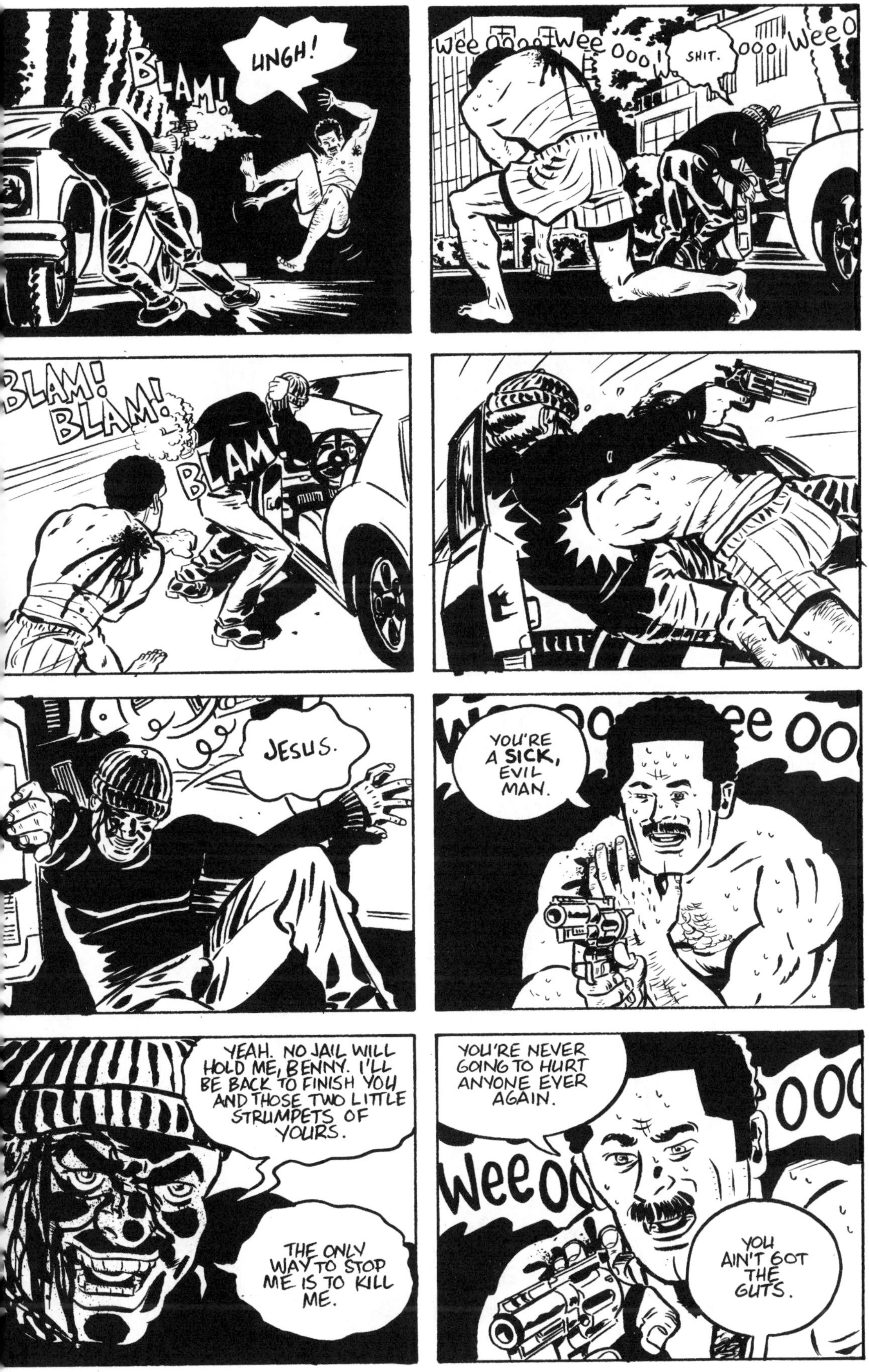
BLAM!
UNGH!
Wee oooo Wee ooo!
SHIT.
ooo Wee o
BLAM! BLAM!
BLAM!
JESUS.
YOU'RE A SICK, EVIL MAN.
YEAH. NO JAIL WILL HOLD ME, BENNY. I'LL BE BACK TO FINISH YOU AND THOSE TWO LITTLE STRUMPETS OF YOURS.
THE ONLY WAY TO STOP ME IS TO KILL ME.
YOU'RE NEVER GOING TO HURT ANYONE EVER AGAIN.
Wee o
YOU AIN'T GOT THE GUTS.

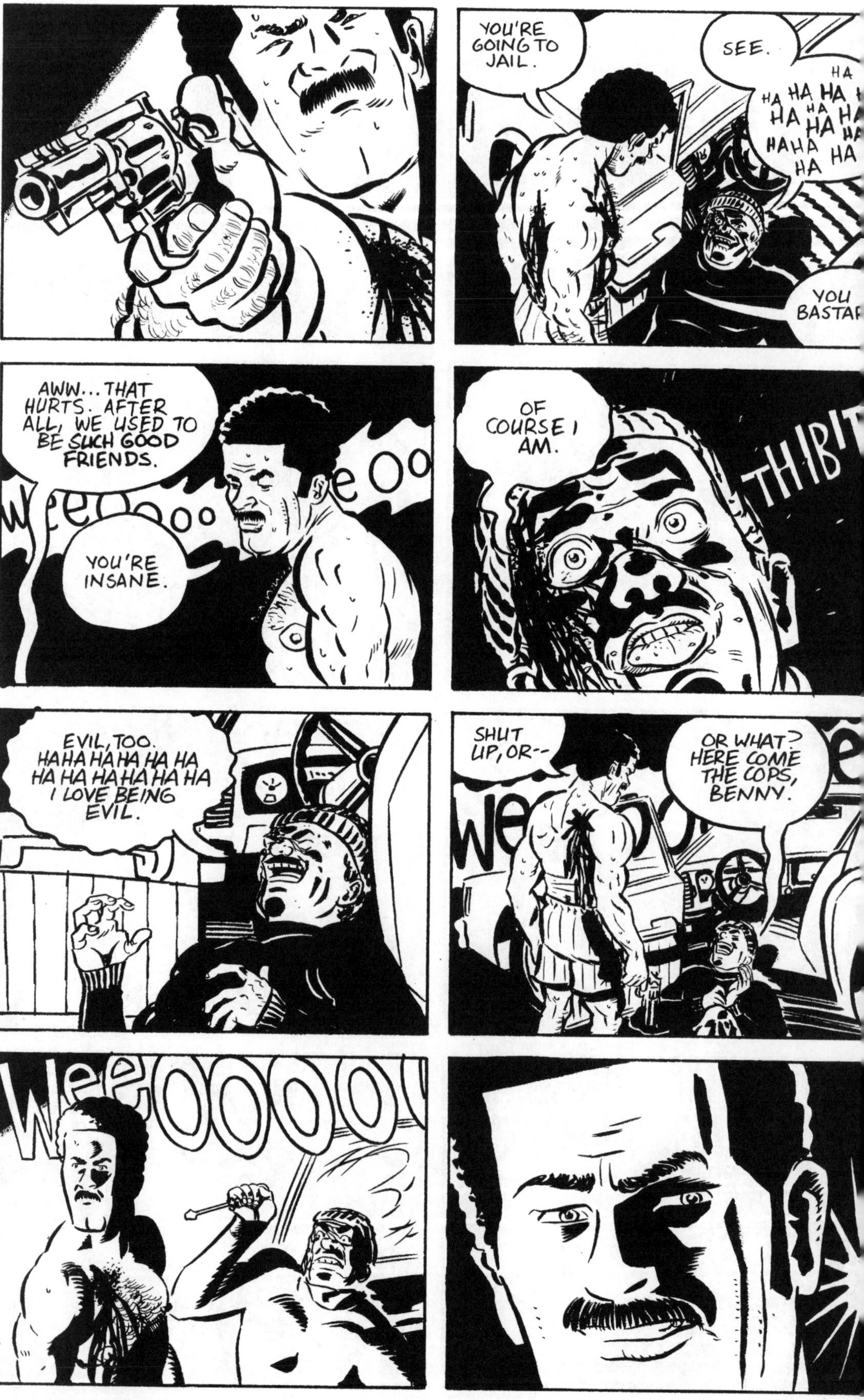
YOU'RE GOING TO JAIL.
SEE.
HA HA HA HA HA HA HA HA HA HAHA HA HA HA
YOU BASTAR
AWW... THAT HURTS. AFTER ALL, WE USED TO BE SUCH GOOD FRIENDS.
WeeOooo
eOo
YOU'RE INSANE.
OF COURSE I AM.
THIBIT
EVIL, TOO. HAHAHAHAHAHA HA HA HA HAHAHAHAHA I LOVE BEING EVIL.
SHUT UP, OR--
OR WHAT? HERE COME THE COPS, BENNY.
Weeoooooo

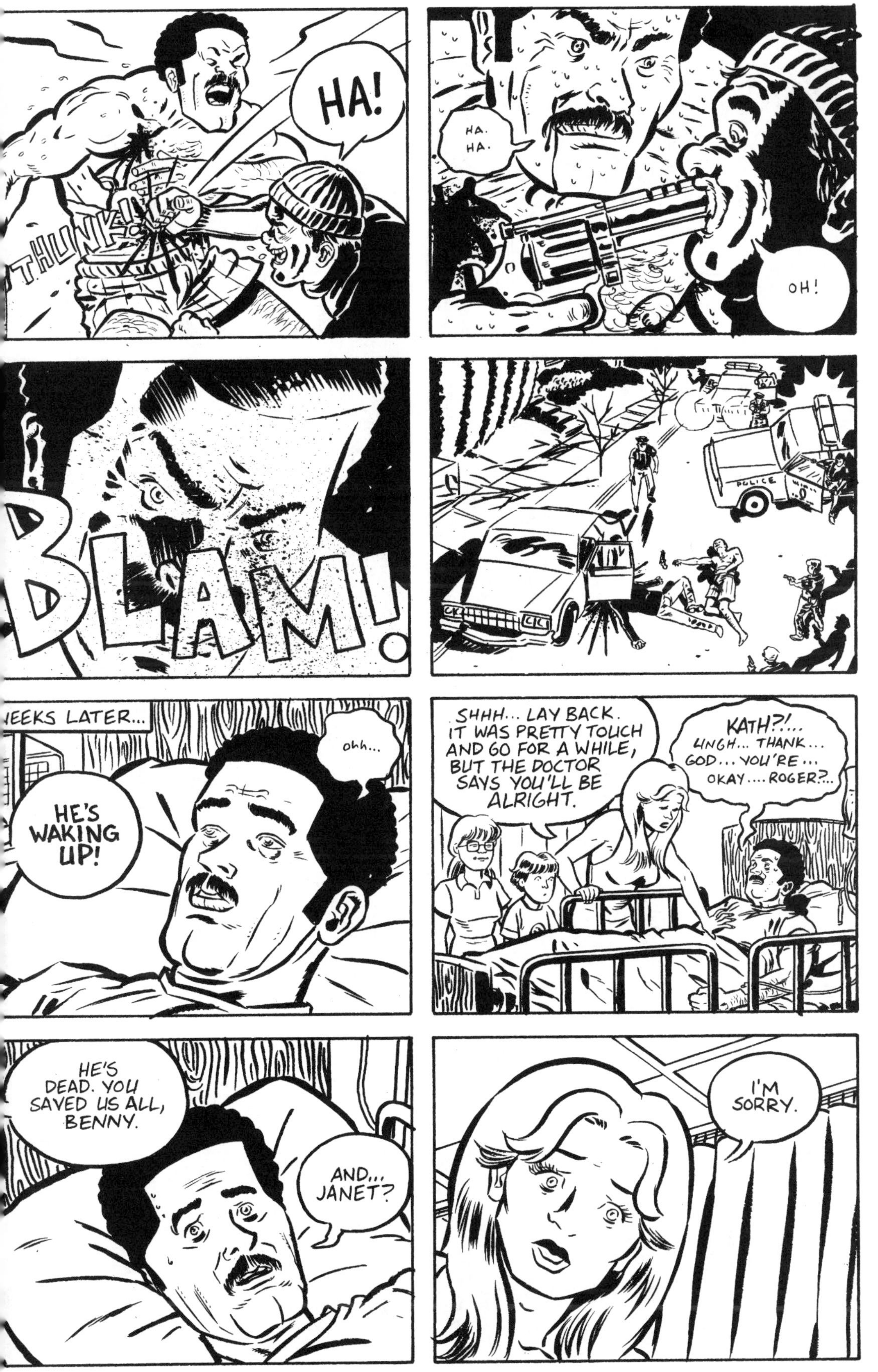

HA!
THUNK!
HA. HA.
OH!
BLAM!
POLICE
WEEKS LATER...
ohh...
HE'S WAKING UP!
SHHH... LAY BACK. IT WAS PRETTY TOUCH AND GO FOR A WHILE, BUT THE DOCTOR SAYS YOU'LL BE ALRIGHT.
KATH?!... UNGH... THANK... GOD... YOU'RE... OKAY.... ROGER?...
HE'S DEAD. YOU SAVED US ALL, BENNY.
AND... JANET?
I'M SORRY.

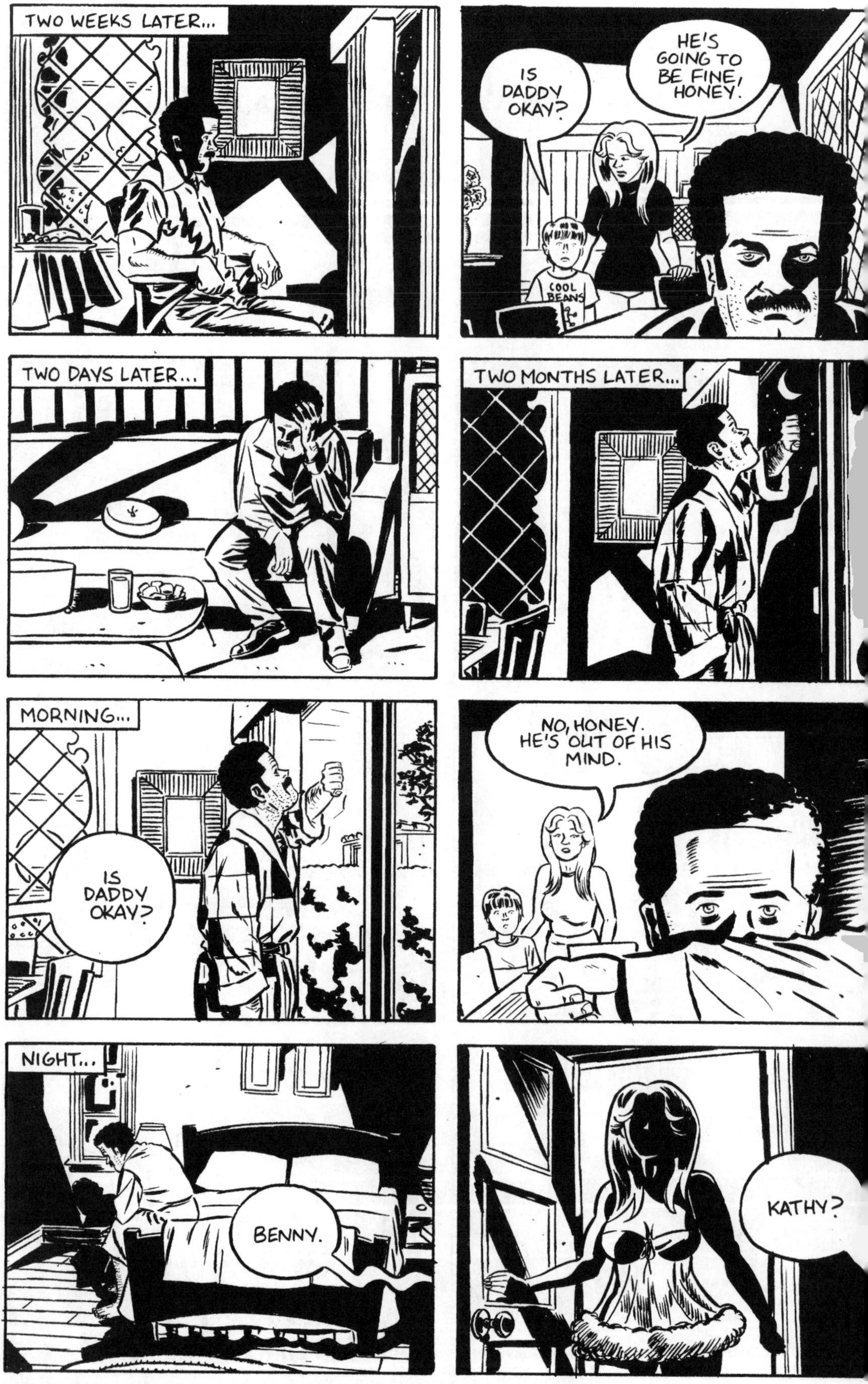
TWO WEEKS LATER...
IS DADDY OKAY?
HE'S GOING TO BE FINE, HONEY.
COOL BEANS
TWO DAYS LATER...
TWO MONTHS LATER...
MORNING...
IS DADDY OKAY?
NO, HONEY. HE'S OUT OF HIS MIND.
NIGHT...
BENNY.
KATHY?

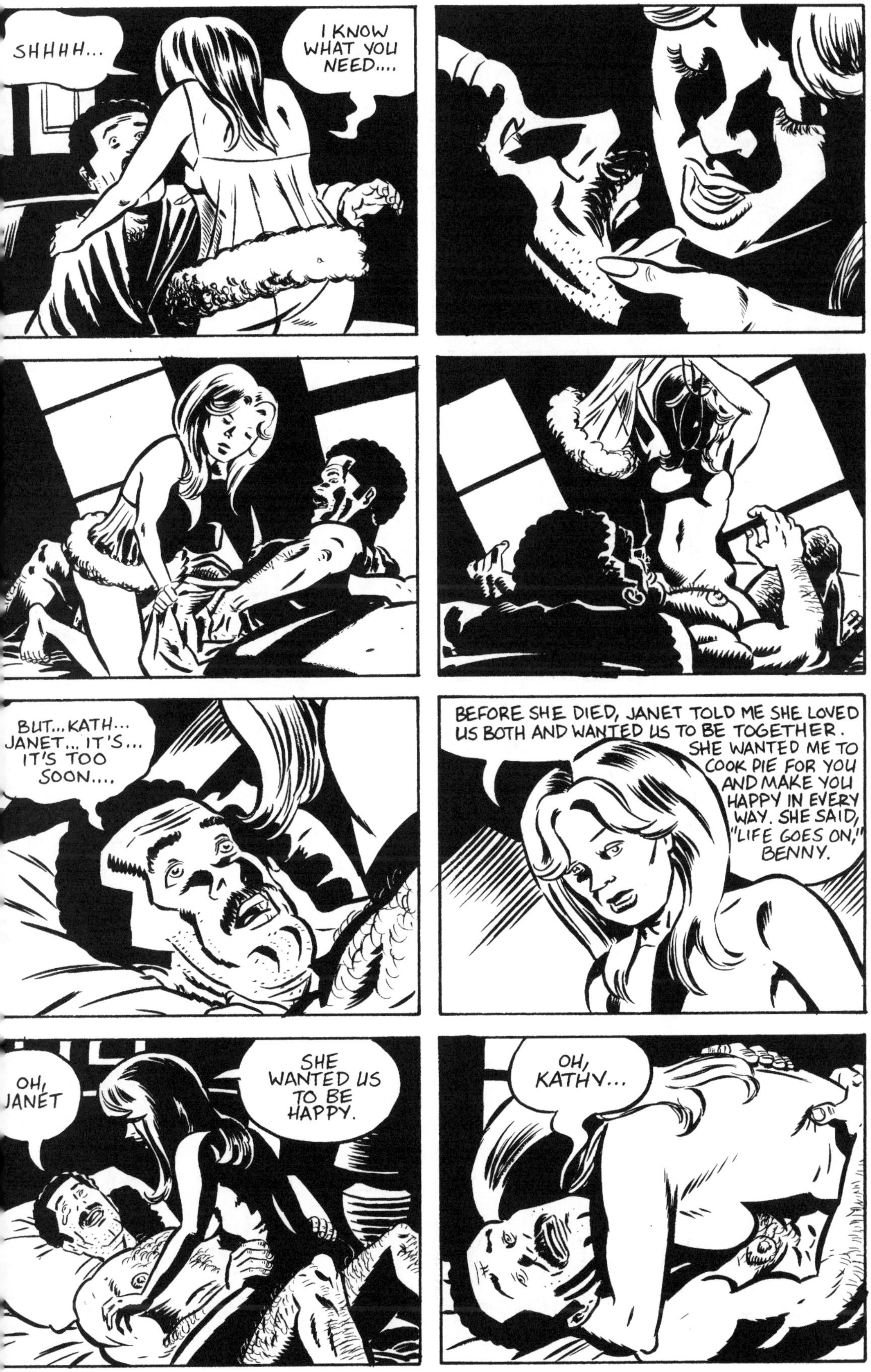
SHHHH...
I KNOW WHAT YOU NEED....
BUT... KATH... JANET... IT'S... IT'S TOO SOON....
BEFORE SHE DIED, JANET TOLD ME SHE LOVED US BOTH AND WANTED US TO BE TOGETHER. SHE WANTED ME TO COOK PIE FOR YOU AND MAKE YOU HAPPY IN EVERY WAY. SHE SAID, "LIFE GOES ON," BENNY.
OH, JANET
SHE WANTED US TO BE HAPPY.
OH, KATHY...

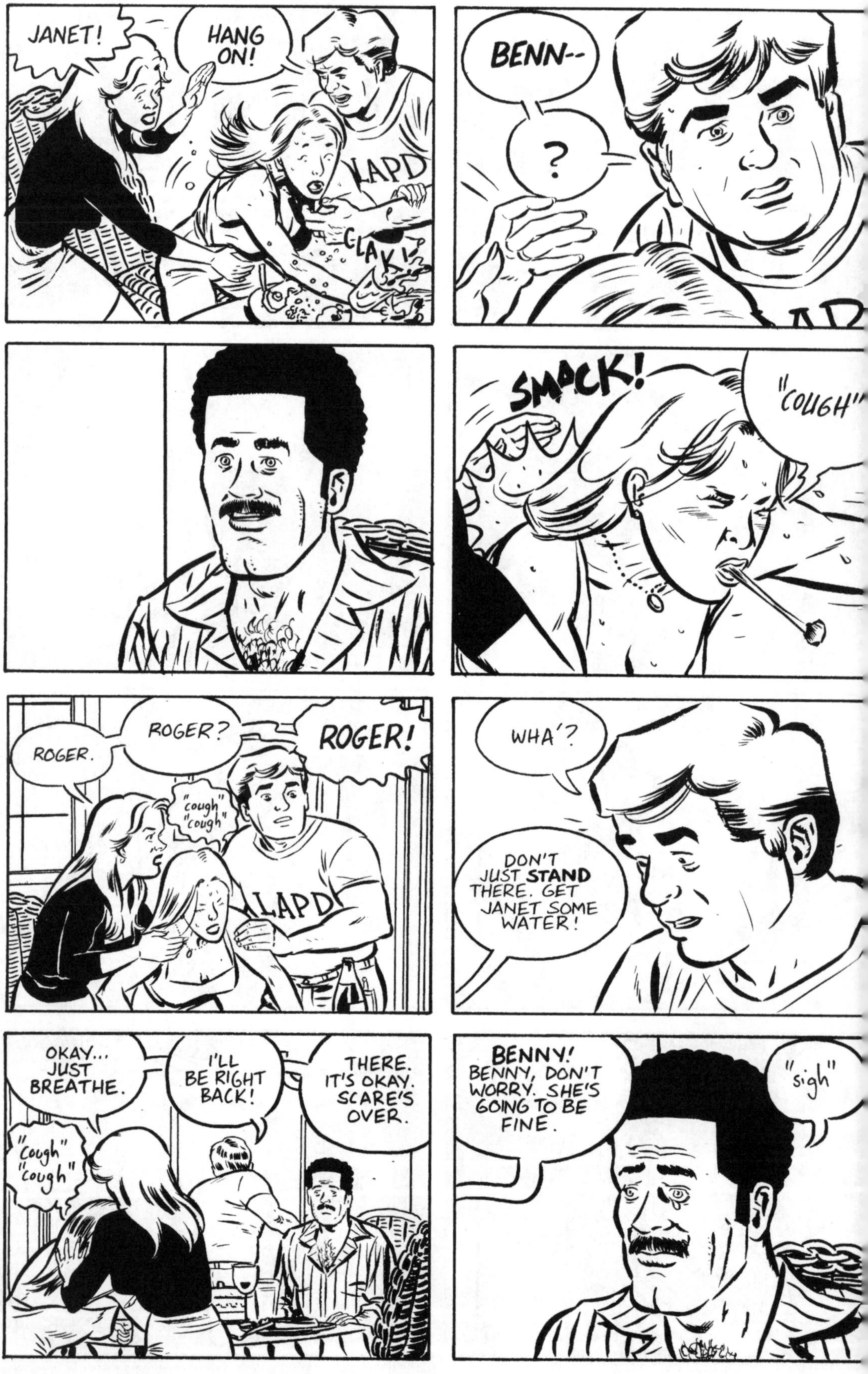
JANET!
HANG ON!
CLAK!
BENN--
?
SMACK!
"COUGH"
ROGER.
ROGER?
ROGER!
"cough" "cough"
WHA'?
DON'T JUST **STAND** THERE. GET JANET SOME WATER!
OKAY... JUST BREATHE.
I'LL BE RIGHT BACK!
THERE. IT'S OKAY. SCARE'S OVER.
"cough" "cough"
BENNY! BENNY, DON'T WORRY. SHE'S GOING TO BE FINE.
"sigh"



**THE END.**

# 8

## "BRING HOME THE DEVIL"

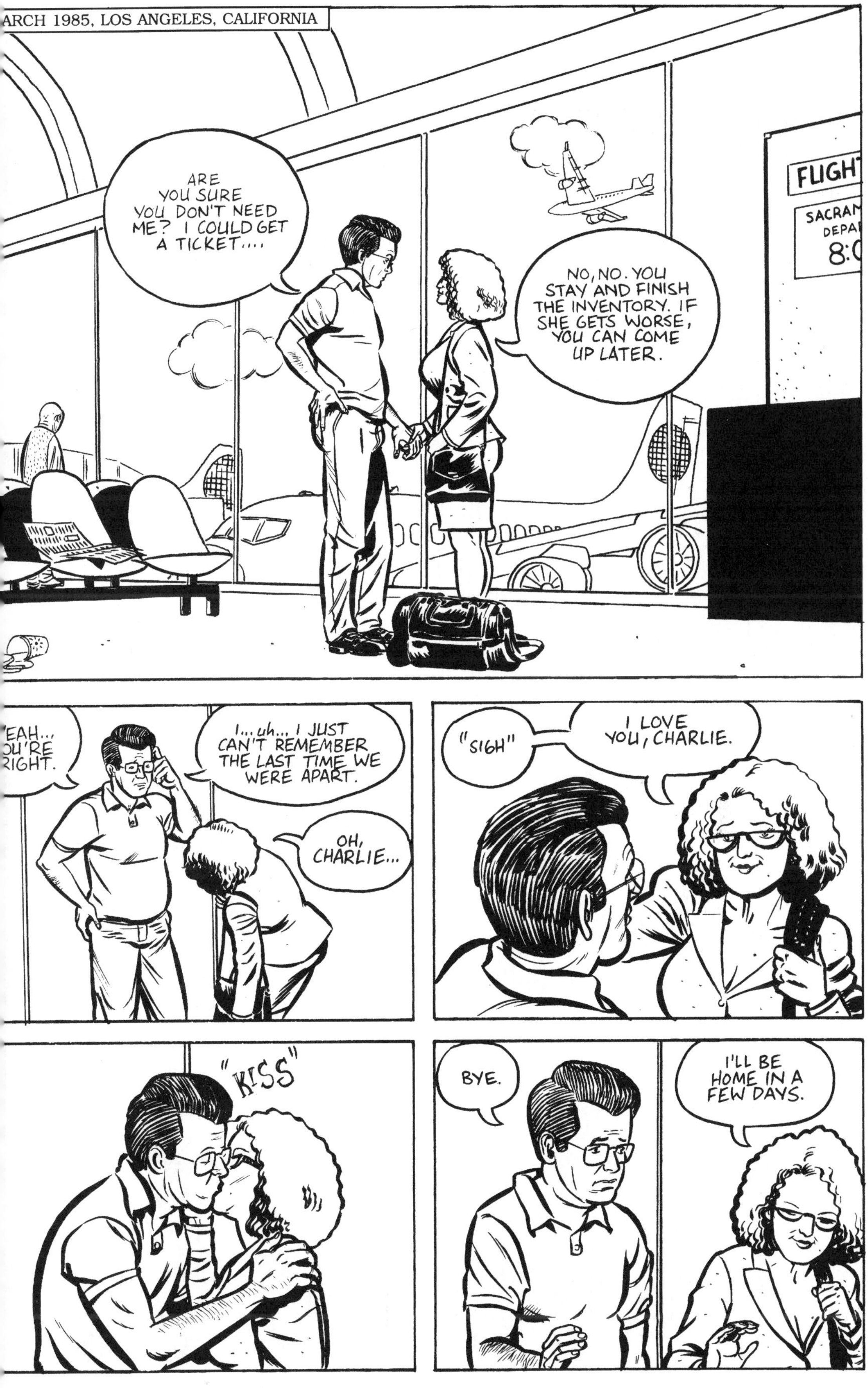
ARCH 1985, LOS ANGELES, CALIFORNIA
ARE YOU SURE YOU DON'T NEED ME? I COULD GET A TICKET....
NO, NO. YOU STAY AND FINISH THE INVENTORY. IF SHE GETS WORSE, YOU CAN COME UP LATER.
FLIGHT
SACRAM
DEPAR
8:0
EAH... OU'RE RIGHT.
I... uh... I JUST CAN'T REMEMBER THE LAST TIME WE WERE APART.
OH, CHARLIE...
"SIGH"
I LOVE YOU, CHARLIE.
"KISS"
BYE.
I'LL BE HOME IN A FEW DAYS.

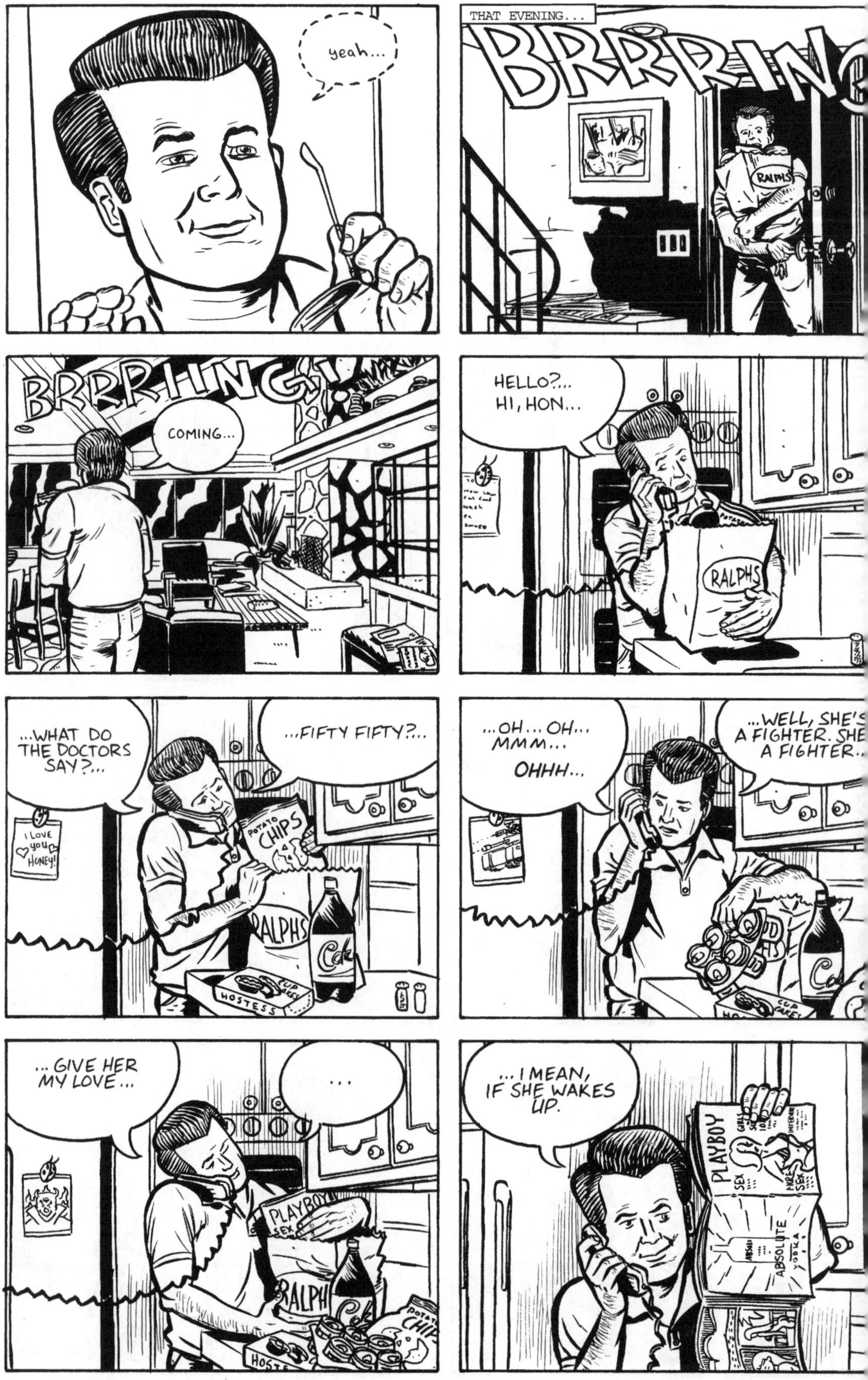
yeah...
THAT EVENING...
BRRRING
RALPHS
BRRRING!
COMING...
HELLO?...
HI, HON...
RALPHS
...WHAT DO THE DOCTORS SAY?...
...FIFTY FIFTY?...
I LOVE YOU HONEY!
POTATO CHIPS
RALPHS
HOSTESS
CUP CAKES
...OH... OH... MMM...
OHHH...
...WELL, SHE'S A FIGHTER. SHE'S A FIGHTER...
... GIVE HER MY LOVE...
...
PLAYBOY
SEX
RALPH
...I MEAN, IF SHE WAKES UP.
PLAYBOY
SEX
ABSOLUTE VODKA

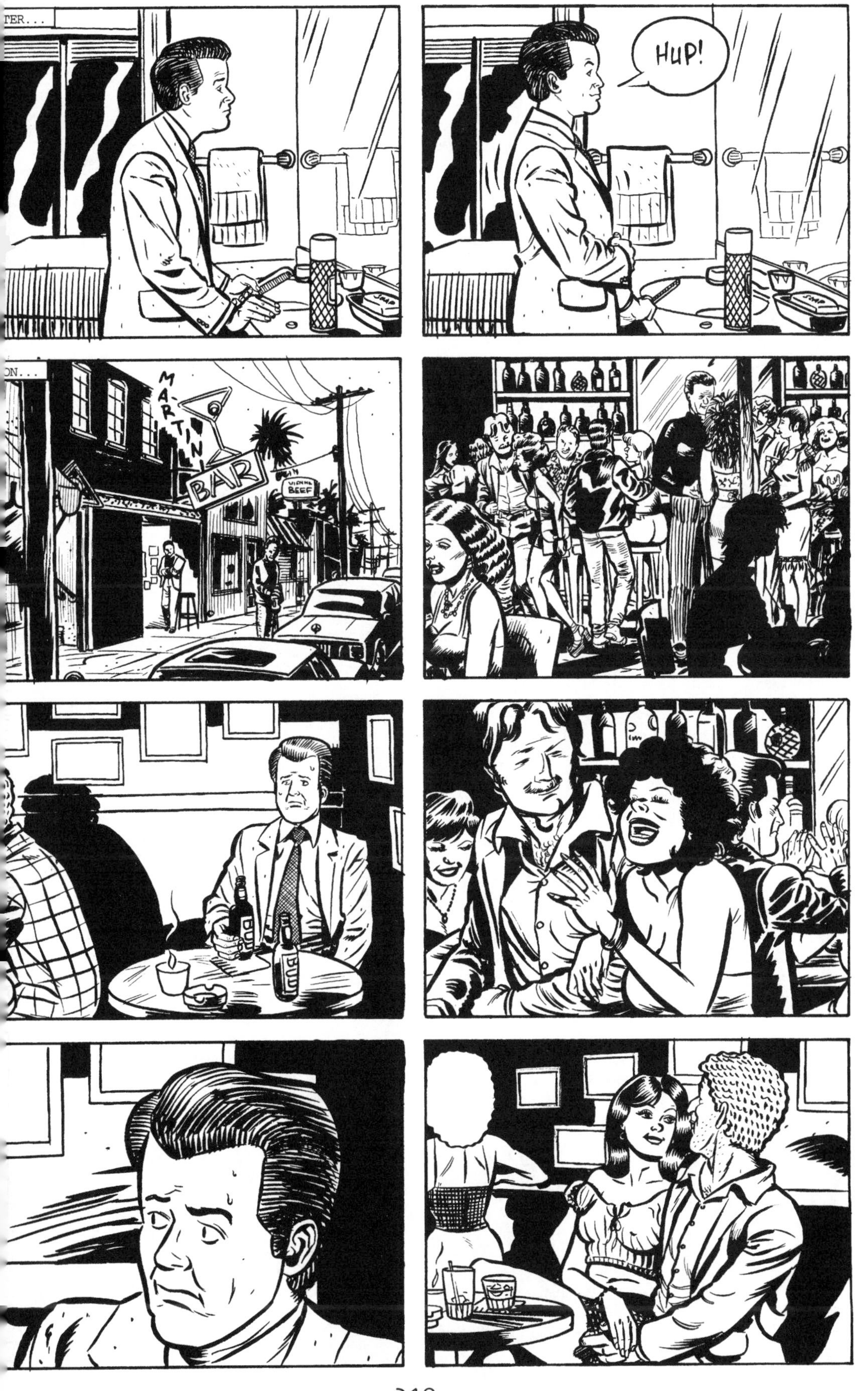
TER...
HUP!
ON...
MARTINI
BAR
VIENNA BEEF
BUD
BUD

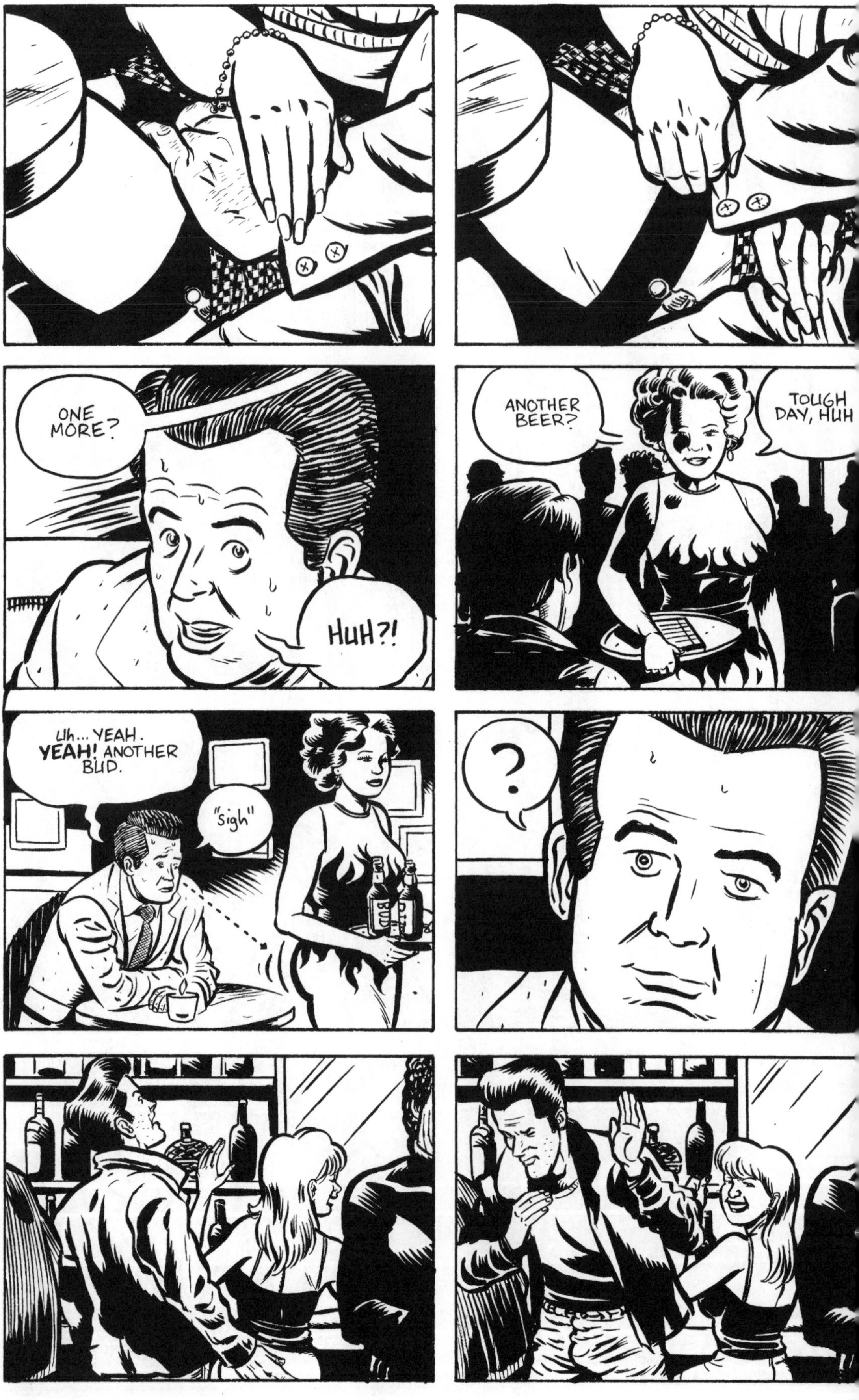
ONE MORE?
HUH?!
ANOTHER BEER?
TOUGH DAY, HUH
Uh... YEAH. YEAH! ANOTHER BUD.
"Sigh"
?

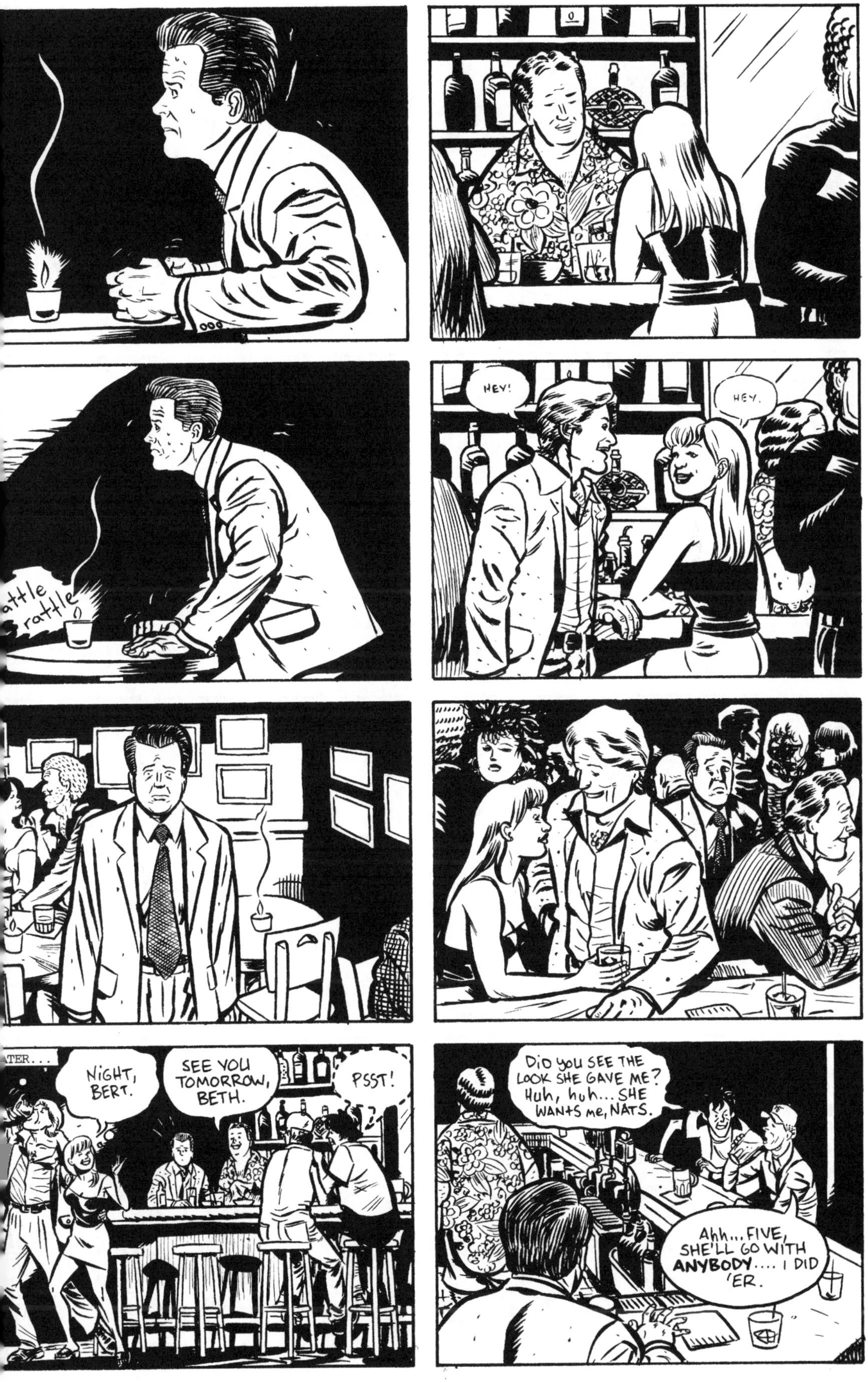
rattle rattle
HEY!
HEY.
LATER...
NIGHT, BERT.
SEE YOU TOMORROW, BETH.
PSST!
DID YOU SEE THE LOOK SHE GAVE ME? HUH, HUH... SHE WANTS ME, NATS.
AHH... FIVE, SHE'LL GO WITH ANYBODY.... I DID 'ER.

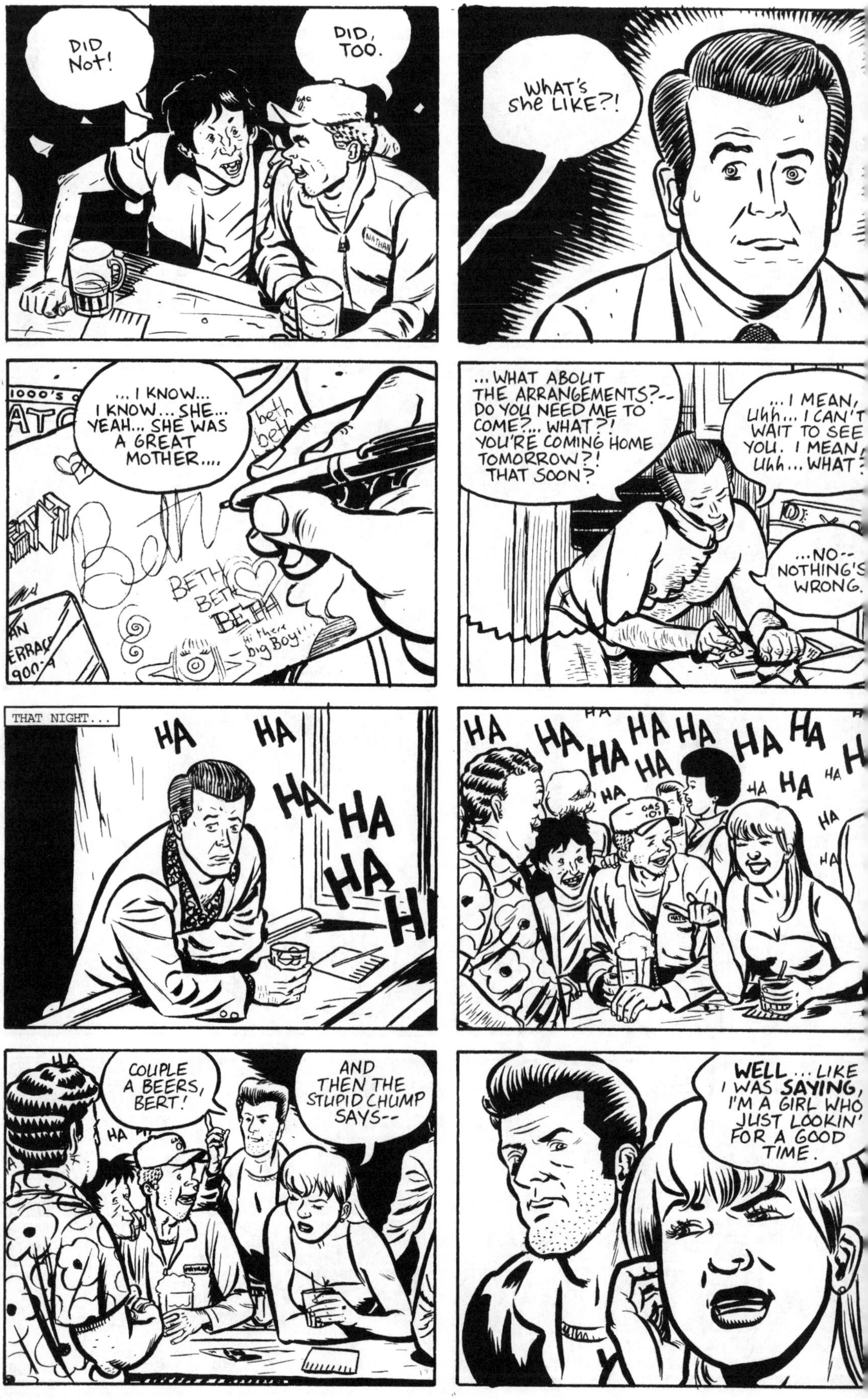
DID Not!
DID, TOO.
WHAT'S she LIKE?!
... I KNOW... I KNOW... SHE... YEAH... SHE WAS A GREAT MOTHER....
... WHAT ABOUT THE ARRANGEMENTS?-- DO YOU NEED ME TO COME?... WHAT?! YOU'RE COMING HOME TOMORROW?! THAT SOON?
... I MEAN, Uhh... I CAN'T WAIT TO SEE YOU. I MEAN, Uhh... WHAT?
...NO-- NOTHING'S WRONG.
THAT NIGHT...
HA HA HA HA HA
HA HA HA HA HA HA HA HA HA HA HA
COUPLE A BEERS, BERT!
AND THEN THE STUPID CHUMP SAYS--
WELL... LIKE I WAS SAYING, I'M A GIRL WHO JUST LOOKIN' FOR A GOOD TIME.

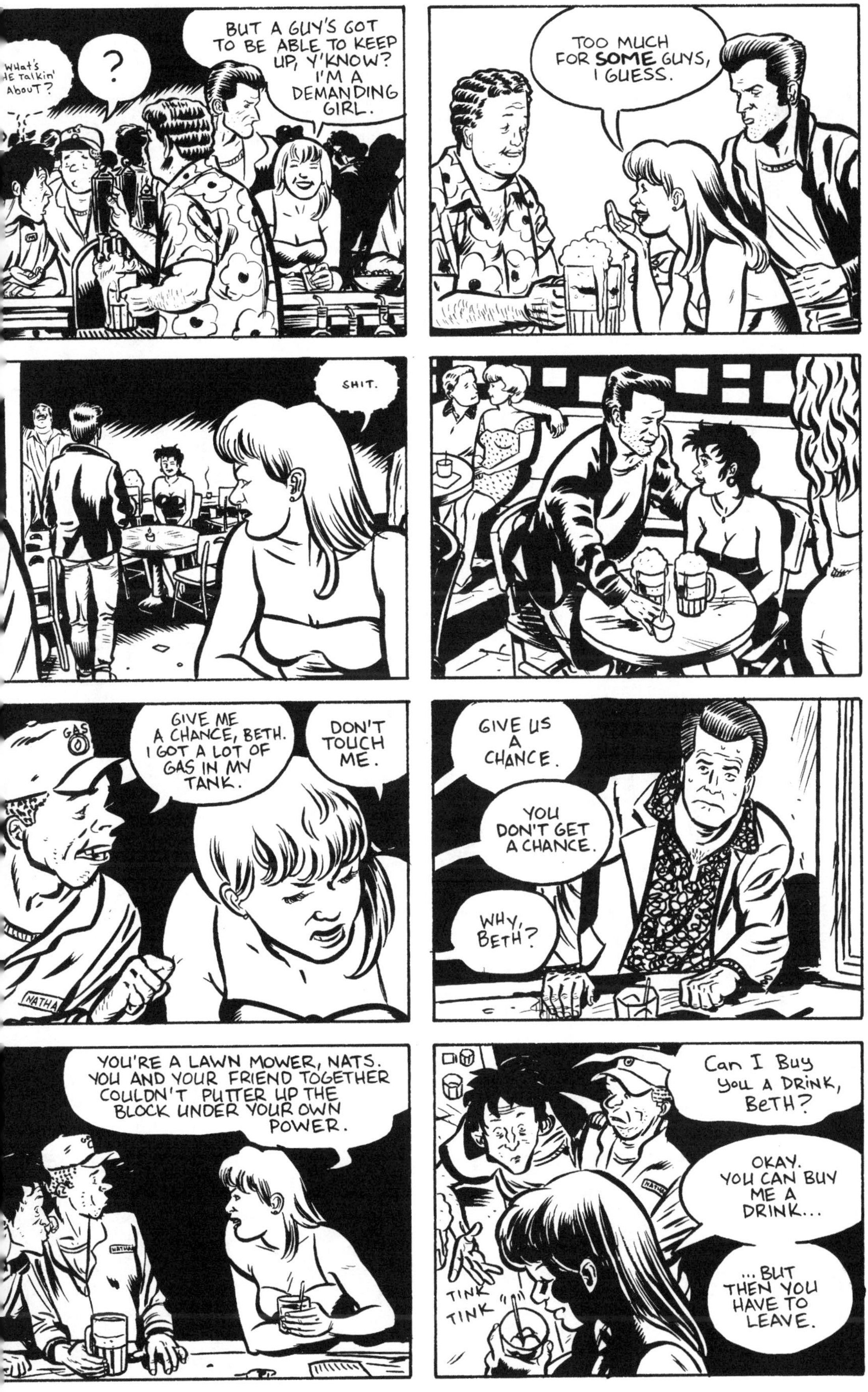
What's HE Talkin' AbouT?
?
BUT A GUY'S GOT TO BE ABLE TO KEEP UP, Y'KNOW? I'M A DEMANDING GIRL.
TOO MUCH FOR SOME GUYS, I GUESS.
SHIT.
GIVE ME A CHANCE, BETH. I GOT A LOT OF GAS IN MY TANK.
DON'T TOUCH ME.
GIVE US A CHANCE.
YOU DON'T GET A CHANCE.
WHY, BETH?
YOU'RE A LAWN MOWER, NATS. YOU AND YOUR FRIEND TOGETHER COULDN'T PUTTER UP THE BLOCK UNDER YOUR OWN POWER.
Can I Buy you a DRINK, BeTH?
OKAY. YOU CAN BUY ME A DRINK...
...BUT THEN YOU HAVE TO LEAVE.
TINK TINK

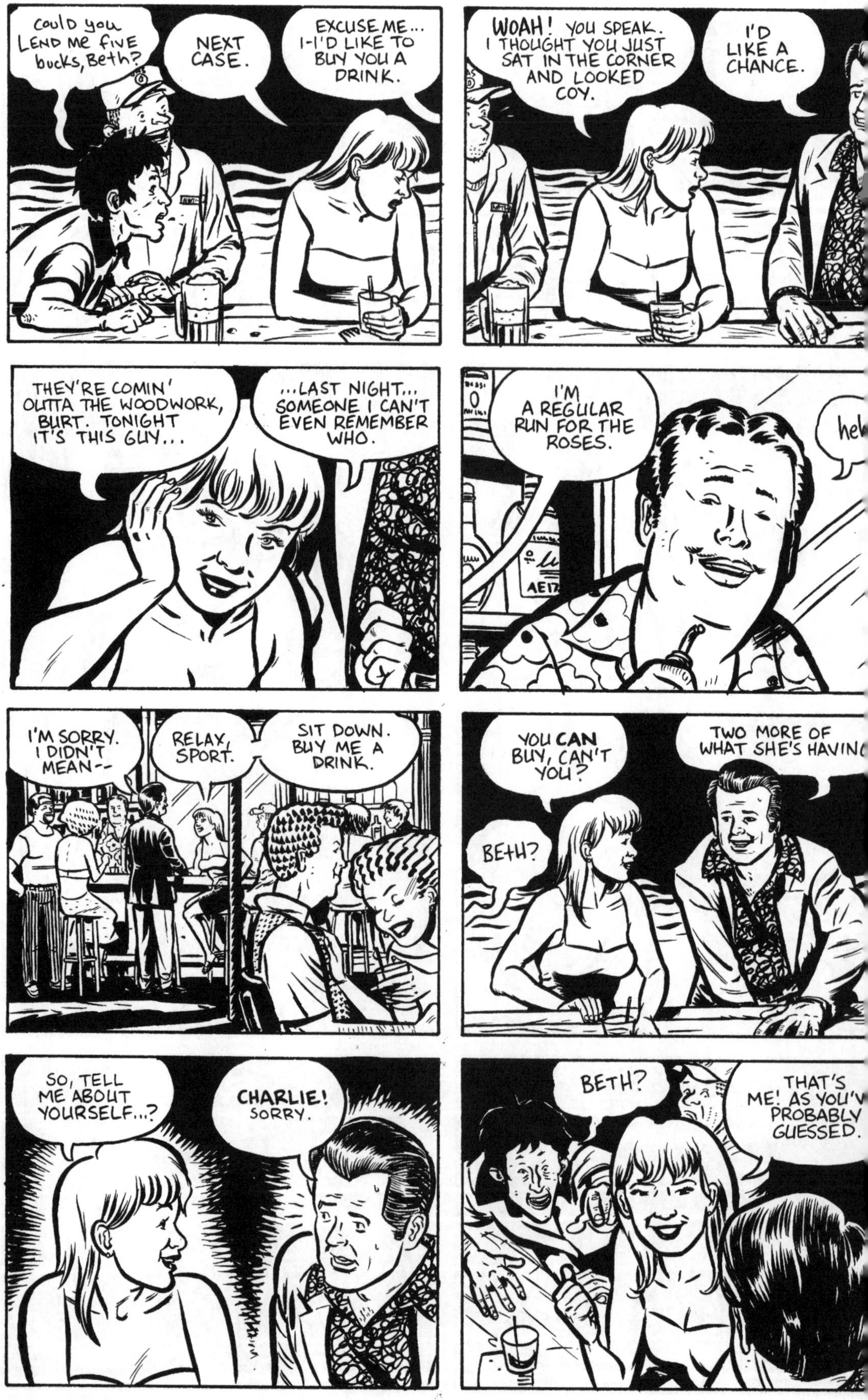
Could you Lend me five bucks, Beth?
NEXT CASE.
EXCUSE ME... I-I'D LIKE TO BUY YOU A DRINK.
WOAH! YOU SPEAK. I THOUGHT YOU JUST SAT IN THE CORNER AND LOOKED COY.
I'D LIKE A CHANCE.
THEY'RE COMIN' OUTTA THE WOODWORK, BURT. TONIGHT IT'S THIS GUY...
...LAST NIGHT... SOMEONE I CAN'T EVEN REMEMBER WHO.
I'M A REGULAR RUN FOR THE ROSES.
I'M SORRY. I DIDN'T MEAN--
RELAX, SPORT.
SIT DOWN. BUY ME A DRINK.
YOU **CAN** BUY, CAN'T YOU?
TWO MORE OF WHAT SHE'S HAVIN
BETH?
SO, TELL ME ABOUT YOURSELF...?
**CHARLIE!** SORRY.
BETH?
THAT'S ME! AS YOU'V PROBABLY GUESSED.

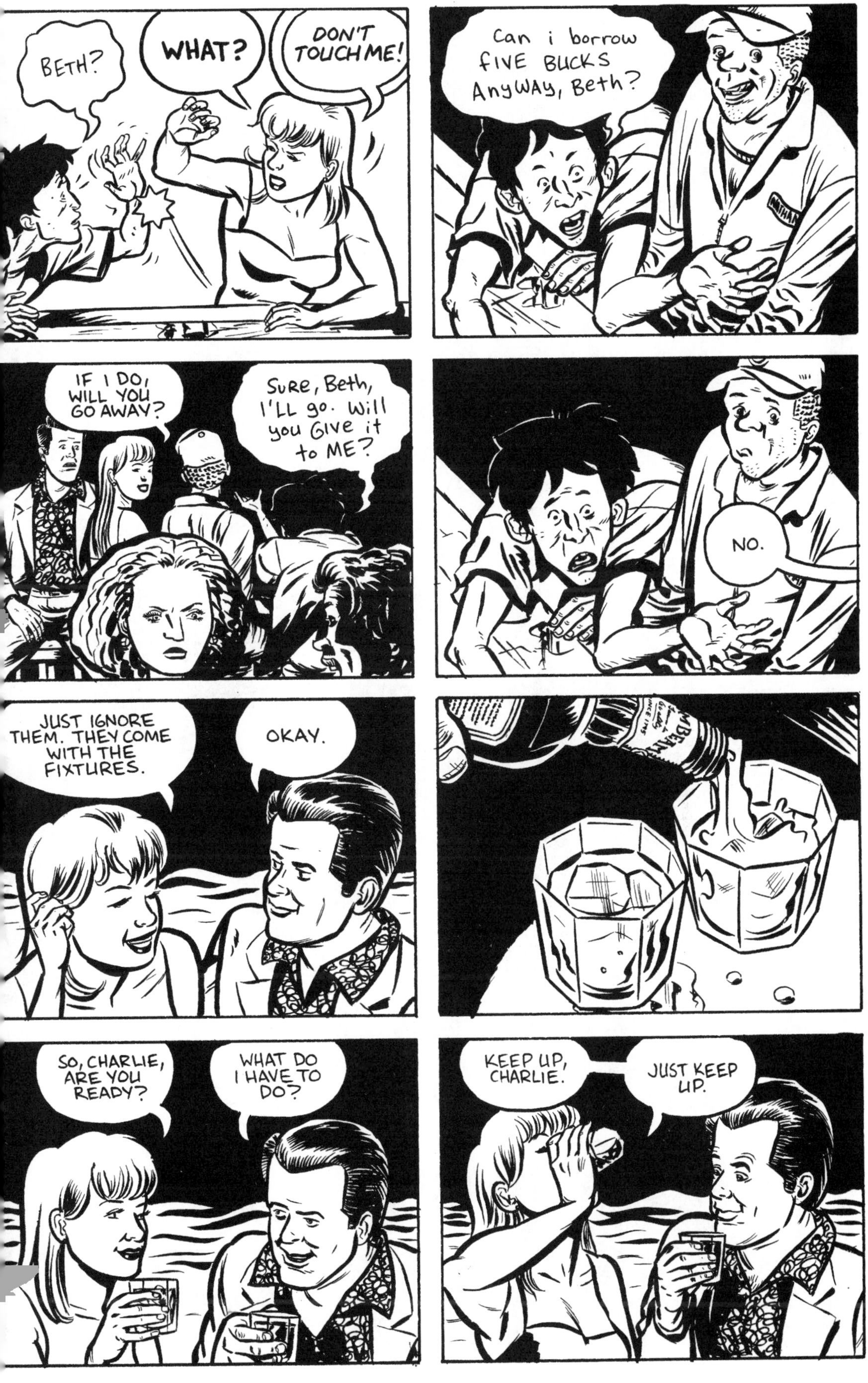
BETH?
WHAT?
DON'T TOUCH ME!
Can i borrow FIVE BUCKS Anyway, Beth?
IF I DO, WILL YOU GO AWAY?
Sure, Beth, I'LL go. Will you Give it to ME?
NO.
JUST IGNORE THEM. THEY COME WITH THE FIXTURES.
OKAY.
SO, CHARLIE, ARE YOU READY?
WHAT DO I HAVE TO DO?
KEEP UP, CHARLIE.
JUST KEEP UP.

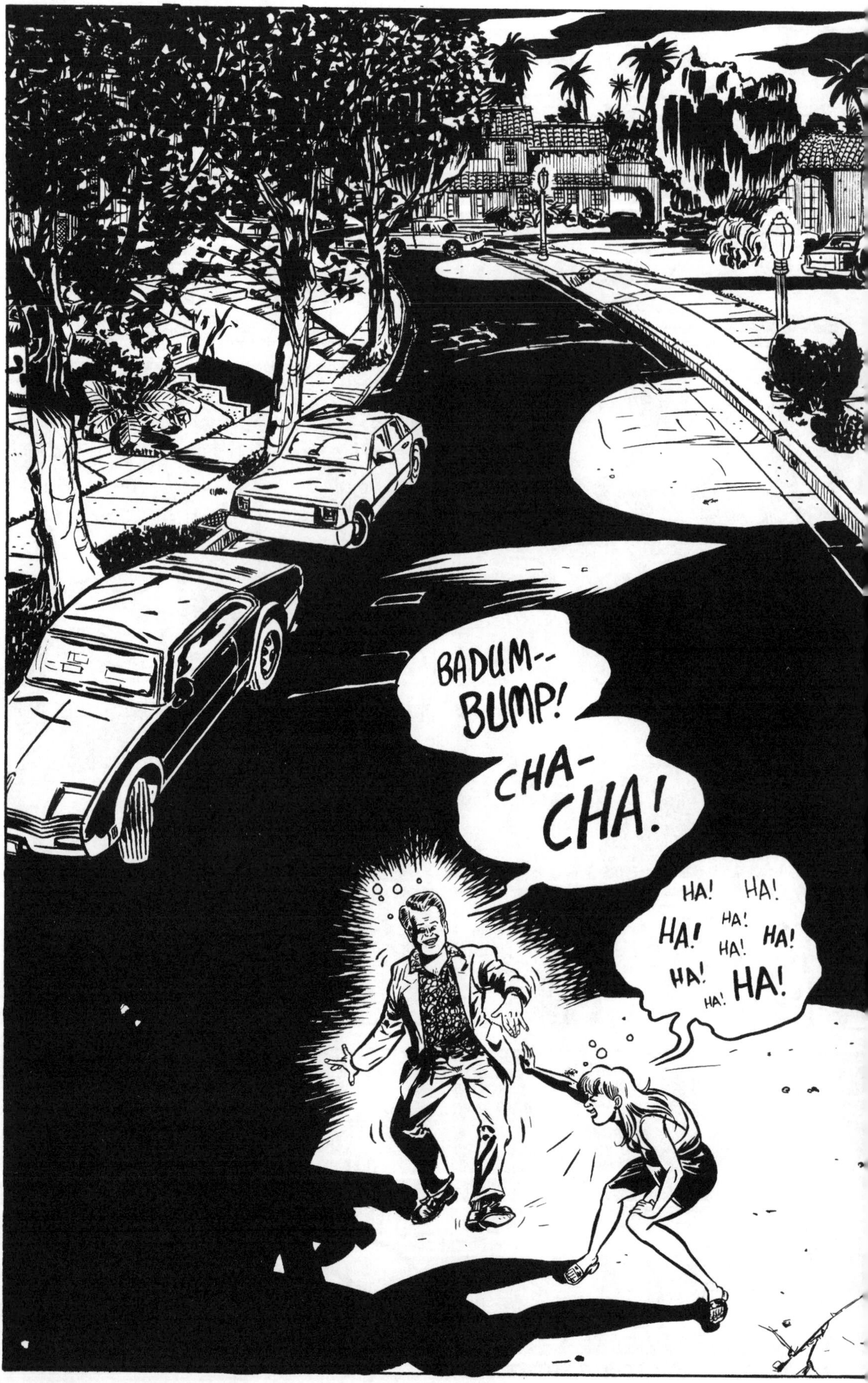
BADUM--
BUMP!
CHA-
CHA!
HA! HA! HA! HA! HA! HA! HA! HA! HA! HA!

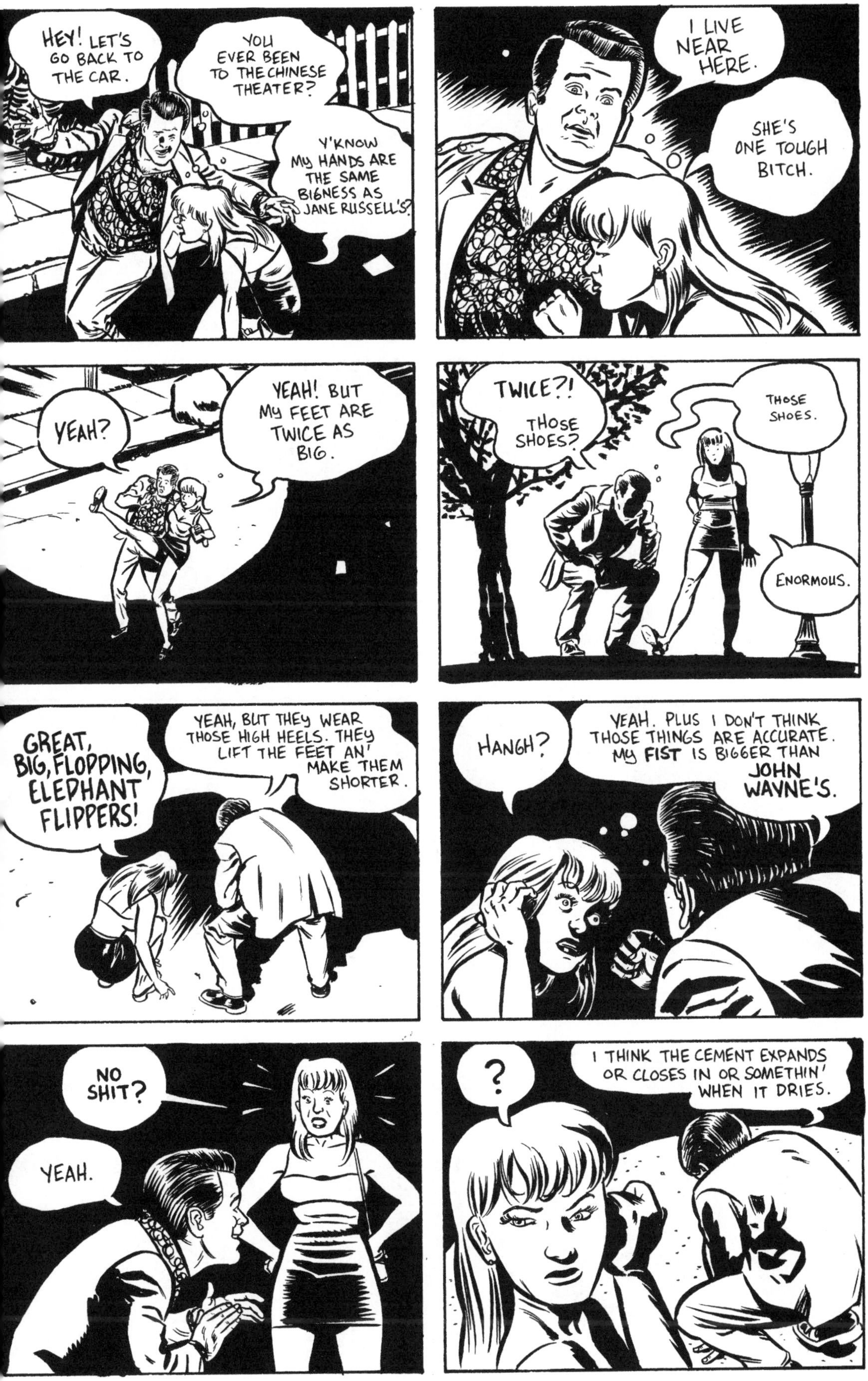
HEY! LET'S GO BACK TO THE CAR.
YOU EVER BEEN TO THE CHINESE THEATER?
Y'KNOW MY HANDS ARE THE SAME BIGNESS AS JANE RUSSELL'S?
I LIVE NEAR HERE.
SHE'S ONE TOUGH BITCH.
YEAH?
YEAH! BUT MY FEET ARE TWICE AS BIG.
TWICE?! THOSE SHOES?
THOSE SHOES.
ENORMOUS.
GREAT, BIG, FLOPPING, ELEPHANT FLIPPERS!
YEAH, BUT THEY WEAR THOSE HIGH HEELS. THEY LIFT THE FEET AN' MAKE THEM SHORTER.
HANGH?
YEAH. PLUS I DON'T THINK THOSE THINGS ARE ACCURATE. MY FIST IS BIGGER THAN JOHN WAYNE'S.
NO SHIT?
YEAH.
?
I THINK THE CEMENT EXPANDS OR CLOSES IN OR SOMETHIN' WHEN IT DRIES.

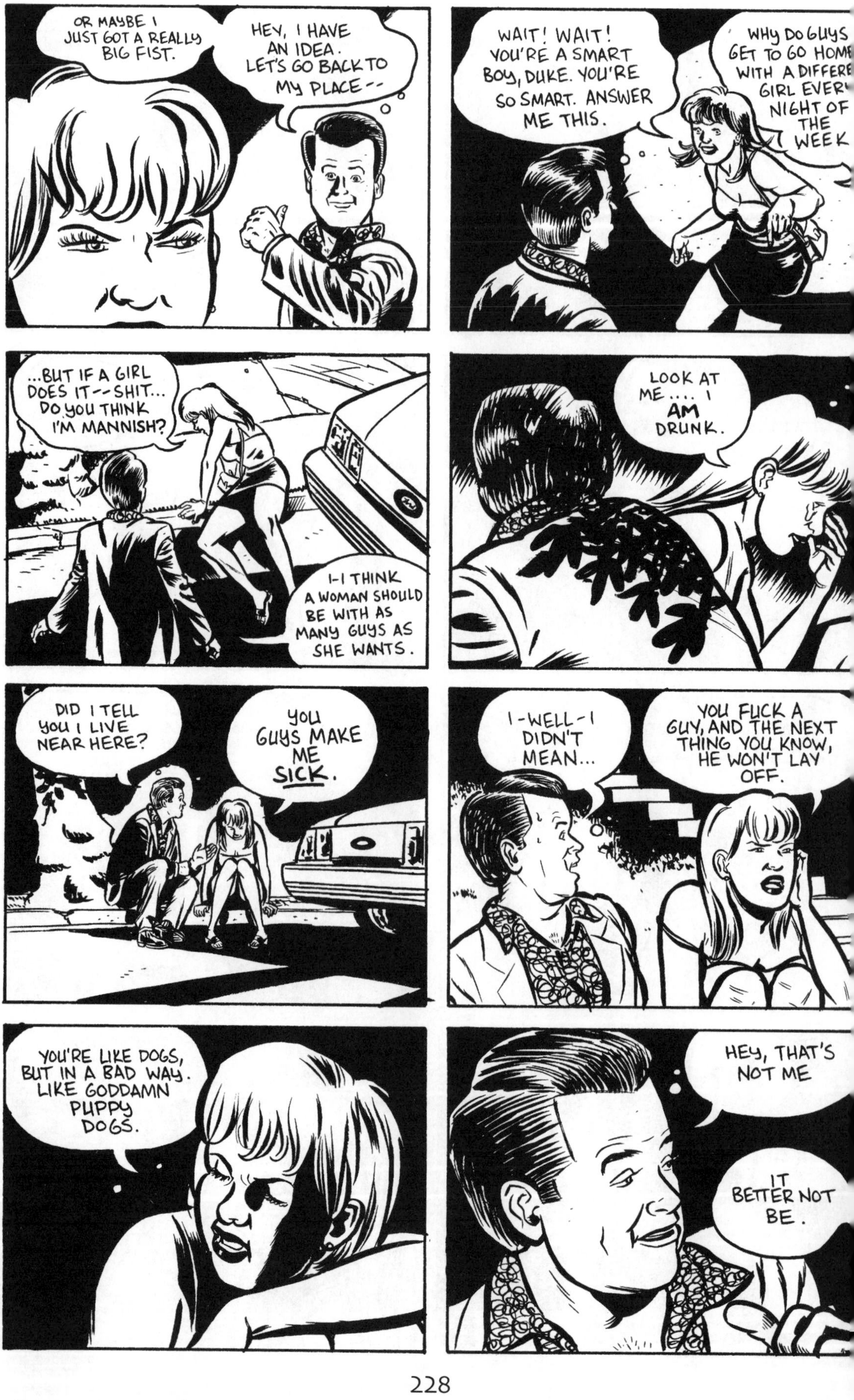
OR MAYBE I JUST GOT A REALLY BIG FIST.
HEY, I HAVE AN IDEA. LET'S GO BACK TO MY PLACE--
WAIT! WAIT! YOU'RE A SMART BOY, DUKE. YOU'RE SO SMART. ANSWER ME THIS.
WHY DO GUYS GET TO GO HOM WITH A DIFFERE GIRL EVER NIGHT OF THE WEEK
...BUT IF A GIRL DOES IT--SHIT... DO YOU THINK I'M MANNISH?
I-I THINK A WOMAN SHOULD BE WITH AS MANY GUYS AS SHE WANTS.
LOOK AT ME.... I AM DRUNK.
DID I TELL YOU I LIVE NEAR HERE?
YOU GUYS MAKE ME SICK.
I-WELL-I DIDN'T MEAN...
YOU FUCK A GUY, AND THE NEXT THING YOU KNOW, HE WON'T LAY OFF.
YOU'RE LIKE DOGS, BUT IN A BAD WAY. LIKE GODDAMN PUPPY DOGS.
HEY, THAT'S NOT ME
IT BETTER NOT BE.

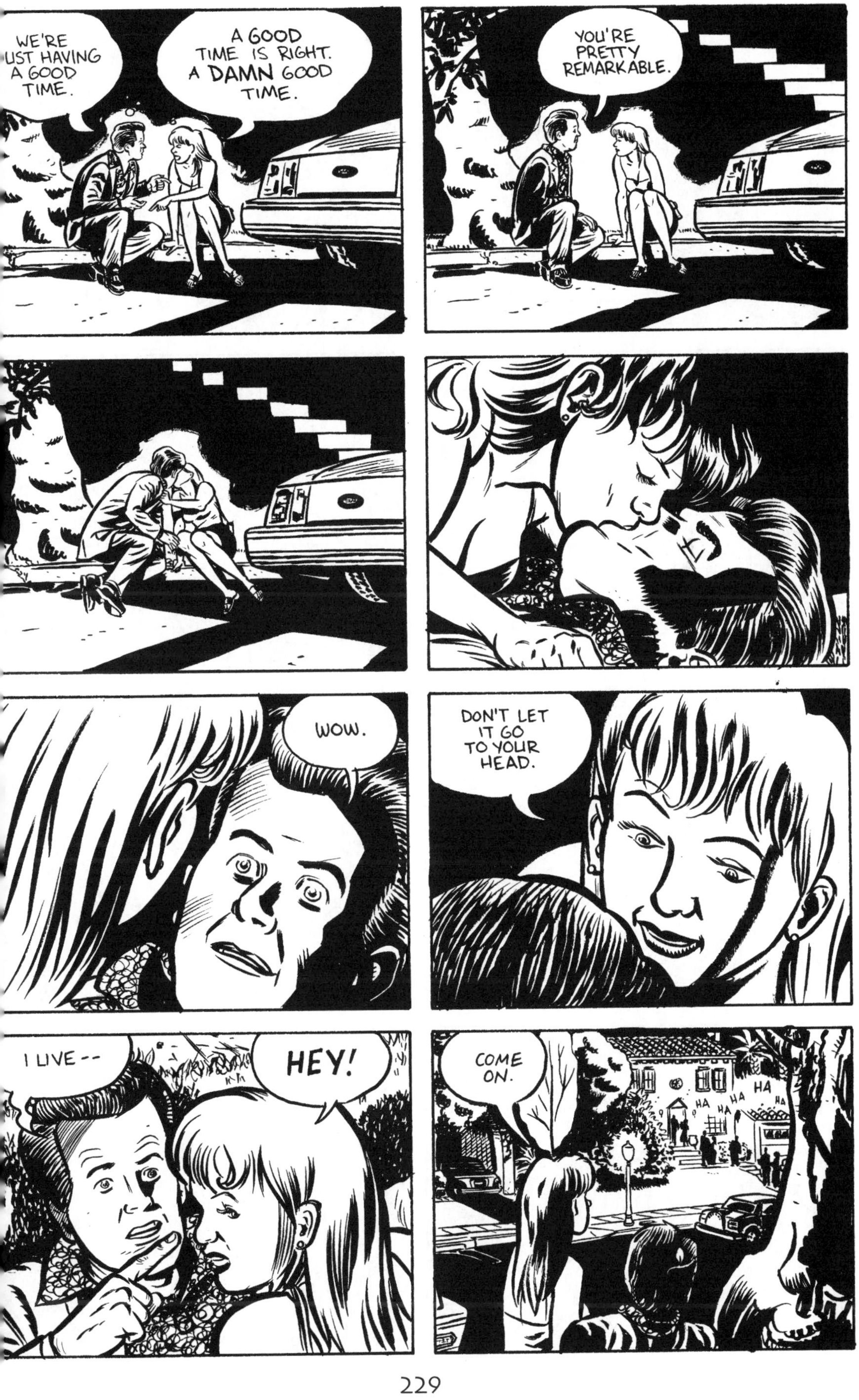
WE'RE UST HAVING A GOOD TIME.
A GOOD TIME IS RIGHT. A DAMN GOOD TIME.
YOU'RE PRETTY REMARKABLE.
WOW.
DON'T LET IT GO TO YOUR HEAD.
I LIVE --
HEY!
COME ON.
HA HA HA HA HA

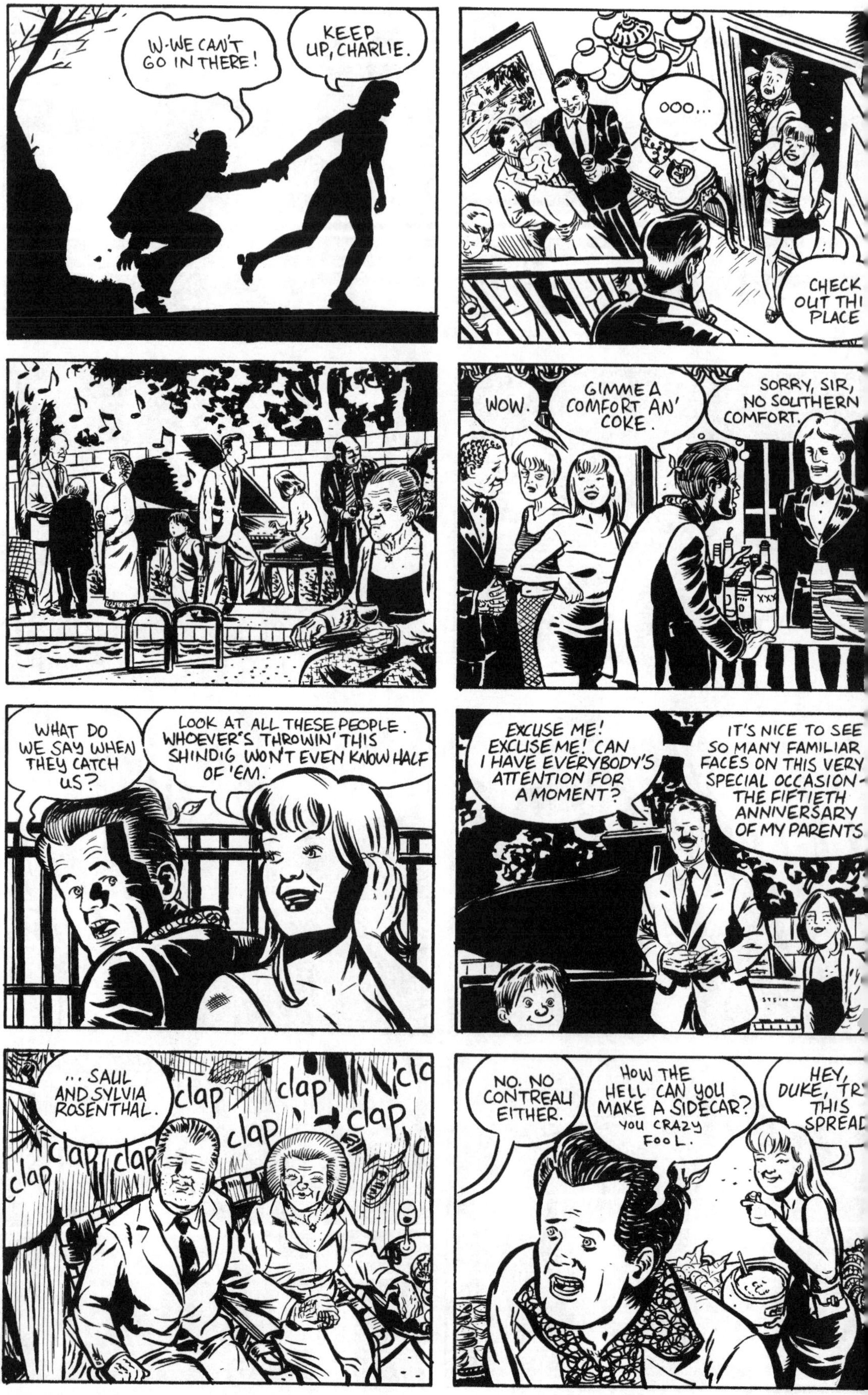
W-WE CAN'T GO IN THERE!
KEEP UP, CHARLIE.
OOO...
CHECK OUT THI PLACE
WOW.
GIMME A COMFORT AN' COKE.
SORRY, SIR, NO SOUTHERN COMFORT.
WHAT DO WE SAY WHEN THEY CATCH US?
LOOK AT ALL THESE PEOPLE. WHOEVER'S THROWIN' THIS SHINDIG WON'T EVEN KNOW HALF OF 'EM.
EXCUSE ME! EXCUSE ME! CAN I HAVE EVERYBODY'S ATTENTION FOR A MOMENT?
IT'S NICE TO SEE SO MANY FAMILIAR FACES ON THIS VERY SPECIAL OCCASION- THE FIFTIETH ANNIVERSARY OF MY PARENTS
...SAUL AND SYLVIA ROSENTHAL.
clap clap clap clap clap clap clap clap
NO. NO CONTREAU EITHER.
HOW THE HELL CAN YOU MAKE A SIDECAR? YOU CRAZY FOOL.
HEY, DUKE, TR THIS SPREAD

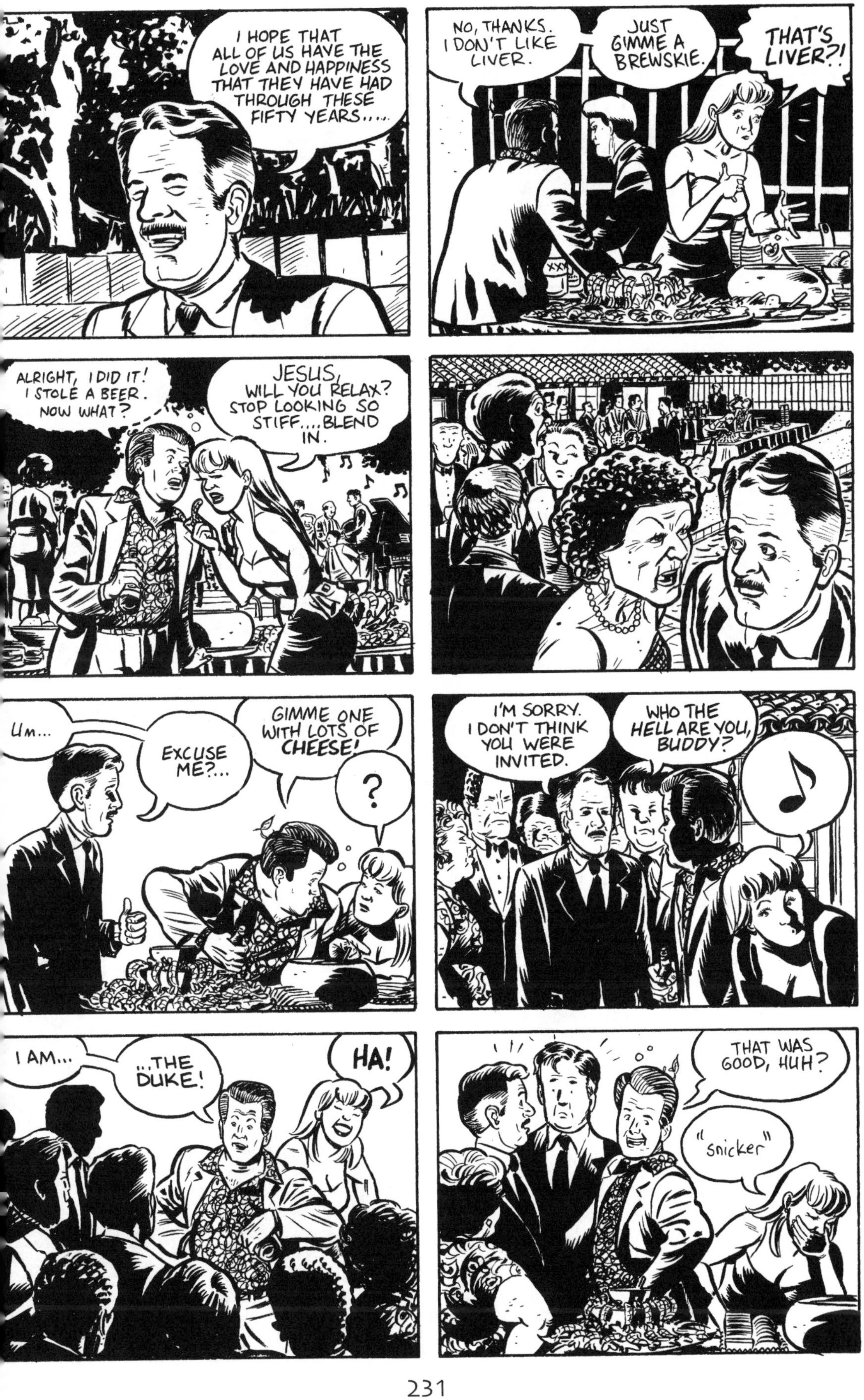
I HOPE THAT ALL OF US HAVE THE LOVE AND HAPPINESS THAT THEY HAVE HAD THROUGH THESE FIFTY YEARS....
NO, THANKS. I DON'T LIKE LIVER.
JUST GIMME A BREWSKIE.
THAT'S LIVER?!
ALRIGHT, I DID IT! I STOLE A BEER. NOW WHAT?
JESUS, WILL YOU RELAX? STOP LOOKING SO STIFF....BLEND IN.
Um...
EXCUSE ME?...
GIMME ONE WITH LOTS OF CHEESE!
?
I'M SORRY. I DON'T THINK YOU WERE INVITED.
WHO THE HELL ARE YOU, BUDDY?
I AM...
...THE DUKE!
HA!
THAT WAS GOOD, HUH?
"snicker"

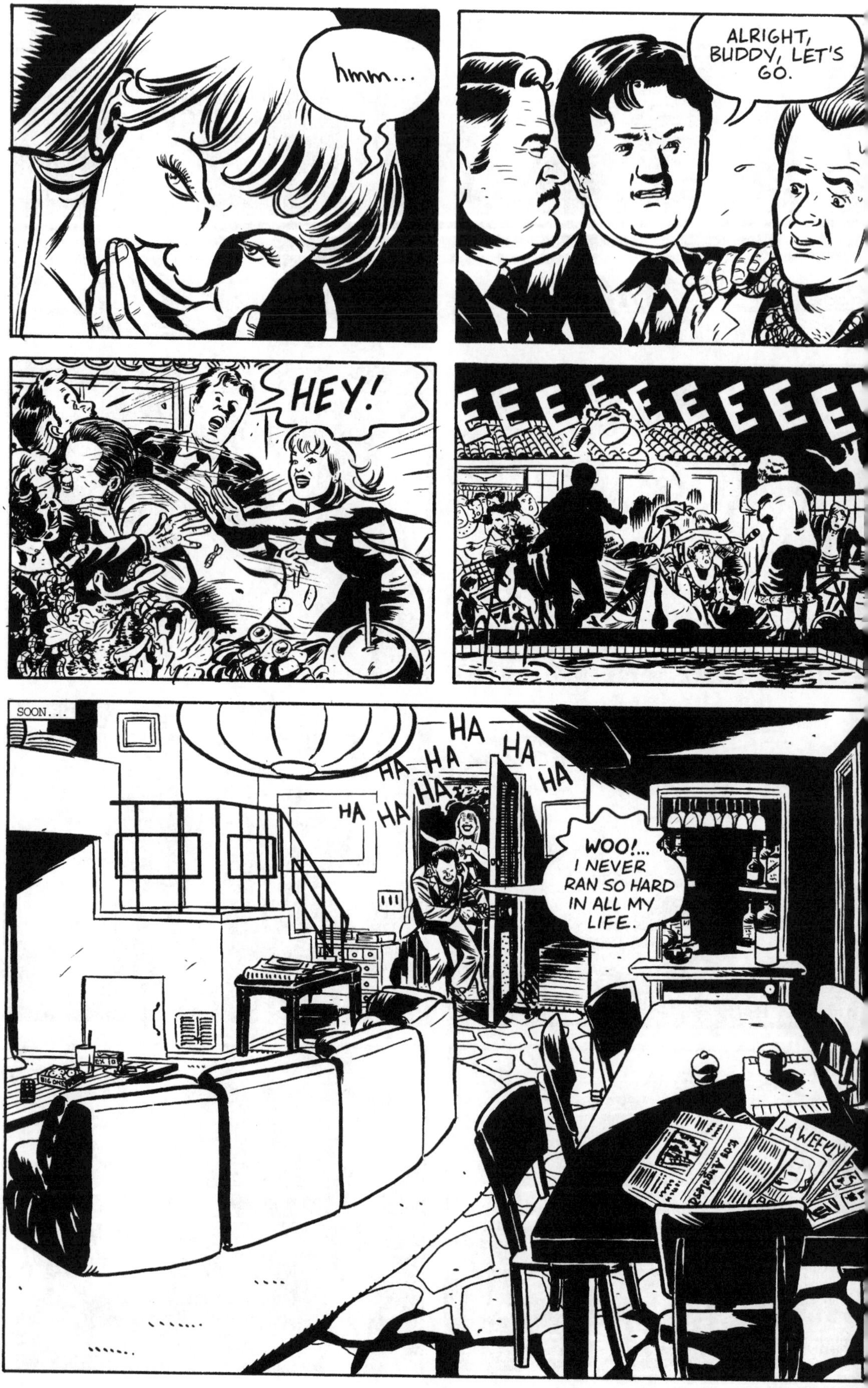
hmm...
ALRIGHT, BUDDY, LET'S GO.
HEY!
EEEEEEEEE
SOON...
HA HA HA HA HA HA HA HA
WOO!... I NEVER RAN SO HARD IN ALL MY LIFE.
LA WEEKLY

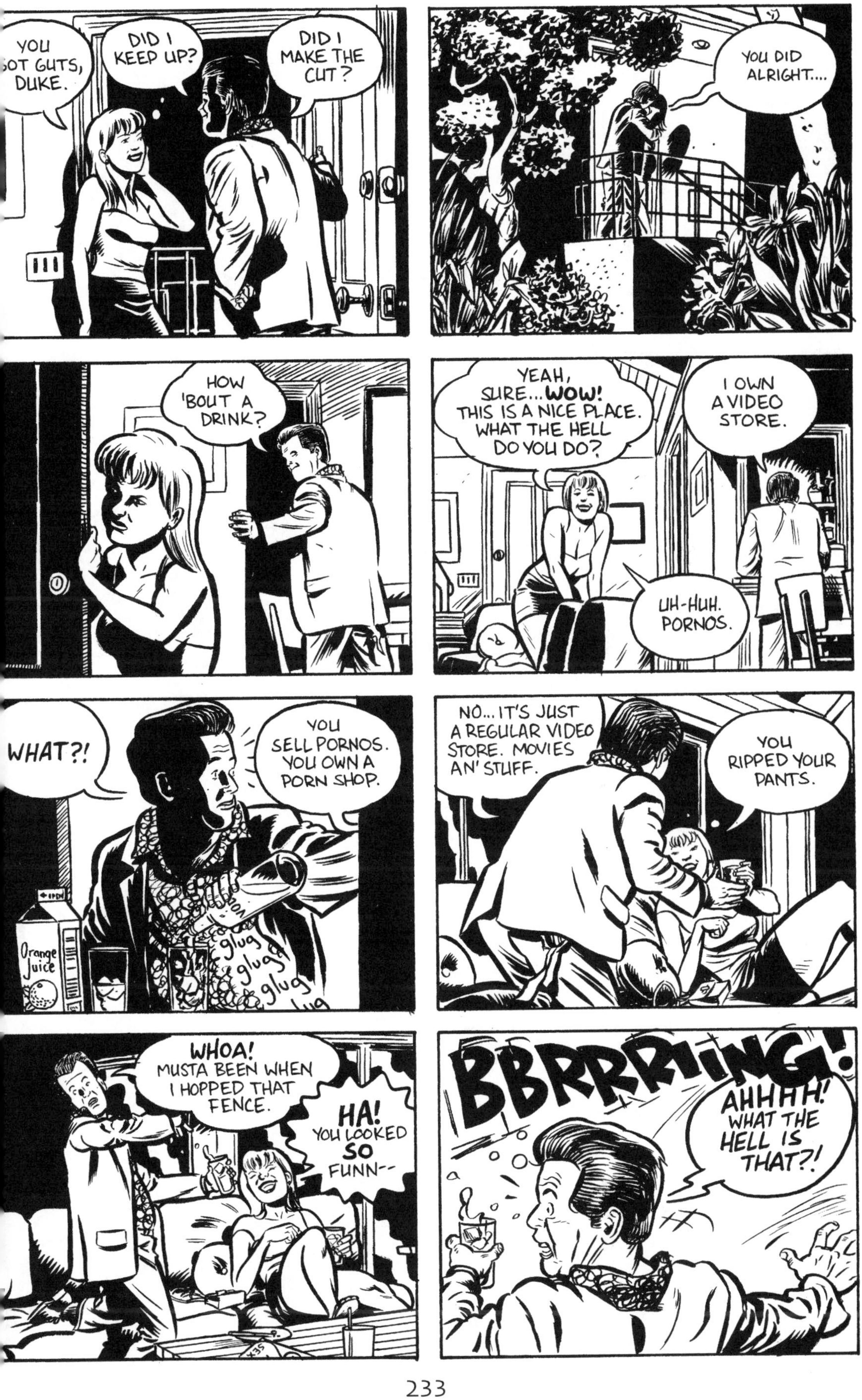
YOU GOT GUTS, DUKE.
DID I KEEP UP?
DID I MAKE THE CUT?
YOU DID ALRIGHT....
HOW 'BOUT A DRINK?
YEAH, SURE... WOW! THIS IS A NICE PLACE. WHAT THE HELL DO YOU DO?
I OWN A VIDEO STORE.
UH-HUH. PORNOS.
WHAT?!
YOU SELL PORNOS. YOU OWN A PORN SHOP.
Orange Juice
glug glug glug lug
NO... IT'S JUST A REGULAR VIDEO STORE. MOVIES AN' STUFF.
YOU RIPPED YOUR PANTS.
WHOA! MUSTA BEEN WHEN I HOPPED THAT FENCE.
HA! YOU LOOKED SO FUNN--
BBRRRING!
AHHHH! WHAT THE HELL IS THAT?!

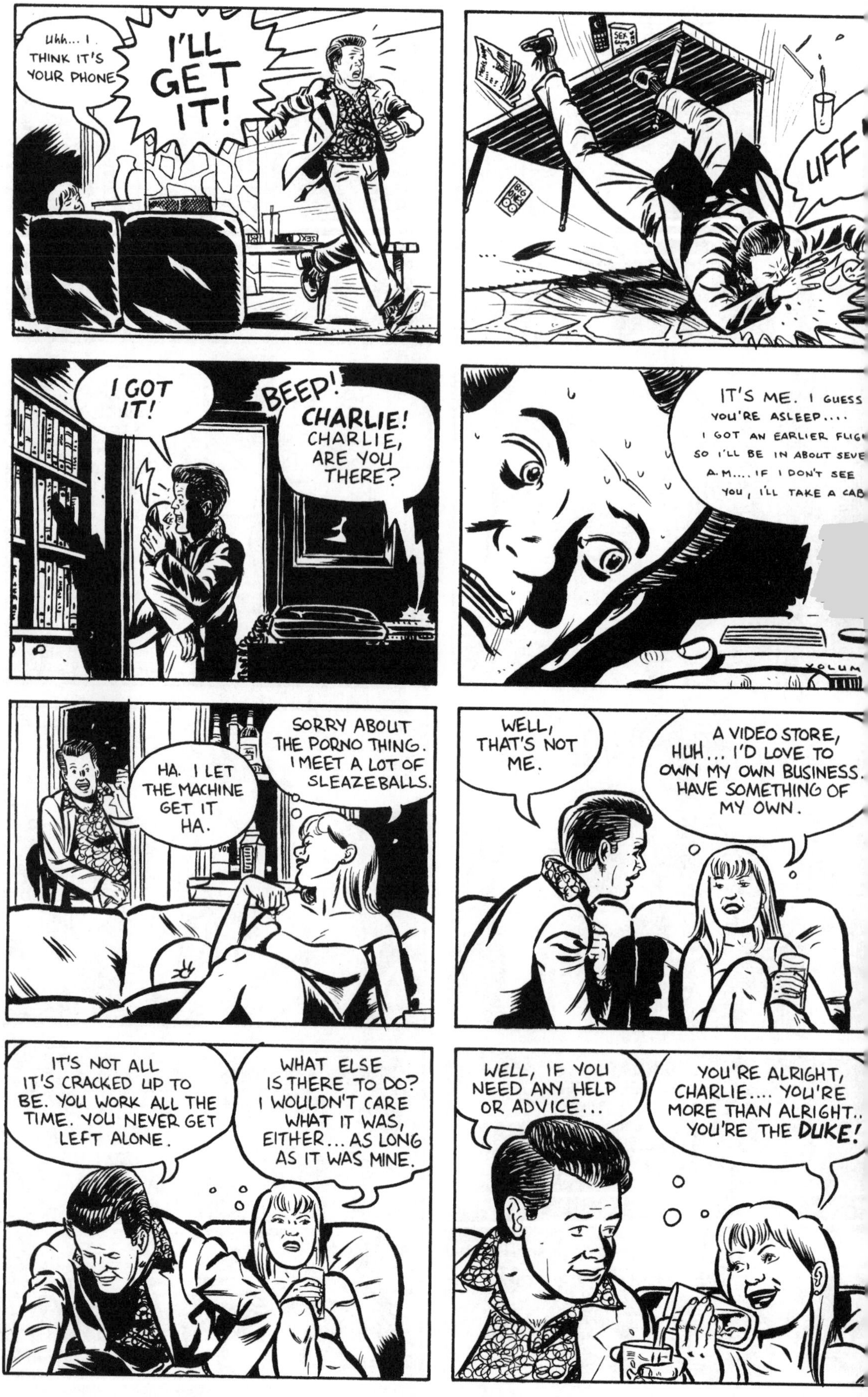
Uhh... I THINK IT'S YOUR PHONE
I'LL GET IT!
UFF
I GOT IT!
BEEP!
CHARLIE! CHARLIE, ARE YOU THERE?
IT'S ME. I GUESS YOU'RE ASLEEP.... I GOT AN EARLIER FLIG SO I'LL BE IN ABOUT SEVE A.M.... IF I DON'T SEE YOU, I'LL TAKE A CAB
HA. I LET THE MACHINE GET IT HA.
SORRY ABOUT THE PORNO THING. I MEET A LOT OF SLEAZEBALLS.
WELL, THAT'S NOT ME.
A VIDEO STORE, HUH... I'D LOVE TO OWN MY OWN BUSINESS. HAVE SOMETHING OF MY OWN.
IT'S NOT ALL IT'S CRACKED UP TO BE. YOU WORK ALL THE TIME. YOU NEVER GET LEFT ALONE.
WHAT ELSE IS THERE TO DO? I WOULDN'T CARE WHAT IT WAS, EITHER... AS LONG AS IT WAS MINE.
WELL, IF YOU NEED ANY HELP OR ADVICE...
YOU'RE ALRIGHT, CHARLIE.... YOU'RE MORE THAN ALRIGHT.. YOU'RE THE DUKE!

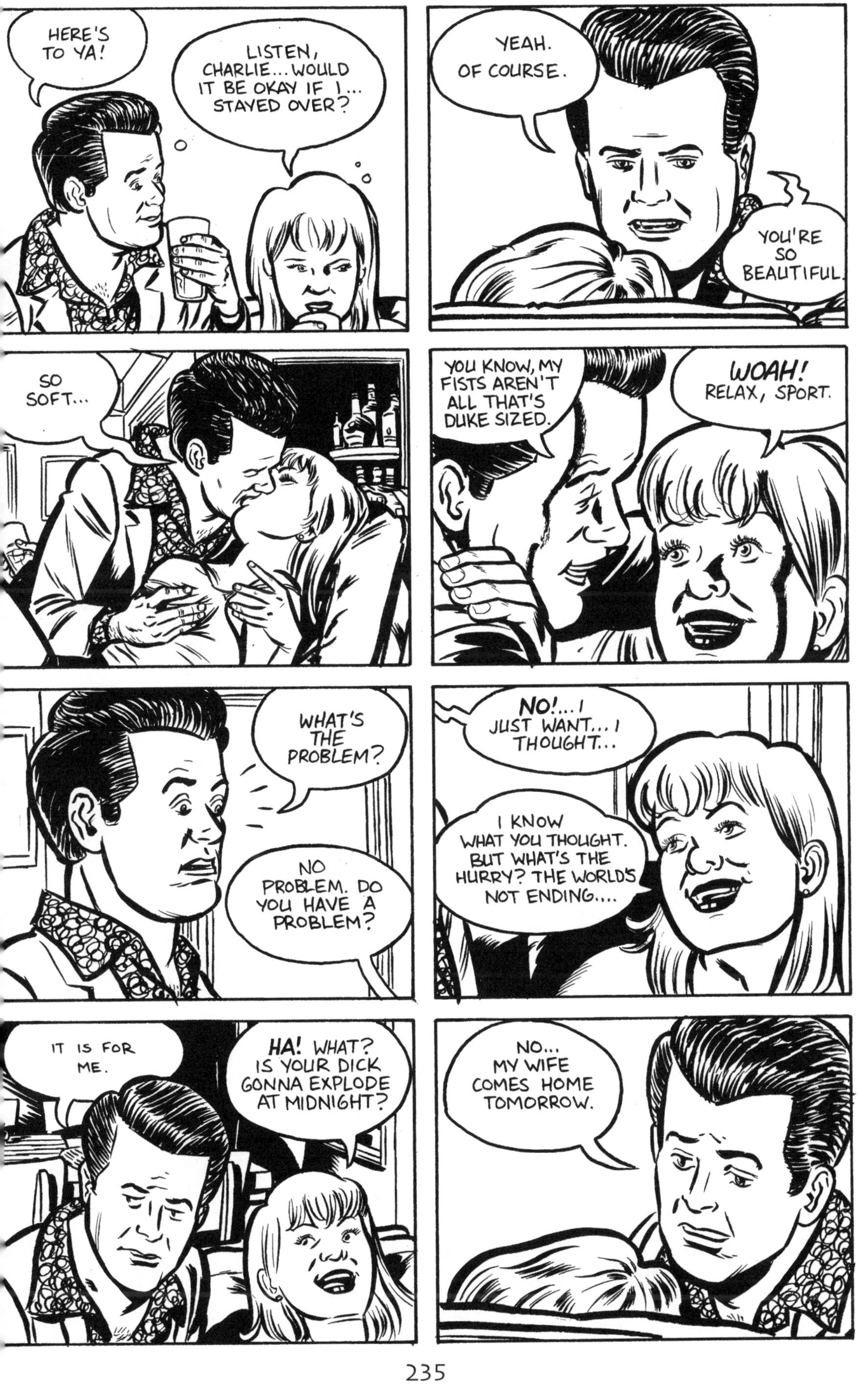
HERE'S TO YA!
LISTEN, CHARLIE... WOULD IT BE OKAY IF I... STAYED OVER?
YEAH. OF COURSE.
YOU'RE SO BEAUTIFUL.
SO SOFT...
YOU KNOW, MY FISTS AREN'T ALL THAT'S DUKE SIZED.
WOAH! RELAX, SPORT.
WHAT'S THE PROBLEM?
NO PROBLEM. DO YOU HAVE A PROBLEM?
NO!... I JUST WANT... I THOUGHT...
I KNOW WHAT YOU THOUGHT. BUT WHAT'S THE HURRY? THE WORLD'S NOT ENDING....
IT IS FOR ME.
HA! WHAT? IS YOUR DICK GONNA EXPLODE AT MIDNIGHT?
NO... MY WIFE COMES HOME TOMORROW.

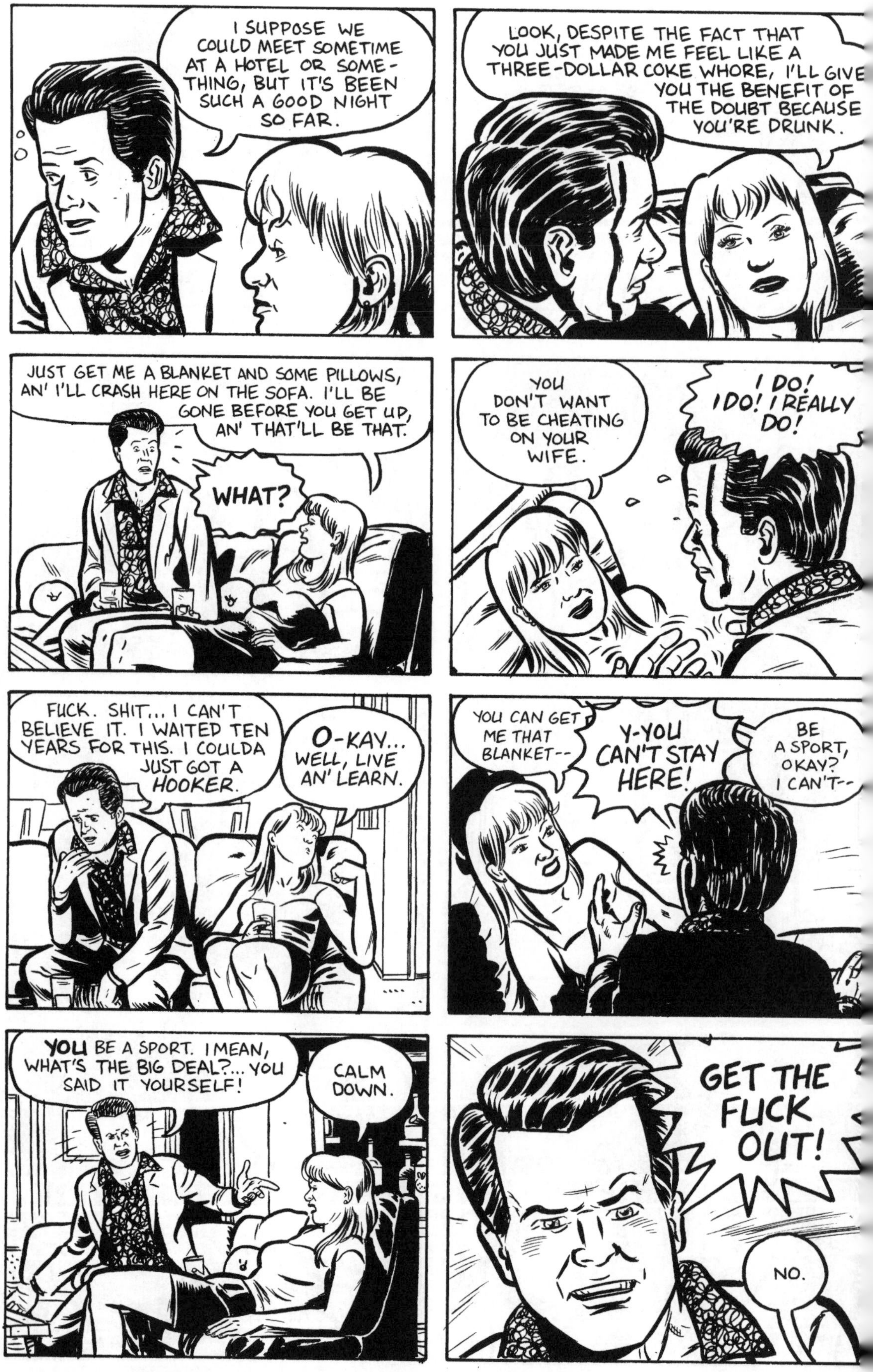
I SUPPOSE WE COULD MEET SOMETIME AT A HOTEL OR SOME-THING, BUT IT'S BEEN SUCH A GOOD NIGHT SO FAR.
LOOK, DESPITE THE FACT THAT YOU JUST MADE ME FEEL LIKE A THREE-DOLLAR COKE WHORE, I'LL GIVE YOU THE BENEFIT OF THE DOUBT BECAUSE YOU'RE DRUNK.
JUST GET ME A BLANKET AND SOME PILLOWS, AN' I'LL CRASH HERE ON THE SOFA. I'LL BE GONE BEFORE YOU GET UP, AN' THAT'LL BE THAT.
WHAT?
YOU DON'T WANT TO BE CHEATING ON YOUR WIFE.
I DO! I DO! I REALLY DO!
FUCK. SHIT... I CAN'T BELIEVE IT. I WAITED TEN YEARS FOR THIS. I COULDA JUST GOT A HOOKER.
O-KAY... WELL, LIVE AN' LEARN.
YOU CAN GET ME THAT BLANKET--
Y-YOU CAN'T STAY HERE!
BE A SPORT, OKAY? I CAN'T--
YOU BE A SPORT. I MEAN, WHAT'S THE BIG DEAL?... YOU SAID IT YOURSELF!
CALM DOWN.
GET THE FUCK OUT!
NO.

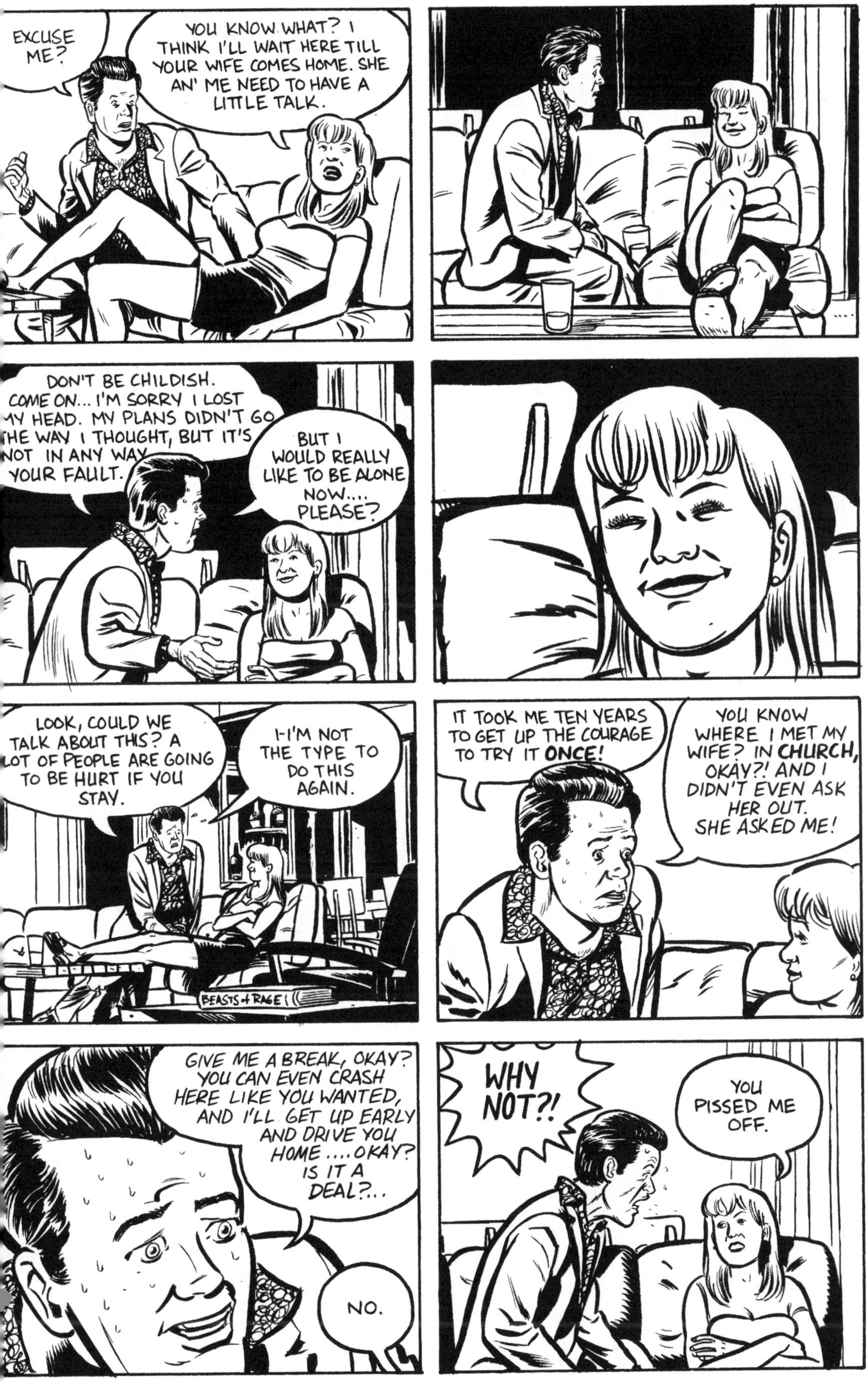

EXCUSE ME?
YOU KNOW WHAT? I THINK I'LL WAIT HERE TILL YOUR WIFE COMES HOME. SHE AN' ME NEED TO HAVE A LITTLE TALK.
DON'T BE CHILDISH. COME ON... I'M SORRY I LOST MY HEAD. MY PLANS DIDN'T GO THE WAY I THOUGHT, BUT IT'S NOT IN ANY WAY YOUR FAULT.
BUT I WOULD REALLY LIKE TO BE ALONE NOW.... PLEASE?
LOOK, COULD WE TALK ABOUT THIS? A LOT OF PEOPLE ARE GOING TO BE HURT IF YOU STAY.
I-I'M NOT THE TYPE TO DO THIS AGAIN.
BEASTS of RAGE
IT TOOK ME TEN YEARS TO GET UP THE COURAGE TO TRY IT **ONCE**!
YOU KNOW WHERE I MET MY WIFE? IN **CHURCH**, OKAY?! AND I DIDN'T EVEN ASK HER OUT. SHE ASKED ME!
GIVE ME A BREAK, OKAY? YOU CAN EVEN CRASH HERE LIKE YOU WANTED, AND I'LL GET UP EARLY AND DRIVE YOU HOME.... OKAY? IS IT A DEAL?...
NO.
WHY NOT?!
YOU PISSED ME OFF.

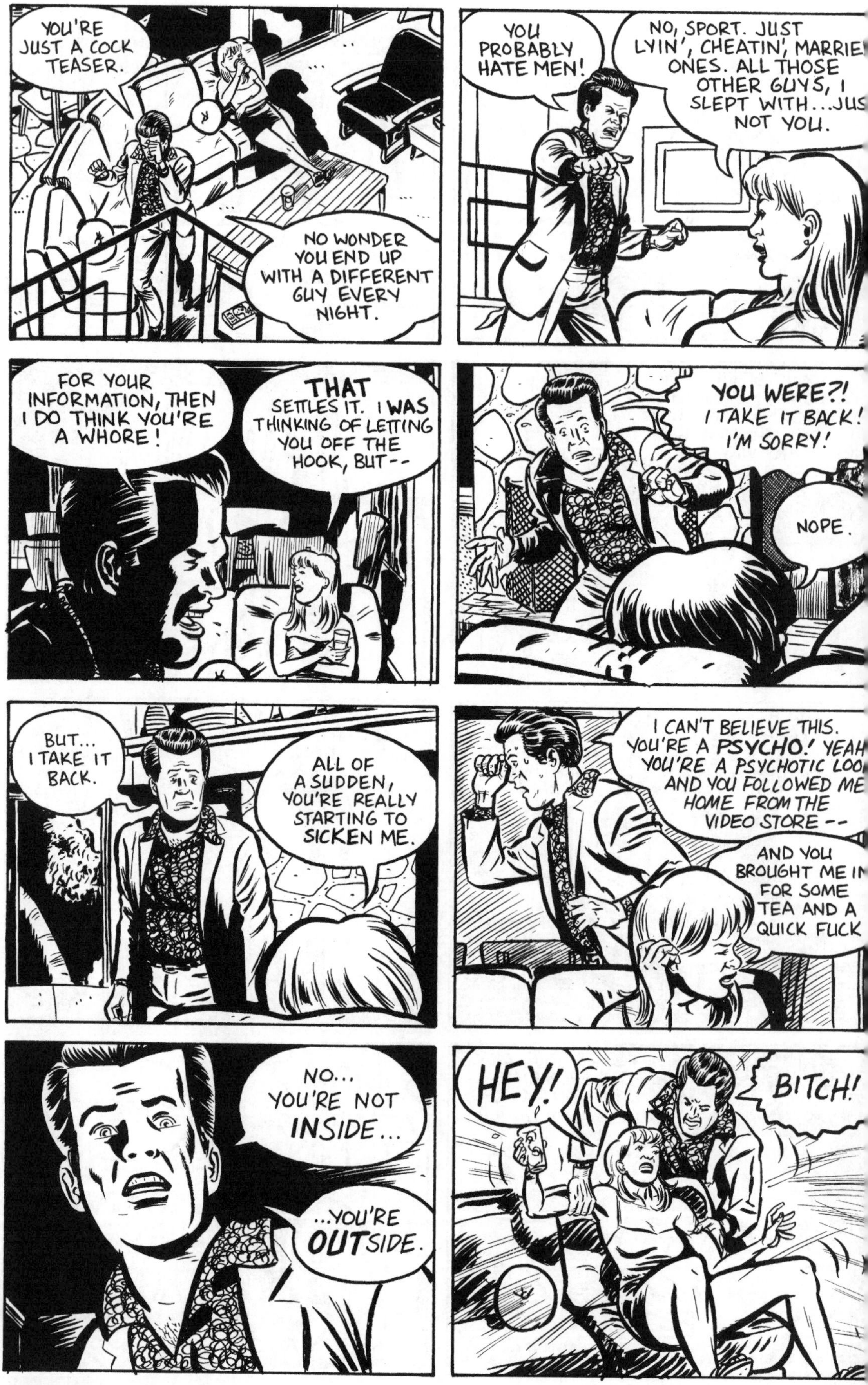
YOU'RE JUST A COCK TEASER.
NO WONDER YOU END UP WITH A DIFFERENT GUY EVERY NIGHT.
YOU PROBABLY HATE MEN!
NO, SPORT. JUST LYIN', CHEATIN', MARRIE ONES. ALL THOSE OTHER GUYS, I SLEPT WITH...JUS NOT YOU.
FOR YOUR INFORMATION, THEN I DO THINK YOU'RE A WHORE!
THAT SETTLES IT. I WAS THINKING OF LETTING YOU OFF THE HOOK, BUT--
YOU WERE?! I TAKE IT BACK! I'M SORRY!
NOPE.
BUT... I TAKE IT BACK.
ALL OF A SUDDEN, YOU'RE REALLY STARTING TO SICKEN ME.
I CAN'T BELIEVE THIS. YOU'RE A PSYCHO! YEAH YOU'RE A PSYCHOTIC LOO AND YOU FOLLOWED ME HOME FROM THE VIDEO STORE--
AND YOU BROUGHT ME IN FOR SOME TEA AND A QUICK FUCK
NO... YOU'RE NOT INSIDE...
...YOU'RE OUTSIDE.
HEY!
BITCH!

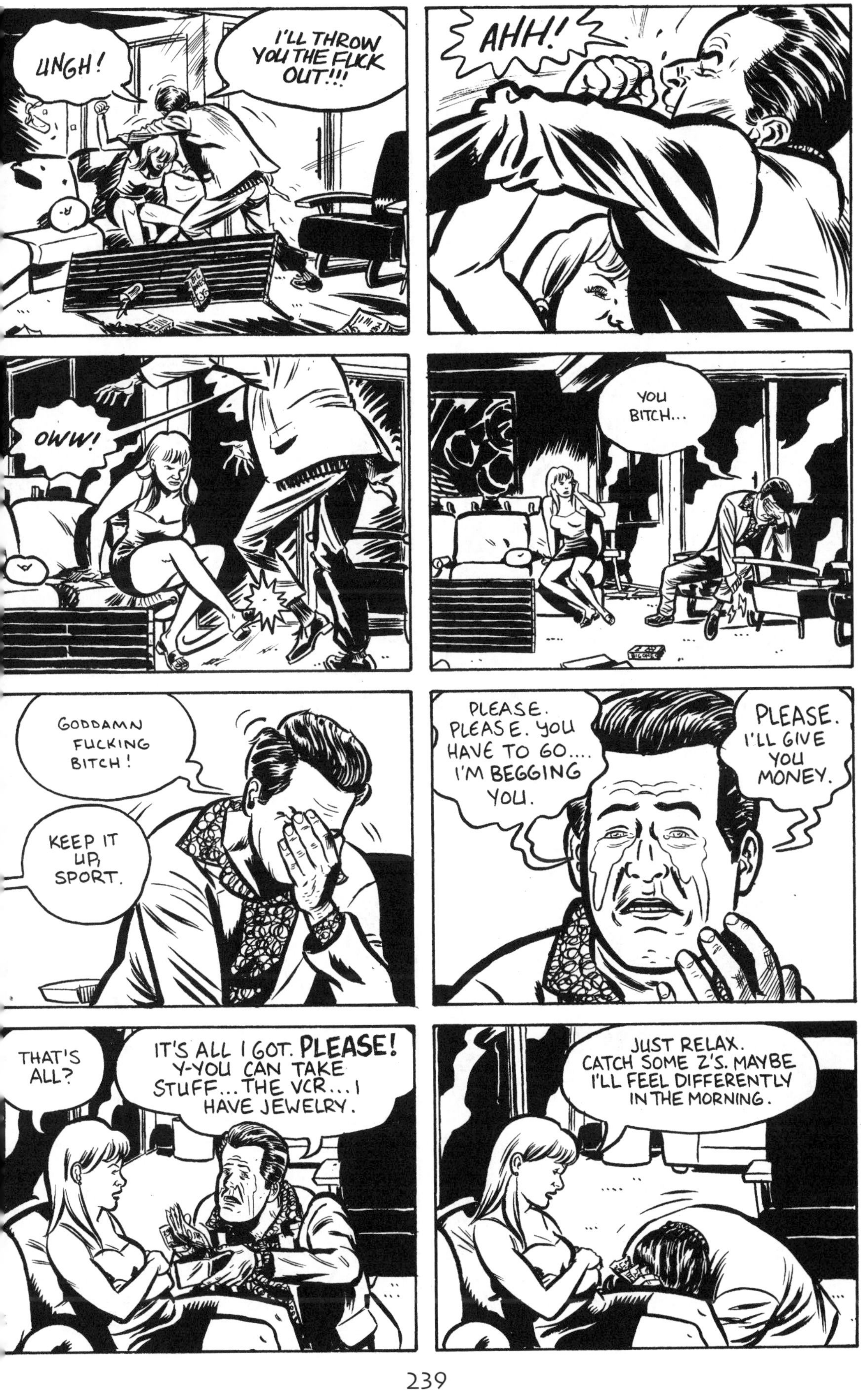
UNGH!
I'LL THROW YOU THE FUCK OUT!!!
AHH!
OWW!
YOU BITCH...
GODDAMN FUCKING BITCH!
KEEP IT UP, SPORT.
PLEASE. PLEASE. YOU HAVE TO GO.... I'M BEGGING YOU.
PLEASE. I'LL GIVE YOU MONEY.
THAT'S ALL?
IT'S ALL I GOT. PLEASE! Y-YOU CAN TAKE STUFF... THE VCR... I HAVE JEWELRY.
JUST RELAX. CATCH SOME Z'S. MAYBE I'LL FEEL DIFFERENTLY IN THE MORNING.

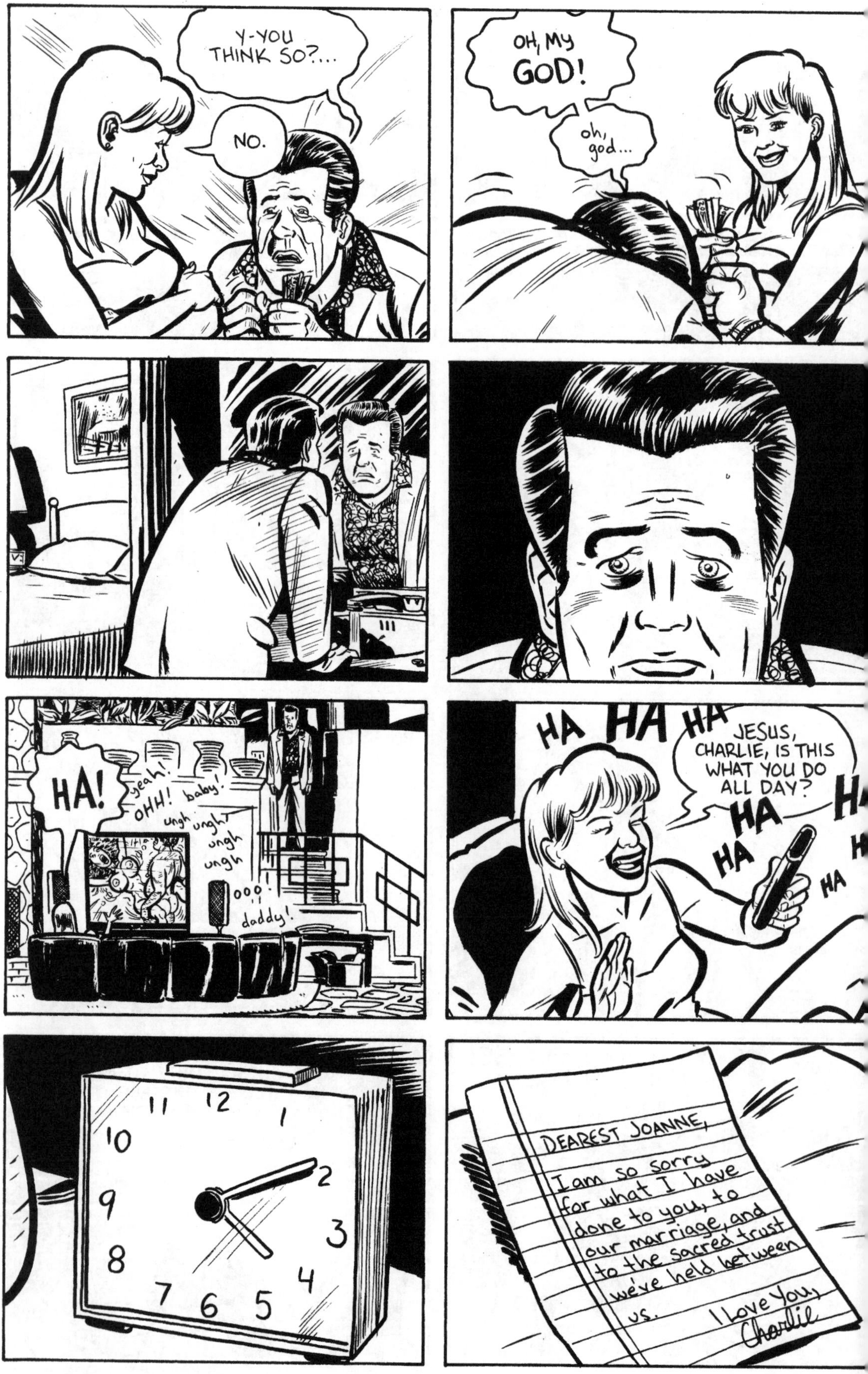
Y-YOU THINK SO?...
NO.
OH, MY GOD!
oh, god...
HA!
yeah!
OHH! baby!
ungh
ungh!
ungh
ungh
ooo!
daddy!
HA HA HA
JESUS, CHARLIE, IS THIS WHAT YOU DO ALL DAY?
HA
HA
HA
12
1
2
3
4
5
6
7
8
9
10
11
DEAREST JOANNE,
I am so sorry for what I have done to you, to our marriage, and to the sacred trust we've held between us.
I Love You,
Charlie

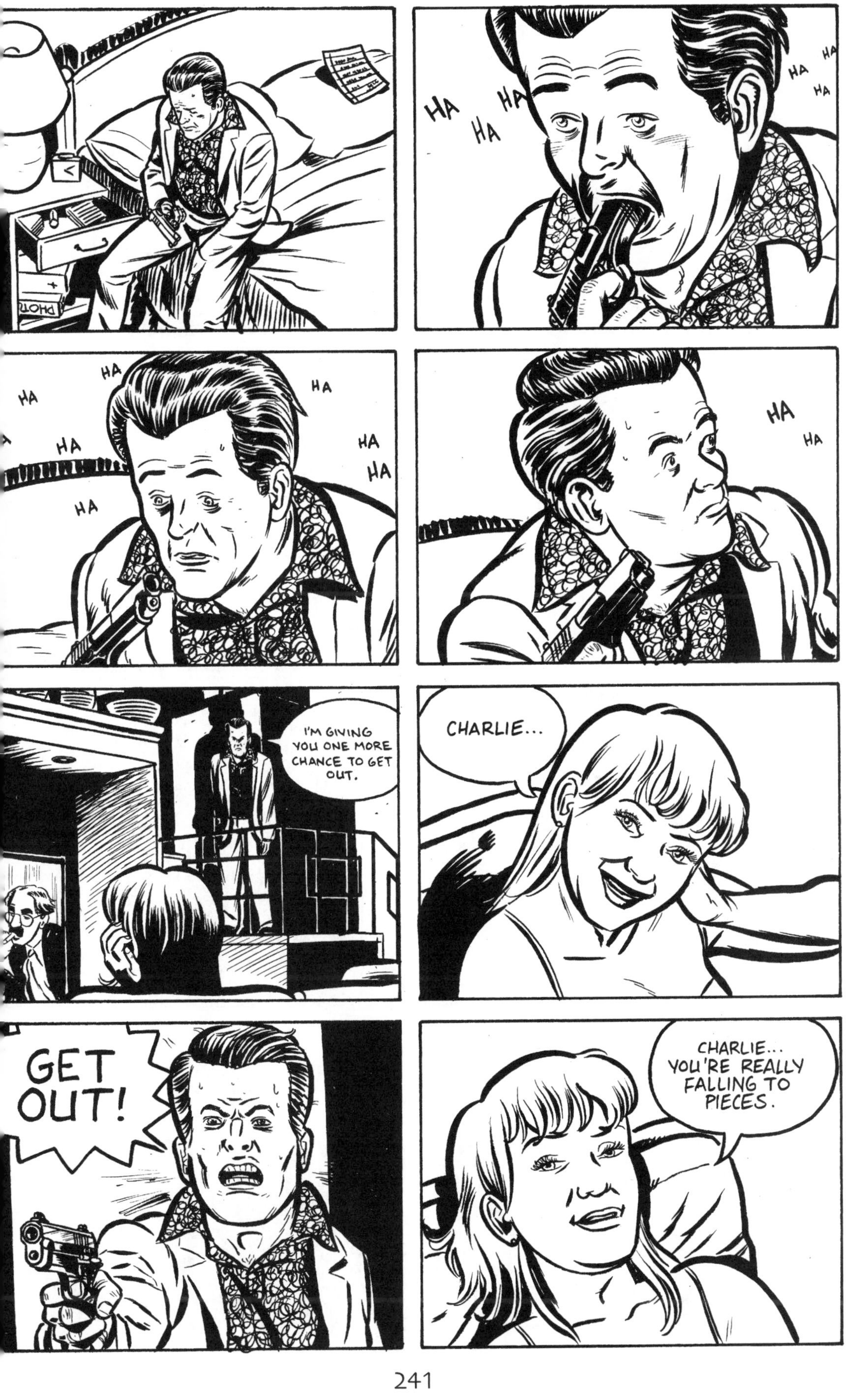
HA HA HA
HA HA HA
HA HA HA HA HA HA HA
HA HA
I'M GIVING YOU ONE MORE CHANCE TO GET OUT.
CHARLIE...
GET OUT!
CHARLIE... YOU'RE REALLY FALLING TO PIECES.

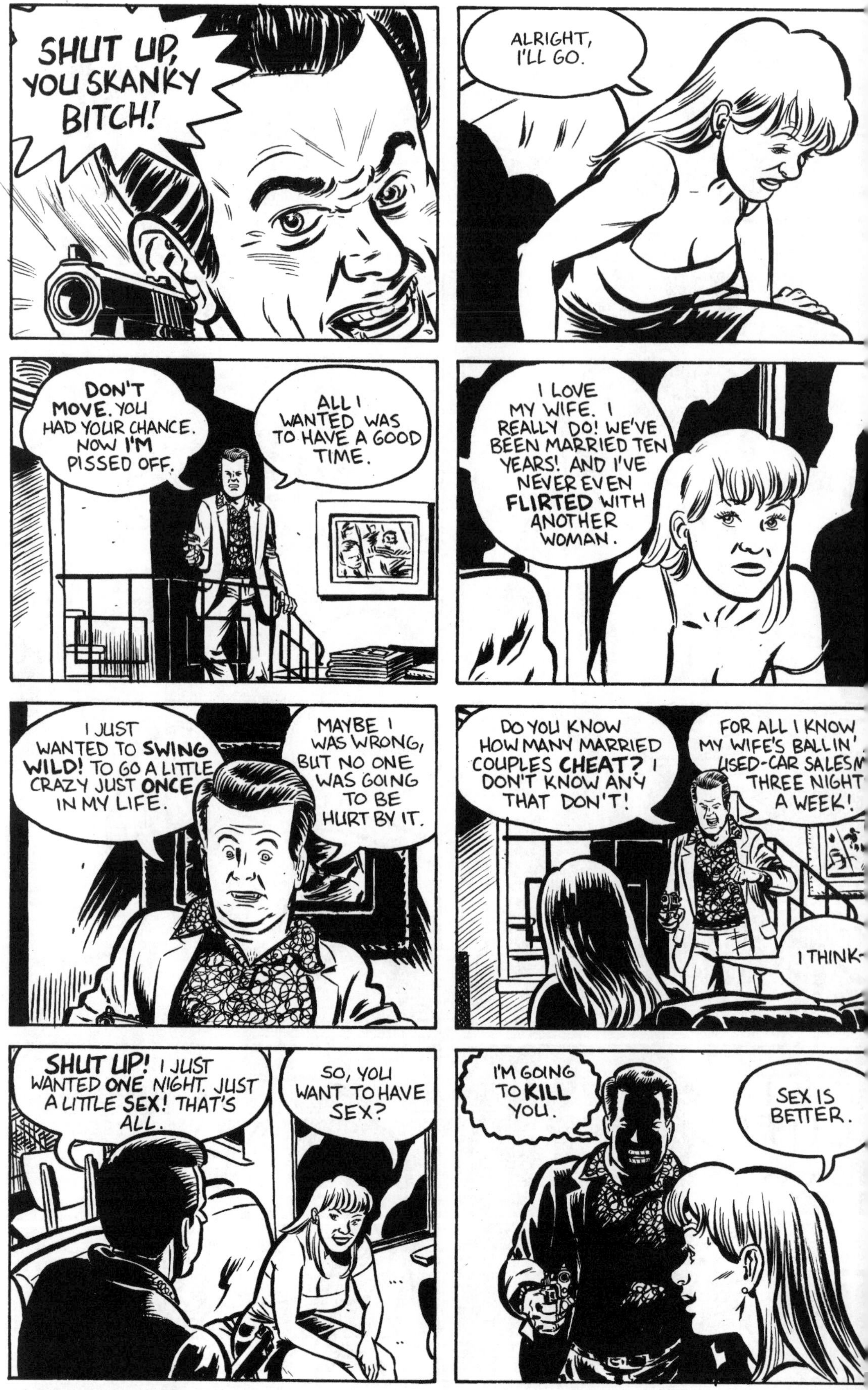
SHUT UP, YOU SKANKY BITCH!
ALRIGHT, I'LL GO.
DON'T MOVE. YOU HAD YOUR CHANCE. NOW I'M PISSED OFF.
ALL I WANTED WAS TO HAVE A GOOD TIME.
I LOVE MY WIFE. I REALLY DO! WE'VE BEEN MARRIED TEN YEARS! AND I'VE NEVER EVEN FLIRTED WITH ANOTHER WOMAN.
I JUST WANTED TO SWING WILD! TO GO A LITTLE CRAZY JUST ONCE IN MY LIFE.
MAYBE I WAS WRONG, BUT NO ONE WAS GOING TO BE HURT BY IT.
DO YOU KNOW HOW MANY MARRIED COUPLES CHEAT? I DON'T KNOW ANY THAT DON'T!
I THINK-
SHUT UP! I JUST WANTED ONE NIGHT. JUST A LITTLE SEX! THAT'S ALL.
SO, YOU WANT TO HAVE SEX?
I'M GOING TO KILL YOU.
SEX IS BETTER.

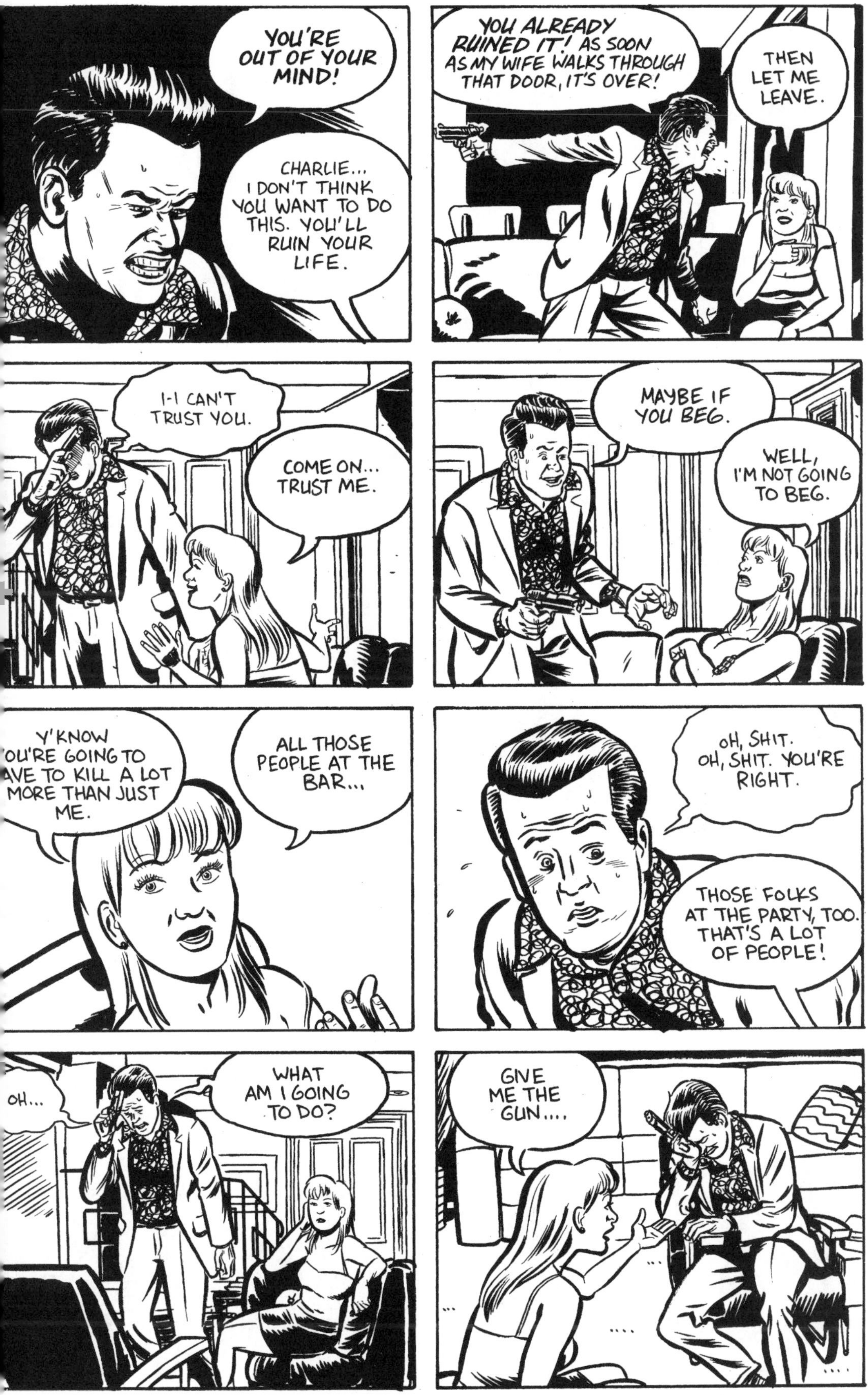
YOU'RE OUT OF YOUR MIND!
CHARLIE... I DON'T THINK YOU WANT TO DO THIS. YOU'LL RUIN YOUR LIFE.
YOU ALREADY RUINED IT! AS SOON AS MY WIFE WALKS THROUGH THAT DOOR, IT'S OVER!
THEN LET ME LEAVE.
I-I CAN'T TRUST YOU.
COME ON... TRUST ME.
MAYBE IF YOU BEG.
WELL, I'M NOT GOING TO BEG.
Y'KNOW OU'RE GOING TO AVE TO KILL A LOT MORE THAN JUST ME.
ALL THOSE PEOPLE AT THE BAR...
OH, SHIT. OH, SHIT. YOU'RE RIGHT.
THOSE FOLKS AT THE PARTY, TOO. THAT'S A LOT OF PEOPLE!
OH...
WHAT AM I GOING TO DO?
GIVE ME THE GUN....
...
...
....
....

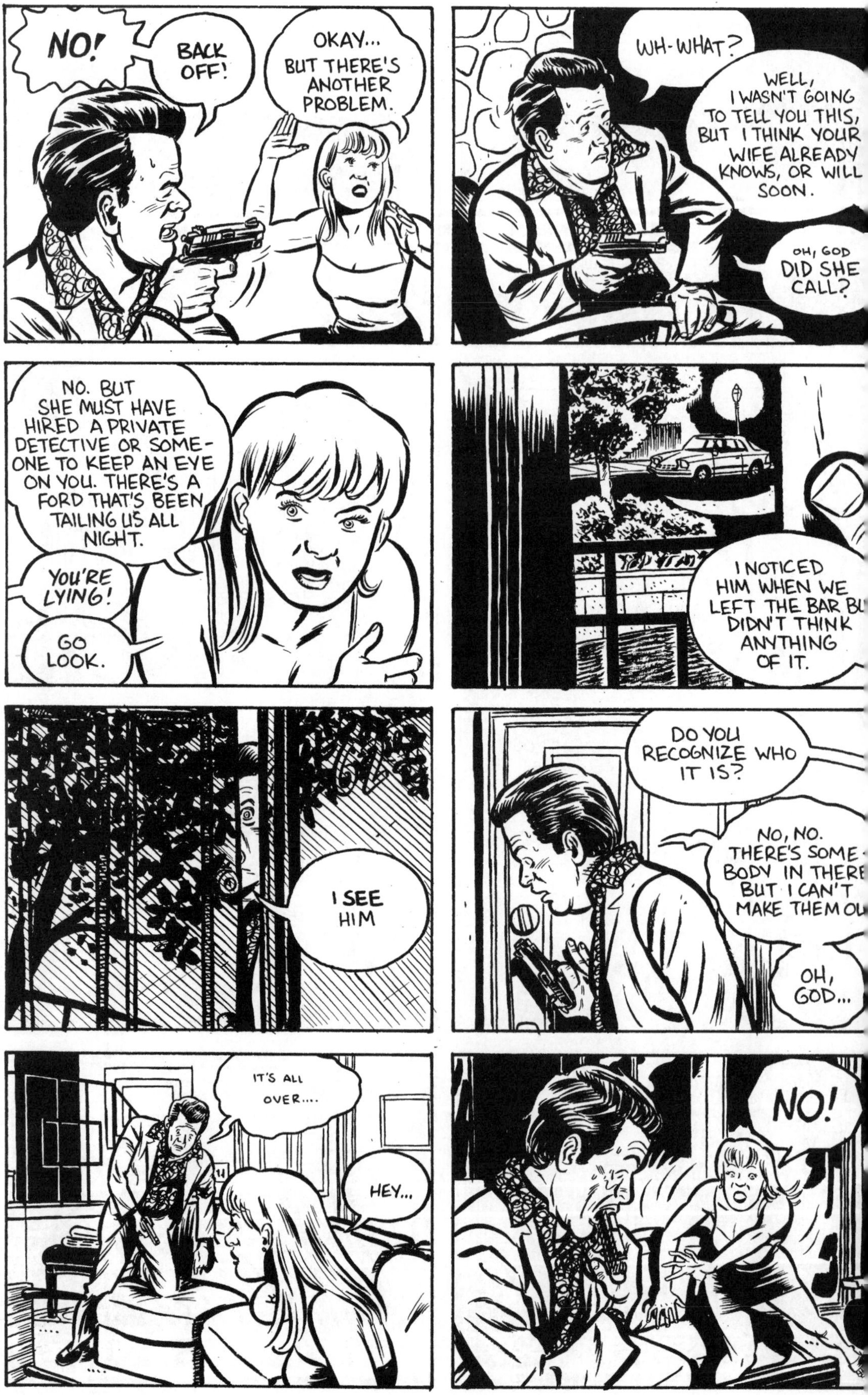
NO!
BACK OFF!
OKAY... BUT THERE'S ANOTHER PROBLEM.
WH-WHAT?
WELL, I WASN'T GOING TO TELL YOU THIS, BUT I THINK YOUR WIFE ALREADY KNOWS, OR WILL SOON.
OH, GOD DID SHE CALL?
NO. BUT SHE MUST HAVE HIRED A PRIVATE DETECTIVE OR SOME-ONE TO KEEP AN EYE ON YOU. THERE'S A FORD THAT'S BEEN TAILING US ALL NIGHT.
YOU'RE LYING!
GO LOOK.
I NOTICED HIM WHEN WE LEFT THE BAR BU DIDN'T THINK ANYTHING OF IT.
I SEE HIM
DO YOU RECOGNIZE WHO IT IS?
NO, NO. THERE'S SOME-BODY IN THERE BUT I CAN'T MAKE THEM OU
OH, GOD...
IT'S ALL OVER....
HEY...
NO!

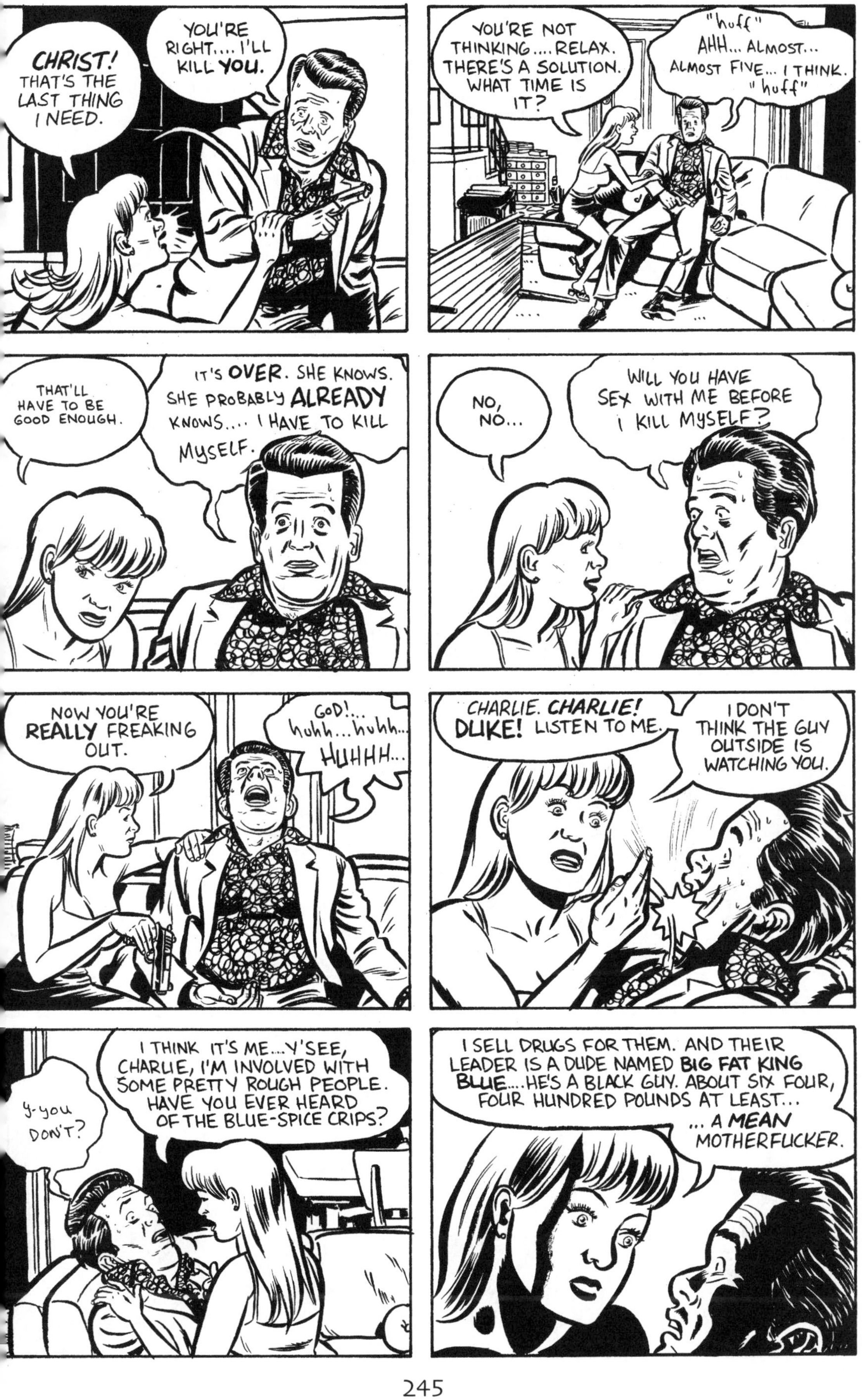
CHRIST! THAT'S THE LAST THING I NEED.
YOU'RE RIGHT.... I'LL KILL YOU.
YOU'RE NOT THINKING.... RELAX. THERE'S A SOLUTION. WHAT TIME IS IT?
"huff" AHH... ALMOST... ALMOST FIVE... I THINK. "huff"
THAT'LL HAVE TO BE GOOD ENOUGH.
IT'S OVER. SHE KNOWS. SHE PROBABLY ALREADY KNOWS.... I HAVE TO KILL MYSELF.
NO, NO...
WILL YOU HAVE SEX WITH ME BEFORE I KILL MYSELF?
NOW YOU'RE REALLY FREAKING OUT.
GOD!... huhh... huhh... HUHHH...
CHARLIE. CHARLIE! DUKE! LISTEN TO ME.
I DON'T THINK THE GUY OUTSIDE IS WATCHING YOU.
I THINK IT'S ME... Y'SEE, CHARLIE, I'M INVOLVED WITH SOME PRETTY ROUGH PEOPLE. HAVE YOU EVER HEARD OF THE BLUE-SPICE CRIPS?
Y-YOU DON'T?
I SELL DRUGS FOR THEM. AND THEIR LEADER IS A DUDE NAMED BIG FAT KING BLUE.... HE'S A BLACK GUY. ABOUT SIX FOUR, FOUR HUNDRED POUNDS AT LEAST...
... A MEAN MOTHERFUCKER.

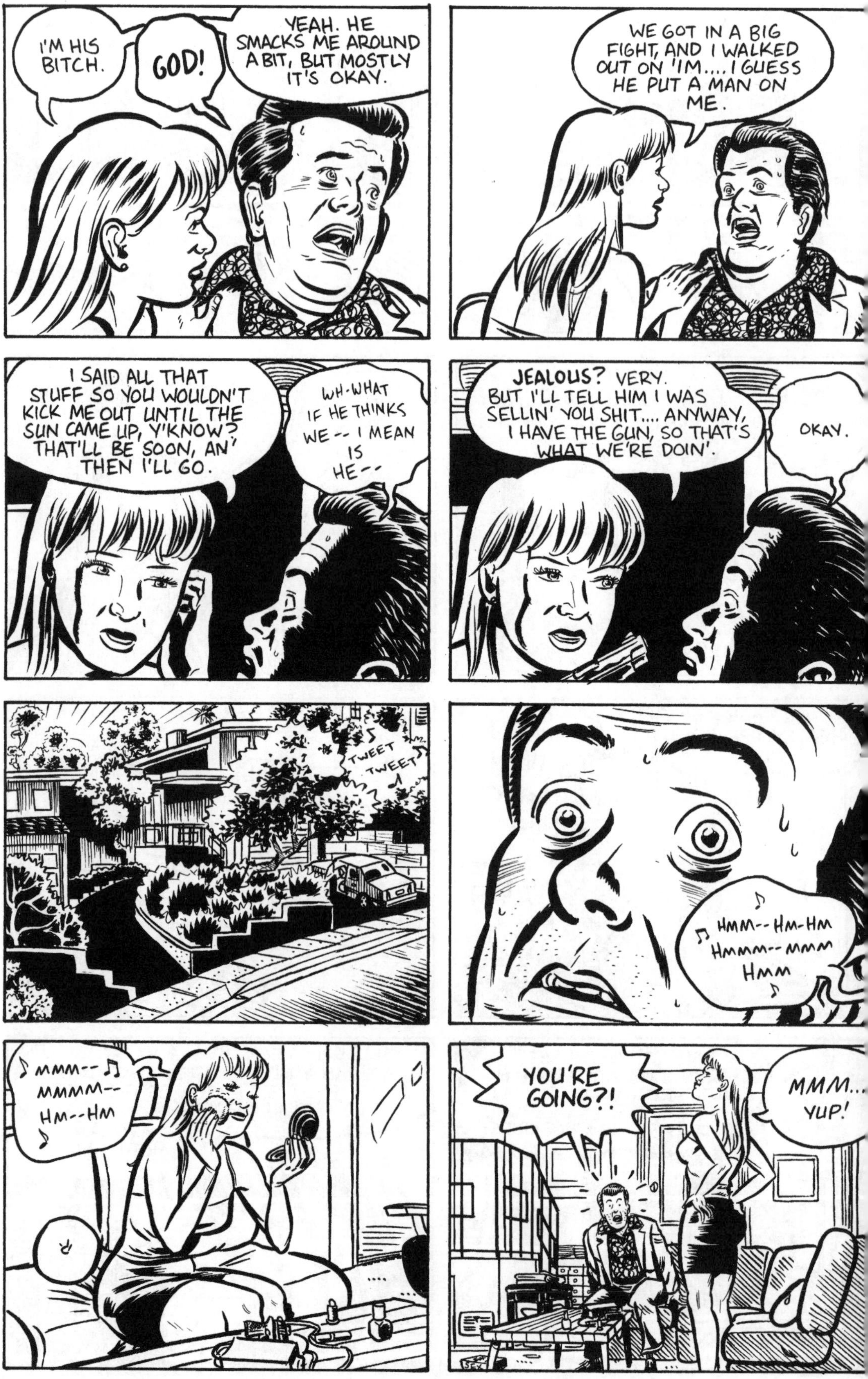
I'M HIS BITCH.
GOD!
YEAH. HE SMACKS ME AROUND A BIT, BUT MOSTLY IT'S OKAY.
WE GOT IN A BIG FIGHT, AND I WALKED OUT ON 'IM.... I GUESS HE PUT A MAN ON ME.
I SAID ALL THAT STUFF SO YOU WOULDN'T KICK ME OUT UNTIL THE SUN CAME UP, Y'KNOW? THAT'LL BE SOON, AN' THEN I'LL GO.
WH-WHAT IF HE THINKS WE -- I MEAN IS HE--
JEALOUS? VERY. BUT I'LL TELL HIM I WAS SELLIN' YOU SHIT.... ANYWAY, I HAVE THE GUN, SO THAT'S WHAT WE'RE DOIN'.
OKAY.
TWEET TWEET
HMM--HM-HM HMMM--MMM HMM
MMM-- MMMM-- HM--HM
YOU'RE GOING?!
MMM... YUP!

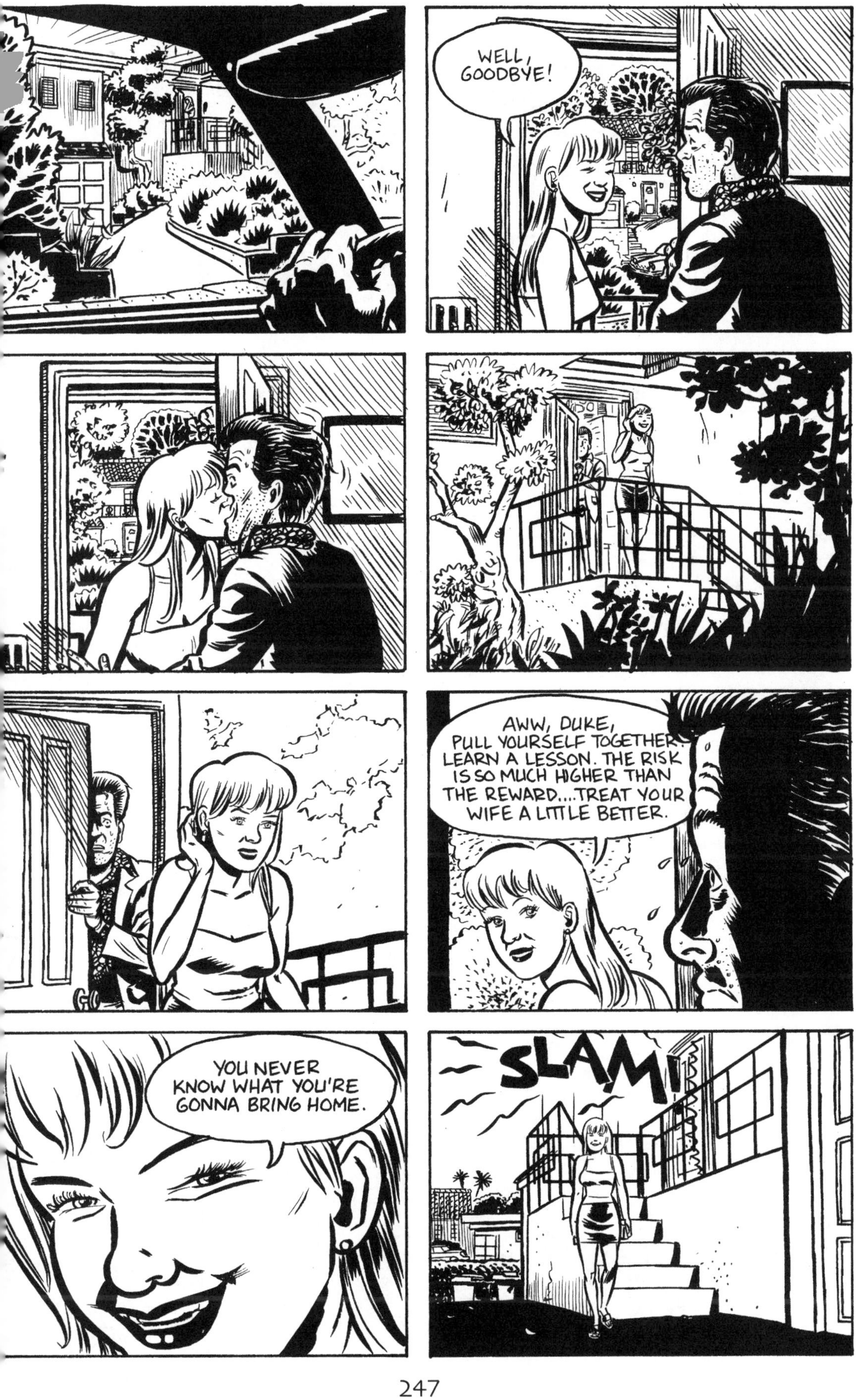
WELL, GOODBYE!
AWW, DUKE, PULL YOURSELF TOGETHER. LEARN A LESSON. THE RISK IS SO MUCH HIGHER THAN THE REWARD....TREAT YOUR WIFE A LITTLE BETTER.
YOU NEVER KNOW WHAT YOU'RE GONNA BRING HOME.
SLAM!

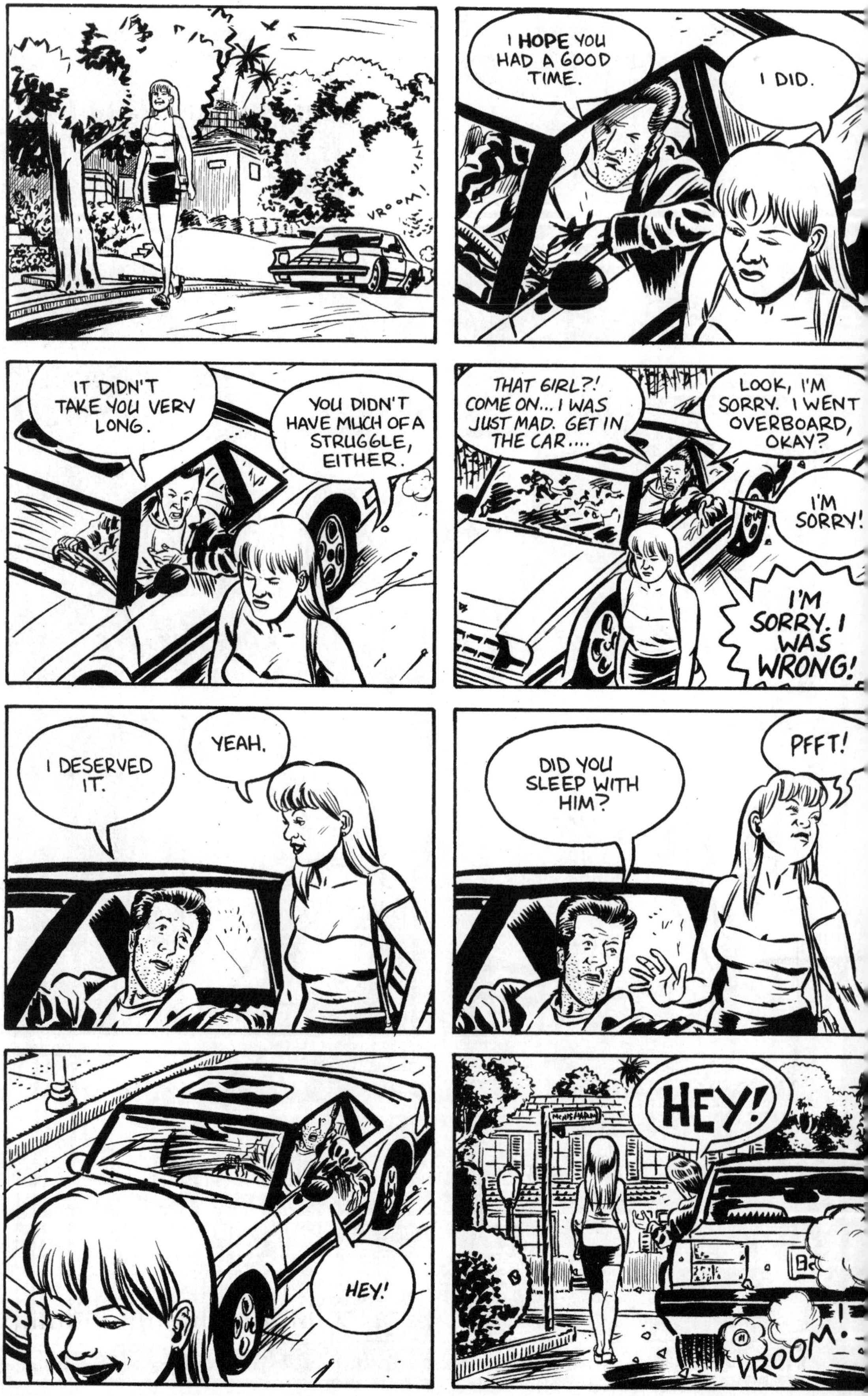
VROOOM!
I HOPE YOU HAD A GOOD TIME.
I DID.
IT DIDN'T TAKE YOU VERY LONG.
YOU DIDN'T HAVE MUCH OF A STRUGGLE, EITHER.
THAT GIRL?! COME ON... I WAS JUST MAD. GET IN THE CAR....
LOOK, I'M SORRY. I WENT OVERBOARD, OKAY?
I'M SORRY!
I'M SORRY. I WAS WRONG!
I DESERVED IT.
YEAH.
DID YOU SLEEP WITH HIM?
PFFT!
HEY!
HEY!
VROOOM!

**THE END.**

STAFFORD TOWNSHI
POLICE DEPT.
3720

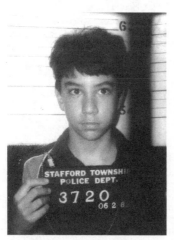

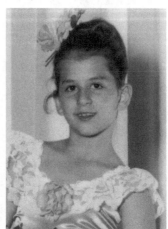

**David Lapham** is the multi-award-winning creator of the groundbreaking comic book series *Stray Bullets*. He won an Eisner Award, the comic industry's highest honor, as the best writer/artist of 1996, and has been nominated five times in that category. He currently resides in Carefree, Arizona with his wife and creative partner, Maria Lapham, and their four daughters. Please ignore their playful cries for help.

**Maria Lapham** formed El Capitán Books at the age of twenty to co-create and publish the seminal comic book series *Stray Bullets.* In 1997, she won an Eisner Award, the comic industry's highest honor, for the collection *Stray Bullets: Innocence of Nihilism,* the innovation and design of which has set the standard for prestige format books since. She currently lives in Carefree, Arizona with her husband and four young daughters.